European Economic Law

Kluwer Law International

European Economic Law

SECOND EDITION

by

Alberto Santa Maria

Wolters Kluwer
Law & Business

AUSTIN BOSTON CHICAGO NEW YORK THE NETHERLANDS

Published by:
Kluwer Law International
PO Box 316
2400 AH Alphen aan den Rijn
The Netherlands
Website: www.kluwerlaw.com

Sold and distributed in North, Central and South America by:
Aspen Publishers, Inc.
7201 McKinney Circle
Frederick, MD 21704
United States of America
Email: customer.care@aspenpubl.com

Sold and distributed in all other countries by:
Turpin Distribution Services Ltd.
Stratton Business Park
Pegasus Drive, Biggleswade
Bedfordshire SG18 8TQ
United Kingdom
Email: kluwerlaw@turpin-distribution.com

Printed on acid-free paper.

ISBN 978-90-411-2536-1

Printed in Great Britain.

Table of Contents

Foreword to the Second Edition **xi**

Introduction **xiii**

Chapter I
Companies' Right of Establishment and Freedom to Provide Services: Mutual Recognition of Eligible Companies **1**

1. The Treaty of Rome and Private International Law on Companies 2
2. The Brussels Convention of 29 February 1968 on the Mutual Recognition of Companies and Bodies Corporate within the EEC 9
3. General Considerations about the 'Recognition' of Foreign Companies: A Historical Overview 12
4. The Double Meaning of 'Recognition' as Applied to Companies 24
5. The Import of Clauses in Establishment Treaties and Friendship, Commerce and Navigation Treaties 28
6. The Treatment of Foreign Companies within the Community: Article 12 and Articles 43 et seq., 49 et seq. and 56 et seq. EC 31
7. The Principle of the Direct Applicability of the Rules of the Treaty on Establishment and Services 38
8. The Notion of Companies' Freedom of Establishment within the European Union 41
9. The Scope of a Company's Right of Establishment 44
10. Private International Law on Companies and the Establishment Rules 46
11. Critical Remarks on the Daily Mail judgment 52
12. Case-Law on Cross-Border Mergers and Its Impact on the Transfer of Seat within the European Union: Directive 2005/56/CE 57

13. The above Principles as Applied in Practice 64
14. The 'National' Treatment: Scope and Limits under Community Case-Law 66
15. The Impact of Article 43 et seq. of the Treaty on: (a) the Italian Rules of Private International Law in Regard to Companies 71
16. More: (b) Mandatory Rules of Italian Law When Companies Formed in Other Member States Set Up Branches in Italy 76
17. More: (c) Applicability of Legislative Decree 231/2001 to 'Community' Foreign Companies 79
18. More: (d) Mandatory Rules of Italian Law Relating to Multinational Groups of Companies 89
19. More: (e) The Rules Applicable to Listed Companies 98
20. Jurisdiction Criteria Relating to Companies in the EC Regulation on Jurisdiction and the Recognition of Foreign Judgments 102
21. EC Regulation No. 1346/2000 on Insolvency Proceedings 106

Chapter II
Harmonization of Company Law within the EU **115**
1. Conflict of Laws and Uniformity: Two Techniques Compared 115
2. General Considerations about the Harmonization of Company Law in the European Union 120
3. Legal Basis of Company Directives 126
4. The Value of Harmonization Directives: The Direct Applicability Issue 129
5. Company Directives and Community Developments: Interpretational Issues 139
6. The Commission's Current Activity in Codifying the Matter 147
7. Directives Concerning General Rules of Member States' Company Laws 149
8. Mergers of Companies Governed by the Laws of Different Member States 157
9. The Draft Directive on Groups of Undertakings and the Seventh Directive on Consolidated Accounts 162
10. The Eleventh Directive 166
11. The Statute for the European Company 167
12. The Regulation on the European Economic Interest Grouping (EEIG) 172

Chapter III
Free Movement of Capital in an Open Economy: The Monetary Eurosystem **181**
1. The Evolution of Economic and Financial Relations in the New World Order 182
2. The Euro and the Free Movement of Capital and Payments 184

3. The Complex Set of Rules on Capital and Payments in Their Original Formulation in the Treaty of Rome 189
4. The Conflict between the Economic Integration Process and Member States' Economic and Monetary Policies: The Werner Report and the 22 March 1971 Resolution 195
5. From the 'European Monetary Snake' to the European Monetary System ('EMS'). The Re-Launch of Financial Integration: Subsequent Commission Communications to the Council Up to the (Delors) Report on the Economic and Monetary Union 197
6. The Economic and Monetary Union and the Maastricht Treaty 200
7. The Criticalities of the European 'Rigid' System 208
8. A Criticism of the Double Standard: Serious Distortions Across the Eurosystem. The UK case 211
9. The Impact of the Euro on Contracts of Duration 213
10. Private Parties and the Full Liberalization of Capital Movements and Payments in the European Union 219
11. The Fundamental Freedoms and the Exercise of 'Special Powers': The Terms of the Problem 223
12. The Legal Bases of the Conflict Over 'Golden Shares' between the Commission and Member States 224
13. The Permitted Scope of the National States' and Their Agencies' Intervention 229
14. The Saga of the Commission's Scrutiny of the Italian Rules on Special Powers 231
15. The 'Proportionate' Exercise of Control in the ECJ's Recent Case-Law 233

Chapter IV
The Role of the European Union in the Organization of International Economy **241**

1. Introductory Remarks 242
2. International Economic Cooperation: From GATT 1947 to the WTO 250
3. The WTO's Relationships with the Other International Economic Organizations: (a) with the United Nations 256
4. More: (b) with the International Monetary Fund: 'Monetary Dumping' 256
5. More: (c) with the G7 Finance 262
6. More: (d) with the International Labour Organisation ('ILO') 263
7. The European Union and 'Social Dumping' 268
8. The Globalization Process: The Widening Gap Between Industrialized Countries and Less Developed Countries (LDCs) and the Doha Round's Difficulties 270

9. The DSB (Dispute Settlement Body) as Contrasted with the Previous System of International Dispute Settlement within the WTO 272
10. Institutional and Procedural Innovations under the Uruguay Round Final Act 274
11. Settled Legal Principles in DSB/WTO Case-Law 276
12. Protection of Private Interests within the WTO System 280
13. The Role of a Private Party, Enterprise Concerned or Association as Amicus Curiae, and Judicial Protection under the Covered Agreements 284
14. The WTO and the European Union 287
15. The European Commission's 'External' Weaknesses and China 288
16. Trade Defence Instruments: (a) Safeguard Measures in General 294
17. More: Safeguard Measures with Regard to the People's Republic of China 298
18. More: (b) 'Dumping' and 'Subsidies' as Causes of Diversion of International Trade 299
19. The New International Rules on Dumping and Subsidies and their Implementation within the EU 300
20. Legal Nature of Dumping: The Requirements 303
21. Circumvention of Antidumping Duties: The 'Screwdriver Assembly' issue 306
22. Community Interest Falling Outside the Scope of GATT Antidumping Provisions: Critical Remarks 310
23. Implementing WTO Rules on Dumping and Subsidies: (a) in the United States of America 320
24. More: (b) in the Chinese Legal System 323
25. Dumping and Competition in the EU 326

Chapter V
Multinational Enterprises and Globalization **331**
1. Methodological Preamble 332
2. Definitory Elucidation 333
3. Multinational Enterprises and International Law in a Changing World 338
4. Multinational Enterprises and the European Union 351
5. The Features of the Phenomenon in General: Unrestricted Freedom of Choice and the Resulting Basic Distortions of Competition 352
6. Advantages Lawfully Acquired by Multinationals in Some Instances of Daily Practice 356
7. Production Delocation as a Result of Globalization 358
8. The Impact of Globalization on Financial Markets: The USA Financial Crisis 359
9. More: The Sovereign Funds 362

10. Unlawful Conduct of Multinational Enterprises 364
11. Risk Areas: The Problem of the 'Normal' Value of 'Transfer Prices' and of Royalties in Intragroup Transactions 365
12. International Cooperation against Corruption, Pollution, Money Laundering, Financial Crimes and the International Financing of Terrorism 368
13. The Role of Banks in Controlling Transactions at Risk 372
14. International Cooperation in the Supervision of Banking Groups and the Basel Concordat: The Different Levels of Control 373
15. Consolidated Supervision Over Banking Transactions in the Relationships between Legal Systems 378
16. From the Basel II Rules to the Present Rules of the European Union 380
17. Investigations into 'Suspicious Activities' in Context 382
18. The Universal Notion of 'SAR' (Suspicious Activity Reporting) 383
19. Suspicious Activity Reporting Requirements to Prevail over any Other Requirement of Law 387
20. The 'Codes of Conduct' 391
21. 'Social Commitment' and Multinational Enterprises: Consequences on the Relationships with the Home State and with Third Countries 393
22. Multinational Enterprises' Activity in a Regional Perspective: The Limited Scope for Enforcement of Community Rules 395
23. The European Union and 'Corporate Social Responsibility' 399
24. Community Actions in Favour of Small and Medium-Sized Enterprises 403
25. Legal Restrictions on Third-Country-Based Multinationals' Operations in the European Union 408
26. Applying Competition Rules to Non-Community Businesses 410
27. Anti-Dumping and Anti-Subsidy Rules as Applied to Non-Community Multinationals 412

Chapter VI
Competition Law between General Theory and Actual Implementation **413**

1. The Peculiarities of the Rules on Competition in General 414
2. Protection of Interests under European Competition Law 417
3. Competition Law Rules as an Essential Part of EU Formation. The Legal Basis of European Rules. The Limited Scope of this Study 420
4. Objectives and Aims of EU Competition Law Rules 423
5. The 'Relevant' Market and the Significance of Economic Analysis 428
6. The Commission's Role in the EU Competition Law System 433

7. Some Aspects of the Cumulation of the Commission's Functions in Administrative Proceedings 437
8. Immediate and Direct Applicability of Commission Decisions 439
9. Public Enterprise and Competition: Transparency of Financial Relations between Member States and Public Undertakings 441
10. The Alitalia Bailout and European Rules 445
11. A Criticism of the Extensive Application by the Commission of Article 87 EC, Specifically in Respect of State Aid 450
12. State Aid by Legislative Act under US Law and New Possible Approaches in EU Law 457
13. Recovery Decisions and Rights of Defence 461
14. The Community Courts' Control over Commission Decisions 464
15. The Scope of Application of the Community's Rules of Competition Law 468
16. Direct Applicability of the European Rules on Competition and the Member States' Authorities' Competence to Apply Them 477
17. Relationships between Community Rules and National Rules 487
18. Applying the Subsidiarity Principle Having Regard to the 'One-Stop Shop', and the Multi-State Examination of Mergers 491
19. Damages Awarded for Losses Arising from Infringements of Antitrust Rules 496
20. Actions for Damages Brought by Competing Undertakings 497
21. Actions for Damages in Consumer Protection 501
22. A New Collective Redress Action: The So-Called 'Italian Class Action' 506
23. Italian Courts' Jurisdiction in Collective Redress Actions and Community Law 517
24. Assessment of Loss in Antitrust Cases 521

List of Binding Acts of the EC Institutions 525

List of the Rulings of the EC Courts and of the Opinions of the Advocates General 531

List of Authors Cited in this Volume 543

Index 547

Foreword to the Second Edition

To cure the 'new' edition of this volume has proved to be a challenging and demanding task more than what I could imagine.

The reasons for this are various. First of all, the time elapsed since the precedent edition in 1996 (too many years, and I apologise for it) has its evident importance.

But it is also true that, during these last twelve years, we have assisted to a development of the international economy in such relevant terms that a new era, commonly named 'globalisation', has opened. Furthermore, the various events concurring to characterise this new era – to which I will often refer in the text of the volume – in a more or less decisive manner, by combining among each other, have had a multiplier effect on most of the topics I have focused on.

In this context, the 'international' aspects, through this long period of time, have assumed, if possible, an even bigger importance for the reflexes they imply vis-à-vis the European Union legal order and the content of EC law. The development of material EC law, overflowing as occurred in the past, completed the picture.

The fact remains that I have used the precedent drafting of the book mainly as a landmark, not even as a starting point, for planning the new text which will then appear to the reader with contents totally new, in each part.

For logical needs, stemming from my interpretation of the deep changes occurred in the international context, I have modified even the structure of the work: the chapter related to the multinational companies has been inverted in respect to that concerning the developments of the international economy, while the chapter on competition law has been placed at the end of this volume in order to make easier its reading in the light of the new international frame, object of the previous chapters.

Among the topics covered in this work, I was not able to discuss, as I would have wished, the European Constitution, which has definitively expired; notwithstanding its substantial emptiness, of which the renounce to the affirmation of the 'common roots' is the most patent example, its approval would have had an undeniable political relevance, representing it the true, new motor of the European Union realisation. Because of this, it seems difficult to understand why the Commission – which has substantially lead such realisation – has given preference to such a conspicuous enlargement of the European Union rather than to the approval of the Constitution by those member States, consolidated in the same Union for a long time.

The Treaty of Lisbon, which by itself is only a palliative, and its analogous unfortunate events show a feeling of uneasiness among the European people, in my opinion, caused not by a generalised adversity to the European Union, but rather by the gap of indifference created between the present European Union and the European people, which the former cannot and must not disregard. However, I ascribe such progressive detachment, more than to the diffidence in the idea of Europe, rather to the scarce knowledge of the contents and the function of the European machine, by now too complex.

In order to come out from the current impasse, it shall be necessary to have the courage to re-draft the structure of the European Union, mainly in relation to the management of the executive and legislative powers for making up the overall confidence for the successful conclusion of the 'democratic' evolutionary process towards the political union started more than fifty years ago.

Without such a 'constitutional' effort, I am afraid it would not be possible to cross the ford, nor I believe desirable that this situation remains unchanged. In this, under various aspects, Europe represents surely more than an economic community, but, under many points of view, it is still far away by a satisfactory model of union of States.

To this aim, I have amended the title of this volume, willing to attain, for once me either, to the magic of the 'power of words', adding to 'Economic' Law – which actually better represents the present content of the book than the previous 'Commercial' Law – the connotation of 'European'.

First of all, I am sincerely grateful to Dr. Raffaele Petrillo that, with devotion and skill, has more than advised me in the translation from the original Italian version and then to Prof. Claudio Biscaretti di Ruffia and to Avv. Edoardo Gambaro for their patient and stimulating support throughout the entire period I have drafted this volume as well as to Prof. Mario Cattaneo for his comfort given to me in reading my wishful economic considerations.

Milan, 7 October 2008
ALBERTO SANTA MARIA

Introduction

SUMMARY:

1. Preliminary remarks: International origin of the European Union and relationship of EU law to national laws.
2. The Community's material law: Reasons for the title 'European Economic Law'.

1. PRELIMINARY REMARKS: INTERNATIONAL ORIGIN OF THE EUROPEAN UNION AND RELATIONSHIP OF EU LAW TO NATIONAL LAWS

The Treaty of Rome of 25 March 1957 establishing the European Economic Community and the subsequent international agreements amending that Treaty have one characteristic in common, peculiar to them: provisions for adequate regulatory sources to lead to the progressive formation of a derivative law, secondary to the primary law contained in those instruments. Within the scope of application of the Treaty, as subsequently amended by the European Single Act, the Treaty establishing the European Union, the Treaty of Amsterdam, the Treaty of Nice and the Treaty of Lisbon, if and when adopted (without considering former international agreements for further amendment never to take effect), such secondary law is now covering all sectors of the Community's *economic life*. The subjective scope of Community law, too, has expanded considerably, as various accession treaties have increased the number of Member States, from the original six to the present-day twenty-seven States.

The end-result has been a *material* Community law, whose main function is, on the one hand, to modify each Member State's body of laws, by replacing domestic rules with Community rules, and, on the other, to compress their scope more and more effectively as new rules are being introduced at a European level, thus covering vast sectors formerly reserved to each Member State's national law.

Thus, beside Community rules, which are addressed to the Member States, which is typical of any international organization created by treaty, there are many 'primary' rules even introduced by *derivative* acts (Regulations among them), which have a 'direct effect' *per se*, to use a term first coined by the European Court of Justice (ECJ) and now part of everyday language. This means that both primary and derivative rules are addressed direct to the same individual parties that are normally the addressees of each Member State's rules of national law.

It was in this context that the Court of Justice held, well before the notion of 'European citizenship' was introduced,[1] that:

> The European Economic Community constitutes a new legal order of international law ... the subjects of which comprise not only the Member States but also their nationals.[2]

The double thread linking the Community system with international law and the Member States' domestic laws has aptly been stressed by Capotorti in a limpid page he wrote when he still was Advocate General at the ECJ, which I feel it appropriate to reproduce in full below:

> As for international law, there is a connection, since the Communities were established by Treaties, and some later developments still arise from Treaties (just consider the possible accession of other States, such institutional changes as the direct election of the European Parliament, or the regulation of the matters contemplated in Article 220 of the Rome Treaty). There is also, and above all, the fact that Member States' core obligation to comply with, and perform, the Treaties arises from the well-known principle in international law that *pact sunt servanda*. However, the Community system provides institutions, institutional balances, sources, addressees and guarantees that, taken together, differ even profoundly from the traditional layout and legal system of institutional organizations.
>
> As for the Member States' internal laws, two apparently contradictory phenomena occur: reciprocal autonomy and complementariness. By *reciprocal autonomy* I mean the distinction between each national law and Community

1. See Articles 17 ff. EC, under the heading 'Citizenship of the Union', as introduced by the Maastricht Treaty. See also Chapter (Title) V, 'Citizenship', of the Charter of Fundamental Rights of the European Union, as proclaimed by the European Parliament, Council and Commission in Nice on 7 December 2000, in *OJ*, L 364, 18 Dec. 2000, and subsequently made binding by the Lisbon Treaty. For the consolidated version of the Treaty on European Union and the Treaty on the Functioning of the European Union, see *OJ*, C 115, 9 May 2008. See, in particular, Declaration 1 annexed to the Final Act of the Intergovernmental Conference that adopted the Treaty of Lisbon.
2. See Judgment of the Court of 5 February 1963, Case 26/62, *van Gend & Loos*, in *ECR*, 1963, Summary, 3.

> law. This is a quite clear distinction, if one only thinks of the diversity and separateness of the sources of each of them. Yet, one should not forget that Community law *interferes* with the scope of application of the Member States' internal laws, since the territory in which the former effectively operates and the subjects it addresses are nothing but the summation of the Member State's territories and subjects, and many of the matters covered by Community law could be regulated by any of such internal laws as well. Thus, in order to prevent such interference from causing conflicts, and to allow Community law to attain its objectives unobstructed, the Member States have left a free space to it, so to speak, *by recognising its jurisdiction over the matters contemplated by the Treaties and giving up their own entitlement to act in this area, except to the extent permitted by the Treaties.* In this sense, one can speak of the Member States' *limited sovereignty*, and of the delegation or transfer by the Member States of their jurisdiction to the Communities. It is appropriate to add that *the co-existence of Community law with national laws is such as to rule out the transformation of the former into a national law.* If there were such a transformation, Community law would be fragmented into nine [now twenty-seven, ed.] different systems of law, and absorbed by each them. On this point, there is a clear-cut difference with the law created by other international treaties, and such difference is also justified by the fact that *distinguishing between international effects and internal repercussions*, as is the case with the other treaties, *would make no sense in the case of Community Treaties, in which the international aspect and the internal aspect are indissolubly linked to each other.*[3]

Even international conventions concluded at a Community level, whether or not legally sourced by Article 293 EC, which, without amendment, incorporates Article 220 of the Treaty establishing the European Community, are apt, where accompanied with 'protocols' referring their interpretation to the ECJ, to bring about a *uniform community law.*

This peculiarity of the conventions in question – which remain instruments typical of international law – bears witness to an 'encroachment' of community law even on international law.

In fact, the unprecedented growth in international trade helped by a number of new factors, which are discussed in this book, is such that even competition law, already shifted as it has been from the national to the Community ambit, is bound to take into account the 'open' international context in which the undertakings are now operating.[4]

In light of these brief comments, it appears even too obvious that a core problem was posed as far back in time as 1964, about the primacy of Community

3. See Capotorti, *Il diritto comunitario dal punto di vista del giudice nazionale*, in *Riv. dir. int. priv. proc.*, 1977, p. 497 f., p. 500 f. Italics added. The international origin of Community law is emphasized by Monaco, in *Manuale di diritto comunitario* by various authors, Vol. I, Turin, 1983, p. 57 f., p. 59 f.
4. Please refer to Chapter VI of this book for these aspects as well.

law over any national norm found to be in conflict with it – even if introduced at a later time or having constitutional status.

I am referring to the judgment of the ECJ of 15 July 1964, in Case 6/64, *Costa* v *Enel*, which paved the way for a protracted debate with the Italian Constitutional Court during twenty years. Only following the landmark judgment of the ECJ of 9 March 1978, in Case 106/77, *Simmenthal*, did the Italian Constitutional Court, by Judgment No 170 of 1984, accept the principle of the supremacy of Community law, although on the basis of different theoretical presuppositions, and, in its subsequent Judgment No 113 of 1985, recognized prior status also to the ECJ's interpretational decisions.[5]

Also, immediate applicability has been recognized, *in lieu* of conflicting rules of national law, to judgments issued by the ECJ at the end of *infringement procedures*.[6] The Italian Constitutional Court has further recognized the primacy of any provisions in *regulations* with a direct effect under Community case-law. According to the Italian Constitutional Court, direct applicability must be tested

5. About the principle of the supremacy of Community law over national laws generally, and a considered examination of ECJ case-law, see LUZZATTO, *La diretta applicabilità nel diritto comunitario*, Milan, 1980, esp.lly pp 51 f. and 108, in relation to the judgment of 9 March 1978, in Case 106/77, *Amministrazione Finanze v. S.p.A. Simmenthal (Simmenthal)*, in *ECR*, 1978, 629 f. See also Judgment of the Court of Justice of the European Communities of 19 June 1990, Case 213/89, *Factorame Ltd* v *Secretary of State for Transport*, in *ECR*, 1990, 2433 f. In this connection, see Judgments of the Italian Constitutional Court No 170 of 8 June 1984, in *Foro it.*, 1984, I, c. 2062 f., with commentary by TIZZANO, and No 113 of (19 April) 23 April 1985, in *Giur. cost.*,, 1985, I, p. 694. See also: CARBONE, *Il nuovo spazio giudiziario europeo. Dalla Convenzione di Bruxelles al Regolamento CE 44/2001*, Torino, 2002; TESAURO, *Diritto comunitario*, Padova, 2008, pp. 196-219. Judgment No 170/84 crowned a lengthy case-law process by laying down the principle that 'Community regulations are to be applied at all times, irrespective of whether they come before or after ordinary laws incompatible with them. The national court seized with their application can rely on references for preliminary rulings on questions of interpretation pursuant to Article 177 of the EEC Treaty'. A later decision taken by the Italian Constitutional Court in 1985 extended this principle to the *judgments* of the Court of Justice as well. That decision (Judgment No 170) stated: 'Community rules shall enter into, and remain in force in, our territory without their effects being impaired by the State's ordinary law; an this shall be the case whenever they meet the requirement of immediate applicability. As indicated above, this principle applies non only to the rules produced by EEC organs by regulations, but also to any rules resulting, as in the case at issue, from the Court of Justice's interpretative judgments'. In this regard, the Italian Supreme Court (First Chamber), stated in its Judgment No 634 of 23 January 1987: 'The national court's power and duty to disapply a rule of domestic law if its is found incompatible with Community law must be acknowledged – including in accordance with the principles laid down by the Constitutional Court in Judgments No 170 of 1984, and No 113 of 1985, both in case a conflict arises with rules produced by EEC organs by regulation and in case it is in contrast with general rules of Community law resulting from an interpretation of that law given by the Court of Justice of the European Communities in performing its institutional tasks under Article 177 of the Treaty'. Along the same lines, see Judgments of the Italian Constitutional Court No 389 of 11 July 1989, in *Foro it.*, 1991, I, c. 1076 f., and No 168 of 18 April 1991, ibid., 1992, I, c. 660 f.
6. See Judgment of the Italian Constitutional Court No 389 of 11 July 1989, *Provincia autonoma di Bolzano*, in *Foro it.*, 1991, I, 1076.

by national judges from time to time, on the basis of substantive grounds, not only on the basis of how the relevant act is formally qualified.[7]

Finally, the Italian Constitutional Court has held that, in a main proceeding as to constitutionality, the conflict of internal rules with Community rules can and must be settled by the Constitutional judges by a declaration of *unconstitutionality*.[8]

It should be noted that, in the progressive establishment of the EU, special recognition must be awarded to the ECJ for the powerful momentum it has historically provided to all sectors of Community life.

The ECJ's function has had an institutionally fundamental impact: The EU's political and legislative efforts to set up a wider internal market – and a 'single' one for the Member States' individuals and undertakings – would have been done to no avail without the guarantee of a correct implementation of the provisions of the European Treaties and of the acts deriving from them, or without the possibility afforded since the very beginning to any individual to resort to the ECJ whenever he or she perceives that his or her rights are jeopardized by any of the Community institutions' binding acts of his or her 'direct' and 'individual' concern, or when any such institution has 'failed to issue an act which is not a recommendation or an opinion addressed to him or her'.

Within the Community judicial framework, precisely in relation to the protection of individual rights, the Court of first Instance has been added, as a result of which the Court of Justice has been empowered as a court of appeal.

In this respect, the first paragraph of Article 220 EC (which superseded, with amendment, Article 164 of the Treaty of Rome) provides:[9]

> The Court of Justice and the Court of First Instance, each within its jurisdiction, shall ensure that in the interpretation and application of this Treaty the law is observed.

Thus, the ECJ has played a propelling role in more than one respect, from the original Economic Community to the present-day EU, Its judgments have led to so highly innovative solutions in Community law as to anticipate many of the changes later made to the original text of the Rome Treaty, first by the European Single Act,

---

7. See Judgments of the Italian Constitutional Court No 64 of 2 February 1990, *Referendum pesticidi*, in *Foro it.*, 1990, I, 747, and No 168 of 18 April 1991, *Industria dolciaria Giampaoli*, in *Foro it.*, 1992, I, 660.
8. It is so because, since the procedure in question is a main proceeding as to constitutionality, no judge on the merits is there to decide the relevant relationship or to rule for the disapplication of national rules. See Judgments of the Italian Constitutional Court No. 384 of 10 Nov. 1994, *Regione Umbria*, in *Foro it.*, 1994, I, 3289, and No. 94, of 31 Mar. 1995, *Regione Sicilia*, in *Foro it.*, 1995, I, 1081. About the suitability of Community rules to alter the jurisdictional relationships between the State and the Regions, see the Judgments of the Constitutional Court of 17 Apr. 1996, *Province di Trento e Bolzano*, in *Giur. it*, 1977, I, 76, and of 11 Apr. 1997, *Regione Umbria*, in *Foro it.*, 1998, I, 1382. Let me also mention the case-law approach under which the Italian Constitutional Court has restricted the admissibility of referenda for the abolition of rules related to Community commitments, See Judgments Nos 31, 41 and 45 of 7 Feb. 2000, in *Foro it.*, 2000, I, 712, 701 and 699.
9. The jurisdictional scope of the Court of First Instance is specified in Article 225 EC.

then by the Maastricht Treaty. And so, it will not come as a surprise that the ECJ's constant invaluable contribution to the solution of various problems is emphasized throughout this book – even in connection with some of its decisions I do not feel inclined to share.

The Commission, too, has played a highly professional role, through its members, from the Commissioners to the officials of its various Directorates who have been appointed over time, in building the EU, far above its qualification as a 'technical' body that seems to emerge from the Treaties. It has been so because of the ways in which it has discharged its multiple institutional functions, from its activity as a lookout watching over compliance with the Treaties and the rules deriving from them, to its general law-making efforts and its work as the protector of free competition and the body essentially responsible for managing the EU's trade policy – all of which combine to have made the Commission the driver of the Community engine. The Commission's members will certainly bear with me if some criticism is offered at some points of this volume as to the cumulation of its functions. This is essentially due to my belief that the jump in quality the EU will hopefully make requires that its institutions' powers and duties be adequately reallocated.

2. THE COMMUNITY'S MATERIAL LAW: REASONS FOR THE TITLE 'EUROPEAN ECONOMIC LAW'

Thus, there is a Community law made up of material rules that now cover most sectors of juridical life across the Continent, within the scope of the EU's expanding jurisdictional powers, in subjective and spatial terms, but also in terms of material contents, from the Treaty of Rome to the European Single Act, the Maastricht Treat, the Amsterdam Treaty and the Nice Treaty – and to the Lisbon Treaty as well, if it is ever to enter into force. Accordingly, we can now speak of, inter alia, European civil law, commercial law, industrial law, tax law and even criminal law.

Common to all areas of the law qualified with the antecendent '*Community*' or 'European' – the latter now taken as synonymous with the former, partly because of the territorial extent gradually covering the whole Continent – is the fact that they are systems set up by an international organization. Therefore, although the rules composing them are addressed, more or less directly, to subjects of internal laws, whether natural or legal persons, 'internationality' is the overriding element in each of the Community or European (or EU) laws.

This phenomenon has even wider implications, though. I am referring to that peculiar aspect of *present-day* international law so aptly emphasized by P. Ziccardi as having developed because of:

> the significance and novelty of the phenomenon of international society being organised through institutions operating at all levels and in all sectors of the States' activity.

Accordingly:

> The sphere of the States' exclusive jurisdiction is narrowing, not because of abstract proclamations, which would no longer be fit for the purpose, but because of the effective exercise by international institutions of functions in many fields formerly reserved to the States' jealous exclusivity. The formidable growth of these functions is a result of the intrinsic internationality that characterises social activity in modern times.... [10]

These words, especially in light of the incredible developments that have occurred in the international economy for the last few years, show the sharp intuition of the scholar who wrote them nearly thirty years ago, based on thoughts rooted in even more remote studies. The fact is that such words now describe the new setting of the rules of international law, most of them introduced on the basis of multilateral agreements of an unprecedented reach – in both the number of signatories and the quality of contents – within which first the States, then, albeit at a different level, the undertakings, both multinational and national, are made to recognize, and to deal with, one another.[11]

Now, the impact of internationality is also most evident in the relationships between Community law and Member States' laws: This applies not only when EU law, through primary or derivative rules, eliminates the conventional distinction between a Community foreigner and a Community citizen, thereby guaranteeing the exercise of rights to individual subjects and imposing corresponding obligations on other subjects of internal law in any one Member State's national system, but also when EU law introduces rules of uniform law replacing those of national law in the various sector of juridical commerce.[12]

These plain observations most clearly apply to the areas attributed to Community jurisdiction on an exclusive basis, and thus precluded to national law-makers. Just consider the area of monetary policy with regard to the States participating in the *Eurozone*[13] or to that of common trade policy, especially the rules on international trade, in respect of which internationality has become an absolute value. This is because the Community legislator himself is bound by other international instruments and cannot but comply with obligations undertaken under the World Trade Organization (WTO)/General Agreement on Tariffs and Trade (GATT) 1994 – a 'worldwide' organization, in fact, to which the EU as well as its Member States are parties.[14]

Yet, at a closer look, these comments have a more general reach. It should be remembered that any Community rule of derivative law – even if in the form of a

---

10. See Ziccardi, *Ordinamento giuridico (dir. intern.)*, article in *Enciclopedia del Diritto*, Vol. XXX (Milan, 1980), pp. 766 f., pp. 835 and 836. Id., *Vita giuridica internazionale* (Milan, 1992), Tome I, p. 105 f.
11. Please, refer to Chs IV and V, *passim*, of this book.
12. In this connection, see the considerations offered in Chs I and II, *passim*, of this book.
13. Please, refer to Ch. III, *passim*, of this book.
14. On this topic, see Ch. IV of this book.

directive, i.e. of an act addressed in principle to the States – must first be interpreted in light of the norm of the international instrument providing its source (the Treaty of Rome, that is, with its multiple subsequent amendments), and then by looking at the letter and purpose of the relevant Community act.

Also consider that it is now settled case-law of the ECJ – i.e. of the supranational judicial body that has *exclusive* jurisdiction over the enforcement and interpretation of EU law – that any internal law not conforming to EU law must be disapplied, and EU law applied instead, not only in the relationships between private individuals and a Member State's public authorities, but also, by growing extension in national practice, in respect of inter-subjective relationships.[15]

Further, this 'internationality' operates in such a way that the contents of a material Community law cannot closely match those which traditionally make up the corresponding national law.

It must be clear, though, that the choice of a title is never too easy, and no title can ever be as comprehensive as one would have it.

Thus, to provide immediate emphasis to the novelties introduced in this book from the contents of previous editions, and also as a token of 'good wish' at a particularly difficult time for the EU, I have substituted 'European' for 'EC' as a more fitting adjective in the title of the volume.

In addition, it seemed to me that referring to a European 'Economy' law was the most synthetic way to express contents ranging from the frame of the global economy and its international rules to the structure and vicissitudes of bodies corporate and the enterprises' activities in the present-day European economy open to the whole world and leading to ever-new situations governed by the rules contained in, or even derived from, the EC Treaty.

It seemed to me that the glue fastening together the various topics considered below, such as the right of establishment and the free provision of services by business companies, the harmonization of company laws, the free movement of capital, the regulation of international trade, multinationals' operations, and the aspects of competition law I consider most significant, is a new view of the present aspects of the life of companies and firms under international law – a 'European view', in fact. There will certainly be topics and issues other than those I have considered here, but the aspects examined and studied in this book have seemed to me to be the most challenging.

15. It is appropriate to mention that the new Article 117 of the Italian Constitution provides: *The legislative power shall be exercised by the State and by the Regions in compliance with the Constitution and of the constraints arising from Community law and from international obligations.*

Chapter I

Companies' Right of Establishment and Freedom to Provide Services: Mutual Recognition of Eligible Companies

SUMMARY:

1. The Treaty of Rome and private international law on companies.
2. The Brussels Convention of 29 February 1968 on the mutual recognition of companies and bodies corporate within the EEC.
3. General considerations about the 'recognition' of foreign companies: A historical overview.
4. The double meaning of 'recognition' as applied to companies.
5. The import of clauses in establishment treaties and friendship, commerce and navigation treaties.
6. The treatment of foreign companies within the Community: Article 12 and Articles 43 et seq., 49 et seq. and 56 et seq. EC.
7. The principle of the direct applicability of the rules of the Treaty on establishment and services.
8. The notion of companies' freedom of establishment within the European Union.
9. The scope of a company's right of establishment.
10. Private international law on companies and the establishment rules.
11. Critical remarks on the Daily Mail judgment.
12. Case-law on cross-border mergers and its impact on the transfer of seat within the European Union: Directive 2005/56/CE.
13. The above principles as applied in practice.
14. The 'national' treatment: Scope and limits under Community case-law.

15. The impact of Article 43 et seq. of the Treaty on: (a) the Italian rules of private international law in regard to companies.
16. More: (b) mandatory rules of Italian law when companies formed in other Member States set up branches in Italy.
17. More: (c) Applicability of Legislative Decree 231/2001 to 'Community' foreign companies.
18. More: (d) Mandatory rules of Italian law relating to multinational groups of companies.
19. More: (e) The rules applicable to listed companies.
20. Jurisdiction criteria relating to companies in the EC Regulation on jurisdiction and the recognition of foreign judgments.
21. EC Regulation No. 1346/2000 on insolvency proceedings.

1. THE TREATY OF ROME AND PRIVATE INTERNATIONAL LAW ON COMPANIES

It has recently been observed:[1]

> European law still does not directly affect Member States' free choice of their respective conflict rules so long as its principles are observed.

This observation is essentially correct and contains two statements, the first of which requires some qualification.

True, Community law lacks a system of private international law for general and uniform application, a matter which is left, as a whole, to the competence of each of the Member States. Yet, the implementation of certain rules set out in the original text of the Treaty of Rome which reflects the needs to complement fundamental rules of Community law, and the evolution of generally applicable principles of Community have led to significant derogations in this respect.

Under a broader, increasingly widespread interpretation of 'private international law', the Brussels Convention *on jurisdiction and the enforcement of judgments in civil and commercial matters* was signed as early as 27 September 1968. Its extensive original text, as supplemented by the Protocol of 3 June 1971, which referred it to the European Court of Justice for interpretation,[2] and as subsequently amended by the Luxembourg Convention of 9 October 1978, following the accession of the Kingdom of Denmark, the Republic of Ireland and the United Kingdom of Great Britain and Northern Ireland, as well as because of later accessions resulting in a

---

1. Thus Advocate General Ruiz-Jarabo Colomer, in his Opinion submitted on 4 Dec. 2001, Case C-208/00, *Überseering BV v. NCC Nordic Construction Company Baumanagement GmbH*, [2002] ECR I-9919, 40.
2. The consolidate version of the Brussels Convention, as updated following the accession of Austria, Finland and Sweden, is available in [1998] O.J. C27, p. 1. The Protocol of 3 Jun. 1971 entered into force for Belgium, the Federal Republic of Germany, France, Italy, Luxembourg and the Netherlands on 1 Sep. 1975.

considerable enlargement of the Community, has become so relevant over time as to hint at a new, distinct and fundamental freedom – *the free movement of judgments across the Community*. The legal basis of the Brussels convention was Article 293 EC (originally Article 220 of the Treaty of Rome).

More recently, the matter already covered by the Brussels Convention of 1968 has been made the object of Regulation (EC) No 44/2001 of the Council of 22 December 2000,[3] which has reproduced the text of the Brussels Convention with amendments, especially with a view to adjust it to the ECJ's substantial case-law that had built up about the most consequential issues, and in furtherance of Article 65 EC, as newly introduced under Article 73 M of the Amsterdam Treaty, which requires:[4]

> Measures in the field of judicial co-operation in civil matters having cross-border implications, to be taken in accordance with Article 67 and insofar as necessary for the proper functioning of the internal market, shall include:
>
> (a) improving and simplifying:
> – the system for cross-border service of judicial and extrajudicial documents;
> – co-operation in the taking of evidence;
> – the recognition and enforcement of decisions in civil and commercial cases, including decisions in extra-judicial cases;
>
> (b) promoting the compatibility of the rules applicable in the Member States concerning the conflict of laws and of jurisdiction;
>
> (c) eliminating obstacles to the good functioning of civil proceedings, if necessary *by promoting the compatibility* of the rules on civil procedure applicable in the Member States. [*Emphasis added*].

Yet other regulatory instruments were adopted on the matter under Article 65 EC: Regulation (EC) No 1436/2000 of 29 May 2000 on insolvency proceedings;[5] Council Regulation (EC) No 2201/2003 of 27 November 2003 concerning jurisdiction and the recognition and enforcement of judgments in matrimonial matters and the matters of parental responsibility;[6] Council Regulation (EC) No 1348/2000 of 29 May 2000 on the service in the Member States of judicial and extrajudicial documents in civil or commercial matters;[7] and, lastly, Council Regulation (EC)

---

3. [2001] O.J. L12, p. 1.
4. About this provision, see, in general: Kohler, 'Interrogations sur les sources du droit international privé européen' [1999] Revue critique dr. int. privé, p. 1; Carbone, *Il nuovo spazio giudiziario europeo* (4th edn, Turin, 2002); Carbone, Frigo, Fumagalli, *Diritto processuale civile e commerciale comunitario* (Milan, 2004); Baratta, 'Art. 65 CE', in *Trattati dell'Unione Europea e della Comunità europea*, ed. Tizzano (Milan, 2004), p. 452; Leroyer, Jeuland, *Quelle coherence pour l'espace judiciaire européen?* (Paris, 2004), and Isaac, Blanquet, *Droit général de l'Union européenne* (Paris, 2006), p. 461.
5. [2000] O.J. L160, p. 1.
6. [2003] O.J. L338, p. 1. This Regulation superseded Regulation (EC) No. 1347/2000.
7. [2000] O.J. L160, p. 1.

No 1206/2001 of 28 May 2001 on cooperation between the courts of the Member States in the taking of evidence in civil or commercial matters.[8]

Furthermore, private contractual law found a uniform solution for universal application in the Convention on the law applicable to contractual obligations signed in Rome on 19 June 1980 among the contracting parties to the Treaty establishing the European Economic Community, and now in force in every Member State of the enlarged Community.[9] In the Preamble of the 1980 Convention, the contracting parties, aware of the lack of an appropriate legal basis in the Treaty, represented they were:

> anxious to continue, *in the field of private international law*, the work of unification of law which has already been done within the Community, in particular in the field of jurisdiction and enforcement of judgments. [*Emphasis added*].

Again in the context of the expansion of Community law also in relation to private international law, mention should be made of Regulation (EC) No 864/2007 of the European Parliament and of the Council of 11 July 2007 on the law applicable to non-contractual obligations (Rome II).[10] This Regulation specifies that the law applicable to a non-contractual obligation arising out of a tort/delict shall be the law of the country in which the damage occurs irrespective of the country in which the event giving rise to the damage occurred and irrespective of the country or countries in which the indirect consequences of that event occur (Article 4).

However, Regulation No. 864/2007 requires that, where the person claimed to be liable and the person sustaining damage both have their habitual residence in the same country at the time when the damage occurs, the law of that country shall apply.

Regulation No. 864/2007 will enter into force on 11 January 2009.

With respect to companies, firms and other legal persons, the need or, at least, the wish to introduce uniform conflict rules in this area had already surfaced in the original version of the Treaty of Rome, specifically in Article 220 – which has remained unchanged in contents, though re-numbered as Article 293 in the Treaty,

---

8. [2001] O.J. L174, p. 1. The following Regulations have their legal basis in Articles 61(c) and 67(5), second indent, *both expressly referring to Article 65* EC: (i) No. 805/2004 of the European Parliament and of the Council of 21 Apr. 2004, creating a European Enforcement Order for uncontested claims [2004] O.J. L143, p. 15; (ii) No. 1896/2006 of the European Parliament and of the Council of 12 Dec. 2006, creating a European order for payment procedure [2006] O.J. L399, p. 1; and (iii) No. 861/2007 of the European Parliament and of the Council of 11 Jul. 2007, establishing a European Small Claims Procedure [2007] O.J. L199, p. 1.
9. See [2005] O.J. L334, p. 1 (consolidated version), under Title I, with regard to the scope of application of the Convention, Article 1(2)(e) exclude the application, with a broad formulation, of the Convention to issues concerning companies, association and other legal persons. Proceedings are underway within the European Union to change this Convention into a 'Regulation'. In this connection, see the Draft Regulation of the European Parliament and of the Council relating to the law applicable to contractual obligations (Rome I), as submitted by the Commission on 15 Dec. 2005 (COM (2005) 650, final).
10. See [2007] O.J. L199, p. 405.

thus providing the legal basis for the Brussels Convention of 27 September 1968 – where it is stated, at the third indent:

> Member States shall, *so far as is necessary*, enter into negotiations with each other with a view to securing for the benefit of their nationals:
>
> – (. . .)
> – (. . .)
> – *the mutual recognition* of companies or firms within the meaning of the second paragraph of Article 58 [now 48], the *retention of legal personality* in the event of *transfer of their seat* from one country to another, and the possibility of *mergers* between companies or firms *governed by the laws of different countries*. [*Emphasis added*].

The explicit reference to Article 48(2) EC – one that has also remained unchanged in its whole, though re-numbered from the original Article 58 – which, in the first paragraph, restricts the subjective and spatial scope for application of the provisions governing freedom of establishment and the free provision of services, and, in the second paragraph, defines the 'companies or firms' and 'other legal persons' indicated as the beneficiaries of such fundamental freedoms, confirms the relevance given since the very beginning to a uniform solution of the main problems of private international company law, ultimately with a view to allow companies, firms and other legal persons within the meaning of Article 48(2) EC governed by the laws of one Member State, so long as at least one of the contact factors specified in the first paragraph of the same article occurs, to benefit from freedom of establishment and the free provision of services (because of the reference made to Article 48 in Article 55 of the Treaty), thereby ensuring fully equal treatment of legal with natural persons national of a Member State as prescribed by Article 48(1) EC itself.

The explicit indication in Article 293 EC of the objectives of 'mutual recognition of companies', 'retention of legal personality' in case a company's seat is transferred from one country to another, and the validity of mergers between 'companies or firms governed by the laws of different countries', seems to suggest that the Treaty was intended, through these provisions, 'so far as is necessary', to overcome any conflicts between the laws of different Member States as might hinder the full, effective enjoyment by a Member State's *national companies*[11] of the freedom of establishment and/or the freedom to provide services.

It must be acknowledged that the compilers of the Treaty had clearly identified the *recognition* of companies, the *transfer by a company of its seat* from one State to another within the Community without *being wound up*, and the very possibility

11. The adjective 'national' and the noun 'nationality', as referred to companies or other entities here and further below in this Chapter 1, are used in a figurative sense to mean companies or other entities governed by another country's national law, thus being *nationals* of such other country, in the same way as when reference is made to a *national* inheritance or a *national* marriage, or even to a *national* judgment in its being delivered by the courts of a given country.

to enter into *international* mergers as the problems to solve which international conventions between Member States were to be used expressly with a view to overcoming them by introducing common rules of appropriate private international law to ensure uniform solutions.

This need seems to be borne out by a sentence in the European Court of Justice judgment of 27 September 1988 in *Daily Mail*, where it is stated:[12]

> It must therefore be held that the Treaty regards the *differences* in national legislation *concerning the required connecting factor* and the question whether – and if so how – *the registered office or real head office* of a company incorporated under national law *may be transferred* from one Member State to another *as problems which are not resolved by the rules concerning the right of establishment* but must be dealt with by *future legislation or conventions*. [*Emphasis added*].

The way the provision in Article 293 of the Treaty is worded would seem to hint that – to the extent actually necessary, i.e. if and insofar as any of the objectives indicated therein has not been attained or is not attainable otherwise through other provisions in the Treaty, legislative acts based thereon or the Court of Justice's judgments for interpretation of primary or secondary rules of Community law, or else through other international conventions between Member States (as is the case, in relation to the last indent of Article 293 EC, with *international arbitration* under the New York Convention of 10 June 1958 on the recognition and enforcement of foreign arbitral awards, or the European Convention on international commercial arbitration done at Geneva on 21 April 1961),[13] or when any such objective has not been accomplished through any of the national laws of each of the Community's Member States – the Member States' commitment may not be construed as just an *option* to enter into negotiations with each other, but in the stricter sense of an actual *obligation to contract*, thereby attaining, through the residual tool of *ad-hoc* international conventions between Member States, the results Article 293 EC expressly states to be necessary to secure the benefits essential for the Community's life to all nationals within the European Union.[14]

Let me stress again that, with respect to conventions now nearing completion or even appearing in agreed texts already executed by the (original) Member States following appropriate negotiations, all problems about the need to establish conventional rules on any one specific issue referred to in Article 293 EC seem to have been finally solved. In other words, it would be logical to assume, in each such case, that the phrase 'so far as is necessary' in Article 293 has already been positively assessed both by the Council of the Member States and by the European Commission.

---

12. See ground 23 of the judgment in Case 81/87, *Daily Mail* [1988] ECR 5483. In a similar sense, see also Advocate General Ruiz-Jarabo Colomer's Opinion in *Überseering BV*, cit., point 40.
13. Both Convention have a general scope. Both are also addressed to countries outside the EU's was signed and ratified by all six original EC Member States and made enforceable in such borders. The former Member States' internal legal systems.
14. This was my contention in previous editions of this book.

Yet, the Court of Justice, in examining the issue from an entirely different perspective in its *Überseering* judgment, referred to the observations put forward by Advocate General Ruiz-Jarabo Colomer[15] in that case to exclude that Article 293 EC is of a 'preceptive' nature, and so it found that the relevant provision *merely gives Member States the opportunity* to enter into negotiations solely '*so far as necessary, that is to say if the provisions of the Treaty do not enable its objectives to be attained*'.[16] In the Advocate General's strong words:

> Unlike Article 295 EC ([t]he Treaty shall not prejudice in any way . . .) which, without the slightest doubt, excludes from application of the EC Treaty the rules governing the system of property ownership, *Article 293 EC contains only an invitation* to Member States to enter into negotiations and, what is more, '*only so far as is necessary*'. Article 293 EC *is not* therefore comparable to *a true exclusion from the legislation* and is rather *an admonition* to Member States to overcome the inevitable problems which will arise from the disparity of legislation on the mutual recognition of companies, on the retention of their legal capacity in the event of cross-border transfers of their head office and on mergers. *Being thus an admonition it cannot*, as such, *hinder the effectiveness of one of the fundamental freedoms*. [*Emphasis added*].

If the provision in question conveys a mere 'invitation' or an 'admonition' at most, without entitling individual Member States to exclude the matters set out in Article 293 EC from Community solutions, then it may not be deemed to require the Member States to perform an obligation in this respect under the Treaty.

Further, under international law, a bilateral or multilateral treaty only enters into effect if and when the contracting parties have exchanged or filed their ratification instruments in the number and manners specified in the treaty itself. Accordingly, where unanimous adoption is required, as in the cases provided for by Article 293 EC, just one Member State's failure to comply is enough to prevent that treaty from taking effect.

On this basis, the use of international conventions is viewed by the Commission to be a means beyond control and considered, as such, less effective than a Community 'act' in settling issues of Community law. Hence, the recent tendency to avoid conventions or even to replace individual international conventions already in force pursuant to Article 293, or otherwise originated from within the Community, with that Community act by excellence, the 'regulation' or, in some cases, the other generally applicable act, the 'directive'. The former approach was taken by the Council though Regulation (EC) No 44/2001 of 22 December 2000, as amended (Brussels I), concerning jurisdiction and the recognition and enforcement of judgments in civil and commercial matters,[17] departing from both the Brussels

15. See Ruiz-Jarabo Colomer's Opinion, cit., point 42.
16. See *Überseering BV* Judgment, cit., ground 40.
17. Published in [2001] O.J. L12, p. 1. Corrigendum in [2001] O.J. L307, p. 28. Amended by Commission Regulation (EC) No. 1496/2002 of 21 Aug. 2002 ([2002] O.J. L225, p. 13, by the Act concerning the conditions of accession of the Czech Republic, the Republic of Estonia,

Convention of 27 September 1968 in the same matters, as amended, and the related Protocol.[18] It should also be noted that work is underway in preparation for the issuance of a Regulation intended to supersede the Rome Convention of 1980 on the law applicable to contractual obligations.

Likewise, the Draft Convention on international mergers (or, rather, 'cross-border' mergers in the case of mergers between companies constituted in different Member States of the European Union) was long laboured through on the same legal basis (Article 293 EC) and then submitted, with its accompanying report, to the Member States as early as Autumn 1973. Yet, it was subsequently withdrawn by the Commission precisely because of doubts and misgivings arising among its members about the use of conventions under Article 293 of the Treaty. Thereupon, the Commission again put forward the issue of mergers between companies subject to Member States' different laws in the form of a *draft tenth directive* in company matters, pursuant to Article 44(2)(g) of the Treaty, which was submitted to the Council on 8 January 1985.[19] In 2003, the Commission submitted yet another draft directive on cross-border mergers, which ultimately found its way into Directive No 2005/56/EC of 26 October 2005, as adopted by the European Parliament and Council.[20]

It does not come as a surprise in this context that, though the Brussels Convention on the recognition of companies and other legal persons had been signed by

---

the Republic of Cyprus, the Republic of Latvia, the Republic of Lithuania, the Republic of Hungary, the Republic of Malta, the Republic of Poland, the Republic of Slovenia and the Slovak Republic and the adjustments to the Treaties on which the European Union is founded ([2003] O.J. L236, p. 33), by Commission Regulation (EC) No. 1937/2004 of 9 Nov. 2004 ([2004] O.J. L334, p. 3), and by Commission Regulation (EC) No. 2245/2004 of 27 Dec. 2004 ([2004] O.J. L381, p. 10).

18. At the time of the entry into force of the Regulation, jurisdiction between Denmark and the other Member States was still governed by the Brussels Convention of 27 Sep. 1968. This exception is provided for by Protocol No. 5 on Denmark's position in 1997 ([1997] O.J. C340) annexed to the treaties establishing the European Communities and to the treaty on the European Union. On 19 Oct. 2005, the Community signed an agreement with Denmark, extending the provisions of the Regulation to the Kingdom of Denmark ([2005] O.J. L299, p. 61; see Council Decision of 20 Sep. 2005, to which the agreement is annexed). The Agreement between the European Community and the Kingdom of Denmark on jurisdiction and the recognition and enforcement of judgments in civil and commercial matters was approved by a Council Decision of 27 Apr. 2006 ([2006] O.J. L120, p. 22) and entered into force on 1 Jul. 2007.
19. COM (84) 727, final. Please, refer to para. 2 of Chapter II of this book. The proposal was scrutinized by several committees of the European Parliament, including the Committee on Legal Affairs, which approved the report on the merits on 21 Oct. 1987. However, the Parliament refrained from giving an opinion, lest the undertakings should take advantage of cross-border mergers to evade their obligations under the rules on employees' participation that were then in force in some Member States. The standstill had to do with the proposed Statute for a European Company and lasted more than fifteen years. In 2001, faced with the prospect of outright withdrawal of the proposals that had been underway for several years or become useless, the Commission withdrew its own original proposal for a tenth directive on company law.
20. [2005] O.J. L310, p. 1. For a detailed discussion of this directive, see para. 15 of this chapter and para. 2 of Chapter II.

all the original six Member States, it has never entered into force, not even among those States,[21] since the Netherlands had failed to file the instrument of ratification required to be deposited pursuant to Article 13 of the Convention.[22]

Not even a study has been initiated so far for the drafting of a convention concerning the '*the retention of legal personality* in the event of *transfer of a company's seat* from one country to another' within the Community, much as a uniform solution of the matter had already been postulated, as indicated above, at the third indent of Article 293 of the Treaty.[23]

2. THE BRUSSELS CONVENTION OF 29 FEBRUARY 1968 ON THE MUTUAL RECOGNITION OF COMPANIES AND BODIES CORPORATE WITHIN THE EEC

In effect, on 29 February 1968, following negotiations started in June 1962 pursuant to Article 220 as then numbered in the Rome Treaty, the plenipotentiaries of the Community's Member States had signed, in Brussels, a Convention on the mutual recognition of companies and bodies corporate.[24] On that same day, in Luxembourg, the same Contracting States had signed a Protocol which referred the Convention to the Court of Justice of the European Communities for interpretation.[25]

As just mentioned above, neither that Brussels Convention nor the Protocol annexed to it ever came into effect. Today, forty years or so from the signature of the Convention, that text must be considered finally abandoned,[26] much as it had extensively been debated in doctrine.[27]

Nevertheless, to get a better grasp of the significance and extent of the Court of Justice's recent case law on major issues of private international law on companies, with a view to the proper observance of the fundamental principles of Community law, I believe it appropriate to provide an overview of the solutions that Convention had incorporated.

---

21. This goes a long way to explain why, notwithstanding the commitment stated in Article 3(2) of the Treaty of Accession of the United Kingdom, the Kingdom of Denmark and the Irish Republic of 22 Jan. 1972, no negotiations for the accession of these States to the Convention on the mutual recognition of companies and other legal persons have been started yet.
22. Accordingly, the limit period set out in Article 14 for its entry into force on the 'first day of the third month following the deposit of the instrument of ratification by the last signatory State to take this step', has not even begun to run.
23. About this issue, a draft harmonization directive has been pressed for. Please, refer to the public consultation promoted by the Commission in Feb. 2004 (See Press Release IP/04/270 of 26 Feb. 2004).
24. The Italian internal law for accession to the Convention is Act No. 220 of 28 Jan. 1971, in [1971] Italian O.J. L113.
25. In *Bull. Suppl.* No. 2-1969, p. 15.
26. See my study: 'Problemi interpretativi della Convenzione CEE sul reciproco riconoscimento delle società e persone giuridiche', in *Comunicazioni e Studi* (vol. XIII, 1969), p. 291 ff.
27. Not all hopes had been forsaken in the second edition of my book, *Diritto Commerciale Comunitario* (Milan, 1995), p. 63 ff.

It should preliminarily be noted that, in a quick overall assessment made soon after the final text had been signed, the results attained by the Convention seemed to me to be satisfactory in substance,[28] in spite of the many uncertainties and inaccuracies that made it something less than a model editorial product. True, not always did the wording of its various articles make simple or easily intelligible reading for the interpreter. But the effort to put in place an actual system of private international law concerning companies and legal persons generally could certainly be considered in positive terms in itself. That system appeared to be based on criteria uniformly applied across the Community,[29] alongside such provisions for the treatment of foreign companies and firms in the Community, which appeared to have a far richer content and wider reach than the existing rules of the Treaty of Rome on free establishment and the free provision of services then being implemented to just a limited extent.

The subjective and spatial scope for application of the Convention was essentially the same as Article 58 (now Article 48) of the Treaty,[30] and Articles 4, 6, 9 and 10 of the Convention provided rules of private international law.

In requiring that all companies or bodies corporate recognized under the Convention should have the capacity accorded to them by the law under which they were incorporated, Article 6 introduced an actual rule of private international law, which was based on the connecting factor of the place of incorporation and dealt with business companies' very existence and functioning. For it was my view that the term 'capacity' in Article 6 is related not only to companies' general capacity, but to their capacity to act as well, i.e. to all aspects of their functioning as well as their organization.[31]

---

28. Please, refer to my article: 'Problemi interpretativi della Convenzione CEE sul reciproco riconoscimento', cit., p. 315 ff., and to my book: *Le società nel diritto internazionale privato* (2nd edn, Milan, 1973), pp. 197 ff., 222 ff.
29. See my article: 'Problemi interpretativi', cit., p. 307 ff., and my book, *Le società*, cit., p. 211 ff.
30. In fact, while Article 2 of the Convention essentially followed the definition contained in Article 58(2) of the Rome Treaty, where only the phrase 'non-wage-earning' had been replaced by 'in fact continuously exercise' 'an economic activity normally exercised for reward', Article 1 of the Convention departed from the wording of the first paragraph of Article 1 of the Treaty establishing the EEC in respect of the requirement of a link with the Community as a whole, which was only identified as the 'statutory registered office in the territories to which this Convention applies'. As I observed in my article 'Problemi interpretativi', cit., in *Comunicazioni e Studi* (1969) since, as a rule, a statutory registered office is initially located in the State of incorporation, the essential effect of both provisions was equivalent, Article 3 provided for a convenient qualification to allow any Contracting State to declare that it would 'not apply the present Convention to any companies or bodies corporate ... which have their real registered office outside the territories to which this Convention applies, if such companies or bodies corporate have *no genuine link* with the economy of one of said territorie'. In substance, as I observed in 'Problemi interpretativi', cit., in *Comunicazioni e Studi* (1969) this wording was equivalent to the *effective continuous link* required, for various purposes, by the two General Programmes for the for the removal of restrictions on freedom of establishment.
31. See Santa Maria, *Le società nel diritto internazionale privato*, cit., p. 212 f.

An exception to the *general rule* set out in Article 6 was, however, provided by Article 4, where it was stated that, any companies or bodies corporate, though validly incorporated in accordance with the law of another Contracting State, could also be subjected by the State of their real registered offices to the provisions of its own substantive legislation. A distinction was made, in this respect, between *essential* provisions (not allowing for derogation) and *suppletory* provisions (allowing for derogation). The Convention considered a company's real seat or real registered office to be 'the place in which its central administration is established' (Article 5).

The provision set out in Article 4 was not directly applicable in itself. It would only come into operation subject to a specific qualification mechanism similar to that provided for by Article 3, which was intended to restrict the scope for application of the Convention, whereby each Contracting State could make a declaration in the terms prescribed by the first paragraph of Article 15. Each of Belgium, France, Italy and Germany had made such a declaration. As was the case with the qualifying declaration provided for in Article 3, the declaration making Article 4 applicable could be withdrawn at any time, and such withdrawal should be deemed to be final (Article 15, second paragraph).

The combined effect of the place of incorporation as a general rule and the place of central administration as a just potential exception, was such that, from the standpoint of the legal system of incorporation, but also from the opposite standpoint of a Member State in which the company so established had not also set up its central administration – whether or not such State had made the relevant declaration – the governing law for such company would *only* be deemed to be the law of the place of incorporation.

However, as this conclusion was clearly a compromise between the advocates of the real seat criterion and the advocates of the incorporation criterion, it was not enough to prevent the conflict possibly arising from that company being required to observe the contrasting essential provisions of the material laws of two different jurisdictions, the place of incorporation and the place of central administration – the latter criterion in its being applicable as a result of a declaration made as discussed above. Such a conflict was made harsher by the consequences of any breach of law or of the company's own memorandum of association as might jeopardize the company's very existence in either competent legal system, thereby necessarily generating effects in yet another system as well. And this was the most serious weakness of the Convention.[32]

Lastly, Articles 9 and 10, as poorly worded as they were, required that 'contravening' a Contracting State's public policy was sufficient cause to prevent the recognition in that State of the existence or even just the functioning of a company incorporated in another Contracting State. In this respect, most telling was the phrase in the second paragraph of Article 9, which excluded that conflict with public policy could be invoked in relation to the recognition of 'single member or shareholder'.[33]

32. See Santa Maria, 'Problemi interpretativi', cit., p. 318 ff.
33. Id., 'Problemi interpretativi', cit., p. 316, body and footnote 40.

In conclusion, notwithstanding the criticisms offered above, the failure to put into effect the Brussels Convention of 29 February 1968 undoubtedly had an adverse impact for years on the full implementation of the rules of the Treaty on the fundamental freedoms, particularly the freedom of establishment and the free provision of services with regard to companies and legal persons generally – much as full implementation had been postulated by the Court of Justice since the end of the transitional period and subsequently imposed by the Single European Act.

The resulting legislative gap has only recently been filled – following a first negative judgment in *Daily Mail* – by the Court of Justice's far-reaching case-law, which, at least in some respects, as discussed further below, has gone quite beyond the results that could have been attained by the text of the Convention I have briefly outlined above if the convention had ever entered into force.

3. GENERAL CONSIDERATIONS ABOUT THE 'RECOGNITION' OF FOREIGN COMPANIES: A HISTORICAL OVERVIEW

Today, no matter what legal system is considered, the rules of private international law relating to companies and other legal persons are based on an express or even silent principle of mutual recognition.

In a judgment of 1963, precisely because this principle is generally accepted in modern legislations, the Tribunal of Rome took the view[34] that the recognition of the existence of foreign companies was founded on a generally applied principle of international law, which, as such, had even been incorporated automatically into the Italian legal system pursuant to Article 10 of the Italian Constitution.[35]

Whether such view was or was not correct, the very presence of private international law provisions in every State's legal system and the functions assigned to the related instrumental conflict rules – which are intended both to restrict the application of internal substantive provisions of law and, because of the presence of extraneous elements, to have the relevant legal system recognize requirements typical of foreign systems' *substantive* laws – show that the resulting complex structure is at work alongside elements of 'internationality'. This is because the 'extrovert' or renvoi function typical of any domestic system of

34. Judgment of 2 May 1963, in Case *Fragiacomo c. Società Zauberberg*, [1964] Giust. civ. I, p. 698 f., p. 701.

35. Abrahams, *Les sociétés en droit international privé, recherche du principe d'extraterritorialité* (Paris-Liège, 1957), p. 169 f., equally holds the view that the extraterritoriality principle in the Belgian system is based on a generally accepted international law principle. An entirely different view is taken by: Sereni, 'La cittadinanza degli enti morali nel diritto internazionale' [1934] Riv. dir. int., pp. 171 f., 437 f., p. 456 f., and Grossfeld, 'Die Anerkennung der Rechstfahigkeit juristischer Personen' [1967] Rabels Zeitschrift fir ausländisches und internationales Privatrecht, p. 1 f., p. 7 f.

conflict rules can be explained as a result of the recognition by each State of the other States' international subjectivity, then as a result of each State's awareness of the existence, beside its own national legal system, of other States' internal bodies of substantive laws different from its own, which it has to reckon with, subject to mutual observance of sovereignty, in taking the most appropriate legal view in connection with the specific case at hand.

The extraterritorial recognition of bodies corporate as a generally accepted principle, whether it has or has not arisen as a matter of customary law, is a comparatively new achievement in the domain of law.

The question whether or not to recognize a foreign company in a country other than a its home country first surfaced in the continental Europe in mid 1800s,when international trade were beginning to scale up and private capital to be allocated to commercial activities also in relation to the operation of public utilities that were vital at that time, such as water and gas lighting supplies or the management of the earliest railways.

In those days, the greatest difficulties arose from the impact of the more general issue of the nature and scope of 'legal person'. In relation to the very approach to it and because of its potentially strong impact on contrasting solutions, the issue of the recognition of foreign entities was increasingly raised whenever the exercise of commercial rights by corporate foreigners was argued for or against before French and Belgian tribunals or higher courts. In fact, it came into play within the context of the involved, long-debated theoretical problem of the nature of legal persons as legal entities parallel with, though distinct from, natural persons.[36] In other words, the recognition of a foreign corporate person was then favourably or adversely decided upon depending on whether the *fiction* or the *reality* of a legal person was the approach of choice. Only in the view of the advocates of the latter approach – depending on an assumed parallelism of *personae morale* with physical, natural beings – was the applicability of the extraterritoriality principle generally believed applicable to the latter extended to the former. In the eyes of the supporters of the fiction approach, a body corporate could only exist in the system that had created it. Hence, the non-existence of foreign entities outside their domestic domain implied that they were not deemed to be 'capable' to operate in any respect in any legal system other than the system of their incorporation.[37]

36. For a wide historical overview of this topic, please refer to the first chapter of my book *Le società nel diritto internazionale privato* (2nd edn, Milan, 1973), p. 11 ff.

37. Santa Maria, *Le società*, cit., p. 14 ff.; many references to the legal literature of that time are contained in footnote 7, p. 15 f. In addition, for an historic view of the same issue related to the English legal system, than adopted by American law, see Blumberg, *The Multinational Challenge to Corporation Law, The Search for a New Corporate Personality* (New York-Oxford, 1993), p. 3 ff. 'With the Revolution, the nascent American legal system adopted the English law of corporations without change' (Id., p. 7). Blumberg underlines that, whilst the recognition of a corporation like a 'legal unit', with its own rights and responsibilities separate from those of its shareholders, 'become firmly established in England countries before the emergence of limited liability' (Id., cit., p. 14 f.), finally the Limited Liability Act of 1855

Indeed, in its decision, taken in 1839, in the case *Bank of Augusta* v. *Earle*,[38] Chief Justice Taney stated:

> . . . that a corporation can have no legal existence out of the boundaries of the sovereignty by which it is created.
>
> it exists only in contemplation of law, and by force of the law, and where that law ceases to operate, and is no longer obligatory, the corporation can have no existence.[39]

Let me specify that, at that time, the entire issue only concerned companies-as-*persons*, in their being autonomous legal entities.[40] The system did not, however, include 'non-person' businesses or – to use a later term – 'companies of (natural) persons', such as those known as *società in nome collettivo* (collective companies) and *società in accomandita semplice* (commandite partnerships simple, roughly equivalent to general partnerships in Britain) under the laws first of Piedmont, then of unified Italy. At that point in time, the lack of personhood of companies of this type prevented any related issues of private international law from arising and developing along the same lines as in respect of other forms of corporate persons. In other words, the question of whether to recognize or not to recognize did not arise for 'non-person' companies, which were recognizable outright. For the rules of private international law relating to companies 'of persons', i.e. entities without legal personhood, originated from that essentially different source, *lex contractus*.[41]

At that time, at least in continental Europe's system of law, corporate persons, as well as foundations and associations, were generally chartered 'by concession' in most jurisdictions, i.e. by virtue of an express authorization issued by government on a case-by-case basis. Such authorization was issued at the end of an involved administrative procedure, which was an eminently discretional process, in that it consisted of not only an investigation as to legitimacy, but also of a

---

and the Joint Stock Companies Act of 1856, adopting general limited liability principle, 'ended the debate once and for all' (Id., cit., p. 17). Accordingly, at the start of the 1800, limited liability was not a leading issue in the United States law. On the first American case-law of this subject, see Blumberg, cit., p. 11.

38. V. in *Peter's U.S. Supreme Court Reports*, [1839], XIII, 519.
39. On this case which can likely be considered the first one on the subject matter seemed not to have had influence on the case law before the Belgian and French courts of ten years later, see: Young, 'The Legal Personality of Foreign Corporations' [1906] LQR 178, at 181; Badr, *Alien Corporation in Conflict of laws, a Study of Comparative Law* (Cairo, 1953), p. 65.
40. Id., *Le società*, cit., p. 60 f.
41. Id., *Le società*, cit., p. 61. The private international law norm on companies now includes companies of all and any types, following the removal of the territorial limits formerly set to the notion of legal person and through the extension of the phrase intended to get closer to a concept of 'subjectivity' as synonymous with 'autonomy', which is also a quality of unlimited companies and partnerships. In Italian positive law, a private international law norm including any type of companies can ultimately be inferred from Articles 230 to 232 of the 1882 Code of Commerce. For the inapplicability of Articles 6 and 3, preliminary provisions, of the 1865 Civil Code, see Santa Maria, *Le società*, cit., p. 61 ff. Please, also refer to the considerations offered below, especially in paragraph 11 of this Chapter 1.

judgment as to the 'convenience and opportuneness of the new entity'. The purport of the authorization and *ex-nunc* recognition in the State of creation was twofold. For it was both a necessary requirement for the entity concerned to be considered as an 'entity' (person) in its relationships with other persons in the relevant legal system, and an indispensable condition for its operations to be deemed relevant to the State's legal system, so that an entity so authorized could benefit from judicial protection in such legal system. Thus, the authorization system with its prerogatives made the automatic recognition of a foreign company even more problematic in a different system.[42]

Quite beyond the theoretical arguments put forward by the scholars of those days, the general trend against the recognition of foreign companies was rooted more deeply in considerations of economic policy than in a congenital bias against foreign laws. While it was feared by most lest foreign economic penetration into the State should result in the formation of centres of power so strong as to escape the central authority's control or even impinge upon the political life of the country of establishment, it was also feared that referring to the substantive laws of the company's home-country to govern its existence, structure and functioning might result in inadequate guarantees for the protection of the interests of any nationals entering into business relationships with that foreign company.[43]

Conversely, the belief that the development of trade and foreign investments across an increasingly wide area would bring significant benefits to the national economy supported the case for the recognition in one country of companies formed in another country, though subject to appropriate guarantees.[44]

In the war between Belgian and French courts – often waged by one country withholding recognition of the other country's national corporate persons, the closing argument against the recognition of foreign countries that Mr Leclercq, General Prosecutor at the Belgian Court of Cassation, had delivered in *Société La France* v *Tongre-Hambursin*[45] sent huge waves into other countries as well, much

42. Santa Maria, *Le società*, cit., p. 29 ff. See also *ibid.*, p. 58, footnote 120, showing that the English system provided an exception, since it, even then, at mid nineteenth century, by no means made the formation of commercial companies subject to government clearance in the sense of a discretional, distinctly political act. On this subject, see Blumberg, *The Multinational Challenge*, cit., p. 3ff.
43. The judgment of the Civil District Court of Naples of 20 Sep. 1871, in *Municipio di Napoli* v. *Società d'Assicurazioni Generali di Venezia*, [1971-1972] Gazz. del proc., p. 488 ff. and p. 489, refers to the dangers of foreign companies' 'overpower' and of their 'eventual sudden disappearance'. In Mancini's Report on the *Progetto*, the problem was viewed in yet another respect. 'What is useful for one Nation could be not so useful for another, and it could even be harmful and incompatible with the latter's public law; it should then be for each country's law-makers to decide whether or not its is appropriate to recognize the existence of bodies corporate created in other States, thereby allowing them to exercise their rights [in that country]'.
44. In this sense, see von Bar, *Theorie und Praxis des internationales Privatrechts* (vol. I, Hannover, 1889), p. 300 f., and Italian translation by Buzzati (Turin, 1915), p. 306 ff.
45. The plaintiff was a French company which had applied to the Belgian district court of Namour seeking settlement of certain claims it had on the defendant, its agent in Belgium. By a decision

as the Court had held a different view and reformed a judgment formerly rendered by the Tribunal of Namur, thereby granting recognition to the French company in Belgium.

Closely following Savigny's thought,[46] Leclercq had emphasized the *fictious* nature of 'civil', 'moral' or 'legal' persons, as opposed to natural persons, in the different but equivalent phrases used at the time, to point out that a legal person was also distinguished from a natural person in the way it came into existence:

> [I]t is created by law and, as such, it can only exist in the territory where the original law is in force.

In his opinion:[47]

> Tout concours donc pour fixer les limites du principe de la personnalité fictive, et par conséquent le titre d'existence de cette personnalité; ce principe, la *fiction*, dont elle dérive et hors de la quelle elle n'est pas, n'a de vie, soit qu'on la considère dans *son origine*, soit qu'on la considère dans *son sujet*, soit qu'on la considère dan *son but*, c'est-à-dire dans tout ce qui peut lui donner l'être, que *là où la loi l'autorise*, la loi de chaque pays est donc aussi *dans ce pays mais pas plus loin que ne s'étendent ses frontières*, le titre d'existence d'une personne civile: *au-delà, cette personne n'est point si elle ne s'est fait reconnaître par la loi qu'elle y rencontre*; en d'autres termes, *si elle ne s'est conformée aux prescriptions, dont cette loi fait dépendre la formation d'une personne civile*; vis-à-vis de cette loi, et en dehors de ses prescriptions, il n'y a que des personnes réelles et responsables agissant à ce titre et sous leurs responsabilité, et dont les actes n'ont d'effet qu'à ce titre aussi, et dans les limites qu'ils comportent, on ne peut y avoir d'actes d'une personne fictive qui n'existe pas. [*Emphasis added*].

The fact that no entity could exist outside the national jurisdiction in which it was created – reasoned Leclercq in his conclusions – implied that it might have legal life in another State *only if it were created afresh* pursuant to the laws in force in such other State (if, in the specific case, the French company had newly been granted the Royal charter pursuant Article 37 of the *Code de Commerce Belge*.

Yet other contrasting judgments were handed down by Belgian and French courts, until the conflict that threatened to upset the commercial relationships between the two countries was satisfactorily resolved by statutes the legislatures of both countries passed – following a declaration made by the Belgian government and annexed to the Treaty of Commerce concluded between France and Belgium

---

of 10 Jun. 1846, the Namour court had dismissed the case, on the ground that, since the French company was not authorized by the Belgian authority pursuant to Article 37 of the Code of Commerce, was to be deemed non-existing in Belgium, and did not, accordingly, have standing before Belgian courts. For the latter holding, see Santa Maria, *Le società*, n. 11.

46. Cfr. Savigny, *Sistema del diritto romano attuale* (1840), transl. by V. Scialoja (Turin, 1888), vol. II, p. 239 ff., 279 ff., 325 ff. and 348 ff.

47. In *Pasicrisie belge* (I, 1847), p. 403; see also, ibid., p. 399 and Santa Maria, *Le società*, cit., p. 19 f., n. 19 and 20.

in 1854[48] – in the form of the Belgian Act of 14 February 1855 and the French Act of 30 May 1857.[49]

The former allowed any corporate persons duly authorized in France to exercise their rights and to stand in court in Belgium, subject to reciprocity, and empowered the Belgian government to extend such treatment to any companies belonging to other countries, also subject to reciprocity.[50]

---

48. The following is the content of the Belgian declaration: 'La faculté de faire valoir leurs droits devant les tribunaux belges étant contestée aux sociétés anonymes françaises, et des inconvénients sérieux pouvant résulter de cet état de choses pour les associations commerciales, industrielles ou financières des deux Etats, le gouvernement de Sa Majesté le Roi des Belges s'engage à présenter au Chambres législatives, dans le délai d'un an, un projet de loi qui aura pour objet d'autoriser les sociétés anonymes et les autres associations qui sont soumises à l'autorisation du gouvernement français, et qui l'auront obtenue, à exercer tous leurs droits et à ester en justice, en Belgique, conformément aux lois du pays, et moyennant réciprocité de la part de la France'. (*S. Lois annotées*, (1854), p. 66). Article 1 of the Belgian Act of 14 Mar. 1855 allowed unlimited companies to exercise their rights and to have standing in Belgium so long as they were duly authorized in France. Articles 1 and 2 of the French Act had similar contents.
49. About the 1855 Belgian Act and the 1857 French Act, partly with reference to their historical origins, see, in particular: Namur, 'De la situation légale des sociétés étrangéres en Belgique' [1877] Jour. dr. int. privé, p. 381 ff.; Weiss, *Traité élémentaire*, 1890, vol. II, p. 443 ff.; Buchere, "Des actions judiciaires exercées en France par les sociétés anonymes étrangères" [1882] Jour. dr. int. prive', p. 37 ff.; Lyon-Caen, "Des divers systèmes législatifs concernant la condition légale des sociétés étrangères par actions et des réformes à apporter à la législation française" in [1885] Jour. dr. int. privé, p. 265 ff., p. 267 f.; Laine, *Des personnes morales en droit international privé*, [1893] Jour. dr. int. privé, p. 303 ff.; Leven, *La nationalité des sociétés* (Paris, 1900), p. 151 ff.; Bossert, *Les sociétés étrangères en France, Loi du 30 mai 1857* (Nancy, 1900); Von Bar, *Theorie and Praxis* cit., vol. I, p. 305 ff.; Despagnet, *Précis de droit international privé* (Paris, 1904), p. 123 ff.; Gaetano, 'Società estere', voce in *Il digesto italiano*, Enciclopedia metodica e alfabetica di legislazione, dottrina e giurisprudenza, ed. L. Lucchini Chief (vol. XXI, Part III, Turin, 1903-1906), p. 545 ff., p. 547; Niemeyer, "Les sociétés de commerce" [1924] Recueil des cours de l'Academie de droit international de la Haye, vol. III, p. 1 ff., p. 26 ff.; Ruhland, "Le problème des personnes morales en droit international privé" [1933] Recueil des cours de l'Académie de droit international de la Haye, vol. III, p. 387 ff., p. 451; Nyboyet, *Traité*, cit., Tome II, p. 439 ff.; Badr, *Alien Corporation in Conflict of Laws*, cit., p. 63 ff.; Loussouarn, "Sociétés étrangères en France, Reconnaissance et jouissance de drafts" in Jur, class. dr. intern., fasc. 564 b, n. 13 ff.; Loussouarn "La condition des personnes morales en droit international privé" [1959] Recueil des cours de l'Académie de droit international de la Haie, vol. I, p. 513 ff.; Abrahams, *Les sociétés*, cit., pp. 11 and 93 ff.; Beitzke, *Parere legale relativo all'art. 220, capoverso 3 del Trattato di Roma*, Parte prima, cit., p. 26 f.; Batiffol, *Droit international privé* (Paris, 1967), p. 235 ff.; Loussouarn and Bredin, *Droit du commerce international* (Paris, 1969), p. 314 ss. Per l'analisi dei decreti collettivi francesi e dei trattati esistenti fra gli Stati membri della CEE e la Francia, cfr.: Goldman, "La reconnaissance mutuelle des sociétés dans la Communauté Economique Européenne", in *Etudes juridiques offertes a L. Juillot de la Morandière* (Paris, 1964); p. 175 ff., p. 177, fn. 2.
50. Article 1 of the Belgian Act provided: 'Les sociétés anonymes et autres associations commerciales, industrielles ou financières, qui sont soumises à l'autorisation du Gouvernement français, et qui l'auront obtenue, pourront exercer leurs droits et ester en justice en Belgique, en se conformant aux lois du royaume, toutes les fois que les sociétés ou associations légalement établies en Belgique jouiront des mêmes droits en France'; and Article 3 required: 'Cette réciprocité sera constatée soit par les traités, soit par la production des lois ou actes propres à en établir l'existence'. Article 2 authorized the Government to extend the treatment of French

As for the latter, Article 1 of the French Act of 30 May 1857 was quite similar in contents with regard to companies originally authorized in Belgium, except that, unlike the Belgian Act – which had, in fact, been adopted earlier – it made no mention of reciprocity. Further, Article 2 of the French Act delegated the French government to issue appropriate *collective decrees* extending the benefits contemplated in Article 1 to companies belonging to any other country as well.[51]

It was precisely against this background that Act No 1564 of 30 June 1853 was introduced in the legal system of the Sardinian States, to be followed by Act No 4387 of 27 October 1860, which were later made part of the positive law of the Kingdom of Italy after Unification.[52]

Act No 1564/1853 was clearly affected by Leclercq's closing argument as well as by the negative aspects of the French and Belgian case-law precedents indicated above. Its subject matter was stated in the quite unspecific heading 'Provisions relating to anonymous [limited] companies, whether mutual or otherwise, and to partnerships limited by bearer shares'.[53,54] It was subdivided into six chapters with

---

companies under Article 1 to other States' companies *subject to reciprocity*. See my book, *Le società*, cit., p. 22, n. 27.

51. Article 1 of the 1857 French Act required: 'Les sociétés anonymes et les autres associations commerciales, industrielles et financières qui sont soumises à l'autorisation du Gouvernement beige et qui l'out obtenue, peuvent exercer tous leurs droits et ester en justice en France, en se conformant aux lois de l'Empire'. Article 2 provided: 'Un décret impérial, rendu au Conseil d'Etat, peut appliquer à tous- autres pays le bénéfice de l'article I'. See my book, *Le società*, cit., p. 23, n. 28. In this connection, it should be noted that French case-law has taken the view that the existence of a treaty with France could perform the same function as the decree both in case the authorization was expressly required by the Treaty and in case the contracting State could benefit therefrom under the most favoured nation clause. On this, see Arminjon, *Précis de droit international privé commercial*, (Paris, 1948), p. 111 f., body and footnotes. See also Diena, *Trattato di diritto commerciale internazionale, ossia il diritto privato commerciale*, vol. I, *Parte generale* (Firenze, 1900), p. 247, n. 4.
52. About these legislative measures, only repealed upon the entry into force of the 1882 Code of Commerce (Santa Maria, *Le società*, cit., pp. 24 ff., para. 12 of Chapter I and paras 1 and 2 of Chapter II) see Gianzana, *Lo straniero*, cit., p. 117 ff.: Gabba, 'Società di fatto: validità ed efficacia di contratti posti in essere in Italia da una società estera non ancora autorizzata ad operare nel Regno' [1886] Foro it., I.C. 808; Danieli, 'De la condition des sociétés étrangères en Italie' [1888] Jour. Dr. Int. Privé, pp. 17 ff. e 330 ff., pp. 17-23; Caberlotto, *Commento del nuovo codice di commercio, testo, fonti, motivi, commenti, giurisprudenza. Del commercio in generale*, libro primo, titolo IX, *Delle società e delle associazioni commerciali* (articoli 76 e 250) (Turin, 1899), p. 371; Diena, *Trattato di diritto commerciale internazionale*, cit., p. 239 ff.; Gaetano, *Società estere*, cit., p. 546; Fiore, *Delle disposizioni generali sulla pubblicazione, applicazione ed interpretazione delle leggi* (vol. II, Naples-Turin, 1908), p. 55 ff.; Biscottini, *Diritto amministrativo internazionale*, cit., Tome I, p. 354 ff., body and footnotes; Caruso, 'Le società nella Comunità economica europea', cit., p. 128 ff.
53. Leclercq statements had a decisive impact on the Italian environment. Suffice to say that Mancini, in his report, 'Relazione alla Camera dei deputati sulla legge 27 ottobre 1860, Atti parlamentari, Sessione 1860', n. 90, considered Belgian case-law, later made to conform to Leclercq's view, to be the logical antecedent to the 1853 Italian Act.
54. The 1853 Act is published in *Collezione celerifera delle leggi, decreti, circolari, manifesti, e istruzioni pubblicati nell'anno 1853 ed altri provvedimenti anteriori* (Turin, 1853), p. 602 ff. That legislation pursued a dual purpose. First, foreign companies were made subject, *in the*

the following contents: Chapter 1, provisions relating to Government Authorisation; Chapters 2, 3 and 4, provisions relating to taxation of companies; Chapter 5, penal provisions in case the Act was violated; and Chapter 6, transitional and final provisions. Act No 1564 was immediately followed by regulations for its implementation, as issued under a Royal Decree of 7 July 1853.[55]

Article 2 of the Act, under the subheading 'About Government Authorisation' in Chapter 1, required:

> Mutual companies formed abroad as well as any other foreign limited associations or partnerships limited by bearer shares shall not operate in the State unless authorised to do so in the manners expressed in the Article next preceding above. [*Emphasis added*].

Article 1 explicitly referred to in the above provision required:

> Anonymous limited companies, whether mutual or otherwise, and partnerships limited by bearer shares shall be authorised by the Government approving their Articles of Association in the manners set out in Articles 46 and 47 of the Code of Commerce.

Article 46 of the 1842 Code of Commerce of the Sardinian States provided that:

> No anonymous company *may exist unless authorised* by Royal Letters Patent, subject to the opinion of the State Council, and unless its Memorandum of Association is likewise approved. [*Emphasis added*].

The second paragraph of Article 47 extended these treatment to partnerships limited by bearer shares.[56,57]

---

interest of any third parties that were to enter into contracts with such companies, to the Italian laws and courts, and were required to give adequate guarantees to secure performance of their contractual obligations. Moreover, *in the national companies' best interests*, foreign companies' competition with them was restricted, by subjecting the latter to the same tax treatment as national companies. See: Cavour, 'Rapporto alla Camera dei deputati', in *Actes du parlament subalpin, Chambre des députés, session de 1852, documents* (Turin, 1853), p. 403 ff.

55. Royal Decree 1578 of 7 Jul. 1853, containing the 'Regulation for the implementation of the Act of 30 Jun. 1853 relating to Anonymous Companies and Mutual Associations' is published in *Collezione celerifera*, cit. (1853), p. 630 ff.
56. Article 47(2) required: 'Where the capital is subdivided into *bearer shares*, a partnership may exist without the authorization or approval required by the article next preceding above'.
57. The partnership with capital subdivided into *registered shares* were not, however, subject from the authorization rules. Under the 1807 Napoleon *Code de Commerce* was still in force, the Article 37 government authorization was required for anonymous companies alone, while no controls or limitations were provided for in the case of partnerships limited by shares. On this rules, see, in particular: Pailliet, *Manuel de droit civil, commercial et criminel*, Tome II (Brussels, 1833), Code de commerce, p. 12 ff., fn. (c) n. 7; Pardessus, *Cours de droit commercial*, Tome II (Brussels, 1836), p. 314 ff., and Levy-Bruhl, *Histoire juridique des sociétés de commerce en France aux XVII et XVIII siècles* (Paris, 1938), p. 51 f. In fact, the draft code de commerce had proposed that limited partnerships should also be required to obtain authorization as was the case with anonymous companies, even the more so as the French legislator identified the rationale behind the prior authorization requirement in the trading of shares, a

Thus, based on the provisions of the Code of Commerce of the Sardinian States, any company of one of the above types which was chartered according to the laws of the Kingdom of Sardinia, could only exist subject to *royal authorization* and to the government's prior approval of the company's memorandum of association. For Article 1 of the 1853 Act simply re-stated the validity of the system provided for by Articles 46 and 47 of the Sardinian Code of Commerce.[58]

---

circumstance deemed to concern public policy. On this, see: Troplong, *Commentaire du contrat de société en matière civile et commerciale* (Brussels, 1843), p. 174, fn. 449; Montanelli, *Ragionamento intorno alle società commerciali, in Annali delle Università Toscane*, Part 1, Tome I (Pisa, 1846), p. 238 ff., now published in [1969] Riv. soc., p. 73 ff., p. 87. This proposal was, however, met with strong opposition, especially from maritime circles. Therefore, with admittedly poor logical consequentiality, it was not to be followed up. In this respect, see Fischer, 'Die Aktiengesellschaft', in *Ehrenbergs, Handbuch des gesamten Handelsrechts* (Leipzig, 1916), vol. III, Part I, p. 24 fn. 10. The discrimination introduced by Article 37 between anonymous companies and partnerships limited by shares for authorization purposes entailed the proliferation of the latter organizations, which became a 'bastard form without either the advantages of an anonymous company nor those of a genuine partnership'. (Montanelli, *Ragionamento intorno alle società commerciali, in Annali delle Università Toscane*, Part 1, Tome I (Pisa, 1846), p. 88). Further, if one considers that 'a figurehead' was usually appointed to hold office as the acting partner having unlimited liability, even though he invariably had no assets of his own, such liability was 'utter sham'. (Montanelli, *Ragionamento intorno alle società commerciali, in Annali delle Università Toscane*, Part 1, Tome I (Pisa, 1846), p. 89), one can readily understand the reasons that led the French government to request, in 1838, that the partnerships limited by shares be abolished. On this point, beside Montanelli, *Ragionamento intorno alle società commerciali, in Annali delle Università Toscane*, Part 1, Tome I (Pisa, 1846), see also: Borsari, *Codice di commercio del Regno d'Italia*, Part I, (Turin, 1868), p. 471 ff., p. 472 and, more recently, Costi, *L'azionista accomandatario* (Padua, 1969), p. 21 ff. By extending the prior governmental authorization requirement to the partnerships limited by bearer shares, the 1842 Sardinian law-maker had intended to overcome the practical rather than conceptual difficulties entailed by such requirement being applied to the anonymous companies alone. In other words, he intended to curb the spreading of 'disguised anonymous companies'. About the second paragraph of Article 47 of the Sardinian States' Code of Commerce, see Parodi, *Lezioni di diritto commerciale* (Genoa, 1854), vol. II, p. 81. Although the fact that the partnerships limited by registered shares required no authorization implied an exception not easily justified at a conceptual level, it still met the need to make the smaller enterprises' operations less burdensome, since share registration did not, in itself, provide adequate guarantees vis-à-vis third parties. Later on, though, even the provision of Article 47 of King Charles Albert's Code of Commerce was deemed inadequate. As a result, that discrimination was removed by Article 156 of the 1865 Code of Commerce, which required that 'neither a partnership limited by shares nor an anonymous company may exist unless it is authorized by a Royal Decree and its memorandum of association is likewise approved'. Article 156 of the attendant ministerial report reads: 'The time has not yet come to weaken, but to strengthen, the defences against such dangers (as outlined hereinabove); and so, there has been no hesitation in extending the requirement of governmental authorization to the partnerships limited by registered shares'. (In Borsari, *Codice di commercio del Regno d'Italia*, Part I, (Turin, 1868), p. 472).

58. In this respect, Article 1 of the 1853 Sardinian Act is worded quite explicitly, to the point that its full consistency with the system provided for, first, by the 1842 Code of Commerce, then by the 1865 Civil Code, has never been called into question by anyone – at least in relation to companies established in Italy since inception.

The innovating thrust of that Act was, in fact, borne out by Article 2, which extended the treatment of domestic companies to foreign companies as well. Article 4 of the same Act required *foreign* companies to apply to the government for the prescribed authorization within thirty days of the publication date of the Act. It also gave the government discretion to *suspend* any operations already started by such companies pending the review of the relevant application for authorization. Unless the applicable provisions of law were complied with, fines were imposed under Article 21, which considered a company's officers and agents to be jointly liable with their corporate principal for the payment of any such fine.

A subsequent statute dated 27 October 1860 closely mirrored the contents of the previous Belgian law of 1855 and French law of 1857,[59] whereby the lengthy confrontation in case-law mentioned above had eventually been put to an end in a liberal frame of mind. Article 1 of the Sardinian statute required:

> Any public limited companies and other commercial, industrial and financial companies that are subject to governmental authorisation in the French Empire *may, upon obtaining such authorisation, operate in the State and exercise any rights and stand in court therein* so long as they comply with the laws thereof. [*Emphasis added*].

Article 2 fully endorsed the liberal opening of the previous Belgian and French laws in stating:

> The King's Government shall have the authority to apply the provisions of Article 1 hereof to any other State.[60]

As a result, a number of international agreements were entered into first by the Kingdom of Sardinia then by the Kingdom of Italy with other States, to whose companies the treatment provided for by Article 1 of the 1860 Act was thereby extended on a bilateral basis and in compliance with the reciprocity principle.[61]

---

59. The Sardinian legislation in question followed, after slightly over a month, a similar French law of 8 Sep. 1860, which implemented Article 2 of the 1857 Act and 'allow out own anonymous companies to exercise any rights in France without requiring additional empowerment'. Thus, for the Sardinian government, 'it became a *pleasant duty* to lay before the Parliament a law granting reciprocity to France'. See *Relazione sulla legge 27 ottobre 1860 al Principe Eugenio di Savoia, luogotenente del re*, in *Collezione celerifera*, cit. (1860), 1775 f.
60. The 1860 Act as reproduced in *Collezione celerifera*, cit. (1860), 1775. Implementation Decree No. 4388 of the same date contained an additional indication of 'the duties French companies are required to discharge in order to exercising commerce in the States of the Kingdom'. That decree is published in *Collezione celerifera*, cit. (1860), 1775 f. About the limited character of such duties, which led to an 'enablement' of foreign companies, see my book, p. 41 ff.
61. Many agreement were reached by the Kingdom of Italy, most of them in the simplified form of an exchange of declarations with other European countries in furtherance of Article 2 of the 1860 Act, notably with Greece, the United Kingdom, Saxony, Belgium, Spain, Holland (excluding colonies), Switzerland, Russia and Austro-Hungary. For an extensive review of the different contents of individual agreements, see Santa Maria, *Le Società*, cit., p. 56 ff., body and footnotes.

The fact that the 1860 Act statutorily allowed any French companies already authorized in France to 'operate in the State, and exercise any rights and stand in court therein', indicates that no foreign companies to which that statute did not apply were allowed to operate, to exercise rights or even to stand in court in the Kingdom of Italy.[62]

In fact, it is certain that the 1853 Act had codified a general principle of *non-recognition* of foreign companies, and that the application of this principle was not, accordingly, limited to companies formed abroad that were engaged or intended to engage in business activities in the Kingdom without possessing the required authorization, but extended to any foreign company, irrespective of how it entered into contact with the Kingdom's legal system, thereby resulting in that company being denied existence anywhere within the State's jurisdiction. In other words, the 1853 Act was not only intended to prevent foreign companies from engaging in any, even just occasional, business activity in the Kingdom, but it also implied that any rights as foreign companies might have validly acquired in another country were denied recognition,[63] and that no such company was afforded judicial remedy before the King's courts.[64]

Under both the 1860 Act and the many international treaties and declarations entered into pursuant to its Article 2, the system of rules governing foreign companies' *eligibility* to carry out their operations in the Kingdom was only to apply to them so long as they existed in the home jurisdictions by virtue of proper authorization.

That the Act of 27 October 1860 made a foreign company's eligibility to operate in Italy, pursuant to the Implementation Decree of the same date, conditional upon *the relevant foreign authority's authorization* may only mean

---

62. This is an obvious consequence of corporate bodies lacking standing before the courts of the State. 'Denying foreign legal persons' capacity to stand as plaintiffs or defendants in court – states von Bar, *Theorie und Praxis des internationales Privatrechts* (vol. I, Hannover, 1889), p. 300 f., Italian transl., p. 306 – is tantamount to denying them not only the capacity, for example, to purchase or sell to or from us, but even their right to buy in the very foreign State to which they belong whenever the effective realization of such right entails our Court's action. It is clearly so because denying judicial protection (unless in the event that such denial is the result of merely arbitrary measures or of penalties, an event which is not appropriate to discuss here) can only be the result of the unwillingness of recognizing such claim for protection as a genuine right'. The denial of the right to stand in court in a State other than the home State is a direct consequence of the non-existence (caused by non-recognition) of the foreign company concerned in that State's legal system.
63. In this sense, by reference to the French positive law following the 30 May 1857 Act, see: Aubri e Rau, *Cours de droit civil francais d'après la méthode de Zachariae* (Paris, 1869), Tome I, p. 188, n. 23, and Niboyet, *Trattato*, cit., Tome II, p. 455. Likewise, Buchere, *Des actions judiciaire*, cit., p. 43.
64. This is also the approach taken in French case-law. See, essentially: Cour imp. d'Orleans (*1ère ch.*), 19 May 1860, in *Boucher* v *Caisse Franco-Suisse*, [1860] Rec. Sirey 1, c. 866, fn.; Cour de cassation (*Ch. req.*), 1 Aug. 1860, in *Caisse Franco-Suisse* v *Ramillon*, [1860] Rec. Sirey 1, c. 865 ff. (the judgment is at c. 869 f.); Cour imp. d'Aia *(1ère ch.)*, 17 Jan. 1861, in *Beaucourt* v *Soc. di Trieste, etc.*, [1861] Rec. Sirey II, c. 335 f.; Cour de Paris (*1ère ch.*), 15 May 1863, *Chemins de fer russes c. Jourde et Trône*, [1863] Rec. Sirey I, c. 352 f., fn. (a).

that, in derogation of the general contrary principle incorporated into the 1853 Act, that company was recognized to be in existence, as a foreign company subject to foreign laws, in a State other than the State where it had first been constituted by authorization, by virtue of renvoi – a feature typical of private international law.[65]

In conclusion, bodies corporate belonging to States that had entered into bilateral international agreements first with the Kingdom of Sardinia, then with the Kingdom of Italy, pursuant to the 1960 Act, as successively implemented, were treated *pari passu* with Italian citizens, though they remained entirely subject to the substantive laws of their place of incorporation.

In other words, the 1860 Act had initiated an actual rule of private international law applicable to bodies corporate, a peculiarity of which was that its scope for application in space was limited, by virtue of specific bilateral international arrangements, to companies validly incorporated in the other contracting State. In fact, as indicated elsewhere,[66] it only worked subject to reciprocity.

The manners in which legal persons came into life in any given legal system, at the end of an involved administrative procedure, explain why the connection factor used at that time could only be the place where the entity concerned was incorporated, i.e. constituted by authorization.

Conversely, since the 1853 Act was based on the *non-recognition approach*, the conceptual distinction between *recognition* of foreign companies' existence and their *eligibility* to operate within the territory of the State – that is, as discussed below, the distinction between an issue of private international law and the problem of how to treat foreign companies – could not even be hinted at, since such a distinction was both impracticable and unnecessary *as far as a non-recognized entity was concerned.*[67]

As for the evolution of law in Italy, only in the 1882 Code of Commerce and in the rules on the treatment of foreign companies under Articles 230 to 232, as well

65. In Case *Mackenzie v. Compagnia dei Tramways Piacenza-Bettola and others*, which the Milan Court of Appeal decided by judgment of 19 Sep. 1882 [1882] Mon. trib., p. 1032, p. 1032, ff., it was held that English companies were subject, pursuant to the Convention of 26 Nov. 1867 between England and the Kingdom of Italy, to the provisions of the 1860 Act. 'Hence, the legal being of these companies in either country shall be determined by the law of origin, and it shall not be subject to the sovereign's consent'. The same approach was taken by the Genoa Court of Appeal in its judgments of 22 Sep. 1882 and 23 Jul. 1886, cited above. The only one judgment to the contrary was delivered by the Modena Court of Appeal on 2 Sep. 1881, in *Società Union des Gas di Parigi c. Municipio di Modena*, [1881] Riv. leg. parm. mod., p. 270 ff. This judgment even denied that the 1860 Act contained an explicit principle of recognition and held that that legislation contained 'only one amendment to the previous law of 1853, and one only addressed to companies which have had to obtain the governmental authorization to come into, and stay, in existence, in that it was believed that it was enough for such companies, in order to exist lawfully in the State, to certify their having been authorized by the foreign State, without the need, in this case, for a royal decree to recognize their existence, subject to that other provision, that the instruments of their incorporation have been approved'.
66. See Santa Maria, *Le Società*, cit., p. 59 ff.
67. See Santa Maria, *Le Società*, cit., p. 45.

as following the shift from constitution by concession to recognition by law, was the system eventually based on the general principle of recognition of foreign companies (incorporated in a foreign jurisdiction, that is), as a direct result of the operation of the recall of private international law operated by those provisions.

4. THE DOUBLE MEANING OF 'RECOGNITION' AS APPLIED TO COMPANIES

As such general principle of recognition set in over a wider reach beyond our country's borders, through a number of bilateral international agreements, it became possible to consider the issue of corporate persons from the standpoint of Italian conflict of laws' system, in quite the same way as any other legal relationships.[68]

In an other respect, that principle points up the fundamental distinction between the private international law question of how to identify the material provisions of law governing a company's capital structure and existence, and the treatment of that company as a foreign company.

This twofold issue must, however, be qualified somewhat against the historical background discussed above.

First of all, the private international law standard, first formed with regard to corporate persons, then extended to all legal persons, has developed along tracks entirely separate from the rules intended to identify the proper laws governing natural persons' general capacity and capacity to act. Consequently, the parallelism between a natural person and a legal person by no means affects the way in which either is dealt with in private international law.

Secondly, once the general principle of recognition had set in and displaced the contrary principle upheld by Leclercq and codified into the Sardinian Kingdom's Act of 1853, the quality of the treatment of foreign companies was further extended – in accordance, in fact, with the international customary rule that grants a foreign person, whether natural or legal, standard minimum rules for treatment at least equivalent to those applied to nationals.[69]

The derogations from the general rule for the treatment of foreign persons have been reduced over time, down the point that they are only allowed for the exercise of activities of special national interest or with a view to regulating *special* activities, such as banking or insurance, in a *special* way, by making the exercise thereof by a foreign person, in Italy as well as in other countries, subject to

68. This is confirmed, in relation to the Italian legal system, by Article 25 of Act No. 218/1995 containing an express norm of private international law on companies and other legal persons for the first time in Italy. This norm is entirely similar in contents to that already implied in Articles 2505 and 2509, Civil Code, on the treatment of foreign companies in Italy (see my book *Le Società nel diritto internazionale privato* (2nd edn, Milan, 1973)), which provisions have expressly been repealed by Article 74 of the private international law reform act.

69. About the international rules on the treatment of foreign companies and the exercise of diplomatic protection, see Chapter V of this book.

compliance with authorization requirements (essentially not different, in fact, from those addressed to nationals) and to more or less strict conditions and regular supervisory controls as provided for by law.

Thirdly, reference to the competent foreign laws allows the existence of a corporate person to be *recognized* outside its home country. This clearly clashes with the opposite view that a legal person's operating scope is bound to be restricted to the territory of its State of incorporation, and that its exit therefrom, and subsequent entry into another State in which it intends to establish itself, should be penalized through its purportedly mandatory *winding up* in the system of origin and its consequent re-incorporation in the State of its new establishment. In theory, there is no reason why this twofold logical proposition should be granted, since maintaining such an entity's continuity, as any legal relationship, is an obvious result of the private-international-law approach.

What is meant by '*recognition*' of companies clearly points to two conceptually distinct, though mutually connected problems – one involving issues of private international law, the other relating to the treatment of foreign companies.[70]

As for the former problem, the solution can be found, as usual, by referring to the linking criteria designed to make foreign provisions of law contained in the system of origin applicable in the system of destination, such provisions being thereby recognized to be capable to govern a given legal relationship in the latter system as well. Obviously, foreign provisions may only be recognized in the host legal system so long as they do not conflict with a principle of international public policy set out in that system.

The distinction between the actual problem of private international law and that concerning the treatment of foreign companies is spelled out quite specifically in the *Rapport du sous Comité* presented to the *Comité d'experts pour la codification progressive du droit international* at its third session in May-April 1927, about the recognition of the legal personhood of foreign commercial companies.[71]

The private international law issue certainly comes first in logical priority, in the sense that it must first be established whether a company exists, with a given

70. See Santa Maria, '*Problemi interpretativi*', cit., p. 295 f.; Id., *Le società*, cit., pp. 46 f., n. 81 e 199 f., and Id., *Problemi attinenti*, cit., p. 1473 f.

71. This document, better known as Rapport Rundstein, is published on *ASIL*, [1928] Am. Jour. Int. Law, spec. suppl., p. 158 and on *Conférence de La Haie de droit international privé, Actes de la septième session tenue du 9 au 31 octobre 1951* (The Hague, 1952), p. 129 f. In the same sense, see also: Balossini, *Nazionalità delle società commerciali* (Turin, 1935), p. 27 f.; Id., "La condition des personnes morales en droit international privé, p. 447 f., pp. 487 f. and 533 f.; Id., *Dispositions du traité de Rome relatives aux sociétés* [1959] Rev. trim. dr. comm., p. 247 f.; Beitzke, *Parere legale relativo all'art. 220, capoverso 3 del Trattato di Roma, Parte prima: il riconoscimento della personalità giuridica delle società straniere* (1962), p. 4 f. (Doc. 4958/IV/62-I); Id., 'Anerkennung und Sitzverlegung von Gesellschaften und juristischen Personen in EWG-Bereich" in *Zeitschrift fuœr das gesamte Haœndelsrecht und Wirtschaftsrecht* (1964), p. 31 f.; Grossfeld, *Die Anerkennung*, cit., p. 3; Drobnig, "Kritische Bemerkungen zum Vorentwurf eines EWG-Ubereinkommes ìber die Anerkennung von Gesellschaften", in *Zeitschrift fuœr das gesamte Haœndelsrecht und Wirtschaftrecht* (1966-1967), p. 93 f., p. 104 f.

structure, in a given system – that of origin or of jurisdiction – before granting it 'recognition' within the former meaning of the term, obviously from the standpoint of the different system in which the company operates or intends to operate.

If this two-step logical test is successful, then, and only then, will it be possible to determine under what conditions and subject to what limitations the company so recognized as foreign may be allowed to act outside the system of its incorporation in the system in which it intends to operate.

For the sake of clarity, assume a controversy between two foreign banks not authorized to operate (then not recognized) in Italy comes before an Italian judge. Undoubtedly, their unfavourable position will not prevent the Italian judge from considering them to be in existence by reference to rules of private international laws, and, to be obviously '*recognized*' accordingly. Think of a foreign bank formed in a State which is not a member of the European Union. In order for that bank to be enabled to open a branch in Italy, it will have to obtain prior authorization pursuant to Article 13 et seq. of the Consolidating Banking Act adopted under Legislative Decree No 385 of 1 September 1993. Therefore, even assuming the bank operates in Italy without the prescribed authority, it will still be recognized as existing in the Italian legal system out of its being duly incorporated in its home State. This will be the case in relation to any rights that bank has acquired abroad, whenever any such right is challenged before an Italian court having jurisdiction as the *forum loci* to decide the controversy. Further, this bank will even be liable, in the Italian legal system, for any of its Italian subsidiary's operations as might be deemed invalid lacking the prescribed authorization to engage in banking activities within the State.[72]

The problem of the recognition of companies in the terms indicated so far remains unchanged even when the private international law issue relating to companies is approached in terms of legal subjectivity. Under this approach, the company concerned is not considered to be subject to one single governing law (that provides for both the company's general capacity in law, i.e. personhood, and its capacity to act, i.e. its functioning), but the possibility is accepted that the rules governing the company's existence and the rules governing its actual operations and affairs may not be one and the same law. However, if the latter approach is granted, it must be specified that the question of the recognition of a company would clearly not cover all the related issues of private international law, and so, since recognition would imply identification of the law regulating that company's existence, it would have no impact on that other question, the determination of the law that governs the functioning of companies.

Acknowledging the considerable practical difficulties the acceptance of the latter view would involve[73] is not apt, in itself, to dispose of the problem. The

72. The opposite case, in which a foreign company's legal capacity and *locus standi* was not recognized, is the object of the ECJ's judgment in *Überseering BV*.

73. On this issue, see Aubert, Le statut international des sociétés anonymes, A propos d'une arrêté du Conseil fédéral du 12 avril 1957, in *L'entreprise, Mémoires de l'Université de Neuchâtel, vol. XXVIII, (Neuchâtel, 1960), p. 177 ff., esp.lly p. 180.*

choice between the two proposed solutions cannot correctly be approached and made in the abstract, but in the light of the positive law ruling in any given system of laws.[74,75]

With regard to the Italian legal system in particular, the second paragraph of Article 25 of Act 218 of 31 May 1995 relating to the reform of the (Italian) system of private international law incorporates the 'single-law' approach and contains a long list, presented in fact as non-exhaustive,[76] of specific occurrences governed

74. There seems to be no doubt that, at least in the original EEC Member States' legal systems, bodies corporate are covered by a single norm of private international law. In this respect, see Beitzke's survey, conducted within the European Economic Community, *Parere legale relativo all'art. 220, capoverso 3 del Trattato di Roma, parte prima: il riconoscimento della personalità giuridica delle società di commercio straniere* (1962), (Doc. 4958/IV/62-I), p. 4 f. In particular, for the approach to the problem and its standard solution in Italian law, please refer to my study, *Le società nel diritto internazionale privato*, cit., p. 12 f. Beside its being not mandatory, this formulation is quite broad, since it includes both requirements for existence and requirements relating to the life and events of companies and other bodies corporate.
75. In fact, the same conclusion could be reached with regard to the Brussels Convention on the mutual recognition of companies and bodies corporate. The more restrictive solution patently clashed with the belief held – mistakenly in my view – both by Goldman, the author of the official report on the Convention, and by other commentators of that instrument, that the State in whose territory a company had its real registered office, pursuant to Article 4, was allowed to subject that company's existence and operation to its own laws. Therefore, either the provisions of Articles 4 and 6 only concerned companies' lives – and that assumption was clearly in conflict with the spirit and the letter of Article 4 –, with the consequence that the Convention would have had a quite narrow scope, or neither article contemplated both the existence and the functioning of companies. In fact, even the provisions of Article 9 and 10 of the Convention, which conveyed the criterion of public policy, clearly supported the idea that the Convention had a wider scope. On this subject, see Goldman, "Le projet de convention entre les états membres de la Communauté européenne sur la reconnaissance mutuelle des sociétés et personnes morales", in Rabels Zeitschrift fuœr auslaœndiches und internationales Privatrecht, (1967), p. 201 f., esp.lly pp. 204 f. and 208 f.; Cerexhe, "La reconnaissance mutuelle des sociétés et personnes morales dans la Communauté Economique Européenne" [1968] Rev. marché comm., p. 578 f., p. 586 and Dieu, "La reconnaissance mutuelle des sociétés et personnes morales dans la Communauté européenne" [1968] Cahiers dr. eur., p. 532 f., p. 536. See also Drobnig, *La convenzione della CEE*, cit., p. 539 f., p. 542 f. It is these authors' view that the rules of private international law contained in the Convention would only concern a company's existence, not its organizational aspects, or in the words of Goldman, *Le projet*, cit., p. 209, 'la répartition des compétences et les rapports entre les organes, les conditions dans lesquelles ceux- ci doivent deliberer et decider, leur pouvoirs de représentation à l'égard des tiers', which were assumed to be not included in the subject matter of the Convention. For a more extensive criticism of this view, see Santa Maria, *Le società*, cit., p. 211 f. In agreement with my opinion, see: Ubertazzi, "Riconoscimento e stabilimento delle società nella Comunità Economica Europea" [1970] Riv. società, p. 532 f.; Stein, 'Conflict-of-Laws Rules by Treaty: Recognition of Companies in Regional Market' [1970] Mich. Law Rev., p. 1327 f.; Id., *Harmonization of European Company Laws, National Reform and Transnational Coordination*, (Indianapolis, 1971), f. 416; Perrin, *Le droit international privé des sociétés dans la CEE* (Genéve, 1971), f. 31.
76. See Santa Maria, 'Società', 'Diritto internazionale privato', in *Enciclopedia giuridica Treccani*, vol. VII, Rome, 1998, p. 1 ff.

by the law applicable to a company, as identified in the first paragraph of Article 25, expressly in regard of:

(a) legal status;
(b) business name or style;
(c) creation, transformation and winding up;
(d) legal capacity;
(e) appointment, powers and workings of governing bodies;
(f) legal representation;
(g) the manners in which the quality of member or shareholder is acquired or forfeited, and the rights and duties inhering in such quality;
(h) liability for the entity's obligations; and
(i) the consequences of infringing the law or the entity's own articles of association.

Much as this list has a merely descriptive character, it indicates that, while all the points relating to a company's legal status (a), business name or style (b), formation, transformation and dissolution (c) and capacity (d), as well as the consequences of infringing the law or the company's articles of association (i), relate to the entity's existence, the remaining points are concerned with its structure, life and events in external and internal relations, including relationships between members.

In a more general respect, the scope for application of *lex societatis* may be inferred by contrast from Article 1(2)(e) of the Rome Convention of 1980 on the law applicable to contractual obligations, which uses a broad formulation to exclude the application of its rules to questions governed by the law of companies and other bodies corporate or unincorporate such as the creation, by registration or otherwise, legal capacity, internal organization or winding up of companies and other bodies corporate or unincorporate and the personal liability of officers and members as such for the obligations of the company or body.[77]

5. THE IMPORT OF CLAUSES IN ESTABLISHMENT TREATIES AND FRIENDSHIP, COMMERCE AND NAVIGATION TREATIES

The clauses concerning companies and other legal persons either in treaties of establishment or in treaties of commerce or commerce and navigation or in treaties of friendship, commerce and navigation, essentially provide for the treatment of foreign companies and other legal persons. However, they seem to imply that the

77. Yet, such topics not necessary falling within the scope of the *lex societatis*, as shareholders' agreements or even, according to some, certain relationships between a company and its owners, could well remain outside the exclusion, then be caught by the purview of the Rome Convention. In this sense, see Zonca, 'Convenzione di Roma e diritto delle società', in Sacerdoti e Frigo, *La Convenzione di Roma sul diritto applicabile ai contratti internazionali*, cit., p. 201 f.; about the Rome Convention, see also Carbone, Luzzatto, *Il contratto internazionale* (Turin, 1994).

problem of private international law of how to identify the law governing a company or another body corporate has already been solved through the operation of the relevant rules of private international law each of the contracting parties to any given international convention has introduced.

This conclusion is patently correct in case the relevant conventional clause itself makes full reference to the private international law rules applicable to companies and legal persons under each contracting State's system of conflict of laws. In fact, in that case, there is full coincidence of criteria both for the purposes of private international law and in terms of the treatment of foreign companies and other legal persons.

Thus, the *formation of companies according to one contracting party's legislation* is assumed to be the linking factor in Article 4 of the Treaty of Commerce and Navigation of 11 December 1882 between Italy and Belgium, as reinstated pursuant to Article 44 of the Peace Treaty of 10 February 1947, with a Belgian diplomatic note,[78] and in Article 7 of the Franco-Belgian Convention of Establishment of 6 October 1927.[79] An especially interesting provision is Article 1 of the Convention of 11 April 1868 between Italy and the Netherlands, relating to *sociétés anonymes* (roughly, limited public companies) and other commercial, industrial and financial associations, as reinstated pursuant to Article 44 of the Peace Treaty, with a Dutch diplomatic note of 16 August 1949.[80] Article 1 of this Convention reads as follows (translated from the French original):

> Each of the High Contracting Parties hereby declare it shall mutually recognise the power of any companies limited by shares and other commercial, industrial and financial associations formed and *authorised* under the other country's own laws to exercise all their rights and to stand in court . . . [*Emphasis added*].

Likewise, among the treaties concluded by Italy, see Article 5 of the Thai-Italian Treaty of Friendship, Commerce and Navigation of 3 December 1937.[81]

In other cases, where the treaty clauses themselves contemplate *explicit linking criteria*, it being understood that the answer to the private international law question must have absolute priority, the solution of this problem is bound to have an impact on the different problem of how to determine the scope for the application in practice of any given treaty. Considering that the general principle underlying the treatment of foreigners is equality with nationals, so that the former must be accorded the same rights as are accorded to the latter, whether or not a company is subject to the national law will solely be determined, as a result of each domestic system's autonomous determination of the scope for application of its own laws, by the rules of private international law that govern companies, including for the purpose of applying that treaty.

78. [1882] J.O. 305, and in *Mon. belge*, 31 Dec. 1882.
79. [1927] J.O.
80. [1869] J.O. 138, and in *N.U. Recueil des Traités*, vol. 98, p. 27 f.
81. [1938] J.O. 107.

However, with regard to the application of the relevant treaty to a company recognized as foreign (non-national, that is), the problem is solved direct by applying the criteria set out in the treaty. For example, from the standpoint of the Italian legal system, whether or not a company is subject to Italian law, i.e. whether it is national or foreign, is determined by the Italian rules of private international law. Once it has been found that it is not Italian, it is on the basis of the criteria set out in that treaty that it is decided, from the standpoint of the Italian system of laws as well, whether it belongs to the other contracting State, in which case it will be accorded in Italy the treatment applicable under the treaty to the companies belonging to that other State.

In the latter case, it might happen that either contracting party's companies are required to be constituted in the other party's territory (*direct criterion*).[82]

It may also occur that the requirement of the constitution of either party's companies in the other party's territory is accompanied by the express requirement that their registered offices should be located in that territory.[83]

Along these lines, certain treaties require the existence of a further factor of contact with either contracting State' territory in addition to constitution according to each contracting State's laws (*indirect criterion*).[84] In these cases, the requirement of the presence of the company's registered office in the territory of the State of incorporation is usually added to the requirement of its constitution under the laws of a contracting State.[85]

---

82. In this sense, for example: Article 23, indent 3, of the Treaty of Friendship, Commerce and Navigation of 27 Mar. 1956, between the Netherlands and the United States (published in the appendix to Kollewijn, 'American-Dutch Private International Law', in *Bilateral Studies in Private International Law* (New York, 1961), p. 79 f.)
83. In this sense, see Articles 3 and 4 of the Convention between France and Luxemburg concerning conditions of residence and business of 31 Mar. 1930, ([1931] J.O.); Article 7 of the Convention on establishment between Italy and France of 23 Aug. 1951 ([1953] J.O. 85 and [1958] J.O.); Article 6 of the Convention on establishment and navigation between Germany and France of 27 Oct. 1956 ([1959] J.O., and in BGBl., 1957, II, p. 1661). For treaties and conventions signed by Italy which contain similar recognition clauses, please reefer to Capotorti, *La nazionalità delle società*, cit., p. 167 f. and to Lanfranchi, 'Il trattamento dello straniero nelle clausole relative allo stabilimento degli accordi bilaterali in vigore tra l'Italia e gli Stati esteri' [1968] Riv. dir. int. priv. proc., p. 331 f., p. 346, body and fn. 54.
84. In this sense, see Article 1 of the Treaty between Germany and the Netherlands of 11 Feb. 1907 on the mutual recognition of public limited companies (Martens, *Nouv. Rec. Gén. Traités*, Third Series, vol. I, p. 729 f.); Article 10(1) of the Convention on establishment and employment between Luxembourg and the Netherlands of 1 Apr. 1933 (*Mém. Gran Duché Luxembourg*, 26 Aug. 1933, p. 610 f.); Article 10(1) of the Convention on establishment and employment between Luxembourg and the Netherlands of 20 Feb. 1933 (*Mon. Belge*, 22 Jan. 1934); and Article 33 of the Treaty of friendship, commerce and navigation between Germany and Italy of 21 Nov. 1957.
85. In the same sense, see Article 35 of the Treaty of friendship, commerce and navigation between Italy and Panama of 7 Oct. 1965, [1968] Riv. dir. int. priv. proc., p. 953 f., p. 963. For treaties and conventions signed by Italy which contain similar recognition clauses, please reefer to Capotorti, *La nazionalità delle società*, cit., p. 167 f., and to Lanfranchi, 'Il trattamento', p. 346, body and fn. 55.

A provision quite similar in nature and content to the clauses just considered above is to be found, *prima facie*, in Article 48(1) EC, as expressly referred to in Article 55 EC. Article 48, too, apparently considers the rules concerning the freedom of establishment or the free provision of services to be applicable to companies or firms '*formed in accordance with the law of a Member State, and having their registered office, central administration or principal place of business within the Community*', without even remotely hinting at the issue of the identification of the law governing those companies, which law should, in fact, be referred to the private international law rules specifically adopted in individual Member States.

It is appropriate to point out in advance that the quite peculiar nature recognized in many respects to the provisions of the EC Treaty relating to the four fundamental freedoms, among which *freedom of establishment* and *free provision of services*, makes the provisions of Article 48(1) EC look quite different from the similar provisions that indicate the beneficiaries of treaty rules in establishment treaties and other similar instruments, of which more below.

6. THE TREATMENT OF FOREIGN COMPANIES WITHIN THE COMMUNITY: ARTICLE 12 AND ARTICLES 43 ET SEQ., 49 ET SEQ. AND 56 ET SEQ. EC

The principle underlying the rules relating to the treatment of foreign companies in the Treaty of Rome is to be found in Article 12 EC.[86] The prohibition of 'any discrimination on grounds of nationality' contemplated in that article as falling 'within the scope of application of this Treaty, and without prejudice to any special provisions contained therein' – though subject to the restrictive interpretation given to it by the Court of Justice, which has limited its application to the sectors specifically considered by other provisions of the Treaty[87] – implies that 'Community foreigner' must be put *entirely on the same footing as* 'Community nationals' in each of the Member States.

This principle underlies the provision enshrined in Chapter II and Chapter III of Title III, concerning the 'right of establishment' and 'services', respectively.

86. Article 12(1) EC reproduces, without amendments, Article 6(1) of the EEC Treaty, itself reproducing former Article 7(1). Article 12(2) was amended by the Amsterdam Treaty, which introduced the co-decision procedure under Article 251 EC, replacing the co-operation procedure under Article 252 EC, which was contemplated in the previous version of the borm, as already amended by Article 8 of the Maastricht Treaty. As a result, the European Parliament's role in issuing acts implementing the non-discrimination principle has been strengthened.

87. According to the ECJ, the general non-discrimination principle laid down in that article can only be applied subject to the special provisions contained in the Treaty (see, among many, Judgments of 14 Jul. 1977, Case 8/77, *Sagulo* & others, [1977] ECR 1495, ground 11 and of 1 Feb. 1996, Case C-177/94, *Perfili*, [1996] ECR I-161, ground 14). This means that Article 12 EC refers, in particular, to other provisions of the Treaty which apply the general principle the Treaty applies to specific cases. See Judgments of the Court of 2 Feb. 1989, Case C-186/87, *Cowan*, [1989] ECR, ground 195, and of 1 Jul. 1993, Case C-20/92, *Hubbard*, [1993] ECR I-3777, ground 10.

The same principle has been the main driver of the gradual implementation of the requirement of unrestricted movement of capital in Chapter IV of Title III of the Treaty. In the original text of Chapter IV, this requirement was, in fact, laid down in far 'softer' terms than the other fundamental freedoms.[88]

As regards the free movement of capital, the criterion of '*nationality*' of a Member State was supplemented with two additional contact factors, namely '*residence*' in a Member State and '*the place where (. . .) capital is invested*', both factors being typical of the rules governing currency transactions. Much as the new provisions are still contained in Chapter IV, Article 56 et seq., they were extensively altered by the Maastricht Treaty from the original text to provide a unified whole to include '*payments*' as well as '*capital*'. Yet, they lack any reference to the non-discrimination principle otherwise laid down in Article 12 EC. This omission was most likely due to the fact that the Treaty as newly amended was deemed adequate to ensure fully unrestricted movements of capital and payments within the internal market.[89]

Article 48 EC is also applicable as a whole to the matter of the free provision of services through the express reference made to it in Article 55. Its first paragraph requires that 'companies and firms' – within the meaning comprehensively specified in the second paragraph of the same Article 48 – be treated in the same way as 'natural persons' who are *nationals* of Member States, so long as they are constituted under a Member State's laws, thus being *nationals* of that State, and satisfy at least one of the prescribed factor of contact with the whole Community in order to be eligible for the application of the provisions in Chapter II and Chapter III.

The first paragraph of Article 48 reads as follows:

> Companies or firms *formed in accordance with the law* of a Member State and having their *registered office, central administration or principal place of business within the Community* shall, for the purposes of this Chapter, be treated in the same way as natural persons who are nationals of Member States. [*Emphasis added*].

The second paragraph provides the following definition:

> 'Companies or firms' means companies or firms constituted under civil or commercial law, including cooperative societies, and *other legal persons* governed by public or private law, save for those which are *non-profit-making*.[90] [*Emphasis added*].

As for the purport of the companies' right of establishment, the second paragraph of Article 43 of the Treaty specifies that:

> Freedom of establishment shall include the right to take up and pursue activities as self-employed persons and to set up and manage undertakings, in

88. Please, refer to Chapter III of this book.
89. On this subject, please see Chapter III of this book.
90. The phrase 'non-profit making companies' is now taken as fully equivalent to the other, more general phrase that refers to the exercise of any 'economic activities'. In this connection, see by book *Le società*, cit., p. 209 f., n. 17, including extensive references to literature.

> particular companies or firms within the meaning of the second paragraph of Article 48, under the conditions laid down for its own nationals by the law of the country where such establishment is effected (. . .).

The first paragraph of Article 43 further provides for the gradual abolishment of any 'restrictions on the setting-up of agencies, branches or subsidiaries by nationals of any Member State established in the territory of any Member State'.

Within the same framework, Article 294 EC, which was introduced to complement the provisions concerning free establishment and the free provision of services, requires:

> Member States shall accord nationals of the other Member States *the same treatment as their own nationals* as regards participation in the capital of companies or firms within the meaning of Article 48, without prejudice to the application of the other provisions of this Treaty.

The 'establishment' notion that emerges from the EC Treaty and appears to be averred by the General Programme for the abolishment of restrictions to freedom of establishment of 18 December 1961,[91] is solely addressed to the exercise of entrepreneurial activities and various forms of self-employed persons' work, while the enjoyment and exercise of civil rights and the judicial protection of such rights have been left unregulated under the EC Treaty. This is, in fact, implicitly confirmed by exclusion in the first attempt made at a conventional regulation under Article 293 EC with a view to securing 'the protection of persons and the enjoyment and protection of rights under the same conditions as those accorded by each State to its own nationals'.[92]

Article 49 EC provides for the gradual abolition of any restrictions existing in any Member State on the freedom to provide services in respect of *nationals* of other Member States – or, subject to the Council's extension, in respect of nationals of a third country as well, based on an amendment introduced by Article 16(3) of the Single Act – who are *established* in a State of the Community other than that of the person for whom the services are intended.

Services are, in turn, defined *in just residual terms* in Article 50 EC, as follows:

> Services shall be considered to be 'services' (. . .) where they are normally provided for remuneration, in so far as they are not governed by the provisions relating to freedom of movement for goods, capital and persons. 'Services'

91. [1962] O.J. L2, p. 32 f.
92. It should be noted, though, that the Charter of fundamental rights of the European Union was proclaimed in Nice in Dec. 2001. At the time of writing, that document, subdivided into chapters concerning dignity, freedom, equality, solidarity, citizens' rights and justice, has no binding juridical value, much as it is frequently referred to in ECJ case-law as a core benchmark in matters of human rights. Should the Lisbon Treaty ever come into force, it would confer *binding value* on the Charter of Fundamental Rights (see Declaration No. 1 annexed to the Treaty). Therefore, for the time being, the Charter suffers from the same standstill as the Lisbon Treaty.

> shall in particular include: (a) activities of an industrial character; (b) activities of a commercial character; (c) activities of craftsmen; (d) activities of the professions.

The General Programme of 18 December 1961[93] should also be referred to in respect of the notion of 'provision of services'. In the terms of Title III ('Restrictions') of the Programme, the restrictions on the free provision of services to be abolished during the transitional period are not only those put in place direct by the provider, but also those affecting him '*indirectly* through the recipient of the services'.

According to the judgment of the Court of Justice of the European Community of 31 January 1984, Joined Cases 286/82 and 26/83, *Graziana Luisi and Giuseppe Carbone* v *Ministero del Tesoro*:[94]

> The freedom to provide services includes the freedom, for the recipients of services, to go to another member state in order to receive a service there, without being obstructed by restrictions, even in relation to payments, and that tourists, persons receiving medical treatment and persons travelling for the purpose of education or business are to be regarded as recipients of services.

The distinction between freedom of establishment and the freedom to provide services accorded to self-employed persons within the internal market can be identified by the different intensity of the linkage of the person accorded either freedom with the host Member State.

For the exercise of the rights recognized by Article 43 EC requires the trader concerned to move out and *establish* himself in a Member State other than the Member State of which he is a national, in order to engage in his activities in such other Member State on a *continuous permanent basis*. Therefore, the inter-State factor only operates in the initial stage of the exercise of the freedom of establishment.

The free movement of the provision of services is, however, of a dynamic nature and is based on the assumption that the linkage with the host Member State remains *discontinuous and occasional*. Thus, the inter-state quality of the relationship has been allowed to stand, and it comes up from time to time as the provider or the recipient of the services, or else the services themselves, transfer or are transferred, as the case may be, from one Member State to another.

Although the distinction between establishment and the provision of services is very clear in the abstract, it may lend itself to serious difficulties in actual cases. For example, think of a German heart surgeon residing in Hamburg, who travels to Verona two days a week to operate on heart patients in a hospital there. Also consider a paediatrician also living in Hamburg, who travels to Padua on the

93. [1962] O.J. L2, p. 36 f.
94. The Judgment of the Court of Justice of the European Communities is published in [1984] ECR, p. 377 f.

same days as his colleague, to see and treat his patients in another hospital. Obviously, despite the apparent analogies, the two German doctors' positions differ from each other, because of the different relationship of each practitioner with his patients, much as both professionals pursue activities as self-employed persons providing services to their respective clients. In the former case, the services provided by the heart surgeon are characterized by his patients' 'mobility', in the sense that they will most likely be different from one week to the next. In the latter case, however, the patients, at least those visiting on a regular basis, remain the same for a considerable length of time – perhaps until each of them develops into an adult. In this respect, the relationship between the paediatrician and his little patients is characterized by the 'continuity' or, at least, the 'periodicity' of the services he provides. This is the decisive aspect to settle the question: the heart surgeon moves within the scope of the free provision of services, while the children's doctor practises in Italy within the scope of freedom of establishment.

The first paragraph of Article 56 of the EC Treaty (former Article 73b), in Chapter 4 headed '*Capital and Payments*', requires:

> Within the framework of the provisions set out in this chapter, all restrictions on the movement of capital between Member States and between Member States and third countries shall be prohibited.

And the second paragraph reads:

> Within the framework of the provisions set out in this chapter, all restrictions on payments between Member States and between Member States and third countries shall be prohibited.

Even certain aspects of the rules on establishment can hardly be distinguished from those concerning the free movements of capital. In this connection, the European Court of Justice has specified:

> Furthermore, it must be borne in mind that as a general rule the acquisition by one or more natural persons residing in a Member State of shares in a company incorporated and established in another Member State is covered by the *Treaty provisions on the free movement of capital*, provided that the shareholding does not confer on those natural persons definite influence over the company's decisions and does not allow them to determine its activities. By contrast, where the acquisition involves all the shares in a company having its registered office in another Member State and the shareholding confers *a definite influence over the company's decisions* and allows the shareholders to determine its activities, *it is the Treaty provisions on freedom of establishment which apply.*[95] [*Emphasis added*].

95. In this sense, see Judgment of 13 Apr. 2000, Case C-251/98, *Baars*, [2000] ECR I-2287, grounds 21 e 22. Still, in this connection, see paragraph 12 of Chapter III of this book.

Under different profiles, a fuzzy reference made by the European Commission to the Treaty provisions governing the freedom of capital movement underlies case-law on the 'golden share' issue, in respect of which, at least in general and notwithstanding the Commission's statements to the contrary, the really material rules are those relating to the right of establishment.[96,97]

Since the provisions on establishment and services have been deemed by the Court of Justice, since the expiry of the transitional period, to be '*directly applicable*', as will be discussed in more details below, if no discrimination was admissible in these areas since as early as 1 January 1970, it has been even the less so since 1 January 1993, following the full establishment of the internal market postulated by Article 14 EC (as rephrased pursuant to Article 7a of the Single European Act signed by the then twelve Member States in Luxembourg on 17 February 1986). This proposition now appears to be further reinforced by the provisions for the establishment of citizenship of the European Union in Articles 17 to 22 of the Treaty of Rome, which, though slightly modified, duplicate the text of Articles 8 and 8a through 8e of the Maastricht Treaty.

This does not amount, though, to outright liberalization, but, as observed above, to a *guarantee of equal treatment* for the nationals of the different Member States. Thus, its seems that the nationals of individual Member States are not accorded any guarantee by the Treaty for the purposes of compliance with the fundamental freedoms. This was, in fact, the answer the Commission gave to Question No 21 by Mr Galland (Doc. H-486/81) at the European Parliament in connection with the alleged incompatibility of French provisions on the nationalization of banks with the Treaty of Rome.

Mr Galland's question was:

> Pursuant to Article 7 of the Rome Treaty (now Article 12 EC), within the scope of application of the Treaty, any discrimination on grounds of nationality is prohibited. Now, Title II of the French draft law on nationalisations of 23 September 1981, concerning the nationalisation of banks, provides, specifically in Article 13(2)(3), that any banks most of whose share capital is owned directly or indirectly by natural persons not residing in France or to legal persons not having their registered offices in France shall not be nationalised. Are these provisions not discriminatory in the terms of Article 7 of the Treaty (now Article 12 EC) against the banks most of whose capital belongs to French natural or legal persons? If it is so, what measures does the Commission intend to take to ensure compliance with Community law?[98]

The Commission's answer was quite to the point:

> In the wording of Article 7 of the EEC Treaty (now Article 12 EC) Member States' duty not to discriminate refers to the nationals of another Member

96. See the *Überseering* Judgment of 5 Nov. 2002, cit., ground 77; likewise, Judgment of 13 Apr. 2000, Case C-251/98, *Baars*, cit. [2000] ECR I-2287, grounds 21 e 22, quoted in the former.
97. Please, refer to the considerations in paragraph 12 of Chapter III of this book.
98. See Doc. H-486/81.

> State. Although some specific rules of Community law may, *in some cases*, prohibit a Member State from *treating its nationals in a less favourable way* than the nationals of another Member State, the Commission's *view is that Article 7 does not, in itself, entail such prohibition*. The French draft law on nationalisations requires that any banks most of whose capital is owned directly or indirectly by natural persons not residing in France or to legal persons not having their registered offices in France shall not be nationalised [*Emphasis added*].

The Commission concluded:

> According to what I have just said and failing specific rules of Community law on the matter, the difference in treatment arising from the draft law quoted by the Honourable Member against banks most of whose capital is owned by French natural or legal persons does not fall within the prohibition of discrimination contemplated by Article 7 [now by Article 6].[99]

Save for one single case of protection relating to alleged reverse discrimination,[100] the Court of Justice's case-law has constantly held the view that a Member State's discrimination against its nationals is essentially not relevant under Community law, but that national courts may be referred to for different views of the matter as are deemed appropriate.

In Judgment No 443 of 30 December 1997,[101] the Italian Constitutional Court, relying on this intimation, left open, in a *decision about equal treatment*, the scrutiny of any discrimination arguably arising from a national measure to the detriment of national undertakings alone, as a logical consequence of a competition-distorting conduct against them, as opposed to foreign 'Community' undertakings, which operated in the same market but were protected by *the non-discrimination principle*. Thus, according to the Italian Constitutional Court:

> Finally, in the absence of uniform rules across the Community, *the principle of non-discrimination among undertakings competing in the same market* operates, therefore, as a means to prevent national enterprises from being burdened by costs, constraints or prohibitions the legislator would be barred from imposing on non-Italian Community manufacturers, which is tantamount to saying that the discriminatory effects the application of Community laws is apt to generate cannot be ignored in the *decision about equal treatment* this Court has been requested to deliver. [*Emphasis added*].

---

99. See *European Parliament Discussion*, 17 Feb. 1982, in [1982] O.J. L43, p. 12.
100. Judgment of the Court of 7 Jul. 1992, Case C-370/94, *The Queen* v *Immigration Appeal Tribunal* e *Surinder Singh, ex parte Secretary of State for Home Department*, [1992] ECR I – 4265.
101. [1998] Foro it. I, c. 697 ff.

7. THE PRINCIPLE OF THE DIRECT APPLICABILITY OF THE RULES OF THE TREATY ON ESTABLISHMENT AND SERVICES

The European Court of Justice delivered judgments about the reach and purport of the rules on freedom of establishment and the freedom to provide services under the Treaty more than thirty years ago, in Cases 2/74, *Reyners*, and 33/74, *van Binsbergen*, of 21 June 1974 and 3 December 1974, respectively.[102]

The innovating significance of both judgments, genuine pillars of the Community's evolution, is well known. It was thought theretofore that the rules of the Rome Treaty in matters of free establishment and free provision of services were not substantive rules, exceptionally save for some of them, and that they were not of a prescriptive nature. In other words, it was surmised that those provisions in the Treaty merely amounted to *programmatic* rules, not intended to place the Member States under real obligations, but just to restate an unspecific need for freedom of establishment and free provision of services. It was believed, in fact, that they were to be implemented through directives to be issued by the Council acting upon proposals from the Commission, when and as specified in the relevant articles and set out in the subsequent two general programmes, and that only such directives, viewed as actual implementation rules, would be adequate – once they had entered into effect and at the end of the adjustment period allowed therein to the Member States – to operate as obligations binding upon Member States, obviously subject to the specific requirements set out in each such directive.

In this context, a Member State's duty to recognize foreign companies that were another Member State's nationals –such duty being enshrined in the rules on establishment and the provision of services – was thought to be not intended for general application, but to be essentially related to the activities already governed in fact by Council directives, and only as such eligible for liberalization.

Further to the many directives designed to govern the position of specific classes of self-employed persons, another instrument was clearly to be reckoned with alongside, and as a supplement to, Council Directive No 68/360/EEC of 15 October 1968 on the abolition of restrictions on movement and residence within the Community for workers of Member States and their families.[103] Such other instrument was Council Directive 73/148/EEC of 21 May 1973 on the abolition of restrictions on movement and residence within the Community for nationals of Member States with regard to establishment and the provision of services in respect of activities as self-employed persons.[104]

---

102. See Judgments *Jean Reyners* v *Belgian State*, 21 Jun. 1974, in Case 2/74, and *Johannes Henricus Maria van Binsbergen* v *Bestuur van de Bedrijfsvereniging voor de Metaalnijverheid*, 3 Dec. 1974, Case 33/74, [1974] ECR, p. 631 f. and p. 1299 f., respectively.
103. [1968] O.J. L257, p. 13.
104. [1973] O.J. L172, p. 14.

In pursuance of Article 1 of Directive 73/148:

> The Member States shall, acting as provided in this Directive, abolish restrictions on the movement and residence of: (. . .) (a) nationals of a Member State who are established or who wish to establish themselves in another Member State in order to pursue activities as self-employed persons, or who wish to provide services in that State;
>
> (b) nationals of Member States wishing to go to another Member State as recipients of services;
> (c) the spouse and the children under twenty-one years of age of such nationals, irrespective of their nationality;
> (d) the relatives in the ascending and descending lines of such nationals and of the spouse of such nationals, which relatives are dependent on them, irrespective of their nationality.

The recognition of the right of natural persons indicated in Article 1 to leave their home-countries is provided for in Article 2:

> Member States shall favour the admission of any other member of the family of a national referred to in paragraph 1 (a) or (b) or of the spouse of that national, which member is dependent on that national or spouse of that national or who in the country of origin was living under the same roof.

In accordance with the first paragraph of Article 4:

> Each Member State shall grant *the right of permanent residence* to nationals of other Member States who establish themselves within its territory in order to pursue activities as self-employed persons, when the restrictions on these activities have been abolished pursuant to the Treaty. [*Emphasis added*].

Further, pursuant to the second paragraph:

> The right of residence for persons providing and receiving services shall be of equal duration with the period during which the services are provided. [*Emphasis added*].

Finally, Article 8 of Directive No 73/148 re-asserts the principle of general protection enshrined in Article 46(1) of the Treaty of Rome:

> Member States shall not derogate from the provisions of this Directive save on grounds of *public policy, public security or public health.* [*Emphasis added*].

The question was posed in *Daily Mail*[105] whether the applicability of the provisions in Directive No 73/148 could be extended, whether by analogy or otherwise, to companies and other legal persons by virtue of the parallelism laid down in Article 48(1) EC. This was, in fact, drastically denied by the Court of Justice in its

105. See *Überseering* Judgment of 5 Nov. 2002, cit., *loc. cit.*

judgment of 27 September 1988, whereby it decided the case, by stating at point 28:

> It need merely be pointed out in that regard that the title and provisions of that directive *refer solely to the movement and residence of natural persons* and that the provisions of the directive *cannot*, by their nature, *be applied by analogy to legal persons*. [*Emphasis added*].

In light of the Court of Justice's judgments in *Reyners*, relating to freedom of establishment, and *van Binsbergen*, relating to the free provision of services, the underlying criteria have repeatedly been re-affirmed by the Court in later judgments without second thoughts. Thus, it can be stated outright that these are settled principles of Community law, which, as such, entail far more than the normal materiality of a case-law approach. Therefore, all the rules on establishment and services, *including the provisions that have not been implemented at the end of the transitional period*, must be deemed to have been *directly applicable* since 1 January 1970. In other words, all the provisions in Chapters 2 and 3 of Title III of the Treaty, including those believed to be merely programmatic theretofore, must be deemed to be directly enforceable in themselves under each Member State's internal legal system.

The Court's approach has remained constant in the sense just discussed. In this respect, suffice it to reproduce some of its statements, as follows:

> Article 52 [now Article 43] of the Treaty constitutes one of the *fundamental provisions* of Community law and *has been directly applicable* in the Member States since the end of the transitional period. Under that provision, freedom of establishment for nationals of a Member State on the territory of another Member State includes the right to take up and pursue activities as self-employed persons and to set up and manage undertakings *under the conditions laid down for its own nationals by the law of the country where such establishment is effected*. [*Emphasis added*].[106]

Again:

> (. . .), it must be borne in mind that, as the Court has already had occasion to point out, the freedom of establishment, conferred by Article 43 EC on Community nationals, includes the right for them to take up and pursue activities as self-employed persons and to set up and manage undertakings under the same conditions as are laid down by the law of the Member State of establishment for its own nationals. Furthermore, according to the actual wording of Article 48 EC, *companies* or firms formed in accordance with the law of a Member State and having their registered office, central administration or principal place of business within the Community shall, for the purposes of

106. See Judgment of the Court (Fifth Chamber) of 13 Apr. 2000, *Baars* v *Inspecteur der Belastingen Particulieren/Oondernemingen Gorinchem*, Case C-251/98, [2000] ECR I-2287, ground 27. Also, in the same sense: Judgments of 28 Jan. 1986, *Commission* v *France*, Case 270/83, [1983] ECR 273, ground 13, and 29 Apr. 1999, *Royal Bank of Scotland*, Case C-317/97, [1997] ECR 2651, ground 22, both quoted in Judgment *Baars*.

> [the provisions of the Treaty concerning the right of establishment], be treated in the same way as natural persons who are nationals of Member States.
>
> The immediate consequence of this is that those companies or firms are entitled to carry on their business in another Member State. [*Emphasis added*].[107]

8. THE NOTION OF COMPANIES' FREEDOM OF ESTABLISHMENT WITHIN THE EUROPEAN UNION

The 'superior' rank granted by now to freedom of establishment under Community law has recently been emphasized by the European Court of Justice in quite clear terms:

> The right of establishment is *essential to the achievement of the objectives* set in the Treaty, the purpose of which is to guarantee to all Community citizens alike the *freedom to engage in business activities* through the instruments provided by national law, thus giving them *the chance to enter the market, irrespective of the motives that may actually have prompted the person concerned*. In other words, *it is the opportunity to exercise business activities that* is protected, and with it the *contractual freedom* to make use of the instruments provided for that purpose in the legal systems of the Member States. [*Emphasis added*].[108]

The foundation of the freedom of establishment notion in regard to companies is the now most obvious consideration that, as Advocate General La Pergola clearly stated in his opinion in *Centros Ltd*:[109]

> The rule contained in Article 52 (now Article 43) of the Treaty, *which has been directly applicable since the end of the transitional period*, is intended to ensure that all nationals of Member States who establish themselves in another Member State, *even if that establishment is only secondary*, for the purpose of pursuing activities there as self-employed persons receive *the same treatment as nationals* of that State. [*Emphasis added*].

As for the contents and scope of this fundamental freedom in relation to business activities, Advocate General La Pergola further observed that it had ultimately become apparent to its full extent. For:

> The right of establishment includes *the right to set up and manage undertakings* under the conditions laid down for its own nationals by the law of the host country and *the setting up of agencies, branches or subsidiaries* by

107. See Judgment in *Uberseering BV*, cit., grounds 56 and 57 and 59 and 60.
108. See Opinion of Advocate General La Pergola, filed on 16 Jul. 1998, Case C-212/97, *Centros Ltd* v *Erhvers – og Selskabsstyrelsen*, [1999] ECR I-1459, ground 20, The ECJ's judgment, in line with this opinion, is dated 9 Mar. 1999.
109. See Opinion of Advocate General La Pergola, cit., point 12.

> Community nationals having their principal establishment in the territory of another Member State. And under Article 58 [now 48] of the Treaty, the right of establishment also includes *the right* of companies or firms formed in accordance with the law of a Member State and having their registered office, central administration or principal place of business within the Community *to do business in another Member State through a secondary establishment. Three further rights are a logical corollary of this fundamental freedom:* first, company business may be conducted in a Member State through a company incorporated in that State or in another Member State; second, companies have the right to decide whether a secondary establishment is to be a subsidiary or a branch; and lastly, *foreign companies have the same rights* in the State in which the secondary establishment is set up *as the companies of that State*. [*Emphasis added*].

Following this general representation of the object of freedom of establishment, Mr La Pergola referred to companies not bearing really Community-specific interests to comment:

> As the liberal provision of Article 58 [now Article 48] could be interpreted as meaning that the freedom to set up a secondary establishment is also extended to legal persons having their registered office but not their 'real' head office, that is to say their central administration or principal place of business, within the Community, it very soon became clear that the conditions governing that freedom in the case of companies *whose principal establishment was outside the Community* would have to be defined. For that purpose, as explained in the *General programme* for the removal of restrictions on freedom of establishment adopted by the Council on 18 December 1961, it is necessary to satisfy the further criterion of an economic connection, an '*effective and continuous*' *link with the economy of a Member State*. [*Emphasis added*].

Similar contents were to be found in the General Programme for the abolition of restrictions on freedom to provide services adopted on the same date.[110] It is appropriate to note that the presence of that further contact factor solely concerned companies that were *not* effectively Community-based.[111] That was not a novel issue, and, meaningfully enough, the need for corrections to the criterion of the place of constitution as such – which were, in fact, present in Articles 3 and 4 of the Brussels Convention of 29 February 1968, as well as in some laws of the Member States,[112] though incompatible with the Treaty rules on establishment and services

110. In cases of establishment based on the relevant general programme, the requirement of an 'effective and continuous' link is limited to the opening of agencies, subsidiaries or branches by a company with statutory registered office within the Community's jurisdiction.
111. See Judgment of the Court of 13 Dec. 2005, Case C-411/03, *SEVIC Systems AG*, [2005] ECR I-10805 and Advocate General Tizzano's Opinion of 7 Jul. 2005 in that case, point 31.
112. As for the Italian, Belgian and Luxembourg laws, please refer to my book *Le società*, cit., p. 221 ff., n. 44. The same layout has been kept in the later Italian and Belgian legislation on reforms of private international law in both systems. Likewise, see Article 25 of Act No.

at that level – was again pointed up in the General Programme, obviously by way of exception, with a view to protecting the Community system as a whole, in order to avoid an *artificial* extensive application of the rules on establishment and the provision of services.

Both General Programmes only define such additional requirement in the negative. The statement that the required link shall not 'depend on nationality, particularly of partners, members of managing or controlling bodies or shareholders' expressly dismisses the so-called 'control' criterion, but by no means contributes towards a positive interpretation of that phrase.[113]

Thus, there can be no doubt that, as a general rule, meeting the requirements set out in Article 43 of the Treaty allows any company – a 'Community' company, in fact – to enjoy freedom of establishment, and implies that company's right to carry on *even all* of its business activities in any Member State other than its State of origin through a subsidiary, a branch, an agency or even a representative office.[114]

In respect of the concepts of 'branch' and 'subsidiary', Advocate General La Pergola, in stating he chose to use the Italian word '*affiliata*' rather than '*filiale*', as a term more appropriate to indicate a legally independent company constituted in the State of establishment of its parent company belonging to another Member State of the European Union, wondered:

> What is the criterion for distinguishing between these two forms of *permanent* territorial division that a company may set up, possibly in the territory of Member States other than the State of origin, generally with the intention that they should deal with third parties? The essential difference is that *a branch has no independent legal personality* but is defined as part of a de facto whole or simply as a limb of the company, allowing a measure of decentralisation. A *subsidiary*, on the other hand, *is legally independent of the parent company* by which it is controlled. As learned writers have observed, the distinction between these two legal devices employed by companies to set up establishments in other countries is important in various respects. Above all, since *nationality* is an attribute of *personality*, a *branch* whose activity is the same as that of its parent company *cannot have a different nationality from that company*; and *its legal status is governed by the legal order to which the parent company*, of which it is merely a limb, *is subject*. The *opposite applies to subsidiaries*. Moreover, although a branch may enjoy a degree of managerial independence, the parent company alone is responsible for the business activity conducted on its behalf by the person appointed to run the branch. A subsidiary, on the other hand, can legitimately conclude contracts, though in some cases the parent company may intervene in the

218/1995, cit., and Articles 110 to 115 of the *Loi portant le Code de droit international privé (belge)* of 16 Jul. 2004, in *Mon. belge* of 27 Jul. 2004.

113. On this subject, see Caportorti, *Il problema*, cit., p. 14.
114. See, one for all, Judgment of the Court of 13 Dec. 2005, Case C-446/03, *Marks & Spencer plc*, [2005] ECR I-10837.

> transaction as a contracting party. And lastly, *on the principle of unity of assets and liabilities, any debts contracted (or, conversely, credits accumulated) by a branch in the course of its activities are chargeable to the company (so that it is incorrect to speak of a branch's debts)* inasmuch as, for reasons of practical convenience, creditors are normally allowed in such cases to bring an action against the company before the court of the place where the branch is established (see point 18 below). A *subsidiary*, on the other hand, *has its own funds to settle any debts it has contracted*; the subsidiary with its own separate legal personality thus acts as a *protective screen* between parent company and creditors. [*Emphasis added*].[115]

9. THE SCOPE OF A COMPANY'S RIGHT OF ESTABLISHMENT

The considerations offered above concern the various ways in which a company or firm caught by the broad definition set out in Article 48 EC and meeting the requirements laid down in the first paragraph of that article may exercise its right of establishment within the European Union. They are not, however, adequate to clarify the actual contents of such right as they are acknowledged today.

Those contents are added or opposed,[116] as the case may be, to those typical of the free provision of services, and their actual exercise has been reinforced by the full implementation of the rules on free capital movements[117] through suitable provisions enacted following significant ECJ precedents.[118] Thus, as shown by the substantial Community case-law that has built up in the last few years, the scope of the right of establishment has been broadened to include any issues as may arise in practice in respect of the treatment of 'Community foreigners', whether natural or legal persons, within the European Union. As for business companies, freedom of establishment encompasses any economic activities actually conducted by a body corporate in one or more Community Member States other than its home country, itself a Member State.

ECJ case-law now ranges from the recognition of legal capacity or even the capacity to file actions in the country of establishment (ECJ Judgment of

---

115. See Opinion in Case *Centros Ltd.*, cit., point 15.
116. See Judgment of the Court of 4 Dec. 1986, Case 205/84, *Commission v. Germany*, [1986] ECR 3755. In matters of insurance, please refer to the second edition of my book *Diritto commerciale comunitario* (Milan, 1995), pp. 32 ff. See also Capitolo III below, *passim.*
117. In relation to the evolution of the matter from Articles 67 ff. of the Treaty and to EJC case-law leading up to the new rules introduced by the Maastricht Treaty, please refer to Chapter III of this book.
118. Full implementation of the free movement of capital and payments has disposed of the inconsistency formerly existing, in insurance matters, between Article 61(2) of the Rome Treaty, now repealed, and the specific provision in the First Directive of 11 May 1960, which liberalized foreign exchange transfers made under insurance policies. Please, refer to the second edition of this book, p. 32 f. See also Chapter III below, *passim.*

5 November 2002 in *Überseering A.G.*[119]), or the recognition of the effects of a cross-border merger (ECJ Judgment of 13 December 2005 in *SEVIC Systems A.G.*[120]), to shopping for the tax system most favourable to an undertaking (ECJ Judgment of 12 September 2006 in *Cadbury Schweppes plc & Cadbury Schweppes Overseas Ltd v Commissioners of Inland Revenue*[121]). Other cases decided in this domain have involved a national company's control in sectors where restrictions on foreign nationals are justified on grounds of public policy, public security or public health (Article 46(1) EC) – better known as 'golden share' issues[122] – or the allegedly unlawful attempt by a Member State of establishment to apply to a foreign company's branch national rules on minimum capital and directors' joint and several liability that are not caught by a directive for the harmonization of company laws within the Community (specifically, the Eleventh Directive pursuant to Article 44(2)(g) EC: ECJ Judgment of 30 September 2003 in *Kramer van Koophandel en Fabrieken voor Amsterdam v Inspire Art Ltd*[123]), especially because the rationale behind such directives is to ensure a more correct application of the right of establishment. Another such case required a decision to be taken about the compatibility of the actions a national (Finnish) trade union, supported by an (English) international association of trade unions of which it was a member, initiated on grounds of social rights, threatening strikes and boycotts if the employer, a Finnish operator of ferry services, had carried through its plan to change its place of establishment to Estonia (and to change its 'flag of convenience') to benefit from lower wage levels for local seamen (Judgment of 11 December 2007 in *The International Transport Workers' Federation and The Finnish Seamen's Union* v *Viking Line ABP and OÜ Viking Line Eesti*[124]).

In summary, the entire matter now embraces any appropriate ways and means to abolish discrimination against a Member State's nationals – or, by virtue of the equal treatment principle laid down in Article 48(1) EC, against another Member State's company meeting the requirements of the same article – in any other Member State across the European Union.

In this connection, Advocate General Tizzano has aptly observed:[125]

> As we know, in order to guarantee full enjoyment of the right of establishment, which is understood as being allowed 'to participate, *on a stable and*

119. See *Uberseering* Judgment, cit.
120. See *SEVIC Systems AG* Judgment, cit.
121. Case C-196/04, [2006] ECR I-7995.
122. Although these last profiles are more specifically connected with the right of establishment of the actual or potential foreign members of a national company in terms of the free provision of services or even free movements of capital, they by no means concern the issue of the recognition of companies, which is discussed extensively in Chapter III on '*Capital*', which is referred to here.
123. Case C-167/01, [2003] ECR I-10155.
124. This was Case C-438/05, Reference for a preliminary ruling from the *Court of Appeal (Civil Division)* of England and Wales. Advocate General Poiares Maduro had filed his Opinion on 23 May 2007.
125. In Opinion in Case *SEVIC Systems AG*, cit., grounds 29, 30 e 31.

> *continuous basis*, in the economic life of [another] Member State', the Court subjected to Articles 43 EC and 48 EC not only the national rules and practices relating directly and specifically to the pursuit of the economic activity in question but also all those '*relating to the various general facilities which are of assistance in the pursuit of those activities*'.
>
> Therefore, the right of establishment covers all measures *which permit or even merely facilitate* access to another Member State *and/or the pursuit of an economic activity* in that Member State by allowing the persons concerned to participate in the economic life of the country effectively and *under the same conditions as national operators*.
>
> In laying down these principles, the Court has almost always referred specifically to the General Programme for the abolition of restrictions on freedom of establishment adopted by the Council on 18 December 1961, under which the following restrictions are to be eliminated: 'provisions and practices which, *in respect of foreign nationals only*, exclude, limit or impose conditions on the power to exercise rights normally attaching to an activity as a self-employed person'. The Programme provides, purely by way of illustration, a list of those 'powers' including, in so far as it is relevant here, *the power to 'enter into contracts' and to acquire, use or dispose of movable or immovable property*. [*Emphasis added*].

In this context, it is even too obvious that the choice as to what means to apply in the pursuit of economic activities in the State of establishment *on a stable and continuous basis* may solely be made by the foreign company involved, and that both the scope of such activities – in that the company has the power to concentrate *even all of its business operations* in the host State – and the reasons behind that choice are entirely irrelevant to the exercise by the company of its rights in that State.

The only one relevant requirement is, instead, that the branch or agency being so set up should not be a '*fictitious*' establishment or that the subsidiary could not be regarded as just a '*letterbox*' or '*front*' operation. Whatever the arrangement chosen, it must be 'an *actual establishment* intended to carry on *genuine economic activities* in the host Member State' [*Emphasis added*].[126]

10. PRIVATE INTERNATIONAL LAW ON COMPANIES AND THE ESTABLISHMENT RULES

The special value recognized to the rules on freedom of establishment and the free provision of services under the fundamental principle sanctioning their general purport and direct applicability – as well as their prevalence over any provisions of national law potentially contrasting with them or even just limiting the unrestricted

126. See Judgment of the Court of 12 Sep. 2006, cit., grounds 54 ff., especially grounds 66 and 68.

exercise of the rights protected in the relevant domains of the Community legal system – only save for any '*frauds or abuses*' on the part of those entitled, the existence of which must, in fact, be demonstrated by the claimant on a *case-by-case basis*, is a fundamental proposition bound to have an impact also on the traditional relationship between the two different concepts of '*recognition*' of companies. One such concept is aimed – as stressed above – at solving the problem in private international law of how to identify the law specifically regulating the existence and structure of a company as a body corporate for such company to be recognized[127] in the legal system from whose point of view the issue is considered. The other concept is to be applied, in principle, at a subsequent stage, in relation to the treatment of the company so recognized as already existing, in the sense indicated above, in a Member State other than that whose laws regulate that company's existence and affairs.

Though the provisions in Articles 43 et seq. and 49 et seq. of the Treaty are worded – as noted earlier – in a similar way as the clauses contained in bilateral establishment treaties, in the various meanings examined above, they are now radically removed from them as a result of substantial changes occurred over time in their interpretation in the Court of Justice case-law, because of the dual requirement as to their direct applicability and their absolute prevalence over national rules, whether substantive or instrumental.

If full enjoyment of the right of establishment in any form under Article 43 et seq. of the Treaty prevails over any contrary provisions of national law, the *recognition* of a 'Community company' from the standpoint of a Member State other then the Member State of origin, may only be ensured by the provision in Article 48(1) EC which dictates the application criteria governing the entire matter.[128]

Only in this way, even in relation to the initial stage of a company's life, may any conflict possibly arising from the preference accorded in a Member State's legal system to the contact factor of the place of central administration – in the various meanings this phrase may take[129] – over the criterion of the place of constitution (i.e. the place where the company is formed, which is, in fact, the same as the place of its statutory registered office, which is, as a rule or by practice, located

127. When referred to a company herein, the adjectives '*foreign*' and '*national*' are obviously used in a figurative sense and are tantamount to references to a company '*subject to a foreign law*' and '*subject to the national law*', respectively, thereby stressing the outcome of the line of reasoning in private international law, in the same way as reference is usually made to a '*national*' contract or to a '*foreign*' marriage.

128. This conclusion should not come as a surprise for those who wrote, as did in my study 'Problemi interpretativi', cit., p. 322 f., that, for the purposes of the rules on freedom of establishment, the recognition of the company was granted in *re ipsa*. At that time, the difference arose from the limited contents of companies' right of establishment, as this right was enshrined in the directives for implementation issued by the Council until then (the landmark judgments of the ECJ in *Reyners* and *van Binsbergen* having been delivered in 1974), in contrast with the consequently wider contents then attributable to the rules on the treatment of foreign companies.

129. See my book *Le società*, cit., p. 99 ff. and p. 141 ff.

in the country of incorporation since the beginning)[130] as adopted under the private international law on companies in force in another Member State, be deemed to be entirely irrelevant to the enjoyment of freedom of establishment. This is because the existence or, if you will, the 'legal capacity' of a company validly constituted in a Member State's legal system must – wherever the further, alternative factor of contact with the Community system may be – be assumed as such in the internal system of any of the other EU Member States. Nor may any conflict with the law of the State of central administration be deemed to prevent, even the less to obstruct, the full exercise of that company's right of establishment, in any of the permitted forms, in another Member State, or the widest possible provision by it of services towards any other Member State, without the company being subjected to whatever burden or required to adjust its articles of association to suit the company law of the State of establishment.

Specifically in connection with the contents of the right of establishment, the distinction between *primary* and *secondary* establishment is itself entirely irrelevant. This is because, as I have observed elsewhere:

> When the two requirements for Community nationality laid down in Article 58 [now Article 48] are satisfied, i.e. when a company is lawfully constituted and belongs to a Member State, *it is entitled to receive the same treatment as companies of a Member State other than the State in which its principal establishment is situated*, even if it carries on its business *solely* in that other State *through* an agency, branch or subsidiary. [*Emphasis added*].[131]

As this proposition applies to any company wishing to set up a *secondary* establishment in such other State, it is applicable *a fortiori* to the setting up of its *principal* establishment in that or any other Member State, even when the company does not conduct nor intends to conduct any activities in its home State. What matters is, rather, that the company does *actually* carry on its business in the host Member State *on a permanent basis* or exercises whatever activity there which a company of that Member State could otherwise carry out in its stead.

Thus, the logical terms within which the 'recognition' of a foreign company is framed are reversed.[132] As the criterion of the valid constitution of a company in any of the EU Member States is satisfied when that company, 'national' of that State, has, within the Community, then in any other Member State, met even only one of the other three requirements of Community law, i.e. registered office, central administration or principal place of business placed within the Community,

---

130. According to Blumberg, *The Multinational Challenge*, cit., p. 171: 'Although some civil law jurisdictions look to the principal place of business, or the *siège sociale*, even these countries require incorporation in the same state, so that in the end the text is much the same.'

131. See Advocate General La Pergola's Opinion in *Centros Ltd.*, cit., point 13. Likewise, Judgment of 10 Jul. 1986, Case 79/85, [1985] ECR 2375, grounds 15 and 16, quoted by AG La Pergola.

132. That is why I have chosen, for the sake of a summary presentation more closely pointing to the contents of this chapter, to change its heading, reversing it formulation from that of the same chapter in previous editions.

it is fully entitled, in the same way as a natural person who is 'national' of a Member State, to establish itself anywhere within the European Union, and to enjoy the fullest prerogatives arising from the exercise of such fundamental freedom, *without being discriminated* from local companies, whatever prescriptions are applied to the constitution, structuring and functioning of domestic companies in the host legal system. The same applies, *mutatis mutandis*, to the exercise of the rights to the free provision of services or to the free movement of capital.

The issue at the core of *Überseering*,[133] a case the European Court of Justice, acting upon reference by the *Bundesgerichthof* for a preliminary ruling, decided by its judgment of 5 November 2001, arose from the conflict between the laws of the Netherlands, the company's place of incorporation, as identified in that country's private international law system based on the *Gründungstheorie*, or incorporation approach, and the German laws, as referred to in the German private international law applicable to companies, which were based on the *Sitztheorie*, or seat principle.

Under the German law, much as the Dutch company had been incorporated under the laws of a Member State (the Netherlands), it should *not*, following the establishment of its central administration in Germany – a fact irrelevant under Dutch law, in that it did not entail the transfer of the company's registered office to a foreign country – have had either *general legal capacity* or the *capacity to bring legal proceedings in a German court to defend its rights* under a contract it had entered into with a company incorporated under the laws of Germany, while it could, surprisingly enough, be sued before a German judge – as it had been, in fact, in a concurring action for the performance of that same contract. For it to enjoy those fundamental rights – to 'exist', that is – under the German laws, the Dutch company would have had no other choice than *to wind up its activities* in the Netherlands and *reincorporate itself* in Germany.[134]

However, as aptly observed, since such requirement applied to the case in issue, the consequence would have been unacceptable under Community law, because:

> The requirement of reincorporation of the same company in Germany is therefore tantamount to outright negation of freedom of establishment. [*Emphasis added*].[135]

Therefore, the following statement is one of the essential points of the Court's decision, which conformed to Advocate General Ruiz-Jarabo Colomer's Opinion:

> In those circumstances, the *refusal* by a host Member State ('B') to *recognise the legal capacity* of a company formed in accordance with the law of another Member State ('A') in which it has its registered office on the ground, in particular, that the company moved its actual centre of administration to Member State B following the acquisition of all its shares by nationals of that State residing there, with the result that *the company cannot*, in Member

133. See *Überseering* Judgment, cit.
134. See *Überseering* Judgment, 79
135. *Ibid.*, ground 82.

> State B, *bring legal proceedings* to defend rights under a contract *unless it is reincorporated under the law of Member State B, constitutes a restriction on freedom of establishment which is, in principle, incompatible with Articles 43 EC and 48 EC.* [*Emphasis added*].[136]

The Court's 'interpretative' judgment – which, as such, has the same prevalence as a Community rule over a conflicting rule of national law – is adequate to confirm that the phrase '*formed in accordance with the law of a Member State*' in Article 48(1) EC does not, in its present correct interpretation, entail reference to the law to be identified on the basis of the relevant conflict rule set out in the legal system of the EU Member State concerned, but is itself representative of a *criterion of direct link* with the State in which a company's constituting process takes place.

In summary, for the rules on free establishment and the free provision of services to generate useful effects in relation to an entitled company, the phrase 'companies or firms formed in accordance with the law of a Member State' should be construed as an instrumental rule capable to confer a Member State's *nationality* on a company, as a result of the law by which that company is governed, as referred to on the basis of that contact factor, the place of constitution.

Thus, that phrase takes the same import as I have identified in the similar phrase used in the Brussels Convention of 29 February 1968,[137] yet with the added advantage over the conventional provision that it is the Court of Justice's settled case-law that the mandatory rules of a Member State where a company incorporated under another Member State's laws has established its central administration shall not apply to that company. And so, the conflicts the 1968 Convention seemed to be inadequate to remove have radically been disposed of, along with the resulting denial of a company's existence, then of its recognition.[138]

In a different respect, the logical process implied in Article 48(1) of the Treaty is by no means a novel occurrence in this domain. For it matches a shift from the previous Italian system of private international laws relating to companies, as a result of which the relevant bilateral conflict rule based on the place of incorporation approach was identified in the provisions on the treatment of foreign companies, i.e. in the original text of Articles 2505 to 2509 of the Italian Civil Code (and, yet earlier, in the 1860 Act of the Sardinian States and the Kingdom of Italy, then in Articles 230 to 232 of the 1882 Code of Commerce).

Article 25 of Act No 218/1995 eventually established that rule by statute, under the caption '*Società ed altri enti*' (Companies and other Bodies Corporate), thus taking it for the first time into the body of Italian private international laws, and accordingly superseding Articles 2505 and 2509 of the Civil Code.

The end result has been a set of 'uniform' rules of private international law for the purposes of the enjoyment of freedom of establishment and the free provision

---

136. *Ibid.*, ground 83.
137. Please, refer to Santa Maria, 'Problemi interpretativi', cit., p. 308 f. and Id., *Le Società*, cit., p. 213 f.
138. See above, paragraph 2 of this chapter.

of services, based on the criterion of the place of constitution in a Member State of the Community, i.e. the State *freely chosen* as the one having the legal system most favourable to the relevant case by the founding partners of a given company who are Community citizens and, as such, direct beneficiaries of the freedom of establishment.[139] Needless to say, the company so formed will, in its turn, have the right to carry on its main, or indeed entire, business *on a permanent*, even exclusive, *basis* in any other Member State or States of the European Union, to freely provide there whatever services, and to be treated on an equal foot with the nationals of the host State – nothing more, nothing less. Still, subject to compliance by it with the laws of its home country, it will always be *exempted from any rules* as that prescribed by the host country's company law – or, *a fortiori*, by the laws in force in the different Member States in which the company provides services – in matters relating to capital, articles of association, the workings of governing bodies generally, and the relationships between the company and its shareholders, even in connection with personal liability for individual violations, much as such other rules may well be different from its home country's.

In fact, quite irrespective of any exceptional instance of 'abuse' by such company or its beneficiaries, or the protection of national interests that are vital to the State of establishment (of which more below), this approach would still, at the two different levels at which it operates, be subject to one limitation, at least in the present state of Community case-law. This would be the case with the transfer of a company's seat abroad, from its State of origin to another Member State of the European Union, in relation to which the former State's law would result in that company's *winding-up*. In this case, according to the *Daily Mail* precedent, the question would be less whether a foreign company's existence should be recognized by the State of establishment, than whether the original law of the Member State of constitution considers the company to have been *wound up as a result of the transfer of its registered office and/or real head office abroad*, even if to another Member State. This would prevent the company in question to benefit, '*in the present state of Community law*' (but the relevant judgment dates as far back as to 27 September 1998), from the right of establishment.

In fact, though the *Daily Mail* judgment has been referred to, albeit just incidentally, in subsequent cases decided by judgments of the opposite (open-minded) sign, just to distinguish each specific case then in issue from the *Daily Mail* case, it was later substantially reversed in *SEVIC*, the only one case that, as discussed below, concerned an issue – a *cross-border merger*, in fact – essentially similar to the *transfer of seat abroad* in *Daily Mail*. Further, some of the grounds relied upon by the ECJ in that twenty years' old judgment have been criticized or somewhat qualified by several advocates general in opinions rendered in later cases.

139. This is basically the conclusion that emerges from the entire Community case-law on the subject. See, esp.lly, *Centros* Judgment, cit., grounds 17 and 18, and Advocate General Alber's Opinion in *Inspire Art*, cit., point 81.

11. CRITICAL REMARKS ON THE DAILY MAIL JUDGMENT

One of the grounds relied upon by the European Court of Justice in support to its negative determination of the *Daily Mail* case in the judgment of 27 September 1988, was that:

> [U]nlike natural persons, companies are creatures of the law and, in the present state of Community law, creatures of national law. They exist only by virtue of the varying national legislation which determines their incorporation and functioning. [*Emphasis added*].

Based on this proposition, the Court stated that a requirement was lacking for the company in question to be deemed validly constituted in the relevant system, i.e. the subsequent removal of its (registered) office from that territory, which, by causing its *winding-up*, would not even give rise to the problem of whether it should be 'recognized' abroad, in another Member State of the European Union. Only in that case, therefore, would the want of a uniform Community rule requiring the *retention of legal personality* be really felt,[140] thus making the actual implementation of the equal treatment of individuals and companies under Article 43 EC necessarily partial for the purposes of the exercise of the right of establishment – though in that respect alone, as observed above.

The Court's line of reasoning appears to be conceptually correct only in the sense that, as a rule, remission under private international law must be made to the competent foreign system as a whole, so that due account must be taken, in the referring legal system, of a rule of the legal system referred to, which considers the relevant legal relationship *extinguished* upon the occurrence of certain facts or the failure of certain presuppositions.

Still, some doubts also arise from the purview of the EJC judgment in *Daily Mail* in relation to the allegedly negative provisions in the legal system of origin, even irrespective of the standard indicated above in terms of the prevalence of the Community rules on establishment and services over any contrasting national rules in force in any Member State.

To begin with, the statement that, unlike natural persons, corporate persons are 'created by a legal system, in which, alone, they exist', is inadequate by itself to rule out the parallelism of the former with the latter type of persons as postulated by Article 48(1) EC. It is also tautological in hinting at the succession in time of each group's creation, which the compilers of the Treaty were certainly well aware of. As for the effect so identified, it is quite surprising that that statement could be a blueprint, even in the way it is worded – more than one hundred fifty years later – of the contents of the concept based on the 'fiction' theory applied to legal persons, which General Prosecutor Leclercq had put forward before the Belgian Supreme

---

140. On Article 393, second indent, EC, please refer to the first paragraph of this Chapter I.

Court in support to his contention that a French company should not be recognized in Belgium.[141]

So many changes have occurred since then, though. A the present time, business companies are brought to life, in any Member State's legal system, by law, not on a case-by-case basis under a royal or government charter, and a general principle of recognition has superseded the initial contrary principle. Thus, there is no longer any reason why a person, whether a 'legal person' or a '*personae morale*', which has come to exist in a given legal system, in the same way as any other legal relationship, such as a contract or a marriage, may not move across the boundaries of that system. In fact, the existence of that general positive principle of recognition postulates quite the opposite. Were it not so, what would be the sense of the rule of English law whereby the legal relationships arising from a trade agreement or a marriage – both being contracts of duration – 'initially' governed by that law are considered 'extinguished' if either party to the agreement or both spouses, as the case may be, have moved their residence to a foreign country? The law governing that relationship may well have changed, but never ever may the relationship itself be deemed extinguished.

It is patently clear that, regardless of whether the choice to establish oneself elsewhere within the European Union is specifically made by the shareholders (as in *Centros* and in *Überseering BV*) or by the company or, in the latter case, whether it is the company which sets up a new business organization (a subsidiary) or establishes its central administration or a secondary office (a branch) or even an agency in another Member State, these are all *manners* in which freedom of establishment can become fact.

It is freedom of establishment alone which is the object of legal protection. To say it in Community terminology, only through the full implementation of freedom of establishment in any of the many forms it may materialize will Articles 43 et seq. EC attain *the useful effect* they are intended to ensure.

In fact, the ultimate addressees of the rights arising from freedom of establishment or the free provision of services are individual natural persons, in their being 'citizens of the European Union'. For they are those who are, whether directly or through companies caught by the provisions of Article 48 of the Treaty, accorded the fullest power of choice for the utilization of a corporate tool already existing or to be newly formed in any of the European Union's Member States. The flexibility of the corporate tool to be so used – which, as indicated above, can be either an entirely new company, a subsidiary (a company's company, that is), a branch, an agency or even a representative office – is borne out by the European Court of Justice's case-law, which has invariably dealt with such various instances in the same way.

Therefore, beside the requirement of equal treatment of legal and natural persons laid out in Article 48(1) EC, the relevance of being a company has radically changed. For it has lost its time-honoured place among 'legal entities' to become one of the occurrences to be dealt with in the domain of 'legal relationships'.

---

141. See paragraph 3, above, in this Chapter I.

Fully in accordance with the historical evolution of the rules of private international law relating to companies in the Italian legal system, it is perfectly useless in the system of Community laws to embark on a scrutiny intended to establish whether, in any one case, the company in question is treated as a corporate 'person' or a corporate 'non-person' in the relevant jurisdiction of incorporation.

This conclusion conforms to the reasoned rethinking of the matter by the most alert scholars in the field of Italian civil law. They have long admonished that the role played by the concept of legal person in legal dogmatism is less in pointing to the existence of an entity, whether fictitious or real, than, essentially, 'in concealing the existence of special sets or rules'.[142] They have also specified that, under the Italian company law currently in force, the 'subjectivity' typical of any body corporate is a notion by now distinct from the notion of 'legal person' understood as an indication of 'limited liability' – itself an exceptional qualification recognized by law to certain types of companies, albeit within an ever-narrowing scope in common law or, according to some, even falling outside any applicable provisions of law. In this last respect, '*Legal person* now sounds as a term, or looks as a symbol, deprived of meaning, since there is no way to find any meaningful description of such symbol'.[143] In this perspective, to say that 'a limited company is a legal person' is to say nothing different from saying 'a limited company is a limited company'. Likewise, saying that 'an unlimited partnership simple' is not a 'legal person' merely means that an unlimited partnership simple is neither a partnership limited by shares or a company limited by quotas, nor a company limited by shares, nor even a cooperative company with limited liability.[144]

Clearly enough, 'subjectivity' is not in question in the sense of the 'autonomy' of any company, whatever its corporate status. The company is a *third party* vis-à-vis its members, and its assets do not, even just indirectly, belong to the members in proportion to their holdings, but they belong to the company. This is true even in the case of a sole owner, in which case, too, such assets belong to the company, with a view to meeting its obligations and to the protection of its stakeholders, and must be managed in the company's best interests, which may even not coincide with the sole owner's.

---

142. Please, refer in full to the considerations offered and the authors cited in footnote 59 to the third chapter of my book *Le società nel diritto internazionale privato*, cit., for an extensive criticism of the various schools of thought about the content of the 'legal person' notion.
143. In this sense, expressly, G. Rossi, *Persona giuridica, proprietà e rischio d'impresa* (Milan, 1967), esp.lly p. 51 ff. and 76 ff.
144. This assumption exceeds the boundaries of our positive law. In the same sense, see David, 'Rapport général', in *La personnalité morale et ses limites études de droit comparé et de droit international public* (Paris, 1960), and p. 7, where he states that the phrase 'legal person' is now there merely to indicate a '*simple formule*'. Likewise, Serick, *Forma e realtà della persona giuridica*, (Milan, 1966), Italian transl., Vitale Ed, cit., p. 84, body and fn. 37, where bibliographic references, reports, with regard to US law, that the main distinction between legal persons and associations without legal personality (e.g. '*partnerships*') is essentially that only a legal persons is created through recognition by the State. For more extensive considerations on the subject, see footnote 60 in the third chapter of my book *Le società*, cit.

None of the issues that may correctly be raised in case a company's seat and/or principal place of business or interests is transferred abroad may entail the company's purported dissolution, either in the host legal system neither in the home legal system. That is to say that the transfer does not affect the company's continuing existence, but only comes into play in relation to any possible change in the governing law or even to the fact that, in general, the host legal system may, in recognizing the foreign company, want to make it liable to mandatory rules of national law.

The latter case would, in fact, entail what is provided for in the Italian system of private international law – specifically in Article 25(1), second sentence, of Act 218 of 31 May 1995 – in relation to companies constituted abroad, then foreign entities, which establish their central administration or main business object in Italy. As for the former case, the question is generally settled by renvoi elsewhere, to another legal system that accepts renvoi, as allowed under a specific provision newly introduced in Article 13 of Act No 218/1995.

However, neither solution applies to 'Community companies'. By virtue of the primacy of EC Treaty rules on freedom of establishment and of the relevant EJC interpretative judgments, these companies are *automatically* recognized in the legal system of establishment and are only subject to the provisions that govern their incorporation, structure, functioning and winding-up in their home legal system, while the relevant rules of the State of establishment, whether or not mandatory, *must be disapplied*. Likewise, the *Daily Mail* precedent notwithstanding, the relevant substantive internal provision of the Member State of incorporation, if any is in force, and/or any provision of tax law as may equally prevent the company from leaving the country and settling in another country within the Community, *must* also *be disapplied*. As the home State's law alone remains applicable in any event, not even Article 13 of the Italian Act No 218/1995 has any role to play in this respect.

I think it appropriate to point up that Advocate General Ruiz-Jarabo Colomer thought the distinctions made by the Court of Justice in the *Daily Mail* judgment to be '*artificial*'.[145]

Serious doubts remain, though, about the real facts put forward by the Court in the grounds for that judgment. Mention is made there of the consent (withhold) by the British Treasury's to the English company's movement out of the United Kingdom (thereby effectively preventing the transfer of its registered office to the Netherlands). Therefore, what appeared to be at issue was not conflict with a prohibitory rule of material law, but the application of a provision of tax law. This view is borne out by the Court of Justice itself, whose *Daily Mail* judgment states:

> *Certain States* require that *not merely the registered office but also the real head office*, that is to say the central administration of the company, should be situated on their territory, and the removal of the central administration from that territory thus presupposes the winding-up of the company with all the

145. See his Opinion in *Überseering*, cit., point 37.

> consequences that winding-up entails in company law and tax law. *The legislation of other States* permits companies to transfer their central administration to a foreign country but certain of them, such as the United Kingdom, *make that right subject to certain restrictions, and the legal consequences of a transfer, particularly in regard to taxation, vary from one Member State to another.* [*Emphasis added*].[146]

In fact, English case-law has it that a legal person's 'domicile', as opposed to its 'residence', determines the applicable 'law of incorporation', and it remains so throughout that legal person's existence.[147]

Lacking the English tax authority's consent, the transferring company would have been treated 'as if' it had been wound up, without actual winding – up, then dissolution, being imposed upon it. As the Court of Justice aptly put it, though in a later judgment and without taking it into account in *Daily Mail*:

> It should be remembered that, according to settled case-law, although direct taxation falls within their competence, Member States must none the less exercise that competence *consistently with Community law*. [*Emphasis added*].[148]

If, therefore, dissolution is outright denial of the right of establishment, and retaining the entity's legal personality is a necessary requirement to permit actual implementation of freedom of establishment within the European Union, then, even in a case like *Daily Mail*, any conflict between Community law and national legislation was, and is, to be resolved in favour of the company, i.e. in the only suitable way to avoid such adverse effect. Likewise, the tax tinsel occasioned by the 'simulated' effects of winding-up was, and is, a quite heavy burden intended to discourage a company's free establishment in a Member State other than the home Member State, and must, as such, be permitted. The end result is, in principle, that the final national norm is disapplied.

As has aptly been noted,[149] lacking harmonization rules on the transfer of company seats between Member States, Member States must still '*comply with substantive Community law*', for the reasons extensively explained above.

---

146. See *Daily Mail* Judgment, cit. ground 20.
147. See, essentially: *Gasque* v. *Inland Revenue Commissioners*, [1940] K.B., II, p. 80 f., p. 84, and *Carl Zeiss Stiftung* v. *Rayners & Keeler Ltd*, [1970] Ch. I, p. 506 f., p. 544. For the distinction between '*domicile*' and '*residence*' of a company, a criterion that, because of the coincidence of 'residence' with the place in which '*its central management and control is exercised*', is relevant to corporation tax treatment in the United Kingdom, see: Cheshire & North, *Private International Law* (7th ed., London, 1987), p. 177, Dicey & Morris, *Conflict of Laws* (11th ed., London, 1987), vol. II, pp. 1130 f. and 1132 f.
148. See *Marks & Spencer plc* Judgment, cit., ground 29. See also, in particular, the judgment of 8 Mar. 2001, Joined Cases C-397/98 and C-410/98, *Metallgesellschaft and others*, [2001] ECR I-1727, ground 37, and case-law quoted therein.
149. See Advocate General Ruiz-Jarabo Colomer's Opinion, in *Überseering*, point 39.

12. CASE-LAW ON CROSS-BORDER MERGERS AND ITS IMPACT ON THE TRANSFER OF SEAT WITHIN THE EUROPEAN UNION: DIRECTIVE 2005/56/CE

The transfer of a company's seat to another country certainly makes one of the toughest, most critical issue in private international law on companies.[150]

As a rule, when reference is made to the transfer of a company's seat from one country to another, what is meant is the transfer of its *registered* office as stated in that company's articles of association, whether or not it is the same as the *real head office*. This is because, as observed above, whether according to practice or by express provision of law, the initial location of a company's registered office, according to its Articles, in a Member State that has adopted the 'incorporation approach'[151] is one of the elements to be specified in the complex incorporation procedure. In principle, the intensity of the problems arising from a proposed transfer can vary depending on whether the company moves between countries whose conflict rules relating to companies imply the same contact factor, or it moves its seat from a system based on the place of incorporation approach to a system based on the real seat approach, or the other way round.

However, beyond any solutions as may be available in any one case – which may or may not imply a change in the law governing that company – it is thought that, as a rule, *for a body corporate to retain legal personality*, the transfer of its seat to another country requires a positive determination by both the home-country and the host-country.[152] In other words, the transfer must take place in accordance with both countries' legislation *without* resulting in the company being *dissolved* and later *re-incorporated*.

---

150. About the possibility for a company governed by Italian law to move its registered office abroad without becoming extinguished thereby, see Capotorti, 'Il trasferimento di sede di una società da uno Stato all'altro' [1958] Foro it. IV, c. 209 f.; Id., 'Sulla continuità delle società di persone che trasferiscono la sede in un altro Stato' [1958] Riv. dir. int., p. 613 f.; Id., *Il diritto di stabilimento*, cit. p. 19 f.
151. See Goldman, *Rapport*, cit., para. 16. Under The Hague Convention of 1 Jun. 1956, the law of origin is identified as that of the place in which registration and publicity formalities were carried out and the company's statutory seat is located. According to van Hecke, *Rapport provisoire et projet de résolution* sul tema *Les sociétés anonymes en droit international*, to the Varsaw Session, in *Annuaire*, cit., p. 232, 'comme, à la connaissance du rapporteur, tous les pays qui pratiquent le système de l'incorporation exigent que leurs sociétés aient une adresse où elles puissent être officiellement touchées dans le territoire, l'incorporation s'accompagne nécessairement du siège statutaire de la société'. That incorporation in the State, according to Italian law, necessarily implies that a company's statutory seat is in Italian territory is contented by Capotorti, *La nazionalità*, cit., p. 200 s., esp.lly p. 204 s. The same view had been taken, with reference to the former Italian code of commerce, by: Anzilotti, *Il mutamento di nazionalità delle società commerciali* [1912] Riv. dir. int., p. 6 of the abstract; Cavaglieri, *Il diritto internazionale commerciale* (Padua, 1936), p. 152 and 156; and by Lefebvre d'Ovidio, *La nazionalità delle società commerciali* (Milan, 1939), p. 153. Please, also refer to my book, *Le società*, cit., p. 141, body and n. 103.
152. This the approach expressly provided for by Article 25(3) of Act No. 218/1995. In this regard, see below, paragraph 15 of this Chapter 1.

As far as Court of Justice case-law goes, only the lack of consent under the law of the State of incorporation would generate a hampering effect, while a negative determination by the State of establishment would certainly be unconsequential. Nor can the latter's demand to make the company liable to additional rules be granted, for any such demand would, according to well-established case-law, result in denying the right of establishment or, in any event, in placing (inadmissible) restrictions on the exercise of such right.

As involved is – in private international law generally – the issue of cross-border mergers, because of the necessary combination of the laws governing the acquirer and the acquiree, respectively.

A case of *cross-border* merger between a German company, SEVIC Systems AG (the absorbing party, or acquirer) and a Luxembourg company, Security Vision Concept SA (the absorbed party, or acquiree), was examined by the ECJ for a preliminary ruling on reference by the Landegericht Koblenz, and the relevant judgment was handed down by the Court on 13 December 2005.[153]

Advocate General Prof. Tizzano delivered his Opinion on the case on 7 July 2005,[154] and argued there against the German government's contention that, based on the *Daily Mail* precedent, the approach first taken by a German district court rejecting the registration in the national commercial register of the merger between the German company and the company established in Luxembourg was correct, and that the merger operation was to be deemed void as a result. Mr Tizzano argued as follows:

> For my part, I should state immediately that I do not share this view. That is primarily because it appears to me that it follows an *inverted logic* in the sense that it concludes that a consequence of the merger, namely the dissolution of the incorporated company, is the reason why that company is unable (even before it is dissolved!) to carry out the merger and therefore the justification for the prohibition on registration which precisely precludes this operation. However, the truth of the matter is that *throughout the stage preceding the merger* and up to the registration thereof *both companies exist and operate as legal persons* entirely capable of negotiating and entering into the merger contract. It is only when the merger is completed, and in particular when this act is registered, that *one of the two persons ceases to exist*. However, until such time that is not the case because *if the operation has not been completed the* company which was to have been incorporated *would continue to exist* as an autonomous legal person. [*Emphasis added*].[155]

153. See the judgment in *SEVIC Systems AG*, cit. That judgment clearly crossed with Directive No. 2005/56 (of which more below), which was not even mentioned in the judgment. It should be remembered that the deadline for implementing Directive No. 2005/56 in Member States' systems pursuant to Art. 19 was 15 Dec. 2007.
154. See AG's Opinion in *SEVIC Systems AG*, cit.
155. *Ibid.*, points 24, 25 and 26.

On this basis, Advocate General Tizzano concluded:

> Therefore, the contested national legislation affects legal entities in full possession of their legal capacity which precisely this legislation, and this legislation alone, bars from benefiting from freedom of establishment. Consequently, only by confusing cause and effect is it possible to justify the claim that the Treaty provisions are not applicable to cross-border mergers on the grounds that the incorporated company is purportedly devoid of legal personality. [*Emphasis added*].[156]

In other words, according to Prof. Tizzano, the 'dissolution' was a false problem in the case in issue, because, *if vesting a Community company with all possible rights arising from freedom of establishment ranks first in priority*, the fact that the company is deemed dissolved in the State of incorporation as a result of the enjoyment by that company of any such right goes contrary to Community law. Therefore, *dissolution cannot be correctly relied upon as a ground for denying the company's operations* in any one specific case. Nor has Advocate General Tizzano any doubts as to the fact that '*cross-border mergers*' (as well as *the transfer of a company's seat* from one country to another within the European Union) are operations falling *optimo jure* within the scope of freedom of establishment. Thus:

> To sum up, the right of establishment does not concern only the right to move to another Member State in order to purse an activity there, but also all the aspects which are linked in any way in complementary or functional terms with the pursuit of that activity and thus the exercise in full of the freedom laid down by the Treaty.
>
> It appears to me evident that this is so also in the case of the national legislation in question. It relates to *aspects* which are not complementary but *actually essential* to the activity of an economic operator since it precludes the conclusion of specific legal transactions (mergers) and in particular operations relating to acquisition/disposal or formation of new companies. [*Emphasis added*].[157]

Therefore, based on the broad definition of freedom of establishment that is evident from Community case-law, Prof. Tizzano concluded that withholding consent to the registration in the German commercial register of a merger between a company established in Germany and a company established in another Member State amounted to an *unlawful restriction* on freedom of establishment. In fact, he referred to the Court of Justice's judgment of 5 October 2004, C-442/02, *Caixa Bank France*, paragraph 26,[158] to point out that:

> 'all measures which prohibit, impede or render less attractive the exercise of that freedom' (...) must be regarded as restrictions thereof. *Consequently,*

156. *Ibid.*, points 27.
157. *Ibid.*, points 32 and 33.
158. [2004] ECR I-8961.

> *national measures which are merely likely to 'discourage' an operator from availing himself of the right of establishment can also be covered by this prohibition.* [*Emphasis added*].[159]

Based on the ECJ judgments in *Baars*[160] and *Hughes de Lasteyrie*,[161] Prof. Tizzano then added:[162]

> Furthermore, it is evident from this case-law that Article 43 EC does not merely prohibit a Member State from *impeding or restricting the establishment of foreign operators in its territory*, it also precludes it from *hindering the establishment of national operators in another Member State.*[163] In other words, *restrictions 'on entering' or 'on leaving' national territory are prohibited.*
>
> When these principles are applied to the present case, there would appear to be no doubt that legislation such as that at issue in the main proceedings is likely at least to discourage exercise of freedom of establishment both by national and foreign operators. [*Emphasis added*].

These considerations were conformed to by the European Court of Justice in *SEVIC* Judgement of 13 December 2005, in which it accommodated Advocate General Tizzano's Opinion.[164]

If, therefore, freedom of establishment does not only entail the capacity of a natural or legal person belonging to a Member State to benefit from the national treatment in another Member State to which it has transferred its business, but also requires that person's home State to refrain from raising obstacles apt to make his stable establishment in such other State impossible or just more difficult, then, based on this undeniable presupposition, the *transfer of a company's (registered) office from one country to another, or even the establishment of its central administration or real head office* in a State other than the State of its constitution, within the European Union's internal market, *cannot but be freely allowed in both directions*, without this resulting in that company's *dissolution* in any event, thereby avoiding the consequent need for it to be re-incorporated – which would, in fact, be tantamount, according to the Court of Justice, to 'outright negation of freedom of establishment'.[165]

It is now an established fact that, when the original logical approach to the relationship between the two different conceptions of recognition is reversed, the full implementation of the rules on free establishment (or free capital movements or the free provision of services) takes absolute priority. And the prevalence of

159. See AG's Opinion in *SEVIC Systems AG*, cit., point 40.
160. See *Baars* Judgment, cit., ground 28.
161. See Judgment of the Court of 11 Mar. 2004, Case C-9/02, *Hughes de Lasteyrie du Saillant*, [2004] ECR I-2409, ground 45.
162. See AG's Opinion in *SEVIC Systems AG*, cit., points 45 and 46.
163. See, esp.lly, judgments in *Baars*, cit., ground 28, e *Hughes de Lasteyrie du Saillant*, cit., ground 42.
164. [2005] ECR I-10805.
165. See *Überseering* Judgment, cit., ground 81.

such rules is such as to overcome, and dispose of, any restrictions in respect thereof, even those resulting from a possible conflict in private international law.

The way in which Article 48(1) EC is worded, in referring to the laws of the State of constitution and specifying three alternate contact factors in relation to Community law as a whole, implies a positive solution with a view to ensuring '*the retention of legal personality*' to a company moving its seat from one State to another within the Community, i.e. the essential requirement for it to benefit, *ipso facto*, from the rights freedom of establishment is all about.

To sum up, in general and in principle, except for exceptional instances in which the right of establishment may be restricted in practice, Member Sates are – it must be stressed once more – bound to conform to the applicable substantive rules of Community law.[166]

Accordingly, any provision of a company's home State's internal law requiring the company to be *dissolved* because of the transfer of its registered (or even real) head office to the host Member State, as well as any rule of the host Member State as may require amendments to be made to the company's articles of association or may otherwise affect its functioning – irrespective of whether or not such rules are considered mandatory under the latter country's national legislation – are *both* bound to be *disapplied*, in their being in conflict with the provisions of Articles 43 et seq. of the Treaty, by virtue of usual mechanism that regulates the relationships between Community law and national legislations.

Likewise, in a case of cross-border merger – one that is caught, in fact, by the rules on freedom of establishment – *no rule of national legislation may lawfully prevent* recognition, in either the acquirer's or the acquiree's legal system, of the effects typical of merger in respect of either of the 'Community companies' involved.

This is the principle underpinning Directive 2005/56/EC of the European Parliament and of the Council of 26 October 2005 on cross-border mergers of limited liability companies.[167]

Presumably because of the express reference in Article 293 of the Treaty to this matter as the potential subject of an international convention, Directive 2005/56 is not numbered as one of the directives relating to companies with Article 44(2)(g) EC as their legal basis. Nonetheless, except for the express reference in the first sentence of the preamble:

> Having regard to the Treaty establishing the European Community, and in particular Article 44 thereof,

it is the contents of the Directive which place it among the harmonization directives.[168] An even clearer link with those directives is to be found in Whereas 5 and 8

166. See AG Ruiz-Jarabo Colomer's Opinion in *Überseering*, cit., point 39.
167. [2005] O.J. L310, p. 1.
168. The essential contents of this directive will be discussed in paragraph 7 of Chapter II of this book. It should be noted that the matter had originally been covered by a draft international convention developed pursuant to Art. 220 of the Treaty, now Art. 293 EC (in *EC Bull.*

and in Article 2(1)(b), in relation to the determination of appropriate solutions, where reference is made to the phrase 'the protection of the interests of members and others', which expressly uses the same wording as is used in Article 44(2)(g) of the Treaty to indicate the rationale behind the need for adequate coordination of the safeguards required by Member States with a view to securing freedom of establishment to companies or firms.

Thus, the linkage of Directive 2005/56 with freedom of establishment has been expressly set out, and again emphasized in the second sentence of Whereas 3:

> In order to facilitate cross-border merger operations, it should be laid down that, unless this directive provides otherwise, each company taking part in a cross-border merger, and each third party concerned, remains *subject to the provisions and formalities of the national law which would be applicable in the case of a national merger.* None of the provisions and formalities of national law, to which reference is made in this directive, *should introduce restrictions on freedom of establishment or on the free movement of capital* save where these can be *justified in accordance with the case-law of the Court of Justice* and in particular by requirements of the general interest and are both *necessary for, and proportionate to,* the attainment of such overriding requirements. [*Emphasis added*].

In general, as the applicability of the directive is expressly restricted to 'limited liability companies', as these are defined in its Article 2(1),[169] it is fully consistent with recent Court of Justice case-law in relation to the possibility to proceed to cross-border mergers so long as at least two of the mergees belong to different Member States. For:

> This Directive shall apply to mergers of limited liability companies formed in accordance with the law of a Member State and having their registered office, central administration or principal place of business within the Community, provided at least two of them are governed by the laws of different Member States (hereinafter referred to as crossborder mergers). [*Emphasis added*].[170]

Suppl. 13, of 1973). Later on, such draft convention was withdrawn and re-submitted in the form of a proposal for a directive, numbered as the 'tenth', relating to companies, and, as such, included among harmonization directives pursuant to Article 54.(3)(g) of the Treaty (now Article 44(2)(g) EC).

169. 'For the purposes of this directive, "limited liability company" means: (a) a company as referred to in Article 1 of Directive 68/151/EEC, or (b) a company with share capital and having legal personality, possessing separate assets which alone serve to cover its debts and subject under the national law governing it to conditions concerning guarantees such as are provided for by Directive 68/151/EEC for the protection of the interests of members and others'. (Article 2(1), *ibid.*, p. 3).

170. See Article 1, *ibid.*, p. 3.

The wording of this provision, which restricts the 'scope' of Directive 2005/56, patently matches the wording of Article 48(1) EC, thereby implying the same interpretation as the Court of Justice has given of the latter. For it is as conducive to a *direct* determination, based on the place of incorporation approach, as to whether each of the parties to a merger belongs to a Member State, and, if such further factor of connection with the European Union as a whole is established, it is similarly bound to replace the applicable rules of private international law in the sense more comprehensively discussed above.

The principle underlying Directive 2005/56 is that, from each Member State's point of view, cross-border mergers between limited companies formed in different Member States are admissible if they would be so permitted in events of domestic mergers in each of the Member States. This confirms the principle of national treatment underlying the entire matter of free establishment.

In particular, in the terms of Article 4(1)(b):

> [A] company taking part in a cross-border merger shall comply with the provisions and formalities of the national law to which it is subject. The laws of a Member State enabling its national authorities to oppose a given internal merger on grounds of public interest shall also be applicable to a cross-border merger where at least one of the merging companies is subject to the law of that Member State. This provision shall not apply to the extent that Article 21 of Regulation (EC) No 139/2004 is applicable.

Exceptions are provided in any of the events of disapplication set out in Article 3. The first such exception is set out in paragraph 2 to provide an option:

> Member States may decide not to apply this Directive to cross-border mergers involving a cooperative society even in the cases where the latter would fall within the definition of 'limited liability company' as laid down in Article 2(1).

The second exception, however, requires outright exclusion under paragraph 3:

> This Directive shall not apply to cross-border mergers involving a company the object of which is the collective investment of capital provided by the public, which operates on the principle of risk-spreading and the units of which are, at the holders' request, repurchased or redeemed, directly or indirectly, out of the assets of that company. Action taken by such a company to ensure that the stock exchange value of its units does not vary significantly from its net asset value shall be regarded as equivalent to such repurchase or redemption.

Obviously, cross-border mergers entail the dissolution of the acquiree or of all the mergees, as the case may be, though *without winding-up being required* in any of the events provided for by Article 2. Since the date of entry into effect of the cross-border merger will fall after the scrutiny referred to in Article 11, pursuant to the law of the Member State to whose jurisdiction the company resulting from the merger is subject, the following consequences will ensue:[171]

> A cross-border merger carried out as laid down in points (a) and (c) of Article 2(2) shall, from the date referred to in Article 12, have the following consequences:
>
> (a) all the assets and liabilities of the company being acquired shall be transferred to the acquiring company;
> (b) the members of the company being acquired shall become members of the acquiring company;
> (c) the company being acquired shall cease to exist. (Paragraph 1)
>
> A cross-border merger carried out as laid down in point (b) of Article 2(2) shall, from the date referred to in Article 12, have the following consequences:
>
> (a) all the assets and liabilities of the merging companies shall be transferred to the new company;
> (b) the members of the merging companies shall become members of the new company;
> (c) the merging companies shall cease to exist. (Paragraph 2).

13. THE ABOVE PRINCIPLES AS APPLIED IN PRACTICE

The starting point is the correct observation indicated above, that the *dissolution* of a company as a legal entity upon its registered office or central administration being moved from one to another Member State of the European Union would be tantamount to outright negation of freedom of establishment. Therefore, the essential element deserving protection for the purposes discussed so far is the *retention of the corporate entity's legal personality* following the transfer of its registered office to another Member State within the European Union.

It is settled case-law that a company eligible for the enjoyment of the right of establishment may set up a 'branch' or even an 'agency',[172] but also its 'central administration' or 'principal place of business' in another Member State, and thereby pursue its activity *optimo iure* in the host Member State, where it will be treated on the same footing as national companies.

In exercising the rights arising to it from freedom of establishment, the 'Community company' will also be entitled to incorporate a new autonomous company (a 'subsidiary') in another Member State. In this case, too, it will secured the same treatment as that accorded to nationals of such other Member State, but

171. See Article 14, *ibid.*, p. 6 f.

172. See ECJ Judgments of 21 Sep. 1999, Case C-307/97, *Saint-Gobain ZN*, [1999] ECR I-6161, ground 35, of 13 Dec. 2005, Case C-446/03, *Marks & Spencer plc*, cit., ground 30; and of 16 Jul. 1998, Case C-264/96, *ICI*, [1998] ECR I-4695, ground 21.

solely, at its free election, through a company whose incorporation, structure and functioning shall be governed by the legislation of the host country.

In the case of a *branch*, it is the company governed by the law of one Member State that moves its own activity to another Member State, where it can well be made subject to the disclosure, direction and supervision requirements set out in the *Eleventh Directive* concerning disclosure requirements in respect of branches opened in a Member States, *but to no other requirement.* It should be stressed that, according to Community case-law, such company's right of establishment also extends to cover its decision to set up in, or transfers to, the host country not a secondary establishment, but even its principle place of business, to conduct even all of its business activities there.

Therefore, a Community company may transfer its registered office (assumedly being also its central administration) to another Member State. In this case, in principle – against the *Daily Mail* precedent, but in line with *SEVIC* – and because of the two-pronged requirement of Community case law, that freedom of establishment cannot be restricted by either any obstacles ruling in the host legal system or any obstacles raised in the home legal system,[173] such transfer of seat from one Member State to another may not be hampered by the legislation of the company's home country under a rule applying which would result in the company being dissolved following the establishment of its seat outside the Member State of constitution.

Assume that the legal system of the company's home country (say the Netherlands) provides that the Dutch law as the law governing a company no longer applies upon that company's registered office being moved to another country (say Italy). One outright solution would be for the company to leave its registered office where it was in the first place, and to set up its 'administrative office' or 'its main business object' in Italy (pursuant to the second sentence of Article 25(1) of Italian Act No 218/95). In this way, retention of status would be secured to that entity, which would remain subject to the home Member State's applicable law, without the host Member State's mandatory rules becoming binding on it (i.e. the provision in Article 25.1 just quoted above, which must be disapplied pursuant to Community case-law).

Further, that company would be considered to be Dutch both in the Dutch and in the Italian legal system. The same result would be achieved from the standpoint of yet another legal system, whatever approach is taken (whether the *Sietztheorie* or the *Grundungstheorie*) under the rules of private international law of such other legal system. And so the benefit of freedom of establishment for the legal entity in our example would be full and real.

If this is the conclusion that emerges from Community case-law in the case a secondary seat is established in a Member Country, the same conclusion applies to the exercise by a company incorporated in any one Member State of the European Union of its right of establishment in another Member State in case the original location of one or the other, or of all the three contact factors specified in the first

173. See, in particular, *ICI* Judgment, cit., ground 21.

paragraph of Article 48 EC changes, so long as at least one of them remains within the Community. In each such event, as well as in the event a branch or an agency is set up in another Member State, the company in question will remain entirely subject to the law of the place of constitution, without the legislation of the State of establishment requiring it to comply with any local rules in matters of articles of association, liability or corporate operations in general as may have contents different from, or even impose requirements in addition to, the laws of that company's home country.

As amply indicated in several instances of the Court of Justice's new case-law – whereas any rule of the legislation of the country of constitution possibly requiring a company's dissolution on exit should be disapplied as contrasting with the provisions of Article 43 et seq. EC – it is *the company's members* who, in principle, must have free choice between the home country, if it affords the more favourable rules of incorporation, and the host country if this is regarded as the system most favourable to the conduct of this or that business activity among the various possible arrangements actually available in different Member States. Accordingly, the company's members or the company itself will be free to determine where to transfer *some* or even the *whole* of the company's operations.

The rule laid down in the first paragraph of Article 48 EC must then be viewed as a conflict rule replacing that provided for by any one Member State's national system of private international law for the *only* purpose of securing the benefit of the rules on freedom of establishment or on the free provision of services to eligible companies. Only outside any situations that, *ratione materiae*, involve the exercise of either fundamental freedom within the wide objective scope for application indicated in ECJ case-law or even where, *subjectively*, the relevant community rules are not applicable in that the company concerned fails to meet the requirements prescribed by Article 48 EC as a whole, the national provisions of private international law relating to companies, and the usual conflicts and suitable technical instruments to solve them, will remain applicable.

14. THE 'NATIONAL' TREATMENT: SCOPE AND LIMITS UNDER COMMUNITY CASE-LAW

The national treatment ensured by establishment rules concerns any activity that a company meeting the contact requirements under Article 48(1) EC, in the same way as any natural person, intends to carry on in any Community legal system other than the system of origin.

This having been said, it should preliminary be noted that the contents of freedom of establishment are bound rather to expand further than to shrink over time, because of the progress towards more and more open-minded solutions compatible with the EC Treaty that usually accompanies its course in relation to major issues of Community interest. The opposite is obviously true in the case of restrictions likely to pose serious obstacles to the exercise of freedom of establishment, which are bound to fade away over time.

This goes a long way to explain why, in answering questions posed by national judges for the Court of Justice to deliver interpretative judgments on a wide range of issues, the Court has often used limiting phrases, such as 'in the present state of Community law'.[174]

As I have pointed out on several occasions, 'liberalization' is a two-pronged process, in the sense that:[175]

> Even though Article 52 of the Treaty, like the other provisions concerning freedom of establishment, is, according to its terms, aimed particularly at ensuring *that foreign nationals are treated in the host Member State in the same way as nationals of that State*, it also *prohibits the Member State of origin from hindering* the establishment in another Member State of one of its own nationals. [*Emphasis added*].[176]

And there is a varied array of prohibited 'discriminations':[177]

> It is also apparent from the case-law that the restrictions prohibited by Article 43 EC may take different forms. There may be *overt* discrimination on the basis of nationality or, in the case of a company, its seat. They can also take the form of '*indirect* discrimination', namely measures which apply irrespective of the company's seat and are based on conditions which apply without distinction which result essentially in *placing nationals from other Member States at a disadvantage*, such as the criterion of fiscal residence. Finally, in its more recent case-law, the Court does not inquire into whether the measure in question is to be classified as direct or indirect discrimination. It merely states that *there is a difference in tax treatment which creates a disadvantage for economic operators who have exercised the rights conferred by Article 43 EC and could deter them from exercising such rights*. [*Emphasis added*].

Conversely, the reasons that drive a trader, whether an individual or a company, to move freely across the territory of the European Union are entirely irrelevant:

> The Court has held that it is *immaterial*, having regard to the application of the rules on freedom of establishment, that the company was formed in one Member State *only for the purpose of establishing itself* in a second Member State, where its main, or indeed entire, business is to be conducted (*Segers*,

---

174. In examining the *Daily Mail* judgment, Advocate General Ruiz-Jarabo Colomer pointed out, in his Opinion of 4 Dec. 2001 in *Überseering AG*, cit., that that ruling only applied, because of the reservation expressed therein, to the extent of 'the state of Community law' as it then stood, and he accordingly argued that it should be established whether any such new changes had occurred since then in Community law, rules and case-law as to justify disregarding that earliest ruling on the matter (see Opinion, points 27, 28, 29 and 30). As a result, he shifted his analysis to the *Centros* judgment (Opinion, point 31).
175. See *Baars* judgment, cit., ground 28.
176. See Judgments of the Court: *Daily Mail*, cit., ground 16; *ICI*, cit., ground 21, and of 18 Nov. 1999, Case C-200/98 [1999] ECR I-8261, ground 26. See also *Baars* judgment, cit., *loc. cit.*
177. See Advocate General Léger's Opinion of 2 May 2006, in *Cadbury Schweppes*, decided by judgment on 12 Sep. 2006 [2006] ECR I-7995, point 63.

> paragraph 16, and *Centros*, paragraph 17). The reasons for which a company chooses to be formed in a particular Member State are, *save in the case of fraud*, irrelevant with regard to application of the rules on freedom of establishment (*Centros*, paragraph 18). [*Emphasis added*].

Up to the point that:

> The Court has also held that the fact that the company was formed in a particular Member State *for the sole purpose of enjoying the benefit of more favourable legislation does not constitute abuse* even if that company conducts its activities entirely or mainly in that second State (*Segers*, paragraph 16, and *Centros*, paragraph 18). [*Emphasis added*].[178]

This view is now settled ECJ case-law, and it has led some scholars to hint derogatorily at a 'Delaware effect', without considering that referring to the company law of that State of the United States may provide a paragon, because of the high specialization and sophistication levels achieved by the Delaware legislation and especially by that State's Courts in matters of company law.

In this connection, and in light of the present state of Community case-law in regard to companies' freedom of establishment, some essential indications can be drawn as to the *legitimate limitations* to liberalization in Member States' national laws.

The starting point is Article 46(1) of the Treaty, according to which:

> The provisions of this chapter and measures taken in pursuance thereof shall not prejudice the applicability of provisions laid down by law, regulation or administrative action providing for *special treatment for foreign nationals on grounds of public policy, public security or public health*. [*Emphasis added*].

It is in connection with this requirement, as well as Articles 56 and 58(1) of the Treaty relating to free capital movements,[179] that conspicuous case-law has developed in the last few years in the matter of 'golden shares', an issue raised within the scope of privatizations now underway or already completed in various Member States of the European Union.[180]

It emerges from ECJ case-law relating to companies' right of establishment that a variety of arguments, often quite unspecific in content, have been put forward in support to, and by way of justification of, restrictive national provisions.

In dealing with such arguments, the Court of Justice has essentially referred to its own settled case-law,[181] based on which any provisions legitimately capable to

---

178. See *Inspire Art* Judgment, cit., grounds 95 and 96.
179. See, one for all, Judgment of 4 Jun. 2002, Case C-483/99, *Commission* v *France*, [2002] ECR I-4781.
180. This subject is extensively discussed below, in Chapter III (on capital) of this book, paragraph 11-15.
181. See Judgments of 31 Mar. 1993, Case C-19/92, *Kraus*, [1993] ECR I-1663, ground 32, and of 30 Nov. 1995, Case C-55/94, *Gebhard*, [1995] ECR I-4165, ground 37.

discourage or hamper the exercise of fundamental freedoms secured by the Treaty must satisfy four conditions. For:

> [A] measure which is liable to hinder the freedom of establishment laid down by Article 52 of the Treaty can be allowed only if *it pursues a legitimate objective compatible* with the Treaty and *is justified by imperative reasons in the public interest*. It is further necessary, in such a case, that its application must be *appropriate to ensuring the attainment of the objective thus pursued and must not go beyond what is necessary to attain it*. [*Emphasis added*].[182]

The arguments, whether specific or unspecific, Member States have put forward in the various cases in support to the legitimacy of national restrictive measures have invariably been dismissed by the Court of Justice.

In particular, in *Centros*,[183] the ECJ held that the conduct of Mr and Mrs Bryde, Danish nationals, did not constitute abuse of the freedom of establishment. According to the Danish authorities, Mr and Mrs Bryde had registered a company in the United Kingdom, which had never traded there since its formation, and had establish just a branch in Denmark, where the UK company intended to carry on all of its business for the sole purpose of *circumventing* the application of the national law governing formation of companies, with regard in particular to minimum capital. Hence, the Danish authorities' refusal to register the company's branch in Denmark. The Danish Government's contention that the case in the main proceedings involved a 'situation purely internal to Denmark', then outside the scope of the rules on freedom of establishment, was firmly rejected by the Court of Justice.

Likewise, in its *Inspire Art* judgment of 30 September 2003, the ECJ held that the Dutch intention to apply the national rules on minimum capital and directors' liability to a UK company, as a result of the establishment by the latter of a branch in the Netherlands, was entirely unjustified.[184]

In the *Überseering* judgment of 5 November 2002, the Court of Justice deemed the restriction on freedom of establishment resulting from the application of the 'seat theory', to be equally unjustified, much as the German government had argued:

> that the restriction applies without discrimination, is justified by overriding requirements relating to the general interest and is proportionate to the objectives pursued.[185]

The Court similarly rejected justifications based on the principles of legal certainty, creditor protection[186] and the protection of minority shareholders,[187] circumvention

182. See Judgments: of 15 May 1997, Case C-250/95, *Futura Participations SA*, [1997] ECR I-2471, ground 26, and *De Laysterie du Saillant*, cit., ground 49. See Judgment of 9 Mar. 1999, *Centros*, cit., ground 34.
183. *Ibid.*, cit.
184. See *Inspire Art Ltd* Judgment, cit., esp.lly ground 95 ff.
185. See *Überseering* Judgment, cit., ground 84.
186. *Ibid.*, ground 87.
187. *Ibid.*, ground 88.

of the *Mitbestimmung*,[188] and the risk of tax advantages being granted,[189] though it acknowledged that:

> It is not inconceivable that overriding requirements relating to the general interest, such as the protection of the interests of creditors, minority shareholders, employees and even the taxation authorities, may, *in certain circumstances and subject to certain conditions*, justify restrictions on freedom of establishment. [*Emphasis added*].

But even under such exceptional circumstances will any national restrictions be limited by a general bar. For:

> [S]uch objectives cannot, however, justify *denying the legal capacity* and, consequently, *the capacity to be a party to legal proceedings* of a company properly incorporated in another Member State in which it has its registered office. *Such a measure is tantamount to an outright negation of the freedom of establishment conferred on companies by Articles 43 EC and 48 EC.* [*Emphasis added*].[190]

In its *Cadbury Schweppes plc* judgment of 12 September 2006, the ECJ again considered the tax issue to specify:[191]

> the fact that a Community national, whether a natural or a legal person, sought to profit from tax advantages in force in a Member State other than his State of residence cannot in itself deprive him of the right to rely on the provisions of the Treaty.
>
> As to freedom of establishment, the Court has already held that the fact that the company was established in a Member State for the purpose of *benefiting from more favourable legislation does not in itself suffice to constitute abuse of that freedom.* [*Emphasis added*].

Based on the consideration that the concept of establishment emerging from the Treaty involves the actual pursuit of an economic activity through a fixed establishment in that State for an indefinite period,[192] the ECJ concluded that:

> in order for a restriction on the freedom of establishment to be justified on the ground of *prevention of abusive practices*, the specific objective of such a restriction must be to prevent conduct involving the creation of *wholly artificial arrangements which do not reflect economic reality*, with a view to *escaping the tax normally due on the profits* generated by activities carried out on national territory. [*Emphasis added*].[193]

188. *Ibid.*, ground 89.
189. *Ibid.*, ground 90.
190. *Ibid.*, ground 91.
191. See *Cadbury Schweppes plc* Judgment, cit., grounds 36 and 37, respectively, and judgments in *Centros*, ground 27, and *Inspire Art*, ground 96, referred to in ground 37 of that ruling.
192. See *Cadbury Schweppes* Judgment, cit. *ibid*, grounds 54 e 56.
193. See same, *ibid.*, ground 55.

Further, the intention to obtain tax relief does not suffice to conclude 'that there is a wholly artificial arrangement intended solely to escape that tax'.[194] To this end, there must also be objective factors contrasting with the requirement of actual establishment, e.g. in the case of a 'letterbox' or 'front' subsidiary,[195] a test which – the ECJ held – was for the referring (national) court to make.[196]

It should be noted, though, to avoid misunderstandings, that *actual* establishment and the quality of *letterbox* or *front* only apply, in Community case-law, to the subsidiary or branch in the State of establishment, *not* in the home State, where the company may well have no business at all.

15. THE IMPACT OF ARTICLE 43 ET SEQ. OF THE TREATY ON: (A) THE ITALIAN RULES OF PRIVATE INTERNATIONAL LAW IN REGARD TO COMPANIES

I have already referred to the Italian Private International Law Reform Act No 218 of 1995, in particular Article 25 which, under the caption 'Legal Persons' in Chapter III of the Act, has codified the rules of Italian private international law in the matter to 'Companies and other entities'.

Allow me to stress that, for the first time in the Italian legal system, the conflict rule governing both partnerships and limited companies has been explicitly formulated and included within the same context as the other rules of private international law in the Italian system.

For the way such a rule as is worded out explicitly joins the solution set forth by the historical process discussed above from the provisions applicable to foreign companies first in the 1860 Act and the following bilateral treaties, then in the Articles 230 to 232, inclusive, of the 1882 Code of Commerce,[197] and again in Articles 2505 to 2509, inclusive, of the Italian Civil Code of 1942, all of them essentially with the same contents.[198]

Because of the breadth of the 'category' provided for in Article 25 of Act No 218/1995, the solution initially applied to the recognition of the existence of

194. See same, *ibid.*, ground 63. Emphasis added.
195. See same, *ibid.*, ground 55. See also the Judgment of 2 May 2006, Case C-341/04, *Eurofood IFSC*, [2006] ECR I-3813, grounds 34 and 35, referred to therein. In the latter ruling, for the purpose of determining the concept of 'centre of main interests' in *applying Regulation No. 1346/2000 on insolvency*, company not carrying out any business in the territory of the Member State in which its registered office is situated is defined as 'letterbox company'. This notion is immaterial, as we have already seen, to the right of establishment in relation to the registered office sited in the home State. See judgments in *Segers*, cit., ground 16, and in *Centros*, ground 29.
196. *Ibid.*, ground 72.
197. See above, paragraph 3 of this Chapter I.
198. Please, note that Article 2505 and 2509 of the Italian Civil Code are listed among the 'incompatible rules', expressly repealed by Article 74 of Act 218/1995 on the reform of private international law.

bodies corporate has been extended in equally explicit terms to companies of any type, including any 'collective body' or 'entity' occurring in any form, 'even if not of an associative nature', in the Italian legal system as well as in any other legal system being referred to.[199]

No question arises here as to compatibility with the Community rules discussed so far, as interpreted by the Court of Justice, in respect of the general rule of private international law set out in the first sentence of the first paragraph of Article 25 of the Italian Act No. 218/1995:

> Companies, associations, foundations and any other public or private entities, even if not having the nature of associations, shall be governed by *the law of the State in whose territory the constitution procedure was perfected.* [*Emphasis added*].

First, there are quite apparent, material analogies between the definition contained in Article 48(2) EC and the 'category' provided for in the rule of private international law in Article 25(1) of Act No 218/1995.

With regard to the term 'companies', both sets of rules include 'companies' of any type – though Community law requires them to be *profit-making*.[200] And so, the term is taken to include partnerships as well as limited and unlimited companies governed by public or private law, companies consisting of several members as well as companies with a single member from the time of their formation,[201] and companies or firms constituted under civil or commercial law.

A for 'legal persons', the phrase in Article 25(1) of Act No. 218/1995 is essentially equivalent to, though more extensively worded than, that used in Article 48(2) EC, which refers to 'other legal persons governed by public or private law'.

Secondly, the rule of private international law caught by Article 25, which is based on the criterion of the company or other entity's place of constitution – as this writer resolutely insisted on having it set out in that article – appears to be quite in line with the Community rules on freedom of establishment and the free provision of services.

---

199. Please, refer to the many judgments handed down by Italian courts in the 1970s in the relation to the refusal to recognize Lichtenstein-based *Anstalten* and *Treuunternehmen* in Italy, chiefly on the ground of an assumed conflict with international public policy under Article 31, prel. prov., of the Civil Code. See, for all: Luzzatto, 'L'Anstalt e l'ordinamento giuridico italiano' [1976] Giur. Comm. II, p. 58 ff.; Carnevali, 'Intestazione fiduciaria', in *Dizionario del diritto privato*, edited by Irti (Milan, 1980), p. 455 ff.; and Biscaretti di Ruffia, 'Sul riconoscimento della personalità giuridica in Italia ad un'Anstalt titolare di un brevetto per invenzione industriale' [1980] Riv.dir.civ. II, p. 481 ff.
200. For the 'profit-making' notion, see footnotes 30 and 90 in this Chapter I.
201. Single-member private limited-liability companies are the object of Directive 89/667/EEC of 21 Dec. 1989, as amended, about which reference should be made to Chapter II of this book. The same result is arrived at by the phrase 'whether or not of an associative nature' in Article 25.

This is not the case, though – as I have stressed elsewhere – with the second sentence of the same paragraph, where an exception is provided to the effect that:

> The Italian law shall, however, apply if the *place of administration* is in Italy or the *principal object* of such entities is in Italy. [*Emphasis added*].

Italian doctrine and case-law are essentially in agreement as to the fact that 'the place of administration' means the place in which the company is actually organized and managed, or the place in which decisions vital for the company's administration are made.

The phrase 'principal object', essentially equivalent to 'the enterprise's main business object' indicated as a factor of contact with our country in Article 2505 of the Civil Code, is related less to the abstract notion of 'corporate purpose' as to the *actual* principal economic activity that substantiates a company's purpose.

In other words, what really matters for this criterion as well as for the one just discussed above is not the abstract provision made in the company's articles of association for its business object – which is, as a rule, deliberately set out in rather broad, unspecific terms – but 'the place where the company's business activity is objectively carried out'.[202]

Clearly enough, the degree of difficulty of the investigation the judge will have to conduct will depend on the actual type of activity a company is actually engaged in. Thus, there will be no difficulty in the case of a single-purpose company, in which case the main business object will be located in the place where the one activity intended to accomplish the company's single business object has been or is about to be completed. Equally easy will be the judge's task when that activity is carried out in several places, all of which falling under the jurisdiction of one and the same State. And so, only the case of a conglomerate operating on the international scale will ultimately be difficult to settle. In this case, too, it will be for the judge alone to decide, *after taking into account all the relevant elements, to be assessed according to the prevalence in value and the ancillary or instrumental character of each of the economic activities actually performed by that company.*

With regard to the contact factors provided for by Article 48.1 EC, the criterion of central administration or *real* head office, as distinguished (if need be) from the *statutory* registered office, is fully matched by the criterion stated in the relevant Italian legislation. As for the other criterion, it is my view that the phrases 'principal place of business' and 'main business object' are essentially equivalent, in their being equally intended to indicate the real, actual prevalence of the exercise of the relevant economic activity.

---

202. See Rome Court, 2 May 1963, cit., p. 103. Patently enough, this does not mean that providing for the business object in a company's articles of association should be overlooked outright. 'However, – held the judges in that ruling – the starting point of any investigation into the matter remains the provision in the contained in the company's Articles, in the sense that it also provide indications of a territorial nature in relation to the "places" where the company's business is conducted, and those indications must be referred to in order to identify the place of the company's main business object, obviously to be assessed in its overall aspect'.

A derogation from the Italian general conflict rule based on the place of incorporation has been introduced by Article 17 of the Italian Act No 218/1995. Such derogation makes mandatory rules of Italian law applicable to any company formed in another country and governed, as such, by the law of the place of constitution with a positive function, i.e. without excluding reference to, and the application of, the home country's legislation so long as this is not in conflict with any such Italian mandatory rule, subject to renvoi back pursuant to Article 13.

However, such dual exception is patently incompatible, for the reasons extensively put forward above, with establishment rules, and it cannot, therefore, be applied to any companies incorporated in another Member State that are entitled to benefit from freedom of establishment, the free provision of services and, to the extent applicable, on the free movement of capital.

Thus, in this context, the rule set out in the second sentence of Article 25(1) of Act No 218/1995 must be disapplied in the terms indicated above, but it will be applied both to *non-Community* foreign companies and to Community companies falling outside the broad scope of the rules on the freedom of establishment, on the free provision of services.

It should be remembered that the general argument of the formation of a company in another State *for tax-avoidance purposes* – so strongly felt as well in the work preparatory to the provisions of the 1882 Italian Code of Commerce applicable to foreign companies operating in Italy, as in the proceedings of the commissions preparing the 1942 Civil Code – has been invoked to justify the use of the criterion of the place of central administration and/or that of the main business object as a limiting factor, in case, that is, either occurs within the Italian territory, in which event the appropriate *corrective* will be the application of Italian law to the company so incorporated abroad.[203]

The use of the criteria of 'the place of administration' and 'the main business object' in the Report to the Italian Civil Code of 1942 was justified by the purpose 'to prevent incorporation abroad from becoming a convenient device to circumvent

203. According to Vivante, 'Le società estere in Italia, una nuova costruzione di questo istituto' [1910] Foro it., p. 3 ff., p. 14, the reference to the criterion of the seat and main business object in the last paragraph of Article 230 of the Civil Code was due to the fact that, although Italian law did not recognize the 'foreign disguise' of a company which, while incorporated abroad, had both the main object of its business and its general centre of its activity, it did treat that company as a *national* company in its own right, in respect both of the requirements for its existence and of its functioning and events. 'Such a company – observed the scholarly Author, *op. cit.*, p. 9 f. – will have, for example, to include in its Articles or, failing this, suffer *ope lege*, those rules that are written in our code for the protection of the owners and cannot be derogated from, so that the owners may: claim the nullity of any of the general meeting's resolutions on matters not stated in the agenda (Article 155); as a majority, resolve the company's transfer to Italy pursuant to the rules established by Article 158, Civil Code; seek a court's intervention to establish the directors' misuse of power (Article 153); bring any actions for director liability which the code allows a majority of the owners to bring (Article 152), etc.' Please, refer to my book, *Le società*, cit., p. 173 ff.

our law'.[204] With reference to a provision setting out the same factors of contact with the Italian territory, which was written into the draft reform released by the Royal Commission in 1925, the D'Amelio Report annexed to the draft submitted that:

> This provision was deemed necessary with a view to prevent the Italian substantive and tax laws from being avoided *through the well-known subterfuge* of setting up a more or less fictitious corporate seat abroad.... [*Emphasis added*].[205]

However, the 'tax-avoidance' argument now appears – in the unspecific, abstract terms it was put forward as a justification by the Italian legislator – to be immaterial, because of the express statements made to the contrary in the Court of Justice's case-law in dealing with claims put forward, in as unspecific and abstract terms, by Member States' authorities in support to the application of national laws, with a view to denying an eligible company the actual exercise of a right arising to it from freedom of establishment.

This does not mean, however, that a company formed in another Member State, which sets up its central administration or its main business object (or place of business) in Italy by exercising its right of free establishment, is invariably denied the application of one or another mandatory rule of Italian law. For the general presumption of the inapplicability of mandatory rules of Italian law to that company, as a result of the ECJ's case-law discussed above, could be *exceptionally* overcome in relation to any specific case. This can only be done after the interested party – a public authority, that is – has discharged the onus placed on it to prove that a specific Italian rule *neither precludes* the enjoyment by that company of its right of free establishment nor makes the exercise thereof *unjustifiably heavier*, or that its disapplication would, in view of national interests deserving protection, entail a cost disproportionately high if compared with the achievement, in the relevant case, of the intended useful effect pursued by the Community rules on the matter.

---

204. *Emphasis added.* See *Relazione alla Maestà del Re Imperatore del Ministro Guardasigilli* (Grandi), *presentata nell'udienza del 16 marzo 1942 per l'approvazione del testo del 'codice civile'*, n. 1024. An essentially similar statement was made in relation to this paragraph in *Relazione al Re sul Libro del lavoro*, n. 216. The same purpose had already been stated in: *Relazione* dello Scialoja (Antonio), *sugli artt. 301-303 del progetto preliminare per il nuovo codice di commercio, elaborato dalla Commissione ministeriale per la riforma della legislazione commerciale*, chaired by C. Vivante (Milan, 1922), p. 98 f., for the text of the draft, and p. 302 ff., for the report; in *Relazione* by D'Amelio *sugli artt. 292-294 del progetto della Commissione reale per la riforma dei codici – Sottocommissione B, codice di commercio*, vol. I, cit., p. 109 f., for the text of the draft, e vol. II, Rome, 1925, p. 120 f., for the report; and in *Relazione sugli artt. 357-361 del progetto preliminare del codice di commercio*, in *Ministero di grazia e giustizia, lavori preparatori del codice civile (anni 1939-1941), progetti preliminari del libro delle obbligazioni, del codice di commercio e del lavoro*, cit., vol. III, p. 103 f., for the text of the report, vol. IV, p. 118 f., for the text of the articles.

205. See D'Amelio *Relazione*, cit.

In conclusion, only such specific provisions of Italian law relied on in each relevant case as might fall within the limits allowed under Community case-law,[206] as indicated above, can be applied to a company incorporated abroad in another Member State. This is clearly a narrow, uphill path, which is quite hard for any national authority to walk on.

Article 25(3) of Act No 218/1995 specifies that:

> Transfers of registered offices to another State and mergers with entities having their seats in different States shall only be deemed effective if made in compliance with the laws of such other States. [*Emphasis added*].

Let me preliminary observe that the first part of this provision, in referring to the transfer of 'registered offices' abroad, concerns itself with a typical issue debated in literature for years.

What especially matters is, in fact, that such provision also remain *inapplicable*, in any instance of 'Community' transactions, in the part where it subordinates the legitimacy of the relevant operation to mutually consistent positive determinations to be made in both the legal systems involved. This is because – irrespective of whether the company concerned is one established in Italy intending to move its *statutory* office (and/or also its administrative office, which is usually the same thing) to another EU Member Country or is a foreign company incorporated in any one Member State intending to move its administrative office (the only one that matters under Article 25.3) to Italy – in either case, if that company is eligible for the application of the Community establishment rules, both the home State's and the host State's consent to transfer is presumed, the retention of that company's legal personality being secured by Article 48(1) EC. And the applicable law will solely be the law of the place of incorporation.

Likewise, *in cross-border mergers*, Article 48 EC ensures the retention of legal personality by the entity resulting from the merger, whatever law governs either mergee, so long as each company belongs to a different Member State of the European Union.

16. MORE: (B) MANDATORY RULES OF ITALIAN LAW WHEN COMPANIES FORMED IN OTHER MEMBER STATES SET UP BRANCHES IN ITALY

With regard to the provisions set out under the heading '*About Companies Constituted Above*' in Chapter XI of the Italian Civil Code, Article 2510, as renumbered (following the repeal of Articles 2505 and 2509 by Act 218/1955), let me first point out the provision newly introduced in Article 2507, concerning '*Relationships with Community Law*'. By a reference to be found more and more frequently in new Italian legislative measures, as if it were capable, by itself, to

206. See above, paragraph 14 of this Chapter I, and, in particular, ECJ case-law mentioned in footnote 187, above.

protect the Italian law-maker against the risk of promulgating rules contrary to Community law, the provision so newly introduced reads:

> The provisions set out in this Chapter shall be construed and applied pursuant to *the principles of the legal system of the European Communities*. [*Emphasis added*].[207]

Such statement apparently avers that the norm that subordinates the contents and effects of national mandatory rules to the ever-evolving principles of Community law also apply to the mandatory rules contained in Chapter XI of the Italian Civil Code. Such principles are sourced, firstly, by *primary* rules, i.e. those contained in the EC Treaty, among which the provisions of Article 43 et seq. EC and Article 49 et seq. EC, secondly, by *secondary* rules, i.e. those set out in regulations or directive, among which the harmonization directives adopted in furtherance of Article 44(2)(g) EC, and, thirdly, by the interpretative judgments handed down by the European Court of Justice.

However, since the interpretation of any rule of law must be conducted on the attempt that it could make sense, the large wording of Article 2507 c.c. combined with the breadth of the implementation given to (as usual in the Italian system) the XI Directive, what provisions all the articles of Chapter eleven of the Italian Civil Code expressly rely upon, it ensues that the EC harmonization rules as applied in the Italian system of law are extended to *all* the foreign companies and *not only* to the ones incorporated in another Member State.

Thus, the new Article 2508, Civil Code, entitled 'Foreign Companies with Secondary Establishments in the Territory of the State', has aptly been rephrased from the previous text of Article 2506 by Article 2 of Legislative Decree No 516 of 29 December 1992 for the implementation of EEC Council Directive 89/666 (the Eleventh Directive concerning disclosure requirements in respect of branches opened in a Member State by certain types of company governed by the law of another State), against which the entire matter considered here should be measured in relation to any company eligible for the right of establishment.[208]

The provisions contained in that and in the following articles provide a typical example of mandatory rules on companies pursuant to Article 17 of Act No 218/1995. Article 2508 also performs this function in connection with the new rule of private international law on companies and other entities, which is contained in Article 25(1), Act No 218/1995.

---

207. The phrase is part of a broader presentation of the relationships between internal law and Community law as it emerges from the new wording of Article 117 of the Italian Constitution, according to which 'the law-making powers of the State and of the Regions' shall be exercised in compliance with, *inter alia* 'the constraints arising from Community law'.

208. Eleventh Directive No. 89/666 of the Council of 21 Dec. 1989, concerning disclosure requirements in respect of branches opened in a Member State by certain types of company governed by the law of another State [1989] O.J. L395, p. 36. It should be noted that Directive is also applicable to companies established in any State participating in the Agreement on the European Economic Area pursuant to Annex XXII thereto.

Therefore, the mere fact that a foreign company establishes a secondary office for permanent representation in Italy generally makes the rules enshrined in Article 2507 et seq., Civil Code, applicable to it forthwith from the point of view of the Italian legal system. In this case, because of the customary operation of mandatory rules, the Italian provisions contained in Article 2507, Civil Code, within the limits specified in the next article, will *necessarily*, then positively, be added to the foreign substantive law applicable to the company in question according to the place of the incorporation criterion.[209]

Likewise, a patent example of mandatory rules can be found in Spanish company law, specifically in Chapter IV, Section 4 ('*De los negocios sobra las proprias acciones*', transactions related to treasury shares) of the law governing limited companies (Real Decreto Legislativo n. 1564 of 22 December 1989). Following two paragraphs providing for the determination of 'control' under Spanish law – in respect of the controlling company, not of the controlled company as is the case in Italian law – paragraph 4 of Article 87 requires (translated from the Spanish original):

> Las disposiciones de esta sección referidas a operaciones que tienen por objeto acciones de la sociedad dominante serán de aplicación *aún cuando la sociedad que las realice no sea de nacionalidad española.* (The provisions of this section that relate to transactions having the controlling company's shares as their object shall also apply *where the company making such transactions is not a national of Spain*). [*Emphasis added*].

Pursuant to Article 5(1) of the law on companies limited by shares and to Article 6(1) of the law on companies limited by quotas, companies of both classes are deemed to be Spanish if they have their '*domicilio*' in the Spanish territory, '*cualquiera que sea el lugar en que se hubieren constituido*' (whatever the place of their formation), and the second paragraph of Article 5 specifies:

> Deberán tener su domicilio en España las sociedades anónimas, cuyo principal establecimiento o explotación radique dentro de su territorio. (Companies limited by shares whose principal establishment or business activity is located within the Spanish territory shall have their domicile in Spain).[210]

It has already been seen[211] that, the consequences of non-compliance with formalities may by no means be different from (and the extent and quality of penalties not

209. About such positive value, in relation to the similar problem concerning the former text of Article 2506 of the Civil Code, see my study *Le società nel diritto internationale privato*, cit., pp. 99 ff. and 182 ff., especially n. 203.

210. About Articles 5 ('*Nacionalidad*') and 6 ('*Domicilio*') of the Act., see: J. Carrera-Giral & E. Carrera-Lazaro, *Ley de Sociedades Anónimas* (5th edn, Barcelona, 1995), vol. II, p. 305 f.; A.J. Sanchez-Crespo-Casanova, *Ley de Sociedades Anónimas, Legislación camplementaria, resoluciones, jurisprudencia y comentarios* (Granada, 1997), p. 19 f.; F. Sanchez-Calero, *Istituciones de Derecho Mercantil, I, Introducción Empresa y Sociedades*, (19th ed., Madrid, 1996), pp. 271 f. and 656 f.

211. See paragraph 9, above, with regard to the ECJ's judgment in *Inspire Art*, cit.

more severe than) those allowed by the Eleventh Directive. This consideration applies, in particular, to the foreign company's directors' liability referred to in Article 2509 and the liability of those who have acted on the company's behalf pursuant to Article 2509-*bis* of the Italian Civil Code.[212]

17. MORE: (C) APPLICABILITY OF LEGISLATIVE DECREE 231/2001 TO 'COMMUNITY' FOREIGN COMPANIES

A special problem has been raised by a recent judicial measure in criminal matters[213] intended to make the consequences provided for in Legislative Decree No 231 of 8 June 2001 ('Decree 231')[214] applicable to companies formed in any EU Member State whenever the free provision of services or the free circulation of goods is at issue in Italy.

Decree 231 has introduced the notion of 'administrative' liability in the Italian legal system with respect to bodies corporate in cases of criminal violations committed by 'subordinates', such as a company's employees, directors or contractors.

Initially, the main offence considered was corruption of public officials, whether Italian or foreign, pursuant to Articles 318 to 320 of the Criminal Code. Following later amendments to the relevant rules of law, a company's liability for the failed adoption or effective implementation of suitable organizational and governance models to prevent such offences was first extended to corporate offences then to offences in matters of environmental pollution and workplace safety.[215]

---

212. Please, refer again to the *Inspire Art* judgment, cit.

213. This is an order applying inhibitory measures adopted by the judge for preliminary investigation of the Milan Criminal District Court of 27 Apr. 2004, as confirmed on the point by an order of the Court of Review dated 28 Oct. 2004 against a German company, *Siemes AG* (see Fusco, 'Applicabilità del d. lgs. 231/2001 alle banche estere', in *La responsabilità amministrativa delle società e degli enti* (2007), p. 179 ff., p. 182), recently referred to in the decree of commitment to trial of some foreign banks' officers, as adopted by the Milan Criminal District Court, Second Chamber, in which each of the banks was held 'liable for the administrative violation under Articles 5(1)(b) and 7(25)(*ter*)(2) of Legislative Decree No. 231/2001' allegedly committed by its employees, 'thereby drawing substantial profit from the criminal conduct of its subordinates, who did not act in their own or any other persons' interest'.

214. A vast literature has been produced on this decree. With regard to private international law issues, see: Di Giovine, 'Lineamenti sostanziali del nuovo illecito punitivo', in AA.VV., *Reati e responsabilità degli enti. Guida al d.lgs. 8 giugno 2001, n. 231* (Milan, 2005), p. 39. Along the same lines, Alessandri, 'Attività d'impresa e responsabilità penali' [2005] Riv. it. dir. proc. pen., p. 559; Razzante, Toscano, *La responsabilità amministrativa delle persone giuridiche. Profili teorici e pratici connessi all'applicazione del D.lgs. 8 giugno 2001, n. 231* (Turin, 2003), p. 73; Gennai, Traversi, 'La responsabilità degli enti per gli illeciti amministrativi dipendenti da reato, Commento al D. lgs. 8 giugno 2001, n. 231' in *Teoria e Pratica del diritto*, sez. III, Diritto e Proc. Pen., (Milan, 2001), p. 31; Paolozzi, *Vademecum per gli enti sotto processo. Addebiti 'amministrativi' da reato (D.Lgs. n. 231 del 2001)*, (Turin, 2006), p. 43 and, in particular, fn. 106.

215. Legislative Decree No. 231/2001 has been amended by the following provisions: Article 6 of Legislative Decree No. 350 of 25 Sep. 2001, as converted, with amendment, into Act No. 409

The line of reasoning followed by the judge for preliminary investigation in a recent case of commitment to trial of certain foreign banks in the so-called 'bankers' section' of the *Parmalat* trial[216] is straightforward and can be summarized as follows: Article 1(2) of Decree 231 specifies the subjective scope for application of the decree to be addressed to

> entities having juridical personality and companies and associations with or without juridical personality,

and paragraph 3 of Article 2 specifies exclusions to the effect that the provisions of the decree

> shall not apply to the State, to local public bodies, other non-economic public bodies and entities discharging functions of constitutional import.

The breadth of the former provision and the lack of any reference to foreign companies in the latter led the court to infer that any foreign company choosing to carry out any activity in Italy, even if casually or just occasionally, such as the sale or purchase of goods or services, whether with or without a permanent connection with the Italian territory, is required to adjust its structure to the provisions of Decree 231/2001.

The same reasoning had been adopted by the judge for preliminary investigation of the Criminal District Court of Milan in *Siemens AG*, who had issued his order by resorting to the following simile:

> An even too plain, yet quite telling, example could be that of road traffic rules. The German rules or those of any other country may well not require motor vehicles registered and travelling in that country to be fitted with safety belts, but this clearly does not imply that they are relieved of the requirement to be so fitted for them to have access to Italian roads. The *lex loci* standard shall apply to road safety measures as well as to any accident prevention measures which, if not adopted, may entail legal liability under internal law.

Quite beyond the question of whether or not Italian criminal jurisdiction exists with respect to the court orders just cited, a different line of reasoning should be followed, and the example offered by the Milan court is by no means appropriate.

The first reason for this is one of method. Whether or not Italian *criminal* jurisdiction exists, the very argument about the outright applicability of Decree 231

of 23 Nov. 2001; Article 3 of Legislative Decree No. 61 of 11 Apr. 2002; Article 299 of The President of the Republic Decree No. 115 of 30 May 2002; Article 52 of The President of the Republic Decree No. 313 of 14 Nov. 2002; Article 3 of Act No. 7 of 14 Jan. 2003; Article 5 of Act No. 228 of 11 Aug. 2003; Article 9 of Act No. 62 of 18 Apr. 2005; Articles 31 and 39(5) of Act No. 262 of 28 Dec. 2005; Article 3 of Act No. 7 of 9 Jan. 2006 and Article 10 of Act No. 38 of 6 Feb. 2006. For a summary of the contents of Decree 231 as amended, please also refer to fn, 85 of Chapter V of this book.

216. The text of the order is reproduced in full in Fusco, 'Applicabilità del d. lgs. 231/2001 alle banche estere', cit., 2007, p. 179 ff.

to foreign companies appears to be not supported on a correct reasoning in point of private international law.

On a different plane, the conclusion drawn by the Milan judge in respect of a company belonging to a EU Member State fails to provide a correct view of the terms of the problem in relation to Community law. In fact, it is in contrast with the ECJ doctrine extensively discussed in the preceding paragraphs of this Chapter, which is intended to ensure to any companies meeting the requirements of Article 48 EC both the right of free establishment and the right to the free provision of services in any Member State – and of course to the free circulation of goods along with them, which is the mainstay of the customs union on which the Community is based (Articles 23 et seq. EC).

As for the first point, pursuant to the private international law rule contained in the first sentence of Article 25 of Act No 218/1995, a company incorporated abroad, in Frankfurt, Germany, in London, United Kingdom, or in New York, N.Y., will be subject to the laws of Germany, of the United Kingdom or of the New York State, as the case may be.

Thus, it is for the *lex societatis* so identified, and for it alone, to govern all the aspects of the existence, structure and functioning of the body corporate in question.

As aptly highlighted, albeit by way of indication only, in the list contained in Article 25(2) of Act 218/1995, the following items are regulated by such governing law in respect of the entity concerned:

(a) its [juridical] capacity;
(b) the formation, powers and manners of functioning of its [managing] organs, and
(c) the consequences of violations of the law or of its Articles of association.

Therefore, in relation to the subjective scope of application of the *lex societatis*, this law provides for as well a company's genetic process as its validity or invalidity, existence or non-existence, and structure and internal organization generally,[217] from inception until dissolution.

If it is indisputably true that the law of the place of incorporation governs that company's organization, then all aspects relating to the adoption of *organization and management* models (Article 25(2)(d) and (e) of Act 218/1995), it is as true that it also clearly governs the *consequences* of any (alleged) *law violations* (Article 25(2)(i) of Act 218/1995).

---

217. Santa Maria, 'Art. 25', in *Riforma del sistema italiano di diritto internazionale privato: legge 31 maggio 1995 n. 218 – Commentario* [1995] Riv. dir. int. priv. proc. 4, p. 1041. The wide scope of application of the *lex societatis* is confirmed, by contrary converse, by Article 1(2)(e) of the Rome Convention of 19 Jun. 1980 on the law applicable to contractual obligations. That provision requires the *lex contractus* be not applied to '*questions governed by the law of companies and other bodies corporate or unincorporate such as the creation, by registration or otherwise, legal capacity, internal organization or winding up of companies and other bodies corporate or unincorporate and the personal liability of officers and members as such for the obligations of the company or body*'. See Santa Maria, 'Spunti di riflessione', cit.

In this respect, besides the (*negative*) international public policy limit of the recognition of foreign judgments – one quite immaterial to the point – the application of the *lex societatis*, and the consequent reference to a foreign legal system's juridical values, can only meet the (*positive*) limit – as indicated above – of the operation of the so-called *mandatory rules of law* (Article 17 of Act 218/1995).

As pointed out above, mandatory rules of law are overriding material provisions of the *lex fori* that must '*mandatorily*' be applied, quite irrespective of any remission to foreign laws under the rules on conflict of laws. For mandatory rules *are capable by themselves – explicitly as a rule, and only exceptionally because of their implied object and specific purpose – to define direct their own scope of application*, in which case they are commonly referred to as *self-limited* or *spatially conditioned* rules.

The examples quoted in literature of rules likely to fall within this category refer to certain provisions in matters of adoption, parental custody, marriages of foreigners in Italy, the capacity to perform certain acts, the protection of incapacitated persons, companies operating through a permanent establishment in Italy, tax and foreign-exchange laws generally, and provisions relating to competition-distorting practices and also *road traffic* rules.[218]

Clearly enough, these are rules of an *exceptional* character, in their being capable to impose their own application, and apt, as such, to result in precluding the application of a foreign law, even if this is referred to by renvoi under private international law. Thereby, the harmony and uniformity of any solutions afforded by the consistent functioning of the conflict-of-laws system are most likely to be jeopardized. That is why the logical process leading to mandatory rules of law must be very strict and *restrictively* applied,[219] and why the use of the whole notion in case-law is approached quite warily.[220]

A mandatory rule of company law can only be identified at the time it is ascertained, *in light of the links established by the body corporate involved with the Italian corporate system*, that that was the effect really 'intended' by the Italian legislator.[221]

Thus, there are two essential features to mandatory rules of law. One is the 'imperative' character of their contents, which cannot be waived or derogated from

---

218. See Mosconi, *Diritto Internazionale Privato e Processuale. Parte generale e contratti* (Turin, 2006), p. 247. About the qualification of the rules on road traffic as 'mandatory rules of law', see Venice District Court Order of 21 May 2002, in [2003] Foro it. I, 2181.

219. See Treves, 'Art. 17', in *Riforma del sistema italiano di diritto internazionale privato: legge 31 maggio 1995 n. 218 – Commentario* [1995] Riv. dir. int. priv. proc. 4, p. 989; Davi, 'Le questioni generali del diritto internazionale privato nel progetto di riforma' [1990] Riv. dir. int., p. 137 ff.; Benedettelli, 'Art. 25', in *Le nuove leggi civili commentate, la riforma del sistema italiano di diritto internazionale privato: commentario alla l. n. 31 maggio 1995, n. 218* (1996), p. 1137; Boschiero, 'Art. 17', in *Le nuove leggi civili commentate*, cit., p. 1065. For the same view, see Venice District Court Order of 21 May 2002, cit.

220. Treves, op. cit., p. 989. According to Treves, a more extensive use of this category would be 'blameworthy'.

221. Benedettelli, op. cit., p. 1137.

by private parties. The other is 'self-limitation', meaning that each such rule must itself provide for when and to whom it is to be applied.

That Legislative Decree No 231/2001 does not contain any mandatory rules emerges from several observations.

First of all, the entire approach taken by the Milan criminal court must be reversed. Article 1 of Decree 231 is not a 'self-limiting' rule *vis-à-vis* foreign companies, precisely because it makes no reference to them and provides no justification for the need to apply the norm to foreign bodies *on the mere ground that they operate in Italy.*

It has aptly been observed that the need to apply certain rules 'mandatorily' with a view to a specific purpose should not be recognized where any solutions available by remission to the competent foreign law are conducive to essentially the same outcome.[222] In other words:

> Mandatory rules of law tend to perform a supplementing function by filling any gaps as might be found in foreign laws, so that it has been stated that internal material rules that are internationally mandatory can *only* be justified when it can reasonably be assumed that the outcome they are intended to achieve cannot be achieved as effectively by reference to the foreign law.[223]

There is more, though. A company's failure to equip itself with suitable organizational and management models to prevent the crimes contemplated in Article 7 of Decree No 231/2001 does not result, by law, in direct corporate liability. For the relevant provision is merely *optional*, in that the company will, even lacking such models, be held exempt, in case a crime is committed by its subordinates, of any administrative penalties, insofar as it can show, against presumption to the contrary, that the commission of that crime could not have been made possible by non-compliance with the company's ordinary duties of direction and supervision. In fact, there are no imperative rules or reasons of (internal) public policy at stake, lacking which there could be no mandatory rules of law.

Assuming that the provisions in Decree 231 can not be categorized as a mandatory rule of law, the applicability of such provisions to a company formed abroad could find its rationale in another mandatory rule of Italian law, if available.

Such a rule is conveyed, in fact, by the second sentence of Article 25(1) of Act No 218, pursuant to which, if a company incorporated abroad has its 'administrative seat' or its 'main business object' in Italy, in the sense specified above, it will still be subject to *all rules* of Italian law.[224]

A quite different case would be that of a company formed abroad that falls under another mandatory rule of law, i.e. Article 2508 of the Civil Code, captioned

222. Boschiero, op. cit., p. 1065.
223. See Venice District Court Order of 21 May 2002, cit. For the same view, see Treves, *op. cit.*, p. 989.
224. It should be remembered that, in this case, the Italian rules to be mandatorily applied are not capable *per se* to exclude the application of, but to operate in addition to, the relevant foreign law. See Santa Maria, *Le società*, cit.

'*Foreign companies with branches within the territory of the State*'.[225] Article 2508 requires that any companies incorporated abroad and having one or more branches *permanently established* in Italy be *mandatorily* subject to certain rules on the publicity of corporate acts (paragraph 1) and on entrepreneurial operations (paragraph 3). In this case, the factor of connection with the Italian territory is provided by the presence of a branch having permanent establishment, by derogation from the criterion of the place of incorporation abroad. This justifies the application of such rules instead of the *lex societatis*, but of only those specified in Article 2508(3), which can hardly be viewed, *ratione materiae*, as including any of the provisions of Decree 231– because of the parenthetic clause 'as for branches' – at least insofar as it refers to 'organizational models', which, by their sheer nature, concern that foreign company's entire structure.[226]

In light of the foregoing, it clearly appears that, *a fortiori*, the law applicable to a foreign company *without any specific link with the Italian territory* cannot but be the law of the place of incorporation on an exclusive basis.

This is not enough, though. It should be noted that Article 49 EC, to the extent it ensures the freedom to provide services, must be understood in its broadest meaning of a general rule. For it prohibits the issuance and application of discriminatory national rules, i.e. any rules that provide more unfavourable conditions for the nationals of another Member State or that, although appearing to be generally applicable, still have the effect to prevent or to make more difficult the provision of services by a person established in another Member State.

This principle has aptly been stressed by the European Court of Justice as follows:

> It is settled case-law that Article [49] of the Treaty requires *not only the elimination of all discrimination* on grounds of nationality against providers of services who are established in another Member State, *but also the abolition of any restriction*, even if it applies *without distinction to national providers of services and to those of other Member States*, which is liable to prohibit, *impede or render less attractive* the activities of a provider of services established in another Member State in which he lawfully provides similar services.[227] [*Emphasis added*].

225. See above, paragraph 16 of this Chapter 1.
226. Enriques, 'Società costituite all'estero', in *Comm. Scialoja-Branca* (Bologna-Roma, 2007), p. 77, with regard to Article 2508, Civil Code, reads: '*Mention is usually made in literature to the rules on representation, employers, employed workers, permits and licences as some among the rules referred to paragraph 3 of the article in question. To the rules so mentioned could be added those on taxation, third-party liability (think, in particular, of manufacturer liability), consumer protection, insolvency, and financial markets (just think of the provisions in matters of foreign bank branches and subsidiaries, insurers or other financial intermediaries, the protection of public savings or door-to-door offers, or of the rules on banking transparency, and so on)*'. As can readily be seen, no reference is made to Decree 231.
227. See ECJ Judgments of 25 Jul. 1991, Case C-76/90, *Säger* v *Debbemeyer*, [1991] ECR I-4221, grounds 12 e 13; of 5 Jun. 1997, Case C-398/95, *Syndesmos ton en Elladi Touristikon kai Taxidiotikon Grafeion* v *Ypourgos Ergasias*, [1997] ECR I-3091, ground 16; of 24 Jan. 2002,

The underlying rationale is quite clear. Indeed:

> the freedom to provide services would become illusory if national rules were at liberty to restrict offers of services.[228]

This also applies only by reference to any national legislative measures 'having the effect simply of laying down a number of additional obligations classified as administrative . . . '.[229]

For it is consistent Community case-law that national legislation which makes the provision of certain services on the national territory by an undertaking established in another Member State subject to *the issue of an administrative authorization* constitutes a *restriction* on the freedom to provide services within the meaning of Article 49 EC.[230]

Thus, for example, a national scheme has been held to be restrictive under which a Member State (France) subjected the professional activity of granting loans within its territory to prior authorization where the company concerned had neither its head office nor a branch in that territory.[231]

Likewise, requiring an insurer to have a permanent establishment in another Member State's territory for him to be allowed to sell policies to residents in that territory was deemed to be contrary to the freedom to provide services.[232]

I would have no doubts about the essentially restrictive character of Legislative Decree No 231/2001. It has aptly been pointed out:[233]

> *The non-existence of an imperative rule* requiring models to be formally set up does not seem to be enough to rule out the *restrictive nature* of the decree as a

---

Case C-164/99, *Portugaia Construções*, [2002] ECR I-787, ground 16; of 21 Oct. 2004, Case C-445/03, *Commission* v *Luxembourg*, [2004] ECR I-10191, ground 20. As for bankers, see Judgments: of 12 Dec. 1996, Case C-3/95, *Reiseburo Broede*, [1996] ECR I-6511, ground 25; of 9 Jul. 1997, Case C-222/95, *Parodi* v *Banque de Bary*, [1997] ECR I-03899, ground 18; of 15 Jan. 2002, Case C-439/99, *Commission* v *Italy*, [2002] ECR I-305, ground 22 and the judgment of 3 Oct. 2006, Case C-452/04, *Fidium Finanz*, [2006] ECR I-9521.

228. Thus, expressly, ECJ Judgment of 10 May 1995, Case C-384/93, *Alpine Investments*, [1995] ECR I-1141, ground 19.
229. See ECJ Judgment of 10 May 1995, Case C-167/01, *Inspire Art*, [2003] ECR I-10155, ground 99.
230. See ECJ Judgments of 9 Mar. 2000, Case C-355/98, *Commission* v *Belgium*, [2000] ECR I-1221, ground 35; of 15 Jan. 2002, Case C-439/99, *Commission* v *Italy*, [2002] ECR I-305, ground 26.
231. See the *Fidium Finanz*. Judgment, cit., ground 46; see also the *Parodi* Judgment, cit., ground 19: 'Even if a national rule such as the 1984 Law is not discriminatory and applies without distinction to national providers of services and to those of other Member States, it none the less makes it more difficult for a credit institution established in another Member State and authorized by the supervisory authority of that Member State to grant a mortgage loan in France in so far as it requires that institution to obtain a fresh authorization from the supervisory authority of the State of destination. Such a national rule thus creates a restriction on the freedom to provide services'.
232. See ECJ Judgment of 4 Dec. 1986, Case 205/84, *Commission* v *Germany*, [1986] ECR 3755.
233. Pernazza, *I modelli di organizzazione*, cit., p. 1286.

> whole. The severe penalties an Italian court may inflict, the strict interim measures than can be ordered in the proceeding and the relevance of the formalisation of crime-prevention models to the applicability of such interim measures *are such as to impose* de-facto *the implementation of those models upon foreign business entities operating in Italy*, if only in order for them not to be forced to compete at a disadvantage with Italian undertakings. [*Emphasis added*].

Yet, this is not the real problem. For one should wonder whether the provisions of Decree 231, generally applicable as they are *per se*, are lawful if applied to traders belonging to another Member State and operating in Italy by merely selling and purchasing goods or providing services, or whether those provisions are to be disregarded in their being contrary to the EC rules on the free movement of goods or the free provision of services, as the case may be.

As for the former freedom, as ensured by Articles 23 et seq. EC, the answer is straightforward, because of the overriding principle stated by the Community Courts as to its full realization, with respect to which any reference to any of the limits set by Article 30 EC would seem to be quite immaterial, since Article 30 EC only applies to specific, exceptional situations, and is certainly not intended to make an entire national law also applicable to 'Community' foreign situations.

As for Articles 28 and 29 EC, which prohibit quantitative restrictions on either *imports* or *exports* between Member States, or any measures having equivalent effect, Article 30 EC provides:

> The provisions of Articles 28 and 29 shall not preclude prohibitions or restrictions on imports, exports or goods in transit justified on grounds of *public morality, public policy or public security; the protection of health and life of humans, animals or plants; the protection of national treasures possessing artistic, historic or archaeological value; or the protection of industrial and commercial property*. Such prohibitions or restrictions *shall not, however, constitute a means of arbitrary discrimination or a disguised restriction* on trade between Member States. [*Emphasis added*].

With regard to the liberalization of services, it should preliminarily be noted that *expressly discriminatory* national measures may only be considered compatible so far as they fall within any of the derogations expressly provided by Article 46 EC, as made applicable because of the reference made to it in Article 55 EC, thus only on grounds of *participation in the exercise of public powers, public policy, public security* or *public health*.

When, however, hindrances to the free provision of services arise from *generally* applicable national measures – such as those allegedly caught by Decree 231 according to the Milan Courts' precedent – such measures may only be deemed lawful on grounds of *imperative requirements* the Treaty has not provided for, so long as they are otherwise related to the *general interest* of the Member State concerned.

Yet, since these are exceptions to general principle that ensures full application of the freedom to provide services, the Court of Justice has restricted to the utmost the pleading of public interest by the Member State to which the provision of services is addressed, and has, instead, stressed the exceptional character of the derogations allowed to be made from the fundamental principle of the free provision of services.[234]

In this perspective, the notion of 'imperative requirement' justifying a limiting national measure has only been deemed to be met if *all* of the following necessary conditions are cumulatively fulfilled: (i) the measure must be capable to secure the attainment of the stated *general interest*; (ii) it must be *proportionate* to the objective so pursued; (iii) and that general interest must not be safeguarded by any rules of the relevant home Member State.[235]

In particular, with regard to the last condition, the Court has specified that it is for the national authority requesting its application to show that the measure in issue does not 'duplicate equivalent provisions in the home Member State'.[236]

In light of the foregoing comments and of the rules and principles of Community law intended to give all Community citizens, whether individuals or corporate bodies, equal rights in exercising the fundamental freedoms, the following conclusions can be drawn.

Beside the correct argument in private international law according to which Legislative Decree No 231/2001 should generally not be applied to a company incorporated in another EU Member State when its right of establishment in Italy is in issue, and according to which the operation of the decree should be restricted to the case of *non-EU countries' foreign companies* wishing to base their administrative seats or main business objects in Italy, the restrictive purview of Decree 231, certainly intended to discourage other EU Member States' companies from seeking permanent establishment in Italy, leads to the assumption that the decree *should not*, in principle, be applied to the company in question because of the

234. See, of many, the ECJ Judgment of 3 Oct. 2000, Case C-58/98, *Corsten*, [2000] ECR I-7919, ground 35. In literature, v. Tesauro, *Diritto comunitario*, cit., pp. 563-564.

235. See ECJ Judgments in *Parodi*, cit., ground 21; of 12 Dec. 1996, Case C-3/95, *Reiseburo Broede*, cit., ground 28; of 9 Mar. 1999, Case C-212/97, *Centros*, [1999] ECR I-1459, ground 34, and *Inspire Art Ltd*, cit., ground 133. Likewise, see Tesauro, cit., p. 565.

236. See the Opinion of Advocate General Stix-Hackl, Joined Cases C-346/02 and C-347/02, cit., ground 83, quoting the ECJ judgment of 4 Dec. 1986 in Case 205/84, *Commission* v *Germany*, cit., above. Se also Judgments of the Court: of 28 Mar. 1996, Case C-272/94, *Guiot* [1996] ECR I-1905, ground 11; of 9 Aug. 1994, *Vander Elst* v *Office des migrations internationals*, [1994] ECR I-03803, ground 16; of 26 Feb. 1991, Case C-180/89, *Commission* v *Italy*, [1991] ECR I-709, ground 17; of 26 Feb. 1991, Case C-198/89, *Commission* v *Greece*, [1991] ECR I-727, ground 18, and of 18 Jan. 1978, Joined Cases C-110/78 and C-111/78, *van Wesemael*, [1979] ECR I- 35, ground 28. The Court of Justice has also stressed this principle in respect of *detachement des travailleurs*: see Judgments of 9 Mar. 2000, Case C-355/98, *Commission* v *Belgium*, [2000] ECR I-1221, ground 38; of 29 May 2001, Case C-263/99, *Commission* v *Italy*, [2001] ECR I-4195, ground 24; of 9 Mar. 2000, Case C-358/98, *Commission* v *Italy*, [2000] ECR I-1255, ground 13; of 7 Feb. 2002, Case C-279/00, *Commission* v *Italy*, [2002] ECR I-1425, grounds 32 and 34.

patent conflict likely to arise with the provisions of Articles 43 et seq. EC, according to the interpretation given in ECJ case-law.

Further, I believe that such assumption can hardly be overcome by way of *exception*, i.e. by alleging that the rules laid down in Decree 231 are definitely relevant to the protection of public interests in terms acceptable to Community institutions.

It is an uphill path in any case, and one along which the Italian courts have not only to ensure actual proportionality to any restrictive measures taken against Community foreign companies on the basis of Decree 231, but also to establish the lack of similar rules in each relevant home Member State that are capable to safeguard the general interest pursued by the decree.

I have no doubts about the *non*-applicability of Decree 231 to a company that sells or purchases goods or services in Italy without any permanent connection with our country.

For in a case as this there is no convincing argument capable to let the provisions of the decree prevail over any of the European Union's *fundamental rights*.

This is because, first, the application of such provisions would meet an insurmountable obstacle in the two fundamental freedoms of the free movement of goods and the free provision of services, respectively, in the single market, the former being regarded, in fact, as the main 'pillar' of the entire European construction.

Secondly, neither type of derogations from such freedoms – much as they appear, in their being *exceptional*, to relate to the specificity of an actual situation – seems to be capable to work when referred to legislative measures with such broad, unspecific contents.

In other words, expecting that Decree 231 may be applied to any foreign company incorporated in another Member State and having no permanent connection with Italy – then not even the least defence under the law – would lead up to an unjustified exercise of extraterritorial application of national legislative measures, which may appear to most to be 'arbitrary discrimination' within the meaning of Article 30 EC.

Finally, in respect of the banking system, as a consequence both of national rules implementing the Basel soft law provisions[237] and of the Community's harmonization directives (notably Directive 2006/48 EC[238]), there is a nearly perfect equivalence among Member States' internal rules on banking supervision, which is sufficient by itself to deny application of Legislative Decree No 231/2001, as amended, to banks belonging to other EU Member States.

---

237. See the considerations offered in paragraphs 13-15 of Chapter V of this book.
238. See paragraph 16 of Chapter V of this book, where I emphasize that the harmonization pursued by Directive No. 2006/48/EC is intended to avoid 'multinational' banks habitually serving clients established in the territory of more than one Member State from being forced to comply with the procedures of a 'multitude' of different jurisdictions instead of merely the rules of their home States, under to the so-called 'Home Country Control' system.

18. MORE: (D) MANDATORY RULES OF ITALIAN LAW RELATING TO MULTINATIONAL GROUPS OF COMPANIES

More than fifty years after the signing of the Treaty of Rome by the six Founding States, partly as a result of the present size of the European Union enlarged to twenty-seven States, it is necessary, *in the present state of Community law*, to consider the issues arising from the functioning of 'Community' multinational conglomerates, including in respect of conflict rules.

In other words, beside the studies currently underway for the development of a uniform body of substantive rules on corporate groups (I am referring to the solutions submitted in the Communication from the Commission to the Council and the European Parliament, '*Modernising Company Law and Enhancing Corporate Governance in the European Union – A Plan to Move Forward*', of 21 May 2003),[239] it is my view that the search for uniform solutions to the problems of private international law on companies, with a view to the full achievement of the freedom of establishment and the free provision of services should not overlook the impact the economic uniqueness of a 'group of companies' is bound to have not only on the choice of the most appropriate criterion to identify the law governing the parent or holding company,[240] but also on the operating scope of that law in relation to the law that governs the life and events of a daughter-company, whether a subsidiary or a branch, and the other way round. If, in principle, it is the law governing the parent company which operates as the law governing the group, due account should be taken of the overriding rules of the national law that governs a subsidiary, with a view to protecting the interests of its 'stakeholders', i.e. its minority shareholders, bondholders, employees and creditors.

Under the Italian company law, one such issue is the treatment of '*società unipersonali*', single-member limited companies. The Italian Supreme Court, sitting in Joint Chambers to establish jurisdiction, has, on many occasions, delivered judgments about whether or not Italian jurisdiction should apply in the case of the US-based company *Raytheon* – the sole shareholder in fact of an Italian public limited company, Elettronica Sicula SpA ('Elsi') – which had been sued by third-party creditors, pursuant to Article 2362 (former version[241]) of the Civil Code, to answer for the debts of its wholly controlled company, itself declared insolvent.

239. COM (2003) 284 final. See paragraph 9 if Chapter II of this book.

240. See Angelici, *Appunti*, cit., p. 32 f.

241. Clearly, I am referring to the original version of Article 2362, which automatically implied the joint (subsidiary) liability of the sole member, whether a natural or legal person, if insolvency were declared against a company wholly controlled during the period when its shares were held by that sole member. Partly under Community pressures, this provision was subsequently amended to require compliance with certain disclosure requirements, failing which the sole member is held jointly liable pursuant to Article 2325(1), Civil Code, in case the company is declared insolvent. About the former norm, see Supreme Court, Joined Chambers, Judgment No. 12683 of May 1971 in *Raytheon Company* v *Banca Commerciale Italiana*, [1972] Giur. it. I, 1, c. 378 f., with a note by Franchi, and the judgments delivered to the same effect on that

With regard to the application of the jurisdiction criterion then applicable,[242] pursuant to Rule 4(2) of the Italian Code of Civil Procedure, the Supreme Court held:

> The shareholder's obligation is sourced both from the fact that the company's obligation arose at a time when the shareholder was its sole member, and from the shareholder's position as a single member. Therefore, such obligation arose in the place where the shareholder took on its position as a single shareholder, i.e. in the place where the company was established. The claim brought pursuant to Article 2362, Civil Code, qualifies, therefore, as the exercise of a right of obligation, and it is, as such, caught by the provision of Article 4(2). Pursuant to this provision, the obligation in issue falls within the scope of the Italian jurisdiction, in its being *an obligation of an Italian company whose single member is a foreign national.* For the position of shareholder, which is, in fact, integral part of the specific case that generated that entity's obligation, has occurred in Italy, and the foreign national's obligation has, accordingly, arisen in Italy. Therefore, according to Rule 4(2) of the Code of Civil Procedure, the Italian Judicial Authority shall have jurisdiction over the claim so brought, pursuant to Article 2362, Civil Code, against a foreigner who is assumed to be the single shareholder of an Italian limited company, and Italian jurisdiction must be declared over the controversy in issue in these proceedings. [*Emphasis added*].[243]

As is know, in the *Raytheon* case, the United States exercised the right of diplomatic protection of citizens abroad against Italy, claiming that Italy had violated the international legal obligations which it undertook by the Treaty of Friendship, Commerce and Navigation between the two countries concluded on 2 February 1948 and the Supplementary Agreement thereto concluded in Washington on 26 September 1951, by reason of its acts and omissions in relation to, and its treatment of, two United States corporations, the *Raytheon Company* and its wholly owned subsidiary *The Machlett Laboratories Incorporated*, in relation to the bankruptcy of the Italian corporation Raytheon-Elsi S.p.A. (previously Elettronica Sicula S.p.A. ELSI, whence the name of the case decided by The Hague International Court of Justice in its judgment of 20 July 1989).[244]

The International Court of Justice unanimously rejected the objection of non-exhaustion of local remedies in judicial proceedings Italy had raised, because Italy

---

same date, Nos 1269 and 1270); Supreme Court, Joined Chambers, Judgments No. 952 of 27 Mar. 1972, *Raytheon Company* v *Cassa centrale di Risparmio Vittorio Emanuele per le provincie siciliane*, [1972] Giust. civ. I, p. 1615 f.

242. Article 4 of the Code of Civil Procedure was repealed together with Articles 2, 3, 37(2), and Articles 796 through 805 of the Code of Civil Procedure, by Article 73 of Act No. 218/1995.

243. Under the same approach: Supreme Court, Chamber I, No. 28799, May 1985, *Credito italiano S.p.A.* v *The Machlett Inc.*; *Raytheon Company* v *Credito italiano S.p.A,*. [1986] Giur. comm. II, p. 537 f.; Supreme Court, Joined Chambers, No. 1088, 24 Feb. 1986, *Soc. Chocolat Tobler* v *Banca nazionale del lavoro*, *ibid.*, II, p. 537 f.

244. See *Elettronica Sicula S.p.A. (ELSI)*, [1989] ECR, p. 15 f.

had failed to supply evidence to that effect,[245] and, in the framework of the merits, rejected the United States' claim by a wide majority, found that Italy had not committed any breaches of the Treaty with the United States and, accordingly, by the same majority, rejected the claim for reparation made against the Republic of Italy by the United States of America.[246]

Still, even in relation to these issues, one could hardly, within the European Union, ignore the case-law of the Court of Justice in respect of the principles laid down in its judgments on the freedom of establishment and the free provision of services.

It is appropriate to specify that the liability of the shareholder, whether a natural or legal person, of a single-member limited company falls within the traditional code-based approach to Italian company law. As the contract of association was viewed as the only suitable legal instrument to form a company, whether one of persons or one of capital (or body corporate, to use a term so often used above), that law by no means allowed a company to be formed by just one proprietor.

It was on the requirement that a plurality of members (binding themselves, in fact, to the *contract* of association) must be present at the time of incorporation, that Article 2497, Civil Code (in respect of limited liability companies), and Article 2362, Civil Code (in respect of shares limited companies), introduced specific rules to govern the liability of an owner who had become the 'sole member' *at a later time*, when the company was already in operation, for the obligations of a subsidiary *in the event this became insolvent*, so long as those obligations had been undertaken by it prior to that time. A derogation was thereby introduced from the core principle of company law, according to which any limited company is only liable for its obligations up to the extent of its assets.

This approach has, however, changed over time, in view the general belief that the way in which Italian law had supposedly solved the problem of single-member companies was *disproportionate*. Even the more so, as so radical a solution was not, and is still not, matched by any other Member State's rules of company law, to the extent it made the single member, whether a natural or legal person, liable for the company's debts.

It was objected, in fact, that the Italian rules governing limited companies already provided for a vast array of tools (autonomy of equity, organizational structure with a plurality of managing bodies, strict disclosure requirements for the protection of creditors, *etc.*), which were capable in themselves to mitigate, if not outright to remove, any distortions impairing the protection of a single-member company's creditors.

Following an earlier opening resulting from the implementation of the Twelfth Council Directive in 1993 – whereby single-member limited liability companies (*società unipersonali a responsabilità limitata*) were be permitted to be formed,

---

245. *Ibid.*, pp. 42 f., 47 f., and 81.
246. *Ibid.*, pp. 48 s. and 81. About the exercise of diplomatic protection, see paragraph 2 of Chapter V herein below.

only subject to the requirement that *suitable forms of disclosure* should be ensured – the Italian Company Law Reform Act of 2003 extended this approach to shares limited liability companies (società per azioni).

As a result of the amendments made under the 2003 Company Law Reform Act, Article 2325(1), Civil Code, has introduced a general rule applicable to any company limited by shares, whatever its shareholding structure, according to which '*the company shall alone be liable for its obligations to the full extent of its assets*'. There is an exception to this general rule, though. For the second paragraph of Article 2325 requires:

> *In case the company becomes insolvent*, if a person has come to be the sole owner of its shares, such person shall be *unlimitedly* liable for any liabilities as the company may have *undertaken in the period in which its shares were owned by that person*, either if equity has not been contributed pursuant to Article 2342 or until the disclosure requirements under Article 2362 are duly met. [*Emphasis added*].

Article 2342(2), Civil Code, in providing for the case of a sole shareholder, requires that capital contributions must be paid in (ordinarily to the extent of 25% of the share capital) upon the company being formed.

The first paragraph of the revised Article 2362 reads as follows:

> When the shares are found to belong to only one person or the person of the sole owner changes, then the directors shall *file with the registrar of companies a declaration containing the indication* of the family name and given name or business style, date and place or birth or *State of constitution*, and domicile or *seat* and nationality, as the case may be, *of such sole owner*. [*Emphasis added*].

The third paragraph specifies:

The disclosure duties provided for in the preceding paragraphs may be discharged by the sole owner or by the person that ceases to be the sole owner.

In other words, failure to make full payment of the share capital or to comply with disclosure requirements has been provided for as a deterrent, for it entails a (subsidiary) liability of the sole shareholder pursuant to Article 2325(2) as well as a liability of the single-member company's directors.

It is appropriate to stress that the rules on the liability of the parent company as another company's sole shareholder have been introduced to secure the protection of a wholly owned subsidiary's creditors. Clearly, the focus of this entire set of provisions is the protection of the subsidiary's balance of economic interests.

As a result, the new rules so introduced will only be applied in case it is the *wholly owned subsidiary* which is *subject to Italian law*, while whether or not the controlling company is also subject to Italian law is quite immaterial. For granting a non-Italian company's creditors rights they do not have under the substantive law applicable to that company would make no sense.

Conversely, in furtherance of the European Court of Justice's case-law principles, the provisions of Italian company law discussed above cannot apply to a wholly owned subsidiary formed in another Member State of the European Union, which is entitled to freedom of establishment pursuant to Article 48 EC, *even if it has its central administration or principal business object in Italy or has transferred either to Italy*, in which case the applicable law would solely be the law of the place of its incorporation.

Likewise, the Italian rules on single-member companies cannot be applied even if a company incorporated in another Member State of the European Union and wholly owned by a foreign or even an Italian company establishes a *secondary office* or a branch in Italy, in that no additional prescriptions or penalties for breaching rules not set out in the Eleventh Company Law Directive can be imposed in the State of establishment further to those contained in the *lex societatis*.

Similar issues arise in connection with the scope for application of the rules of company law to companies performing *direction or coordination activities* on other companies.

Here again, the starting point is the assumption that – in principle and in general – the daughter company, irrespective of the extent and manners of control, is an entity legally separate from, and independent of, the parent or holding company. And it is so even in respect of any sub-holding and, *a fortiori*, of sister companies, if any. In general, therefore, the principle is one and the same: each company will be liable for its own obligations.

Still, pursuant to the first paragraph of the revised Article 2497 of the Italian Civil Code:

> Any company or entity which, in performing direction and coordination activities on other companies, acts in its own or others' business interests in breach of such other companies' principles of corporate governance and enterprise, shall be directly liable to such other companies' shareholders for any prejudice made to their profitability or shareholder value, as well as to their creditors for any injury caused to the wholeness of their assets. There shall be no liability when the damage is found to be lacking in light of the overall result of such direction and coordination activities or to have been removed in full whether following measures taken to that effect or otherwise. [*Emphasis added*].

The second paragraph of that same article requires:

> *Whosoever has participated in whatsoever manner* in the injurious act or has consciously benefited therefrom, shall be held jointly liable therefor, though only to the extent of the relevant benefit in the latter case. [*Emphasis added*].

The third paragraph further provides that:

> None of the company's owners or creditors may bring action against the company or entity performing direction and coordination activities unless their claims have not been satisfied by the company subject to such direction and coordination. [*Emphasis added*].

These provisions assume the parent company's liability for the relevant violation, as specified at paragraph 13 of the Report on Legislative Decree No 6 of 17 January

2003. Thus, Aquilian liability is deemed only to occur because of the holding company's *negligent* conduct consisting of acts made in violation of the principle of correct corporate governance and business management, in 'its own or others' interests', for example in the interests of the parent company's shareholders or any 'related' parties.

Pursuant to Article 2391-*bis*, Civil Code, transactions with 'related parties' are relevant in respect of companies that rely on risk capital for their operations. By using a *per-relationem* formulation, Article 2(h) of the Regulation adopted by Consob by Resolution No 11971 of 14 May 1999, as subsequently amended ('Regulation of Issuers'), provides that 'related parties' shall mean:

> persons so defined by the international financial reporting standard for the disclosure of transactions with related parties in financial reports, adopted under the procedure referred to in Article 6 of Regulation (EC) 1606/2002,

namely, IAS (International Accounting Standard) 24.[247]

The notion of *related parties* offered by IAS 24, which the EC Regulation refers to, should be construed by taking into account the whole Standard, which, much as it comes in three sections, i.e.:

- an *introductory* section, which specifies the purpose of the disclosures about transactions with related parties, and the scope for application and objective of the Standard;
- a substantive section, which provides a definition of related parties; and
- a residual section, which provides information supplementing the above items;

  only permits to identify the information required if it is considered as a whole.

This preliminary observation is a fundamental basis on which an interpretation can be given, because, if only the section captioned 'Definitions' were focused on, there would be the risk of considering situations indicated just by way of example, but certainly not mandatory, to be conclusive.[248]

---

247. According to Article 6 of the Directive 2006/46 EC by European Parliament and the Council of 14 Jun. 2006 which modifies the following Directives: 78/660 EEC on annual accounts, 83/349 EEC on consolidated accounts, 86/635 EEC on annual and consolidated accounts of the banks and 91/674 EEC on annual and consolidated accounts of insurance companies ([2006] O.J. L224), '*"related party" has the same meaning as in international accounting standards adopted in accordance with Regulation (EC) No 1606/2002*'. On this issue, see Pozzoli & Vitali, *Guida operativa ai principi contabili internazionali*, 310 ff.

248. In fact: *A party is related to an entity if: (a) directly, or indirectly through one or more intermediaries, the party: (i) controls, is controlled by, or is under common control with, the entity (this includes parents, subsidiaries and fellow subsidiaries); (ii) has an interest in the entity that gives it significant influence over the entity; or (iii) has joint control over the entity; (b) the party is an associate (as defined in IAS 28* Investments in Associates) *of the entity; (c) the party is a joint venture in which the entity is a venturer (see IAS 31* Interests in Joint Ventures); *(d) the party is a member of the key management personnel of the entity or its parent; (e) the party is a close member of the family of any individual referred to in (a)*

An additional requirement is that the liability in question must have caused an *unjust* damage to the controlled company's owners and/or creditors, which damage must consist of either an injury to the owners' right to profits or shareholder value, or to the creditors' claims secured by the company's assets.

Further, that such a damage exists must be assessed in light of the *overall result* of the direction and coordination activity, and it must also be established that the alleged damage has not been removed *in its whole* through subsequent compensatory measures taken within the same fiscal year, which would entail full discharge of liability.

It is for the injured persons to prove the *causal relationship* between the parent company's *careless conduct* and the *damaging event*, as well as such conduct and the alleged damage. This is to say that they will have to prove that the damage was not caused, say, by an adverse trade cycle, a third party's act or even an unsuccessful business choice, but that the damage was the result of a specific violation of the duty of care by the controlling company's managing body in furtherance of their own or other persons' advantage, in performing direction and coordination activities over the controlled company. This implies that the prejudice alleged by the shareholders or by the creditors must have been caused by operations the controlled company carried out *on the basis of directions from* the controlling company. The complainants must, in brief, also prove that specific directions were actually imparted to the controlled company from the top, and that the compliance therewith was the cause of the damage allegedly incurred by it.

Though so heavy a burden of proof is quite hard to discharge, it is made lighter by the disclosure requirements to be met under the last paragraph of Article 2497-*bis* and under Article 2497-*ter* of the Italian Civil Code. Article 2497-*bis* requires the controlled company's directors to disclose its transactions with the parent company and the other sister companies in the report on operations attached to the controlled company's financial statements, specifying the economic impact the parent company's direction and coordination activities have had on the controlled company's business operations and results.

Article 2497-*ter*, Civil Code, requires that the decisions made by a company subject to another company's direction and coordination must, when influenced by the latter, be based on reasonable grounds, and the reasons and interests behind them adequately specified. Each such decision must be accounted for in the directors' report on operations pursuant to Article 2428 of the Civil Code.

Article 2497-*ter* of the Civil Code provides the necessary complement to the liability system framed within Article 2497, because, on the one hand, the fulfilment of the duty to give grounds facilitates the onus placed on the complainants to assert

---

or (d); (f) the party is an entity that is controlled, jointly controlled or significantly influenced by, or for which significant voting power in such entity resides with, directly or indirectly, any individual referred to in (d) or (e); or (g) the party is a post-employment benefit plan for the benefit of employees of the entity, or of any entity that is a related party of the entity. However, this by no means implies that a relationship meeting the above qualifications must necessarily be one of correlation or that a relationship that does not so must automatically be excluded.

the parent company's liability, and, on the other hand, such fulfilment permits determining *ex post* the existence of the compensatory advantages which, *if obtained in the same financial year*, pursuant to the first paragraph of Article 2497 are apt to prevent a liability action from being brought against the holding company.

According to Article 2497-*ter*, no liability can be placed on the parent company where the damage alleged by the controlled company or any of its owners or creditors is *made up for* by the advantages – whether achieved or reasonably predictable – that accrue to the subsidiary from its belonging to the group. Nor can any such liability exist if the alleged prejudice has been removed through measures specifically taken to that effect – for example, through cash payments or contracts or paid professional assignments to the controlled company in compensation for the acts by which it alleges to have been damaged.

Mention should be made of the second paragraph of Article 2497, Civil Code, which requires that, if the parent company's liability is established, *those who participated in the injurious act* – such as the parent company's *directors* or *general manager* who authored the direction prejudicial to the subsidiary, and those of the subsidiary who carried it out – be held jointly liable.

Equally liable will be held, though only to the extent of the benefit received, the persons who knowingly received a benefit, such as the parent company or a sister company to which resources were arbitrarily transferred.

Obviously, the heavier the weight of control (for example, the sameness of both board of directors or of directors holding special offices in both companies), the more difficult will be to contend that the controlled company acted rather of its own accord than under the influence of the parent company's direction and coordination activities, because the directors of the former were elected by the shareholders' meeting through which control is exercised by the latter.

In conclusion, the entire system described above bears out the fact that, even if there is a dominant or a single shareholder, the controlled company may well take *decisions independent* of the controlling company. This fact is further confirmed by the power vested in the subsidiary's directors to refrain from complying with any directions they may be given by the parent company's directors.

In general, the problem of the subjective and spatial scope for application of the newly introduced rules to any company subject to another company's coordination and direction must be solved in the same way as the problem arising from the new rules on the sole shareholder's liability. It will be so even though, as I have observed above, the former problem arises in connection with a case of *ex-lege* liability, while Article 2497, Civil Code, provides for events relevant to the law of torts.

In both cases, the interests Italian law protects are the *controlled company's*: in the former case, for the protection of its creditors in an event of insolvency, and, in the latter case, for the protection of its stakeholders generally.

As a consequence, as is the case with the combined effects of the second paragraph of Article 2325 and Article 2362, Civil Code, the provisions of Article 2497 will likewise only be applied if and when it is *the controlled company which is subject to Italian law*.

Let me add, for the sake of completeness only, that it is my view that Italian law can hardly be assumed to be applicable, not for its being the law governing the controlled company – which I assume to be foreign in the terms of Article 25(1) of Act No 218/1995 – but because of the other rule of private international law contained in Article 62 on the law applicable to liability for violations. This result could only be achieved, in fact, only if the damaging event or the act that caused the event, within the scope of direction and coordination activities, had occurred in Italy – for example, in the place of the meeting of the subsidiary's board of directors at which the relevant resolution was adopted at the parent company's instigation. I do not think this could be a practicable solution (even after the Regulation Rome II will become effective), for the forceful reason that, as submitted above, the case of a foreign controlled company is hardly caught by Article 2497, Civil Code, and is accordingly unrelated to Aquilian (torts) liability.

The same line of reasoning applies to the applicability of the rule of private international law enshrined in Article 61 of Act No 218/1995 (on *obligations arising from the law*) in respect of cases of *ex-lege* liability arising from violating Article 2362, Civil Code. The disclosure duties laid down in that article essentially concern the controlled company (much as they may be discharged by the controlling company's directors acting in lieu), and the duty to pay in the whole share capital is equally placed on the controlled company. Therefore, only if the controlled company is Italian (subject to Italian law, that is), will any violation of those duties be deemed to have occurred within the Italian territory. If the wholly owned subsidiary is foreign and lacking permanent connections of it with the Italian territory, no violation of either Article 2362 or Article 2342(2), Civil Code, may be deemed to have occurred.

Now, in the case of a holding company formed in any other Member State of the European Union, the question is whether applying the provisions of Article 2497, Civil Code, to its Italian subsidiary or subsidiaries may result in an unendurable regulatory obstacle to the full exercise by the holding company of its rights under both the rules on freedom of establishment and the rules on the free provision of services.

I have some doubts, though. The cooperation that must invariably exist between the directors of a holding company exercising direction and coordination activities on a subsidiary and the directors of such subsidiary is bound to result in an overall balance that deserves outright protection. It should not be forgotten that the essential aim of Article 44(2)(g) EC, which provides the legal foundation of all harmonization directives relating to companies in the field of freedom of establishment, is precisely *the protection of the interests of members and others*.

In fact, if the foreign holding company in our example were unwilling to be subjected to the provisions of Article 2497 et seq. of the Italian Civil Code, it would suffice for it to refrain from subjecting its Italian subsidiary to direction and coordination measures, and to maintain just arm's length relations with it.

This much having been said, it is quite clear that, in the case of a Community group of companies, the only criterion available to determine whether a controlled company is subject to the laws of Italy is whether it has or has not been incorporated in Italy.

19. MORE: (E) THE RULES APPLICABLE TO LISTED COMPANIES

Under the caption 'Scope', Article 119 of Legislative Decree No 58 of 24 February 1998, as amended, providing the consolidated law on finance, commonly referred to as the '*TUF*' or Draghi Act, which article is the first in Chapter II ('Listed Companies') of Title III in Part IV, requires:

> Unless specified otherwise, the provisions of this chapter shall apply to Italian companies with shares listed on regulated markets in Italy or other EU countries (listed companies). [*Emphasis added*].

Therefore, in principle and from a general point of view, this rule provides – unless 'specified otherwise' in individual articles of Chapter II – for two concurring, equally mandatory requirements to be met for the rules on listed companies to be deemed applicable: (i) the company concerned must be an *Italian* company; and (ii) its shares must be listed *in regulated markets in Italy or in other Member States of the European Union.*

What does '*Italian company*' mean, though? An answer to this question is provided by the rule of private international law set out in Article 25(1) of Act No 218/1995. As we already know, a company is in general subject to Italian law, and is accordingly *Italian,* if it has been incorporated in Italy or, as an exception to the general rule, has its central administration or main business object in Italy even if incorporated abroad.[249] In the presence of either factor of contact with the territory of the Republic of Italy, subject to *renvoi* back or elsewhere under Article 13 of Act No 218/1995, that company will still be governed by the law of its home country *as well*, and can, subject to this qualification, be treated as '*Italian*' from the point of view of Italian law.

Clearly enough, this proposition is immaterial under Community law, in the sense that, since the listing of foreign 'Community' companies in Italy falls within the scope of freedom of establishment, *only* a company incorporated in Italy may be deemed to be 'Italian' for these purposes.

And so, in this as in other respects, based on the same simplifying formulation as is used for Italian companies, a company applying for an IPO procedure, i.e. the initial public offer for first listing in the Italian stock exchange, is assumed to be *French, Spanish or German* or a national of any other EU country, depending on whether its was incorporated in France, Spain, Germany or such other EU country, respectively.

In principle, for it to be subjected to the rules here under scrutiny, it is not enough for it to be *Italian* in the alternate meaning of a company governed by the laws of Italy, but it must also be listed in a stock exchange in Italy or in another regulated market of the European Union.

---

249. See Santa Maria, 'Società' (dir. int. priv.), in *Enc. giur, Treccani*, cit., p. I ff.; Id., 'Spunti di riflessione sulla norma di diritto internazionale privato in materia di società ed altri enti' [1996] Riv. soc., p. 1093 ff.

Article 119 of Legislative Decree No 58 of 1998 contains no mandatory rules in the terms of Article 17 of Act No 218/1995, for the simple reason that mandatory rules are only those that '*must be applied notwithstanding remission to foreign laws*'.[250] The rule we are concerned with here has, however, been expressly declared to be applicable *only* to companies subject to Italian law – and listed in Italy or elsewhere in the EU, *at that*.

More simply put, most of the provisions set out in the Chapter II of the Draghi Act are 'rules of internal public policy', in the sense that they cannot be derogated by those to whom they are addressed, and their purviews must be applied to any case of reference to the Italian legislation in terms of private international law, *but not* in a case of remission to a foreign law – obviously except in case that foreign law is in contrast with a principle of international public policy laid down in the Italian legal system.

As a consequence, none of the rules on listed companies contained in the *TUF* (the Consolidating Financial Services Act) is applicable in itself to foreign companies assumedly listed in Italy (which is, in fact, something hard to understand). Nor can any such rule be applied to 'Community' companies – incorporated, that is, in a EU Member State other than Italy – even if listed in another regulated market within the Community, whether or not in addition to an Italian stock exchange. Nor can it be applied to *non*-Community foreign companies, whether or not listed in a Community or a *non*-Community market.[251]

The comments offered above are true in general. In theory, some derogations may occur in view of the exception expressed in Article 119 for any individual clauses as may provide otherwise, in that same chapter, in respect of the addressees of the rules on listed companies.

For avoidance of doubts, let me first observe that this is not the case where the legislator uses the term 'listed companies' in paragraphs 2 and 3 of Article 120, paragraph 3 of Article 121, and paragraphs 1 of Articles 122, 132 and 134. In each such case, the term has clearly been used *elliptically*, as expressly indicated where it is mentioned in parentheses, at the end of Article 119. Its extended form would be '*Italian* companies with ordinary shares *listed* on regulated markets in Italy or other EU countries'.

This longer wording has been used, in fact, only in paragraph 1 of Article 145, in respect of the issue of non-voting shares with preferential rights.

Other provisions in the chapter of the Draghi Act that contains rules on listed companies have a narrower scope for application to the addressees broadly indicated in Article 119. Paragraph 4 of Article 149, paragraph 3 of Article 152, and paragraph 3 of Article 157 expressly exclude the application of a given provision to 'companies with shares listed only on regulated markets in other EU countries'.

---

250. So in Article 17 of Act No. 218/1995.

251. For a contrary view entirely disregarding the problem in private international law, see CONSOB Note No. 99075915 of 18 Oct. 1999 [2000] Giur. Comm., p. 213 ff., reproduced at the end of my article, 'Sulla legittimità della struttura di un progetto di alleanza internazionale con assunzione di partecipazioni reciproche', *ibid.*, p. 186 ff., esp.lly from paragraph 6, p. 200 ff.

Obviously, the companies covered by the three provisions are '*Italian* companies with shares listed only on regulated markets in other EU countries'. This is the phrase used by the legislator in Article 124 in vesting CONSOB, in the case of Italian companies whose shares are listed *only* in other countries of the European Union, with the power to declare Article 120, 121, 122 and 123(2) inapplicable, '*in consideration of the legislation applicable to such companies by virtue of their being listed*'.

In other words, the legislator expressly wanted to provide an exceptional device capable, on a case-by-case basis, to remove any conflicts of law as might arise in respect of a company as a consequence of its being subject both to Italian law pursuant to Article 25(1) of Act 218/1995, and to the rules regulating the EU market in which its shares are listed – i.e. mandatory rules of foreign laws.

In fact, there is *only one mandatory rule* in Chapter II of the Draghi Act. Such rule is set out in Article 165, captioned 'Auditing of Group', which expressly requires that the provisions in Section VI of Chapter II, 'Auditing', be 'also' applied, except for Article 157, 'to subsidiaries of companies with listed shares'. Clearly enough, though not so explicitly stated, the companies referred to in this provision are clearly *controlled companies, whether Italian or foreign*. For Article 150 of the CONSOB Regulation issued under Resolution No 11971 of 14 May 1999, pursuant to Article 165(2) of the Draghi Act, correctly provides for the 'auditing of *foreign subsidiaries*'.

The only two references to foreign companies in the Draghi Act have a different import, though. Neither the provision in Article 120(3) nor that in Article 161(3) are mandatory rules. Article 120(3), in stating that notification requirements apply to 'listed companies that hold more that 10 per cent of the capital of an Italian *or foreign* unlisted company', refers to foreign companies only with a view to providing for the duties arising from acquiring the quality of shareholder in a listed company caught by the general definition provided by Article 119, which duties fall, *in themselves*, within the scope of application of the *lex societatis* applicable to such listed company.

Paragraph 3 of Article 161, in permitting 'auditing firms constituted abroad' to be entered in the special register of authorized auditing firms – if they satisfy certain mandatory requirements, in fact – is solely intended to extend the area of the firms eligible for auditing listed companies as broadly defined in Article 119, and subject, as such, to the rules of Chapter II, Title III, Part IV of the Draghi Act.

Therefore, save for the provision contained in Article 165, the addressees of the rules on listed companies set out in the Draghi Act are *invariably Italian companies* that are *listed in regulated markets in Italy or in other EU countries* and, in the specific instances indicated above, listed *only* in regulated Italian markets or *both* in these markets *and* in one or more regulated markets in other EU countries.

There is more to it, though. For the revised body of rules on listed companies has been so structured as to provide a *special law*, relating to listed companies alone, in addition to the *general rules* on companies contained in the Civil Code, which rules remain applicable, in principle, to Italian listed companies as well.

In fact, the Draghi Act often refers expressly to Civil Code provisions, whether in order to exclude or to affirm their applicability, or in order to identify any explicit modifying profiles thereof.[252]

In light of Community rules safeguarding freedom of establishment and the free provision of services, it is quite clear that, partly for the purpose of the application of Article 119 *TUF* to situations material to Community law, only a company *constituted* in Italy can be subjected to Italian legislation and categorized as an *Italian* company.

Specifically in regard to cross-holdings, the different limits set in other European countries, which the Draghi Act takes into no account, and the fact that, in other legislations as well as in our own, correctives are only applied when *both prescribed limits* are exceeded – a mandatory element for the relevant event to be deemed prohibited and the resulting duties to be imposed only on the company that was the last to exceed the limit (under Italian law) or on the company that was the last to give notification (under Spanish law) – or no limits are imposed (under English law), combine to generate conflicts that are quite difficult to settle.

While the reader is referred to another study of mine for the analysis and solution of problems arising from the acquisition of cross-holdings by two companies, one Italian within the meaning just provided above, the other subject to the governing law of another EU Member State,[253] let me submit a basic observation.

The two different governing laws respectively applicable to each of the two companies entering into a cross-holding deal must be combined, with a view to a 'balanced' application, without either being made to prevail in such a way as to hamper or even prevent the transaction. For such an adverse occurrence would patently clash with the Community rules on freedom of establishment and free movements of capital.[254] This would be the case especially when cross-holdings are effected just as a temporary move in preparation for a merger (or a legally equivalent, strongly integrated transaction), with a view to their cancellation upon merger or their termination if the merger (or equivalent transaction) has not been completed by the end of the stated interim period. In addition, a cross-holding deal is an international operation obviously intended, within the European Union, to contribute significantly towards the achievement of full integration in furtherance of both the Maastricht Treaty and the Amsterdam Treaty.

---

252. For example, the norm on 'control' referred to in those provisions is that contained in Article 2359 of the Civil Code, not in Article 93 of the of the *TUF*, which, by express reference to that article, added two more cases. See, for all, Spolidoro, 'Disciplina delle partecipazioni reciproche' [1998] Riv. soc., p. 1039 ff., esp.lly. p. 1044 ff.

253. See Santa Maria, 'Sulla legittimità della struttura di un progetto di alleanza internazionale', cit., p. 200 ff.

254. It is appropriate to note the Article 2 of the *TUF* specifies that 'The Ministry for the Economy and Finance, the Bank of Italy and CONSOB shall exercise their powers *in harmony with Community rules* and apply the regulations and decisions of the European Union'. Emphasis added.

20. JURISDICTION CRITERIA RELATING TO COMPANIES IN THE EC REGULATION ON JURISDICTION AND THE RECOGNITION OF FOREIGN JUDGMENTS

It has been observed above that Council Regulation (EC) No 44/2001 of 22 December 2000 on jurisdiction and the recognition and enforcement of judgments in *civil and commercial matters*[255] has superseded the Brussels Convention of 27 September 1968 on the same subject matter. Regulation No. 44/2001 states:

> In order to attain the objective of free movement of judgments in civil and commercial matters, it is necessary and appropriate that the rules governing jurisdiction and the recognition and enforcement of judgments be governed by a Community legal instrument which is binding and directly applicable.[256]

Regulation No. 44/2001 has retained the layout of the Brussels Convention it has superseded – initially except for Denmark[257] – although it has refined its contents in several places, following the experience made with the Court of Justice's interpretative judgments and with a view to adjusting closer to new needs that had emerged over the years.

Because of the object common to both instruments, the scope for application of the rules set out in the Regulation has remained essentially unchanged from the Convention, except for a qualifying statement added in the first paragraph of Article 1:

> This Regulation (. . .) shall not extend, in particular, to revenue, customs or administrative matters.

The list of exclusions set out in paragraph 2 of Article 1 has also remained unchanged.[258]

---

255. The Regulation in question, cit., *loc. cit.*, in the first paragraph of this Chapter 1 was subsequently amended by Regulation No. 1496/2002/EC of the Commission of 21 Aug. 2002, in [2002] O.J. L225, p. 13, by Regulation No. 1937/2004/EC of the Commission of 9 Nov. 2004, in [2004] O.J. L334, p. 3, by Regulation No. 2245/2004/EC of the Commission of 27 Dec. 2004, in [2004] O.J. L381, p. 10, and by Regulation No. 1791/2006/EC of the Council of 20 Nov. 2006, in [2006] O.J. L363, p. 1, as amended by the Act concerning the conditions of accession of the Czech Republic, the Republic of Estonia, the Republic of Cyprus, the Republic of Latvia, the Republic of Lithuania, the Republic of Hungary, the Republic of Malta, the Republic of Poland, the Republic of Slovenia and the Slovak Republic and the adjustments to the Treaties on which the European Union is founded, in [2001] O.J. L307, p. 28 (44/2001).
256. See the sixth Whereas in Regulation No. 44/2001.
257. Though Denmark was still expressly excluded from the application of Regulation No. 44/2001 at the end of the transitional period generally allowed for the accession of a new State to the Community, pursuant to Article 1(3) of the Regulation, it then acceded under the agreement of 19 Oct. 2005.
258. The paragraph 2 of Article 1 requires: The Regulation shall not apply to: (a) the status or legal capacity of natural persons, rights in property arising out of a matrimonial relationship, wills and succession; (b) bankruptcy, proceedings relating to the winding-up of insolvent companies or other legal persons, judicial arrangements, compositions and analogous proceedings; (c) social security; (d) arbitration.

It should be remembered that, in order to attain the objective of an actual free movement of judgments within the Community – i.e. a 'judicial union' of a sort, which provided the rationale behind the original Convention in the first place, and which is still a token of excellence of the Community's progression in the judicial domain – the criterion of a Member State's *nationality* has not been considered as the fundamental standard by which jurisdiction should be recognized.

A more open-minded approach has been taken, perhaps for the sake of fairness, by according foreigners who are domiciled within the Community, 'thereby participating in its economic activity and prosperity', the right to benefit from the common rules and to be heard by the 'natural' court, i.e. the judicial body 'most qualified from a territorial point of view'.[259]

The fundamental criterion remains the jurisdiction of the court of the defendant's *domicile*, although alternative or even exclusive jurisdictions is also contemplated:

> [J]urisdiction is generally based on the defendant's domicile and jurisdiction must always be available on this ground save in a few well-defined situations in which the subject-matter of the litigation or the autonomy of the parties warrants a different linking factor. The *domicile of a legal person* must be defined *autonomously* so as to make the common rules more transparent and avoid conflicts of jurisdiction [*Emphasis added*].[260]

Article 60 in Chapter V ('General Provisions') lays down a highly innovating concept of how to determine the domicile of a company and other legal person.

It should be remembered that the wording of Article 53 of the Brussels Convention, after stating that the 'seat' of a company or other legal person should be treated in the same way as a natural person's 'domicile', specified that, in order to determine 'that seat', the court seised of the relevant case was to apply its rules of private international law – an approach that had not gone by without criticism. First, it was argued that, since the seat identification criteria under the *lex societatis* differed from one State to another, depending on the norm of private international law of the court seised of the matter, the approach so taken did certainly not contribute to either legal certainty or the uniform application of the Convention.[261]

Secondly, it was pointed out that more inconsistency might arise from the different notions of a company's 'seat' to be found across different national legislations. For it could be viewed as a *direct* linking factor, ordinarily in the sense of 'actual' or 'real' seat, or it could be associated with the criterion of the place of incorporation in the meaning of '*statutory seat*', or even be used, in any of its

259. See Jenard, 'Relazione sulla Convenzione concernente la competenza giudiziaria e l'esecuzione delle sentenze in materia civile e commerciale' [1972] EC Bull. Suppl. 2, pp. 14 and 27 f. See also Nascimbene, *Il trattamento dello straniero*, cit., p. 386 f., body and footnote 77.
260. See Whereas 11 of the Regulation in question.
261. See Santa Maria, 'Problemi in tema di applicazione alle società della Convenzione della C.E.E. sulla competenza giurisdizionale e sul riconoscimento e l'esecuzione delle sentenze in materia civile e commerciale', in *L'efficacia delle sentenze straniere nelle Convenzioni multilaterali dell'Aja e della C.E.E.* (Padua, 1969), p. 245 ff.

meanings, as one of the pre-requirements arising from that different, *indirect* linking factor, a company's '*nationality*'.

Such criticisms appear to have been overcome by the present text of Article 60 through the determination of three alternative criteria set at one and the same level. The first paragraph of Article 60 states:

> For the purposes of this Regulation, a company or other legal person or association of natural or legal persons is domiciled at the place where it has its: (a) statutory seat, or (b) central administration, or (c) principal place of business.

It is patently clear that the use of the same criteria as those contained in Article 48(1) EC has caused them to be treated as Community-wide notions, which are not for any Member State's national law to determine. Therefore, this qualification – thanks to a rich case-law in matters of the companies' freedom of establishment and right to free provision of services – allows the outright eradication of any conflict as to the interpretation of such three notions.

Article 5 of Regulation No. 44/2001 provides for certain *special criteria* alongside the principal jurisdiction criterion, i.e. the criterion of the domicile of natural persons and legal persons as set out in Articles 2 and 60, respectively.

Thus, a person bringing action is granted one of seven options under Article 5(5), as an alternative to the basic criterion, in the sense that a person domiciled in a Member State may, in another Member State, be sued:

> as regards a dispute arising out of the operations of a branch, agency or other establishment, in the courts for the place in which the *branch*, *agency* or *other establishment* is situated. [*Emphasis added*].

The suing party may only rely on this jurisdictional criterion so long as it has proven that the company being sued has its 'domicile', under one of the three possible provisions set out in Article 60 of the Regulation, in the territory of whatever Contracting State.

Likewise, if a company sued in the place of establishment of a branch, agency or subsidiary wants to plead the provision in Article 5(5) to challenge the Court's jurisdiction, by denying that the relevant issue is caught by such provision, then that company will have to give proof, under the combined provisions of Articles 2 and 60, of its having 'its statutory seat', 'its central administration' or else 'its principal place of business' in one of the EU Member States.

Failing such proof, the provisions of the Regulation are no longer applicable, and jurisdiction will again be determined, pursuant to Article 4(1) of the Regulation, by the ordinary criteria contemplated by the national law of the court seised of the case, only except for any of the events of *exclusive jurisdiction* listed in Article 22, which will apply regardless of the defendant's domicile, or for the case of a prior agreement between the parties as to which court is to have jurisdiction, in accordance with Article 23, in which case it is necessary and sufficient that just one of them is domiciled in territory of a Member State.

By its judgment of 22 November 1978, in regard to the application of the Brussels Convention, Case 33/78, *Somafer SA v Saar-Ferngas AG*,[262] the European Court of Justice clarified that the terms '*branch, agency or other establishment*' as used in Article 5(5) of the Convention are *Community* concepts, which, as such, require an interpretation independent of the Contracting States' national laws. Such concepts imply the existence of a place of business which has the appearance of permanency, such as the extension of the parent body, has a management and is materially equipped to negotiate business with third parties so that the latter, although knowing that there would, if necessary, be a legal link with the parent body, the head office of which is abroad, should not have to deal directly with such parent body but may transact business at the place of business constituting the extension.

The concept of '*operations*' is relevant to actions relating to rights and contractual or non-contractual obligations concerning the management properly so-called of the agency, branch or other establishment, and actions concerning undertakings entered into in the name of the parent body, as well as non-contractual obligations arising from the activities in which the branch, agency or other establishment has engaged at the place in which it is established on behalf of the parent body.

Likewise, the concept of '*matters relating to a contract*', in the terms of Article 5(1), should be regarded as an independent concept of Community law, which, for the purpose of the application of the Regulation, must be interpreted by reference chiefly to the system and objectives of the Regulation, in order to ensure that it is fully effective.[263] The same principle of independence has provided the basis for ECJ case-law also in connection with the '*prorogation of jurisdiction clause*' in the terms of Article 17 of the Brussels Convention (as superseded by Article 23 of the Regulation).[264]

Of course, these concepts are intended to stand if referred to the corresponding rules enshrined in the Regulation.

As for the provisions for '*exclusive jurisdiction*' in Article 22 of the Regulation, paragraph 2 of that article has introduced a derogation from the criterion of natural or legal persons' domicile, by requiring that:

> in proceedings which have as their object the validity of the constitution, the nullity or the dissolution of companies or other legal persons or associations of natural or legal persons, or of the validity of the decisions of their organs,

the courts of the Member State in which the company, legal person or association has its seat shall have exclusive jurisdiction 'regardless of domicile'.

---

262. [1978] ECR 2183.
263. See ECJ Judgment of 22 Mar. 1983, Case 34/82, *Martin Peters Bauemternehmung GmbH* c. *Zuid Nederlandse Aaunemers Vereniging*, reference for a preliminary ruling from the *Hoge Raad der Nederlanden*, [1983] ECR, p. 987 f., p. 1002, ground 10.
264. In this respect, see Judgment of the Court of 10 Mar. 1992, Case 214/89, *Powell Duffryn plc* v *Wolfgang Petereit*, acting as liquidator of the company *IBH-Holding AG*, esp.lly grounds 13 f., as published in [1992] ECR, p. 1745 f. The judgment was later rectified, due to a material mistake in paragraph 29 and in ground 2, by an order dated 25 Mar. 1992.

While this provision is identical with the former corresponding wording in the Convention up to this point, it departs from it in the sentence next following:

> In order to determine that seat, the court shall apply *its rules of private international law*. [*Emphasis added*].

In this respect, the Community legislator has duplicated the much-criticized formulation of the last sentence of Article 53 of the Convention, which had been in fact, as I have observed above, removed from the corresponding wording of Article 60 of the Regulation, as a result of the well-taken choice to remove from it the general jurisdictional criterion of a *company's seat* and to replace it with the three 'Community' criteria, to which the same terminology was applied to reflect the long-settled concepts contained in Article 48(1) EC.

True, the broader approach to the determination of the domicile of companies and other legal persons has a precise rationale behind it, in that it is referred to the *general rule*, but would by no means be justified in relation to the determination of cases of *exclusive jurisdiction*, which are *exceptions* by nature and, as such, hardly conducive to an extensive application for obvious reasons of legal certainty.

Some coordination problems may, in fact, arise in connection with the ECJ case-law I have extensively commented on above about the exercise of the fundamental freedoms by companies and other legal persons. For the significance given by case-law to the provision of Article 48(1) EC as a typical rule of private international law – so that, as observed earlier, the phrase 'Companies or firms formed in accordance with the law of a Member State' is assumed to imply actual reference to the *law of the place of incorporation* with a view to allowing them to benefit from freedom of establishment and the free provision of services – is bound to affect remission to the national court's rules of private international law in determining the seat as the relevant jurisdiction criterion according to Article 22(2) of Regulation 44/2001.

It is my view in this respect that, where the proceedings have as their object rights arising from such fundamental freedoms as are secured by the EC Treaty, the court seised of the case will have, for the purposes of Article 22(2) of the Regulation, to determine the *seat* jurisdictional criterion by reference to private international law rules as is required under the first paragraph of Article 48 EC, thus under an approach conforming to that caught by Article 60 of the Regulation. In this case, should that court apply its own rules of private international law, it would go against the Treaty rules on freedom of establishment and the free provision of services.

21. EC REGULATION NO. 1346/2000 ON INSOLVENCY PROCEEDINGS

Council Regulation (EC) No 1346/2000 of 29 May 2000 on insolvency proceedings[265] falls within the aim set out by the European Union 'of establishing an area of

265. In O.J. L160 cit., p. 1. The Regulation in question had been preceded by a draft convention of 1970 on bankruptcy and similar procedures, to be later set aside.

freedom, security and justice', with a view to which other Regulations were adopted in addition to Regulations No 1346/2000 and No 44/2001 over a short period of time, to provide for several aspects of judicial cooperation in civil matters in accordance with Article 65 EC.[266]

The instrument under scrutiny provides an effective Community-wide 'tool' to govern the pathologic condition affecting any companies having establishments and assets in more than one Member State of the European Union, which are, as such, subject to insolvency rules in force in several legal systems, most of them in conflict with one another. Within this framework, since many business operations are increasingly 'cross-border', there has been a pressing need for rules of Community law to govern *cross-border* insolvency proceedings efficiently and effectively.

Regulation No. 1346/2000 has failed to provide a comprehensive definition of '*insolvency proceedings*'. In fact, it does not pursue the goal of providing uniform rules of substantive law – one so difficult to attain in the face of so many different national substantive laws. Its aim is narrower than that, because it is merely an attempt, in furtherance of the mutual recognition principle, at solving conflicts as to jurisdiction and to the applicable law in respect of insolvency proceedings, as these are expressly identified on a country-by-country basis in annexes to the Regulation, the substantive regulation of which is left to the individual Member States' rules of law.

The Regulation does contain a definition of '*winding up proceedings*' as insolvency proceedings involving realizing the assets of the debtor, including where the proceedings have been closed by a composition or other measure terminating the insolvency, or closed by reason of the insufficiency of the assets.[267] In any event:

> This Regulation should set out, for the matters covered by it, *uniform rules on conflict of laws* which replace, within their scope of application, national rules of private international law. [*Emphasis added*].[268]

In summary, as stated in its 'whereases', the Regulation is intended: (a) to govern international competence in matters of insolvency in accordance with uniform rules in all of the European Union's Member States; (b) to set out uniform rules

---

266. Please, refer to the first paragraph of this Chapter 1.
267. Initially, insolvency and liquidation procedures were listed for each Member State in Annex A and Annex B, respectively, of the Regulation in question. Following the reform laws on the matter enacted in Member States, No. 603/2005 of 12 Apr. 2005, in [2005] O.J. L100, p. 1 ff., and Regulation No. 694/2006 of 27 Apr. 2006, in [2006] O.J. L121, p. 1 ff., were introduced to amend in sequence the annexes to the 2000 Regulation, by replacing the first two with Annex I and Annex II, respectively. The *insolvency procedures* available in Italy are: *fallimento* (bankruptcy), *concordato preventivo* (composition), *liquidazione coatta amministrativa* (forced liquidation by administrative, as contrasted with judicial, authorities), and *amministrazione straordinaria* (special administration of large enterprises to preserve their assets) (Annex I); *liquidation procedures* are: *fallimento* (bankruptcy), *liquidazione coatta amministrativa, concordato preventivo*, and *cessione dei beni* (assignment of assets) (Annexe II).
268. See *ibid.*, Whereas 23.

to determine the law applicable to insolvency proceedings opened in Member States; and (c) to ensure the mutual recognition and enforcement, in the EU Member States, of judgments concerning the opening, conduct and closure of insolvency proceeding.[269]

As for its scope for application on a sector-by-sector basis, the Regulation is intended, pursuant to Article 1(1), to 'apply to collective insolvency proceedings' opened in Member States on the basis of the debtor's insolvency 'which entail the partial or total divestment of a debtor and the appointment of a liquidator'.[270]

From a subjective standpoint, the Regulation is not, pursuant to Article 2(2), intended to 'apply to insolvency proceedings concerning insurance undertakings, credit institutions, investment undertakings which provide services involving the holding of funds or securities for third parties, or to collective investment undertakings'.

As for its application over time, Article 43 requires that its provisions shall apply only to insolvency proceedings opened after its entry into force, i.e. 31 May 2002.

Against this background:

> This Regulation acknowledges the fact that as a result of widely differing substantive laws it is not practical to introduce insolvency proceedings with universal scope in the entire Community. The application without exception of the law of the State of opening of proceedings would, against this background, frequently lead to difficulties. [*Emphasis added*].
>
> This Regulation should take account of this in two different ways. On the one hand, provision should be made for special rules on applicable law in the case of particularly significant rights and legal relationships (e.g. rights *in rem* and

---

269. On this Regulation, see: Lupone, 'La convenzione comunitaria sulle procedure d'insolvenza e la riforma del sistema italiano di diritto internazionale privato' [1999] Contr. Impr. Eur., p. 429 ff.; Fumagalli, 'Il regolamento comunitario sulle procedure di insolvenza: competenza internazionale, legge applicabile e riconoscimento delle decisioni straniere' [2001] Riv. dir. proc., p. 677 ff.; Daniele, 'Legge applicabile e diritto uniforme nel regolamento comunitario relativo alle procedure d'insolvenza' [2002] Riv. dir. int. priv. proc., p. 33 f. Id., 'Il regolamento n. 1346/2000 relativo alle procedure di insolvenza: spunti critici' in *Diritto internazionale privato e Diritto comunitario*, Picone Ed. (Padua, 2004), p. 289 ff.; Queirolo, 'L'evoluzione dello spazio giudiziario europeo: in particolare la disciplina comunitaria delle procedure d'insolvenza', in *Comunicazioni e Studi*, XXII, (2002), p. 903 ff.; Starace, 'La disciplina comunitaria delle procedure di insolvenza: giurisdizione ed efficacia delle sentenze straniere' [2002] Riv. dir. int., p. 295 ff.; De Cesari, 'Giurisdizione, riconoscimento ed esecuzione delle decisioni nel regolamento comunitario relativo alle procedure di insolvenza' [2003] Riv. dir. int. priv. proc., p. 55 ff.; De Cesari & Montella, *Le procedure di insolvenza nella nuova disciplina comunitaria: commentario articolo per articolo del Regolamento CE n. 1346/2000* (Milan, 2004); Carbone, 'Il Regolamento (CE) n. 1346/2000 relativo alle procedure di insolvenza', in Carbone, Frigo, Fumagalli, *Diritto processuale civile e commerciale comunitario* (Milan, 2004), p. 89 ff.
270. It should be remembered, though, that Denmark is not bound, save at its express request, by Community acts approved within the scope provided for by Title IV of the EC Treaty (see Whereas 33 of Regulation No. 1346/2000).

> contracts of employment). On the other hand, *national proceedings* covering only assets situated in the State of opening should also be allowed *alongside main insolvency proceedings with universal scope*, [*Emphasis added*].[271]

Thus, one same company may be subjected to insolvency proceedings more than once, in a succession of actions and in different Member States. For:

> This Regulation enables the *main insolvency proceedings* to be opened in the Member State where the debtor has the *centre of his main interests*. These proceedings have *universal scope and aim at encompassing all the debtor's assets*. To protect the diversity of interests, this Regulation permits *secondary proceedings to be opened to run in parallel* with the main proceedings. Secondary proceedings may be opened i*n the Member State where the debtor has an establishment*. [*Emphasis added*].[272]

Courts with jurisdiction over secondary proceedings pursuant to Article 3(2) are not competent for dealing with the debtor's state of insolvency.

The effects of *secondary proceedings* are limited to the assets located in the Member State where the debtor has an establishment. Binding rules of coordination with the main proceedings satisfy the need for uniformity in the Community.

The 'centre of main interests' should correspond to the place where the debtor conducts the administration of his interests on a regular basis and is therefore ascertainable by third parties.[273]

As used in the Regulation, '*establishment*' is taken to mean any place of operations where the debtor carries out *a non-transitory economic activity with human means and goods*. Because of such unspecific definition, an establishment can be any place where economic activities are carried on in the territory of another Member State through a business firm or a going concern, but also through individual assets principally owned by the insolvent company.

In the time-worn conflict between the *universality* and the *territoriality* conceptions of insolvency proceedings – for the purposes of both the determination of jurisdiction over bankruptcy declarations (i.e. the determination of one or more bankruptcy forums) and the determination of the law applicable (singleness or plurality of applicable laws) – the Community legislator has opted for a half-way approach, the so-called *limited universality*.

Under this solution, the main proceeding brought in the place where the debtor has the 'centre of its main interests' has a basically universal reach, but it coordinates with a (potential) whole of territorial proceedings arising from the debtor's steady and continuous operations abroad, through 'establishments' located in other Member States, where the debtor's company has assets or investments available to it.

---

271. See *ibid.*, Whereas 11.
272. See *ibid.*, Whereas 12 and Article 27.
273. See *ibid.*, Whereas 16.

As for the law applicable, Article 4(1) of Regulation No. 1346/2000 reads:

> Save as otherwise provided in this Regulation, the law applicable to insolvency proceedings and their effects shall be *that of the Member State within the territory of which such proceedings are opened*, hereafter referred to as the 'State of the opening of proceedings'. [*Emphasis added*].

The applicable law so defined determines the conditions for the opening of those proceedings and their conduct, the respective powers of the debtor and the liquidator, the effects of insolvency proceedings on contracts and on proceedings brought by individual creditors, the claims which are to be lodged against the debtor's estate, the distribution of proceeds from the realization of assets and the ranking of claims, the rules relating to the voidness, voidability or unenforceability of legal acts detrimental to all the creditors, and the closure of insolvency proceedings.

Based on a similar principle, Article 28 requires that the law applicable to *secondary proceedings* be that of the *Member State* within the territory of which *the secondary proceedings are opened.*

In this connection, it appears appropriate to stress the prominence of the administrator, official receiver or provisional liquidator[274] in main proceedings over their counterparts in secondary proceedings, without prejudice to the significance of the requisite coordination between different insolvency proceedings pending in respect of one and the same undertaking, with a view to their effectiveness. In fact:

> Main insolvency proceedings and secondary proceedings can, however, contribute to the effective realisation of the total assets only *if all the concurrent proceedings pending are coordinated.* The main condition here is that *the various liquidators must cooperate closely*, in particular by exchanging a sufficient amount of information. In order to ensure the *dominant role of the main insolvency proceedings*, the liquidator in such proceedings should be given several possibilities for intervening in secondary insolvency proceedings which are pending at the same time. For example, *he should be able to propose a restructuring plan* or *composition* or *apply for realisation of the assets in the secondary insolvency proceedings to be suspended.* [*Emphasis added*].[275]

In particular, the liquidator in the main proceeding may exercise all the powers conferred on him by the law of the State of the opening of proceedings in another Member State, so long as no preservation measure to the contrary has been taken further to a request for the opening of insolvency proceedings in that other State. He may also, through the courts or out of court in any other Member State, claim the rights in a moveable asset that was removed from the territory of the State of the

274. See Annex III to Regulation No. 1346/2000, cit., *loc. cit.*
275. See *ibid.*, Whereas 20.

opening of proceedings after the opening of the insolvency proceedings. He may also bring any action to set aside which is in the interests of the creditors.

Pursuant to Article 3 of Regulation No. 1346/2000, the courts of the Member State within the territory of which the *'centre of a debtor's main interests* is situated' shall have (international) jurisdiction to open insolvency proceedings. In the case of a company or legal person, the place of the registered office shall be presumed to be the centre of its main interests in the absence of proof to the contrary.[276]

The European Court of Justice has handed down a judgment on a conflict over jurisdiction between the High Court of Dublin, Ireland, and the Tribunal of Parma, Italy, concerning *Eurofood*, a subsidiary of the *Parmalat* Group.[277]

The reference for a preliminary ruling from the Supreme Court of Ireland to the European Court of Justice posed four specific questions, essentially concerning the issue of whether proper application of Regulation No. 1346/2000 implied that *Eurofood IFSC Ltd*, a subsidiary of the Italian company *Parmalat SpA*'s, should be placed under liquidation in Ireland, where it had its registered office, or in Italy, where its parent company had its own registered office and where the economic choices concerning the Irish subsidiary's operations were assumedly made.

In the specific case at issue, the Irish Supreme Court had appointed a 'provisional liquidator' for the liquidation of *Eurofood*, by decision of 27 January 2004, which decision was subsequently confirmed by decision of 23 March 2004, whereby the Irish Court took the view that the 'centre of main interests' of *Eurofood* was in Ireland.

In the meanwhile, on 9 February 2004, the Italian Ministry of Production Activities had admitted *Eurofood* to the extraordinary administration procedure, and, on 20 February 2004, the Tribunal (District Court) of Parma, had declared that *Eurofood* was in a state of insolvency, taking the view that *Eurofood's* 'centre of main interests' was in Italy.

In answering these questions, the European Court of Justice held that a decision to open insolvency proceedings for the purposes of that provision is a decision handed down by a court of a Member State to which application for such a decision has been made, based on the debtor's insolvency and seeking the opening of proceedings referred to in Annex A to the Regulation, where that decision involves the divestment of the debtor and the appointment of a liquidator among those listed in Annex C to the Regulation.

---

276. See *ibid.*, Article 3(1).

277. *Eurofood* Judgment of 2 May 2006, Case C-341/04, [2006] ECR I-3813. For criticisms in point of substantive law in this case, see: Gismondi, 'La nozione di "centro degli studi interessi principali del debitore" (COMI) nella giurisprudenza della Corte di giustizia: il caso Eurofood', on http://www.dircomm.it/2006/n.7.8/01.html, pointing out that substantive rather than formal factors should have been emphasized in order to avoid companies from stating fictitious places of business; Bariatti, 'Il regolamento n. 1346/2000 davanti alla Corte di giustizia: il caso Eurofood' [2007] Riv.dir.proc., p. 203 ff., points out that, in light of this judgment, it will be more difficult to conduct an authorized management of corporate groups' insolvency, and suggests that a remedy could be found through amendments to the text of the Regulation.

Further, after pointing out that, based on Regulation No. 1346/2000, where the debtor is a subsidiary whose registered office is situated in a Member State other than the Member State where its parent company has its own registered office, that subsidiary's centre of main interests *is presumed to be situated in the place of its registered office*, the Court of Justice took the view that such presumption:

> (...) can be rebutted only if factors which are *both objective and ascertainable by third parties* enable it to be established that *an actual situation exists which is different* from that which location at that registered office is deemed to reflect. That could be so in particular in the case of a company *not carrying out any business* in the territory of the Member State in which its registered office is situated. By contrast, where a company carries on its business in the territory of the Member State where its registered office is situated, *the mere fact that its economic choices are or can be controlled by a parent company in another Member State is not enough* to rebut the presumption laid down by that Regulation. [*Emphasis added*].

Although the general rule is that a *main* insolvency proceeding is opened in the first place, and any secondary insolvency proceedings can be opened in other EU Member States at a later time, national insolvency proceedings may still be opened prior to the opening of main insolvency proceedings: (a) where insolvency proceedings cannot be opened because of the conditions laid down by the law of the Member State within the territory of which the centre of the debtor's main interests is situated; or (b) where the opening of territorial insolvency proceedings is requested by a creditor who has his domicile, habitual residence and/or registered office in the Member State within the territory of which the establishment is situated, or whose claim arises from the operation of that establishment.

A number of special provisions concern, *inter alia*, third parties' rights *in rem*, the set-off of the creditors' claims against the debtor's, reservation of title, payment systems and financial markets, contracts of employment, the effects on rights subject to registration, Community patents and trademarks, acts detrimental to all the creditors, the protection of third-party purchasers, and the effects of insolvency proceedings on lawsuits pending.

In principle, any judgment opening insolvency proceedings handed down by a court of a Member State which has jurisdiction pursuant to Article 3 is deemed to be *automatically* recognized in all the other Member States, without the need for specific formalities, 'from the time that it becomes effective in the State of the opening of proceedings'.[278]

Article 25 further specifies that judgments handed down by a court whose judgment concerning the opening of proceedings is recognized in accordance with Article 16 and which concern the course and closure of insolvency proceedings, and compositions approved by that court shall also be recognized with no further formalities.

278. See *ibid.*, Article 16(1).

However, any Member State may withhold recognition of insolvency proceedings opened in another Member State or enforcement of a judgment handed down in the context of such proceedings:

> where the effects of such recognition or enforcement would be manifestly contrary to that State's public policy, in particular its fundamental principles or the constitutional rights and liberties of the individual.[279]

---

279. See *ibid.*, Article 26.

Chapter II

Harmonization of Company Law within the EU

SUMMARY:

1. Conflict of laws and uniformity: Two techniques compared.
2. General considerations about the harmonization of company law in the European Union.
3. Legal basis of Company Directives.
4. The value of harmonization directives: the direct applicability issue.
5. Company Directives and Community developments: interpretational issues.
6. The Commission's current activity in codifying the matter.
7. Directives concerning general rules of Member States' company laws.
8. Mergers of companies governed by the laws of different Member States.
9. The draft directive on groups of undertakings and the Seventh Directive on consolidated accounts.
10. The Eleventh Directive.
11. The Statute for the European Company.
12. The Regulation on the European Economic Interest Grouping (EEIG).

1. CONFLICT OF LAWS AND UNIFORMITY: TWO TECHNIQUES COMPARED

Conflict of laws can be overcome through international agreements by either of two techniques.

One technique is to establish a norm of private international law based on the same connection criterion or criteria in relation to the same legal situations. Except where the criterion or criteria so selected imply duality, as is the case with double citizenship or double residence, using connection criteria with identical contents immediately results in full uniformity of outcomes across the contracting States' legal orders. Even the exceptions just indicated have usually been dealt with successfully in international conventions by using sub-criteria to be applied sequentially. Thus, when any class of legal relations governed by an international agreement is considered in whatever contracting State's legal system, the private international law approach will lead up to 'uniform' outcomes, in the sense that the same substantive norm will be applied throughout as the law governing the legal relation in question.

Therefore, the solution achieved through this technique by no means implies that the contents of the substantive laws regulating any one legal issue should be the same from one State to another, as a result of which such laws could well lead to substantive assessments even considerably different from one another. What this technique can only do is to solve conflict of laws by univocally, thus 'uniformly', pointing to which law should apply among the different substantive laws in force in different legal orders possibly competing with one another.

In other words, uniformity *does not*, in this context, amount to dictating *substantive* norms of identical contents with one another, but implies the contracting States' choice of a common connection factor applicable to a given class of relationships across their legal orders, thereby achieving legal certainty through uniform solutions.

This is the sense of the private international law rules contained in the Brussels Convention of 29 February 1968 in connection with the mutual recognition of companies and other legal persons within the Community. And this is the sense of the Rome Convention of 19 June 1980 on the law applicable to contractual obligations,[1] as well as of any international convention on conflict of laws.

A far different technique envisages uniformity of substantive laws, by the introduction of substantive rules with identical contents to govern the same legal relations in different national legal systems under international conventions.

Appropriate examples are the UN Convention on contracts for the international sale of goods signed in Vienna on 11 April 1980[2] and the two Hague Conventions of 1 July 1964 relating to a Uniform Law on the International Sale of Goods, and a Uniform Law on the Formation of Contracts for the International Sale of Goods, respectively.[3] Within the scope of application of

---

1. About these conventions and related events, refer to Chapter I, ss 1 and 2, of this book.
2. See text in *Conference on Contracts for the International Sale of Goods, Final Act (10 April 1980)*, in *UN Conf. on Contr. for the Int. Sale of Goods – Official Recs. (UN Doc. A/CONF. 97/18)*, and *Int. Legal Mat.* [1980], vol. XIX, p. 668 f.
3. The two Hague Conventions of 1 Jul. 1964 took effect in Italy on 23 Aug. 1972, following the adoption of the Act of Ratification and Implementation No. 816 of 21 Jun. 1971. Italy was first

each convention of this type, irrespective of the criterion capable to identify the law governing any one relation or class of relations, the substantive laws applicable to such relation or class of relations have the same contents and bring about *uniformity* in this sense and in this direct way, thereby achieving legal certainty.[4]

Could law be reduced to mathematical formulas and could the laws of the States concerned be so fully integrated as to include any aspects of those States' private international laws, and, further, should such laws be made univocally to apply in judicial proceedings – as is the case, for example, within the Community legal system – the latter technique would certainly be a better choice than the former, if only because of its straightforwardness in use.

This is not the case, though. On the one hand, rules of private international law are at work in legal systems which can widely differ from one another – just think of Civil Law as opposed to Common Law systems. On the other hand, a uniform body of substantive rules cannot but be partial and sector-specific, so that some, even the most general aspects of any one legal issue – then the most relevant to the proper assessment of any one case – are bound either to remain outside such uniform rules or to be predicated on any 'reservations' as one or more of the State parties to a multilateral convention may have about one or more provisions of that convention. The end result is that, in practice, any legal relationship not covered by any such provision remains, in general, governed by the law of the legal order of one or another of the contracting States.

In this connection, just consider the impact that the different rules which, in the different legal orders of the States acceding to the Vienna Convention, govern the transfer of ownership title in an asset being sold can have on uniform law, for example in respect of defects found in that asset.

In fact, it often happens that, even in wide areas of uniform substantive law, the technique based on the rules of conflict of laws must be used anyhow in order to determine the governing law capable to regulate any aspects which are not covered by rules of uniform law or are not otherwise applicable to the relevant case. And the

---

among the contracting parties to the two 1964 Hague Conventions to accede to the Vienna Convention of 11 Apr. 1980, soon after filing the relevant ratification instrument on 11 Dec. 1986 pursuant to the Act of Ratification and Implementation No. 765 of 11 Dec. 1985, in compliance with the obligation provided for by Article 99(3) of the UN Convention. It then notified the denunciation of the two Hague Conventions to the Ministry of Foreign Affairs of the Netherlands, effective as from 31 Dec. 1987, because the validity of both instruments – which were to cease from effect on 11 Dec. 1987, pursuant to Articles XII and X, respectively – had been postponed, at the Italian Government's request, until the entry into force of the Vienna UN Convention. As a result, from the point of view of the Italian legal order, the older provisions still apply to all contracts for the international sale of goods concluded up to 31 Dec. 1987, while the new provisions apply to all such contracts entered into as from 1 Jan. 1988. For a discussion of the subject, see Bonell, 'L'entrata in vigore della Convenzione di Vienna sulla vendita e le sue conseguenze nella prassi delle contrattazioni commerciali internazionali' [1987] Dir. comm. int., p. 415 f.; and, generally, see Carbone & Luzzatto, *Il contratto internazionale* (Turin, 1994).

4. For the relationships between uniform law and conflict of laws, see Malintoppi, 'Les rapports entre droit uniforme et droit international privé' [1965] Rec. des Cours, vol. III, p. 5 f.

choice so made is bound to have some influence on the overall assessment of the case.

Moreover, it is an essential characteristic of multilateral conventions providing for uniform laws that, when it comes to application, the norms contained therein either concur with the domestic law of each country acceding to that convention, thereby operating as special norms independent of that domestic law, or entirely replace the applicable sector-specific rules of domestic law.

In the latter case, the application of uniform substantive law in any one legal system will depend on how jurisdiction is allocated under that system's rules of private international law, which operate as a delimitating factor. Where this is the case, the uniform norms laid down in the relevant international agreement will apply anyhow, even if either party to a private legal relationship does not belong to a State party to that agreement, which agreement will thereby deemed to be of 'universal' application.

In any one system, uniform substantive law can only be applied if reference is made in that system's private international law to the rules of another system. It cannot, however, be applied where reference is made there to the legal system of yet another State not acceding to the relevant convention, whose law will obviously not contain any such norm of uniform law.

Conversely, where a uniform law is applicable concurrently with, and does not replace, the domestic rules of law on the same subject matter – which means that it has rules of its own entailing automatic application – that uniform law must be treated as a body of *mandatory rules* designed to apply along with, or even to exclude, any reference to conflict of laws. The result is that, from the point of view of the system accommodating the relevant rules of uniform law, such rules will be applied at all appropriate times, regardless of whether the home State of either party to the private law relationship at issue has or has not acceded to the relevant international convention on uniform law.[5]

Moreover, these difficulties are usually compounded by the fact that the different framework rules that, in any one system, fall outside the scope of application of uniform law are ultimately bound to influence its interpretation by the national courts of the different States in which that uniform law is applicable.

This is not the case, as indicated above, with the European Union, whose Commission can rely on appropriate devices to force any Member State, upon the ECJ's final assessment, to comply with EU law. Further, Article 234 EC requires the Court of Justice itself to ensure uniform interpretation of the rules of Community treaties and of any acts deriving therefrom.

---

5. For the connotation of mandatory rules typical of uniform law, see, for all, Malintoppi, 'Diritto uniforme e diritto internazionale private' [1955] Riv. dir. int., p. 79 f. For the relationship between conflict of laws and uniformity in the sense essentially indicated above, see Bariatti, *L'interpretazione delle convenzioni internazionali di diritto uniforme*, (Padua, 1986), p. 20 f.

The EC Treaty provides several devices for unifying Member States' laws in matters falling within its scope of application. One of the devices expressly listed in Article 3(h) of the Treaty is:

> [T]he approximation of the laws of Member States to the extent required for the functioning of the common market.[6]

Further, Article 94 et seq. EC in Chapter 3 of Title VI ('Approximation of Laws') requires the Council, acting unanimously, to issue directives:

> for the approximation of such laws, regulations or administrative provisions of the Member States as directly affect the establishment or functioning of the common market.[7]

Moreover, on the legal basis of Article 61(c) and 67(5) EC, second indent, Regulation (EC) No 805/2004 of the European Parliament and of the Council of 21 April 2004 was issued to create a *European Enforcement Order for uncontested claims.*[8]

Likewise, Article 44(2)(g) EC provides for coordination, through directives, of:

> the safeguards which, for the protection of the interests of members and other, are required by Member States of companies or firms within the meaning of the second paragraph of Article 48 with a view to making such safeguards equivalent throughout the Community.[9]

---

6. For the notion of 'the extent required for the functioning of the common market', please refer to the considerations offered in Section 3 of Chapter III of this book.
7. The wording is identical with the one referred to in the footnote next preceding above.
8. [2004] O.J. L143, p.15. See also Regulation (EC) No. 1896/2006 of the European Parliament and of the Council of 12 Dec. 2006, creating a European order for payment procedure in [2006] O.J. L399, p. 1, and Regulation (EC) No. 861/2007 of The European Parliament and of The Council of 11 Jul. 2007, establishing a European Small Claims Procedure, in [2007] O.J. L199, p. 1.
9. For the notions of 'unification', 'harmonization' and 'approximation' of laws, generally, see Malintoppi, 'Il ravvicinamento delle legislazioni come problema di diritto internazionale' [1959] Riv. dir. int., p. 239 f., especially p. 248 f.; Id., 'Les relations entre l'unification et l'harmonisation du droit et la technique de l'unification ou de l'harmonisation par la voie d'accords internationaux' in Unidroit, Annuaire 1967-68, p. 43 f.; Id., 'Unification et harmonisation du droit. Un essai de systematisation', in *Istituto italo-africano, L'harmonisation du droit en Afrique* (Milan, 1974), p. 81 f.; Bariatti, *L'interpretazione delle convenzioni internazionali di diritto uniforme*, cit., p. 1 f., and 18 f. For the notions of 'harmonization', 'approximation' and 'coordination' of laws under Community law, see Monaco, 'L'adeguamento delle legislazioni nazionali nell'ambito del mercato comune europeo' [1957] Dir. economia, p. 1147 f.; A. Migliazza, 'I problemi di diritto internazionale relativi alla creazione di una società commerciale europea' [1970] Riv. dir. int. priv. proc., p. 761 f., 768 f.; von der Groeben, 'Die Politik des Europäischen Kommission auf dem Gebiet der Rechtsangleichung' [1970] Neue juristische Wochenschrift, p. 358 f.; Goldman, *Droit commercial européen* (Paris, 1971), p. 589 f.; Ipsen, *Europäisches Gemeinschaftsrecht* (Tübingen, 1972), p. 686 f.; Id., *Le droit de la Communauté economique européenne, Commentaire du Traité des textes pris pour son application*, edited by Mægret, Louis, Vignes, Waelbroeck & Wagenbaur, vol. V, (Brussels, 1973), p. 152 f. In particular, for the problems related to the 'harmonization' and 'coordination' of company laws within the Community, please refer to Lanza, 'Attività e tendenze della Comunità economica europea in tema di società' [1966] Riv. società, p. 1034 f., and in *La riforma delle società di capitali in Italia. Studi e dibattiti*, Fenghi & Santa Maria eds (Milan, 1966), I, p. 187 f.; Scholten, 'L'unification du droit des

On the legal bases just cited above, the Community institutions' activity has brought about a major 'harmonization' of the Member States' company laws through the many directives already issued or about to be defined.

In fact, once harmonization is completed, the uniform law created within this context will be fully implemented throughout the EU, and made part of the individual Member States' laws, yet without losing its original quality as 'Community' law, subject, as such, to the rules of interpretation of Community law.

Further below in this chapter, I will discuss the outcomes of harmonization of company laws throughout the EU, which, although falling short of completeness – because of the usual issue-by-issue process – have gone a long way in regulating economic relations between Member States.

It should be clear that such effort of harmonization is by no means an end to itself, in the sense that it must chiefly be viewed with *the right of establishment in the background*. Thus, it can by no means be expected to address the entire body of company laws, not even in prospect.[10]

In a different respect, notwithstanding any reference to freedom of establishment, the subjective scope of application of harmonization directives is far narrower than that implied in the definition contained in the second paragraph of Article 48 EC. This is because, as discussed in details further below, very few directives are addressed to companies of whatever type. Most are, in fact, concerned *solely* with limited companies or even just public companies limited by shares, and only one directive is addressed to private limited liability companies.

2. GENERAL CONSIDERATIONS ABOUT THE HARMONIZATION OF COMPANY LAW IN THE EUROPEAN UNION

The first real turnabout in the European Community's life took place in the early 1970s, ahead of the time scheduled under the Treaty of Rome, with the shift from the so-called transitional period to the final period.

---

sociætæs dans les Pays du Marchæ Commun', *ibid.*, I, p. 235 f.; Loussouarn, 'Le rapprochement du droit des sociétés dans le cadre de la Communauté économique européenne', in *L'harmonisation dans les Communautés* (Bruxelles, 1968), p. 29 f.; Leleux, 'Harmonisation du droit des sociétés', in *Europäische Handelsgesellschaft und Angleichung des nationales Gesellschaftsrechts* (Frankfurt-Berlin, 1968), p. 37 f.; Lutter, 'Die Rechtsangleichung im Gesellschaftsrecht', in Europäische Handelsgesellschaft, cit., p. 5 f. (there, p. 6, fn. 4, extensive references); and Caruso, *Le società*, cit., p. 345 f.; Migliazza, *I problemi di diritto internazionale*, cit., especially p. 282, f.; Bar Mann, *Europäische Integration im Gesellschaftsrecht* (Köln-Berlin-Bonn-München, 1970); Stein, *Harmonisation of European Company Laws. National Reform and Transnational Coordination* (Indianapolis-Kansas City-New York, 1971), especially pp. 23 f. and 87 f.; Goldman, *Droit commercial européen*, cit., p. 598 f., and Bransbury, 'Company Law and Directives of EEC: a U.K. View' [1974] Riv. int. scienze ec. comm., p. 1143 f.; Portale, 'Armonizzazione' e 'concorrenza' tra ordinamenti nel diritto societario europeo [2003] Corr. giur., p. 95 f.; Miola, 'Lo statuto di Società europea nel diritto societario comunitario: dall'armonizzazione alla concorrenza tra ordinamenti' [2003] Riv. soc., p. 322 f.

10. This assumption is recognised by the Commission itself. See below Section 5 of this chapter, especially fn. 82, and also Section 11.

Yet, by that time, the work for the harmonization of Member States' company laws, which had progressed at a satisfactory pace for several years along with the actual implementation of the freedoms of establishment and provision of services, had come to a standstill.

The process had begun as early as 1961. Specifically, the *General Programme* adopted on 18 December 1961 to abolish restrictions to freedom of establishment[11] contained provisions for a far-reaching activity to harmonize Member States' company laws to be carried out in accordance with Article 54(3)(g) of the Rome Treaty (now Article 4(2)(g) EC) hand in hand with the progressive realization of freedom of establishment.

Pursuant to Article 52 of the Treaty (now Article 43 EC), all restrictions on freedom of establishment ought to have been abolished during the transitional period. Therefore, that General Programme, in conjunction with the other *General Programme* adopted on the same date to provide for the liberalization of services,[12] pursuant to Article 63 of the original version of the Rome Treaty (now Article 52 EC), was intended to establish 'general conditions as regards a particular activity for the attainment of freedom of establishment and, in particular, the timetable of such attainment'.

Although the step-by-step method, along with a pragmatic approach to individual issues sector by sector, was probably the only one process capable to ensure the gradual and smooth attainment of the intended objectives in matters of company law, in relation to which individual Member States might have exhibited rejection crises most acutely *vis-à-vis* the Community – with a predictably disruptive impact on the entire process of European integration – that method forced the Commission to embark on an effort which, though impressive in quantitative terms, still proved dispersive more often than not.

And so, on 31 December 1969, the date of expiry of the transitional period, there was a long way yet to go before reaching the *full* attainment – as postulated by Article 52 (Article 42 EC) and by Article 3(c) of the original Rome Treaty before it – of the freedom of establishment of nationals of a Member State in the territory of another Member State.

Therefore, it should come as no surprise that only the first directive on the harmonization of company law had been issued by that time.

Thereafter, following the first enlargement of the Community pursuant to the Treaty of Accession signed in Brussels on 22 January 1972, fears arose, because of the increased difficulties caused by the impact with legal orders somewhat different from the original Member States', lest an almost definitive standstill should ensue in the development of Community rules capable to remove any obstacles in the different Member States to the full attainment of freedom of establishment and free provision of services.

---

11. For this topic, see Chapter I, above, especially Section 6.
12. See Chapter I, above, especially Section 6.

The new situation had also instilled fears (and hopes in many) that the parallel process of full harmonization of company law should also be delayed to some distant future.

Those fears (or hopes) did not materialize, though. For the picture changed dramatically following the European Court of Justice's steadfast decisions, already mentioned in Chapter I of this book, about the direct effect of the Rome Treaty rules on free establishment and free provision of services, beginning with the well-known judgments in *Reyners*, Case 2/74 of 21 June 1974 (on freedom of establishment) and in *van Binsbergen*, Case 33/74 of 3 December 1974 (on free provision of services), having regard to all the objectives still unattained as at the expiry date of the transitional period.[13]

By applying the so-called 'direct effect doctrine', to at least the so-called 'vertical' relations between private parties and a Member State's authorities, the ECJ reversed what then seemed to be an attitude of widespread acceptance of Treaty rules being regarded as having merely programmatic import.

As noted above, the European Court of Justice relied on the principles laid down chiefly in Articles 2 and 7 of the Treaty of Rome – in the original version then in force – to hold that the rules of the Treaty on freedom of establishment and free provision of services, including the too many clauses still denied implementation following the expiry of the transitional period, had themselves become mandatory norms as a result of the Community's entry into the definitive period, and, as such, *directly applicable* in the Member State's internal orders even in respect of matters not yet liberalized in full through directives.

Around the same time, other judgments of the European Court of Justice were endorsed by the Italian Constitutional Court to affirm the prevalence of Community over domestic norms.[14] Neither jurisprudential streak has changed since then, and both have, in fact, become the drivers of subsequent developments in various areas of Community life.

ECJ case-law has resulted, *inter alia*, in the Commission's activity being resumed to deal with the issues of free establishment of persons and free provision of services.

Moreover, Member States have renewed their efforts towards the full attainment of those freedoms throughout the Community, if only with a view to curbing the reach of the ECJ's intervention based on the 'direct effect' principle.

Such convergence of intents also brought about the Community institutions' renewed commitment to the harmonization of the Member States' company laws, a project closely connected to the full attainment of free establishment.

Nearly half a century after the beginning of the Commission's work on the harmonization of company laws, the picture has become quite impressive. As many as twelve directives sequentially numbered (plus unnumbered instruments on matters not merely complementary with the others), including those finally

13. For these judgments, see Section 2 of Chapter I of this book.
14. For these judgments, see Section 1 of the Introduction to this study.

adopted and those still at the proposal stage, have been issued on many aspects of company law.[15]

Among these, there have been the First Council Directive 68/151/EEC of 9 March 1968[16] on provisions concerning disclosure, the validity of obligations entered into by, and the nullity of, *all limited companies*, and the Second Council Directive 77/91/EEC of 13 December 1976,[17] the scope of which only included provisions for safeguards in respect of the formation of public limited liability companies and the maintenance and alteration of their capital.

Then came the Third Council Directive No 78/855/EEC of 9 October 1978 based on Article 54(3)(g) of the Treaty concerning *(internal) mergers of public limited liability companies,*[18] which was implemented in its original text in all EU Member States. It was later amended, together with the Sixth Directive 82/891/EEC concerning *the division of public limited liability companies*, by Directive 2007/63/EC of the European Parliament and the Council regarding the requirement of an independent expert's report on the occasion of merger or division of public limited liability companies.[19] The Fourth Directive No 78/660/EEC of 25 July 1978

---

15. A number of directives and other Community measures have concerned stock exchanges, banks and other financial institutions. The first instrument relating to stock exchanges was a Recommendation from the Commission to Member States dated 25 Jul. 1977 concerning a European code of conduct relating to transactions in transferable securities (in [1977] O.J. L212, p. 37), which was followed by other documents until the latest directives: Directive 2007/14/EC of 8 Mar. 2007, laying down detailed rules for the implementation of certain provisions of Directive 2004/109/EC on the harmonization of transparency requirements in relation to information about issuers whose securities are admitted to trading on regulated markets (in [2007] O.J. L69, p. 27), and Commission Directive 2007/16/EC of 19 Mar. 2007 implementing Council Directive 85/611/EEC on the coordination of laws, regulations and administrative provisions relating to undertakings for collective investment in transferable securities (UCITS) as regards the clarification of certain definitions (in [2007] O.J. L79, p. 11). As for banks and other financial institutions, the first act was Council Directive 86/635/EEC of 8 Dec. 1986 on the annual accounts and consolidated accounts of banks and other financial institutions (in [1986] O.J. L372, p. 1). Other acts followed until Directive 2004/39/EC of the European Parliament and of the Council of 21 Apr. 2004 on markets in financial instruments amending Council Directives 85/611/EEC and 93/6/EEC, and Directive 2000/12/EC of the European Parliament and of the Council repealing Council Directive 93/22/EEC (in [2004] O.J. L145, p. 1). Then came Directive 2006/49/EC of the European Parliament and of the Council of 14 Jun. 2006 on the capital adequacy of investment firms and credit institutions (in [2006] O.J. L177, p. 201) and Commission Directive 2006/73/EC of 10 Aug. 2006 implementing Directive 2004/39/EC of the European Parliament and of the Council as regards organizational requirements and operating conditions for investment firms and defined terms for the purposes of that Directive (in [2006] O.J. L241, p. 26).
16. [1968] O.J. L65, p. 8. The First Directive was latest amended by Council Directive 2006/99/EC of 20 Nov. 2006 (in [2006] O.J. L363). On 30 Jan. 2008, the Commission submitted a proposal for a directive to codify the First Directive.
17. [1997] O.J. L26, p. 1. The Second Directive has been amended several times, and, of late, by Directive 2006/68/EC of the European Parliament and of the Council of 6 Sep. 2006, in [2006] O.J. L264. As at 15 Apr. 2008, the date of expiry of the implementation period, the amendments to the Second Directive had not yet been implemented by some Member States, Italy among them.
18. [1978] O.J. L295, p. 36.
19. [2007] O.J. L300, p. 47. The period of implementation of this directives expires on 31 Dec. 2008.

on the *annual accounts of limited companies*[20] was then fully implemented, at least in its original text.

Many amendments were made by the Council to the Fourth Directive, even while it was being implemented, for example by: Council Directive 90/604/EEC of 8 November 1990 amending Directive 78/660/EEC on annual accounts and Directive 83/349/EEC on consolidated accounts as regards exemptions for small and medium-sized companies and the publication of accounts in ecus; Council Directive 90/605/EEC of 8 November 1990 amending Directive 78/660/EEC on annual accounts and Directive 83/349/EEC on consolidated accounts;[21] and Council Directive 94/8/EC of 21 March 1994 amending Directive 78/660/EEC as regards the revision of amounts expressed in ecus.[22] The Fourth Directive was amended of late by Directive 2006/43/EC of the European Parliament and of the Council of 17 May 2006, and by Directive 2006/46/EC of the European Parliament and of the Council of 14 June 2006.[23]

Although the deadline allowed for transposition of the provisions contained in Directives 2006/43/EC and 2006/46/EC into the Member States' domestic legislations has already expired, some States have not yet implemented the amendments under the Fourth Directives in their internal systems.

Mention should also be made of the Sixth Council Directive 82/891/EEC of 17 December 1982 concerning the division of public limited liability companies (share companies),[24] and of the Seventh Council Directive 83/349/EEC of 13 June 1983 *consolidated accounts* with regard to undertakings organized in the form of any of the types of limited company in Member States.[25] The Eighth Council Directive 84/253/EEC of 10 April 1984 on the *approval of persons responsible for carrying out the statutory audits of accounting documents of limited companies* was, however, repealed by the subsequent Directive 2006/43/EC of the European Parliament and of the Council of 17 May 2006, which was, in turn, amended by Directive 2008/30/EC of the European Parliament and of the Council of 11 March 2008.[26]

---

20. [1978] O.J. L222, p. 11.
21. Directives No. 90/604 and No. 90/605 are both published in [1990] O.J. L317, p. 57 f. and p. 60 f., respectively.
22. [1994] O.J. L82, p. 33 f. On this topic, see Malesci Baccani, 'La nuova disciplina comunitaria dei bilanci di società, banche e assicurazioni', in *Il processo di formazione dei principi contabili e l'armonizzazione economico-finanziaria d'impresa in alcuni paesi europei*, by various authors (Naples, 1995), p. 285 f.
23. See the text of Directive 2006/43/EC [2006] O.J. L157, and the text of Directive 2006/46/EC [2006] O.J. L224. The Fourth Directive was amended in part by Directive 2006/99/EC of the Council of 20 Nov. 2006, [2006] O.J. L363, p. 137 f., following the accession of Bulgaria and Rumania, which promptly adopted that text.
24. [1982] O.J. L378, p. 47. The Sixth Directive was amended by Directive 2007/63/EC ([2007] O.J. L300), the implementation deadline for which has been fixed at 31 Dec. 2008.
25. [1983] O.J. L193, 18 Jul. 1983, p. 1. The Seventh Directive was amended by Directives No. 2006/43/EC ([2006] O.J. L157), No. 2006/46/EC ([2006] O.J. L224), and No. 2006/99/EC of the Council of 20 Nov. 2006, in [2006] O.J. L363, p. 137.
26. [2008] O.J. L81, p. 53.

Lastly, final instruments are the Eleventh Council Directive 89/666/EEC of 21 December 1989 concerning *disclosure requirements in respect of branches* opened in a Member State by certain types of company governed by the law of another State,[27] implemented in Italy by Legislative Decree No 516 of 29 December 1992, and the Twelfth Council Company Law Directive 89/667/EEC, itself of 21 December 1989, on *single-member private limited-liability companies*,[28] which was implemented in Italy, not without some interpretational problems, by Legislative Decree No 88 of 3 March 1993.

Along with final directives, others are being developed at different stages of completion.

In particular, discussions are underway on the third amended proposal for a fifth directive on the structure of public limited liability companies,[29] in respect of which the Commission developed a study headed 'Employee Participation and Company Structure'.[30] This proposal, which was patterned after German and Dutch laws, has attracted criticisms mostly from British and Italian law scholars.[31] The delay in its approval seems to be due to English hostility, because of the even too obvious consideration that, once a directive bas been approved and become final within the Community, it must be implemented in each Member State's national order by the prescribed time limit, pursuant to Article 189 of the EC Treaty.

The *draft Ninth Directive* is concerned with the law 'of groups of companies', the earliest known text of which dates back to 1977.[32] That text was followed by a new draft by the Commission, in a far more innovative text which has not yet found its way into a 'proposal' and has not yet, therefore, been submitted to the Council.[33] As was the case with the first draft, the second draft is chiefly addressed to undertakings organized in the form of *public limited companies* (share companies), while just a few provisions of limited scope are addressed to the other types of limited company, and its contents are more restrained and less velleitarian than those of the first draft. It only consists of forty-six articles, as contrasted with the one hundred and three of the former text. The whole section containing rules on organic groups and the section containing rules on cross-shareholdings have been removed in the new draft, as the Commission has deferred these matters to a later directive.

---

27. [1989] O.J. L395, p. 36. Please, refer to the considerations offered in Section 10 of this Chapter II.
28. [1989] O.J. L395, p. 40. This directive was amended by Directive 2006/99/EC of the Council of 20 Nov. 2006, cited above, following the accession of Bulgaria and Rumania.
29. [1991] O.J. C321, p. 9.
30. See in *EC Bull., Supplement 8*, of 1975.
31. The introduction of a *monistic* and a *dualistic* system – the former having characteristics not fully conforming to the German model – as novel systems operating along with the *traditional* one in the new Italian company law, has swept away most of the objections Italian law scholars had raised at that time.
32. See Doc. XI/215/77 F, rev. 3.
33. The latest known version, preceded by the relevant Report, has been published in [1985] Riv. società, pp. 1040 f. and 1071 f., respectively.

Following the withdrawal of a draft international convention on cross-border mergers of limited companies, the matter was made the object of a proposal for a tenth directive on 8 January 1985. But only twenty years later did the European Parliament and the Council adopted (unnumbered) Directive 2005/56/EC of 26 October 2005 on *cross-border mergers* of limited liability companies.[34]

Thereafter, an amended proposal for a thirteenth Council directive on company law, concerning takeovers and other general bids, was forwarded to the Council on 14 September 1990. This proposal later found its way into (unnumbered) Directive 2004/25/EC of the European Parliament and of the Council of 21 April 2004 on *takeover bids*.[35]

3. LEGAL BASIS OF COMPANY DIRECTIVES

As pointed out above, the many Directives on company law I have just briefly outlined have an explicit, formal legal basis in Article 44(2)(g) EC.

This provision is included in Chapter II headed 'Right of Establishment' and requires:

> The Council and the Commission shall carry out the duties devolving upon them under the preceding provisions, in particular: . . . by coordinating to the necessary extent the safeguards which, for the protection of the interests of members and other, are required by Member States of companies or firms within the meaning of the second paragraph of Article 48 with a view to making such safeguards equivalent throughout the Community. [*Emphasis added*].

The article at issue is written out in its extended form at the top of all the directives considered here, save for those concerning listing, in which it is only briefly mentioned, either alone or in conjunction with Article 94. Directive 2004/25/EC of 21 April 2004 on takeover bids expressly refers to the entire provision quoted above *as well as* to the provision of Article 44(1), which, in turn, refers to Article 251 EC for the applicable procedure.

Article 48(2) EC referred to in Article 44(2)(g) contains a determination of companies and other legal persons eligible for the treatment provided for by the rules on the right of establishment.

In fact, the formulation of the relevant Treaty rules is far broader than, and only seldom coincides with, the indication of the companies or firms addressed by the individual harmonization or coordination directives mentioned above.

---

34. See the draft tenth directive in [1985] O.J. C23, p. 11 f. Directive 2005/56/EC is published in [2005] O.J. L310, p. 1 ff. By the date of expiry of the implementation period, 15 Dec. 2007, some Member States, Italy among them, had not yet notified the relevant measures for implementation.
35. See the text of the amended proposal for the Thirteenth Directive in [1990] O.J. C240, p. 7 f. The text of Directive 2004/25/CE is published in [2004] O.J. L142, p. 12 f.

Firstly, whereas the phrase 'companies or firms constituted under civil or commercial law' used in the Treaty obviously includes *unlimited* companies as well, none of the harmonization directives concerns companies of this type.

Secondly, just some directives concern *all* limited companies, some concern share companies *alone*, and one, the Twelfth Directive, is *solely* concerned with private limited companies.

It should be noted that, in principle, the limitation as to the types of company is in contrast with the determination of the companies eligible for the right of establishment and the free provision of services under Article 58(2) of the Treaty. Such limitation is to be found, for example, in the Third and Sixth Directives – one on mergers, the other on the division of *public limited companies* (share companies) – in which it is only justified, in practice, in light of a reasonable need for streamlined provisions on issues already complex in themselves, such as corporate mergers or spin-offs.

Particularly in respect of mergers, the unfavourable condition in which companies other than share companies find themselves seems to be assuaged only in part by the fact that, in practice, at least in the Italian legal order, mergers may raise problems mostly in the case of share companies (i.e. large corporations), and by the fact that, in a case of merger of a share company with a company of a different type, the latter may well be transformed into a share company prior to the deal, thereby becoming eligible for harmonized treatment.

In the Italian system, with regard to both mergers and divisions, the problem has been solved drastically by Parliament, which has implemented the Third Directive by replacing all existing code-based provisions in this area and introducing the new rules generally, *without limiting their applicability to share companies alone*.

It was on the basis of Article 44(2)(g) that the Commission undertook to propose to the Council some directives intended to *achieve equivalence of safeguards* by coordinating the devices provided for in each Member State's law to protect company members' and other parties' interests, all of which with a view to the full attainment of the freedom of establishment of natural and legal persons anywhere within the European Union.

In past years, the very wording of Article 44(2)(g) raised criticisms among company law and Community law scholars against the Commission, which many blame for exceeding its powers in submitting proposals for directives in this field to the Council.

It is my view that, however, the ensuing debate has become pointless anyhow, and that the terms of the problem had been mistaken in the first place, resulting in a fruitless terminological dispute about the presumed value of the words 'coordination', 'harmonization' and 'uniformity' in the text of the EC Treaty.[36]

It is a fact that the EC Treaty contains provisions capable to confer the fullest powers on the Community institutions in this domain. It is enough to consider

---

36. See my study: 'L'attuazione negli ordinamenti interni delle direttive comunitarie in materia di società' [1980] Giur. Comm., p. 927 f., p. 938 f.

Article 3(h) as for principles, and Article 94 or even Article 95, to the extent applicable to the matter, to dispel any doubts as to the Commission's standing to act as it does.

Further, it must be considered that, in practice, any controversy about the boundaries of the Community's powers in this matter has become patently pointless in light of the consequential measures already completed or about to be completed.

One problem appears, however, to remain still unsolved, in that, while the Council's resolutions may be taken *by a qualified majority* pursuant to Article 44(2)(g), it is expected to act *unanimously* under Article 94 EC.

In fact, the Second Directive on companies was adopted by a majority of the Council, with the Netherlands voting against. Yet, precisely the Netherlands' subsequent choice to refrain from challenging that directive before the ECJ for misuse of power by the Council, and to implement the directive in its domestic system (by an act of 15 May 1987), shows that the real issue was not, already at that time, one of formally establishing the legal basis of the Council's directives on the harmonization of company laws.

In formal terms, however, the problem cannot be deemed to have been overcome yet. Article 95(1), which the European Single Act as amended by the Maastricht Treaty introduced in the EC Treaty, contains a special derogation from the *unanimity* rule set forth in Article 94 for the achievement of the objectives set out in Article 14. Thus:

> The Council shall, acting in accordance with the procedure referred to in Article 251 [*by a qualified majority*] . . . adopt the measures for the *approximation of the provisions laid down by law, regulation or administrative action* in Member States which have as their object the establishment and functioning of the internal market. [*Emphasis added*].

Still, Article 94(2) provides that Article 94(1) does not apply:

> to fiscal provisions, to those relating to *the free movement of persons* nor to those relating to the rights and interests of employed persons. [*Emphasis added*].

Since there is no doubt as to the fact that the free movement of persons also includes the right of establishment, it seems that also excluded from application should be the harmonization of company laws, which is closely connected with the right of establishment.

Let me further point out that, as stressed in Chapter I of this book, the cornerstone of the Treaty rules on freedom of establishment is *equal treatment* of foreigners with nationals, thus of *foreign companies* with national companies. For this equality to be finally established, there must be full equivalence of the legal safeguards in force in the host State with those in force in the home State, both Member States of the EU.

Therefore, in this respect, the provision of Article 44(2)(g) plays a crucial role in the full attainment of the fundamental freedom in question, and is also part of the wider integration process towards the progressive building of a citizens' Europe.[37]

4. THE VALUE OF HARMONIZATION DIRECTIVES: THE DIRECT APPLICABILITY ISSUE

A crucial requirement is that, where harmonization directives contain *precise and unconditional* norms, and the period of their implementation in national systems has expired, they should be deemed *directly applicable* in the Member States' domestic jurisdictions.

'Direct applicability' of Community directives is an issue falling within the general problem of the legal status of a 'directive' adopted in accordance with Article 249 EC. It is settled ECJ case-law[38] that:

> If, however, by virtue of the provisions of article 189 [now Article 249 EC, third para.] regulations are directly applicable and, consequently, may by their very nature have direct effects, *it does not follow from this that other categories of acts mentioned in that article can never have similar effects.* [*Emphasis added*].

Accordingly, in the ECJ's view:[39]

> it would be incompatible with the binding effect which Article 189 ascribes to directives to exclude on principle the possibility of the obligations imposed by them being relied on by persons concerned;
>
> particularly in cases in which the Community authorities have, by means of directive, placed Member States under a duty to adopt a certain course of action, the effectiveness of such an act would be weakened *if persons were prevented from relying on it in legal proceedings and national courts prevented from taking it into consideration as an element of Community law*;
>
> consequently a Member State which has not adopted the implementing measures required by the directive in the prescribed periods *may not rely, as against individuals, on its own failure* to perform the obligations which the directive entails;
>
> it follows that a national court requested by a person who has complied with the provisions of a directive not to apply a national provision incompatible with the directive not incorporated into the internal legal order of a defaulting member

---

37. For this proposition, see Predieri, *Il legislatore recalcitrante e il rimedio degli effetti diretti delle direttive comunitarie* (Florence, 1987), p. 173 f.
38. See, chiefly: Judgments of 4 Dec. 1974, Case 41/74, *Van Duyn* v *Home Office* [1974] ECR, 1337, and of 1 Feb. 1977, Case 51/76, *Verbond van Nederlandse Ondernemingen* v *Inspecteur der Invoerrechten en Accijinzen* [1977] ECR, 113.
39. Judgment of 5 Apr. 1979, Case 148/78, *Ratti* [1979] ECR, 1629, grounds 20 to 24.

> state, must uphold that request if the obligation in question is *unconditional and sufficiently precise*;
>
> therefore the answer to the first question must be that after the expiration of the period fixed for the implementation of a directive a Member State may not apply its internal law – *even if it is provided with penal sanctions* – which has not yet been adapted in compliance with the directive, to a person who has complied with the requirements of the directive. [*Emphasis added*].

The same view was taken by the European Court of Justice in relation to certain requirements in the Second Directive on companies in its judgment of 30 May 1991, in Joined Cases C-19/90 and C-20/90, *Marina Karella and Nicolaos Karellas* v *Ypourgoviomichanias, Energies & Technologies and Organismos Anasygkrotiseos Epicheririseon AE* (*Velka* case) on reference for a preliminary pursuant to Article 177 (now 234) from Symvoulio Epikrateias (the Greek Council of State).[40]

In particular, according to the ECJ, by providing that any increase in capital must be decided upon by the general meeting, Article 25(1) of the Second Directive lays down provisions which appear to be unconditional and sufficiently precise. (Para. 18 *et seq.*).

As a result, that provision may be pleaded by individuals against public authorities before national courts (Para. 23). On the other hand, the scope of Article 25 of the Second Directive does not allow Member States to retain domestic legislation incompatible with the principle laid down therein, even if that legislation seeks to deal with exceptional situations. The case in dispute was concerned with the subscription by a Greek public-sector body, Anasygkrotiseos Epicheiriseon AE (*Business Reconstruction Organization*, referred to as 'the OAE'), of an increase in the company Klostiria Velka AE's capital which was decided upon without the general meeting's approval, in breach of the shareholders' pre-emptive rights, according to the procedure laid down for undertakings undergoing serious financial difficulties in Article 8(8) of the Greek Law No 1386/1983 of 5 August 1983.[41]

The ECJ then argued that, if, however, the prevalence of the Greek law were recognized, this would be liable to impair the binding nature and uniform application of Community law (Para. 31).[42]

With regard to the directives for the harmonization of company laws, the application of the direct applicability principle has become a topical issue because

---

40. [1991] ECR, 2691 f.
41. See in *Official Journal of the Hellenic Republic* No. 107/A of 8 Aug. 1983, p. 14 f.
42. On this topic generally, see Luzzatto, *La diretta applicabilità nel diritto comunitario* (Milan, 1980), especially pp. 30 f., 32 f. and 45 f. See also the Judgments of the ECJ: of 25 Jan. 1983, Case 126/82, *D.J. Smit Transport BV* v *Commissie Grensoverschrijdend Beroepsgoederenvervoer* [1983] ECR, p. 73 f.; of 22 Sep. 1983, Case 271/82, *Vincent Rodolphe Auer* v *Ministère Public* (*Ordre National des Vétérinaires de France and other*) [1983] ECR, p. 2727 f.; and of 15 Dec. 1983, Case 5/83, Criminal proceedings against *H.G. Rienks* [1983] ECR, p. 4233 f.; 26 Jan. 1984, Case 301/82, *SA Clin Midy* v *Kingdom of Belgium* [1984] ECR, p. 251 f.; and the Judgment of the Court of First Instance of 11 Feb. 1992, Case T-16/90, *Anastasia Panagiotopoulon* v *European Parliament* (unpublished), grounds 42 and 43.

of some Member States' exceedingly slow progression towards implementation in their national systems, even if the period allowed to that end has expired.[43]

Yet, relying on this principle brings about especially sensitive and complex problems, because of some peculiarities of the directives involved.

In particular, directives on company law tend to overemphasize *flexibility*, which is admittedly a quality typical of Community directives. In fact, such directives contain provisions that are for Member States to implement at their own discretion, often to a great extent, so that each Member State is at liberty to choose among two or more alternative manners of implementing individual rules.

According to ECJ case-law, this criterion does not seem to prevent recognition of the direct applicability of any one specific provision contained in a directive of this type, where it is capable of being severed from the context, so long as it meets the general requirements for being qualified as a self-executing rule, and can readily be applied the way it is written out in the relevant Community instrument.

In this respect, the European Court of Justice, when called upon to give a ruling in relation to Sixth Directive No 77/388 of 17 May 1977 amending the common system of value added tax,[44] whose provision for implementation in relation to the exemption of transactions consisting of the negotiation of credit had not timely been adopted by the Federal Republic of Germany,[45] observed:

> Whilst the Sixth Directive undoubtedly confers upon the Member States varying degrees of discretion as regards implementing certain of its provisions, individuals may not for that reason be denied the right to rely on any provisions which owing to their particular subject-matter *are capable of being severed from the general body of provisions and applied separately*. This minimum guarantee for persons adversely affected by the failure to implement the directive is a consequence of the binding nature of the obligation imposed on the member states by the third paragraph of Article 189 of the Treaty. That obligation would be rendered totally ineffectual if the member states were permitted to annul, as the result of their inactivity, even those effects which certain provisions of a directive are capable of producing by virtue of their subject-matter.
>
> Consequently, the general nature of the directive in question or the discretion which, in other areas, it leaves to the Member States may not be relied upon in order to deny any effect to those provisions which in view of their subject-matter may be relied upon to good purpose before a court even though the Directive as a whole has not been implemented. [*Emphasis added*].

After expanding on the relevant exemption provision contained in the Sixth Directive, and establishing that the relevant transposition deadline had expired,

---

43. See Santa Maria, *L'attuazione negli ordinamenti interni*, *op. cit.*, *loc. cit.*
44. [1977] O.J. L145, p. 1.
45. Judgment of the Court of 19 Jan. 1982, *Ursula Becker* v *Finanzamt Münster-Innenstadt* (reference for a preliminary ruling from the *Finanzgericht Münster*) [1982] ECR, p. 53 f., especially p. 72 f.

the Court of Justice held that provision to be *directly applicable*,[46] in the sense that:

> [. . .] as from 1 January 1979 it was possible for the provision concerning the exemption from turnover tax of transactions consisting of the negotiation of credit contained in article 13b(d)1 of the Sixth Council Directive of 17 May 1977 on the harmonization of the laws of the Member States relating to turnover taxes – common system of value-added tax: uniform basis of assessment, to be relied upon, in the absence of the implementation of that Directive, by a credit negotiator where he had refrained from passing that tax on to persons following him in the chain of supply, and the State could not claim, as against him, that it had failed to implement the directive.

As for the profile being considered here, directives in company matters exhibit an added peculiarity, in that, while the enforceability of a Community norm in the form of a directive is usually relied upon by the entitled person *against a Member State's authorities* for failure to perform Community obligations, especially those laid down in Article 10 EC and 249 EC, with a view to having an internal norm conflicting with that Community norm disapplied (as in *Ratti*), in matters of company law a controversy is most likely to arise between private individuals as to the contents of their rights. This is because, in the latter case, a private individual seeks redress against another private individual, by requesting the competent national court to recognize his right based on a provision contained in the directive in question possibly conflicting with a rule of domestic law, thus pleading for the direct application of that provision and the disapplication of that rule.

A case in point would be an Italian company's annual accounts being challenged by a minority shareholder before a national court of competent jurisdiction. Assume that, in this case, merely by way of example, the company in question had chosen to value its financial fixed assets at cost, in compliance with the provision of Article 35 of the Fourth Council Directive of 25 July 1978 on the annual accounts of public and private limited companies, instead of applying the equity method, which was alleged by the plaintiff to be the mandatory valuation method under Article 2425 of the Italian Civil Code.[47]

Although the directive in question is of the type that, in many an article, confers on the Member States discretion and free choices (one of which relates to Article 36, albeit in relation to investment companies alone), it has been maintained that both the provision of Article 35 in itself and the valuation criteria laid down in Articles 34 to 42 of the directive should be regarded, even before any implementing measure is adopted, to be directly applicable under Italian law, resulting in the company concerned being required to comply with those criteria since the expiry of the period for the implementation of the directive in the national system.[48]

---

46. *Ibid.*, ground 49, p. 76.
47. About the Fourth Directive, see below, Section 7 of this Chapter II.
48. Community Directives on company law are considered to be directly applicable by Predieri, *Il legislatore recalcitrante*, cit., pp. 173 f., 180 f. and 186 f.

As for this conclusion, consideration should be given to the ECJ's precedent according to which the direct effect of directives may only be pleaded against the Member State (or its authorities) allegedly responsible for failure to fulfil its obligations. However, the case in question does not involve a *vertical* relationship, i.e. a direct one between the individual and the State, but a private individual's *horizontal* claim that the State, through its judicial bodies, should ensure the assessment of a legal relationship between private parties in compliance with the rules of Community law.

In fact, this is by no means a novel line of reasoning, since it has been followed in judgments the ECJ has delivered in ruling on the direct applicability of competition rules and on the individuals' related rights which national courts are required to safeguard.[49]

The argument that directives have direct effects solely in respect of the so-called *vertical* relationships between the State and an individual person, and not in respect of *horizontal*, interpersonal relationships, was upheld by the European Court of Justice in its judgment in Case 8/81, *Becker*, of 19 January 1982,[50] and reaffirmed by it even more explicitly in its judgment in Case 152/84, *Marshall*, of 26 February 1986,[51] whereby the Court denied that any directive already expired and not implemented could have horizontal effects.

In its judgment of 22 June 1989, in Case 103/88, *Costanzo*,[52] the ECJ widened the number of the State authorities responsible for implementing Community directives, by requiring administrative authorities, too, to disapply any domestic rules found to be conflicting with directive provisions having direct effect.

At nearly the same time, the same view was taken by the Italian Constitutional Court in Judgment No 389 of 4 July 1989, in *Provincia Autonoma di Bolzano* v *Presidenza del Consiglio dei Ministri*,[53] holding that:

> it must be concluded, in the case in issue, that all bodies competent for enforcing laws (and any act having force or validity as a law) in our system – whether such bodies have law declaratory powers, such as the courts of law, or lack such powers, as is the case with administrative authorities – are legally required to disapply internal rules incompatible with the rules laid down in Articles 52 or 59 of the EC Treaty (now Articles 43 and 49 EC) according to the interpretation thereof given by the European Court of Justice. This means, in practice, that those bodies must recognise the Community norm as a legitimate and binding norm of law which, in respect of access to property or location of dwelling or any related claims, demands that self-employed workers who are nationals of other Member States be *treated*

---

49. See the ECJ's judgment of 30 Jan. 1974, Case 127/73, *Belgische Radio en Televisie et Société belge des auteurs, compositeurs et éditeurs* v *SV SABAM and NV Fonior* (*BRT* v *SABAM I*) [1974] ECR, p. 51 f., especially grounds 15, 16 and 17, p. 62 f. See also Chapter VI of this study.
50. [1981] ECR, 53.
51. [1986] ECR, 723.
52. [1989] ECR, p. 1839 f.
53. See in [1989] Dir.com. scambi int, p. 395 f., especially p. 389.

> *equally* with nationals of Italy, while *being required to disapply any State or regional norms of law that recognise the relevant rights and benefits to Italian nationals alone*. [*Emphasis added*].

This view was by no means denied by the Milan District Court in its judgment of 14 July 1983 in *Mezzasalma* v *La Rinascente SpA*,[54] in connection with treasury shares reported on a historical-cost basis among investment held as financial fixed assets pursuant to Articles 9 and 35 of the Fourth Directive. The Milan District Court observed:

> True, Community directive has not yet been implemented in the Italian legal order, but it is obvious that any reference made to the criteria laid down therein by company directors acting with the scope for discretion conferred on them by the laws and regulations in force can hardly be treated as manifestly arbitrary, entirely unreasonable conduct.

Quite correct. Since the dispute was over the annual accounts of *La Rinascente SpA* for fiscal years 1977, 1978 and 1979, the period for implementation of the Fourth Directive had not yet expired (Article 55) and, therefore, the direct applicability of the provisions of that directive had not yet become an issue by that time.

It should also be noted that, as a logical corollary of the principles the ECJ relies on to affirm the direct applicability of Community directives, were a domestic implementing measure is found to be short of adjusting to the Community norm, the latter must prevail in accordance with the third paragraph of Article 249 EC, in order to secure uniform interpretation.

For the national court is required to interpret such domestic implementing measure, and the relevant national law generally, 'in the light of the wording and the purpose of the directive'.

In this respect, in its Judgment of 10 April 1984 in Case 14/83, *Sabine von Colson and Elisabeth Kamann* v *Land Nordrhein-Westfalen*, on reference for a preliminary ruling from *Arbeitsgericht Hamm, Germany*,[55] the ECJ ruled:

> Although that provision [the third paragraph of article 189, now Article 249 EC, third paragraph] leaves Member States to choose the ways and means of ensuring that the directive is implemented, that freedom does not affect the obligation imposed on all the Member States to which the directive is addressed, to adopt, in their national legal systems, all the measures necessary to ensure that the directive is fully effective, in accordance with the objective which it pursues.
>
> However, the Member States' obligation arising from a directive to achieve the result envisaged by the directive and their duty under article 5 of the Treaty [now Article 10 EC] to take all appropriate measures, whether general or particular, to ensure the fulfilment of that obligation, is binding on all the authorities of member states including, for matters within their jurisdiction,

---

54. See in [1984] *Le Società*, p. 35 f., p. 37.
55. [1984] ECR, 1891.

> *the courts*. It follows that, in applying the national law and in particular the provisions of a national law specifically introduced in order to implement Directive No 76/207, *national courts are required to interpret their national law in the light of the wording and the purpose of the directive in order to achieve the result referred to in the third paragraph of article 189)* [now Article 249 EC, third paragraph]. [*Emphasis added*].[56]

Lastly, as again emphasized by the ECJ:

> [W]hen the wording of secondary community law is open to *more than one interpretation*, preference should be given to the interpretation which renders the provision *consistent with the treaty rather than the interpretation which leads to its being incompatible with the Treaty*. Consequently, the directive should not be construed in isolation and it is necessary to consider whether or not the requirements in question are contrary to the abovementioned provisions of the Treaty and to interpret the directive in the light of the conclusions reached in that respect. [*Emphasis added*].[57]

This jurisprudential approach intended to affirm the validity of 'Community' interpretation was also taken by the European Court of Justice in its judgment of 13 November 1990, in Case C-106/89, *Marleasing SA* v *La Comercial Internacional de Alimentacion SA*, on reference for a preliminary ruling from Juzgado de Primera Instancia e Instruccion no 1 de Oviedo, Spain, pursuant to Article 177 of the EC Treaty (now 234 EC).[58]

In that judgment, in relation to the wording of the First Company Directive No 68/151 of 9 March 1968, the ECJ, in examining the question whether an individual may rely on the directive against a national law, reaffirmed its consistent case-law according to which a directive may not of itself impose obligations on an individual and, consequently, a provision of a directive may not be relied upon as such against such a person.

Yet, it was the Court's view that the problem should have been submitted in a different way to provide a substantive solution. According to the ECJ:

> the Member States' obligation arising from a directive to achieve the result envisaged by the directive and their duty under Article 5 of the Treaty

56. For the same view, see again Judgment of the Court of 10 Apr. 1984, Case 79/83, *Dorit Harz* v *Deutsche Tradax GmbH*, on reference for a preliminary ruling from the *Arbeitsgericht* of Hamburg, *ibid.*, 1921 f., especially grounds 26 e 28.
57. See ground 62 of the judgment of 4 Dec. 1986, Case 205/84, relating to the free provision of insurance services, often cited elsewhere in this book (especially in Chapter I). Along the same lines, see also Judgment of the Court of Justice of 13 Dec. 1983, Case 218/82, *Commission* v *Council* [1983] ECR, 4063.
58. This judgment is in [1990] ECR, p. 4135 f. The same principles are also expressed in the ECJ judgments of 16 Dec. 1993, C-334/92, *Wagner Miret* v *Fondo de Garantia Salarial* [1993] ECR, 6911, and of 5 Oct. 2004, Joined Cases C-397/01 to C-403/01, *Pfeiffer and others* [2004] ECR, I-8835, ground 113, and case-law referred to therein. See also the judgment of the Court of 4 Jul. 2006, C-212/04, *Adeneler and others* [2006] ECR, I-6057.

> [now Article 10 EC] to take all appropriate measures, whether general or particular, to ensure the fulfilment of that obligation, is binding on all the authorities of Member States including, for matters within their jurisdiction, the courts. It follows that, in applying national law, *whether the provisions in question were adopted before or after the directive*, the national court called upon to interpret it is required to do so, as far as possible, in the light of the wording and the purpose of the directive in order to achieve the result pursued by the latter and thereby comply with the third paragraph of Article 189 of the Treaty [now Article 249 EC, third para.]. [*Emphasis added*].

By these arguments, albeit following such interpretational effort, the jurisprudential distinction that restricts the direct effect of directive to *vertical* relations, to the exclusion of *horizontal* relations. seems to be overcome. In my view, this is the logical conclusion, since it would be nonsense to expect any one rule to be interpreted in different ways at the same time depending on whether the relevant dispute is concerned with a relationship between an individual and a Member State or with a relationship between individuals.

This approach seems to have been shared by the ECJ in its judgment of 14 July 1994, in Case C-91/92, *Paola Faccini Dori* v *Recreb Srl*,[59] in which the Court, based on precedent, reaffirmed that:

> when applying national law, *whether adopted before or after the directive*, the national court that has to interpret that law must do so, as far as possible, in the light of the wording and the purpose of the directive so as to achieve the result it has in view and thereby comply with the third paragraph of Article 189 of the Treaty [now Article 249 EC, third para.].[60] [*Emphasis added*].

When the European Court of Justice was called upon to examine a specific case in which a Member State's national law referred to the content of a directive provision in order to determine rules applicable to a situation which was purely internal to that State, it excluded that such examination fell outwith its jurisdiction under Article 177 of the Treaty (now Article 234 EC) and held as follows:

> On the contrary, it is manifestly in the interest of the Community legal order that, in order to forestall future differences of interpretation, every Community provision should be given a uniform interpretation irrespective of the circumstances in which it is to be applied.[61]

The same approach was taken by Advocate General Tesauro in the Opinion delivered on 8 April 1992 in Case C-83/91, *Wienand Meilicke* v *ADV/ORGA F. A. Meyer AG*, a case decided by the ECJ's judgment of 16 July 1992.[62] In that judgment, the European Court of Justice, considering that the compatibility of

---

59. [1994] ECR, I-3325.
60. *Ibid.*, ground 26.
61. See Judgment of the Court of 18 Oct. 1990, Joined Cases C-297/88 and C-197/89, *Massan Dzodzi* v *Belgian State* [1990] ECR, p. 3763 f., p. 3793, ground 36 f.
62. [1992] ECR, I-4871.

the doctrine of contributions in kind under German law with the Second Company Directive is a hypothetical one, ruled that it was not appropriate for it to answer the questions submitted by the *Landgericht Hannover* in its reference for a preliminary ruling.

Finally, mention should be made of the decision delivered by the ECJ on 19 November 1991 in Joined Cases C-6/90 and C-9/90, *Andrea Francovich and Danila Bonifaci and others* v *Italian Republic*, in which the principle was laid down, for the first time, that, where the result prescribed by a directive cannot be *achieved by interpretation* in the sense indicated above, then a Member State must make reparation for the consequences of the loss and damage caused to individuals as a result of that Member State's infringement of Community law (failure to transpose a directive).[63]

The two joined cases had been opened following references to the ECJ for preliminary rulings from the *Preturas* (magistrate's courts) of Vicenza and of Bassano del Grappa, on questions about the interpretation of the third paragraph of Article 189 of the Treaty (now Article 249, third paragraph) and of Council Directive No 80/987 of 20 October 1980 on the approximation of the laws of the Member States relating to the protection of employees in the event of the insolvency of their employer.[64]

The purpose of Directive No 80/987 is to provide employed persons with minimum protection Community-wide in respect of their claims outstanding in case their employers become insolvent. Italy had failed to issue the required legislative, administrative and regulatory measures by the stated deadline, 23 October 1993, thereby failing to fulfill the obligations prescribed by the directive, and the ECJ had already established such failure in its judgment of 2 February 1989 in Case C-22/87, *Commission* v *Italian Republic*.[65]

The Court of Justice reaffirmed the *Francovich* precedent, holding that the fact that Articles 3 and 4(1) and (2) give the Member States some discretion as regards the means of establishing that guarantee and the restriction of its amount does not affect the precise and unconditional nature of the result required.[66] However, as for the identity of the guarantor under Article 5 of the directive, the Court observed that such identity cannot be determined without the State's intervention. Accordingly, even as the controversial provisions of the directive in question are sufficiently precise and unconditional as regards the determination of the persons entitled to the guarantee and as regards the content of that guarantee, *those elements are not sufficient*, according to the ECJ, to enable individuals to rely on those provisions before the national courts. This is because those provisions do

63. [1991] ECR, I-5357.
64. [1980] O.J. L283, p. 23. The judgment of the Court is in [1991] ECR, p. 5357 f.; it has also been published in [1992] *Foro it.*, IV, c. 1450 f., with a note by Barone & Pardolesi and commentary by Ponzanelli.
65. [1989] ECR, 143.
66. *Francovich* judgment, cit., ground 18.

not identify the person liable to provide the guarantee, and the State cannot be considered liable on the sole ground that it has failed to take transposition measures within the prescribed period.[67]

Still, the ECJ, in examining the question whether Italy was liable for the loss and damage caused to individuals as a consequence of its failure to transpose Directive 80/987, and was consequently required to make reparation therefor, answered in the affirmative.

Firstly, as indicated above, the Italian State's infringement of the directive in question had already been established in the ECJ's judgment of 2 February 1989.

Secondly, according to the Court, the prescribed result of that directive entailed the grant to employees of a right to a guarantee of payment of their unpaid wage claims, a right the content of which could be identified on the basis of the provisions of the directive. The ECJ then ruled:

> Consequently, the national court must, in accordance with the national rules on liability, uphold the right of employees to obtain reparation of loss and damage caused to them as a result of failure to transpose the directive.[68]

It is appropriate to recall that the Italian Constitutional Court, in Judgment No 160 of 18 April 1991 in *Società dolciaria Giampaoli* v *Ufficio Registro di Ancona*,[69] explicitly extended the principles itself had laid down in Judgment No 170 of 1984, regarding Community Regulations, to directives having direct effect. Specifically, the Constitutional Court held in Judgment No 160/91 that, where unconditional and sufficiently precise directives have been issued, it is for national courts to apply them directly and to disapply any national norm conflicting therewith.

The Italian Constitutional Court held that, precisely because national courts are not required to apply a national provision conflicting with a Community rule, the constitutional question raised as to the legality of a provision subjecting debt issues to registration tax was entirely irrelevant to the case at hand, since Article 11 of Directive No 335/69 requires that Member States must not subject to any form of taxation whatsoever loans raised by the issue of debentures or similar securities.

Instruments supplemental to the directives under scrutiny in this matter are Council Regulation (EEC) No 2137/85 of 25 July 1985 on the European Economic Interest Grouping (EEIG), applicable as from 1 July 1989, and the package of acts relating to the creation of a 'European public limited company'. Neither set of instruments is based on Article 44(2)(g) of the Treaty, but their legal bases are Articles 2 and 308 EC for Regulation No 2137/85 and Article 95 EC for the acts creating a European company.[70]

67. *Ibid.*, ground 26.
68. *Ibid.*, ground 45.
69. [1992] *Foro It.*, I, 660, with note by Daniele.
70. Council Regulation (EEC) No. 2137/85 of 25 Jul. 1985 on the European Economic Interest Grouping (EEIG) is in [1985] O.J. L199, p. 1. See Section 11 of this Chpater II for the European Company (*Societas Europaea*, SE), and Section 12 for the EEIG.

5. COMPANY DIRECTIVES AND COMMUNITY DEVELOPMENTS: INTERPRETATIONAL ISSUES

I have referred above to the significance of the *right of establishment* for the progressive attainment of the harmonization of company laws within the EU. This is not only because the entire matter has its rationale in a norm included in the chapter 'Right of Establishment' in the EC Treaty, but also and above all because the process of harmonization of company law within the EU is closely related to the ever-growing importance every highly advanced legal order ascribes to the protection in whatever form of minority shareholders and any of other persons however *interested* in a company's life, i.e. the parties currently referred to as '*the stakeholders*'.[71]

In fact, for the time being, this not the only benchmark for either thorough harmonization or a correct reading of company directives.

The starting point is that many, even deep changes have occurred across the Community during the nearly fifty-year long process of formation of company directives, thereby affecting Community law, which is itself an ever-changing system.

Consider how competition law has evolved in its various aspects within the Community, both through the introduction of new regulations and as a result of case-law, whether of the Commission, at the end of administrative procedures, or of the Court of First Instance or the Court of Justice in judicial proceedings, through increasingly accurate and sophisticated decisions.

Thus, the Third Whereas of the Fourth Directive on the annual accounts of limited companies explicitly refers to competition.

In more general terms, there are clear coordinating links between the rules on merger control under competition law and the rules on groups of undertakings (in the Draft Ninth Directive) or on cross-border mergers (Directive 2005/56). What is at play are two different aspects of the same choice of Community economic policy to attain the optimum dimension of 'European' undertakings while complying with the rules of competition law.[72]

Further, both reports submitted by the Commission along with the Draft Ninth Directive on groups of undertakings and with the Regulation creating the European Company, respectively, use rather 'undertaking' than the terminologically more correct word 'company' to stress the significance ascribed in both instruments as well to the economics of a merger as to the structure of, and the legal relationships within, a corporate group.

Interferences still exist between the rules on takeover bids (Directive 2004/25/EC) and competition regulations, as show, for example, by the case of *Irish Distillers*.[73]

---

71. See above, Chapter I, especially Sections 18 and 19.
72. Thus was also the thrust of both the *Explanatory Memorandum* accompanying the first draft proposal for a ninth directive, especially at pages 2 and 6, and the *Exposé des motifs* commenting the new text of the directive on groups, particularly at page 36 f.
73. This was a notice of charges the Commission sent on 29 Jun. 1988 in relation to a 'hostile takeover bid' prohibited by the Commission. See the Commission's press releases of 17 Aug. 1988, IP/88/512 and of 2 Sep. 1988, IP/88/526.

Functional links also exists between, on the one hand, the rules on corporate structure (Proposal for a Fifth Directive) and those on corporate groups (Amended Draft Proposal for a Ninth Directive) and on consolidated accounts (Seventh Directive) and, on the other, the Council Regulation on the Statute for a European Company and the Regulation on the European Economic Interest Grouping.

It is so not only because the most serious issues raised by the Fifth Directive and the acts creating on a European Company are the same: (i) the two-tier system of managing bodies, with a management board (*Vorstand*) and a supervisory board (*Aufsichtsrat*); and (ii) employee participation in the supervision of the company (*Mitbestimmung*). It is also (and chiefly) so because such an approach meets the need – one the Commission is highly sensitive to – for the attainment of optimum dimension, while ensuring 'transparency' (of both shareholdings and power relationships within a group's individual companies) through more and more precise forms of disclosure (see the sixth Whereas of the Draft Proposal for a Ninth Directive).

The same line of reasoning applies to the directive on internal mergers (and to that on divisions) in relation to Directive No 2005/56 on 'cross-border mergers'.[74]

In the matter of mergers of public limited companies, the disclosure requirements laid down in the Firs Directive 'must be extended to include mergers so that third parties are kept adequately informed' (seventh Whereas of the Third Directive). Under Article 13 of Directive No 78/855, this task is made the responsibility of Member States, which are required to 'provide for an adequate system of protection of the interests of creditors of the merging companies whose claims antedate the publication of the draft terms of merger and have not fallen due at the time of such publication'. For the protection of the rights of the employees of each of the merging companies, Article 12 of Directive No 78/855 expressly refers to Directive No 77/187.

For the protection of the interests of members and third parties, a provision in Directive No 78/855 (clearly innovating on the present Italian system) requires the directors or managers of each of the companies participating in the merger to disclose the *draft terms* of the merger, which:

> must be published in the manner prescribed by the laws of each Member State in accordance with Article 3 of Directive 68/151/EEC, for each of the merging companies, at least one month before the date fixed for the general meeting which is to decide thereon [Article 6].

The *social policy purpose* has become more and more important within the Community itself. Not by chance, the Whereases of many of the directives considered here expressly mention the need to protect the rights of employees, now definitely counted among a company's 'stakeholders', a notion that also refers to non-shareholders, whose interests are deemed worthy of being protected in the most advanced legal systems.

---

74. For the relationships of Directive No. 2005/56 with the right of establishment, please refer to Section 12 of Chapter I of this book.

This was the approach also taken in Council Directive 77/187/EEC of 14 February 1977 on the approximation of the laws of the Member States *relating to the safeguarding of employees' rights in the event of transfers of undertakings, businesses or parts of businesses.*[75] This directive was expressly referred to in the Third Directive on (internal) mergers, in the Sixth on divisions, in the directive on cross-border mergers, and in the directive supplementing the Regulation on *Societas Europaea.*

It should be noted that, though after the expiry of the period allowed for the implementation, Directive No 77/187 was at long last transposed into the Italian legal system under Act No 428 of 29 December 1990.

Quite interesting instruments in this area have been the amended proposal for a Council directive on procedures for 'informing and consulting the employees of undertakings with complex structures, in particular transnational undertakings', of 13 July 1983, based on Article 100 of the Treaty (now Article 94 EC) and on Article 117 of the Treaty (now Article 136 EC),[76] as well as Council Directive 94/45/EC of 22 September 1994 on the establishment of a European Works Council or a procedure in Community-scale undertakings and Community-scale groups of undertakings for the purposes of informing and consulting employees.

What clearly emerges from the indications offered above is an involved process in respect of which the equivalence of measures for the protection of members' and other parties' interests in Community-based companies with a view to the attainment of full right of establishment is not the only principle underlying the interpretation of company directives. For the different profiles that are closely connected with the wider reach of the European Union must also be taken into account.

Thus, a though task has been imposed on national law-makers (the first interpreters of Community directives because of their peculiar nature), who are required, in adjusting domestic legislations to Community law, to analyse individual provisions very closely in order to identify the interests each of them is intended to protect.

The uniformity of the measures implementing the harmonization directives in different national jurisdictions is guaranteed anyhow by the system of references to the ECJ for preliminary rulings under Article 234 EC.

The considerations offered so far are especially material to the solution of the interpretational problem of establishing the extent to which the directives discussed above are binding upon national legislators.

In other words, what is to be determined is whether or not a national law-maker is allowed to adopt *stricter norms* than those contained in the directives or – which is the same thing in theory – may maintain any existing domestic rules which are *more restrictive* than the rules laid down in the directives.

It is widespread wisdom that Community directives on the harmonization of company laws establish 'minimum equivalent legal requirements' (a phrase

75. This directive is published O.J., cit., p. 26 f.
76. This proposal for a directive is published in O.J. C217, cit., p. 3 f.

contained in the third Whereas of the Fourth Directive), in the sense that they are supposed to provide a minimum solution to any one issue being considered. As a result, the national law-maker would apparently be at liberty to *use a stricter approach* than the *minimum* required by the relevant directive.

In my view, this line of reasoning may be granted in most cases. For example, there is no doubt that the requirement of Article 9 of the Second Directive, according to which shares issued for a consideration must be paid up in cash at the time the company is incorporated, at not less than 25% of their nominal value, entailed amendments to be made to Article 2329 of the Italian Civil Code (which envisaged full payment of at least three tenth of capital among the preconditions for incorporation). Yet, the Italian Parliament, in reforming Italian company law, chose to adopt that minimum 25% by reference to Article 2343(2) of the Civil Code.

Likewise, the requirement in the Second Directive that 'a minimum capital shall be subscribed the amount of which shall be not less than 25,000 European units of account' is by no means in conflict with Italian Legislative Decree No 6 of 17 January 2003, which raised the minimum capital of public limited companies and of partnerships limited by shares to 120,000 euros (Article 2327, Civil Code). Obviously, this applies regardless of the entirely different grounds on which law scholars have raised objections as to the advisability or even the validity of the choice so made by the Italian legislator.

The interpretational rule mentioned above has no absolute value, though. It is only valid in principle, because of the many derogations attaching to it. It has a limited scope, in fact, whenever a 'different' (thus stricter) implementing measure by a Member State is in contrast with the protection of either minority shareholders' or other parties' interests, by postulating the need for full 'equivalence', i.e. for a really 'uniform' solution. Examples can easily be found in the rules on the *nullity* of companies under Article 10 et seq. of the First Directive or in the rules intended to *limit the causes of invalidity* of obligations assumed in a company's name as provided for by Article 7 *et seq.* of the same directive.

Specifically, as the last recital of the First Directive reads, 'it is necessary, in order to ensure certainty in the law as regards relations between the company and third parties, and also between members, to limit the cases in which nullity can arise and the retroactive effect of a declaration of nullity'. This requirement was also stated in quite the same terms in the last recital of the Third Directive on internal mergers.

Thus, in its *Marleasing* judgment of 13 November 1990, the ECJ ruled that the Spanish court was prohibited from declaring that the founders' contract establishing *La Commercial*, a Spanish company, was void on the ground that, based on Articles 1261 and 1275 of Spanish Civil Code, the establishment of the company lacked cause, *was a sham transaction* and was carried out *in order to defraud the creditors* of a co-founder of the defendant company. For the Spanish court's decision was held to be in contrast with Article 11 of the First Directive No 68/151 on company law, since that provision, particularly under paragraph 2(b):

> prohibits the laws of the Member States from providing for a judicial declaration of nullity on grounds other than those *exhaustively* listed in the

> directive, amongst which is the ground that the objects of the company are unlawful or contrary to public policy.[77] [*Emphasis added*].

In this connection, the ECJ observed that:

> According to the Commission, the expression '*objects of the company*' must be interpreted as referring exclusively to the objects of the company *as described in the instrument of incorporation or the articles of association.* It follows, in the Commission's view, that *a declaration of nullity of a company cannot be made on the basis of the activity actually pursued by it,* for instance defrauding the founders' creditors. [*Emphasis added*].

As a result, the ECJ's ruled that:

> That argument must be upheld. As is clear from the preamble to Directive 68/151, its purpose was to limit the cases in which nullity can arise and the retroactive effect of a declaration of nullity in order to ensure '*certainty in the law as regards relations between the company and third parties, and also between members (sixth recital)*'. [*Emphasis added*].
>
> Furthermore, the protection of third parties 'must be ensured by provisions which restrict to the greatest possible extent the grounds on which obligations entered into in the name of the company are not valid' [Emphasis in the text]. It follows, therefore, that each ground of nullity provided for in Article 11 of the directive must be interpreted strictly. In those circumstances the words 'objects of the company' must be understood as referring to the objects of the company as described in the instrument of incorporation or the articles of association. [*Emphasis added*].[78]

It should be noted that, as the provision of Article 44(2)(g) EC is one among the rules on the right of establishment, the equal protection accorded both to a company's members and to third parties is not an end to itself, but it is part of the general design to facilitate the free movement of persons within the Community, by finally removing any discrimination based on nationality and ensuring 'national treatment' to companies as well as to individuals belonging to another Member State.

In Case No 32/74, *Frierich Haaga GmbH*, on reference from the *Bundesgerichtshof* (High Federal Court) of the Federal Republic of Germany,[79] a case decided by the ECJ's judgment of 12 November 1974, the European Court of Justice had been called on to answer questions on the interpretation of Article 2(1)(d) of the First Directive requiring disclosure of certain acts concerning persons or bodies representing a company. Still, the Court went beyond the case then at issue to give reasons for a strict interpretation of that article.

---

77. See *Marleasing* Judgment, cit., ground 10. For the simulation of limited companies in Italian law, see L. Santa Maria, 'Società e simulazione, società e comunione di godimento' [1995] Riv. trim. dir. proc. civ., p. 205 f.
78. *Ibid.*, grounds 11 and 12.
79. [1974] ECR, 1201.

The Court observed:[80]

> [T]his interpretation is in conformity with the objective of the directive, which is to guarantee legal certainty in dealings between companies and third parties *in view of the intensification of trade between member states* following the creation of the common market. In view of this fact, it is important that *any person* wishing to establish and develop trading relations with companies situated in other member states *should be able easily to obtain essential information relating to the constitution of trading companies and to the powers of persons authorized to represent them* in the interest of legal transactions between nationals of different member states. It is therefore important that all the relevant information should be expressly stated in official registers or records, even if certain information follows automatically from national legislation or may appear self-evident. In fact, *third parties cannot be expected to have a full knowledge of the legislations or current commercial practices of other member states*. [*Emphasis added*].

In other cases, in relation to the widening of the scope of company directives, an especially relevant factor may be the protection of employees' interests, for example on a merger or in respect of 'employee participation' under measures implementing the Fifth Directive as and when approved.

In yet other cases, prevalence may be accorded to a general interest in controlling multinational corporations' activity, especially with regard to the implementation of the Seventh and Ninth Directives (in this connection, see the sixth recital in the new draft proposal for a Ninth Directive).

Some conclusions can be drawn from these brief general remarks.

The uniformity already achieved or about to be achieved among company laws is far from being perfect. Nor does the fact that Article 44(2)(g) EC asks for something less, i.e. mere coordination of 'safeguards', diminish the import of such statement.

As observed above, the approach taken first by the Community, then by the European Union, hand in hand with the evolution of Community law, for the attainment of the proposed objective is chiefly based on the *harmonization of company laws*.

Therefore, in this perspective, there appear to be too many alternative solutions among which each Member State may choose from (in particular, see the Fifth Directive or Article 1(2) and (3) of the Third), and too many derogations allowed to them in implementation.

For example, the Seventh Directive on consolidated accounts provides for an impressive number of derogations, which may ultimately impair the 'true and fair view' concept underlying this directive.

Further, the fact that the directives discussed above, save for those on stock exchanges, sometimes concern limited companies in general, once with regard to

---

80. *Ibid.*, ground 6.

private limited companies and often solely with regard to share companies, results in a hardly justified bias in favour of the latter – especially if one considers that the form by far more widely used in Germany is the *GmbH*, a private limited company. This creates quite a few problems in coordinating the different laws, which have resulted in the far broader determination of the companies, both *limited* and *unlimited*, indicated as the addressees of the rules on the right of establishment in Article 48(2) EC, as expressly referred to in Article 44(2)(g).

It is also appropriate to stress that uniformity is not, and cannot be, complete. In the *Memorandum* in which it again advocated a European commercial company,[81] the Commission, taking a view that has essentially remained unchanged over time,[82] recognized that, notwithstanding harmonization, differences will persist in national legislations and administrative practices, and stated that the coordination of national legislations is not intended to abolish different legal systems in different Member States.

I had already raised some doubts as to certain references to conflict of laws contained in these directive,[83] particularly in respect of Article 6, 6(b) and 7 of the Seventh Directive, which, in an earlier version, envisaged different rules depending on whether a company considered as a controlling or a controlled company had or had not its *seat* within the Community. And I had also criticized such reference to the seat, stressing that the failure to specify which of the possible terms (*registered office*, *head office* or *real seat*) should mean in that context was itself a source of considerable confusion.[84]

My doubts about the Seventh Directive have been dispelled, though, since the Commission has modified its previous approach and introduced a reference to a company's 'national law' as I suggested it should do.[85]

In fact, the original version of Article 48(1) EC had contents and purposes other than those typical of a norm of conflict of laws, and, as I have already observed, Article 48(2) EC, in indicating the addressees of the rules on the right of establishment, provides for a wider subjective scope for application of the different company directives, as it has specifically been limited by the directives themselves.

Precisely for these reasons, as the things now stand, the directives discussed here can only apply to companies '*subject to the national law*' of a Member State of the European Union, such phrase being taken as equivalent to the other phrase: 'formed in accordance with the law of a Member State'.

---

81. See *Memorandum* of the Commission of 15 Jul. 1988, cit., p. 9.
82. As shown by the ECJ's entire case-law on companies' right of establishment, as discussed in Chapter I of this book.
83. See my work 'L'attuazione negli ordinamenti interni delle direttive comunitarie in materia di società', in *Il gruppo di società e il bilancio consolidato di gruppo, Direttive comunitarie e diritto nazionale* (Milan, 1981), p. 13 f., especially p. 25 f.
84. About the possible meanings of the phrase 'company seat', please see Chapter I of this book, especially Sections 5 and 6.
85. See 'Relazione' by Niessen, in *Il gruppo di società*, cit., *La proposta di settima direttiva sui conti di gruppo*, p. 28 f., especially paragraph 16.

What remains to do is to establish the reach of such reference to another law. In other words, for our purposes, the question should be asked whether preference should be given to the outcome of the internal process of conflict of laws to identify the law governing companies from the standpoint of a Member State's own legal system, or whether the private international law issue of the relationship between any company and any Member State – further in the presence of least one of the three alternative requirements of connection with the Community under Article 48(1) EC – should uniformly be determined on the basis of the place chosen by the shareholders, as Community citizens, *to form the company.*

Since, as observed above, a company, wherever incorporated within the EU, initially has its statutory seat, whether pursuant to the competent national law or just in fact, in the Member State of its formation, it is quite clear that, in the latter alternative, merely forming a company in a Member State (pursuant to such Member State's law) would automatically determine that company's entitlement to freedom of establishment.

Such entitlement and the rules applicable to it prevail over any restrictions under national laws – save for entirely exceptional cases – both when any such restriction arises from a substantive norm and when it is the result of conflict of laws.

There is more to it, though. With a view to establishing whether or not a national measure restricting freedom of establishment was correct, the ECJ has invariably referred, as a requirement for admissibility, to compliance with the norms contained in Community directives on company law – specifically the rules in the Eleventh Directive.

In conclusion, the close connection of the directives on company law with the issue of establishment, even when the legal basis expressly referred to is not Article 44(2)(g) EC, leads me to choose rather the second among the proposed options. In the sense that, in the case of a conflict of laws, for example between the law of the place of incorporation and the law of real seat, the phrase '*companies subject the law of a Member State*' should, when correctly interpreted, be read otherwise – as is the case in matters of free establishment and provision of services – so that the similar phrase contained in Article 48(1) comes to mean '*companies governed by the laws of the place of incorporation*' of that State.

This is the approach to be taken to the interpretational issue relating to individual directives on the harmonization of company laws. In particular, the Third Directive is concerned with mergers of companies '*governed by* [the] *national laws*' of one Member State (Article 2 of the Directive), whereas the problem of mergers of companies governed by the laws of several Member States is dealt with in the new directive of 2005, no longer numbered.

Setting up the company's seat within the European Union by the other contracting party is still provided for in Article 28(1) of the draft proposal for a ninth directive as the contact factor which requires such other party, under the affiliation agreement, to publish its annual accounts, reports on operations and independent auditors' reports, as approved, throughout the term of the agreement. Further, such documents and their publicity must comply with the principles that govern public limited companies of the Member State in which the other contracting party has its seat.

The comments offered above also apply to this provision, which, for the avoidance of doubts, should itself be amended, even the more so as reference is made in Articles 8(1) and (5), and 11(e) to 'national legislation' or to 'the manners provided for in the legislation of each Member State'.

Let me make one last observation, which is, in fact, a *caveat* for the Italian policy-makers.

A question arises from the various possible choices available under the directives discussed so far. The range of choices offered to each Member State is intended to meet the Commission's need to mediate among the various possible solutions to any problem as they emerge from a review of individual national laws. They are a result of the advisable compromises to be reached when a country's representatives are reluctant to give up a national solution for another that comes from a different legal order, which would be the one of choice within the Community context.

In this way, through the system of alternative choices (though with all the flaws of this approach, especially in terms of uniformity, then of legal certainty), undesirable standstill conditions can be avoided, while positions sternly defended in any one national system can still be safeguarded.

Now, Italy has long been conspicuously absent from the debate underway at Community level in the terms outlined above. For Italian representatives seem to be not in the least worried *ahead* of the possible outcome of such debate. In fact, such an attitude should not come as a surprise in a country in which, until recently, lack of concern for Community problems had been a constant commitment on the part of Italian policy-makers. Nor can it come as a surprise that only in the last few years have some attempts been made in Italy at accommodating the peculiarities of the Community system, due account being taken of the fact that, when the text of a directive has become *final*, the national legislator is merely called upon to *transpose the precise contents thereof* into the relevant national body of laws. For there is no doubt that no initiative can be taken at any time thereafter in implementing Community law in that national system. Once a directive has finally been approved, both the national legislator and the national courts and legal professionals after him will be rigidly bound to the contents and reach of the relevant Community rule, subject first to the Commission's supervision and control, then to any final decision the European Court of Justice may elect to take, regardless of the type of proceeding involved.

6. THE COMMISSION'S CURRENT ACTIVITY IN CODIFYING THE MATTER

The huge amount of acts the Community bodies have approved over time, as each has possibly been amended even more than once, have convinced the Commission of the advisability of codifying Community laws. For example, in 2001, before the accession of the twelve new States, those of Eastern Europe among them, the Community legislative stock amounted to as many as 80,000 pages, already translated into the languages of all candidate States.[86]

In effect, the issue had already been raised by the Commission in its Communication of 1987, whereby its had instructed its offices to codify legislative acts after no more than ten amendments were made to each of them, stressing that such instruction should be understood as a minimum requirement, and that each of the different offices could codify the acts it was responsible for even at shorter intervals.[87]

The need to codify the Community's legislative acts was later reaffirmed in the conclusions of the 1992 Edinburgh European Council with a view to meet the requirement of *legal certainty* in any one matter at any one time.

To that end, on 20 December 1994, the European Parliament, the Council and the Commission signed the Interinstitutional agreement of 20 December 1994 on an *accelerated working method for official codification of legislative texts*, based on which the Commission was entrusted with the task to define and make proposals for codification to be then submitted to the European Council and Parliament for approval.

Another *Interinstitutional Agreement on a more structured use of the recasting technique for legal acts* was entered into by the three institutions in 2001, partly with a view to saving substantial costs through codification of legislative acts, where one only considers that each such act must be translated into the twenty plus official languages of the European Union.

The codification process entails, first, the *consolidation* by the Commission of existing legislative acts, following which the Commission is responsible for reviewing and assessing the legislative texts, abolishing outdated provisions and checking each text to remove overlaps, inconsistencies and errors. The Commission's Legal Service has been made, in turn, responsible for following up that work and recasting the consolidated legal texts in order to bring about *codification*. So complex a work is first carried out in one of the official languages of the EU, and each consolidated text is then translated into all the other official languages.

The codification work currently in progress also covers directives on company law. A proposal for amendments to the First Directive (Directive No 68/151/EEC) was submitted by the Commission on 30 January 2008. The Commission had submitted a similar proposal regarding the Third Directive (Directive No 78/855/EEC) on 29 January 2008. At the time of writing, no other proposals have been brought forward for codification of company directives, while efforts are well underway to consolidate them in preparation for codification.

---

86. See Commission Communication to the European Parliament and to the Council of 21 Nov. 2001, COM(2001)645, final, p. 3.
87. COM (87) 868 PV final of 14 Apr. 1987, as referred to in the Communication cited above.

7. DIRECTIVES CONCERNING GENERAL RULES OF MEMBER STATES' COMPANY LAWS

As stressed above, Community directives on companies, whether final or not, irrespective of the underlying legal basis, concern many of the traditional domains of company law.

Some of them relate to limited liability companies in their general and structural aspects, others are concerned with specific aspects of corporate life.

Of the former group of directives, the first to be issued, then to be officially assigned an ordinal number according to the Commission's original practice, was the directive of 9 March 1968 *on co-ordination of safeguards which, for the protection of the interests of members and others, are required by Member States of companies within the meaning of the second paragraph of Article 58 of the Treaty* (Article 48(2) EC), *with a view to making such safeguards equivalent throughout the Community.*[88] It was transposed in Italy under The President of the Republic Decree No 1127 of 29 December 1969, and, pursuant to Article 1 of this decree, it applies to '*società per azioni*' (public limited companies), '*società in accomandita per azioni*' (limited partnerships), and '*società a responsabiltà limitata*' (private limited companies).[89]

The First Directive was amended by Directive 2003/58/EC of the European Parliament and of the Council of 15 July 2003,[90] and again by Directive 2006/99 of the Council of 20 November 2006 following the accession of Bulgaria and Rumania.[91,92] It essentially contains three distinct sets of provisions.

---

88. In O.J., cit., p. 8 f. About this directive, which has been transposed in every Member State, see.: van Ommeslaghe, 'La première directive du Conseil du 9 mars 1968 en matière de sociétés' [1969] Cahiers dr. eur., pp. 495 f. and 619 f.; Loussouarn, 'L'harmonisation du droit d'établissement' [1969] Rev. trim. dr. eur., p. 280 f.; Loussouarn e Bredin, *Droit du commerce international* (Paris, 1969), p. 514 f.; Wyatt, 'The first Directive and Company Law' [1978] Law Quart. Rev., p. 182 f.; Perret, 'Coordination du droit des sociétés en Europe. La première directive de la CEE en matière de sociétés et le droit suisse', in *Etudes suisses de droit européen*, cit., p. 613 f. For problems in connection with the text of the First Directive in regard of the Member States' different national legislations, see Stein, 'Harmonisation of European Company Laws', cit., p. 237 f.
89. On the implementation of the First Directive in Italy, which has raised much criticism in literature, see essentially: Ferri, 'Disarmonie della legge di armonizzazione' [1970] Riv. dir. comm. I, p. 167 f.; Simonetto, 'Modifica lampo delle norme sulle società con Decreto del Presidente della Repubblica' [1970] Riv. dir. civ. II, p. 794 f.; Lanza, 'Effetti sull'ordinamento interno dell'opera prima comunitaria in tema di società' [1970] Riv. società, p. 794; Scordino, 'Rilevanza nell'ordinamento delle cooperative delle modificazioni alla disciplina delle società di capitale introdotte dal d.p.r. 29 dicembre 1969, n. 1127, in attuazione della I direttiva CEE sul coordinamento del diritto delle società' [1971] Dir. e giur., p. 804 f.
90. [2003] O.J. L221. Even as the relevant transposition deadline was 30 Dec. 2006, this directive has not yet been implemented by Lithuania, while the notifications from Spain and Slovenia are still being examined by the Commission. Italy has notified partial transposition.
91. [2006] O.J. L363. The Directive has been transposed into both countries legal systems.
92. Within the scope of the codification process, the Commission submitted a proposal for a new first directive on 30 Jan. 2008 to replace the previous texts, while preserving the substance, by only making the necessary amendments for codification.

The first group of articles contains rules on disclosure of documents by companies. Article 2 specifies the instruments and data of which Member States are required to ensure compulsory disclosure, and the following articles specify the manners in which disclosure must be so ensured, the persons by whom the disclosure formalities are to be carried out, and the penalties to be applied in case of failure to comply with any of the obligations laid down in the directive.

The provisions in second group govern certain actions carried out in a company's name and the provisions protecting third parties and ensuring the validity of the obligations entered into by the company.

Yet other articles provided for the nullity of the company, specifying the possible causes of invalidity of the instrument of constitution, while ascribing effects as mere grounds for dissolution to the causes of nullity when these are pleaded and established in a court of law.

Some interesting peculiarities are to be found in the rules on nullity of mergers under the Third Directive of 9 October 1978. First, as is the case with the rules of Italian law, nullity must be ordered in a court judgment. Secondly, mergers may be declared void only if there has been no judicial or administrative preventive supervision of their legality, or if they have not been drawn up and certified in due legal form, or if it is shown that the decision of the general meeting is void or voidable under national law. Dictated by obvious reasons of legal certainty is the provision according to which 'nullification proceedings may not be initiated more than *six months* after the date on which the merger becomes effective as against the person alleging nullity or if the situation has been rectified'. In fact, 'where it is possible to remedy a defect liable to render a merger void, the competent court shall grant the companies involved a period of time within which to rectify the situation' – clearly with a view to promoting mergers generally.

It should be noted that approval of the draft terms of merger makes the merger finally effective and its validity cannot be challenged in whatever form.

The Second Directive (of 13 December 1976) provided for the coordination of safeguards which, for the protection of the interests of members and others, are required by Member States of companies within the meaning of the second paragraph of Article 58(2) of the Treaty (Article 48(2) EC), in respect of the formation of public limited liability companies and the maintenance and alteration of their capital, with a view to making such safeguards equivalent. The Second Directive was later amended by Council Directive No 92/101/EEC of 23 November 1992.[93]

It was implemented in Italy by The President of the Republic Decree No 30 of 10 February 1986, after the ECJ had, in its judgment of 12 October 1982, Case 136/81,

93. The Second Directive No. 77/91 is in [1977] O.J. L26, p. 1: Directive No. 92/101 of 23 Nov. 1992 amending the Second Directive is in [1992] O.J. L347, p. 64. For the Second Directive, see, in particular: Iannuzzi, 'Osservazioni nel progetto di seconda direttiva in tema di armonizzazione del diritto societario' [1971] Riv. società, p. 636 f.; Ferri, 'La seconda direttiva comunitaria in materia di società' [1977] Riv. dir. comm. I, p. 58 f.; Houin, 'Droit des sociétés' [1978] Rev. tr. dr. eur., p. 728 f.; Schmitthoff, 'The Second EEC Directive and Company Law' [1978] CMLR, p. 43 f. See also an extensive analysis of the problems that have arisen from this directive in: *La seconda direttiva CEE in materia societaria*, Buttaro & Patroni Griffi, Eds (Milan, 1984). See *Commission* v *Italian Republic* [1982] ECR, 3547.

declared that the Republic of Italy had failed to implement the directive by the original deadline of 16 December 1978.[94] Directive No 92/101 was finally transposed into the Italian system under Legislative Decree No 315 of 2 May 1994.[95]

Within the framework of the Commission's codification efforts, this directive was superseded by Directive 2006/68/EC of the European Parliament and the Council of 6 September 2006,[96] on the same matter, with 15 April 2008 as the transposition deadline.[97]

The Second Directive is solely concerned with *public limited liability companies* or *share companies* and provides for major aspects of such companies' corporate lives. Firstly, it has required Italy and other Member States to raise the amount of minimum capital to be subscribed at incorporation.

Secondly, as regards increases in subscribed capital, it has raised to five years the period during which a company's duly empowered body may resolve capital increases one or more times by issuing common shares.

New provisions were introduced to govern pre-emptive rights, payment of dividends and the acquisition of own shares.

As indicated above, even though the Second Council Directive on company law is only concerned, pursuant to Article 1, with companies limited by shares, the Italian implementation rules, because of reference being made to several rules governing '*società per azioni*', also concern *società in accomandita per azioni* (partnerships limited by shares) and *società a responsabilità limitata* (private limited liability companies).[98]

Among the Directives regulating companies' corporate lives in their general and structural aspects, the following instruments should also be considered: the Fifth Directive, still at the proposal stage, in the text last amended of 20 November 1991, on *the structure of sociétés anonymes and the powers and obligations of their organs*,[99] and the Twelfth Directive No 89/66//EEC of 21 December 1989 on *single-member private limited-liability companies.*[100]

The former was brought forward as a proposal of the Commission to the Council as far back as 1972. Later on, in 1983, a new proposal was submitted

94. See *Commission* v *Italy* [1982] ECR, 3547.
95. For this decree, see Sbisà, 'La (mancata) attuazione della direttiva 92/101/CEE in tema di azioni proprie' [1994] Riv. soc. 4, p. 870.
96. [2006] O.J. L64.
97. As for Belgium, Cyprus, Spain, Italy, Luxembourg, Poland, Portugal, Rumania and Slovenia, the Commission has received no notification. Latvia and Malta have transmitted partial notification. The remaining States have transmitted notifications which are being examined by the Commission.
98. It is appropriate to point out that The President of the Republic Decree No. 30 of 10 Feb. 1986 – as the original decree implementing the Second Directive – was implicitly superseded by Legislative Decree No. 6/2003.
99. The text of the initial proposal for a fifth directive is in [1972] O.J. C131, p. 49, and the text of the first amended proposal of 19 Aug. 1983 (printed opposite to the initial text) is in [1983] O.J. C240, p. 2. The texts of the subsequent amended proposals are in [1991] O.J. C7 p. 4, as to the second, and in [1991] O.J. C321, p. 9, as to the third proposal.
100. [1989] O.J. L395, p. 40. On this Directive, see: Iudica, 'CEE e società impersonali: una proposta in discussione' [1988] Corr. giur., p. 665 f.; Id., 'La direttiva CEE sulla "società a responsabilità limitata con un unico socio" ' [1988]Riv. società, p. 814 f.

after being amended in light of the European Economic and Social Committee's and of the European Parliament's opinions.[101]

The purpose of the Fifth Directive is to make the rules relating to the structure of public limited companies and to employee participation in their decision-making bodies equivalent throughout the Community.

According to the original proposal, employees' rights were to be safeguarded through a two-tier structure consisting of a board of management and a supervisory body in appointing which workers were to participate with a view to a form of joint management based on the German model (*Mitbestimmung*).[102]

The amended proposal that followed still provided for the Member States' discretion to allow companies to choose between the two-tier, German-type system and the conventional, single-body system. but the manners in which workers were to participate in a company's board of management were specified in more details.

It should be observed that the *optional provision* for a single-tier governance system is one of the major innovations in the amended proposal. Yet, the goal was attained only in part, since the executive members of the board of management have been separated from those with merely supervisory responsibilities, and different tasks have been assigned to the two different groups. Thus, the single-tier model appears to be, even in the amended proposal, quite similar to the *monistic* model already introduced in Italian law by Legislative Decree No 6 of 17 January 2003, as amended, relating to the reform of company law effective as from 1 January 2004.

From a comparison with Italy's latest provisions of law, it seems that the '*traditional*' model has been disregarded in the proposal, even as it is still the one most commonly used in Italian corporate practice, even as far listed companies are concerned. That is why it would politically advisable for the Italian government's representatives in Brussels to insist in seeking the extension of the existing *scope for option* to the third model – the traditional one, in fact.

The Twelfth Directive No 89/667/EEC on *single-member private limited-liability companies*, as approved by the Council on 21 December 1989 and amended

101. About the proposal for a fifth directive, see chiefly: Conlon, 'Industrial Democracy and E.E.C. Company Law: A Review of Draft 5th Directive' [1975] Int. Comp. Law Quart., p. 348 f.; Bonell, 'Democrazia industriale e diritto societario nella legislazione comunitaria' [1982] Giur. comm. I, p. 369 f.; Visentini, 'Contro la proposta di quinta direttiva comunitaria; e ancora contro la "cogestione" ' [1982] Riv. società, p. 116 f.; Marziale, 'La proposta di V direttiva CEE sull'armonizzazione del diritto delle società: il fondamento giuridico e l'impatto sull'ordinamento italiano' [1985] Le società, pag. 121 f.; Covelli, 'L'organo amministrativo della S.p.a. nella proposta di V direttiva CEE', *ibid.*, p. 124 s.; Foglia, 'La partecipazione dei lavoratori alla gestione della società nella proposta di V direttiva CEE', *ibid.*, p. 129 f.; Rordorf, 'L'assemblea: funzionamento', *ibid.*, p. 143 f.; Landolfi, 'L'impugnazione delle delibere assembleari', *ibid.*, p. 152 f.; Salafia, 'La revisione dei conti nella proposta di V direttiva CEE', *ibid.*, p. 157 f.; Esteban Velasco, 'La estructura de las sociedades anonimas en el Derecho Comunitario (El proyecto modificado de quinta Directiva)', in *Tratado de Derecho Comunitario Europeo*, cit., p. 111 f.; Dine, 'Implications for the United Kingdom of the EC 5th Directive' [1989] Int. Comp. Law Quart., p. 547 f.
102. For this issue, which was approached in similar terms in the Statute for a European company, see Marletta, *La cogestione delle imprese nella CEE* (Naples, 1981).

by Council Directive 2006/99/EC of 20 November 2006,[103] serves the need to help small and medium-sized companies in using corporate techniques to arrange for separate assets intended for business operations as contrasted with the owner's personal assets. A fair assumption is that, under this approach – as was the case in France through the introduction of the *enterprise unipersonelle à responsabilité limitée* – the exceedingly high number of companies fictitiously held by several owners can be cut substantially.[104]

Underlying the Twelfth Directive is the Commission's and the Council's belief that it is important to provide 'a legal instrument allowing the *limitation of liability of the individual entrepreneur* throughout the Community, without prejudice to the laws of the Member States which, in exceptional circumstances, require that entrepreneur to be liable for the obligations of his undertaking' (fifth recital).

Precisely in furtherance of this primary principle, Article 7 states that:

> A Member State need not allow the formation of single-member companies where its legislation provides that an *individual entrepreneur* may set up an undertaking the liability of which is limited to a sum devoted to a stated activity . . .

so long as safeguards are laid down for such single-member undertakings which are equivalent to those imposed by the Twelfth Directive.

Therefore, the matter is so touchy that it requires national legislators to take a wary approach to the determination of the necessary grounds and limits for a single-member undertaking to be accorded limited liability.

In general terms, albeit to a temporary extent, pending coordination of national laws relating to groups, the Twelfth Directive allows Member States to:

> lay down certain 'special provisions and penalties' for cases where a natural person is the sole member of several companies or where a single-member company or any other legal person is the sole member of a company (*Sixth Whereas and Article 2(2)*).

Further, Member States may, 'in specific cases':

> lay down restrictions on the use of single-member companies or remove the limits on the liabilities of sole members (*Sixth Whereas*).

In my view, this power has been provided to allow single members 'to ensure that the subscribed capital is paid' (last sentence of the sixth Whereas) and to meet the obligations to disclose the holding by a single shareholder of all of the company's shares and the identity of the single member, both of which data must be entered into a register accessible to the public (seventh Whereas and Article 3), in addition to the duty to record information in writing about both any decisions taken by the

---

103. [2006] O.J. L363, p. 137.
104. About the French law, Act No. 85-697 of 11 Jul. 1985 (J.D., 12 Juillet 1985, p. 786 f.), see Flores-Mestre, 'L'entreprise unipersonelle à responsabilité limitée' [1986] Rev. Sociétés, p. 17 f.

sole member in his capacity as general meeting (eight Whereas and Article 4) and any contracts between a sole member and his company as represented by him, subject to Member States' discretion not to provide the latter obligation insofar as such contracts do not relate to current operations concluded under normal conditions (last Whereas and Article 5).

A private limited liability company may be a 'single-member' company either *at the time of its formation* or at any time thereafter (sixth Whereas and Article 2(1)).

The crowning provision is Article 6, pursuant to which:

> Where a Member State allows single-member companies as defined by Article 2(1) in the case of public limited companies as well, this Directive shall apply.

All in all, these rules have been transposed into the Italian body of laws quite correctly, even though the Italian legislator endeavoured to implement the most 'protective' provisions of the European system for the benefits of the undertakings concerned. For paragraph Article 2462(2) of the Italian Civil Code, under the heading '*Liability*', requires that:

> In case the company becomes insolvent, the single member shall have unlimited liability for the obligations the company undertook in the period during which all the shares were held by that single member insofar as capital was not contributed in accordance with Article 2464 or until the disclosures duties under Article 2470 are performed.

In this connection, it should preliminarily be noted that the Italian law-makers have used the discretion under the sixth Whereas of the Twelfth Directive to provide for unlimited liability as a penalty in 'specific cases', i.e. in case the obligation to pay contributions to equity in full or any disclosure obligations have not been performed under Article 2464 and Article 2470, respectively, of the Civil Code.

Moreover, the first implementation instrument (Legislative Decree No 88 of 1993)[105] was later suitably amended by abolishing the provision that excluded natural persons from the benefit of limited liability where a private individual was the sole shareholder of more than one limited company, thereby conforming to the rules already introduced in the French and Belgian laws at the time of transposing Directive No 89/667.

In general terms, the Italian implementation act has also taken into account a major provision newly introduced in the Italian legal system following the transposition of both Directive No 89/667 and of Directive No 82/891 on the 'division' of public limited companies (the Sixth Directive), and so – as indicated elsewhere in this book[106] – any company can now be formed without executing the contractual

105. For a more extensive examination of the issues arising from the first instrument implementing the Twelfth Directive in the Italian company law system, see: Iudica, 'Società di comodo' [1988] Quadrimestre I, p. 147 f., especially p. 156; Mosco, 'La dodicesima direttiva CEE sulle società unipersonali a responsabilità limitata' [1991] Giur. comm., p. 30 f.; Spolidoro, 'La legge sulla s.r.l. unipersonale' [1993] Riv. società, p. 97 f.; and Angelici, 'Società unipersonali: l'esperienza comparatistica' [1993] Le società, p. 893 f.

106. See above, Chapter I of this book.

instrument which must be entered into when a plurality of members join to form a company.

In this connection, the simplest law-making technique was used in wording out Article 1 of Legislative Decree No 88 of 1993, to the effect that, under Article 1, the heading '*Notion*' of Article 2247 of the Civil Code, which conveyed the idea of exclusive applicability, was replaced with '*Company Contract*', which restricts the scope of application to the (general) case of a company formed by contract, thereby implying that a company can also be formed by using different devices.

As for the necessary amendments to Article 2250 of the Civil Code relating to the disclosure obligations of single-member private limited liability companies, one last paragraph has been added, paragraph 4, which requires each such company to disclose its status as a single-member private limited company in its acts and letterheads.

I would be inclined to include the uniform rules on the *drawing-up of annual accounts* and *consolidated accounts* among the provisions relating to a company's structure. I am obviously referring to the Fourth and Seventh Directives. The latter is discussed at section 9 of this Chapter 2, which covers the work still in progress at Community level on the rules on groups of companies. At this time, let me briefly expand on the *Fourth Directive*.[107]

107. See the Fourth Council Directive 78/660/EEC of 25 Jul. 1978 on the annual accounts of certain types of companies [1978] O.J. L222, p. 11. The directive was originally implemented by all Member States, and it was amended by a number of later directives. Last came Directive 2006/43/EC of the European Parliament and of the Council of 17 May 2006 [2006] O.J. L157, the transposition deadline of which expired on 29 Jun. 2008. At the time of writing, it has only been implemented by Belgium, Germany, Latvia, Portugal, the Czech Republic and Slovakia. For the Fourth Directive, see chiefly Clayton & Vallois, 'The fourth company law directive on the annual accounts of limited liability companies' [1978] Droit pr. comm. int., p. 405; Bernard, 'Les incidentes de la 4ème directive CEE sur la reddition des comptes au Luxembourg' [1979] Journ. U.E.C., p. 334; Kaminski, 'Nouvelles prescriptions à la reddition, à la révision et à la pubblication des comptes de clôture annuels des sociétés de capitaux dans la C.E., selon la 4ème directive de la CEE', [1979] *ibid.*, p. 358; Knobbe Kuek, 'Die vierte gesellschaftsrechtliche EG- Richtlinie' [1979] Europarecht, p. 312; Barbaso, 'Les options dans la quatrième directive' [1980] Journ. U.E.C., p. 195; Id., 'Presupposti obiettivi, sviluppi delle direttive comunitarie sui conti annuali delle società' [1979] Dir. com. scambi internaz., p. 733 f.; Bloch, 'Les incidences de la quatrième directive C.E. relative à la presentation et l'établissement des comptes annuels des sociétés de capitaux sur la legislation comptable en Belgique' [1980] Journ. U.E.C., p. 34; Rutteman, 'Mise en application de la quatrième directive en Royame Uni' [1980] *ibid.*, p. 33; Van Hulle, 'The EEC Accounting Directives in Perspective: Problems of Harmonization' [1981] Com. Market Law Rev., p. 121; Irace, 'La quarta direttiva comunitaria in materia di bilanci' [1980] Giur. comm. I, p. 600 f.; Superti Furga, 'L'allegato e la relazione sulla gestione nella IV direttiva CEE' [1980] *ibid.*, p. 662 f.; Cera, 'Quarta direttiva CEE sui conti annuali e adeguamento della normativa italiana' [1980] Riv. società, p. 1148 f.; Pontani, *Il bilancio delle società di capitali nella quarta direttiva CEE* (Milan, 1981), p. 45 f.; Jaeger, 'La "clausola generale" del bilancio nella direttiva comunitaria e nel diritto italiano' [1984] Giur. comm. I, p. 471 f.; Id., 'Problemi tipici del bilancio d'esercizio (nell'evoluzione della giurisprudenza e nella prospettiva dell'attuazione della quarta direttiva CEE)' [1986] Giur. comm. I, p. 984 f.; Pivato, ' "Quadro fedele" e "speciali ragioni" con riferimento ai prospetti di bilancio e alla relazione degli amministratori' [1984] Riv. dott. Comm., p. 603 f.;

The principle that, in the Fourth Directive, underlies the rules on limited companies' annual accounts – comprising a balance sheet, a profit and loss account and the notes on the accounts, which constitute a composite whole – is that such documents must be drawn up 'clearly' and give a '*true and fair view*' of the company's assets, liabilities, financial position and profit or loss.

An added obligation is that 'additional information must be given [. . .] where the application of the provisions of this Directive would not be sufficient to give *a true and fair view* within the meaning of paragraph 3'. Further, 'where, in exceptional cases, the application of a provision of this Directive is incompatible with the obligation laid down in paragraph 3, that provision must be departed from in order to give a *true and fair view*', and 'any such departure must be disclosed in the notes on the accounts together with an explanation of the reasons for it and a statement of its effect on the assets, liabilities, financial position and profit or loss. The Member States *may define the exceptional cases in question* and lay down the relevant *special rules*'.

Plainly enough, although the French phrase '*image fidèle*' has been borrowed in using the words '*quadro fedele*' in Italian, both phrases match the IAS notion of '*true and fair value*' in English.[108,109]

Salafia, 'La IV direttiva CEE e gli effetti dell'inflazione sui bilanci della società di capitali' [1985] Le società, p. 8 f.; Ventura, 'IV direttiva CEE: il bilancio nell'inflazione e il quadro fedele' [1985] Riv. dott. comm., p. 435 f.; Fadda, 'Osservazioni sulle norme generali contenute nella IV direttiva della CEE e nelle relative leggi di attuazione' [1986] *ibid.*, p. 579 f.

108. Jaeger, 'La "clausola generale" del bilancio', cit., p. 474 f., points out that the present wording of the directive, reflecting the true and fair view standard, was first contained in the amended proposal of 1974, after the United Kingdom had acceded to the Community, and that the French, German and Italian corresponding phrases are a mere translation of that English phrase. Jaeger has also made a close survey of the contents and reach of this standard in English law as a 'general clause' – open to discretion as is customary in Common Law systems – which has overriding force, but undetermined contents. Thus, compliance with generally accepted accounting principles is just *prima facie* evidence of compliance with the true and fair view rule (*op.cit.*, p. 475 f.). Hence, the difficulties in adjusting a Civil Law system as the Italian one to the Community's body of rules in the matter, although such difficulties are somewhat mitigated by the fact that, under the scholarly approach far prevailing in Italy, the notion of '*chiarezza e precisione*' (clarity and accuracy) now caught by Article 2423(2) of the Italian Civil Code, seems already to be a clause for general application, as a result of which there would already be an essential closeness of meaning of '*chiarezza e precisione*' with '*quadro fedele*'. See Jaeger, 'La "clausola generale" del bilancio', p. 482 f., and also p. 486 f., where he specifies that a correct Italian translation of the English adjective 'true' is '*vero*' or '*veritiero*', not '*fedele*'. As for the scholarly debate triggered by the first implementation in Italy of the '*quadro fedele*' principle in Article 9 of Act No. 72 of 19 Mar. 1983 (the so-called 'Visentini-*bis* Act'), see also: Minervini, 'Piccola cronaca di due emendamenti legislative' [1983] Riv. società, p. 43 f., a p. 52; and Colombo, 'L'art. 9 legge 19 marzo 1983: una deroga da determinare', *ibid.*, p. 56 s., p. 70. About the same topic, see also: Ferri, 'Le speciali ragioni secondo l'art. 9 della legge n. 72 del 1983', *ibid.*, p. 79 s.; Portale, 'Le "speciali ragioni" rinnovate: dagli "strappi" interpretativi alle "ricuciture" normative', *ibid.*, p. 85 f., and Casella, 'Quadro fedele', contabili e giuristi, *ibid.*, p. 103 f.

109. The Italian instrument for transposition of the Fourth Directive is Legislative Decree No. 127 of 9 Apr. 1991, published in the Official Journal of the Italian Republic No. 90 of 17 Apr. 1991, as supplemented by Article 12 of Legislative Decree No. 1 of 7 Jan. 1995, adding a new paragraph 4-*bis* (concerning value adjustments) to Article 31 of Law Decree No. 127/91, and

A specific instrument, Directive No 86/635 of 8 December 1986, was issued by the Council to regulate the annual accounts and consolidated accounts of banks and other financial institutions.[110] This directive was subsequently amended by Directives No 2001/65/EC, No 2003/EC and No 2006/45/EC.[111]

Also, on 19 December 1991, the Council adopted Directive No 91/674 on the annual accounts and consolidated accounts of insurance undertakings.[112]

The entire regulatory financial accounting and reporting framework was later significantly altered through the adoption of the International Accounting Standards (IAS) under Regulation (EC) No 1606 of 19 July 2002 applicable to all companies listed in regulated markets within the European Union, effective from 1 January 2005.[113]

8. MERGERS OF COMPANIES GOVERNED BY THE LAWS OF DIFFERENT MEMBER STATES

As early as 1 December 1965, the Commission, acting on a proposal from the then Commissioner for Competition, Mr van der Groeben,[114] sent the governments of the Member States a communication providing an extensive, in-depth survey of certain issues relating to the need to promote corporate mergers within the common market, in terms of economic policy, company law, tax law and the legislation on agreements between undertakings.[115] According to the Commission, the creation of

---

repealing indent *o-bis* in Article 38(1) of the same law decree. On this topic, see Salafia, 'Caratteri generali del bilancio e principi di redazione' [1991] Le società, p. 1611 f.; Fortunato, 'Il recepimento della IV direttiva CEE nell'ordinamento italiano' [1992] Riv. società, p. 889, and Viganó, Ed., *Il recepimento della IV direttiva CEE in alcuni paesi europei* (Milan, 1993). Of the many options afforded by the Fourth Directive to the Member States, Article 1(2) provides that, 'pending subsequent coordination, the Member States need not apply the provisions of this Directive to banks and other financial institutions or to insurance companies', and Article 5(1) allows the Member States to prescribe special layouts for the annual accounts of investment companies and of financial holding companies 'provided that these layouts give a view of these companies equivalent to that provided for in Article 2(3)', i.e. a '*quadro fedele*'.

110. [1986] O.J. L372, p. 1.
111. [1986] O.J. L224, p. 1.
112. [1991] O.J. L374, p. 7. This directive was amended by Directives 2003/51/EC and 2006/46/EC, *ibid.*
113. [2002] O.J. L243, p. 1, as amended by Regulation (EC) No. 297/2008 of 11 Mar. 2008, in [2008] O.J. L97, p. 62.
114. See the speech delivered by von der Groeben on 16 Jun. 1965 to the European Parliament on *Competition policy as part of the economic policy in the Common Market*, Doc. 8152/2/VI/1965/5.
115. The document, commonly known as *Memorandum on Mergers*, is also published in [1966] Riv. società, p. 1182 f. On the subject, see Iannuzzi, 'Spunti di riflessione per il legislatore societario italiano nel memorandum della Comunità europea sulle concentrazioni' [1966] Riv. soc., p. 1023 f., and in La riforma delle società di capitali in Italia, Studi e dibattiti, Atti del convegno internazionale di studio sulla riforma della società per azioni, Fenghi & Santa Maria, Eds, cit., vol. II, p. 879 f.

large enterprises was necessary for them to adapt to the new dimension of the common market and to the amount of competition from third countries' large corporations.[116]

Accordingly, the Commission emphasized *mergers* along with such merely economic devices for business concentration as acquisition of shareholdings, the administrative combination of companies through managers common to different undertakings or the amalgamation of enterprises under special agreements (the so-called *Organschaftsverträge* in German law), whereby the management of one firm's business is entrusted with another firm. Thus, merger was identified as a device that, unlike the others, was ideally suited to achieve the amalgamation of several companies into one legal as well as economic unit.[117]

Yet, the domestic laws of the Community's Member States were hardly capable to promote mergers of companies subject to different national legislations, the so-called 'international mergers', precisely because of the existing legal barriers, whether under substantive or even tax laws.[118]

While refraining from taking a position on the many issues of conflict of laws arising in connection with 'international mergers', let me just observe, as to the method, that such issues can only be approached on a case-by-case basis, and any solutions thereto may be found to differ from one another depending on the legal system concerned and on the extent to which the companies being merged are linked to that system. In particular, as observed above, the issues of conflict of laws arising in connection with the acquiree are not dissimilar, in principle, from the problems to be dealt with when a company's seat is moved from one to another State within the Community.[119]

In general, more barriers to 'international mergers' were raised in the past because of differences between company laws, in particular between the rules applicable to mergers in different legal systems or in connection with the different

116. In this sense, see *Memorandum on Mergers*, cit., pp. 1182 and 1183. This need was again stressed in *Rapporto del gruppo di lavoro intergovernativo per la società commerciale europea*, published in [1967] Riv. società, p. 699 f., p. 700 f., preceded by an exhaustive introductory note by De Gennaro, 'Studi per la creazione della società commerciale "europea"', *ibid.*, p. 689 f., and in the *Memorandum* from the Commission to the Council, headed '*Politica industriale della Comunità*' (Bruxelles, 1970). Moreover, many have stressed the significance of concentrations of undertakings (notably mergers) at a Community level as a indispensable tool for the thorough achievement of European Economic integration, thanks to its intrinsic capability to get past national barriers. In this latter sense, see the reports by Lecourt, *Concentrations et fusions, facteurs d'intégration*, and by Marchal, 'Nécéssité économique des concentrations et fusions', in *Atti del Colloquio di Parigi* sulle *Coopérations, concentrations, fusions d'entreprises dans la Cee*, published in [1968] Rev. Marché Com., p. 6 s., p. 10, and p. 25 f., and p. 44 f, respectively. See also below, Chapter IV and V of this book.

117. See again *Memorandum on Mergers*, cit. p. 1190 f., and, in the same sense, the subsequent *Memorandum de la Commission de la Communauté européenne sur la création d'une société commerciale européenne* [1966] Riv. società, p. 1095 f., especially p. 1105.

118. In this respect, see Santa Maria, 'La fusione di società soggette a leggi regolatrici diverse nel progetto preliminare di convenzione della Comunità economica europea' [1968] Riv. società, p. 581 f.

119. Please, refer to the considerations offered in Chapter I of this volume, especially in Section 12.

tax treatment of mergers depending on the different tax laws in force in each State.[120]

Precisely tax issues, notwithstanding the general reservation of national jurisdiction over tax matters, have been dealt with by Directive No 90/434/EEC, and tax regulatory differences have largely been overcome by the adoption of both the Third Directive and the Regulation establishing the European Commercial Company.[121]

Nonetheless, the matter was unsuccessfully approached in an attempt to implement Article 293 EC, third indent (former Article 220), and successfully later on, with a specific directive in the company law harmonization process.

For a committee of national experts assisted by the Community's staff responsible for the matter had already, as early as 1967, developed a preliminary draft convention on 'cross-border mergers' in furtherance of Article 220, third indent, of the Treaty of Rome. The writers of such preliminary draft, in addition to laying down the principle of the validity of mergers between companies governed by the laws of different States and of the recognition thereof by the other contracting States,[122] addressed their work to a far more ambitious solution. With a view to removing the obstacles arising from different national rules on mergers with foreign companies in force in different Member States,[123] they prepared a highly detailed text in an attempt to provide uniform rules on cross-border mergers throughout the Community.

---

120. In Italian literature, with regard to the Code of Commerce previously in force, see: Diena, *Trattato di diritto commerciale internazionale, ossia il diritto internazionale privato commerciale*, vol. 1 (Florence, 1900), p. 379 f.; and Ferri, *La fusione delle società commerciali* (Rome, 1936), p. 97 f. With regard to the rules currently in force, see: Guerra, 'Les fusions des sociétés en droit italien', in *Rapports au Colloque international de droit européen* (Bruxelles, 1962), p. 95 f., p. 99, and in Ann. dir. comp. studi legislat., 3ª serie, vol.36, p. 51 f.; and Santagata, *La fusione tra società* (Naples, 1964), p. 9, fn. 8. In foreign literature, see, in the same sense, Spindler, *Die Wanderungengewerblicher Korperschaften von Staat zu Staat* (Berlin, 1932), p. 70 f.; Beitzke, 'Fusion von Gesellschaft ìber die Grenze?' [1961] Aussenwirtschaftsdients des Betriebs-Beraters, p. 288 f. See also: the comparative law study by Beitzke, 'Les conflits de lois en matière de fusion de sociétés (droit communautaire et droit international privé)' [1967] Rev. crit. dr. int. privé, p. 1 f.; my article, 'La fusione di società soggette a leggi regolatrici diverse nel progetto preliminare di Convenzione della Comunità economica europea' [1968] Riv. società, p. 581 f.; Luzzatto, 'La Convenzione CEE sulla fusione delle società. Il diritto delle società', cit., 1975, p. 101 f.; and Mascardi, 'La fusione di società nel diritto comunitario', cit., p. 1767 f.
121. See below, Section 10 of this Chapter II.
122. Even narrower was the scope of The Hague Convention of 1 Jun. 1956 concerning the recognition of the legal personality of foreign companies, associations and institutions. For Article 4(2) of this Convention requires: 'La fusion d'une société, d'une association, ou d'une fondation qui a acquis la personnalité dans un des Etats contractants, avec une société, une association ou une fondation qui a acquis la personnalité dans un autre Etat contractant, sera reconnue dans tous les Etats contractants, au cas où elle est reconnue dans les Etats intéressés'. This Convention has not yet taken effect, lacking the minimum number of five ratifications required by Article 11 of this instrument.
123. On this, see Santa Maria, 'La fusioni di società soggette a leggi regolatrici diverse', cit., p. 582 f. The preliminary draft Convention and related *Note esplicative*, are published, *ibid.*, p. 737 f.

Later on, in 1973, a draft convention on the international merger of *sociétés anonymes* (share companies) was submitted by the Commission to the Council to amend the previous one.[124] In the event, this draft convention was withdrawn and replaced with the proposal for a Tenth Council Directive concerning *'cross-border mergers' of public limited companies* (share companies).[125]

In this content, a directive is by far the most preferable instrument, not only because it overcomes the problems arising from some Member States' attitude to the Brussels Convention of 29 February 1968, on the recognition of companies and other legal persons, which I have mentioned elsewhere in this book,[126] but also because the entire matter can thereby be regulated by mere references to the rules of the Third Directive concerning mergers of public limited liability companies wherever any such reference can be made.

As a result, under the final text of Directive No 2005/56/EC on 'cross-border mergers' of limited liability companies, as adopted by the European Parliament and the Council on 26 October 2005,[127] any domestic or international merger operation requires the following procedure to be conducted in consecutive steps:

(a) the preparation of common draft terms of merger;
(b) the approval of the common draft terms of merger by the administrative organs of each of the merging companies (in principle, the general meetings);
(c) the drawing-up of a report by the management or administrative organ of each of the merging companies;
(d) the drawing-up of an independent expert report for each merging company; and
(e) legal, judicial or administrative scrutiny prior to the merger, and the execution of the acts approving the merger in a *public instrument* for each merging company.

---

124. The draft and the related *Report* by Goldman are published in *EC Bullettin, Suppl. No 13/73.*
125. See COM(84)727, final, of 8 Jan. 1985. At page 2 of the explanatory memorandum accompanying the proposal for a tenth directive, the Commission observed: 'The major element in this new approach is the priority accorded by Community bodies to the need to facilitate and promore cooperation between undertakings operating in the Community. It had in fact become evidente, particularly in high-investment areas, that adequate means could usually only be found through a pooling of resources by several undertakings. More and more such cooperation involved undertakings which in the internal market were governed by the laws of different Member States'. The Commission added: '. . . cross-border mergers provided public limited companies which wish to do so with the legal means to take international cooperation ot its ultimate conclusion *with the aim of attaining the size and achieving the economies of scale necessary for them to take full advantage of the European economy and strengthen their ability to compete with large undertakings from non-member States*'. [*Emphasis added*]
126. See above, Chapter I of this book, especially Section 2.
127. [2005] O.J. L310, p. 1. The transposition deadline was 15 Dec. 2007. By that date, only fifteen Member States had notified the Commission to have implemented the directive in full; three had delivered a partial notification; and the remaining States, Italy among them, had not yet carried out the required formalities for transposition. On this, see Gurrado, 'Via libera alle fusioni transfrontaliere' [2006] Dir. comm. int., p. 353 f.

At the end of this procedure, the merger may be deemed effective, as of a specified date, against third parties, through appropriate disclosure formalities. It should be observed that both every preparatory operation, save for the common draft terms, and the disclosure formalities must be carried out separately by each merging company, in compliance with the law of the Member State to which it is subject, without the need for uniform rules in this respect.

Major changes from the rules concerning domestic mergers (under the Third Directive) are: the draft terms of the cross-border merger, which must be drawn up and certified as a public instrument 'if so required by the laws governing one or more of the merging companies', thereby giving priority to the law that requires the *greater formal severity* (Article 5(2)); the publication of the draft terms of merger, which cannot be done merely by mention, but requires far wider information and indications (Article 6); the provisions for *nullity*, pursuant to which a cross-border merger *may not be declared null and void* unless the law governing the merging company requires the merger to be annulled lacking a judicial and administrative scrutiny as to legality or lacking the requisite public instrument; and the *date* on which the cross-border merger *takes effect*, which must be determined under the law of the Member State to whose jurisdiction the company resulting from the cross-border merger is subject, provided that that date must be after the prescribed scrutiny and formalities have been carried out (Article 11).

Therefore, in each such case, the purpose of a *greater uniformity* than under the rules on domestic mergers is accomplished either by stating the applicable law or by adopting uniform substantive provisions under the Tenth Directive.

The use of references to conflict of laws through solutions similar to those already provided for in the preliminary draft convention on cross-border mergers can only, also in respect of companies participating in cross-border mergers, emphasize the importance of the application of the uniform standards of private international law that emerge from the ECJ's case-law in relation to Article 48(1) EC.[128]

On 23 July 1990, in the belief that:

> [M]ergers, divisions, transfers of assets and exchanges of shares concerning companies of different Member States may be necessary in order to create within the Community conditions analogous to those of an internal market and in order thus to ensure the establishment and effective functioning of the common market (*first Whereas*),

the Council, pursuant to Article 100 of the Treaty, adopted Directive No 90/434 on the common system of taxation applicable to mergers, divisions, transfers of assets and exchanges of shares concerning companies of different Member States.[129]

---

128. See above, Chapter I of this book, especially Section 12 f.
129. [1990] O.J. L225, p.1, as amended by Directives 2005/19/EC and 2006/98/EC. Directive No. 90/434/EEC was implemented in Italy under Legislative Decree No. 544 of 30 Dec. 1992 (published in the Official Journal of the Italian Republic No. 9, 13 Jan. 1993). By the draft directive submitted to the Council on 26 Jul. 1993 ([1993] O.J. C225, p. 3) designed to amend

This directive was intended to achieve a dual purpose. On the one hand, it was deemed necessary to introduce, with respect to such operations, tax rules which were neutral from the point of view of competition, in order to allow enterprises to adapt to the requirements of the common market, to increase their productivity and to improve their competitive strength at the international level, by removing any tax provisions which, in individual Member States, lacking the directive, worked to the disadvantage of such international operations, in comparison with those concerning companies of the same Member State (last sentence of the first Whereas, second Whereas, and Titles II, III and IV of the directive).

On the other hand, it was deemed necessary to allow Member States the possibility of refusing the 'benefit' of applying the directive where the merger, division, transfer of assets or exchange of shares operation has as its objective tax evasion or avoidance or results in a company, whether or not it participates in the operation, no longer fulfilling the conditions required for the representation of employees in company organs (last Whereas and Title V of the directive).[130]

9. THE DRAFT DIRECTIVE ON GROUPS OF UNDERTAKINGS AND THE SEVENTH DIRECTIVE ON CONSOLIDATED ACCOUNTS

In the process for the progressive establishment of the internal market as 'an area without internal frontiers in which the free movement of goods, persons, services and capital is ensured', a prominent position was assigned to the determination of uniform rules governing groups of undertakings. It was so not only because such rules would essentially promote European integration, but also because they would fill a gap still existing in many Member State's legal systems.

The Commission's 'White Paper',[131] which put forward in great detail all the aspects of an ambitious plan to build a 'Europe without frontiers' by the end of 1992 – a plan which was approved by the Milan European Council of 28-29 June 1985 and later substantiated by the provisions of Article 14 EC – expressly referred to the advisability to put in place uniform rules on groups of companies. In this connection, it was stressed that, beside the need for ensuring transparency in intra-group relations, it was necessary to strike a balance between the interests of the group as a whole and the interests of its individual members, taking into account the interests of the subsidiaries' minority shareholders and creditors. In other words, a fair compromise was to be found between the majority shareholders'

Directive 90/434, the Commission primarily intended to expand the scope for application of the directive to every company with tax domicile in a Member State, irrespective of legal status, and further proposed to make the rule on holdings in the directive on mergers consistent with the rule of minimum shareholding in the parent-and-subsidiaries directive (No. 90/435), itself of 23 Jul. 1990, which is discussed in the section next following below.

130. See Gurrado, 'Via libera alle fusioni transfrontaliere', p. 364 f.

131. See COM (85) 310, final, of 14 Jun. 1985.

needs, as viewed from a group-wide angle, and the needs of the subsidiaries' minority owners, who are obviously interested in upholding the full autonomy (and profitability) of the companies in which they hold shares.

The importance of these issues has aptly been stressed by the Commission in the Report accompanying the latest draft directive in the matter, in which the Commission clarified that its paramount purpose was to remove the legal obstacles that appear, in the Member States' different systems, to prevent groups of undertakings from relying on the necessary scope for action they need to attain economic results. The proposed rules are also intended to fill gaps existing in domestic legislations and to provide corporate groups with a reliable legal basis, thereby ensuring protection to the interests at stake. The Commission further observed that reality had become so far removed from law that the legislation on limited liability companies had come to apply only to an *exceptional form*, i.e. companies operating solely under their own liability. This was an unsatisfactory situation both for the legislator and for the stakeholders, and the directive was just an *early effort to get the law closer to reality*.[132]

Nevertheless, the present text of the draft ninth directive is still as it was before the presentation of the Commission's White Paper and it has not yet found its way into a 'proposal' ready to be submitted by the Commission to the Council.[133]

On 23 July 1990, the Council adopted Directive 90/435/EEC on the common system of taxation applicable in the case of *parent companies and subsidiaries* of different Member States.[134]

---

132. See *Relazione* introducing the draft ninth directive [1987] Le società, p. 1309.

133. The last version of the draft proposal for a directive on groups of undertakings has been published in Italian, introduced by the Relazione [1985] Riv. società, pp. 1041 f. and 1071 f., and in [1987] Le società, pp. 1308 f. and 1326 f. For the Commission's draft ninth directive, see chiefly: Minervini, 'I gruppi di società nella Comunità economica europea. Problemi di diritto societario', in Il diritto delle società nella Comunità economica europea, cit., p. 22 f.; Lutter, 'Lo sviluppo del diritto dei gruppi in Europa' [1981] Riv. società, p. 654 f.; Jaeger, 'I gruppi fra diritto interno e prospettive comunitarie' [1981] Giur. comm. I, p. 916 f.; Id., 'Nozione di "gruppo" nel progetto di direttiva comunitaria e nell'ordinamento italiano', in *Il gruppo di società e il bilancio consolidato di gruppo* (Milan, 1983), p. 42 f.; Immenga, 'L'harmonisation du droit des groupes des sociétés. La proposition d'une directive de la Commission de la CEE' [1986] Giur. comm. I, p. 846 f.; Pavone La Rosa, 'Osservazioni sulla proposta di nona direttiva sui gruppi di società' [1986] Giur. comm. I, p. 831; Embid Irujo, 'Los grupos de sociedades en la Comunidad Economica Europea (Septima y novena Directivas)', in Tratado de Derecho Comunitario Europeo, cit., p. 73 f.; Barbaso, 'Il progetto di IX direttiva CEE' [1987] Le società, p. 1295 f.; Gambino, 'I gruppi in Italia alla luce del progetto di IX direttiva' [1987] Giur. comm., p. 5 f.; Pavone La Rosa, 'I gruppi di imprese nel diritto italiano' [1987] Le società, p. 1239 f.

134. [1990] O.J. L225, p. 6, as amended by Directives 2003/123/EC and 2006/98/EC. This directive was transposed into the Italian legal system under Legislative Decree No. 136 of 6 Mar. 1993 ([1993] GURI 107). A draft Council directive was submitted on 26 Jul. 1993 ([1993] O.J. C225, p. 5) to amend Directive 90/435, both by extending its scope to every company with tax domicile within the Community, regardless of legal status, and in relation to Article 4(1), with a view to abolishing double taxation on earnings distributed by a subsidiary to its parent company.

This directive, as well as the other also adopted on 23 July 1990 on mergers, divisions, transfers of assets or exchanges of shares, had Article 100 of the Treaty as its legal basis and its rationale in the consideration that:

> the grouping together of companies of different Member States may be necessary in order to create within the Community conditions analogous to those of an internal market and in order thus to ensure the establishment and effective functioning of the common market;

and in the belief that:

> such operations ought not to be hampered by restrictions, disadvantages or distortions arising in particular from the tax provisions of the Member States.

Accordingly:

> it is therefore necessary to introduce with respect to such grouping together of companies of different Member States, tax rules which are neutral from the point of view of competition, in order to allow enterprises to adapt to the requirements of the common market, to increase their productivity and to improve their competitive strength at the international level. (First Whereas).

Since such grouping together may result in the formation of groups of parent companies and subsidiaries, and the existing tax provisions which govern the relations between parent companies and subsidiaries of different Member States vary appreciably from one Member State to another and are generally less advantageous than those applicable to parent companies and subsidiaries of the same Member State, it was deemed:

> necessary to eliminate this disadvantage by the introduction of a common system in order to facilitate the grouping together of companies. (Second and third Whereases).

A logical complement to the Ninth Directive is the *Seventh Directive* No 83/349/ EEC, as adopted by the Council on 13 June 1983, on 'consolidated accounts' (or group accounts), which is patterned, at least as to the principles and methods of consolidation, after more the English than the German experience.[135]

In the process of consolidation of company directives, this Directive was amended first by Directive 2006/43/EC of the European Parliament and of the Council of 17 May 2006, then by Directive 2006/46/EC of the European Parliament and of the Council of 14 June 2006.[136]

---

135. See Bianchi, 'L' 'area di consolidamento' nella VII direttiva CEE nella prospettiva della sua attuazione in Italia' [1977] Riv. società, p. 1109 f., and p. 1123. The Seventh Directive was implemented in Italy under Legislative No. 127 of 9 Apr. 1991, published in the Official Journal of the Italiam Republic, *Suppl. Ord.* No. 90 of 17 Apr. 1991.

136. The former is in [2006] O.J. L157, p. 87, with transposition deadline 29 Jun. 2008; the latter is in [2006] O.J. L224, p. 1, with transposition deadline 5 Sep. 2008.

Still, the final version of the Seventh Directive was drawn up, probably because of the great delay in developing a proposal for a directive on groups, in such a way as to make it entirely independent of any other directive, thereby bringing about a radical innovation in legislative methods from both the proposal for a seventh directive of 1976 and the amended proposal of 1978.

In fact, the final text of the Seventh Directive appears, however, to be closely connected with the Fourth Directive (No 78/660) of 25 July 1978, which was intended to coordinate national legislations on limited companies' annual accounts.[137,138]

The need for consolidated accounts arises from the finding that the annual accounts of a company doing business, whether directly or indirectly, though controlling holdings in a number of other companies, are not suitable by themselves to provide an accurate view of the assets, liabilities and profit or loss of the 'group' of undertakings as a whole. It has aptly been observed[139] that, even if the parent's holdings in its subsidiaries were valued by the equity method, the parent's financial statements would still give just a partial, or even distorted, view of the group's financial position. Likewise, because of the business and financial relations between the parent and its subsidiaries or between subsidiaries, not even the annual accounts of individual subsidiaries would allow their shareholders or other parties to make an accurate evaluation of the group's overall shareholders' equity and profit or loss.

As a result, as indicated in the first recital of the Seventh Directive, 'consolidated accounts must be drawn up so that financial information concerning such bodies of undertakings may be conveyed to members and third parties', and 'national legislation governing consolidated accounts must therefore be

137. For this directive, see above, Section 7 of this Chapter II.
138. The Seventh Directive had been worked on for over ten years, from the preliminary draft of 1971 (Comm. XIX/533/71) – the relevant matter being formerly included in the draft fourth directive – to the preliminary draft of 1974 (Comm. XI/333/74) and to the Commission's first 'official' proposal of 4 May 1976 ([1976] O.J. C121, p. 2), as later amended on 14 Dec. 1978 ([1979] O.J. C14, 17 Jan. 1979, p. 2), following the adoption of the Fourth Directive, which is referred to in many parts of the directive under scrutiny. For this act, in its different versions, see essentially: Niessen, 'La proposition de septième directive concernant les comptes du groupe' [1981] Cah. dr. eur., p. 26 f.; Id., 'La proposta di settima direttiva sui conti di gruppo', in *Il gruppo di società ed il bilancio consolidato di gruppo. Direttive comunitarie e diritto nazionale*, cit., p. 28 f.; Gerini, 'Alcune considerazioni tecniche sulla proposta di settima direttiva', *ibid.*, p. 77 f.; Chiaraviglio, 'Derogabilità da parte degli Stati membri della proposta di settima direttiva del Consiglio della CEE', *ibid.*, p. 104 f.; Pevtehin, 'La proposition de septième directive concernant les comptes du groupe' [1981] Cah. dr. eur., p. 38 f.; Petite, 'The Conditions for Consolidation under the 7th Company Law Directive' [1984] Com. Market Law Rev., p. 81 f.; Provasoli, 'I bilanci consolidati dei gruppi di società: la VII direttiva CEE' [1984] Riv. dott. comm., p. 229 f.; Pennington, 'Consolidated Accounts: the Seventh Directive' [1984] The Comp. Lawyer, p. 66 f.; D'Alessandro, 'L'area di consolidamento dei bilanci secondo la settima direttiva CEE' [1985] Giur. comm. I, p. 365 f.; Salafia, 'La settima direttiva CEE sul bilancio consolidato' [1987] Foro it. IV, c. 235 f.; Di Sabato, 'Il bilancio consolidato di gruppo' [1987] Le società, p. 1258 f.
139. See Provasoli, 'Il bilancio consolidato e lo schema di legge per l'attuazione della VII direttiva comunitaria', in *La IV e la VII direttiva CEE nel progetto d'attuazione* (Milan, 1989), p. 207 f.

coordinated in order to achieve the objectives of comparability and equivalence in the information which companies must publish within the Community'.

The consolidation duty applies not only to a company governed by the national law of a Member State (the 'parent') which holds control, based on a majority of voting rights, over a 'subsidiary', but also to a company that holds such control on the basis of agreements, thus even if only relying on a minority holding which provides it with *de-facto* control.[140] This duty is also expected to be discharged by any subsidiary which is also the parent company of other companies.

The consolidated accounts must:

> *give a true and fair view* of the assets and liabilities, the financial position and the profit and loss of all the undertakings consolidated taken as a whole; [. . .] consolidation should in principle include all of those undertakings; [. . .] such consolidation requires the full incorporation of the assets and liabilities and of the income and expenditure of those undertakings and the separate disclosure of the interests of persons outwith such bodies; [and] however, the necessary corrections must be made to eliminate the effects of the financial relations between the undertakings consolidated. (Fifth Whereas).

Therefore, the interests consolidated accounts are intended to protect are the interests of the parent company's shareholders, of the subsidiaries' minority shareholders, and of the creditors of both types of company.

The Seventh Directive applies to limited liability companies and, therefore, as far as the Italian legal order is concerned, to *società per azioni, società in accomandita per azioni* and *società a responsabiltà limitata.*

10. THE ELEVENTH DIRECTIVE

On 21 December 1989, the Council adopted the Eleventh Directive No 89/666/EEC concerning disclosure requirements in respect of branches opened in a Member State by certain types of company governed by the law of another State.[141]

This directive has been implemented in every Member State of the European Union[142] and has not been amended since the date of its adoption. Its objectives are suitably specified in the seventh recital, as follows:

> to ensure the protection of persons who deal with companies through the intermediary of branches, measures in respect of disclosure are required in the Member State in which a branch is situated.

---

140. For the Community notion of 'de facto *control*' please refer, in particular, to Section 15 of Chapter III of this book.

141. [1989] O.J. L395, p. 36. About the Eleventh Directive, see: Benedettelli, 'Le direttive comunitarie sulla pubblicità delle "succursali"' [1990] Riv. dir. comm., p. 845; and Vismara, 'Prime applicazioni giurisprudenziali delle norme attuative dell'undicesima direttiva comunitaria in tema di società' [1995] Riv. dir. int. priv. proc., p. 87.

142. The Eleventh Directive was implemented in Italy under Legislative Decree No. 516 of 29 Dec. 1992.

Since, in certain respects, the economic and social influence of a branch may be comparable to that of a subsidiary company, there is public interest in disclosure of the company at the branch. It is also stated that, to effect such disclosure, it is necessary to make use of the procedure already instituted for companies with share capital within the Community.

The Eleventh Directive has been arranged into four sections. The first and second sections are concerned with branches of companies from other Member States and branches of companies from third countries, respectively. The third section deals with the indication of branches in the company's annual report, and the fourth contains transitional and final provisions.

As provided for in the first section, documents and particulars relating to a branch opened in a Member State by a company which is governed by the law of another Member State and to which Directive 68/151/EEC (the First Directive) applies must be disclosed pursuant to the law of the Member State of the branch, in accordance with Article 3 of that Directive (Article 1).

Under the second section, Article 7 requires that documents and particulars concerning a branch opened in a Member State by a company which is not governed by the law of a Member State but which is of a legal form comparable with the types of company to which the First Directive applies must be disclosed in accordance with the law of the Member State of the branch.

Pursuant to Article 11, the only one in the third section, the existence of branches of the company must be disclosed in the company's report on operations, this being a departure from the Fourth Directive on the annual accounts of certain types of companies.

The fourth section containing transitional and final provisions is concerned with, *inter alia*, penalties to be provided for by the Member States in the event of failure to comply with disclosure obligations.

11. THE STATUTE FOR THE EUROPEAN COMPANY

As an alternative to the harmonization of company law to be carried out under the directives discussed above, the Commission, in the belief that:

> coordination, even if pursued to the maximum extent, will not bring about complete unity of the national conditions under which enterprises are allowed to undertake their business,[143]

considering

> *the difficulties under present company law* in virtually all Member States of *managing a group of enterprises* as a single economic unit rather than in the interests of its individual component companies,

143. See the Commission *Memorandum* of 15 Jul. 1988 to the Parliament, the Council and the two sides of industry on the Statute for the European Company, p. 24.

and acknowledging that:

> entrepreneurs are not as familiar with foreign requirements as with those of their own national system [and this] inevitably poses *psychological difficulties* for effective cooperation across borders,[144]

thought it appropriate to complete its plan in the matter of company law, in furtherance, in fact, of what it had envisaged in the White Paper, by approving the Statute for a European limited liability company. To this end, it proposed:

> the setting up of a single legal framework at Community level, independent from (although not alien to) the – coordinated – national company laws.[145]

The Commission had worked on the prospective setting-up of the so-called 'European commercial company' since 1966. In fact, it was as early as March 1965 that the French government transmitted a note to the Commission,[146] advocating the creation of a new type of commercial company capable to foster capital investments, and commercial transactions generally within the Community, through a Community instrument identical across the Member States. Many years had gone by since the French government's suggestion, during which many studies were produced by the Commission itself and by many law scholars. The problems of how to found a legal basis for a European company in the Treaty of Rome and of whether to create a company 'governed by Community law' or a company of a 'European type' were discussed and solved.[147]

On 30 June 1979, the Commission submitted a proposal for a Council regulation embodying a statute for the 'European' company, pursuant to Article 235 of the Treaty.[148] A new proposal forwarded to the Council on

144. See *Memorandum*, last cit. above, p. 9.
145. The Statute for the SE (*Societas Europaea*) was adopted under Regulation (EC) No. 2157/2001 of 8 Oct. 2001 [2001] O.J. L294, p. 1 ff.
146. *Note du Gouvernement français sur la création d'une société commerciale de type européen* [1966] Riv. società, p. 1091 f.
147. In this respect, see chiefly: *Memorandum de la Commission de la Communauté européenne sur la création d'une société commerciale européenne* [1966] Riv. società, p. 1095 f.; and *Rapporto del gruppo di lavoro intergovernativo, ibid.* See also: the Sanders draft, in doc. COM 16, 205/IV/66-I, and the *prise de position* of the Commission on such draft, in doc. COM 1100/IV/67-I, about both of which see De Gennaro, 'Studi per la creazione della società commerciale "europea"', in Riv. società, p. 1091 f. For the problems concerning the creation of the European company, see essentially: Migliazza, 'I problemi di diritto internazionale relativi alla creazione di una società commerciale europea', cit. p. 775 f.; Renauld, *Droit européen de sociétés* (Bruxelles, 1969), pp. 9 and 31 f., and Capotorti, 'La società commerciale europea: un progetto dall'esito incerto' [1970] Dir. economia, p. 221 f., where, at p. 223 fn. 9, many references are made to the vast literature on the subject.
148. See the text of this proposal for a Council Regulation on the Statute for a European Commercial Company [1970] O.J. C124; see also in [1970] Riv. società, p. 1261 f., with a comprehensive commentary by Allegri, Una proposta della Commissione CEE al Consiglio dei Ministri della Comunità in tema di società anonima europea, *ibid.*, p. 1248 f. About the same text, see: Van Ryn, Le projet de statut des sociétés européennes [1971] Rev. trim. dr. eur., p. 563 f.; Keutgen, *Le droit des groupes de sociétés dans la CEE* (Bruxelles-Louvain, 1973),

13 May 1975[149] was not more successful than either the 'older' or the 'newer' proposals for a regulation and a directive of 25 August 1989 and 16 May (6 April) 1991, respectively.[150] And yet, the White Paper of 1985 listed the Statute for the European Company among the acts that the Council 'should' adopt by 1992 with a view to completion of the internal market, and the issue was again raised by the Commission in its *Memorandum* of 15 July 1988.

At long last, Regulation (EC) No 2157/2001 and Council Directive No 2001/86/EC were adopted on 8 October 2001,[151] and both entered into force on 8 October 2004.

A European Company may be set up in the form of a company having a capital divided into shares and legal personality (Article 1 of Regulation 2157/2001), subject to the conditions and in the manners discussed below.

Public limited liability companies (share companies) formed under the law of a Member State, with registered offices and head offices within the Community, may form an SE *by means of a merger* provided that at least two of them are governed by the law of different Member States.

---

p. 67 f.; and Schmittoff, 'The Role of the Multinational Enterprise in an Enlarged European Community', in Bathurst, Simmonds, Hunnings, Welch, *Legal Problems of an Enlarged European Community* (London, 1972), p. 211 f., especially p. 224 f., offering, inter alia, an interesting comparison between the system proposed in the draft Statute for a European Company and the Canadian system, which provides for a public limited company governed by Federal law along with the public limited company governed by the law of each of the Canadian provinces. See also the Economic and Social Committee's consultation about the proposal for a Council regulation on the creation of a Statute for the European public limited liability company, in [1972] O.J. C131, p. 32, and in [1973] Riv. società, p. 926 f. For the criticism addressed by the Economic and Social Committee, in its opinion just mentioned above, to the text of the 1970 proposal for a regulation on the European company, see Iannuzzi, Considerazioni critiche sulla più recente evoluzione dei lavori della Comunità Economica europea in tema di disciplina delle società per azioni e dei gruppi, in [1973] Riv. società, p. 634 f., p. 671 f. The European Parliament's opinion that originated the amendment made by the Commission to the original text in May 1975, is in [1974] O.J. C93, p. 22.

149. The amended proposal for a regulation, as submitted by the Commission to the Council on 13 May 1975, is published in *EC Bulletin, Suppl. No 4/1975*, p. 13 f., with annexes at p. 119 f., and the related report at p. 136 f.

150. The proposal for a regulation of 25 Aug. 1989 is in [1989] O.J. C263, p. 41. The amended proposal for a directive of 6 Apr. 1991 concerning workers' role is in [1991] O.J. C138, p. 8 f.

151. About the final texts of Regulation (EC) No. 2157/2001, in [2001] O.J. L294, p.1, and of Council Directive No. 2001/86/EC, in [2001] O.J. L294, see: Biscaretti di Ruffia – Gurrado, 'La società europea: un nuovo strumento per investire nell'Europa allargata' [2004] Giur. comm. I, p. 361 ff.; Carbone, 'La corporate governance della "società Europea" nel regolamento n. 2157/2001: tra norme materiali uniformi e tecniche di diritto internazionale privato' [2002] Dir.comm.int., p. 134 ff.; Pocar, 'Le statut de la société européenne: une étape importante dans l'évolution du droit communautarie' [2002] Riv.dir.int.priv.proc., p. 585 f.; Draetta, 'La Società Europea e il federalismo strisciante del diritto comunitario', in *La Società Europea. Problemi di diritto societario comunitario* (Milan, 2002), p. 2 f.; Malatesta, 'Il regolamento n. 2157/2001/CE sulla Società Europea: il difficile parto di una forma societaria comunitaria', in *La Società Europea*, cit., p. 8 f.; Cafari Panico, 'Il regolamento della Società Europea e le fusioni transfrontaliere', in *La Società Europea*, cit., p. 40 f.

Public and private limited-liability companies formed under the law of a Member State, with registered offices and head offices within the Community, *may promote the formation of a holding SE* provided that each of at least two of them:

(a) is governed by the law of a different Member State, or
(b) has for at least two years had a subsidiary company governed by the law of another Member State or a branch situated in another Member State.

Companies and firms within the meaning of the second paragraph of Article 48(2) of the Treaty and other legal bodies governed by public or private law, formed under the law of a Member State, with registered offices and head offices within the Community *may form a subsidiary SE*, by subscribing for its shares, provided that each of at least two of them:

(a) is governed by the law of a different Member State, or
(b) has for at least two years had a subsidiary company governed by the law of another Member State or a branch situated in another Member State.

A public limited-liability company formed under the law of a Member State, which has its registered office or head office within the Community *may be transformed into an SE* if for at least two years it has had a subsidiary company governed by the law of another Member State.

A Member State may provide that *a company the head office of which is not in the Community may participate in the formation of an SE* provided that such company is incorporated in a Member State, has its registered office in that Member State and has a real and continuous link with a Member State's economy.

It must be added that an SE may itself set up one or more subsidiaries in the form of SEs. (Articles 2 and 3).

The subscribed capital of an SE shall not be less than EUR 120,000 (Article 4). The registered office of an SE shall be located within the Community, in the same Member State as its head office (Article 7).

Article 12 requires that an SE be registered in a special registry to be set up in the Member State of its registered office, and Articles 13 and 14, which complete the general provisions in Title I, deal with the forms in which the acts of an SE must be published.

Further, Title II (Articles 15 to 37) is concerned with formation. Title III (Article 38 to 60) regulates the structure of the SE, by providing for the choice between a management organ together with a supervisory organ (the two-tier, German-type system) and an administrative organ (the conventional one-tier system). Title IV (Article 61 and 62) is concerned with annual accounts and consolidated accounts. Title V (Article 63 to 66) has as its object the winding up, liquidation, insolvency and cessation of payments. Title VI (Article 67) contains additional and transitional provisions, and Title VII contains final provisions.

Some phrases in the recitals of Regulation 2157/2001, in indicating Article 100(A) of the Treaty (now Article 95 EC), clarify the purpose of the *Societas Europaea*.

First comes a consideration already expressed in previous instruments, that the legal framework within which business must be carried on in the Community is still based largely on national laws and therefore no longer corresponds to the economic framework within which it must develop if the objectives of the Treaty are to be achieved. That situation forms a considerable obstacle to the creation of groups of companies from different Member States. (Fourth Whereas).

Then, it is essential to ensure as far as possible that the economic unit and the legal unit of business in the Community coincide. For that purpose, provision should be made for the creation, side by side with companies governed by a particular national law, of companies formed and carrying on business under the law created by a Community Regulation *directly applicable* in all Member States. (Sixth Whereas).

In brief, the ultimate purpose of the Regulation is to permit the creation and management of companies with a European dimension, free from the obstacles arising from the disparity and the limited territorial application of national company law. (Seventh Whereas).

It should be noted, though, that, because of the many references made to national legislations, the combined rules of Regulation 2157/2001 and of Directive 2001/86 complementary thereto make the legal structure of individual SEs *variable* in practice and not so *uniform* as it was intended to be.

Further, the text of Regulation 2157/2001 is less than compact, because of a number of regulatory gaps in connection with such issues as the rules on groups, general meetings' resolutions or shareholders' agreements.[152]

Against this background, it comes as no surprise that, for the time being, the SE appears to be a tool with a blunt edge, and used in just a few States, such as Germany (where the Allianz insurance group, one of some fifty German companies, has elected to change into an SE) and the Czech Republic. The new corporate form has not, however, been welcomed in other Member States such as Italy (where no SE has been registered so far) or the United Kingdom and Spain.

As for employees' involvement, the Statute for the SE was completed with Council Directive No 2001/86,[153] whereby the intended social objectives were achieved by indicating three alternative models.[154]

The first model envisages the conclusion of a special agreement between the competent organs of the participating companies and a special negotiating body representative of the employees of the participating companies.

The second model has to do with the application of the provisions for consultation and information of employees already existing in the national legislation(s) of the Member State(s) in which the SE has its employees.

---

152. See Biscaretti di Ruffia-Gurrado, 'La società europea', cit., p. 381.
153. About this, see *ibid.*, p. 376.
154. On this, see Gulotta, *Le relazioni industriali nelle imprese multinazionali. I diritti di informazione e di consultazione dei lavoratori nell'Unione Europea e nel diritto internazionale* (Milan, 2002), p. 62 f.

The third model envisages the application of the uniform rules issued by the Member States concerned in furtherance of the specific provisions contained in the annex to the Directive.

The Commission has supplemented the above arrangements by drawing up Council Regulation (EC) No 1435/2003 of 22 July 2003 on the Statute for a European Cooperative Society (SCE), and Council Directive 2003/72/EC of 22 July 2003 supplementing the Statute for a European Cooperative Society with regard to the involvement of employees.[155]

12. THE REGULATION ON THE EUROPEAN ECONOMIC INTEREST GROUPING (EEIG)

Council Regulation (EEC) No 2137/85 of 25 July 1985 provides for the creation of a European Economic Interest Grouping (EEIG).[156] This the first instrument containing uniform rules of Community law offered to Community undertakings for the conduct of economic activities of common interest. In principle and in general terms, a EEIG should be formed, have legal existence and operate upon the terms, in the manner and with the effects laid down in Regulation No 2137/85.

Even as the legislative instrument chosen by the Council (a regulation, that is) implies that the rules it contains are directly and immediately applicable in the Member States pursuant to Article 249 EC, such directness is attenuated, in the specific case of the EEIG, by the provision of Article 43 of the Regulation, pursuant to which, although the Regulation is to enter into force on the third day following its publication in the Official Journal of the European Communities, it shall apply from 1 July 1989. This peculiar provision is primarily intended to allow individual Member States to implement in their national legislations certain provisions addressed to them alone, such as rules on national registries, registration and publication, and the setting-up of a Contact Committee, pursuant to Articles 39 and 42, respectively, of the Regulation, which articles are to apply directly as from the entry into force of the Regulation according to Article 43.

---

155. See the text of Council Regulation 1435/2003/EC in [2003] O.J. L207, p. 1; the text of Council Directive No. 2003/72 is itself published in [2003] O.J. L207, p. 25.

156. [1985] O.J. L199. See also Communication from the Commission of 9 Sep. 1997, '*Participation of European Economic Interest Groupings (EEIGs) in public contracts and programmes financed by public funds*', COM(1997)434 final, in [1997] O.J. C285, which reads: '*More than 800 groupings are currently developing economic activities in a wide range of sectors. This is an encouraging figure given that the first EEIGs could only be set up from 1 July 1989, the date on which the Regulation came into force. However, a recent conference organized by the Commission (3) showed that optimum use is not yet being made of the EEIG by firms wishing to cooperate at transnational level, particularly where they hope to participate in public contracts and programmes financed by public funds*'. See also Judgment of the ECJ of 18 Dec. 1997, Case C-402/96, *EITO* [1997] ECR I-7515.

Council Regulation No 2137/85 contains mandatory rules establishing the legal structure of the EEIG, and the principles underlying the protection of third parties and the treatment of the relations of a EEIG's members with the grouping. Subject to these core provisions, the contracting parties to a EEIG are afforded wide discretion, so that, lacking specific provisions in the Regulation or where it refers to the grouping's formation contract, it is the latter that must apply. Lacking contractual provisions, the supplemental rules of the Regulation will be resorted to. In some specific instances, the Regulation itself expressly refers to the national law of the Member State in which the EEIG has its seat. This is the case with Article 1(2) and Articles 15 and 36. In other cases, the Regulation allows the Member State to choose any specific regulatory solutions among those provided for in Article 1(3), Article 4(3) and (4), Article 28(1), second sentence, and Article 32(3).

The instrument after which the EEIG has been patterned can readily be identified in the French *Groupement d'intérêt économique*, adopted by *Ordonnance* No 67-821 of 23 September 1967,[157] as amended, and even more so in the similar entity previously provided for by the Spanish Parliament in the *Ley sobre asociaciones y fusiones de empresas* of 28 December 1963, which has, however, been poorly successful because of inadequate tax benefits and of complex and burdensome procedures.[158]

157. [1967] O.J., p. 9537 f.
158. Conspicuous literature has already been devoted to the new Community instrument being discussed here. On this topic, see chiefly: Israel, 'Une avancée du droit communautaire: Le Groupement Européen d'Intérêt Economique (GEIE)' [1985] Rev. Marché Commun, p. 645 s.; Id., 'The EEIG – A major step forward for Community Law' [1988] The Company Lawyer, p. 14 f.; Id., 'Les caractéristiques juridiques du GEIE et son avenir économique' [1988] Fiscalité européenne, p. 3 f.; Gleichmann, 'Europaische Wirtschaftliche Interessenvereinigung' [1985] Zeitschrift fur das gesamte Handelsrecht und Wirtschaftsrecht, p. 633 f.; Guyenot, 'Le groupement d'intérêt économique, nouvelle institution européenne ouverte aux activités des professions libérales: le règlement CEE du 25 Jul. 1985' [1986] Fiscalité européenne, p. 49 f.; Meyer-Landrut, 'Europaische Wirtschaftliche Interessenvereinigung (EWIV) Eine neue Gesellschaftsform europaischen Rechts' [1986] Recht der Internationalen Wirtschaft, p. 107 f.; Proto, 'Il gruppo europeo di interesse economico' [1986] Giur. comm., p. 294 f.; Draetta, 'Problemi di adeguamento della legislazione italiana al GEIE comunitario' [1986] Dir. com. scambi internaz., p. 501 f.; van Gerven, 'Le Groupement Européen d'Intérêt Economique – GEIE' [1986] Rev. prat. des sociétés, p. 181 f.; Sass, 'Les aspects fiscaux du Groupement Européen d'Intérêt Economique (GEIE)' [1986] Fiscalité européenne, p. 43 f.; Kustermann, 'Un contratto tipico: il Gruppo europeo di interesse economico' [1986] Le società, p. 846 f.; Castelli e Napoletano, 'Il Gruppo europeo d'interesse economico (GEIE)' [1986] Dir. com. scambi internaz., p. 461 f.; Keutgen, 'Le Groupement Européen d'Intérêt Economique' [1987] Cah. Dr. Européen, p. 492 f.; Haug-Adrion, 'L'imposition du Groupement Européen d'Intérêt Economique' [1988] Fiscalité européenne, p. 19 f.; Pietrobon, 'Il gruppo europeo di interesse economico (GEIE)' [1989] Riv. dir. civ. II, p. 43 s.; Corapi, 'L'applicazione in Italia del Gruppo europeo di interesse economico' [1991] Le Società, p. 1168 f.; Draetta, 'La normativa italiana di applicazione del GEIE' [1991] Dir. comm. int., p. 487 f.; Beraud, *Le Groupement Européen d'Intérêt Economique (G.E.I.E.)* (Genéve, 1991); Notari, 'L'attuazione in Italia del Regolamento (CEE) sul gruppo europeo di interesse economico (GEIE)' [1991] Riv. soc., p. 1905 f.; Sacerdoti, 'I caratteri del GEIE e il suo impiego

The legal basis of Regulation No 2137/85 is Article 308 EC, and it has accordingly been adopted in furtherance of the general aim laid down in Article 2 EC. For its was the Council's view that:

> a harmonious development of economic activities and a continuous and balanced expansion throughout the Community depend on the establishment and smooth functioning of a common market offering conditions analogous to those of a national market.

Therefore:

> to bring about this single market and to increase its unity a legal framework which facilitates the adaptation of their activities to the economic conditions of the Community should be created for natural persons, companies, firms and other legal bodies in particular.

To that end:

> it is necessary that those natural persons, companies, firms and other legal bodies should be able to cooperate effectively across frontiers. (First Whereas of Regulation No 2137/85).

Accordingly:

> the creation of an appropriate Community legal instrument in the form of a European Economic Interest Grouping would contribute to the achievement of the abovementioned objectives and therefore proves necessary. (Second Whereas).

It should further be pointed out that:

> a grouping differs from a firm or company principally in its purpose, which is only to facilitate or develop the economic activities of its members to enable them to improve their own results; whereas, by reason of that ancillary nature, a grouping's activities must be related to the economic activities of its members but not replace them so that, to that extent, for example, a grouping may not itself, with regard to third parties, practise a profession, the concept of economic activities being interpreted in the widest sense. (Fifth Whereas; see also Article 3(1)).

---

nell'ordinamento italiano' [1992] Giur. comm., p. 876 f.; Dine, 'The European Economic Interest Grouping: Some Private International Law Issues' [1992] The Company Lawyer, No. 1, p. 10; Werlauff, 'The Development of Community Company Law' [1992] Eur. Law Review, p. 207 f.; Vague, 'Le groupement européen d'intérêt économique et les professions juridiques et comptables' [1992] Rev. Marché Commun et de l'Union Européenne, p. 403 f.; Mariani, 'Gruppo europeo di interesse economico (G.E.I.E.)' [1993] Riv. dir. eur., p. 301 f.; Mongiello, *Il gruppo europeo di interesse economico (G.E.I.E.)* (Padua, 1994); and Giuliani Thompson, 'Il conflitto nell'applicazione del diritto di stabilimento primario e secondario delle società europee' [2000] Contratto e Impresa Europa, p. 229 f.

The purpose of creating EEIGs is aptly described in the *Explanatory Memoramdum* that the Commission delivered on transmitting the draft regulation of 21 December 1973 to the Council:[159]

> Unlike a company, the grouping does not constitute an economic entity separate and independent from its members, operating autonomously and seeking to make profits only part of which would be distributed, the rest being retained for its own purposes in the form of reserves, provisions for depreciation *etc.* The grouping does not seek to make profits for itself; it is simply a vehicle for the business of its member. It is created to enable them, by means of the temporary pooling of certain resources, to develop their own business and. if this result is achieve, to increase their own business and, if this result is achieved, to increase their own profits.

There are two overriding, inescapable elements to a EEIG: The first is that it must comprise at least two natural persons or two companies, firms or other legal bodies, which carry on their principal activities and have their central administrations in different Member States (Article 4(2)). The second element is its *auxiliary nature*, in the sense that the relevant formation contract is one of cooperation, as opposed to the contracts for any other forms of company, in that it falls within the area that includes joint ventures, temporary associations of undertakings and consortia. In a sense, it is a device 'half-way between businesses operated as companies and mere forms of not-for-profit association'.[160]

In practice, an EEIG is expected to be used for common activities of research and development, the common production, purchases and sales of goods, and the common provision of specialized services. Think, for example, of several Community-based undertakings from different Member States, active in mutually complementary sectors, participating in a major tender for public works. In this case, using a EEIG allows each participating undertaking to meet the requirements and terms of the tender far more effectively than it could do on an individual basis, whereas, once the contract is awarded, the EEIG will be able to allocate different tasks to its different members, and coordinate and supervise their performance.

A EEIG is only intended for business to be done within the Community, as specifically provided for in Article 4, according to which any entities established outside the Community are barred from participation.[161]

Yet, nothing prohibits non-Community entities from participating in a EEIG through a company formed in a Member State for the intended purpose.

---

159. See in *EC Bull.*, Suppl. 1/74, p. 15 f., especially p. 20.
160. See the report accompanying the Italian draft bill of 1 Mar. 1989 on the creation of the European Economic Interest Grouping (EEIG), implementing Council Regulation 2137/85/EEC, p. 1.
161. Pietrobon, 'Gruppo europeo', cit., p. 45.

For Article 4(1) requires:

> *Only* the following may be members of a grouping:
>
> (a) companies or firms within the meaning of the second paragraph of Article 58 of the Treaty and other legal bodies governed by public or private law, which have been formed in accordance with the law of a Member State and which have their registered or statutory office and central administration in the Community; where, under the law of a Member State, a company, firm or other legal body is not obliged to have a registered or statutory office, it shall be sufficient for such a company, firm or other legal body to have its central administration in the Community;
> (b) natural persons who carry on any industrial, commercial, craft or agricultural activity or who provide professional or other services in the Community.

Further, pursuant to Article 12:

> The official address referred to in the contract for the formation of a grouping must be situated in the Community.

The official address must be fixed either:

> (a) where the grouping has its central administration, or
> (b) where one of the members of the grouping has its central administration or, in the case of a natural person, his principal activity, provided that the grouping carries on an activity there.

According to Article 13:

> The official address of a grouping may be transferred within the Community. When such a transfer does not result in a change in the law applicable pursuant to Article 2, the decision to transfer shall be taken in accordance with the conditions laid down in the contract for the formation of the grouping.

Article 14(1) provides for the opposite case, in that:

> When the transfer of the official address results in a change in the law applicable pursuant to Article 2, a transfer proposal must be drawn up, filed and published in accordance with the conditions laid down in Articles 7 and 8. No decision to transfer may be taken for two months after publication of the proposal. Any such decision must be taken by the members of the grouping unanimously. The transfer shall take effect on the date on which the grouping is registered, in accordance with Article 6, at the registry for the new official address. That registration may not be effected until evidence has been produced that the proposal to transfer the official address has been published.

A EEIG is accorded the capacity, in its own name, to make contracts or accomplish other legal acts, and to sue and be sued (Article 1(2)). It will be for the Member States to determine whether or not groupings registered at their registries, pursuant to Article 6, have legal personality (Article 1(3)).

A EEIG may not exercise a power of management or supervision over its members' own activities or over the activities of another undertaking in the fields of personnel, finance and investment, nor may it hold shares in a member undertaking, whereas the holding of shares in another undertaking shall be possible only in so far as it is necessary for the achievement of the grouping's objects and if it is done on its members' behalf. Nor may it employ more than five hundred persons – a requirement that matches the threshold above which a *Mitbestimmung* become mandatory in the Federal Republic of Germany, thereby finally disposing of a recurring problem in connection with EEIGs. Further, any such grouping may not be a member of another EEIG (in order to avoid diluting the principle of individual members' liability) (Article 3(2)). No grouping may invite investment by the public (Article 23).

The official address referred to in the contract for the formation of a grouping must be situated in one of the Member States (Article 12), and it must be fixed, albeit at its members' full discretion, according to minimum objective criteria. In any event, its seat need not be situated in its main place of business. It will be for the law of the State of its seat (the internal law applicable the EEIG's contract),

> except as regards matters relating to the status or capacity of natural persons and to the capacity of legal persons,

to regulate the contract for the formation of the EEIG and the grouping's own functioning (Article 2). A grouping may also set up branches in other States. In particular, it is the EEIG's national law that determines the consequences of its members' unlimited joint and several liability for the grouping's debts and other obligations (Article 24(1)), and governs its insolvency and cessation of payments (Article 36).

A EEIG's necessary organs are: the *general meeting* and the *individual managers* (Article 16(1)). At general meetings, each member must have one vote, but the contract for the formation of a grouping may give more than one vote to certain members, provided that *no one member holds a majority of the votes* (Article 17(1)).

A unanimous decision by the members is required to alter the objects of a grouping, to alter the number of votes allotted to each member, to alter the conditions for the taking of decisions, to extend the duration of the grouping or to alter the contribution by the grouping's members (Article 17(2)). Subject to these provisions, the contract for the formation of the grouping may prescribe the conditions for a quorum and for a majority, in accordance with which the decisions shall be taken (Article 17(3)).

Each of the managers *severally* binds the EEIG, a provision from which it can be inferred that the managers do not constitute a 'board' (Article 20(1)). A manager's acts bind the EEIG even where they do not fall within the objects of the grouping – in furtherance of the principles of the First Directive on companies, as implemented in Italy by Article 2384 of the Civil Code – 'unless the grouping proves that the third party knew or could not, under the circumstances, have been unaware that the act fell outside the objects of the grouping'.

Since a EEIG's activities are regarded as its individual members' activities performed by the grouping as a whole, *any profits resulting therefrom are deemed to be the profits of the members* and must be apportioned among them in the proportions laid down in the formation contract or, in the absence of such provision, in equal shares (Article 21(1)). The same criteria apply to losses (Article 21(2)). These standards are reinforced by the tax provision in Article 40 of the Regulation, which, in furtherance of the full-disclosure principle, requires that the results from the activities of a EEIG are taxable only in the hands of its members. This requirement cannot be departed from by national law-makers.

As for the creation of the EEIG in Italy, Article 11 of Legislative Decree No 240/1991, under the heading '*Direct taxation*', requires:

1. EEIGs shall not be liable for taxes on income of natural persons, taxes on income of legal persons or local taxes on income.
2. EEIGs residing in the territory of the State and any non-resident EEIGs permanently established in the State shall file tax returns for the purposes of taxes on income of natural persons, taxes on income of legal persons or local taxes on income payable by the EEIG's members, according to the provisions in Title I of The President of the Republic Decree No 600 of 29 September 1973, and maintain the accounting records provided for in Title II thereof.
3. EEIGs shall also be responsible for the withholdings provided for in Title III of The President of the Republic Decree No 600 of 29 September 1973, and return the statement provided for in Article 7 thereof.
4. A EEIG's profits and losses, as determined according to the provisions of the Consolidating Act on Income Tax, as adopted under The President of the Republic Decree No 917 of 22 December 1986, shall, for the purposes of the taxes specified therein, be taxable in the hands of each member irrespective of whether or not any such profit was actually received or ay such loss actually incurred, in the proportions laid down in the formation contract or, lacking such provision, in equal shares. For the purpose of the application of tax to non-residents within the territory of the State, the profits and losses taxable in the hands of non-resident members shall be deemed to have arisen within the territory of the State.
5. Any withholding tax paid by the EEIG shall be deemed to have been paid on account and shall be deducted from the individual tax amount payable by each of its members.
6. The share of profits or losses arising to residents from their membership in a EEIG not residing in the territory of the State shall be deemed to be part of total income for the purposes of income taxes on natural persons or on legal persons, as the case may be. The provisions of Article 15 and 92 of the Consolidating Act on Income Tax, as adopted under The President of the Republic Decree No 917 of 22 December 1986, shall apply.

A EEIG must not have equity of its own, for the Regulation contains no requirement for it to have capital in any form or any endowment fund.

In the absence of assets owned by the EEIG as such, third parties are protected by the requirement that the members of a grouping must have unlimited joint and several liability for its debts and other liabilities of whatever nature (Article 24(1)), a requirement extended to every new member (Article 26) and still applicable to any member who has ceased to belong to the grouping (Article 34) for a period of limitation of five years after liquidation (Article 37).

In this context, the requirement that creditors may not proceed against a member for payment in respect of debts and other liabilities, before the liquidation of a grouping is concluded, unless they have first requested the grouping to pay and payment has not been made within an appropriate period (Article 24(2)), appears to provide less for prior enforcement of claims than for 'a *beneficium ordinis* of a sort being granted to the grouping's members, not a form of separation of assets'.[162]

It is not by chance, therefore, that page 5 of the *Report* on the instrument establishing the EEIG in Italy (Legislative Decree No 240 of 23 July 1991), in implementation of Regulation 2137/85, reads, *inter alia*, as follows:

> The EEIG has not been given legal personality (Article 1(3) of the Regulation). Along with the general reason offered above, it has been deemed advisable not to introduce an element of dishomogeneity with entities having similar status (consortia), to avoid procedural implications of homologation and to exclude from the Italian legal system the singularity of an entity having legal personality and concurrently entailing all of its members' unlimited liability.

Conversely, Article 1 of the French transposition instrument, Act No 89-377 of 13 June 1989, requires that any EEIG registered in the French registry of commerce and enterprises be given legal personality upon registration.[163] A similar provision is contained in Article 1 of the Belgian transposition Act No 89-1480 of 12 July 1989.[164] By contrast, Article 9 of the Italian legislative decree for implementation, which refers to Article 151 of the Italian Insolvency Act for the unlimited liability of EEIGs' members, treats a EEIG's event of bankruptcy in the same way as bankruptcy of unlimited cooperative societies, thereby implicitly denying that the EEIG should have legal personality in the Italian legal system.[165]

---

162. See Pietrobon, 'Gruppo europeo', p. 62. Ms Pietrobon, 'Gruppo europeo', pp. 50 f. and 56 f., criticises the solution of unlimited joint and several liability of a grouping's members, which she believes to be in utter contrast with other rules on the EEIG, specifically the provision allowing national legislations to give legal personality to EEIGs. This provision would make no sense because of the inescapable conflict that would result between the notion of legal person with the notion of a legal person's members' unlimited liability. For the identification, for the time being, of the contents of the concept of legal person in the Italian system, precisely in connection with the benefit of limited liability, see Galgano, 'Struttura logica e contenuto normativo del concetto di persona giuridica' [1965] Riv. dir. civ. I, p. 625 f. For a deeper analysis of this issue, see my work, 'Le società nel diritto internazionale private', cit., p. 118 f., fns 59 e 60.
163. [1989] O.J., p. 7440 f.
164. See in *Moniteur Belge* of 22 Aug. 1989, No. 14385.
165. By inference fron the tenth Whereas of the Regulation, Pietrobon, 'Gruppo europeo', takes the view that the general provision in Article 24 may be departed from under specific derogations

The protection of any third parties entering into contact with a EEIG is also ensured by the provisions for disclosure of EEIGs' acts (Articles 7 to 11 of the Regulation). Such provisions, in respect of whether a grouping's registration or its subsequent acts, closely mirror the formalities imposed by the First Council Directive on limited liability companies.[166]

It has already been observed that Regulation No 2137/85 entered into force on 1 July 1989. Since that date, therefore, it has been possible for EEIGs to be formed with their registered offices in any State whose domestic system provides for registration. Accordingly, any such grouping will be able, without territorial restrictions, to operate anywhere across the Community, without the possibility for a Member State that has not yet transposed the Regulation to curb the activity in its territory of a EEIG having its seat in another State in which it has duly been registered. All the Member States of the Community as at 31 December 1994 have issued rules for the implementation of Regulation No 2137/85 in their systems.

---

agreed on between the grouping and a third party in respect of the lliability of one or more of the grouping's members for any given debt.

166. See above, Section 5 of this Chapter II.

Chapter III

Free Movement of Capital in an Open Economy: The Monetary Eurosystem

SUMMARY:

1. The evolution of economic and financial relations in the new world order.
2. The Euro and the free movement of capital and payments.
3. The complex set of rules on capital and payments in their original formulation in the Treaty of Rome.
4. The conflict between the economic integration process and Member States' economic and monetary policies: The Werner Report and the 22 March 1971 Resolution.
5. From the 'European monetary snake' to the European Monetary System, ('EMS'). The re-launch of financial integration: Subsequent Commission Communications to the Council up to the (Delors) Report on the Economic and Monetary Union.
6. The Economic and Monetary Union and the Maastricht Treaty.
7. The criticalities of the European 'rigid' system.
8. A criticism of the double standard: Serious distortions across the Eurosystem. The UK case.
9. The impact of the euro on contracts of duration.
10. Private parties and the full liberalization of capital movements and payments in the European Union.
11. The fundamental freedoms and the exercise of 'special powers': The terms of the problem.
12. The legal bases of the conflict over 'golden shares' between the Commission and Member States.

13. The permitted scope of the national States' and their agencies' intervention.
14. The saga of the Commission's scrutiny of the Italian rules on special powers.
15. The 'proportionate' exercise of control in the ECJ's recent case-law.

1. THE EVOLUTION OF ECONOMIC AND FINANCIAL RELATIONS IN THE NEW WORLD ORDER

The late 1900s were marked by significant novel events that contributed to a faster progression in economic and financial international relations.

First, upon the entry into effect of the Marrakesh agreements, the new WTO system went into full operation, effectively abating customs duties, equalizing quotas and extending treaty rules to the trade in services, thereby bringing about a far higher degree of trade liberalization worldwide, both in volumes and values, than under the former GATT 1947 arrangements.[1]

Secondly, the contents of the new liberalization rules were further expanded by their wider subjective extension to the new States (there are now 153 GATT 1994 Contracting States) that have been admitted to the system on the presupposition of the acceptance of free-trade rules within each of them, in a process which culminated in the accession of The People's Republic of China to the WTO/GATT effective on 1 January 2002.[2]

Although the whole set of WTO/GATT rules are hardly apt to fill the deep gap between the world's north and south, they now entail and warrant a huge market across the whole world – a 'global' market, in fact, open to the principles of free trade.

This is the context within which, at the dawn of the new century, financial activity and investment capacity are being powerfully enhanced, as they gradually concentrate on 'funds' of all types, operating in every sector of the economy, with the 'sovereign funds' paramount among them.[3]

The mass of capital available for investment moving around and across the international securities and real-estate markets is further augmented as well by the multinational enterprises' *modus operandi*[4] as by the cash amounts made increasingly available to the new Russian mid-upper class through the assistance of bright minds who have given up chess games for the more sophisticated games of international finance.

Lastly, the boom of web communication works as a glue binding together these different fragments of business and financial growth, thereby enhancing the

1. For a discussion of the GATT 1947 system and the amendments introduced in subsequent rounds and of the new arrangements introduced under the Marrakesh agreements in trade matters at a systematic level, please refer to Chapter IV below, in particular paragraphs 2 et seq.
2. On the subject, see paragraphs 11, 12 and 13 of Chapter IV below.
3. See the considerations about the 'sovereign funds' offered in paragraph 8 of Chapter V below.
4. Please, refer to Chapter V below, *passim*, for a discussion of this subject.

new international picture characterized, especially in the last decade, by a more and more powerful drive for every investor, wherever located, to operate in an open economy.

However, along with these favourable factors, there are other, materially adverse factors at work worldwide. Within a global view of economic relations at all levels, a growing demand for 'scarce commodities' and the 'dear oil' are causing serious unbalances, which affect individual countries more or less seriously depending on domestic circumstances.

These unbalances are made even more serious as the existing (outdated) international rules seem incapable of ensuring a well-balanced stability and a consistent progression of exchange rates.[5]

Although currencies and exchange rates mainly entail monetary policy issues which are up to each government to handle, usually in agreement with that State's national monetary authority (with its typically technical tasks), the impact of the applicable rules is by no means restricted to the *macroeconomic* domain, since they are intended to ensure price stability within each country, thus to keep inflation risk under control through such monetary tools as the determination of the official discount rate and the stability of that currency's exchange rates against the main foreign currencies.

Yet, inflation control and exchange rate stability, on the one hand, and the free movement of capital and payments, on the other, both within and outside any economic area, are two facets of the one issue affecting the private individuals' daily lives and the enterprises' business operations, both of which must rely on stability for them to draw actual, properly balanced benefits from a worldwide system of freely moving capital and payments.

Matters seem to be compounded further by the acts of international, mainly Islamist, terrorism, which culminated in the attack to the Twin Towers on 11 September 2001. The need then arose for ever more sophisticated and efficient controls around the world, in relation not only to the movement of persons, but to the lawfulness of cross-border payments and fund transfers as well. This has increasingly required actions to be taken which result in a severe curtailment of human rights, often in contrast with the rules in force in individual domestic legal systems for the protection of personal data, and derogate from the rules governing free trading, by requiring that the ordering parties, the receivers of funds or payments, and even the indication of the related operations for individual transactions be identified to supervisory authorities.[6] At the same time, there is an increasingly shared need for effectively combating the cross-border flows of proceeds from crime or from other unlawful activities generally.

As actions of this type are intended to keep financial transactions and forex transfers between countries under control through the banking system, whether they occur between private individuals, foreign enterprises or States (by 'MT

5. See paragraph 2 of Chapter IV below for a discussion of the crisis of the Bretton Woods agreements and the IMF.
6. See paragraph 11 *et seq.* of Chapter V below.

103s') or even between banks in connection therewith (by 'MT 202s'), they are bound, for them to be really effectual, to require 'cross-border' measures capable to be enforced beyond the boundaries of any one State.[7]

The end-result has been a complex body of prior notifications to the competent supervisory authorities, followed by a number of supervisory tests and checks designed to fight both international terrorism and organized crime, and, specifically, to prevent money laundering.

In other words, the resulting system is one of duties and prohibitions addressed to banks and other financial institutions,[8] the legal basis of which are the rules contained in international agreements or in UN resolutions providing for economic restrictions in accordance with Article 41 of the Charter. Similar rules have also been laid down in individual domestic legislations on financial matters and made enforceable beyond the customary boundaries of national jurisdictions in accordance with a 'novel' notion of 'international public policy' of an essentially *positive* value. I would submit that, by reference to a settled principle applied in international commercial arbitrations, such new international public policy should be based as well on *ius cogens* in international law as on a body of rules of natural law, principles of universal justice and *the general principles of morality recognized by civilized nations.*[9]

2. THE EURO AND THE FREE MOVEMENT OF CAPITAL AND PAYMENTS

Thus, the EU Member States' choice to introduce the euro as the *single currency*, which has already replaced most domestic currencies in those States, was taken within the present complex context of international economics and finance – an entirely new setting, hardly predictable just fifteen years ago. And yet, this has only occurred by virtue of a double system made up of the *euro 'area'* (or '*zone*') and the *non-euro 'zone'* (or '*area*'). The latter includes both the Member States that have not yet met the Maastricht Criteria and those, such as the United Kingdom and

7. Please, refer to the considerations offered in Chapter V, *passim*.
8. See paragraph 11 *et seq.* of Chapter V below.
9. The last phrase is closely reminiscent of the 'general principles of law recognised by civilized nations' expressly referred to in Article 38(1)(c) of the Statute of the Hague International Court of Justice as a provision the Court must apply to any relevant case in performing its function 'to decide in accordance with international law such disputes as are submitted to it'. The phrase 'international public policy' – which obviously has nothing to do with that used to establish e *negative limit* to the reference, under private international law, to a foreign law in a given legal system – is offered by Sheppard in his 'Interim ILA Report on Public Policy as a Bar to Enforcement at the 69th ILA Conference' (London, 2000) [2003] Arb. Int., p. 220. As for its application to international arbitration, see: Lalive, 'Ordre public transnational (ou réellement international) et arbitrage international' (1986) Rev. Arb. p. 329, p. 341; Loquin, 'Les manifestations de l'illicite' in Kan, Kessedjian, *L'illicite dans le commerce international* (Dijon, 1996), pp. 276-278; Hunter, Silva, 'Transnational Public Policy and its Application in Investment Arbitrations' [2003] Jour. World. Invest., p. 378.

Denmark, which have taken their free choice to retain their domestic currencies and Sweden which is still thinking on it.

As the double system is the result of a compromise between conflicting positions and demands, it has not, as will be seen below, provided the optimum solution, and has caused unbalances both within and outside the European Union, the extent of which seems to have been neither adequately understood nor suitably resisted.

Still, the Maastricht Treaty has put an end to a relatively low process of gradual implementation of the free movement of capital.

Although such freedom was initially asserted as one of the four fundamental freedoms, even the rules originally intended to govern it in the Treaty of Rome – and long caught by derivative Community law as well, because of the severe disclosure requirements they imply in matters of economic and monetary policy – have been implemented separately from, and with poorer contents and less pervasively than, the rules governing the other fundamental freedoms.

Notwithstanding some judgments regarded as highly innovative at the time they were rendered, even the European Court of Justice's case-law has, after the end of the transitional period following the first stage provided for by the Treaty of Rome, been far weaker in upholding the rules on the free movement of capital to their full extent than in the case of the other three freedoms.[10]

And so it was, much as it was quite clear to all that the liberalization of the movement of capital throughout the Community was bound to have a decisive weight on the progressive implementation of the internal market as a space without internal frontiers and characterized by the full operation of the four fundamental freedoms. Albeit initially opposed by some Member States in the face of the most thoughtful authors' consensus, this belief had already brought about sweeping innovations in the field by the late 1980s.

In this respect, a decisive role has been played by Council Directive 88/361/EEC of 24 June 1988[11] for the implementation of Article 67 of the Treaty, in the text that was later abrogated (along with that and other directives issued on the same legal basis) by the Maastricht Treaty.

With a view to the establishment of the *internal market* pursuant to Article 14 EC by 31 December 1992 (see the third Whereas of the directive), as discussed in details further below, Directive 88/361 set out the general rule that the financial markets within the Community should be fully liberalized, though at different times according to Article 15 EC: almost forthwith (no later than 1 July 1990) by a majority of the Member States, Italy among them; and somewhat later by other Member States (by 31 December 1990 or 31 December 1992).

It must be noted that, however, the desired outcome was only reached in the late 1980s, after several years' drudgery both at Community level and in some

10. See Chapter I(7) above, specifically in regard of the ECJ's judgments in *Reyners* and *van Bisbergen*.
11. [1988] O.J. L178, p. 5.

Member States' legislatures, through the impetus of the ECJ's consequential precedent in matters of free movement of capital and free payments.

Within that context, a highly significant decision was issued by the Court of Justice on 11 November 1981 in Case 203/80, *Casati.*[12] This is a judgment well known in Italy, where a stringent, most severe currency legislation[13] had been in force since 1976.[14] The applicable law punished any violations by residents of Italy, whether individuals or bodies corporate, with administrative and even criminal sanctions. That was the first judgment in which the Court directly and explicitly tackled many of the issues relating to the free movement of capital within the Community, especially with regard to the restrictive measures typical of Italian law at that time. Still, the peculiarity of the case, together with the wide scope of the questions referred by the District Court of Bolzano,[15] were not enough to make some of the ECJ's statements of principle known to everyone, much as the Court of Justice's express intent had been to establish clear-cut boundaries between Community law and individual domestic laws on the matter.[16]

---

12. [1981] ECR 2595 f. Advocate General Capotorti's Opinion of 7 Jul. 1981 is in [1981] ECR, 2621 f.
13. The OECD described the Italian currency legislation of the time as '*unduly severe*'. See Santa Maria, 'European Financial Integration: Institutional and Legal Aspects' [1981] Giorn. Econom., Annali econ., p. 747 ff., and [1981] Riv. dir. eur., p. 263 f. The study last named was presented as a written report to the 'Colloquium on the European Capital Market Problems and Outlook' held at Università Bocconi on 27-28 Nov. 1980. It was also published in the volume with the same title as the Colloquium (Milan, 1981), p. 747 f. See also the *Commenti* made to that report by Gianviti, *ibid.*, p. 776 s., and by Pecchioli, *ibid.*, p. 775 f.
14. I refer to Act No. 159 of 30 Apr. 1976, as amended. For the Italian currency system of the time, reference should essentially be made to Santa Maria, 'Disciplina valutaria, sanzioni penali e certezza del diritto' [1981] Dir. prat. trib., p. 603 ff. and Id., 'European Financial Integration', cit.
15. The Bolzano District Court's Order of 6 Oct. 1980 has been published in [1981] Riv. dir. int. priv. proc., p. 775 f. to p. 778 f., for the questions referred under Article 177 EC. On the Order, see comments by De Guttry, 'Normativa penale italiana e Trattato CEE', *ibid.*, p. 11 f., and by Ferrari, 'Legge penale e valutaria e Trattato CEE' [1981] Gazz. valutaria, p. 11 f. On 29 Oct. 1979, the District Criminal Court of Bolzano had already issued an order in the same Casati case, whereby it referred questions to the ECJ under Article 177 EC with a view to 'letting the record reflect information about the procedure followed in the matter by the Italian Government vis-à-vis the Community Institutions as provided for by Article 73 of the Treaty'. This order, too, was published in [1980] Riv. dir. int. priv. proc., p. 645 f. At the end of his 'odyssey', Mr Casati was acquitted by the District Court of Bolzano by Judgment dated 1 Mar. 1982, in [1982] Giur. it. II, c. 356.
16. The ECJ's judgment in Casati brought about a number of publications. See: Panico, 'La valutazione della legge penale italiana in materia di infrazioni valutarie alla stregua del diritto comunitario sulla libera circolazione dei capitali' [1982] Gazz. valutaria, p. 104 f.; De Guttry, 'La disciplina penale valutaria italiana e la libera circolazione dei capitali alla luce dell'interpretazione della Corte comunitaria' [1982] Foro it. IV, c. 73; De Vergottini, 'La riserva di competenza statale in materia di normativa valutaria (in margine alla sentenza della Corte di giustizia nel procedimento n. 1973 del 1980)' [1982] Banca, Borsa, ecc. II, p. 492 f.; Telchini, 'Un'occasione perduta: la mancata soppressione delle restrizioni ai movimenti di capitali nella Comunità europea, nota alla sentenza del Tribunale di Bolzano che assolveva il Casati' [1982]

The purpose of the ECJ's decision was not, nor could it be, to determine whether or not the Italian body of criminal laws in currency matters was inherently unlawful by Community legal standards. Nor is any such question to be found among those referred by the Italian judge to the Court for a preliminary ruling. In fact, the questions raised by the District Court of Bolzano concerned a quite specific issue, i.e. whether or not there was a right guaranteed by the Treaty to some Mr Casati, an Italian national residing in Germany, allowing him, upon leaving Italy, to re-export a sum of money he had previously imported into Italy without declaring it by completing Form 'V-1' on entry into Italian territory, as required by the Italian administrative regulations in force at that time for application to non-residents of Italy.[17]

The European Court of Justice had also been requested to establish, *inter alia*, whether, in case that above question had been answered in the affirmative, a violation of the formal requirements set out by the domestic currency legislation was punishable, in the relevant case, by the criminal and administrative sanctions then provided for by the Italian laws on currency matters or, cumulatively: the confiscation of the sum of money involved in the attempt to export, a fine of two up to four times the value of the relevant assets (i.e. the effects exported), a penalty accessory to such fine in an amount of up to five times the amount involved in the infringement, and a term of imprisonment of up to six years, unless increased in case more than one persons participated in committing the offence (Question 4).

The answers to the questions so raised were quite to the point. The ECJ ruled that, whereas, in principle, criminal legislation and the rules of criminal procedure were matters for which the Member States were still responsible, the *proportionality principle* was nonetheless applicable in relation to transactions to be liberalized.

Thus, the domestic penalties that exceeded what was necessary to suppress the infringement in proportion to its gravity were found to be incompatible with Community law. In other words, in the Court's view:

> the administrative measures or penalties *must not go beyond what is strictly necessary*, the control procedures must not be conceived in such a way as to

---

Giur. it. II, c. 519 f.; Louiss, 'Free Movement of Capital in the Community: the Casati Judgement' [1982] Com. Market Law Rev., p. 443 f.; Luzzatto, 'La circolazione dei capitali nella Comunità economica europea: una libertà "dimezzata"? (la Corte delle Comunità europee e la legge valutaria italiana)' [1982] Dir. com. scambi int., p. 403 f.; Mengozzi, 'Un contributo della Corte di giustizia delle Comunità europee al chiarimento del regime della circolazione dei capitali' [1983] Banca, Impresa, Società, p. 223 f.; Santa Maria, 'Norme comunitarie e disposizioni valutarie italiane, Relazione tenuta nel corso della Conferenza di Genova del 28-29 ottobre 1983' [1984] Giur. comm., p. 494 f. In general, about the rules on the free movement of capital within the Community, see my study, European Financial Integration and a summary of the general discussion about the basic report at p. 781 f., containing my considerations on the Casati case, not yet decided by the Court. See also De Guttry, *Verso un mercato finanziario europeo? La disciplina giuridica della circolazione dei capitali nella CEE* (Milan, 1987).

17. For the peculiarities of the case, see the Bolzano District Court's Order of 6 Oct. 1980, cit., p. 775 f.

> restrict the freedom required by the treaty and they must not be accompanied by *a penalty which is so disproportionate* to the gravity of the infringement that it becomes an obstacle to the exercise of that freedom.[18] [*Emphasis added*].

In fact, the Court went further to hold that:

> with regard to capital movements and transfers of currency which the member states are not obliged to liberalize under the rules of community law, *those rules do not restrict the member states' power to adopt control measures and to enforce compliance therewith by means of criminal penalties.*[19] [*Emphasis added*].

It is should also be noted that, precisely in that context of unaccomplished liberalization of the movement of capital and payments within the Community, a principle of paramount significance for a correct interpretation of Community rules in the field was *non-discrimination*, itself the subject, albeit in a peculiar respect, of another question, Question 7, the District Court of Bolzano had referred to the ECJ.

The non-discrimination principle had been laid down in general terms in Article 7 of the EC Treaty (now Article 6 EC), and it was more specifically set out in Article 67(1) of the Treaty of Rome,[20] which extended its scope – for the purpose of the progressive abolition of restrictions on the movement of capital within the Community, through an application typical of currency laws – to '*any discriminatory treatment* based on the *nationality* or *place of residence* of the parties or on the *place in which such capital is invested*' as well as 'any discrimination based on nationality'.

The same principle of *non-discrimination* was further affirmed in Article 68(2),[21] by a reference thought redundant by some, as a limitation set to each State when applying its domestic provisions in respect of the capital market and credit system to the movements of capital freed in accordance with the Treaty.

---

18. The proportionality principle is one of the keystones of Community law. The ECJ had already based its rulings on it on many occasions. In particular, see Judgment of 14 Jul. 1977, Case 8/77, *Sagulo, Brenca and Bakhouche*, [1977] ECR 1495, especially paragraphs 11, 12 and 13. See also Judgments of 7 Jul. 1976, Case 118/75, *Watson*, [1976] ECR 1985; 15 Dec. 1976, Case 41/76, *Criel, née Donckerwolcke and Shou v. Procureur de la République au Tribunal de Grande Instance, Lille and Director General of Customs*, [1976] ECR 1921; and 30 Nov. 1977, Case 52/77, *Cayrol*, [1977] ECR 2261. See also Judgment of 16 Dec. 1992, Case C-169/91, *B & Q*, [1992] ECR 6635, ground 15. In literature, essentially: Tosato, 'I rapporti contrattuali con i residenti nella CEE', in *Il sistema valutario italiano*, vol. I, l'ordinamento valutario (Milan, 1981), p. 377 ff. to p. 410.
19. See ECJ Judgment in *Casati*, cit., paragraph 27. Also see Advocate General Capotorti's Opinion of 7 Jul. 1981, in the same case.
20. Repealed by the Treaty of Amsterdam.
21. Itself repealed by the Treaty of Amsterdam.

In this connection, it should also be recalled that, according to the provisions of Article 54 EC (former Article 65 of the Treaty of Rome), under the title covering services:

> As long as the abolition of restrictions on the free supply of services has not been effected, each Member State shall apply such restrictions without distinction on grounds of nationality or residence to all persons within the meaning of Article 49, first paragraph, who supply services (*i.e. citizens of one Member State residing in another Member State*).

Specifically with regard to the acquisition by citizens of one Member State of ownership interests in companies established in another Member State, the principle of 'national treatment' is invoked by Article 294 EC, as follows:

> Member States shall, within three years from the entry into force of this Treaty, accord nationals of the other Member States the same treatment as their own nationals as regards participation in the capital of companies or firms within the meaning of Article 48, without prejudice to the application of the other provisions of this Treaty.[22]

3. THE COMPLEX SET OF RULES ON CAPITAL AND PAYMENTS IN THEIR ORIGINAL FORMULATION IN THE TREATY OF ROME

As observed above, the original text of the Treaty of Rome also predicated the full establishment of the European Economic Community upon the free movement of capital between Member States, and recognised this as the fourth fundamental freedom.

In fact, only rules on capital movements *stricto sensu* were contained in the original Articles 67 et seq. of the Treaty of Rome, in the chapter entitled 'Capital', as a way to supplement the rules set out to ensure the free movement of persons, goods and services.

As for the manners of making payments and transfers of funds from one country to another within the Community, to the extent they had not yet been freed under Article 67(2), the matter remained governed by the provisions relating to 'balances of payments' until appropriate amendments were introduced by the Maastricht Treaty of 7 February 1992.[23]

---

22. See Chapter I of this book for a discussion of these provisions.
23. Though without overrating a terminology not always used properly (see Maestripieri, *La libre circulation des capitaux dans la C.E.E.*, p. 141), for the essential equivalence of the terms 'payments' and 'transfers' in Community terminology, see Ehlermann, in *Kommentar zum EWG-Vertrag*, edit by Groeben, Boeck e Thiesing (2° ed., Baden, 1974), I, p. 1375 ff. p. 1378; Monaco, 'La libera circolazione dei capitali nella C.E.E. e la disciplina valutaria italiana', in *Imprese industriali e banche di fronte alla nuova disciplina valutaria* (Milan, 1979), p. 29 ff., p. 39. As for such concepts as 'current payments', 'financial operations' and 'invisible transactions' within the meaning of the Treaty of Rome, reference should be made to

In respect of issues concerning private parties, the result was an involved, poorly homogeneous system, in which these provisions were of a merely residual import when contrasted with the rules on capital. For they were only applicable so long as no 'current payments connected with movements of capital between Member States' were involved, while these were to 'be freed from all restrictions not later than at the end of the first stage'.

Quite beyond the macroeconomic issue relating to the then-national currencies, the existing correlation, in respect of both private individuals and undertakings, between the two sets of rules, which was based on a distinction not easily circumscribed in practice, make them neither understandable nor applicable in full.

Nor was the system really improved by the provision of paragraph 2 of Article 106(3) of the Treaty in the original formulation, which considered the progressive abolition of existing restrictions in some respects, in so far as such abolition was not governed by the provisions contained in the two preceding paragraphs or 'by the Chapter relating to the free movement of capital'.

Let me stress again that, in private law relationships, the provisions set out under the heading 'Balances of Payment' were intended as a natural complement to the rules ensuring the free movement of goods, persons, services and capital, as the Court of Justice aptly pointed out in its judgment of 23 November 1978 in Case 7/78 (*Regina v Thomson and others*),[24] and, later on, in Judgment of 31 January 1984, Joined Cases 286/82 and 26/83, *Carbone* and *Luisi*.

Thus, Article 106(1) (repealed) expressly ensured the freedom of:

> any payments connected with the exchange of goods, services or capital, and also any transfers of capital and wages, to the extent that the movement of goods, services, capital and persons is freed as between Member States in application of this Treaty.

In *Regina* v *Thompson* and others, the ECJ ruled:

> The aim of this provision is to ensure that the necessary monetary transfers may be made both for the liberalization of movements of capital and for the free movement of goods, services and persons. (Paragraph 24).

With the same view, Article 106(2) provided:

> To the extent that exchanges of goods and services and movements of capital are limited only by restrictions on payments connected therewith, the provisions of the Chapters relating to the abolition of quantitative restrictions, to the freeing of services and to the free movement of capital shall, for the purposes of the progressive abolition of such restrictions, apply by analogy.

Incidentally, the provision contained in Article 106(2) had already fulfilled its function in that it concerned the transitional period, as the ECJ noted at paragraph 21

Grisoli, 'Commento agli articoli 67 e s.', in *Commentario C.E.E.*, published by Quadri, Monaco e Trabucchi (Milan, 1965), I, p. 509-510.

24. [1978] ECR 2247 ff.

of Judgment 9 June 1982 in Case 95/81, *Commission of the European Communities* v *the Republic of Italy*.[25]

In fact, freedom of payments was recognised to be so important within the framework of the Treaty, in its being preparatory to the full establishment of the other fundamental freedom, as to be even described as the 'fifth freedom'.[26]

As it happens, not only the rules on payments, but those on the free movement of capital, too, were, in turn, complementary to the provisions of the Treaty that ensured the other fundamental freedoms, and were the decisive factor in bringing about their full realization.

For there is no doubt that, unless capital had been allowed to move freely within the Community, the harmonious adjustment of the different Member States' production structures, of which the free movement of goods was a crucial pre-condition, could hardly been achieved.[27] The same was also true for the other freedoms ensured by the Treaty.[28]

It is even too obvious that, had capital flows between Member States remained subject to severe restrictions, some significant provisions of the Treaty – those ensuring the right of establishment and the free provision of services in the first place – would have remained dead letter.[29]

This was the view held by the Court of Justice in *Casati*, where it stressed that:

> [F]reedom to move certain types of capital is, in practice, *a pre-condition for the effective exercise* of other freedoms guaranteed by the treaty, in particular the right of establishment.[30] [*Emphasis added*].

This observation is quite correct now as it was at that time. Only think of someone wishing to move his residence from one Member State to another in exercising his right to free establishment. Such right would have been deprived of any material value unless the person concerned were allowed to take his capital along with him automatically, without restrictions, including the fruits of his personal or even real properties.

This was, in fact, what has specifically been ensured, since as early as 1960, by Article 1 of the First Directive of the Council for the application of Article 67 of the Treaty of Rome in its original text.

---

25. [1982] ECR 2187 f., 2202 f.
26. The statement is in Boerner, 'Die finfte Freheit des Gemeinsamen Marktes: der freie Zahlungs-verker', in W. Hallstein H.J. Schlochauer (Hers), *Zur Integration Europas, Festschrift fir Ophìls* (Karlsruhe, 1965), p. 19.
27. Expressly, in this sense, Segrè, 'Introduzione agli articoli 67 e s.', in *Commentario C.E.E.*, cit., p. 497 f. Also see ECJ Judgment in case *Regina* c. *Thompson and others*, cit., paragraph 22, p. 2273.
28. Also see express references to the provisions for free capital movements in Articles 52(2) and 61(2) of the Treaty.
29. See Segrè, 'Introduzione agli articoli 67 e s.', p. 497 f., also to be referred to for the examples given at p. 505 f.
30. See ECJ Judgment in *Casati*, cit., paragraph 8, last sentence, p. 2613 f.

Likewise, of what use would have been the option granted to every person established within the Community to take out policies with any insurer, whether national of that or of another Member State, under the right to the free provision of services, if any provisions of currency law of any one Member State had otherwise prevented that person from paying his premiums abroad, in another Member State?

And this is not the only one aspect of the issue, mind you.

A well-known fact is that liberalization of capital and payments cannot but be regarded as a matter of public law, concerning each Member State's economic and monetary policy.

In this respect, the ECJ pointed out in *Casati*:

> [C]apital movements are also closely connected with the economic and monetary policy of the Member States. At present [in the early 1980s], it cannot be denied that complete freedom of movement of capital may undermine the economic policy of one of the Member States or create an imbalance in its balance of payments, thereby impairing the proper functioning of the Common Market.[31] [*Emphasis added*].

Advocate General Capotorti, in his Opinion in *Casati*, reversed the terms of the problem as to the priorities stated by the Court, to stress:

> The need to align the liberalisation of movements of capital with the effectiveness of national measures intended to ensure the stability of exchange rates and domestic prices, by conferring on the Member States sufficient room for manoeuvre, is in conformity with the system of the Treaty, under which the *provisions on the movement of capital may not be interpreted independently of those on economic policy.*[32] [*Emphasis added*].

That was a delicate matter, then subject to each Member State's rules on currency control and foreign trade, so that the scope for liberalization was expressly restricted, in the original version of the Treaty, '*to the extent necessary for the proper functioning of the Common Market*' or '*to the full extent necessary for the functioning of the Common Market*', in the certainly equivalent terms of Article 67(1) and of Article 105(2), respectively, both repealed, of the Treaty of Rome.

On the one hand, these terms further confirm the complementary function the matter in question has always had within the common market of goods, persons and services, the actual establishment of which was stated to be a precondition for the establishment of the internal market (Article 8 A, paragraph 2, of the Treaty of Rome, in the text amended by the 1986 European Single Act and renumbered as 7 A by the Maastricht Treaty, and now Article 14 EC). On the other hand, that very wording emphasizes the fact that, within the Community, all enterprises are accorded free access to the capital market at equal terms, and also accounts for the need to complete the admittedly low Community process of economic and

31. See ECJ Judgment in *Casati*, cit., paragraph 9, p. 2614.
32. [1981] ECR 2621 f., 2626.

monetary integration[33] culminating in the daring adoption of the euro as the single European currency.

It is now appropriate to expand upon what must be regarded as the overriding principle the European Court of Justice affirmed in the *Casati* judgment, i.e. that liberalization was the *rule* in respect of capital as well, albeit within the then-limited scope for actual implementation, whereas any domestic restrictions imposed within Member States to protect national public interests were just *exceptions*.

According to the Court, the scope of the restrictions imposed by the articles of the Treaty discussed above on the general duty to liberalize capital movements:

> depends on an assessment of the requirements of the common market and on an appraisal of both the advantages and risks which liberalisation might entail for the latter.[34]

The Court went on to rule that such an assessment was, *first and foremost*, a matter for the Council, which acted thereupon over time through directives having their legal basis in Article 69 of the Treaty (later repealed).[35]

In other words, it was the ECJ's view, *as early as 1981*, that Article 67 must by now be considered *fully and directly applicable within the scope and in the terms of directives* the Council had already issued.[36]

---

33. The Resolution of the Council and of the Representatives of the Governments of the Member States of 22 Mar. 1971 on the attainment by stages of economic and monetary union in the Community ([1971] O.J. C28, p. 1 f.) expressed the wish that, at the end of the process for the establishment of economic and monetary union (to be accomplished by 31 Dec. 1980), 'the Community creates an area within which persons, goods, services and capital will circulate freely *without distorting competition* or cause structural or regional unbalances, under such conditions as to allow economic entities *to develop their activities in a Community area*' (emphasis added). The Werner Report, on which this resolution was based, after noting the presence of factors that delayed the liberalization of capital movement, went on to state: 'Disparities in the cost of credit and the conditions of access to credit resulting therefrom falsify competition and conflict with the institution of economic and monetary union'. (The *Report to the Council and the Commission on the realisation by stages of economic and monetary union in the Community*, Luxembourg, 1970, better known as the *Werner Report*, the contents of which are discussed at some length in paragraph 4 of this Chapter, is published in [1970] O.J. C136, p. 1. *Emphasis added*).
34. See ECJ Judgment in *Casati*, cit., paragraph 10.
35. *Ibid.*, paragraph 11.
36. First, there were *two directives* relating the same matter, one of 11 May 1960, the other of 18 Dec. 1962, No. 63/21, 'adding to and amending the First Directive for the implementation of Article 67 of the Treaty' (the former published in [1960] O.J. 43, p. 921, the latter in [1963] O.J. 9, p. 62). Both referred to *four classes of transactions* each implying a different degree of liberalization. Thus, Articles 1 and 2 required Member States to implement full liberalization of the transactions specified in Lists A and B of Annexe I. Those were transactions related to the free movement of goods, persons and services, of which they were the necessary complement, as frequently indicated in this Chapter III. By Directive 72/156/EEC of 21 Mar. 1972 on regulating international capital flows and neutralizing their undesirable effects on domestic liquidity (as published in [1972] O.J. L91, p. 13 f.), the Council required the Member States to take all necessary steps to prevent capital movements of a speculative nature, thereby

considering certain transactions already included in List D to be excluded from liberalization in any event. This directive marked a regression from the two directives of 1960 and 1962, in that it authorized Member States (under Article 1(6)) to regulate financial loans and credits by derogating from Article 3(1) of the First Directive for the implementation of article 67 of the Treaty, as amended by the Second Directive of 18 Dec. 1962. On Directive No. 72/156, see Tosato, 'I rapporti contrattuali con i residenti nella CEE', cit., p. 387. On 4 Nov. 1987, the Commission submitted to the Council a draft directive intended to amend Directive No. 72/156, in [1988] O.J. C26, p. 12 f. Directive 72/156 was repealed as from 1 Jul. 1990 by Article 9 of Directive No. 88/361 of 24 Jun. 1988. Following approval of the two directive of 1960 and 1962, the Commission began to study any obstacles to free capital movements under Member States' laws other than the obstacles directly concerning foreign exchange controls. On 14 Apr. 1964, based on suggestions from the Monetary Committee, the Commission recommended the Council to adopt a third directive pursuant to Article 69, which concerned the abolition of any other restrictions based upon the issuer's nationality or residence, the issue and placing of foreign securities on national capital markets, the admission of foreign securities to listing on national stock exchange and the acquisition by financial undertakings of foreign securities, all such transactions being subject to conditional liberalization treatment under Article 3 of the First Directive, and included, as such, in List C of the two former directives. The recommendation failed to achieve the hoped-for result in relation to the degree of liberalization existing in fact within the Community, as a consequence of the different use of the discretion Member States were accorded by Article 3(2) of the first 1960 directive. For Belgium, Luxembourg and the Federal Republic of Germany, for which the transactions considered in List C were fully liberalized, thought it fair to subordinate the adoption of the proposed new directive to prior actual reciprocity between all Member States. Taking this into account, the Commission submitted to the Council a new draft directive on 8 Feb. 1967, but this draft, too, was inconsequential. About the two drafts, see Sarmet, 'Capitaux', in *Le droit de la Communauté économique européenne, Commentaire du Traité et des textes*, Megret and others. eds, vol. 3 (Brussels, 1971), p. 210 f., and Maestripieri, *La libre circulation des capitaux dans la C.E.E.*, cit., p. 80 f. Later on, the two directives of 1960 and 1962 were amended, first by Directive No. 85/583 of 20 Dec. 1985 ([1985] O.J. L372, p. 39 f.), then by Directive No. 86/611 of 17 Nov. 1986 ([1986] O.J. L332, p. 22 f.). In particular, Directive 85/583 replaced List B with a new version and made changes to List C, in relation to 'transactions in securities'. The most significant aspect of Directive 85/583 was the introduction in List B of items relating to the acquisition and disposal of units of 'undertakings for collective investment in transferable securities (UCITS)', the subject matter of Council Directive No. 85/611 of 20 Dec. 1985. as amended by Council Directive No. 88/220 of 22 Mar. 1988. (Directive No. 85/611 of 20 Dec. 1985 is in [1985] O.J. L375, p. 3 f, and Directive No. 88/220 of 22 Mar. 1988, where Article 22 amended Directive No. 88/611, concerning the coordination of legislative, regulatory and administrative provisions in the matter of some undertakings for collective investment in transferable securities (UCITS), in relation to the investment policy of some UCITS, is in [1988] O.J. L100, p. 31). Pursuant to Article 2 of Directive 85/583, which supplemented Annex II of the Directive of 11 May 1960, such 'undertakings' were defined as those 'the object of which is the collective investment in transferable securities or other assets of the capital they raise and which operate on the principle of risk-spreading, and the units of which are, at the request of holders, under the legal, contractual or statutory conditions governing them, repurchased or redeemed, directly or indirectly, out of those undertakings' assets'. Action taken by a collective investment undertaking to ensure that the stock exchange value of its units did not significantly vary from their net asset value was to be regarded as equivalent to such repurchase or redemption. In accordance with national laws, such undertakings could be constituted 'either under the law of contract (as common funds managed by management companies) or trust law (as unit trusts) or under statute (as investment companies)'. For the purposes of this directive, the term 'common

4. THE CONFLICT BETWEEN THE ECONOMIC INTEGRATION PROCESS AND MEMBER STATES' ECONOMIC AND MONETARY POLICIES: THE WERNER REPORT AND THE 22 MARCH 1971 RESOLUTION

It has aptly been pointed out by many that, as originally worded, the provisions in the original version of the Treaty of Rome on the movements of capital and transfers of funds between Member States and between Member States and third countries lacked clarity and stood out for their high degree of approximation.

Accordingly, the Treaty had been criticized for years for failing to provide for the manners of implementation of the rules in this sector to the same degree of accuracy as in the case of the other fundamental freedoms.

The reason for such wariness on the part of the Community lawmakers can readily be identified in the close correlation noted above between, on the one side, the liberalization process then underway, which concerned capital *lato sensu*, as a necessary complement to a wider integration, and, on the other side, economic and monetary policy, the latter being, in principle, a matter for individual Member States to provide for (Articles 71(2) and 106(2) and (4) of the original text of the Treaty of Rome).[37] In other words, those conflicts between microeconomic and macroeconomic elements I have oftentimes referred to elsewhere in this book were actively at

---

funds' also included unit trusts. Directive No. 86/566 also introduced a simplification, by repealing Article 2 of the 1960 directive and consolidating the former Lists A and B into List A. As a result, the lists became three following the removal of List D. The same directive made some amendments to the 'Nomenclature of Capital Movements' and to the 'Explanatory Notes'. Lastly, Article 2 introduced time derogations for Spain and Portugal in respect of some operations listed in Annex A, because of the timing (1985) of their accession to the Community. On 24 Jun. 1988, the Council issued Directive No. 88/361 ([1988] O.J. L178, p. 5 f.) 'for the implementation of Article 67 of the Treaty', compliance with which was to be ensured by Member States in their domestic laws no later than 1 Jul. 1990, though some of them were allowed to apply temporary restrictions (Article 6). Article 9 of this Directive repealed the first directive of 11 May 1960, as amended form time to time as indicated above, and Directive No. 72/156 of 21 Mar. 1972, with effect from 1 Jul. 1990. On 31 May 1963, in furtherance of Article 106(2) of the Treaty (in the version repealed by the Maastricht Treaty), the Council had issued Directive No. 63/340, which required Member States to issue all foreign exchange authorizations necessary for payments and transfers arising from the provision of services for which the only existing restrictions related to payments. (Directive published in [1963] O.J. L86, p. 1609). It was quite obvious by then that, as the ECJ ruled in its judgment of 9 Jun. 1982 in Case 95/81, paragraph 21, the rule contained in Article 106(2) of the Treaty, which was chiefly concerned with the transitional period, was no longer applicable, and the directive in question was, accordingly, no longer apt, following the expiry of the transitional period, to limit the elimination of restrictions or prohibitions on payments relating to the trading of goods or provision of services to those cases alone which were considered in that directive. On 30 Jul. 1963, in connection with the standstill requirement in Article 106(3) of the Treaty, the Council had issued Directive 63/474 on the liberalization of transfers relating to certain invisible transactions unrelated to the movement of goods, services, capital or persons, (Directive published in [1963] O.J. L125, p. 2240).

37. See, essentially, Tosato, 'I rapporti contrattuali con i residenti nella CEE', cit., p. 379 f.; and the Opinion of 7 Jul. 1981 of Capotorti, Advocate General, in *Casati*, in ECR, cit., p. 2626.

work, affecting the protection of private parties' interests, whose actual implementation came second in priority behind the overriding needs of public policy typical of foreign exchange controls, then falling within each Member State's jurisdiction.

In principle, whatever legal system is involved, every State's purpose in applying foreign exchange controls is to keep the rates of exchange of its domestic currency stable against the currencies of the States with which it has the largest volume of financial and trade relations, in order to ensure price stability within its own country by fending off dangerous, seriously harmful inflationary pressures.[38]

Thus, the original text of the Treaty of Rome expressly provided:

> Each Member State shall pursue the economic policy necessary to ensure the equilibrium of its overall balance of payments and to maintain confidence in its currency, while ensuring a high level of employment and *the stability of the level of prices*. [*Emphasis added*].

This provision was only partially qualified by the requirement that:

> Each Member State shall treat its policy with regard to exchange rates as a *matter of common interest*. [*Emphasis added*].

This basic approach implied that, in principle, liberalization within the Community should be limited to those payments alone which were connected with the exchange of goods, services or capital, or with transfers of capital and wages, to the extent that the movement of goods, services, capital and persons was freed as between Member States in application of the Treaty.

Nothing was required beyond this minimum duty, except that Member States were asked to declare their willingness to free capital and payments 'in so far as their economic situation in general and the situation of their balance of payments in particular so permit'.

This conflict between intra-Community liberalization and individual Member States' balance of payment exigencies had long been the main reason for the powerful brake applied to the process of implementation of the freedom of movement of capital and payments, which ought, in fact, to have been implemented in full in the transitional period.[39]

The 'Report to the Council and the Commission on the realization by stages of economic and monetary union in the Community' of 8 October 1970, commonly known as the 'Werner Report', acknowledged that:

> The extension of the liberation of movements of capital and the realization of the right of establishment and of the free rendering of services by banking and financial undertakings have not progressed far enough.

---

38. Thus, expressly: my study 'Les critères d'application des règles italiennes des changes', in *Comunicazione e Studi dell'Istituto di Diritto Internazionale e Straniero dell'Università di Milano* (Milan, 1980), vol. XVI, p. 221 f., p. 228 f., where bibliographic notes are also provided. See also my other study, 'Disciplina valutaria, sanzioni penali e certezza del diritto', cit., p. 606.
39. See Grisoli, 'Commento agli articoli 67 e s.', p. 513 f., also for a review of the work preparatory to the Treaty in this matter.

The causes of the delay were identified as:

> the absence of sufficient coordination of economic and monetary policies and . . . local peculiarities of law or of fact [*Emphasis added*].[40]

Further below, the *Werner Report* expressed the hope that:

> The suppression of the obstacles of various kinds should make it possible to arrive at *a true common market for capital* free from distortions. The financial policy of the Member States must be sufficiently unified to ensure the balanced operation of this market [*Emphasis added*].

Yet, the Treaty did not, in its original text, seem to allow for the full attainment of the intended goal. The fifth Whereas of the preamble of the 1971 *Resolution* recognised that some actions entailed a modification of the Treaty of Rome.[41]

It can fairly be concluded from these scanty observations that only the realization of an economic and monetary union within the Community, in far more advanced terms and with far richer contents, could have adequately disposed of the Member States' individualistic drives, by making the Community institutions responsible for a unified management of interests that had by now become a matter of European public policy.

5. FROM THE 'EUROPEAN MONETARY SNAKE' TO THE EUROPEAN MONETARY SYSTEM ('EMS'). THE RE-LAUNCH OF FINANCIAL INTEGRATION: SUBSEQUENT COMMISSION COMMUNICATIONS TO THE COUNCIL UP TO THE (DELORS) REPORT ON THE ECONOMIC AND MONETARY UNION

In the spring of 1971, at the peak of the serious crisis of the international monetary system which had been caused, on the one hand, by the abandonment of the fixed exchange rate system, following the decision by some countries to let the exchange rates of their currencies fluctuate beyond the very narrow margin of 1% of parity prescribed by Article IV, Sections 3 and 4 of the Agreement establishing the International Monetary Fund (IMF), and, on the other hand, by the impending unilateral suspension by the United States of the convertibility of the dollar into gold or other reserve instruments, the Member States of the European Community embarked on an effort to accomplish an economic and monetary union on the basis of the *Werner Plan* and of the consequent *Resolution* of 1971.

Thus, in April 1972, the 'European monetary snake' was established, to be followed up, some years later, by the creation of the European Monetary System

---

40. See the *Report to the Council and the Commission on the realisation by stages of economic and monetary union in the Community (Werner Report)*, cit., p. 4.
41. See Resolution of the Council and of the Representatives of the Governments of the Member States of 22 Mar. 1971.

(the SME) based on the European Currency Unit (the ECU), a 'currency basket' of a sort, effective as from 13 March 1979.

However, despite the significance to be ascribed to that achievement, the progression of the liberalization of the movements of capital and payments within the Community lingered in a standstill for a long time.

Such deadlock in the liberalization process was criticized by the Commission in a Communication to the Council dated 18 April 1983 on the financial integration of the Community,[42] whereby the Commission solicited renewed efforts towards a single 'European financial market'.

In the Commission's view, the time was ripe for a greater freedom of capital movements to provide 'the financial basis for efficient mobilization of Community savings and their allocation to productive investments'. Indeed, the Commission was convinced that suitable conditions already existed at that time for new actions to be taken on the issue of financial flows, while the economic policy considerations that had long 'justified' the absence of a single financial space had now become much less relevant, after four years of successful operation of the EMS.

According to the Commission, this context now made renewed progress toward financial integration possible and as necessary as ever along three different directions.

First, the Commission proposed appropriate measures to be taken with a view to a financial system of more direct service to the Community's economic development through, on the one hand, the gradual removal of barriers preventing the establishment of a European venture capital market and the development of a technical system linking up the main European stock exchanges, and, on the other hand, the creation of a more unified network of financial services in the fields of banking, insurance and stock exchanges, along with the development of new financial instruments to ensure efficient tapping and circulation of capital within a geographically wider financial sector.

The second set of initiatives pointed to by the Commission were intended to contribute to better balanced international financial relations through a greater control of capital flows between the Community and the rest of the world, *the strengthening of international banking supervision* (including through improved cooperation between national credit information exchanges), and the coordination of the foreign borrowing policies of the Member States.

Lastly, the Commission suggested that *the use of the ECU*, the European single monetary unit, *should be promoted* both for borrowings within the Community and in financial markets generally, in the terms already recommended by the Commission in its Communication of 15 March 1982 on strengthening the EMS.

This approach was further confirmed by the Commission in the White Paper of 14 June 1985 on completing the internal market. Section 5 of Part II, under the heading 'Capital movements', reads as follows:

> Greater liberalisation of capital movements in the Community should serve three aims. (Paragraph 124).

---

42. See the Communication from the Commission to the Council of 18 Apr. 1983 on financial integration (COM (83) 207 final).

> First, the completion of a large internal market inevitably involves a financial dimension. The free movement of goods, services and persons must also mean that firms and private individuals throughout the Community have access to efficient financial services. The effectiveness of the harmonisation of national provisions governing the activities of financial intermediaries and markets would be greatly reduced if the corresponding capital movements were to remain subject to restrictions. (Paragraph 125)
>
> Secondly, it must be stressed that monetary stability, in the sense of the general level of prices and exchange rate relations, is essential precondition for the proper operation and development of the internal market. In this regard, action to achieve greater freedom of capital movements would need to move in parallel with the steps taken to reinforce and develop the European Monetary System. Exchange-rate stability and convergence of economic policies help the gradual removal of barriers to the free movement of capital; conversely, greater financial freedom leads to greater discipline in the conduct of economic policies. (Paragraph 126).
>
> Thirdly, the decompartmentalisation of financial markets should boost the economic development of the Community by promoting the optimum allocation of European savings. The task is to set up an attractive and competitive integrated financial system for both Community and non-Community business circles. (Paragraph 127).

Later on, with a view to the establishment of the internal market under the Single Act signed in Luxembourg and The Hague on 17 February and 28 February 1986, respectively, addressed a new Communication dated 23 May 1986 to the Council on 'the programme for the liberalization of capital movements in the Community'.[43]

After acknowledging that Article 130(B) of the Single Act required that the implementation of common policies and of the internal market should take into account the Community's objectives of economic and social cohesion, the Commission proposed liberalization solutions which each Member State could adopt, though each at a different time, depending on that Member State's temporary difficulties in implementing the relevant measures.

Further, based on the existence of a close link between the development of the EMS and the free movement of capital, the Commission recommended two sets of objectives. First, the major phases in the proposed approach should be suitably considered 'so as to arrive at as liberal as possible a Community system of capital movements' (Part 1). Secondly, the resultant implications for the effective integration of the financial markets of the Member States should be set out (Part 2).

Specifically in the latter respect, the Commission stressed that a high degree of capital liberalization was a necessary, but not sufficient, condition for the Community's genuine financial integration. Hence, it was 'important for liberalization

---

43. See COM (86) 292 final.

to be paralleled by provisions designed to ensure the cohesion' of the European financial area. The Commission also pointed out that 'a truly integrated financial market is bound to have consequences for the conduct by the Member States of their monetary policies'.

The close link between the last stage in the liberalization of capital movements and the necessary strengthening of the EMS was further stressed by the Commission in its Communication of 4 November 1987 on the 'Creation of a[n] European Financial Area'.[44] There was something new to it, though. It was the Commission's view that the integration of financial markets could no longer be regarded as a preliminary step in the implementation of the programme for the liberalization of capital movements. In fact, quite the opposite was believed to be true: the accomplishment of full liberalization of capital movement was certainly to result in a major step forward in the integration of financial markets.

A document delivered to the Council as an annex to the Communication of 4 November 1987 was a draft directive for the implementation of Article 67 of the Treaty, introduced by a substantial commentary by the Commission's staff. As indicated above, the proposed directive was approved by the Council as Directive No 88/361 on 24 June 1988, bringing about the *full liberalization* of capital movements within the Community.

The exigencies indicated above were later restated in the *Report on the Economic and Monetary Union*, commonly known as the 'Delors Report' after the name of Jaques Delors, the Chairman of the *Committee on the economic and monetary union* responsible for developing the Report.[45]

6. THE ECONOMIC AND MONETARY UNION AND THE MAASTRICHT TREATY

Then came the Treaty on the European Union signed by the then-EC Member States in Maastricht on 7 February 1992.

The Treaty was, in fact, the result of the work done by the (most capable) compilers who succeeded in overcoming serious practical difficulties when combining the Treaty on the political union with that on the economic and monetary union, both of which had been drawn up as separate texts at the Maastricht meeting of the European Council of 11 December 1991. Thus, the two documents were merged into one treaty, which was presented to the twelve Member States for ratification.

The Treaty on the European Union, which is the name now given to the combination of the two former treaties, along with its protocols and additional instruments (among which the Agreement on Social Policy), as ratified by all

44. See COM 87/550 final.
45. The *Delors Report* dated 12 Apr. 1989 was published on the occasion of the Luxembourg meeting of the Council of 17 Apr. 1989 (see the document in English with the two annexes [1989] Europe 1550). It provided for the accomplishment of the economic and monetary union in three stages. As agreed at the Madrid Summit of 26-27 Jun. 1989, the first stage began on 1 Jul. 1990, concurrently with the full liberalization of capital movements postulated by the directive of 24 Jun. 1988.

Member States and effective as from 1 November 1993, was the key breakthrough in the development of the Community.

Between the Delors Report and the Maastricht meeting of the European Council, an intense preparatory activity was carried out, from the Madrid Summit in June 1989 to the Dublin Summit of 1990. At the latter meeting, the Member States' Heads of State and Government resolved to arrange two intergovernmental conferences on the political union and the economic and monetary union. And so, commencing on 15 December 1990, a number of reports and drafts were developed during both conferences, until the definitive versions were discussed and finally approved at Maastricht in December 1991.

The Community framework changed further from the Single European Act. First, because the original European 'Economic' Community was changed into the 'European Community' under the Maastricht Treaty, through the deletion of that adjective '*economic*' that qualified, but also restricted, the scope of this international organization. Secondly, because the economic union of the States involved now effectively became a genuine political union with new far-reaching opportunities for aggregation.

This was the background against which an attempt was made with a view to the 'progressive' implementation of the Economic and Monetary Union in stages, under an approach patterned after the method already successfully experimented in relation to the internal market since the entry into force of the Treaty of Rome.

It is just fair to observe that the Treaty on the European Union, with its fifty-three article is only partially independent of the Treaty establishing the EEC. For it contains many provisions amending the Treaty of Rome as was the case with the Single European Act. And those amendments were made on essential points, introducing new tasks and further extending the Community's jurisdiction to other sectors of the EC Treaty, even beyond the changes made under the 1986 European Single Act, which were to be implemented in full by 31 December 1992.

It is appropriate to stress that Article 2 EC provided a new version – following ratification by all the States signatories of the Maastricht Treaty – which superseded the original version in the Treaty of Rome to require:

> The Community shall have as its task, by establishing a common market and an economic and monetary union and by implementing common policies or activities referred to in Articles 3 and 4, to promote throughout the Community a harmonious and balanced development of economic activities, sustainable and non-inflationary growth respectful of the environment, a high degree convergence of economic performance, a high level of employment and social protection, the raising of the standard of living and quality of life, and economic and social cohesion and solidarity among Member States.

In fact, it was a challenging programme, of a scope far wider that the original treaty signed as far back in time as 25 March 1957. The tools for implementation have remained as provided for in Article 3, albeit in a version just marginally amended by the introduction of the new sectors contemplated in the latest text of the Treaty supplemented with Articles 4 and 5, which are of paramount importance for the matter discussed here.

In particular, Article 4(1) requires:

> For the purposes set out in Article 2, the activities of the Member States and the Community shall include, as provided in this Treaty and in accordance with the timetable set out therein, the adoption of an economic policy which is based on the close coordination of Member States' economic policies, on the internal market and on the definition of common objectives, and conducted *in accordance with the principle of an open market economy with free competition.* [*Emphasis added*].

The reference made to the need for an open market economy and free competition is a recurring theme throughout those articles.

In the terms of Article 4(2):

> Concurrently with the foregoing, and as provided in this Treaty and in accordance with the timetable and the procedures set out therein, these activities shall include the irrevocable fixing of exchange rates leading to the introduction of a single currency, the ECU, and the definition and conduct of a single *monetary policy* and *exchange-rate policy* the primary objective of both of which shall be to maintain price stability and, without prejudice to this objective, to support the general economic policies in the Community, *in accordance with the principle of an open market economy with free competition.* [*Emphasis added*].

Article 4(3) further requires:

> These activities of the Member States and the Community shall entail compliance with the following guiding principles: stable prices, sound public finances and monetary conditions and a sustainable balances of payments.

These paragraphs provide the key to a correct reading of the contents of the after-Maastricht economic and monetary integration.

Thus, under the Maastricht Treaty, the implementation of the Economic and Monetary Union was to progress gradually and, as resolved at the Madrid meeting of the European Council in June 1989, in three stages, commencing on 1 July 1990.

A high degree of liberalization vis-à-vis third countries had initially been provided on the basis of a *reciprocity standard*, i.e. conditional upon a similar conduct by the third country involved from time to time, or whenever liberalization is mandated by international commitments. The latter is the case with the United States, Canada, Switzerland and Norway – Norway having even remained, following a referendum, excluded from the enlargement of the Community to Sweden, Finland and Austria as from 1 January 1995. A high degree of liberalization has been ensured vis-à-vis the States mentioned above by the provisions in the capital movement liberalization code and by the OECD provisions on invisible transactions.[46]

Merely by way of exception, each State was at liberty, at times of particular balance of payment difficulties, to apply 'safeguard measures' in the first stage.

---

46. This was the original basis of Annex III to the Rome Treaty, itself repealed by the Amsterdam Treaty.

However, while currency liberalization was already fully ensured, to the point that no specific reference was made any longer to a nomenclature of 'classes', certain transactions were still *mandatorily* excepted as identified in Annex II to the Directive of 24 June 1988. All of them were *short-term* and exceptionally allowed to be temporarily barred in foreign trade within the Community, depending on a State's needs, under the control of either the Commission or the Council depending on whether the relevant measure was intended as a preventive or subsequent move. The application of safeguard clauses had already been removed from the national authorities' discretion. Safeguard clauses were, in fact, deemed to be so strictly *exceptional* that they could only be tolerated if justified by especially difficult conditions of that State's balance of payments, and had to be always authorized by the competent Community institution, either before or after introduction, on a *temporary* basis and never for longer than six months.

Concurrently with the liberalization of capital and payments, the monetary integration framework was introduced in the form of the European Monetary System (the EMS).

The SME was severely affected by a crisis in August 1993, when the difficulties brought about by the German unification and international speculation, along with the great uncertainties surrounding the ratification of the Maastricht Treaty by some Member States, generated fears for the possible collapse of the rigid exchange rate system within which the individual currencies had been made to move. As a rule, they could only fluctuate within a narrow band (plus or minus 2.25%), and only exceptionally within a wide band (plus or minus 6%).

The consequences of that crisis were the exit of the Italian lira and the British pound from the EMS, and the introduction of so wide a fluctuation band from central parity (plus or minus 15%) for the other currencies as to make the very use of such restriction doubtful, to say the least.

The ECU had become the single (albeit only *virtual*) European currency since that first stage, and it was referred to as the benchmark currency for international transactions in many Member States, in addition to, or even as a substitute for, their domestic currencies.

The Community's monetary unit was made up of a basket of the EMS currencies. It had a conversion value of its own against each national currency, whose exchange rate was allowed to move within the range of fluctuation established within the EMS.[47]

The second stage, described as 'transitional', began on 1 January 1994, in accordance with Article 109e of the European Union Treaty, now Article 116 EC. During the second stage, monetary policy was to remain the responsibility of each Member State until the beginning of the third and final stage of the Monetary Union. However, Member States were, in the second stage, to 'endeavour to avoid excessive government deficits', and each Member State should, 'as appropriate, start the process leading to the independence of its central bank'.

47. Council Regulation (EC) No. 3320/94 of 22 Dec. 1994 consolidated the existing Community legislation on the definition of the ECU following the entry into force of the Treaty on the European Union. This Regulation is in [1994] O.J. L350, p. 27.

On 1 January 1994, Articles 67 to 73 of the EC Treaty, which concerned the free movement of capital, ceased from effect. And so, the articles of which Council Directive 88/361 of 24 June 1988 was the latest implementation, together with that directive and those preceding it on the same legal basis, were repealed by the Maastricht Treaty and replaced by the new provisions contained in Articles 73b through 73g as from 1 January 1994. These articles, to be later renumbered as Articles 56 through 60 EC, took on force as primary rules to establish full liberalization of capital movements and thoroughly free payments from one country to another within the Community.

Following the Maastricht Treaty, capital flows and payments have, both in form and for the sake of clarity, ceased from being subject to separate sets of rules and have been treated together so as to let them circulate freely both within the Community and from and to third countries.

Under a specific Protocol, the third and final stage was to commence either during 1997, at the earliest, or as from 1 January 1994 at the latest. In fact, it began on the latter date and brought about the full operation of the Economic and Monetary Union (the EMU).

Concurrently, a European System of Central Banks (the ESCB) composed of the European Central Bank (ECB), based in Frankfurt, and of the national central banks of the present-day twenty-seven Member States, was established with the task to orientate the EU's monetary policy towards *stability*.

The system of central banks so established was to be independent of any political influence from any government of a Member State or from Community bodies or institutions, and its primary objective was to cause Member States to observe price stability.

The decision-making procedure for the passage to the final stage was intended to ensure full participation in the EMU to any Member States capable to ensure long-term stability policies. To this end, in order to arrive at the final stage and to overcome the resistances offered by some Member States, it was resolved that only those countries that met the minimum economic requirements set out in details further below should be admitted to the EMU. Moreover, it was agreed that the participating States should be selected in accordance with the principle of accession, and that any State intending to exercise a specific reservation made in advance should be allowed to remain outside the system.

The ECB has two decision-making bodies, the *Governing Council*[48] and the *Executive Board*.[49] The former usually meets twice a month and its primary task is

48. See Article 112 EC and Article 10 of the Statute of the European System of Central Banks and of the European Central Bank. The Governing Council comprises the six members of the Executive Board and the governors of the national central banks of the 15 States members of the euro area. Pursuant to Article 113 EC, the President of the EU Council and one member of the Commission may participate, without voting rights, in the meetings of the Governing Council.

49. See Article 11 of the Statute of the ESCB and of the ECB. The Executive Board comprises the President, the Vice-President and four other members appointed by the Heads of State and Government of the States members of the euro area (meeting at the European Council), upon

to formulate monetary policy for the eurozone. The Executive Committee is responsible for preparing the Governing Council's meetings, implementing monetary policy for the eurozone, managing the ECB's day-to-day business and exercising certain powers delegated to it by the Governing Council, including some of a regulatory nature.

The ECB's General Council[50] performs functions of an advisory nature (carrying out the tasks taken over from the European Monetary Institute) and also represents the twelve countries which are *not members* of the eurozone yet. For it comprises the President and Vice-President of the ECB, plus the governors of the national central banks (NCBs) of the twenty-seven EU Member States. The other members of the ECB's Executive Board may attend the meetings of the General Council, though without voting rights.

The General Council's responsibility is essentially to act as a transitional link between the euro area and the non-euro area countries. It will be dissolved once all EU Member States have introduced the single currency.

Therefore, within this overall picture, there is a 'single monetary area' in respect of which the ESCB has exclusive responsibility for monetary decisions, with the *primary objective* to maintain price stability, and so, pursuant to Article 105(1) of the Maastricht Treaty:

> the ESCB shall support the general economic policies in the Community with a view to contributing to the achievement of the objectives of the Community as laid down in Article 2. The ESCB shall act in accordance with the principle of *an open market economy with free competition*, favouring an efficient allocation of resources, and in compliance with the principles set out in Article 4. [*Emphasis added*].

Pursuant to paragraph 2 of the same article:

> The basic tasks to be carried out through the ESCB shall be:
>
> – to define and implement the monetary policy of the Community;
> – to conduct foreign exchange operations consistent with the provisions of Article 111;
> – to hold and manage the official foreign reserves of the Member States;
> – to promote the smooth operation of payment systems.

It is also empowered to establish the necessary guidelines for the implementation of key interest rates (Article 12 of the Statute of the ECB).

---

recommendation from the Council and consultation with the Parliament and the EBC's Governing Council. At the time of writing, the President of the ECB is Jean-Claude Trichet (France), the Vice-President is Lucas D. Papademos (Greece), and the other four members of the Executive Board are Lorenzo Bini Smaghi (Italy), José Manuel González-Páramo (Spain), Jürgen Stark (Germany) and Gertrude Tumpel-Gugerell (Austria).

50. See Articles 45-47 of the ESCB and ECB Statute.

Beginning on 1 January 2002, the euro has been actual legal tender[51] replacing all the currencies of the Member States participating in the 'euroarea' or 'eurozone', within which conversion is applied at the exchange of rate established for each of them at the beginning of the final stage.[52]

The result has been a 'two-speed' Monetary Union, to account for the other Member States not admitted to the final stage or remained outside the euro area by exercising the reservation stated at the time of signing the Maastricht Treaty. This is still the case with the United Kingdom, Denmark and, *de facto*, though in different terms, Sweden.

As at 30 June 2008, the *euro area* included fifteen, and the *non-euro area* the remaining twelve, of the twenty-seven Member States of the European Union.[53]

The entry of nine of the non-euro area Member States has been scheduled to take place upon them meeting the requisite criteria indicated below. The procedure is more complex for the other three. Sweden lies in a limbo of a sort, with an open-ended derogation it has not yet resolved if, how or when to give up, while the United Kingdom and Denmark have stated reservations on euro membership under specific protocols, thereby benefiting from a special 'opt-out' status, based on which both States will basically remain out of the Monetary Union *sine die*, subject to their option to enter if and when they choose to do so.

Based on specific monetary agreements with Monaco, San Marino and the Vatican City State, each such country had adopted the euro as its domestic currency and has been entitled to issue coins within set limits. Yet, as they are not EU Member States, they are not part of the euro area.

In order to prevent fluctuations in the exchange rates of each of the non-euro countries against the euro from creating disruptions within the internal market, a special exchange rate mechanism (ERM II, or Exchange Rate Mechanism II[54]), based on fixed exchange rates within the permitted fluctuation band. The Danish kroner joined ERM II on 1 January 1999, and observes a central rate to the euro within a 'narrow' fluctuation band of ±2.25%, while the remaining countries (only four, in fact, i.e. Estonia, Latvia, Lithuania and Slovakia, as the four other States

---

51. See Council Regulation (EC) No. 974/98 of 3 May 1998 on the introduction of the euro in [1998] O.J. L139, p. 1 ff., as amended for later accession of new EU Member States by Council Regulations (EC) No. 2596/2000 of 27 Nov. 2000, in [2000] O.J. L300, p. 2 ff., No. 2169/2005 of 21 Dec. 2005, [2005] O.J. L346, p. 1 ff., No. 1647/2006 of 7 Nov. 2006, *ibid.*, 9.11.2006, p. 2 ff., No. 835/2207 of 10 Jul. 2007, [2007] O.J. L186, p. 1 ff., and No. 836/2007 of 10 Jul. 2007, [2007] O.J. L186, p. 3.
52. The conversion rates irrevocably fixed between the euro and the currencies of the Member States that have adopted the euro are contained in Article 1 of Council Regulation (EC) No. 2866/98 of 31 Dec. 1998, in [1998] O.J. L359, p. 1 f.
53. The following Member States have joined the euro zone: Belgium, Germany, Ireland, Greece, Spain, France, Italy, Cyprus, Luxembourg, Malta, The Netherlands, Austria, Portugal, Slovenia and Finland. Slovakia will adopt the euro on 1 Jan. 2009. As from that date, the euro area will include sixteen Member States and the so-called ERM II zone will include only four Member States (Denmark, Estonia, Lithuania and Latvia).
54. The Roman number two has been added to distinguish it from the original ERM under the European Monetary System.

originally not included have joined the euro area) have been allowed a 'wide' fluctuation band of ±15.00%.

Thus, the United Kingdom and Sweden, as well as Hungary, the Czech Republic, Poland, Bulgaria and Romania, have remained out of ERM II since inception.[55]

The position of the United Kingdom is quite another story, if only because of the serious consequences its self-exclusion has had and still has on the whole European Union.

The history of the monetary relations between the United Kingdom and the Community has never been a downhill path. At the time of the establishment of the EMS, the United Kingdom had appeared willing to join, but, as indicated above, it left the system in August 1993.

As the British pound has not joined the euro area, no conversion rate for it has been fixed to the euro, but, as at 2 January 2002, i.e. on the day that the euro became single legal tender in substitution for the participating Member States' currencies, the pound sterling stood at 0.6262 to 1 euro.

The exchange rate has constantly fluctuated since then, with depreciation peaks approximating 30%.

As at 30 June 2008, the exchange rate was 1 euro against 0.79225 pounds sterling, with a depreciation of 20.9%.

Over the period from 4 January 1999 to 30 June 2008, based on ECB official statistics, the British pound fluctuated between a low 0.57110 (on 3 May 2000) and a peak of 0.80610 (on 16 April 2008).[56] On the same dates, the exchange rates of the euro against the dollar were 0.8891 and 1.597, respectively.

Such an anomaly can be understood more easily by looking at the fluctuation of the Danish krone and the Swedish krona against the euro on the same dates. The former (which. as indicated above, is allowed to fluctuate within a narrow band of ±2.25%) went from 7.4388 to 7.4581, and the latter (which has remained out of any scheme) from 9.2825 to 9.3581.

In general, the Treaty requires that the status of the Member States not participating in the euro area be reviewed every two years so that, at the expiry of each two-year period, both the States that have filed and exercised reservation and any other Stare temporarily excluded from the system can be allowed to join.

The criteria initially laid down in the Maastricht Treaty for admission to the euro area concerned: price stability, sustainability of the Government's financial position, the observance of the normal fluctuation margins provided for by the ERM for at least two years, without devaluing against the currency of any other Member State, and long term interest rates reflecting the durability of the convergence achieved by the Member State concerned.

The criteria initially to be fulfilled, obviously only in respect of the States then members of the EU, for testing the achievement by each State of a 'high degree of sustainable convergence', with a view to the admission to the euro area, have

---

55. Only Romania has a commitment to join the euro area by 2014.
56. Source: ECB, <www.ecb.int.stats>. As at 15 Dec. 2008, the exchange rate was 1 euro against 0.8994 GB pounds.

essentially remained unchanged, *mutatis mutandis*, also for the States that acceded to the European Union at a later time. The criteria so stated were:

(1) the achievement of a high degree of price stability; this will be apparent from an average rate of inflation, observed over a period of one year before the examination, that does not exceed by more than 1/2 percentage points that of, at most, the three best performing Member States in terms of price stability;
(2) the sustainability of budgetary position as reflected by a ratio of government deficit to gross domestic product that does not exceed (or 'substantially and continuously' comes close to) 3% as the reference value, and by a ratio of government debt to gross domestic product that does not exceed (or approaches at a 'satisfactory pace') the reference value of 60%;
(3) the observance of the normal fluctuation margins provided for by the Exchange Rate Mechanism of the European Monetary System (by maintaining the exchange rate within the narrow band of fluctuation from central parity), for at least two years, without devaluing against the currency of any other Member State;
(4) the durability of convergence achieved by the Member State and of its participation in the Exchange Rate Mechanism of the European Monetary System as reflected in the long-term interest rate levels; this criterion means that, observed over a period of one year before the examination, a Member State has had an average nominal long-term interest rate that does not exceed by more than 2 percentage points that of, at most, the three best performing Member States in terms of price stability. (In fact, as differences in nominal interest rates essentially reflect different inflation expectations by national governments, this latter criterion is actually intended to reinforce the former).

To get a better grasp of the huge extent, far beyond expectations, of the improvement in individual Member State's general economic situation from that prevailing on the date of the entry into force of the Maastricht Treaty, it is enough to consider that, as at that date, 1 November 1993, only three Member States would have been eligible forthwith for admission to the last stage of the Economic and Monetary Union, i.e. Luxembourg, France and Denmark – Denmark being, in fact, one of the States benefiting from the opt-out provision.

7. THE CRITICALITIES OF THE EUROPEAN 'RIGID' SYSTEM

The complex construction outlined above, which has given rise to the 'Eurosystem', lends itself to some criticism.

Clearly enough, the euro is different from any other currency having legal tender status in any State Member in the non-euro area, such as the British pound, the Danish krone, the Swedish krona and others, or in any third country, such as the US dollar, the Canadian dollar, the Australian dollar, the Chinese yuan or renminbi, the Japanese yen, the Russian ruble and others, all of which are currencies controlled by individual States and subject to the 'political' decisions of individual governments. Unlike these currencies, the euro does not belong to any one State but is an outgrowth of the European Union organization, the so-called Eurosystem.

Yet, the political powers so removed from each of the States participating in the euro zone have not been paralleled by similar powers vested in Community institutions under the ESCB. It has aptly been observed that:

> There are no bodies within the Eurosystem which are vested with political powers identical with, or similar to, those of which the Member States have been deprived. Within the area of fundamental decision, political powers have simply been suppressed.[57]

The end result has been a *sui generis* system without bodies institutionally vested with decision-making powers similar to those exercised in monetary policy by, for example, the President, the Congress and/or the Federal Reserve in the United States, or their counterparts in any other country around the world.

In other words, within the European monetary system, political decisions to be taken on a case-by-case basis, even though they may have major effects on the European peoples' economic and social lives, have been substituted for by rigid and unchangeable treaty rules and standards to be invariably complied with at all times.

Thus, within this context:

> the Council, the Commission and the European Central Bank have names identical with, or similar to, those of governmental bodies in any country. Still, as difficult as it might be to believe, their functions appear to be entirely different. They are not the holders of political powers, and they only exercise merely applicatory functions. Their only one task is to interpret the Treaty and to ensure strict observance of the rules and constraints of the Eurosystem. The Eurosystem is not governed by people, but by the operation of a machine, which has ultimately been cleaned up and freed of any human contribution. Whatever is to be concretely done, even in the distant future, was established at the time of its creation, in a way that is abstract by reason of having been fixed *ex ante* and once for all.[58]

What is certain is that the current power vacuum implies, among other negative effects, the lack of immediate reactivity, which is *per se* able to discourage the phenomenon of international speculation.[59]

57. Thus in Guarino, *Eurosistema: Analisi e prospettive* (Milan, 2006), p. 56.
58. Guarino, *Eurosistema*, cit., p. 60 and also p. 103.
59. As a rule, speculation does not have an autonomous strength, capable to impose its own solutions or even to play an active role on choices made by the main countries of the world, but goes with or, in the most favourable intuitions, precedes the actual course of demand and supply; amplifies the trends of real economy, but it does not seem able to modify its movements, at least in the medium/long term.

It emerges from the foregoing that the powers delegated by the Maastricht Treaty to the Community's governing bodies are not 'political'. They are, in fact, of a typically *technical* nature and are *strictly bound* to that one objective, *price stability*.[60]

If these are the Eurosystem's core deficiencies, there is a pressing need, partly in the wake of more than five years' experience, for some action to be taken to make the application of the Treaty more flexible, a result that is most likely to be attained through an appropriate *ad-hoc* regulation of the Council.

Far more difficult would it be to fill the existing political power vacuum indicated above.[61] Indeed, in light of the firm adoption of the euro as the European single currency, I wonder whether there is any choice between restoring the relevant 'political' powers to the individual national States in the euro area and giving the Council (or the Ecofin?) a greater (discretional) political say in monetary decisions or whether the latter option is the only one remaining approach to be pursued in practice.

Clearly enough, the latter option would find an obstacle in the full freedom of action still available to the national authorities of the States not participating in the euro area.

Nor can the purpose be served by either the Commission or the ECB as possible new proxies. For the latter is a technical body *par excellence*, while the former has no political responsibilities, at least under the Treaty of Rome. There is more to it, though. Precisely because of the essentially political character of the powers in question, the control over compliance with the Treaty in exercising them must, once they have been delegated, be withheld from the Commission in order to avoid such control from sliding back to the formal rigidity that ought be corrected in the first place.

In conclusion, it is my view that the problem could only be effectively overcome if the present Union is changed into an actual 'Union of States', by the establishment of a federal State vested with all political powers.

I do not believe, though, that this goal – which could only be attained after the European Union is re-founded, following a thorough reshuffling of executive and legislative powers at federal level – is within easy reach. For its attainment would require widespread awareness, extensive information and a debate involving every layer of European society about Europe's real objectives, none of which is anywhere to be found for the time being.

60. See Costi, at the presentation of the book by Guarino, *Eurosistema*, cit., in Florence, on 20 Apr. 2007, in *Eurosistema: Omaggio a Giuseppe Guarino*, Morbidelli Ed., (Florence, 2008), p. 49.
61. This issue is particularly pressing today in order to put the EU and its member States in condition to properly face the deep financial crisis arriving from the USA banking system which is already producing dramatic effects on the EU banking system. On the American crisis, see further Section 8 of Chapter V of this book.

8. A CRITICISM OF THE DOUBLE STANDARD: SERIOUS DISTORTIONS ACROSS THE EUROSYSTEM. THE UK CASE

Under an overall, *macroeconomic* view, the benefits for the exports and the drawbacks for the imports of goods and services, both within and outside the EU, could well be balanced off in the medium term, following a substantial creeping devaluation of the pound sterling against the euro and its comparatively low revaluation against the US dollar, as compared with the exchange rate of the euro to the US dollar. In the trade of goods and services with the other Member States and with third countries, the greater cost of the raw materials necessary for production could well be set off, in the large numbers, by the foreign exchange benefits arising to 'British' exporters.

However, this possible basic balance could hardly pass a sector-by-sector test. For there are activities in respect of which there are just marginal or no production costs. In any such sector, exports at a favourable rate of exchange only bring about a competitive edge. Examples are the entire area of trade or the area of the provision of services and, among them, the financial, interbank or insurance services, or the sectors of the manufacturing and trade of high-technology or high-value added products, such as widely popular brand products.

If one considers the shares of the investment banking and financial markets in the last decade, it should come to no surprise that most market leading banks have been English banks or banks otherwise operating on a permanent basis in or by the London financial market.[62] These are known to be two of the most profitable sectors of the banking industry, and the only ones with a geographic scope effectively extending across the European Union.[63]

Whether permanent aid measures are intended for undertakings established within the euro zone or for undertakings established outside it should be duly considered by the Community institutions when assessing each relevant case. This would be both in line with the *non-discrimination principle* – which is the foundation of observance of each of the four fundamental freedoms and the standard against which their full implementation throughout the European market should be measured – and with a correct and balanced application of the rules on free trading and competition, among which the criteria to be met to establish the lawfulness or the compatibility of State aid granted by legislative measures. The end result would simply be that at least one cause of disequilibrium, among others,[64] would be removed from intra-Community relationships, i.e. the disparity of exchange rates within the single market. This would also lead the States which

62. This observation was the subject of my oral discussion of 3 Feb. 2005 before the ECJ in defence of UniCredito about the Ciampi Act (in the joined hearing in Cases C-66/02 and C-148/04).
63. According to the European Commission, some investment banking and financial market segments even have an international dimension.
64. See paragraph 11 of Chapter VI below.

have freely chosen not to join the euro area to refrain from prolonging their positions of exclusive, *de facto* advantage indefinitely.[65]

The concrete advantage for the UK is an addition to the one, of not only a macroeconomic nature, which all Member States not participating in the eurozone enjoy just because of their being abstractly entitled to manage monetary issues with full powers to take political decisions and to set guidelines on the matter. Thus, they are free, if need be, to adopt unilateral measures based on a very wide flexibility of action in the interior and full freedom of action in relation to third countries' currencies. In fact, such unilateral measures are drastically precluded to the Member States participating in the eurozone, which are prevented, even at times of severe crisis of their national economy, from taking any restrictive action on capital movements to protect their domestic economy and are even barred from taking common action to protect the single currency, since any such action may only be taken – except in quite exceptional urgent cases – by the European Council with a necessarily all-embracing view, then regardless of any national differences.

I share the opinion of those who believe that allowing indefinitely for a double standard was a further serious mistake made when the euro and the present European Monetary System were first introduced.[66] I would myself stress that, since these are mechanisms established by international treaty, the lack of any treaty provision setting a time limit to the opt-out system, thereby positively influencing the future behaviours of those States – the United Kingdom, Denmark and Sweden – which could well join the eurozone in their own right at its very inception and declined to do so although they met the Maastricht criteria – may make the double standard anything but provisional and irreversible in fact.[67]

Why, one may wonder, should those very States which have achieved stable exchange rates against the world's major currencies, by admitting other 'virtuous' States to the euro area, become part of a rigid system, with all the faults pointed up above, and give up the advantages intrinsic even in the theoretical flexibility of exchange rates with their own domestic currencies, while being able, for the time being, to rely on their public opinions' and national undertakings' unconditional support to leaving things where they stand?

Still, the present unbalance of consumer good prices in individual national markets brings about serious doubts as to the functioning of the eurozone itself. The structural disparities still lawfully existing even between Member States – beyond any optimistic assumption to the contrary uncritically accepted widely within the Community[68] – show that there is no such thing as a single monetary market and that inflation risk is by no means shared uniformly across the Union. As a member of the ECB's Executive Board, Mr Bini Smaghi, has authoritatively

65. Thereby making the present disequilibrium irreversible in fact. See Guarino, *Eurosistema*, cit., *passim*.
66. See Guarino, *Eurosistema*, cit., *passim*.
67. See Guarino, *Eurosistema*, cit., pp. 41 and 175 f.
68. See Chapter VI of this volume, paragraph 10.

remarked,[69] the same consumer good, a litre of milk in a supermarket, costs 50% more in Rome or Milan than in Frankfurt on the same day, and although:

> not all products differ so widely in prices, but there are substantial differences in many cases. If Italian households were allowed to do their shopping at the prices ruling in Frankfurt instead of those quoted in Rome or Milan, then they would save a considerable portion of their incomes.[70]

If this is true – as it must be, if only because of the authority of the source – in respect of countries which have been members of the euro area for more than six years, one can readily grasp the significance of individual national governments' renouncement of any room for manoeuvre in their exchange rate policies, then of any opportunity to exercise direct influence on prices and inflation rates.

This picture of concrete disparity is compounded by Member States' widely differing expectations of economic growth, even entailing a very real risk of stagnation in some of them. Hence, the question of whether the ESCB would ever, even if modified and reinforced with political powers, be able to allow effective actions to be taken, beside the collective interest, necessarily with an eye to the critical or otherwise different position of any one State already participating in the eurozone, in the same way and as effectively as a non-euro country's national authority which is still required to observe the *common interest.*

This is by no means a marginal question, if one only considers that, even if participation in the eurozone were not an irreversible right in law, it would be bound to be so in fact, because of the serious consequences a State choosing to leave it would understandably incur. Indeed, the opposite approach should be taken. Suitable solutions should be investigated which, lacking any room for manoeuvre on monetary instruments, may give power back to the Member States participating in the euro area and allow them to take effective action, where appropriate, to protect their domestic economies – obviously without disregarding their commitment to act in the common interest, which is a duty to be observed by the non-participating Member States as well.

9. THE IMPACT OF THE EURO ON CONTRACTS OF DURATION

The introduction of the euro as a substitute for national currencies raised some issues in relation to contracts in force as at 1 January 2002 pursuant to which

---

69. See Bini Smaghi, 'Crisi e costo del denaro. Non lasciate sola la BCE', in *Corriere della Sera*, 7 Jun. 2008, p. 40. The topic was taken up and exhaustively discussed by *Sole 24 Ore*, 23 Jun. 2008, p. 15, in a central story by Scarli, *Area euro, l'altalena dei prezzi*, which confirms the substance of the observations offered above.
70. The extension of the Italian phenomenon of excessive prices to 'many' products seems to remove the doubt that the cause of the asymmetry found in the case of milk prices could be the milk quotas imposed years ago by the Community to the advantage of other Member States' milk producers by inflicting fines on the Po Valley farmers.

payments should be made in one or another of the EU Member States' currencies so substituted for.

As aptly implied in the Eighth Whereas of Council Regulation (EC) No 1103/97 of 17 June 1997, the first of several regulations on provisions relating to the introduction of the euro, monetary matters are subject to the *lex monetae* because of the universally accepted principle of the recognition of the monetary law of the issuing State.

Indeed, it is for the issuing State to determine what is to be understood for a currency having legal tender status, what sub-units and multiples it should be composed of and, in general, any provisions relating to the internal and international circulation of that currency.[71] As a consequence, only the substitution of the euro for the original contractual currency, the time of its inception and the other aspects just indicated above fall within the scope of that State's *lex monetae*. Conversely, the determination of interest rates, indexation and the possibility to adjust a contract to devaluation are aspects regulated by the *lex contractus* as identified on the basis of the relevant rule of conflict of laws applicable in the legal system in question.

Thus, the actions taken by the Council of the European Union, which, by Regulation No 1103 of 1997 and subsequent instruments, paramount among which is Regulation No 974/1998 of 3 May 1998,[72] has explicitly confirmed the *principle of the continuity of contracts*, should be analysed within the framework of all provisions of private international law relating to contracts.

Pursuant to Article 3 of Regulation No 1103/1997:

> The introduction of the euro shall not have the effect of altering any term of a legal instrument or of discharging or excusing performance under any legal instrument, nor give a party the right unilaterally to alter or terminate such an instrument.

Still, Article 3 goes on to specify:

> This provision is subject to anything which parties may have agreed.

Thus, the principle of the continuity of contracts has finally been laid down, so that no party is allowed to plead any of the remedies for the termination or alteration of a contract that are available in any jurisdiction upon the occurrence of exceptional or unpredictable events.

---

71. On the subject, generally, see Mann, *The legal aspect of money* (5th ed., Oxford, 1992); Conforti, *L'esecuzione delle obbligazioni nel diritto internazionale privato* (Naples, 1962), p. 261 ff.; Vardi, 'Reflections on Trends and Evolutions' in *The Law of Monetary Obligations in European Private Law* [2007] Eur. Bus. Law. Rev., p. 443 ff.
72. Council Regulation No. 1103/1997 of 17 Jun. 1997 is in [1997] O.J. L162, p. 1 ff.; it was amended by Council Regulation No. 2595/2000 of 27 Nov. 2000 [2000] O.J. L300, p. 1. Council Regulation No. 974/1998 of 3 May 1998 is in [1998] O.J. L139, p. 1 ff, and it was amended by Council Regulation No. 2596/2000 of 27 Nov. 2000 in [2000] O.J. L300, p. 2 f. The matter has been completed with various recommendations from the Commission on specific topics, and with a resolution by the European Parliament on the duration of the transitional period.

The introduction of such an explicit provision is intended 'to fulfil the objective to provide legal certainty and transparency' (Seventh Whereas of Regulation No 1103/1997).

The significance attributed to this issue in international trade is witnessed by the laws whereby the States of California, New York, Illinois, North Carolina, Texas, Arizona, New Jersey and so on have, concurrently with, and in the same way as, Regulation No 1103/1997, laid down the principle of the continuity of contracts following the substitution of the euro for the various European national currencies.[73]

What Community law and similar US statutes intend to ensure, each within its scope for enforcement, is that the introduction of the euro as the single currency in the EU Member States participating in the euro area should not be treated as an alteration capable to make any provision for contingencies applicable to any contract of duration, and to exclude that it may become a cause of 'frustration'. Accordingly, the coming of the euro must be treated as an occurrence immaterial to the contract, and the contract stands as it was at the time of execution subject to anything to the contrary the parties may agree as to the contractual currency.

It is not by chance that the principle of the continuity of contracts has been laid down by the European Council in a *Regulation*, i.e. in an instrument of Community law directly applicable and enforceable *erga omnes* in the legal system of every Member State of the European Union, and one which prevails *per se* over any rule of internal law in contrast with it, even if adopted at a later time.[74] Thus, this principle has been superimposed on the Member States' laws, thereby making any conflicting provisions inapplicable,[75] and, because of the peculiarities of the instrument used – a regulation – it applies not only to contracts governed by the law of a *Member State participating* in the EMU, but to any contracts governed by *a Member State not participating in the EMU*, or at least in the 'senior league' of the euro zone.

Consequently, a monetary obligation requiring payment to be made in the currency of a State in the euro zone after 1 January 2002, must be performed in euros. The creditor must accept payment, without being entitled to raise any objection grounded on any material rule of the *lex contractus* in relation to the change in the contractual currency, since any such objection is expressly barred by Article 3 of Regulation No 1103/1997.

Because of the importance the Council has ascribed to the matter, even *contracts governed by the law of a non-EU State* should, where they require payments to be made in the currency of a Sate in the eurozone, follow the substitution of the euro for the relevant contractual currency, and their other terms should remain unaffected thereby.

---

73. See, for example, New York General Obligation Law, Title 16, para. 5-1602, Continuity of contract. For some of those statutes, see also Pocar & Malatesta, *L'Euro e i contratti internazionali* (Milan, 1999), p. 446 ff.
74. See the Introduction to this book.
75. In this sense, see De Nova, 'Il principio di continuità dei contratti dopo l'introduzione dell' Euro' [1998] I Contratti, pp. 5-6.

Since the euro has legal tender status as the currency issued by the States participating in the EMU, and circulated as such within the euro area, it cannot but be quietly accepted as a new currency substituted for the contractual currency, at the conversion rate adopted by the Community institutions, even from the standpoint of the legal system of a non-EU State. Accordingly, *the substitution of the euro for contractual currencies* occurs automatically even in respect of contracts subject to a third country's law which provide for payments in any of the European domestic currencies.

What will happen, though, in case a contract *governed by the law of a third county* originally required payments to be made in ECU? In this case, neither the official ECU nor, even the less, the 'private' ECU – both being mere 'virtual' units of account, rather than official means of payments having legal tender status – may be deemed to be caught by the definition 'currency issued by a State', i.e. a currency to which the principle of the issuing State's exclusive sovereignty over the regulation of its own currency must apply, as also confirmed by Regulation No 1103/1997. Accordingly, the substitution of the euro for the ECU is legally irrelevant to a contract governed by a third country's law. In this case, each party to the contract will retain *full freedom as to the outcome of the contract*, including the right to withdraw from, or terminate, the contract or to adjust it to any intervening circumstances, obviously subject to the terms permitted by the material rules of the *lex contractus*.

If the approach advocated by some authors is followed, Regulation No 1103/1997 *would not be applicable also to contracts governed by a third country's law*, since Article 3 of the Regulation should not be treated as a mandatory rule of law. It is appropriate to observe that this quality is typical of the rules long identified by Italian private international law scholars and expressly set out in Article 17 of Act No 218 of 31 May 1995 on the *reform of the Italian system of private international law*.

Let me point out here, as elsewhere in this book,[76] that, as mandatory rules of law are intended to protect public interests, they provide a special class of mandatory rules or provisions of domestic public policy of a positive value. That is to say that they must be applied in any event, irrespective of any reference made under private international law to any other governing law.

Now, based on the argument that the last sentence of Article 3 of Regulation No 1103/1997 makes the relevant provision 'subject to anything which parties may have agreed', some have maintained that that article lacks the minimum requirement of cogency for that provision to be construed as an inescapable rule, and it cannot, therefore, and *a fortiori*, be categorized as a mandatory rule of law.

In principle, a rule of law may only be qualified as mandatory if it cannot be waived or derogated from by private autonomous choice, while it is deemed dispositive when it is intended to govern relationships that are not otherwise governed by contract.

---

76. See paras. 11, 15 and 16 of Chapter I, above, and paragraph 1 of Chapter VI below.

If, therefore, the provision in question were deprived of cogency in the EU Member States, in which Regulation No 1103/1997 is directly applicable, it would be all the more inconceivable for it to be treated as a mandatory rule of law in any third country's legal system.

Thus, following this approach in literature,[77] if the contract were governed by a third country's law (obviously subject to any relevant statutory provision adopted by such third country, as is the case with the US laws referred to above), the parties would be free to rely on the material provisions for contingencies applicable to that contract, if and insofar as any are contained in that law, even in case the parties had failed to set out any remedies to that effect in the contract.

If, however, it is maintained – as I do, based on the considerations offered below – that Article 3 qualifies as an actual mandatory rule of law, then, *even in respect of contracts governed by a third country's law*, in any case in which the relevant question *has been referred to a court of any EU Member State*, the court so referred to would be bound to have regard to the principle of the stability or continuity of contract laid down in Regulation No 1103/1997, specifically in Article 3 thereof. This would also be in accordance with Article 7(2) of the Rome Convention of 19 June 1980 on the law applicable to contractual obligations.

Indeed, this conclusion would still hold even if the question were raised before the courts of a EU Member State not participating in the euro zone by its own choice or for failing to meet the relevant requirements.

Such different approach presupposes that the norm contained in Article 3 of Regulation No 1103/1997 has a *cogent* content and should then be treated as a *mandatory rule of law* in each of the EU Member States' legal systems.

This presupposition is supported, first of all, on the fact that the provisions contained in Regulation No 1103/1997 are complementary to the rules on the introduction of the euro, which are themselves mandatory rules of law in their being concerned with monetary matters.[78]

As for Article 3, the reader should not be misled by the wording of the Italian version (*'L'introduzione dell'euro non ha l'effetto di modificare . . .'*) analogous to the French version (*'L'introduction de l'euro n'a pas pour effet de modifier . . .'*). The peremptory character of that provision emerges more clearly from the wording used in the English version ('The introduction of the euro shall not have the effect of altering . . .'), in the German version (*'Die Einfuehrung des euro bewirkt weder . . . noch . . .'*).

Nor seems the above presupposition to be impaired by the second sentence of Article 3, which makes the provision subject to anything the parties may have agreed, thereby attributing an imperative character to any event of conflict or failed agreement between the parties, as provided for in the first sentence of the same

77. See Draetta, 'L'Euro e la continuità dei contratti in corso' [1997] Diritto del commercio internazionale, p. 3 ff, p. 7 ff.

78. See, in general, on currency rules as mandatory rules of law: Santa Maria, 'Les critères d'application des règles italiennes de ch'ange' in *Comunicazioni e Studi*, cit., especially pp. 228, 236.

article. This is, in fact, a matter of contract law, which is rooted in *the core principle of the parties' autonomous wills*. It would be even inconceivable for a rule to go far beyond the principle of neutrality in respect of the introduction of the euro to prohibit termination by mutual agreement or even any mutually agreed amendments to the contract in respect, for example, of interest payments or any other matters not falling within the scope of the *lex monetae*.

As for how the provision in question is to be applied, the relevant criteria are stated, *ratione materiae*, in Regulation No 1103/1997 itself and, generally, in Article 189(2) EC.

It should be noted that, if the *question of the continuity of a payment obligation* arising from a contract governed by a third country's law is raised before the courts of a third country, then the application of the principle in question will depend on whether that country's body of laws recognize such principle as implying a mandatory rule of the *lex contractus* or a mandatory rule of the *lex fori* or else a mandatory rule of a foreign law with which the issue is closely connected. In this last case, the continuity principle may only be considered within the operating scope recognised to the mandatory rules of that foreign law.

A special issue relating to the matter under scrutiny here is how rates of interest should be determined in case the contractual currency changes. It has already been observed that contractual or legal interest rates must be determined in accordance with the *lex contractus*, and so, in the case of legal interest, in accordance with the law the parties have chosen as the governing law, whether before or after the contractual currency has changed.

In this case, under Italian law, the interest rate to be applied will still be the legal rate of interest provided for by the law that periodically alters the norm on legal interest contained in Article 1282 of the Civil Code (as suitably adjusted to the new situation).

This proposition is by no means affected by the last sentence of the Seventh Whereas of Regulation No 1103/1997, which provides:

> ... in the case of fixed interest rate instruments the introduction of the euro does not alter the nominal interest rate payable by the debtor...

Thus, in the case of a fixed-rate mortgage loan, the rate of interest agreed by the parties will remain unchanged even after the introduction of the euro.

This conclusion may, however, be too onerous for either party whenever the official discount rate of the euro is higher or lower than the rate originally agreed to by reference to the relevant national currency. For example, think of a case in which the contractual rate of interest as referred to the Italian lira were 8%, then two and a half percentage points above the official discount rate of the Italian lira in 2001, while the official discount rate of the euro is assumed to be a low 3% or 4%, and this in a legal system as that of Italy or France, where usurious rates are punished as criminal offences.

As indicated above, in the case of fixed-rate mortgage loans, the principle of the continuity of contracts requires that the introduction of the euro should not alter the nominal interest rate payable by the debtor.

However, applying the Italian law on usury (Act No 108/1996), would – according to the Supreme Court's interpretation according to which, for usury to be established, reference should be made not to the time that the contract was first created, but to the time of each interest payment – *mandatorily* alter the debtor-to-creditor relationship between the bank and the borrower, thus breaching the relevant provision in the Council Regulation.

Even after the adoption of the law of authentic interpretation of Act 108/1996 (Act No 49 of 28 February 2001), it is unclear how the Italian (as well as French) rules on usury may operate within a single economic area characterized by a single currency. One should wonder how reference could still be made only to the interest rates applied in the Italian market, while the very concept of an *Italian* financial and banking market has lost any meaning, since the relevant market is now the European single market alone.

If that specific Italian norm were still to be applied, if only within the Italian territory, a disparity of treatment would occur on an essentially regional basis, limited to the Italian territory, that is, which appears incompatible with the design of a European economic and monetary union.

What would then happen if the parties have failed to provide by contract for a fixed interest rate payable under any payment obligations, and have, instead, referred to the official discount rate or to the legal interest rate for the contractual currency without any qualification? It is my view that, in the former case, the official rate for the euro should automatically apply, though it may be considerably lower than that for the national currency.[79]

And what if the parties have referred by contract to instruments no longer existing in the international market? In this case, the law-maker will have to take over, as was the case, for example, with a decree adopted for the introduction of the euro in Italy (the Ministry of the Treasury Decree of 23 December 1998), whereby the RIBOR was replaced by the EURIBOR as the new indexation rate applicable to legal instruments and relationships – an instance of substitution of contractual provisions by statute.

10. PRIVATE PARTIES AND THE FULL LIBERALIZATION OF CAPITAL MOVEMENTS AND PAYMENTS IN THE EUROPEAN UNION

As observed above, the full liberalization of capital flows and payments within the Community had already been achieved during the first stage of the Economic and Monetary Union. This accomplishment was chiefly due to the entry into force, on

79. Pursuant to the Ministry for the Economy and Finance Decree of 12 Dec. 2007, updating Article 1284, Civil Code, the legal interest rate has been determined at 3 percent *per annum*. That rate was: 5 percent in the original version of the Code; 10 percent as from 16 Dec. 1990; 5 percent as from 1 Jan. 1997; 2.5 percent as from 1 Jan. 1999; 3.5 percent as from 1 Jan. 2001; 3 percent as from 1 Jan. 2002; and 2.5 percent as from 1 Jan. 2004.

1 July 1990, of Council Directive No 88/361 of 24 June 1994, which repealed all previous directives on the matter, thereby bringing about a veritable Copernican revolution.

It was then that *full liberalization* was imposed as a general rule. For paragraph 1 of Article 1 required:

> Without prejudice to the following provisions, Member States shall abolish restrictions on movements of capital taking place between persons resident in Member States.

Article 1 was supplemented by Annex I headed 'Nomenclature of the capital movements referred to in Article 1 of the Directive'. Annex I contained a list of liberalized capital movements, though the last paragraph of the Nomenclature specified that the list *only had an indicative purpose*. Indeed:

> *This Nomenclature is not an exhaustive list for the notion of capital movements* – whence a heading XIII-F. 'Other capital movements – Miscellaneous'. It should *not* therefore be interpreted as restricting the scope of the *principle of full liberalization of capital movements* as referred to in Article 1 of the Directive. [*Emphasis added*].

In furtherance of the principle of full liberalization that has governed capital movements within the Community since 1 July 1990, any relationships between persons residing in different EU Member States, as well as any transaction entered into by a resident of a Member State with anyone residing in a third country, have been entirely free since then, *without any reference to specifically authorized transaction.*

Exceptions have been allowed, though, under the restrictions *expressly* and *mandatorily* stated in the Directive and under any restrictions on the exercise of a different fundamental freedom as might indirectly affect capital movements in special instances complementary to the realization of such fundamental freedom.

In this respect, the Court of Justice, in its Judgment of 28 January 1992, *Hanns-Martin Bachmann* v *Belgian State*, Case C-204/90,[80] observed that:

> ... Article 67 [in the original version of the Rome Treaty] does not prohibit restrictions which do not relate to the movement of capital but which result indirectly from restrictions on other fundamental freedoms ...

During the period of application of Directive No 88/361, which expired upon the entry into force of the Maastricht Treaty on 31 December 1993, each Member State retained the option, as an exception to the general liberalization principle, to apply protective measures in respect of *those transactions alone which were listed in Annex II*,

> where *short-term capital movements of exceptional magnitude* impose *severe strains* on foreign-exchange markets and lead to serious disturbances in the

80. [1992] ECR 249 f., para. 34.

> conduct of a Member State's monetary and exchange rate policies, being reflected in particular in substantial variations in domestic liquidity (Article 3(1), *emphasis added*).

In principle, under the conditions so stated, it was for the Commission, after consulting the Monetary Committee and the Committee of Governors of the Central Banks, to authorize a Member State to take protective measures the conditions and details of which the Commission would determine, *so long as, and only if, the relevant transaction was one of the capital movements listed in Annex II.*

Further, by way of exception and on grounds of urgency, such protective measures might be taken by the Member State concerned itself, but remained subject to the Commission's scrutiny on the merits at any subsequent time as well as on the date of their entry into force (Article 3(2)). The decisions taken by the Commission in this respect might be set aside or amended by the Council acting by a qualified majority (Article 3(3)). In no event might the period of application of such protective measures *exceed six months* (Article 3(4)).

As can plainly be seen, in respect of both the provision of Article 73 and the contents of Article 108 of the Treaty – in the original text of both articles later repealed by the Maastricht Treaty – the rules on protective measures introduced by the 1988 Directive were primarily based on very strict requirements which greatly restricted their use. It was so, essentially because of the preconditions for application, since the transactions concerned were to be 'short-term capital movements of exceptional magnitude' capable to 'impose severe strains' and to 'lead to serious disturbances'. It was so also because of the object, since the taking of protective measures was – as observed above – *mandatorily* limited to 'the capital movements listed in Annex II' to the Directive.

Moreover, since 1 July 1990,[81] national authorities have been under a prohibition to carry out any preventive, or even the less subsequent, currency controls beyond:

> all requisite measures to prevent infringements of their laws and regulations, inter alia in the field of taxation and prudential supervision of financial institutions, or to lay down procedures for the declaration of capital movements for purposes of administrative or statistical information. [*Emphasis added*].

Nevertheless, in order to reaffirm the exceptional character of this provision as contrasted with the general rule, Article 4 of the Directive required:

> Application of those measures and procedures may not have the effect of impeding capital movements carried out in accordance with Community law.[82]

81. Directive No. 88/361 was implemented in Italy by a Ministerial Decree of 27 Apr. 1990 ([1990] O.J. No. 100).
82. This approach has been confirmed by the ECJ's settled case law. In its judgment of 14 Jul. 1977, Case 8/77, *Sagulo, Brenca, Bakhouche*, cit., paragraph 5, the Court ruled: '. . . a member state . . . must naturally not adopt administrative or judicial measures which would have the

By the Maastricht Treaty, the principles laid down in Directive No 88/361 became rules of primary law contained in Articles 56 through 60 newly introduced in Chapter 4 under the now consolidated heading 'Capital and Payments'.

Quite briefly, it is the text of the Treaty which has provided that the general rule underlying the new European monetary system is full liberalization of capital movements across the Union, and this also applies in relation to capital inflows or outflows from or to third countries.

Derogations are restricted to the cases provided for in Article 58(1) EC, where Member States are allowed:

> (a) to apply the relevant provisions of their tax law which distinguish between taxpayers who are not in the same situation with regard to their place of residence or with regard to the place where their capital is invested;
>
> (b) to take all requisite measures *to prevent infringements* of national law and regulations, in particular *in the field of taxation* and the *prudential supervision* of financial institutions, or to lay down procedures for the declaration of capital movements for purposes of *administrative or statistical information*, or *to take measures which are justified on grounds of public policy or public security*. [*Emphasis added*].

Paragraph 2 specifies:

> The provisions of this chapter shall be without prejudice to the applicability of restrictions on the right of establishment which are compatible with this Treaty.

Paragraph 3 further states:

> The measures and procedures referred to in paragraphs 1 and 2 shall not constitute a means of arbitrary discrimination or a disguised restriction on the free movement of capital and payments as defined in Article 56.

As for protective measures, safeguard may only be taken, in principle, by the Council (Article 59 EC), or, by way of exception, by the Member State concerned, but only on grounds of urgency and on a temporary basis (Article 60 EC).

Thus, the entire 'list nomenclature' system has been abandoned, in respect of any transactions, whether authorized or granted by derogation, not allowed or subject to reservation. Following full liberalization, the former are no longer necessary and the latter are no longer admissible. In other words, no specific derogations from the basic principle of the freedom of capital movements and payments exist any longer, not even within the scope of mandatory lists.

---

effect of limiting the full exercise of the rights which the Community law guarantees to the nationals of other Member States' ([1977] ECR 1504, cit.). The same view was taken by the ECJ in the following judgments: 3 Feb. 1983, Case 29/82, *Van Luipen*, cit., p. 151, and 4 Dec. 1986, Case 205/84, *Commission* v *Federal Republic of Germany*, cit., p. 3810, para. 54.

The only possible exceptions arise from Article 58(1) EC just quoted. Of the two points stated there, let me stress the right recognised to Member States:

> to take measures which are justified on grounds of public policy or public security. [*Emphasis added*].

This provision is a transposition, even among the rules on free capital movements, of the derogation expressed (albeit by a broader formulation) in Article 30 EC, in respect of the general prohibition of quantitative restrictions on imports and exports, under the general principle of the free movement of goods, which derogation has been extended under Article 46 EC to grounds of 'public health', in respect of the right of establishment, and restated by reference in Article 55 EC, where such derogation is also applicable within the scope of the freedom to provide services.

The right in question, in respect of one or another fundamental freedom, is peculiarly relevant – as a legal basis pleaded by Member States to justify application of the rules on the so-called 'golden share' discussed below – to the privatization of companies operating in sectors considered to be especially important for the national economy.

11. THE FUNDAMENTAL FREEDOMS AND THE EXERCISE OF 'SPECIAL POWERS': THE TERMS OF THE PROBLEM

Clearly enough, the primary objective of the full implementation of all of the EU's four fundamental freedoms has been achieved through the full realization of the free movement of capital and payments.

One major effect of that achievement has been the freedom for any person within the Community, whether natural or legal, to acquire control over, or even to purchase a substantial holding in, any company, whether privately or publicly held, listed or unlisted in a regulated market in the EU, in compliance with the rules of the Members State in which the 'target' is established. However, such rules must not be *discriminatory* against a different Member State's citizens, and they must not generate such an impact, in whatever manner, as to *discourage* a potential acquirer who is a citizen of another Member State.

Hence, the conflicts that have arisen between the governments of various Member States and the Commission in recent years, especially in respect of such major sectors of the national economy as energy, electricity, telephony, natural gas and oil products generally.[83]

On the one hand, Member States are wary of acquisitions in their national economies' most delicate industries by 'foreigners', even if Community citizens, or, more frequently, by companies treated as Community 'companies or firms'

83. About the interpretation of the derogation to restrictions on capital movements, see the ECJ's recent judgment of 14 Feb. 2008, Case C-274/06, not yet published in ECR.

within the meaning of Article 48 EC. Such wariness has often led the government of this or that Member State, especially in respect of privatization transactions and after *losing control*, to secure a number of governance prerogatives, loosely referred to as 'special powers' or 'golden shares'.

On the other hand, the Commission has constantly take a strong position in the matter, waging a 'crusade' of a sort to reaffirm the general value of the fundamental freedoms, among which the free movements of capital – albeit by way of rather shaky references.

The end result has been a situation of harsh conflict in respect of which, in an attempt to curb and restrict the exercise by Member States' governments of 'special powers', the Commission has repeatedly summoned each Member State concerned before the Court of Justice, pursuant to Article 226 EC, requesting, often successfully, that that Member State be punished for failure to fulfil its obligations under the Treaty. Consequently, substantial case-law has built up on the entire matter, providing sufficient clarity to all but a few cases and essentially endorsing the exceedingly stringent rules of conduct imposed on Member States along the lines advocated by the Commission.

12. THE LEGAL BASES OF THE CONFLICT OVER 'GOLDEN SHARES' BETWEEN THE COMMISSION AND MEMBER STATES

What is commonly known as 'golden share', or *action spécifique*, is a core of prerogatives a privatizing government authority retains, being thereby given more or more effective rights – the so-called 'special powers' – than those it would be given, as any private party, by statute or common law.[84]

Such powers to act *are not necessarily associated with the capacity of shareholder* vested in the State or in any government authority. In fact, the 'golden share' institute, one of Anglo-Saxon origin, seems to be grounded on the actual, full disposal by the State of its holdings. Under English law, the relevant legal framework consists in making a company's capital include a *special share*, preferred and convertible, of one pound nominal value, the 'golden share' in fact, which is held by the government or a government agency and capable to allow its holder to retain control over the company even after disposing of the other shares of different classes representing the whole or a majority of that company's capital.

The influence the State can exercise pursuant to the national rules on golden shares is, therefore, of an exceptional nature only, and it is only intended to protect public interests in sectors of a peculiar strategic importance, on the basis of the derogation granted to Member States by the last sentence of Article 58(1)(b) EC, which gives them the right 'to take *measures which are justified on grounds of public policy or public security*' in the matter of the free movement of capital and payments.

---

84. See Libonati, 'La faticosa "accelerazione" delle privatizzazioni' [1995] Giur. comm., 39.

The Italian legislator itself has even gone beyond the British golden share model (according to which the government retains ownership of at least *one* share carrying special rights) to separate the government's privileged position from its status as a shareholder, by assigning the golden share direct to the State, without qualification, so long as certain requirements are met.[85]

The restrictions posed by Community law to any Member State's or national authority's attempted influence in the sense just indicated, have firmly been supported by the Commission. The Commission's starting point is the recognition of its own neutrality under Community law, in furtherance of Article 295 EC, which states that the Treaty 'shall in no way prejudice the rules in Member States governing the system of property ownership', and of the consequent regulatory power accorded on an exclusive basis, in principle, to the national law-makers.[86]

In fact, the only relevant distinction under Community law between *private* and *public* ownership is that the latter is subject to the rules on State aid, in the classic sense of the phrase. In this respect, the principle still applies, as laid down in the ECJ's early case-law in the matter of State aid, that a *public* undertaking's conduct should be deemed lawful where it acts, for example in respect of an injection of capital, 'as if' it were a *private* undertaking.[87]

However, this statement cannot be true at all times. For the granting of such powers does not allow Member States or any national public bodies to retain any influence on the governance of privatized companies, regardless of whether their capital has been transferred to private investors in full or only in part, since, in the latter case, there will still be the tough problem of the 'proportionality' of the 'public' shareholder's rights arising from its remaining holding. How this problem should be correctly approached and solved under Community law will be discussed further below.

---

85. See Law Decree No. 332 of 31 May 1994, as converted, with amendment, into Act No. 474 of 30 Jul. 1994. This Act was amended, in accordance with the principles laid down by the ECJ, by Art. 4 of Act No. 350 of 24 Dec. 2003 (Finance Act 2004). For an exhaustive discussion of the Commission's and the Court's actions in respect of the Italian legislation on golden shares, see paragraph 14 of this Chapter 3.
86. In its Communication on services of general interest in Europe ([1996] O.J. C281, p. 3), the Commission specifies: 'The Community has nothing to say on whether companies responsible for providing general interest services should be public or private and is not, therefore, requiring privatisation.' See also the Communication of the Commission on certain legal aspects concerning intra-EU investment (97/C 220/06), footnote 1. The foregoing has also been confirmed by the approach taken by most authors in literature, which assumes, more or less broadly, that Art. 295 EC entails the neutrality of the Treaty in respect of national 'systems' of property ownership, including all acts of nationalization and privatization. See, for all, Mégret, *Le Droit de la CEE*, Vol. 15, (Brussels), p. 421; Groeben, Thiesing, Ehlermann, *Kommentar zum EU-/EG-Vertrag* (1997), p. 5/383; Various Authors, *Commentaire article par article des traités UE et CE* (Paris, Brussels, 2000), p. 1878; Pocar, *Commentario breve ai Trattati della Comunità e dell'Unione Europea* (Padua, 2001), p. 988.
87. See Judgment of the Court of 21 Mar. 1991, Case C-305/89, *Italian Republic* v *Commission*, [1991] ECR I-1603.

The legal basis on which the Commission's position is supported consists, first, of the EC Treaty rules on the free movements of capital and, secondly, of the rules protecting the right of establishment or the free provision of services.

In both cases, the Commission is well aware of the derogations allowed, with essentially equivalent formulations, by the last sentence of Article 58(1)(b) EC, relating to capital and payments (as quoted in full above), and by Article 46(1) EC, relating to freedom of establishment, as also referred to in Article 55 EC in relation to the free provision of services. In particular, the first paragraph of Article 46 requires:

> The provisions of this chapter and measures taken in pursuance thereof shall not prejudice the applicability of provisions laid down by law, regulation or administrative action providing for special treatment for foreign nationals *on grounds of public policy, public security or public health.* [*Emphasis added*].

What appears incorrect to me is the Commission's central reference to the need to abide by the freedom of capital movements to justify its position.

Quite obviously, the Maastricht Treaty has led to the full recognition of the freedoms of capital movement and payments in terms of *primary rules*, in same way as the other fundamental freedoms, thereby completing the veritable revolution brought about by Council Directive No 361 of 24 June 1988 – a genuine act of full liberalization.

Thus, nobody could ever dispute the ECJ's statement in its judgment of 13 May 2003, Case C-463/00, *Commission* v *Kingdom of Spain*,[88] that the nomenclature and explanatory notes appearing in Annex I to Directive 88/361 *are of a just indicative value*, as the notion of liberalized 'capital movements' had become commonplace by then.

In particular, the Court refers to both the transactions under Points I, 1 and 2, '*Direct Investment*' (characterized by 'a view to establishing or maintaining lasting economic links') and those contemplated at Point III, '*Operations in securities normally dealt in on the capital market*' (the so-called 'financial or portfolio investments').

Yet, such a distinction was crucially important only in the former system of partial liberalization under the repealed Articles 67 et seq. of the Treaty of Rome, in order to distinguish the class 'direct investment', as already liberalized pursuant to the Directives of 1960 and 1962, from the class 'portfolio investment', which was only liberalized by the directive of 1988.

In fact, that distinction has lost its significance, because of primary rules introduced since the entry into force of the Maastricht Treaty. This is because, under the new set of rules on capital and payments, *all* operations have been fully liberalized.

Thus, referring to itemized lists of transactions was of real use only under the former system, in order to distinguish between operations authorized and

88. See [2003] ECR I-4581, point 52.

unauthorized under the annexes to subsequent implementation directives relating to *movements of capital and payments.*

For such liberalization only covers the free movement of capital and payments, and by no means entails the granting of rights of any different type in the conduct of the underlying transactions or any change in the existing rules of private law or commercial law in force in national jurisdictions from time to time.

Thus, by way of example only, in respect of the item 'Inheritances and legacies', i.e. personal capital movements liberalized since the 1960 Directive, it is quite clear that such liberalization by no means required the testate to comply with specific choices or special forms of will, but only to vest someone residing in a Community country other than the testate's own, and designated by the testate in a will as the legatee of a cash amount, with the right to receive any cash owing to him, not from a bank in the deceased's country, but from a bank in the legatee's country or wherever else he might have chosen, obviously in compliance with the substantive and taxation laws of the deceased's country, *without any specific restriction being imposed on the relevant transfer of money* from one Member State to another within the EU. It goes without saying that, had the will been invalid under the relevant governing law, invoking the free movement of capital under Community law would have been of no avail to the legatee.

Likewise, express reference to a '*direct investment*' or a '*portfolio investment*' in any domestic company entitles a Community foreign investor to enter into the transaction without any restriction on the associated capital movement, obviously along with the right freely to receive the fruits of his investment and any proceeds from a subsequent disinvestment. The substantive rules governing the relevant acquisition and the Community investor's related rights – beyond and above contractual provisions – are those established by the applicable national laws, whether general of special, *the contents of which must be consistent with the right of establishment* (pursuant to Article 43 ff. and Article 58(2) EC).

This is the sense, in fact, of the belief expressed by Mr Advocate General Ruiz-Jarabo Colomer in his Opinion of 6 February 2003, in Case C-463/00, *Commission* v *Kingdom of Spain*, where he stated (at paragraph 36):

> First, I continue to hold the view that the natural and appropriate framework within which to consider the various restrictions deriving from what can, very imprecisely, be described as golden shares is *freedom of establishment*. In each case, what the defendant Member State is seeking to control, using powers of intervention as regards share structure, transfer of assets or certain management decisions, is *the formation of the privatised company's corporate will* (either by intervening in the composition of the membership or by influencing specific management decisions), *an aspect which has little to do with the free movement of capital referred to in Article 56 EC*. Such powers *may affect the right to freedom of establishment* and make it less attractive, either directly where they impinge on access to share capital, or indirectly, where they reduce its allure by restricting the powers of the board of directors relating to the ownership or management of the company. Contrary to the Court of Justice's

> finding, the resulting restriction of the free movement of capital is *incidental*, rather than inevitable. If that is the case as regards measures affecting the composition of the membership, it is even more true as regards *measures restricting the adoption of company resolutions* (change of company object, disposal of assets). In the latter cases, *the link with the free movement of capital is hypothetical or very tenuous*. [*Emphasis added*].[89]

Advocate General Ruiz-Jarabo Colomer restated his thought in his Opinion of 13 February 2007, in Case C-112/05, *Commission* v *Federal Republic of Germany*[90] (the so-called 'Volkswagen Law Case'), and further specified at paragraph 58:

> I have not altered my view that the natural and appropriate framework within which to consider the various restrictions deriving from what can, very imprecisely, be described as 'golden shares' is *the freedom of establishment*, since the defendant Member State *is generally seeking to control*, using powers of intervention as regards share structure, the formation of *the privatised companies' corporate will* (either by intervening in the composition of the membership or by influencing specific management decisions), an aspect which has little to do with the free movement of capital. (*Emphasis added*).

In both cases, the Advocate General saw 'no point in delving any deeper into an incorrect legal classification of the alleged infringement... since the Court of Justice subjects both Community freedoms to similar scrutiny'.

Though this observation was quite correct in relation to the two cases mentioned above, each of which was an Article 228 EC dispute between a Member State and the Commission, it is by no means correct if made in relation to a case referred by a national judge to the European Court for a preliminary ruling, pursuant to Article 234 EC, in which the ECJ is *only* required to interpret the Community rule indicated by the referring national judge, and has *no* power to replace it with another Community rule. Therefore, in this case, a request for having national rules hold to be incompatible with Article 56 EC, *instead of* Articles 43 et seq., ought not to be granted and, indeed, it should be rejected by the ECJ, for its being related not to an issue of foreign exchange transfer but to a purported substantive restriction.[91]

---

89. [2003] ECR I-4581.
90. [2007] ECR I-8995.
91. Although the point was expressly made in the oral discussion before the ECJ, in Joined Cases C-463/04 and C-463/04, *Federconsumatori* and Others, and *Associazione Azionariato Diffuso dell'AEM SpA* and Others v *Comune di Milano*, with the intervention of *AEM S.p.A.* and *Edison S.p.A.*., concerning reference for a preliminary ruling pursuant to Art. 234 by the Tribunale amministrativo regionale (TAR) per la Lombardia, Italy, the Court disregarded the question in its judgment of 6 Dec. 2007 (paras 19-21), and uncritically repeated the statements put forward by the Commission and referred to its own precedents in which it had shared the Commission's (mistaken) arguments. Here again, this bears witness to the ECJ's 'psychological submission' to the Commission so often exhibited by the EU judges, as I have mentioned in many parts of this book.

13. THE PERMITTED SCOPE OF THE NATIONAL STATES' AND THEIR AGENCIES' INTERVENTION

Under the approach recommended by the Commission, the European Court of Justice has laid down guiding principles for the adoption of national laws on golden shares over time.

Thus, in respect of French law,[92] the ECJ stated the incompatibility with Community law of a decree of 1993 vesting in the State a golden share in *Société National Elf-Aquitaine* active in the energy sector, whereby the State was accorded power of approval, to be exercised by the Minister for Economic Affairs, on the acquisition of rights and claims which exceeded certain shareholding ceilings and the right to oppose any decision to transfer or use as security the company's assets.

According to the Court:

> The investors concerned are given no indication whatever as to the specific, objective circumstances in which prior authorisation will be granted or refused.

It was so, in the Court's view, because a prior administrative authorization scheme:

> must be based on objective, non-discriminatory criteria which are known in advance to the undertakings concerned. . . .[93]

The Court did, however, rule that the Belgian golden share system was admissible, in that the regime in issue:

> . . . is predicated on the principle of *respect for the decision-making autonomy of the undertaking concerned*, inasmuch as, in each individual case, the exercise of control by the minister responsible requires an initiative on the part of the Government authorities. *No prior approval is required.* Moreover, in order for that power of opposition to be exercised, the public authorities are obliged to adhere to *strict time-limits*. Next, the regime is *limited to certain decisions* concerning the strategic assets of the companies in question, including in particular the energy supply networks, and to such specific management decisions relating to those assets as may be called in question in any given case.[94] [*Emphasis added*].

In another judgment relating to Spanish law,[95] the *prior authorization scheme* for the acquisition of substantial holdings was held to be deprived of any protection for the investors concerned, since they had been given no indication of the specific,

---

92. See Judgment of the Court of 4 Jun. 2002, Case C-483/99, *Commission* v *French Republic*, [2002] ECR I-4781.
93. *Ibid.*, para. 46. See also Judgment of the Court of 20 Feb. 2001, Case C-205/99, *Asociación Profesional de Empresas Navieras de Líneas Regulares and Others* v *Administración General del Estado*, [2001] ECR I-1271, para. 38.
94. See Judgment of the Court of 4 Jun. 2002, Case C-503/99, *Commission* v *Belgium*, [2002] ECR I-4809, paras 49-50.
95. See Judgment of the Court of 13 May 2003, *Commission* v *Spain*, cit.

objective circumstances in which prior approval would be granted or withheld. According to the Court:

> Such lack of precision does not enable individuals to be apprised of the extent of their rights and obligations deriving from Article 56 EC, with the result that such rules must be regarded as contrary to the principle of *legal certainty*... The rules concerned therefore go beyond what is necessary to attain the objective relied on by the Spanish Government, namely preventing any impairment of supplies of petroleum products or electricity or of telecommunication services.[96] [*Emphasis added*].

In providing grounds for the incompatibility of the Spanish law, the Court compared that case with the case of the Belgian law, stating that it was clear first that:

> the system examined in that judgment [*Kingdom of Belgium*] was one of *ex post facto* opposition, which is less restrictive than a system of prior approval such as that in the present case....[97] [*Emphasis added*].

It also appropriate to note that some of the Court's rulings highlighted that anyone affected by restrictive measures, such as the application of an authorization regime, must be allowed to rely on a *judicial remedy*. Yet, this fact alone is not sufficient to ensure legal certainty, since it will be the regime at issue which must 'provide the national courts with *sufficiently precise criteria* to enable them to review the way in which the administrative authority exercises its discretion' (*Emphasis added*).[98]

In particular, whatever the scope for application of the rules on golden shares, the Commission's view is that any national provisions allowing a State to exercise an influence over an undertaking *irrespective of its own shareholding* are in contrast with Community law.

In its Communication concerning intra-EU investment, the Commission stated the view that the powers given to national authorities, such the right to veto certain decisions or the imposition of a requirement for the nomination of some directors, *could 'present several problems'*, in connection with the fundamental principles laid down in the EC Treaty, *only in cases where the State does not hold a controlling stake*.[99]

---

96. *Ibid.*, paras 75-76.
97. *Ibid.*, para. 78.
98. *Ibid.*, para, 79.
99. See footnote 8 to the Communication, cit., [1996] O.J. C281, p. 3. The Commission had explained, in its complaint against France (Case C-483/99), that Art. 295 EC was not relevant for the purposes of those proceedings, '*since what is at issue in infringement proceedings is not the State's participation in the control of the privatised company, but certain rights and powers relating to the distribution of the ownership [of that company] between private persons*'. (So were the contents of the Commission's application summarized by Advocate General Ruiz-Jarabo Colomer in his Opinion, cit., para. 41). Thus, '*[f]or the Commission, ... ownership can be exercised only by having a sufficient holding in the capital of the company concerned*'. (AG Ruiz-Jarabo Colomer's Opinion, cit., para. 42). It should be noted that the Advocate General's view was that the Commission's interpretation of Art. 295 EC was 'reductionistic'.

The ECJ itself, in declaring several national provisions to be incompatible with Community law, only looked at some cases which had the following facts in common:

> *the State [had] released its strategic shareholding in the undertakings concerned*, the same shareholding which allowed the public authorities to participate in the determination of the undertaking's financial objectives through its decisive influence on the shaping of the will of the company organs.[100] [*Emphasis added*].

14. THE SAGA OF THE COMMISSION'S SCRUTINY OF THE ITALIAN RULES ON SPECIAL POWERS

Law Decree No 332 of 31 May 1994, as converted, with amendment, into Act No 474 of 30 July 1994, introduced 'Provisions for the speeding-up of the procedures for the sale of ownership interests held by the State and public authorities in public limited companies'. The Ministry for the Economy and Finance was thereby granted 'special powers' in companies active in certain strategic sectors, as expressly identified in a Decree of the President of the Council,[101] in order for the State to acquire control over such companies, irrespective of the amount of its shareholdings in them.

By express regulatory extension,[102] *special powers* also apply in respect of companies directly or indirectly controlled by publicly owned (local and economic) entities operating in strategic sectors, as such companies are identified in a regulatory instrument to be issued by the public entity concerned.

By a first judgment of 23 May 2000, the European Court of Justice held that, by adopting Act No 474/94, the Italian Republic had failed to fulfil its obligations in matters of right of establishment, free provision of services and free movement of capital.[103]

While the case was pending before the Court, the national legal framework had already changed, as the newly adopted Finance Act No 488, of 23 December 1999 for financial year 2000, had already amended the articles of Act 474/1994, under the subsequent Decree of the President of the Council of Ministers of

---

Accordingly, he proposed that the Court should dismiss the Commission's two applications against France and Belgium, since the special prerogatives of the public authorities in both cases, though unrelated to each State's shareholding, constituted a matter for the Member States, and so they were not contrary to the Treaty.

100. See Advocate General Ruiz-Jarabo Colomer of 3 Jul. 2001, Cases C-367/98, C-483/99 and C-503/99 [2001] ECR I-4731, point 60.
101. Special powers have also been introduced in the articles of associations of privatized companies ENI, ENEL, Telecom and Finmeccanica, while none have been provided in those of Autostrade, Aeroporti di Roma, Lloyd Triestino or Italia di Navigazione.
102. Art. 2(3) of Law Decree No. 332/94, unchanged since Finance Act 2004.
103. Judgment of the Court of 23 May 2000, Case C-58/99, *Commission of the European Communities* v *Italian Republic*, [2000] ECR I-3811.

11 February 2000, which specified the scope of the special powers provided for by Act 474/1994 and the related criteria for implementation.[104]

However, the ECJ referred in its judgment to settled case-law, as the Commission had specifically requested, and accordingly declined to take into account the changes so newly introduced, on the ground they were adopted by the Italian lawmaker *after* action had been brought by the Commission pursuant to Article 226 EC, following notification of reasoned opinion on 10 August 1998.

Moreover, in its judgment of 23 May 2000, the Court of Justice did not even consider the original version of Act 474/1994 on the merits, and merely acknowledged the Italian Government's failure to argue against the Commission's complaint.

On 5 February 2003, the Commission opened a *second* infringement procedure against Italy pursuant to Article 226 EC, noting that, though both the Finance Act of 1999 and the Decree of 2000 had amended significantly the Privatisation Law of 1994, the criteria provided in the 2000 Decree still seemed to be disproportionate to meeting overriding general interest requirements that, in accordance with the ECJ's case-law, would justify control of the ownership structure of the capital of an enterprise and its management.[105]

The Italian Parliament took action on the matter once again by adopting Article 4 of Act No 350 of 24 December 2003 (Finance Act 2004) further amending Act No 474/94, specifically in respect of the special powers provided for in Article 2, according to the principles laid down by the European Court of Justice in the matter of golden shares. Act No 474/94 required that the criteria for the exercise of special powers be defined by a decree of the President of the Council of Ministers. The decree for implementation was issued on 10 June 2004.[106]

---

104. Article 2(2) of this decree laid out five criteria for the exercise of special powers. No shareholdings should be sought which: (a) are not transparent or do not otherwise ensure disclosure of the ownership of participating interests relevant to the purposes of the direct or indirect corporate control and of the acquirer's objectives and business plans; (b) impair liberalization and market-opening processes, are inconsistent with the company's choice to privatize or lead up to such conflicts of interest as to prejudice the pursuit of the company's mission in terms of public interest; (c) entail objective risks of encroachment of organized crime or the company's involvement in unlawful activities; (d) may jeopardize the preservation of special powers; or (e) may involve substantial hazards seriously prejudicial to the State's interests in relation to: (i) the autonomy or security of supplies of raw materials or goods essential to the community; (ii) the continuity of public utilities essential to the community or the security of public utility facilities or networks; or (iii) the development of technologically advanced sectors.
105. See Press Release IP/03/177 of 5 Feb. 2003.
106. Following the entry into force of Finance Act 2004, the following special (golden share) powers have been made available to the Italian Minister for the Economy and Finance: (a) opposition (to be raised within 10 days of the directors' relevant notification made upon applying for registration in the book of members) to the acquisition of holdings representing at least one twentieth of the company's capital or any lower fraction the Minister for the Economy shall have determined by decree; (b) opposition to the conclusion of agreements or arrangements under Art. 122 of the Consolidating Act No. 58 of 24 Feb. 1998, in case at least one twentieth of the company's capital or any lower fraction the Minister for the Economy shall have determined by decree is a party thereto; (c) the right, on reasonable grounds of prejudice to the State's vital interests, to veto any resolutions for the dissolution

The saga went on, though. On 13 October 2005, the Commission announced it had sent a *reasoned opinion* to the Italian Government, assuming that the Italian legislation that provided for the exercise of special powers in privatized companies was *still* in breach of the EC Treaty rules on the free movement of capital and the right of establishment (Articles 56 and 43 EC, respectively).[107]

In the press release published in that respect, the Commission acknowledged the 'improvements compared to the 1994 law'. Nevertheless, it took the view that the criteria introduced by the authorities were 'vague and indeterminate' and that 'the wide discretionary powers given to the authorities to judge the risks to the vital interest of the State involved' prevented 'any effective judicial review of the decision-making process'. In any event, the Commission's objections only concerned the Decree of 10 June 2004, not the amendments introduced by Act No 350/2003.

On 28 June 2006, in relation to the relevant procedure, the Commission announced it had decided to refer Italy once more to the Court of Justice.[108] The complaint filed by the Commission on 13 July 2007 was registered as Case C-326/07.[109]

15. THE 'PROPORTIONATE' EXERCISE OF CONTROL IN THE ECJ'S RECENT CASE-LAW

In Judgment of 13 May 2003, Case C-98/01, *Commission* v *United Kingdom*,[110] the Court of Justice provided an invaluable distinction between 'national rules', which

---

of the company, the transfer of business, mergers, spin-offs, the transfer abroad of the company's registered office, changes in the company's business object, amendments to its articles of association for the abolition or alteration of such special powers, and (d) the appointment of a director without voting rights. It should be noted that the exercise of opposition or veto powers can be challenged before the Regional Administrative Tribunal of Lazio within 60 days. The companies concerned (as expressly identified by decree) are required to amend their articles of association for compliance. This requirement has not an indefinite scope, though. Art. 2(1) of Act No. 474/94 provides, *inter alia*, that the articles of association of the companies concerned '*shall be supplemented with a clause vesting the Minister of the Economy and Finance with one or more of the following special powers . . .*' (There follows the listing of items (a) to (d) above). Art. 4 of Act No. 474/94 provides, *inter alia*, that: '*[. . .] minority lists shall have at least one fifth, in the aggregate, of the directors not appointed pursuant to Article 2(1)(d), to be rounded up, in the case of a fractional number lower than one, to the nearest integer . . .*'.

107. See Press Release IP/05/1270 of 13 Oct. 2005. Thus, the reasoned opinion came about two and a half years after the Commission had opened the relevant procedure against the Italian government in Feb. 2003.
108. See Press Release IP/06/859 of 28 Jun. 2006.
109. [2007] O.J. C247, p. 3. 'The Commission takes the view that the criteria referred to by Article 1(2) of the Decree of 10 Jun. 2004 for the exercise of special powers, laid down by Article 4(227)(a), (b) and (c) of Law No. 350/2004, are not precise or specific enough to enable an investor in another Member State to know when the special powers under Article 4(227)(a), (b) and (c) of Law No. 350/2004 will be used'. See Advocate General Ruiz-Jarabo Colomer of 6 Nov. 2008, Case C-326/07, nyp.
110. [2003] ECR I-4641.

can only be adopted within the limits discussed in the preceding paragraph above, and a company's articles of association, which are admissible '*per se*' in their being the result of a choice under private law. Point 48 and 49 of that judgment read:

> The United Kingdom Government's argument that what is concerned here is solely the application of private company-law mechanisms cannot be accepted. The restrictions at issue do not arise as the result of the normal operation of company law. BAA's Articles of Association were to be approved by the Secretary of State pursuant to the Airports Act 1986 and that was what actually occurred. In those circumstances, the Member State acted in this instance *in its capacity as a public authority. Consequently*, the rules at issue constitute a restriction on the movement of capital for the purposes of Article 56 EC. . . . [*Emphasis added*].

This ruling was subsequently confirmed, albeit expressed *a contrariis*,[111] in the Judgment of the Court of 23 October 2007, Case C-112/05, *Volkswagen, Commission* v *Federal Republic of Germany*, paragraph 40 of which reads:

> . . . as the Commission has correctly noted, there is a *difference* between a *power made available* to shareholders, who are free to decide whether or not they wish to use it, and a *specific obligation imposed* on shareholders *by way of legislation*, without giving them the possibility to derogate from it. [*Emphasis added*].

And paragraphs 45 and 46 further specify:

> As the Federal Republic of Germany has observed, the percentage of 75% of the share capital provided for in the Law on public limited companies may be increased and fixed at a higher level by the particular company's articles of association. *However*, as the Commission has correctly noted, *it is open to shareholders to decide whether or not to make use of that power*. Conversely, the fact that the threshold of the required majority has been fixed by Paragraph 4(3) of the VW Law at more than 80% of the capital results, *not from the will of the shareholders, but*, as was held in Paragraph 29 of the present judgment, *from a national measure*. This requirement, derogating from general law, and *imposed by way of specific legislation*, thus affords *any shareholder* holding 20% of the share capital a blocking minority. [*Emphasis added*].

As the Advocate General pointed out in his Opinion in those same proceedings,[112] the situation was such that:

> Even if an investor obtained sufficient power to amend the articles of association and repeal those clauses, he would then face the difficulty of amending

111. In fact, in connection with this same case, the Commission had stated, in its press release of 30 Mar. 2004 (IP/04/400), that the restrictions 'have been imposed by the State *acting in its capacity as a public authority* rather than as the result of the *normal operation of company law*. They therefore fall under the scope of application of Article 56 EC'. (Emphasis added). A similar statement had been made by the Commission in connection with proceedings brought against the Netherlands (IP/03/1733 of 17 Dec. 2003).

112. See points 71 and 72 of the Opinion, cit., para. 42.

the Volkswagen Law, which would require the approval of the national parliament.

In its Judgment of 6 December 2007 in *Comune di Milano* (*AEM*), i.e. little more than one month after the *Volkswagen* judgment, the Court (with only five judges to hear the case, instead of thirteen sitting as Grand Chamber) seemed to go far beyond the criteria laid down in past case-law. Granting the plaintiffs' submissions – this time with the Commission's full endorsement[113] – the Court, called upon to deal with references for a preliminary ruling under Article 234 EC from the *Tribunale amministrativo regionale per la Lombardia* (Italy), ruled as follows:

> Article 56 EC must be interpreted as precluding a national provision, such as Article 2449 of the Italian Civil Code, under which the articles of association of a company limited by shares may confer on the State or a public body with a shareholding in that company the power to appoint directly one or more directors which, on its own or, as in the main proceedings, *in conjunction with* a provision such as Article 4 of Decree Law No 332 of 31 May 1994, which became, after amendment, Law No 474 of 30 July 1994, as amended by Law No 350 of 24 December 2003, which grants that State or public body the right to participate in the election on the basis of lists of the directors it has not appointed directly, is such as to enable that State or public body *to obtain a power of control which is disproportionate to its shareholding in that company*. [*Emphasis added*].

On its way to such a conclusion, the Court held it irrelevant:

(1) that the former text of Article 2449, Civil Code, to which the judgment referred, *did not impose* an obligation, for the benefit of the public shareholder, on a company controlled by a public body (the *Comune di Milano*

113. In fact, the Commission had maintained until then that any national rules allowing a Member State to influence a company *regardless of its holding* were in conflict with Community rules. In particular, in its Communication on certain legal aspects concerning intra-EU investment (97/C/220/06), it had held the view that the powers granted to national authorities (such as veto rights or the appointment of directors) might 'raise compatibility problems', in relation to the fundamental principles laid down in the EC Treaty, *only in cases where the State did not hold a controlling stake.* See footnote 8 to the Communication, cit., para. 42. The Commission had explained, in its application against France (Case C-483/99), that Article 295 EC was not relevant for the purposes of those proceedings, '*since what is at issue in infringement proceedings is not the State's participation in the control of the privatised company, but certain rights and powers relating to the distribution of the ownership [of that company] between private persons*'. (So were the contents of the Commission's application summarized by Advocate General Ruiz-Jarabo Colomer in his Opinion, cit., para. 41). Thus, '*[f]or the Commission, . . . ownership can be exercised only by having a sufficient holding in the capital of the company concerned*'. (AG Ruiz-Jarabo Colomer's Opinion, cit., para. 42). It should be noted that the Advocate General's view was that the Commission's interpretation of Art. 295 EC was 'reductionistic'. Accordingly, he proposed that the Court should dismiss the Commission's two applications against France and Belgium, since the special prerogatives of the public authorities in both cases, though unrelated to each State's shareholding, constituted a matter for the Member States, and so they were not contrary to the Treaty.

in the relevant case), but *allowed it the option* to resolve that the company's articles of association, in compliance with Community law and as long as the *Comune di Milano* retained its 33.4% shareholding, should provide the power to appoint directly a number of directors who, together with those appointed by voting on the basis of lists, would have been a majority of the board of directors;

(2) that such resolution, approved by the favourable vote of 99.78% of the shareholders present at the general meeting, in accordance with the rules of private law, required a qualified majority of shareholders, which majority had been reached through the necessary vote of 'private' shareholders representing over 10% of the company's capital;

(3) that a 33.4% holding in a listed public company such as *AEM S.p.A.* was enough *to give control over the company* pursuant to Article 2359(1) and (2) of the Civil Code;

(4) that, as the things stood, a 'private' shareholder, would, in the normal exercise of the powers associated with control, have had the *right* to appoint *all* the members of the board, except any as might be attributed to the minority by law or under the company's Articles;

(5) that the fact that one shareholder, whether public or private, owned such holding in excess of 30% in a listed company's capital, i.e. above the ceiling required by law (the Consolidating Financial Services Act) for a Mandatory Takeover Bid, indicated that holding any percentage of shares exceeding such ceiling was considered adequate to confer control over the company – even though the percentage giving control over a public company could well be far lower than 30% in practice;

(6) that, in such a setting, it was even doubtful that the plaintiffs, as the holders of just a tiny proportion of shares, had an 'actual interest' in bringing action, something which, if the Court – which is certainly not called upon to decide hypothetical questions – had duly considered the issue, would have precluded a ruling in the first place, *for lack of the actuality requirement*; and

(7) that, much as an explicit question had been submitted in writing by the ECJ to the parties in the letter fixing the date for the next hearing, it abundantly emerged at that hearing that 'analogous' powers were accorded by Italian common company law to any private shareholder owning 33.4% or even less of the shares representing a listed company's capital. It is enough, in this respect, to refer to the new Article 2348 of the Civil Code, which has introduced several classes of shares in the Italian system as well.

There is more to it, though. The Court's entire reasoning rested on the presumption that the opposite approach were correct under Italian law. For the Court noted:

> First of all, it should be stated that the *questions referred by the national court are based on the premiss* that the rule set out in Article 2449 of the Civil Code, although falling within the scope of the general rules of company law contained

> in that code, *derogates* from ordinary company law in so far as the latter does not provide *an identical rule applicable to all shareholders*, in particular to private shareholders. It is for the Court to give the interpretation sought in the light of that premiss. [*Emphasis added*].

Such presumption clearly implied that an assessment should be made of Italian laws, which could only be done by the national court *ratione materiae*. Moreover, it was by no means included among the questions referred by the Regional Administrative Tribunal of Lombardy, and it was even misstated by the Court, since the 'identicalness' of the measures at issue was of no use as a yardstick, and their 'equivalence' was, instead, clearly sufficient.[114]

By the judgment in question, the Court also introduced a criterion of *proportionality of control*, based on a notion of 'control' that cannot possibly be shared.

Control, whether in fact or in law, is 'control' altogether, and cannot, as such, be subject to any limitations whatsoever. Since it is obvious that the shareholder 'legally' controlling a company because of his 50.01% stake in the company's capital has the right to appoint the entire board of directors, except any member(s) that must be appointed by the minority shareholders under the law or under the company's Articles, it is as obvious that the same right must be deemed vested in any private or public shareholder who has control 'in fact' over a public company, even if only through a stake equal to, or lower than, one half of the company's whole capital.

It is worth noting, though, that, under the system of judicial cooperation established by Article 234 EC, the interpretation of Member States' rules of law *is not a matter for the Court of Justice*.[115]

The Information Note on references from national courts for a preliminary ruling expressly requires:[116]

> Under the preliminary ruling procedure, the Court's role is to give an interpretation of Community law or to rule on its validity, not to apply that law to the factual situation underlying the main proceedings, which is the task of the national court. [*Emphasis added*].

The same view was taken by Advocate General Ruiz-Jarabo Colomer in his Opinion of 13 June 2002 in Case C-206/01, *Arsenal Football Club plc*,[117] where he stated:

> When use of a trade mark by a third party is use of it as such is a question of fact which falls to the national court to determine in the light of the

---

114. See Judgment in *Comune di Milano*, cit. point 17.
115. See Order of the Court of 27 Jun. 1979, Case C-105/79, *Hyange* (I), [1979] ECR, 2257, and Judgments of the Court of 12 Oct. 1993, Case C-37/92, *Criminal proceedings against José Vanacker and André Lesage*, [1993] ECR I-4947, point 7, and of 13 Jun. 1996, Case C-144/95, *Criminal proceedings against J.L. Maurin*, [1996] ECR I-2909.
116. [2005] O.J. 143, p. 1 f., especially paragraph 5.
117. [2002] ECR I-10273.

> information available to it for the purpose of deciding the case ... [E]xamination of these matters falls outside the jurisdiction of the Court of Justice. [*Emphasis added*].

Yet, the Court of Justice failed to comply with that principle in qualifying the facts at issue at paragraph 56 of the judgment delivered in that case on 12 November 2002.[118] As a consequence, the referring judge (the English High Court) correctly decided it was not bound by the ruling of the European Court, which had exceeded the limits of its jurisdiction.[119]

When these observations are applied to the case of the Comune di Milano (*AEM*), it is fair to conclude that the very 'premiss' of Italian law on which the Court expressly based its interpretative decision undermined that judgment, under the weight of the overriding principle of Italian common company law that the shareholder having control over a company, whether in law or in fact, is entitled to appoint all the members of its board of directors, save for any that must be appointed by minority shareholders under the law or under the company's Articles.

Let me point out that the well-known *principle of proportionality in EU law* – according to which any national measure restricting any of the rights guaranteed by the Treaty must be *proportionate* to the intended objective – operates quite in the opposite direction, in the sense that such measures are only allowed if the objective pursued cannot possibly be achieved by less severe means.[120] Therefore, the reference to the principle of proportionality in the matter discussed here only concerns the need for each national measure to be adequate in relation to overriding requirements of general interest (such as national defence or secure raw material supplies).

However, for the notion of 'proportionality' of control to make any sense in relation to shareholdings, it must essentially be referred to national law. In *Comune di Milano*, it ought to be interpreted and assessed within the exclusive jurisdiction of Italian courts.

Moreover, even if a 'community notion' of *control* were to be referred to a *public undertaking* – a proposition which the ECJ's judgment in *Comune di Milano implicitly* ruled out – that line of reasoning would not change. For Article 2 of Commission Directive 2006/111/EC of 16 November 2006 on the transparency of financial relations between Member States and public undertakings[121] offers so broad a definition of 'public undertaking' as to include any type of public control. In the sense that:

> 'public undertakings' means any undertaking over which *the public authorities may exercise* directly or indirectly *a dominant influence* by virtue of their

118. *Ibid.*
119. See England and Wales High Court (Chancery Division) Decision, 12 Nov. 2002 [2003] CMLR III, p. 753 f.
120. See, among others, *Commission* v *France*, cit., para. 46.
121. The directive, which was 'overlooked' by the Commission in upholding the applicants' case, and not considered by either the Advocate General or the Court's judges, has been published in [2006] O.J. L318, p. 17. Please, refer to para. 9 of Chapter VI of this book.

ownership of it, their financial participation therein, or the rules which govern it. [*Emphasis added*].

The notion of 'dominant influence' (equivalent to that of 'control'), when exercised by public authorities on an undertaking, is quite meaningful in this respect. It includes *both* any case where governance powers are exercised by a central, regional or local authority or any other public body directly or indirectly holding a majority of the capital of a company or firm acting as a business undertaking, relying on a majority of the votes carried by the shares or quotas of such company or firm, *and* any case where a public authority, as defined above, *is otherwise empowered to designate more than one half of the members of the board of directors or management and of the supervisory body of that company.* It is even too clear that, under such notion, the two cases must be treated in the same way, since both imply control both in law and in fact.

Nevertheless, upon a pressing request from the Commission – which had opened new infringement proceedings against Italy concerning compatibility of Article 2449 of the Italian Civil Code with Community law[122] – Article 2449 had, to ensure compliance with the principles laid down in the ECJ's case-law, to be replaced with Article 13 of Act No 34 of 25 February 2008 (Community Law 2007).[123] The fact that the new version of Article 2449 has introduced, *inter alia*, the concept of *proportionality* in relation to 'public' ownership interests in companies or firms, specifically in connection with the appointment of directors and statutory auditors of unlisted companies, is quite likely to bring about serious misunderstandings in practical implementation.

In fact, Article 3(1) of Law Decree No 10 of 15 February 2007, as converted into Act No 46 of 6 April 2007, had already superseded Article 2450 of the Civil Code.

---

122. These were infringement proceedings 2006/2104. The Commission opened the procedure against the Italian Government by issuing two letters of formal notice on 4 Apr. 2006 and on 12 Dec. 2006. At the hearing held on 29 Jun. 2006 in Joined Cases C-463/04 and C-464/04, the Commission had, as an intervening party, 'alerted' the Court, so to speak, to an infringement procedure pending in relation to compatibility of Art. 2449 of the Italian Civil Code with Community law.

123. In *Gazzetta Ufficiale della Repubblica Italiana*, n. 56, 6 Mar. 2008, *Suppl. Ordinario n. 54*. As early as 6 Dec. 2007, Ms Emma Bonino, the Italian Minister for Community Policies, had stated that Art. 2449, Civil Code, '*has been amended and the revised text is now part of Community Act 2007*'. See Emma Bonino's statement of 6 Dec. 2007, available on the website <www.politichecomunitarie.it>. The then-Minister specified that 'The European Commission's view has been granted and the infringement will be remedied as soon as the Community Act enters into force'.

Chapter IV

The Role of the European Union in the Organization of International Economy

SUMMARY:

1. Introductory remarks.
2. International economic cooperation: From GATT 1947 to the WTO.
3. The WTO's relationships with the other international economic organizations: (a) with the United Nations.
4. More: (b) with the International Monetary Fund: 'Monetary Dumping'.
5. More: (c) with the G7 Finance.
6. More: (d) with the International Labour Organisation ('ILO').
7. The European Union and 'social dumping'.
8. The globalization process: The widening gap between industrialized countries and less developed countries (LDCs) and the Doha Round's difficulties.
9. The DSB (Dispute Settlement Body) as contrasted with the previous system of international dispute settlement within the WTO.
10. Institutional and procedural innovations under the Uruguay Round Final Act.
11. Settled legal principles in DSB/WTO case-law.
12. Protection of private interests within the WTO System.
13. The role of a private party, enterprise concerned or association as amicus curiae, and judicial protection under the covered agreements.
14. The WTO and the European Union.
15. The European Commission's 'external' weaknesses and China.
16. Trade defence instruments: (a) Safeguard measures in general.

17. More: Safeguard measures with regard to the People's Republic of China.
18. More: (b) 'Dumping' and 'subsidies' as causes of diversion of international trade.
19. The new international rules on dumping and subsidies and their implementation within the EU.
20. Legal nature of dumping: The requirements.
21. Circumvention of antidumping duties: The 'screwdriver assembly' issue.
22. Community Interest falling outside the scope of GATT antidumping provisions: Critical remarks.
23. Implementing WTO rules on dumping and subsidies: (a) In the United States of America.
24. More: (b) In the Chinese legal system.
25. Dumping and competition in the EU.

1. INTRODUCTORY REMARKS

Since the introduction of the GATT system in 1947, world trade has grown more than exponentially. The following are figures accounting for the progression of *world merchandise exports* by value:[1]

– 59 billion dollars	in 1948
– 84 billion dollars	in 1953
– 157 billion dollars	in 1963
– 579 billion dollars	in 1973
– 1,838 billion dollars	in 1983
– 3,675 billion dollars	in 1993
– 7,369 billion dollars	in 2003
– 10,159 billion dollars	in 2005
– 11,783 billion dollars	in 2006.

Although no statistics have been made available for 1995 onward, i.e. since the WTO-GATT system 1994 first came into effect, and taking the overall figures published for 2003 and 2005 as the relevant benchmark, the figures shown above bear out the huge leap forward in world merchandise exports in this last period. The most conspicuous rate of growth *in value* was recorded precisely in 2003 though 2005 (+51.9%).[2]

---

1. Source: WTO, *Selected long-term trends International Trade Statistics*, Table I.6, 2007.
2. Source: WTO, *Selected long-term trends*, Table II.1, 2006. In general, on the world-wide growth of the trading transactions after the formation of the WTO since 1 Jan. 1995, see Panitchpakdi, 'The WTO at ten: building on ten years of achievements', in *The WTO at Ten – The Contribution of the Dispute Settlement System*, Sacerdoti, Yanovich and Bohanes (Eds), Cambridge [2007], 7.

World exports grew at a very fast pace, 75% from 1993 to 2005, *in terms of volumes* as well.[3] The most significant growth, at rates around 10% each year, was recorded in 1997, 2000 and 2004.

The proportion of exports from the United States to the world's total declined steadily from 21.7% in 1948, to 12.6% in 1993, down to 8.8% in 2006.

The proportion of *European* exports, to be understood as all exports from the entire geographic area of the European continent, grew from 31% in 1948 to 42.1% in 2005, though they declined 2.4% from 1993 to 2005.[4] As for the European Union, exports rose from 36.1% in 1993 to 39.4% in 2005.[5]

The People's Republic of China recorded a considerable increase in its merchandise exports, which grew from 0.9% of the world's total exports in 1948 to 2.5% in 1993, until they amounted to three times as much (8.2%) in 2006.

A progression quite similar to that shown in the world's export table was recorded in the values of *world merchandise imports*, as follows:[6]

– 66 billion dollars	in 1948;
– 84 billion dollars	in 1953;
– 153 billion dollars	in 1963;
– 589 billion dollars	in 1973;
– 1,882 billion dollars	in 1983;
– 3,769 billion dollars	in 1993;
– 7,647 billion dollars	in 2003;
– 10,511 billion dollars	in 2005;
– 12,113 billion dollars	in 2006.

A similar trend was also observed in individual countries' imports by region, as a percentage of the world's total.

In 2006, the GATT/WTO Members accounted for 93.9% of world exports and 95.8% of world imports.

Such huge results, which have reached a peak in the last few years, were affected by a number of factors.

I refer to such far-reaching political events as the implosion – first economic then political – of State-planned economy countries, with the almost simultaneous collapse of the Soviet Union and the East European countries, the breakdown of German Democratic Republic and the resulting reunification of Germany within the European Community, all of which events combined to open those economies to the free market economy.

The evolution within the European Union has also had an impact. While the recent increase in the number of its partners – which almost doubled to become as many as twenty-seven – has more than made up for a moderate decline in the

3. The growth was still lower than in terms of value over the same years.
4. Source: WTO, *International Trade Statistics*, Table I.6, 2007.
5. *Ibid.* Note that the Member States were 12 in 1993 and 25 in 2005.
6. Source: WTO, *International Trade Statistics*, Table I.7, 2007.

Community's balance of trade in the last two years, it has provided a safeguard of political stability not only for Europe, but for other regions as well. What matters more for the European Union has been the extension of its authorities' jurisdiction over such matters as environment protection, social welfare policy and, albeit with the deficiencies pointed up elsewhere in this book, economic and monetary policies.[7]

A major event in the economic and monetary arena was the introduction of the 'Euro' as a result of the substitution of primary rules of the Maastricht Treaty for the former unspecific provisions of the Rome Treaty, whereby the freedom of capital movements and payments was fully achieved both within the European Union and from the European Union to other countries. The Euro has become the single currency directly used in an area of direct utilization now including 16 States as from 1 January 2009, following the decision the ECOFIN adopted in its session of 8 July 2008 on the entry of Slovakia into the so-called *Euro zone*. In a macro-economic perspective, the Euro, though ranking somewhat below the US Dollar, is now being widely used for international payments. When compared with such events, the political setbacks suffered by the European Constitution – and only slightly overcome by the Lisbon Treaty, itself at risk following the adverse outcome of the Irish referendum – entail a pause for serious thought, in the hope that, as it has often been the case in the past, this may lead up, from pluckily different bases in a climate of renewed transparency and better information to the European public opinion, to the full achievement of European unity.[8]

Let me add that the remarkable growth in international trade transactions, both in number and in value, has greatly been contributed by the significant economic expansion of the People's Republic of China, whose GDP has steadily grown at rates around two digits in the last five years (following its entry into the GATT/WTO system on 11 December 2001, though only effective as from 1 January 2002)[9] – an unprecedented feat on the global scale.

Exports of goods and services *from China* rose from approximately 5.4% of total world trade in 2001 to around 11.5% in 2005 and over 12.5% in 2006. *Chinese imports* grew from about 4.1% of total world trade in 2001 to about *8.4%* in *2005*.[10]

7. See above, Chapter III of this volume, *passim*, esp.lly paragraphs 7 and 8.
8. On 13 Dec. 2007, the European Union's leaders signed the Treaty of Lisbon, putting an end to several years' negotiations on the institutional reform. The Treaty of Lisbon amended, without superseding, the Treaty on European Union and the Treaty establishing the European Community, which are still in force. As at 30 Nov. 2008, 25 Member States had already ratified the Lisbon Treaty by parliamentary means. Parliamentary ratification was still underway in Czech Republic. However, on 26 Nov. 2008, the Czech Constitutional Court has given a positive verdict on the compatibility of the Treaty of Lisobn with the Czech constitutional order. As is known, Ireland rejected ratification at a referendum on 12 Jun. 2008, with 53.4% voting 'no', which prevents the Lisbon Treaty from coming into force.
9. In effect, China had been an original member State of the GATT 1947, before the creation of the Communist State. See the first Whereas in the *Preamble* to the *Protocol on the Accession of the People's Republic of China* at the WTO-GATT meeting of 10 Nov. 2001.
10. Source: EUROSTAT. Statistics provided by DG Trade of the European Commission, 15 Sep. 2006.

Exports have constantly been on the increase in value as well, almost doubling over the 2001-2006 timeframe:[11]

– 292,205 million euro	in 2001
– 337,461 million euro	in 2002 (+15.5%);
– 379,567 million euro	in 2003 (+12.5%);
– 466,133 million euro	in 2004 (+22.8%);
– 599,460 million euro	in 2005 (+28.6%);
– 752,846 million euro	in 2006 (+25.6%).

Imports into China performed quite at the same pace in the same period:[12]

– 241,420 million euro	in 2001
– 272,113 million euro	in 2002 (+12.7%);
– 321,317 million euro	in 2003 (+18,1%);
– 399,264 million euro	in 2004 (+24.3%);
– 470,673 million euro	in 2005 (+17.9%);
– 559,248 million euro	in 2006 (+18.8%).

The balance of trade of the People's Republic of China recorded a steady surplus, more than doubling in the period, from +50.7 billion euro in 2001 to +128.7 billion euro in 2005 and +193.5 billion euro in 2006.[13] This was a proportionally growing performance, that resulted in a figure three times as high as in 2001.

China's demand for *commodities* grew impressively from 2002 to 2005, especially if compared with the most economically advanced WTO Members. The following are some statistics which appear quite meaningful, particularly because of the significance of the commodities involved:[14]

– China's demand for copper:	+31.6%;	Other States':	+3.4%
– China's demand for cotton:	+59.5%;	Other States':	+3.0%
– China's demand for natural rubber:	+46.6%;	Other States':	+11.9%
– China's demand for oil:	+32.0%;	Other States':	+5,8%
– China's demand for soybeans:	+49.9%;	Other States':	+5.2%

In 2005, China's consumption of copper accounted for 22.2% of world consumption; consumption of cotton, 39%; consumption of natural rubber, 21.6%; consumption of oil, 7.9%; and consumption of soybeans, 17.3%.[15]

According to IMF statistics, China was the European Union's topmost trading partner in 2006 (displacing the United States, which ranked first in 2003). The

11. Source: IMF, *Evolution of the China's Trade Balance*, Statistics provided by DG Trade of the European Commission, 7 Aug. 2007.
12. Source: IMF, cit., *ibid.*
13. Source: IMF, cit., *ibid.*
14. Source: UNCTAD, *Handbook of Statistics 2006/2007.*
15. Source: UNCTAD, cit., *ibid.*

European Union was, in turn, China's second largest export market (after the United States). As for imports into China, the EU ranked second, ahead of South Korea (first was Japan, fourth was the United States).

Foreign direct investments in China also grew in quantity, from 16,918 contracts in 1999 to 41,485 contracts in 2006.[16]

On 22 July 2005, following resolute international pressures, the People's Republic of China shifted from the *de-facto* fixed peg of the yuan exchange rate to the dollar to a currency-basket formed from four major currencies (US Dollar, Euro, Korean Won and Japanese Yen) and six minor currencies (Singapore Dollar, Australian Dollar, Canadian Dollar, Rouble, Malaysian Ringgit, and Thai Baht).

In the face of inquiries from the competent international monetary institutions and the criticisms raised by many economists, the Chinese currency-basket mechanism and the weight of each currency within the basket are still unknown,[17] and, as a result, there has been a just token revaluation of the yuan, around 2.1% against the US dollar. Far higher appear to be the exchange rates needed to re-balance international trade relationships:

> The yuan would have to increase in value by as much as 20% or 30% against the dollar – much larger than today's 2% shift – to have a material impact on the trade deficit.[18]

In the few weeks before Chinese President Hu Jintao's visit to Washington (April 2006), the revaluation rate of the Chinese currency against the dollar kept rising by as much as 6 to 9%,[19] only to fall back again in line with the former figure, much as it was the analysts' view that a considerably revaluated yuan would be desirable to restore international trade to a fair balance. Yet, the opinion is widespread that:

> China will allow the [currency] to appreciate only enough to appease critics but not enough to affect its economy or those of its trading partners.[20]

The People's Republic of China took a very active part in adopting antidumping measures throughout 2005, and turned out to be the State that brought most of the trade defence actions on dumping against WTO Members in the second half of that year.[21] Yet, only three Chinese antidumping investigations were initiated in respect of European products in 2005.[22]

As at 31 March 2007, ten defence actions had been brought by China (all of them on grounds of dumping) against undertakings from the European Union or

---

16. Source: US-China Business Council, *FDI in China (Total and US) 1995-2006.*
17. A similar mechanism is applied by the Singapore authorities: See *Business Week on line, A Yuan-Revaluation Surprise*, 21 Jul. 2005.
18. See Wall Street Journal *on-line*, *FAQ: China's Yuan Revaluation*, 22 Jul. 2005.
19. Source: Deutsche Bank.
20. Source: *US-China Business Council.*
21. See *Overview of Third Country trade defence actions against the Community* on 1 Nov. 2006, edited by the European Commission, DG Trade, B.2.
22. The cases concerned were: *Octanol*, *Butanol* and *Wear resistant overlay.*

some of the EU Member States. Most definitive measures related to the *chemical industry* – one of the areas in which the Chinese economy is growing the fastest.

Faced with these initiatives and with a relatively 'new' user of trade defence instruments, the European Commission has taken a wary approach to the matter, while reassuring the European public opinion that:

> all new Chinese investigations are closely monitored in order to anticipate and avoid serious and large scale problems.[23]

The most serious problems European exporters encounter in proceedings such as these arise from the involved, oftentimes vague structure of the official forms released by Chinese authorities,[24] widespread lack of proper disclosure and – in the substance – inadequate 'injury/causation analyses' in the investigation stage.

Quite different from China's are the international trade figures for India, the other big Asian country which is so often, though just superficially, compared to China in terms of economic growth. This is not the case, though.

Exports of goods and services *from India* grew from 0.93%, approx., of total world trade in 2001, to about 1.32% in 2006.[25] *Indian imports* increased from about 1.1% of total world trade in 2001 to approximately 1.99% in 2006.[26]

Exports were steadily on the rise in terms of value (though falling far behind Chinese exports in absolute values), growing at an average annual rate of 15.8% in 2002 through 2006, as follows:[27]

– 50,004 million euro	in 2001
– 52,838 million euro	in 2002
– 53,549 million euro	in 2003
– 60,143 million euro	in 2004
– 78,210 million euro	in 2005
– 94,863 million euro	in 2006

Imports performed in value along the same lines as China's, growing at an average annual rate of 24.7% from 2001 through 2005:[28]

– 65,1238 million euro	in 2001
– 61,617 million euro	in 2002
– 64,823 million euro	in 2003
– 79,469 million euro	in 2004
– 107,217 million euro	in 2005
– 149,071 million euro	in 2006

23. See *Overview of Third Country trade defence actions against the Community*, cit., p. 10.
24. Nardelli, 'Anti-dumping cinese e anti-dumping CE a confronto: una minaccia per le imprese comunitarie' [2006] Dir. comm. Int., p. 369, pp. 388-389 and 394-395.
25. Source: IMF (*Direction of Trade Statistics*), DG Trade document dated 24 Aug. 2007.
26. Source: IMF, cit., *ibid.*
27. Source: IMF (*Direction of Trade Statistics*), DG Trade document dated 7 Aug. 2007.
28. Source: IMF, cit., *ibid.*

India posted a *passive* balance of trade with the rest of the world, with a deficit increasing from -15.1 billion euro in 2001 to -54 billion euro in 2006.

Likewise, India's balance of trade with the European Union has posted a moderate *deficit* since 2006 onward (about 6 billion euros in 2006).

The European Union is India's first largest trading partner, followed by the People's Republic of China and the United States.[29]

In the second half of 2005, on a global level, India was overtaken by China as the leading initiator of new antidumping cases. Nevertheless, India still remains one of the largest users of TDIs world wide.[30]

The number of measures in place against the EU significantly decreased from 36 in 2004 to 22 at the end of 2005. This was the outcome of the successful dispute brought by the EU before the WTO Dispute Settlement Body against India's twenty-seven measures at the end of 2003, and which resulted in the termination by India of ten of the main problem cases during 2005.[31]

As at 31 March 2007, nineteen defence measures were in force in India against the EU or some of the EU Member States, all but one of them antidumping. Most definitive measures concerned the *chemical* and *pharmaceutical industries*.

When compared with these major events in the economic arena, the Iraqi and Afghanistan wars and other local war foci in Africa and Asia, and even the fierce confrontation between Islamic countries and the rest of the world, with the resulting outgrowth of terrorism on the global scale, as dramatically harmful as they may be to international life, have by no means had a crippling impact on the steady growth of international trade in the last few years.

Another reason for this development – its main driver, in fact – has been the spreading of web-based communication systems, which, at almost no cost for the user, contribute to the abatement of boundaries, by allowing everyone to 'navigate' without time or space limits, thereby creating a level playground equally, on the supply side, for the smallest and the biggest trader, say a USA enterprise as opposed to a Thai enterprise, all of them being afforded the same conditions in the search for the most favourable solution worldwide for the accomplishment of any economic venture, thereby enabling consumers, wherever located, to shop for the lowest-cost goods or services.

Within the scope of a widespread mutual recognition of free capital movements, at least between the world's biggest States, this opportunity also generates real-time financial flows from one regulated market to another, and from one listed company to another within each market. This is brought about by a variety of assessment factors whereby, in a boundless financial game, the figures for one individual enterprise as well as the macroeconomic statistics concerning a whole market are oftentimes mere, not even decisive, elements based on which both small and large investors will make their choices.

---

29. Source: IMF (*Direction of Trade Statistics*).
30. See *Overview of Third Country trade defence actions against the Community*, cit., pp. 10-11.
31. See *Overview of Third Country trade defence actions against the Community*, cit., p. 11.

It is within this context, now of a 'global' size, that the interests of all of the world's countries basically confront one another in a *macroeconomic* contest in which – as directly evidenced by the figures offered above – private entities cannot, whatever their size and purpose, but play roles as second leading actors, certainly not as leads in the drama of trade.

This comment must be further qualified. In general, while a State acts for the protection of national economic positions, which it represents abroad as a whole body, as a result of its political choices depending on its preferential view of the frequently conflicting interests of this or that sector of the *national economy*, a multinational enterprise, as large as it may be, represents only itself, and its interests are usually in conflict, or in competition, if you like – unless industry-specific interests are at stake – with the interests of other enterprises in the same industry as its own, whatever their size, be they domestic or foreign.

The same applies even when lobbying pressures, fully lawful in some systems, lead the government of any one country to seek international protection for only certain manufacturing or commercial sectors, through actions that may concern even a large number of national enterprises united by common sectoral interests. It is still at an international level that the relevant complaint will be filed and discussed – before the WTO pursuant to the Dispute Settlement Understanding – by the State concerned against whichever other country the complaining country alleges to be liable for an infringement of international obligations. The fact that sometimes the complaining country may use the legal assistance of specialists designated and also paid by the enterprises concerned, in addition to its own counsel, does in no way change the terms of the dispute or the basic view of it as an international controversy between States.[32]

Therefore, the real players on the stage of the world economy cannot be but individual States, among which I venture to count the European Union – the just seeming inaccuracy of this statement being dealt with below.

With regard to the international economy, the applicable set of rules, most of them laid down in a number of multilateral conventions – supported on a thick mesh of complementary bilateral agreements covering other aspects of the international economic life – is the most advanced, widely spread and effective among all sets of sectoral rules in the international legal system.

Obviously, the overall result of international economic cooperation is by no means perfect, nor can it be deemed to be adequate to today's exigencies in many respects – if you only think of the monetary issues I will consider below. Yet, this is a lag which the law physiologically suffers from in all of its branches. Conversely, at least as far as international commercial law is concerned, that same legal framework provides for a whole set of regular, concerted reviews and updates that have secured its progress – at least so far – in contents as well as in the growing number of addressees.

---

32. See below, paragraph 13 of this Chapter IV, for a recent dispute between the United States and China over alleged violations of the TRIPs.

I respectfully disagree with those who maintain that so broad a framework of international rules on matters of international trade is good proof of the crisis of State sovereignty.[33] The contrary is true, in fact. My contention is based on two observations. First, if it is true that international rules confine individual States' choices to within national systems, they arise from agreements between States and are founded on the reciprocity principle. Secondly, the necessarily gradual adjustment of such rules to ever-new economic realities is not forced upon any one State from the outside, but is the result of cooperation between States.

In fact, international law is now, as never before, playing a major role in individual States' internal legal systems as well, precisely because national laws have been adjusted to international rules in the economic arena.

Now, if 'sovereignty' is to be understood with a view to 'domestic jurisdiction', as a function, that is, of the wider or narrower scope of the matters over which each State has exclusive jurisdiction, there could be no doubt as to the fact that, in the economic field – as well as in those of pollution or human rights – the proliferation of international rules invariably causes this scope of internal jurisdiction to narrow even further. If, however, the *sovereignty* concept is associated, as I submit it should, with a person's capacity to exercise rights and to comply with obligations within the international system, and to generate, negotiate and settle disputes between entities subject to international law, then individual States have never before had a more significant role to play in the formation and, through the international organizations they have set up, the application of the international law rules that govern economic issues.

The international law system so newly developed has also had an impact, in the matter under scrutiny, on the traditional hierarchy of sources, since the most commonly used instrument, then the one most relevant under the new international rules, has now become rather the international treaty than custom.

2. INTERNATIONAL ECONOMIC COOPERATION: FROM GATT 1947 TO THE WTO

The vision of the achievement of 'international co-operation in solving international problems of an economic, social, cultural, or humanitarian character' already emerged as one of the institutional purposes stated in Article 1(3) of the Charter of the United Nations, which came into force on 24 October 1945 and whose entire Chapter IX was devoted to 'international economic and social co-operation'.

---

33. In this sense, see Goldsmith, 'Sovereignty, International Relations Theory, and International Law: Organized Hypocrisy' [2000] 52 Stan. L. Rev. 959, 959; Raustiala, 'Sovereignty and Multilateralism' [2000] 1 Chi. J. Int'l L. 401, 418-19; Trimble, 'Globalization, International Institutions and the Erosion of National Sovereignty and Democracy' [1997] 95 Mich. L. Rev. 1944, 1948.

That was the context, in fact, within which the United Nations Conference on Trade and Development ('UNCTAD') was established as a permanent institution, primarily with the task to prepare analyses and reports about the most significant topical issues in international trade relations.

A similar purpose was stated among others in Article 1(2) of the Articles of Agreement of the International Monetary Fund ('IMF'). Further, Article 1(3) of the Articles of the International Bank for Reconstruction and Development specified the Bank's function even more extensively and with greater emphasis, thus:

> To promote the long-range balanced growth of international trade and the maintenance of equilibrium in balances of payments by encouraging international investment for the development of the productive resources of members, thereby assisting in raising productivity, the standard of living and conditions of labor in their territories.[34]

However, the international rules on economic and commercial relations were actually introduced through the General Agreement on Tariffs and Trade (the 'GATT') under a multilateral convention signed in Geneva on 30 October 1947, within the scope of a conference called by the Economic and Social Council of the United Nations, which proposed to develop a far more ambitious project for the establishment of a far-reaching international economic cooperation institution, the International Trade Organisation ('ITO'), by adopting the 'Havana Charter'.[35] After that project was abandoned following the US State Department's resolution not to lay the ratification of the Havana Charter before the US Congress, the Geneva General Agreement was first signed by 23 States, and subsequently entered into by a number of other States. It was affected by two adverse features, though. First, only the first two articles, which formed Part I of the Agreement, were binding on the contracting parties, while all the remaining articles were intended for 'provisional application'. Secondly, Part II provided for a number of derogations and exceptions that allowed any contracting party to introduce *temporary* restrictions in case the need arose to restore equilibrium in its balance of trade.

The General Agreement became increasingly important in the development of international trade and in the regulation of its Members in this area, until, at the end of the Uruguay Round, the GATT 1994 Agreements were annexed to the World Trade Agreement establishing the World Trade Organisation ('WTO') signed in Marrakech.

The present GATT/WTO membership includes almost all of the world's countries whose economic systems are based on free trade. Specifically, there are currently 153 Members, after the accession of the Socialist Republic of Viet Nam, Tonga (27 July 2007), Ukraine (16 May 2008) and Capo Verde (23 July 2008) as the last signatory in time, while negotiations are still pending in preparation of the accession of some other countries, the Russian Federation among

34. See U.N. Treaties Series, vol. 2, 134.
35. Santa Maria, 'Il diritto internazionale dell'economia' in *Istituzioni di diritto internazionale*, Carbone, Luzzatto & Santa Maria (Eds), 3rd ed., Turin, 2006), p. 480.

them.[36] Thus, it can be said that the GATT/WTO system provides the 'general' framework for the regulation of international trade.[37]

In fact, it was within this framework that the commercial relations between the United States, EC Member States and market-economy Third States were increasingly dealt with and regulated through a series of agreements, from the first revision of the GATT 1947 in the Kennedy Round of 1967, to the Tokyo Round in 1979, until the present text came into effect at the end of the Uruguay Round, when the Final Act and Agreement were signed by 111 States in Marrakech on 15 April 1994.

The work on the rules of international trade is still in progress at the Doha Round, from the name of the capital city of Qatar where it was opened, much as it was slowed down abruptly following the 'suspension' of negotiations in 2006. In the discussions at the Doha Round, the globalization issue has heightened the contrasts between industrialized and developing countries, also and above all in agricultural matters, thus making it more difficult to find solutions agreeable to all Members.[38]

The present text of the GATT 1994/WTO Agreements has been formed from a number of treaties, protocols and annexes – more than sixty among them. They include, *inter alia*, the revised text of the Tokyo Round antidumping and anti-subsidy 'codes', intended to provide for equitable and open antidumping proceedings, to reduce discretion in the determination of the margin of dumping and injuries, and to clarify the very notion of 'subsidy' to a substantial extent. The relevant instruments are the Agreement on Implementation of Article VI of the General Agreement on Tariffs and Trade 1994 (on dumping), and the Agreement on Subsidies and Countervailing Measures, both included in Annex IA ('Multilateral Agreements on Trade in Goods') to the Agreement establishing the World Trade Organisation.[39]

---

36. Save for the Holy See, the States that have 'observer status' are under an obligation to start negotiations for accession to the WTO within five years from achieving that status. In Dec. 2008, the 'observer governments' were 30: Afghanistan, Algeria, Andorra, Azerbaijan, Bahamas, Belorussia, Bhutan, Bosnia Herzegovina, the Comoros, the Vatican City, Ethiopia, the Russian Federation, Equatorial Guinea, Iran, Iraq, Khazakstan, Liberia, Libya, Montenegro, the Lebanese Republic, the Peoples' Democratic Republic of Laos, Samoa, Sao Thomé and Principe, Serbia, Seychelles, Sudan, Tajikistan, Uzbekistan, Vanuatu and Yemen. See WTO's website.
37. See Ruggiero, 'The WTO: ten years after its establishment', in *The WTO at Ten*, cit., 13, who underlines that the exceptional growth of the number of Contracting Parties is a clear proof of the success of the institution. He also emphasizes that, 'at the beginning, when the *General Agreement on Tariffs and Trade* (GATT) was established in 1947, there were only 23 Contracting Parties, half of which were developed countries. Nowadays, by contrast, developing countries constitute 80 per cent of the membership'.
38. On the growing difficult issues on the development of WTO see: Barón Crespo, 'From Doha to Hong Kong: a parliamentarian perspective', in *The WTO at Ten*, cit., 23 ff., at 29 ff.
39. Although the whole package of the agreements by which the Uruguay Round is written in the three official languages, English, French and Spanish – which alone may be used in interpreting those agreements internationally – (unofficial) translations into the various languages of the then fifteen Member States of the EC (including Italian) are contained in an appendix to Council

> The 'Final Act' signed in Marrakech in 1994 is like a *cover note*. Everything else is attached to this. Foremost is the Agreement Establishing the WTO (or the WTO Agreement), which serves as an *umbrella agreement*. Annexed are the agreements on goods, services and intellectual property, dispute settlement, trade policy review mechanism and the plurilateral agreements. The schedules of commitments also form part of the Uruguay Round agreements. [*Emphasis added*].[40]

The original text of the 1947 General Agreement, based on the general principle of free trade, was aimed at pursuing the *harmonious development* of international trade according to the following principles:

(a) *non-discrimination* in international trade, to be achieved by applying: (i) the most-favoured nation clause; and (ii) national treatment;
(b) '*tarification*', a term used today particularly in respect of the agricultural sector, but one reflecting a principle laid down at the very beginning (when agriculture was not caught by the GATT rules), one with a general reach and intended to permit tariff-based duties solely in international trade, out of their being certain and transparent by nature, and to exclude any other measures with equivalent effects;
(c) general prohibition of quantitative restrictions; and
(d) *reciprocity* (already firmly established in the 'case-law' practice of the GATT 1947 panels), pursuant to which compliance with international trade rules was not required as a value in itself, but as the expression of a *balance of commercial advantages* mutually accorded to the contracting parties, i.e. within a framework of mutual trading opportunities arising from the abolition of tariffs and other barriers to trade and the equivalence of the advantages actually obtained by the contracting parties in terms of quantities of goods exported.

All these principles have firmly been retained, as *ius receptum*, in the GATT 1994 agreements, then in the WTO system of which they are part (based on the 'continuity principle').[41]

Still, the whole of the agreements signed in Marrakech at the end of the Uruguay Round gave a new face to the Organisation, by substantially reinforcing the institutional structure governing trade between countries, establishing an advanced system for the settlement of disputes in international trade, and greatly

---

Decision of 22 Dec. 1994, concerning the conclusion on behalf of the European Community, as regards matters within its competence, of the agreements reached in the Uruguay Round multilateral negotiations (1986-1994), [1994] O.J. L336, 1 ff., for the decision, and 3 ff. for the text of the Agreements in question.

40. See the list *ratione materiae* of the Agreements and related annexes, and of the obligations undertaken by the Member States with the Uruguay Round, in *WTO Legal Texts*, at website http://www.wto.org/english/docs_e/legal_e/legal_e.htm.
41. Please, refer to Art. XVI of the agreement establishing the WTO and to Art. 3(1) of the Dispute Settlement Understanding.

expanding the scope for application of sector-specific rules (just think of the extension to services, through the GATS, and to industrial property rights, through the TRIPs).

The international rules on world trade were crowned with the WTO system. The agreement establishing the World Trade Organisation is based on the recognition, common to all Members, that:

> [T]heir relations in the field of trade and economic endeavour should be conducted with a view to raising standards of living, ensuring full employment and a large and steadily growing volume of real income and effective demand, and expanding the production of and trade in goods and services, while allowing for the *optimal use of the world's resources* in accordance with the *objective of sustainable development*, seeking both to protect and preserve the environment and to enhance the means for doing so in a manner consistent with their respective needs and concerns at different levels of economic development (. . .). [*Emphasis added*].

The Agreement is underpinned by the other recognition, that:

> there is need for positive efforts designed to ensure that developing countries, and especially the least developed among them, secure a share in the growth in international trade commensurate with the needs of their economic development. [*Emphasis added*].

Therefore, the WTO is:

> the *common institutional framework* for the conduct of trade relations among its Members in matters related to the agreements and associated legal instruments included in the Annexes to this Agreement. [*Emphasis added*].[42]

The WTO's essential task is to facilitate the implementation, administration and operation, and further the objectives, of the *General Agreement* establishing it and of the *multilateral trade agreements*, and it also provides the framework for the implementation, administration and operation of the *plurilateral trade agreements* as well.

One among the WTO's tasks is to provide the forum for negotiations among its Members concerning their multilateral trade relations even beyond the matters expressly provided for in the relevant agreements. It also administers the Dispute Settlement Understanding ('DSU') and the Trade Policy Review Mechanism ('TPRM'). While the former mechanism is an essentially juridical tool, the latter provides political control over the impact of each Member's economic policies on the multilateral trade system. Such control is exercised over a short timeframe in respect of the industrialized countries and for a longer period in respect of the developing countries.

---

42. See paragraph 1 of Art. II of the Agreement establishing the WTO.

The structure of the WTO includes a *Ministerial Conference*, which meets at least once every two years, and a *General Council*, both composed of representatives of all the Members (Article IV). The General Council's functions are to discharge the responsibilities of the *Dispute Settlement Body*, in cooperation with the *Panels* and then the *Appellate Body* under the revised Dispute Settlement Understanding, and to act as the mechanism for the review of Members' trade policies.

The WTO's administrative functions are performed by a *Secretariat* headed by a *Director-General*, appointed by the Ministerial Conference, which is also responsible for adopting regulations setting out 'the powers, duties, conditions of service and term of office of the Director-General'. The responsibilities of the Director-General and of the staff of the Secretariat are 'exclusively international in character'. This implies their full independence of any governments or other authorities outside the WTO, and the WTO's Members 'shall respect the international character of the responsibilities of the Director-General and of the staff of the Secretariat and shall not seek to influence them in the discharge of their duties' (Article VI).

> In the terms of Article XI(1) of the Agreement, the original WTO Members are the contracting parties to GATT 1947 as of the date of entry into force of the Agreement, and the European Communities.[43]

An important provision, the actual reach of which may only be determined by practice, is set out in the second paragraph of Article XI of the Agreement, according to which:

> The least-developed countries recognized as such by the United Nations will only be required to undertake commitments and concessions to the extent consistent with their individual development, financial and trade needs or their administrative and institutional capabilities.[44]

Finally, Article VIII(1) states:

> The WTO shall have *legal personality*, and shall be accorded by each of its Members such legal capacity as may be necessary for the exercise of its functions. [*Emphasis added*].

Although this provision, which was not set out in the GATT 1947 text, is not decisive in itself because – as was correctly observed in connection with a similar

---

43. This clarifies the sense of the extension to the European Union of each Member State's powers for the purpose of the international rules on this matter, which I discussed in the first paragraph of this Chapter IV.
44. In 1971, the United Nations acknowledged the nee to identify category of low-income States facing serious hindrances to development, the Least Developed Countries ('LDCs'). Twenty-four LDCs were identified in that year. Since 2006 their number has increased to 50 (34 African and 9 Asian States, 6 Pacific Islands and 1 Latin American country). The list is updated every three years according to the following criteria: (i) GNI *per capita*; (ii) weak Human Asset Index ('HAI'), a composite index based on health, nutrition and education indicators; and (iii) high economic vulnerability.

issue raised in regard to the EEC Treaty – international personality cannot be accorded by charter, but must be established on a case-by-case basis in light of the whole of the Organisation's rules and of its capacity to operate upon an international plane,[45] it is aimed at securing a *strong* position to the WTO within the international community.

3. THE WTO'S RELATIONSHIPS WITH THE OTHER INTERNATIONAL ECONOMIC ORGANIZATIONS: (A) WITH THE UNITED NATIONS

The first question to be examined in reviewing the WTO's relationships with the other international organizations it how it relates to the UNO system. Though the WTO operates outside the scope of the United Nations Organisation, its operations are coordinated with the UNO's with a view to establishing an orderly and peaceful system of international relations based on close cooperation among countries.

In this respect, the letters exchanged between the WTO Director-General with the UN Secretary, the text of which was subsequently approved by the UN General Council,[46] provide both for the exchange of information and documentation and cooperation between the two organizations' respective administrative bodies, and for the admission of each organization's representatives to participate as 'observers' in the other's work.

4. MORE: (B) WITH THE INTERNATIONAL MONETARY FUND: 'MONETARY DUMPING'

The second question concerns the WTO's relationships with the International Monetary Fund (the 'IMF'),[47] the world organization for international monetary cooperation.

The idea to create such an organization first surfaced in July 1944, when the representatives of forty-five countries met at Bretton Woods, New Hampshire, to approve a framework agreement on international monetary cooperation. They recognized that this was necessary to prevent the return of the disastrous economic policies that had brought about the 'Great Depression' in the 1930s. The Fund was

45. See the International Court of Justice's opinion of 11 April 1949 on the 'Reparation of injuries suffered in the service of the United Nations', in C.I.J. [1949] *Recueil*, 174 ff.
46. See WTO doc. WT/GC/W/10.
47. For the relations between the WTO and the IMF, see Matsushita, 'Governance of International Trade Under World Trade Organization Agreements. Relationships Between World Trade Organization Agreements and Other Trade Agreements' [2004] Journal of World Trade, p. 185 ff.; Dukgeun, 'Linkages between International Financial and Trade Institutions – IMF, World Bank and WTO' [2000] Journal of World Trade, p. 2 ff.; Gianviti, 'Les rapports entre l'Organisation Mondiale du Commerce et le Fond Monétaire International' in *La réorganisation mondiale des échanges (problèmes juridiques)* (Paris, 1996), pp. 75-86; Schlitzer, *Il Fondo Monetario Internazionale* (Bologna, 2000).

formally set up in December 1945, when the twenty-nine original member countries signed the 'Articles of Agreement'. Their number has increased exponentially since then, up to 185 members today.[48]

The first of the Articles of Agreements states the main purposes of the Organisation, as follows:

(i) To promote international monetary cooperation.
(ii) To facilitate the expansion and balanced growth of international trade.
(iii) To promote exchange stability.
(iv) To assist in the establishment of a multilateral system of payments.
(v) To provide members with financial resources (under adequate safeguards), thus an opportunity to correct any maladjustments in their balance of payments.

The IMF's general aim is to secure stability to the international financial and monetary system (i.e. the system of international payments and exchange rates between currencies). By encouraging its members to adopt serious economic policies, the IMF also attempts at preventing financial crises.[49]

What especially matters for our purposes is that Article IV, including Section I, 'General obligations of members', Section II, 'General exchange arrangements', and Section III, 'Surveillance over exchange arrangements', requires that each member shall:

> avoid manipulating exchange rates or the international monetary system in order to prevent effective balance of payments adjustment or to gain an unfair competitive advantage over other members. [*Emphasis added*].

Each member shall, instead, follow exchange policies compatible with its undertakings under the IMF Agreement. Each member country is also required to 'notify the Fund promptly of any changes in its exchange arrangements', and the IMF is expected, in turn:

> [to] exercise *firm surveillance* over the exchange rate policies of members, and shall adopt *specific principles for the guidance* of all members with respect to those policies. [*Emphasis added*].

Lastly, Article X of the IMF Agreement requires the Fund to cooperate

> with any general international organization and with public international organizations having specialized responsibilities in related fields,

then with the WTO/GATT 1994 as well.

---

48. The number of accessions to the IMF increased substantially during the 1960s (when several former colonial territories gained independence) and the 1990 (when the IMF was joined by States of the former 'Soviet bloc'. The People's Republic of China has been a member of the IMF since 17 April 1980.

49. About the IMF's tasks and history, generally, see Comba, *Lezioni di diritto internazionale monetario* (Turin, 2007), esp.lly p. 61 ff.

In order to accomplish its purposes, the IMF uses some fundamental tools, as follows:

- *Country surveillance*: This activity involves the monitoring of economic and financial developments, and the provision of policy advice to each member country at least once a year. This activity consists of 'Article IV consultations', during which IMF economists visit the member country to gather information and hold discussions with government and central bank officials, and often private investors and labour representatives, members of parliament, and civil society organizations. Upon its return, the mission submits a report to the IMF's Executive Board for discussion. The Board's views are subsequently summarized and transmitted to the country's authorities.
- *Global surveillance*: The Fund puts together the information collected in bilateral consultations and publishes it in the *World Economic Outlook* and in the *Global Financial Stability Report* twice a year.
- *Regional surveillance*: The IMF continuously reviews regional economic trends. It regularly examines economic developments and policies pursued under regional arrangements such as the euro area, the West African Economic and Monetary Union, the Central African Economic and Monetary Community, and the Eastern Caribbean Currency Union.
- *Multilateral consultations*: Consultations between the IMF and a group of countries about specific economic and financial problems (a tool first introduced in 2006)).
- *Lending to countries with balance of payments difficulties*: Loans are granted to countries unable to raise funds in the market to the extent necessary to meet their international payment obligations or to maintain adequate reserves.[50] This is a function in performing which the IMF acts neither as a subsidy agency nor as a development bank.[51]
- *Technical assistance and training*: This activity is chiefly intended to help underdeveloped countries or countries just coming out of a state of war.

The IMF has a Board of Governors, composed of one Governor for each member country (totalling 185). Typically, Governor is a country's Minister of the Treasury or the Governor of its Central Bank. The Board meets in September or October each year, on the occasion of the IMF/World Bank's annual meeting. Twenty-four Governors meet as the International Monetary and Financial Committee (the 'IMFC') twice a year.

---

50. In the first twenty years of the IMF's life, over one-half of all loans were addressed to industrialized countries. Since the mid-1970s, however, IMF borrowers have been developing countries, countries in transition from a command economy to a free-market economy or emerging countries.
51. Most IMF loans account for a tiny fraction of a Member State's requirements to fund its balance of payments. Still, since the IMF's intervention indicates that a country's economy is 'on the right track', this reassures the investors and helps in generating loans from other lenders. In this way, the INF acts as a catalyst to attract funds from other public or private institutions.

The IMF's business is conducted by an Executive Board of 24 members[52] whose seat is in Washington, D.C. The Executive Board elects a Managing Director, who remains in office 5 years (unless re-elected), is chief of the Fund's operating staff and is assisted by three Deputy Managing Directors.

Unlike other international organizations, the Fund has a weighted voting system. Resolutions are usually adopted in the form of mere 'recommendations', which are not binding in themselves, but are generally recognized as 'soft law'.[53]

Most of the IMF's financial *resources* come from *quota subscriptions* Members are required to pay in full upon joining the Fund. Quotas reflect a country's relative size in its own economy. The largest quotaholder of the IMF is obviously the United States. Quotas are reviewed by the Board of Governors at regular intervals, and may be increased on proposal by it.

The relations of the IMF with the WTO are governed by a Cooperation Agreement signed on 18 November 1996.[54] The Cooperation Agreement is intended to ensure proper and effective implementation of the rules contained in the 'Covered Agreements', which allow any member to apply quantitative restrictions on trade if a deficit occurs in its balance of payments. Correct assessment of the conditions that may justify the application of such restrictions requires that, along with commercial considerations, the WTO's technical bodies should also consider the relevant monetary aspects. Hence, the need for a close cooperation linkage between the IMF and the WTO.

To this end, Article XV of the GATT 1994 requires that in all cases in which the WTO is called upon to consider or deal with problems concerning monetary reserves, balance-of-payments or foreign exchange arrangements, *they shall consult fully with the International Monetary Fund.* In all such consultations the WTO is required to justify its decisions based on all findings of statistical and other facts presented by the Fund, and on the Fund's own determinations in respect of the financial position of a contracting party and as to whether action by that contracting party in exchange matters is in accordance with the Articles of Agreement of the International Monetary Fund.

A provision almost identical in content is set out in Article XII of the GATT 1994.

The following are the main tools of cooperation between the WTO and the IMF:

- *Regular consultation*: The IMF has observership status at the WTO, and participates actively in many meetings of WTO committees, working groups, and bodies. The WTO Secretariat attends meetings of the IMF Executive Board or the Board Committee on Liaison with the WTO on matters of common interest (which often occurs in the Fund's surveillance and lending activities). The WTO is required to consult the IMF when it

52. Eight of the 24 members of the Executive Board are appointed by individual States (the 5 largest quotaholders, i.e. the USA, Japan, France, Germany and the United Kingdom, plus China, Russia and Saudi Arabia). The remaining 16 members are appointed for a two-year term.

53. On the topic, see Comba, *Lezioni di diritto internazionale monetario*, cit., p. 1 ff. About the notion of 'soft law', see footnote 105 in Chapter V of this book.

54. WTO, doc. WT/L/194, of 18 Nov. 1996. On 28 Apr. 1997, the WTO signed a similar agreement with the World Bank.

deals with issues concerning monetary reserves, balance of payments, and foreign exchange arrangements. In particular, when a WTO member country intends to apply trade restrictions in the event of balance of payments difficulties, the WTO's Balance of Payments Committee is required to base its assessments of restrictions on the IMF's determination of a member's balance of payments situation.
- *High-level coordination* (e.g. between the IMF's Managing Director and the WTO's Director-General).
- *Technical assistance and training*: in respect of developing countries, based on the Integrated Framework for Trade-Related Technical Assistance to Least-Developed Countries.
- *Fund assistance for trade liberalization*: In an effort to support progress under the WTO's Doha round of trade talks, the IMF established the Trade Integration Mechanism ('TIM') in April 2004. The TIM is available to all Fund member countries whose balance of payments positions might suffer, *albeit temporarily*, as a result of multilateral trade liberalization.

Notwithstanding these provisions, and beyond the overemphasized significance of working together and making individual member countries' economic policies comply with both organizations' technical requirements, the cooperation agreement between the IMF and the WTO essentially *contributes little* to the coordination of national and supranational instruments of economic policy. For it only provides for the use of *conventional cooperation tools*, such as the mutual exchange of information and documentation, each organization's possibility to participate as an observer in the other's meetings and the creation of close links between their respective administrative bodies.

The end result is a difficulty in trying and reconciling the rules that govern international trade – quite unspecific by nature in the way they are worded in both general provisions and exceptions – with the needs arising from the new conditions of the world's economic order. In *this respect*, the problem is compounded by the fact that exceptions to the general rules are merely intended to operate in relation to the consequences of *unlawful imports of individual products into closely determined areas*. In other words, there are rules for exceptional application, which are inadequate in themselves to offset the effects of *general anomalous situations*.

Such inadequacy becomes especially apparent in cases of 'monetary dumping' or 'exchange rate dumping'. Either phrase is used to indicate the *anomalous* situation that affects a market where:

> the lower price of a foreign product than that of a *similar* domestic product arises from an artificial exchange rate between the currencies of the country of origin and the country of sale of the merchandise.[55]

---

55. See Comba, *Il neo liberismo internazionale – Strutture giuridiche a dimensione mondiale dagli accordi di Bretton Woods all'Organizzazione Mondiale del Commercio* (Milan, 1995), p. 113. About the merely definitional import of the phrase 'monetary dumping', see footnote 64 of this Chapter IV.

In this event, and until the prices within a country with an underappreciated currency increase to such an extent as to offset the difference in exchange rates, the exports from the country with the weaker currency gather great momentum, since its production costs are lower than those in countries with 'healthy currencies' just because of such difference in exchange rates.

Unlike price dumping, which is voluntarily used by individual enterprises for specific products, *monetary dumping* is an automatic consequence – a general one, in fact, as it extends to all industries and all markets – of a monetary policy choice made by a given country with a view to the depreciation of its national currency. It is also so, though, with far worse effects, when unilateral exchange rate control measures are taken by a country's government to keep its exchange rates with the world's major currency *constantly* weak. Such 'creeping' devaluation measures compound their general impact on all foreign industries and markets with that other feature, continuity over time, which makes them even more harmful.[56]

Such measures have been applied through outright unlawful means, such as:[57]

- *competitive devaluation* of national currencies, basically resulting in lower prices of a country's merchandise in international markets through manipulated exchange rates; or
- *multiple exchange rates* favourable to the selling of domestic products in foreign markets, and conversely unfavourable to the purchasing of imported products,[58] which, as such, reflect an approach unacceptable to the international community.

The real problem lies somewhere else, though. Despite the rather 'generic' than 'general' requirements set out in Section 1 of Article IV of the IFM Agreement discussed above, the real difficulty is the IMF system's persisting inadequacy and inability, as many as sixty years later, to give practicable answers to newly emerged exigencies. Such a gap especially concerns a regulation of the manners in which the exchange rates between major currencies should ordinarily be determined. The IMF system's predicament has far-reaching consequences, which have aptly been exposed by E. Truman, the economist who, in considering the document released in the matter at the end of a recent IMF multilateral consultation to be unsatisfactory, has pointed out that:

> It essentially ignored the role of exchange rates in the adjustment process; however, we know that if there is to be a substantial adjustment of global imbalances – not just the US deficit but also the oversized surpluses

56. For attempts to provide an international legal framework to the so-called 'foreign exchange dumping practices', see Santa Maria, 'Cina: regole internazionali e dumping sociale e monetario' [2003] Dir. com. int., p. 667 ff.
57. See Gerbino, 'Dumping', in *Enciclopedia del diritto* (Milan, 1965).
58. See Picone & Ligustro, *Diritto dell'Organizzazione Mondiale del Commercio* (Padua, 2002), p. 6.

elsewhere – substantial real effective exchange rate changes for the Chinese Yuan, the Japanese yen, and other currencies will be part of the process.[59]

In addition, in spite of the large number (185) of State members of IMF, today are still lacking international rules in the financial field.

First and in general, there are no rules apt both to prevent any 'systemic' financial crises and to manage and soothe the negative effects of them over foreign markets.[60] Besides, there is no international regulation at all on the activity of the so called 'sovereign wealth funds' as hereinafter described.[61]

5. MORE: (C) WITH THE G7 FINANCE

As is known, major macroeconomic and monetary policy issues are examined and discussed in periodical meetings by the 'Group of Seven', or '*G7 Finance*', whose members are Canada, France, Germany, Japan, the United Kingdom, Italy and the United States. The G7 is not an international organization in the technical sense of the term. The group is not founded on an international treaty and does not have an autonomous structure, with respect to member countries, nor does it have a permanent secretariat. The Group of Seven was created in 1975 by a Franco-German initiative (Giscard d'Estaing and Schmidt) with the objective of setting up a forum, at the highest decisional level and having formalities reduced to a minimum, in which to discuss important macroeconomic and monetary issues. The group was established with the intent of filling the gap created in the management of the monetary system which occurred following the breakdown of the Bretton Woods agreements in 1971. Thus, it is rather a forum in which the member countries participate, chiefly through their senior financial officials and often at the same time as their Central Bank Governors' meetings.

The G7 Finance[62] monitors the evolution of the world economy, and also intervenes in the resolution of financial crises, preparing financial aid packages in support to countries with balance of payments difficulties, in collaboration with the IMF. In the last few years, the G7 has also been involved in the strengthening of the international financial system, in the emerging countries' economic performance, in development financing, in the cancellation of debt to the poorest countries, and even in capital movement control within the scope of the fight against terrorism. 'Communications' very carefully written out and often containing *recommendations*

59. Truman, 'The role of US and EU Financial Markets in the Global Economy', a paper presented to the Conference of 17 April 2007, at the Fed. Reserve Bank, NY, concerning '*The Euro and the Dollar: Pillars in Global Finance*'.
60. I obviously refer to the present financial crisis in USA on which, see section 8 of Chapter V of this book.
61. See again section 8 of Chapter V.
62. Wider powers not restricted to the economic and financial areas are vested in the G8, which, since the Birmingham Summit of 1998, has also included the Russian Federation, and which chiefly operates through annual summit meetings of Heads of State and Government.

to the members of the IMF or other international economic bodies are published at the end of each meeting.

6. MORE: (D) WITH THE INTERNATIONAL LABOUR ORGANISATION ('ILO')

What is meant by 'social dumping' is a practice whereby the retail price of a specific imported foreign product is lower than that of a *similar* domestic product, and such difference is due to 'social' conditions affecting production.[63]

The phrase[64] is mainly used in a derogatory sense, in that it describes the special position in international trade that favours countries in which the working conditions are less safeguarded than in others, and the advantage those countries gain from the free trade rules (on the most favoured country or national treatment) over countries in which more protective labour rules are in force.[65]

That this is unlawful conduct becomes most clearly apparent when such practices as exploitation of child labour or forced labour are ignored and so permitted in any given country. Detecting any actual instance of social dumping and assessing it for unlawfulness at an international level is less easy, though, when it occurs under a general approach to workers' treatment and safety on the workplace less favourable than, or even far remove from, those guaranteed to workers in more economically developed countries.[66] In any such instance, adequate yardsticks against

---

63. Comba, *Il neoliberismo*, cit., p. 113.
64. It should be noted that the phrases 'social dumping' and 'monetary dumping' have an essentially definitional import because, notwithstanding the analogy with the word 'dumping' as applied to the distorting effects both occurrences have on international trade, neither falls under the GATT/WTO's antidumping rules. On this subject, see Santa Maria, 'Il diritto internazionale dell'economia', cit., p. 460. See also the extensive analysis of the difficulties in framing foreign-exchange dumping and social dumping within the WTO system, in Santa Maria, 'Cina: regole internazionali e dumping sociale e monetario', cit., p. 681 ff.
65. See Venturini, *L'Organizzazione Mondiale del Commercio* (Milan, 2000), p. 47, and G. Porro, 'Disciplina del lavoro e commercio internazionale: quali relazioni?' [1999] Il diritto dell' economia I, pp. 161 ff.
66. As per China, it has to be underlined that, in the most recent years, the Chinese government attaches great importance to the issue of employment moving from the assumption that 'employment has a vital bearing on the people's livelihood. It is the fundamental prerequisite and basic approach for people to improve their lives'. Since 'China has a population of nearly 1.3 billion', it recognizes that 'to solve the employment task in China is strenuous, arduous and pressing task'. See 'China's Employment Situation and Policies' (April 2004), in (4) *White Papers of the Chinese Government (2002-2004)*, compiled by the Information Office of the State Council of the People's Republic of China, Foreign Language Press [2005], 457-491. To give an idea of the great difficulty of the challenge suffice it to say that: 'In 2003, the total population of China reached 1.292 billion (excluding Hong Kong Special Administrative Region, Macao Special Administrative Region and Taiwan Province). The population over the age of 16 was 998.89 million, of which the urban population was 423.75 million and the rural population was 760.75 million and the workforce participation rate was 76.2 percent. Among the population over the age of 16, the population with junior middle school education

which to make negative assessments or to apply actual remedies can hardly be found in international rules.

The entire issue is worsened by multinational corporations' interest in failing to make good for lacking or poor labour standards in any one country, and by its interest, in fact, in benefiting from weak national legislation or control in this area.[67]

Although some among the most highly developed countries look at 'low-cost countries' as a source of global growth, there is growing concern in others about competition from manufacturers operating in countries with legal systems that provide for exceedingly low labour standards. This concern also extends to social matters, since social dumping may give rise to an international 'race to the bottom' of a sort in *de minimis* wages and benefits – in addition to higher unemployment rates and stagnant wages of unskilled workers in industrialized countries.[68]

In this perspective, the welfare state may well turn into a 'competition state', with a government forced to adjust its social policy to other countries' policies unfair to workers, in an attempt at making its economic system look more attractive to foreign capital.[69]

---

level and above took up 61.7 percent, and that with junior college education and above, 6.6 per cent. Among the population of technical workers, those of the elementary grade took up 61.5 percent, those of the intermediate grade, 35 per cent and those of the advanced grade, 3.5 percent'. See 'China's Employment Situation', cit., 459-460. The numbers of the continuous growth are impressive: 'At the end of 2003, there were 744.32 million people in employment in China, 6.92 million more than the number at the end of 2002. They included 256.39 million urban people, an increase of 8.59 million from the previous year. In 2003, 4.4 million people laid off from state-owned enterprises were re-employed. At the end of 2003, the nationwide registered urban unemployment rate was 4.3 percent'. See 'Progress in China's Human Rights Cause in 2003 (Mar. 2004)', in *White Papers*, cit., 415. Since social security is recognized to be 'one of the most important socio-economic system for a country in modern times' and it is also 'an important guarantee for the social stability and the long-term political stability of a country', the Chinese Government declares that it 'devotes every effort to establishing and improving its social security system'. See 'China's Social Security and Its Policy (Sep. 2004)', in *White Papers*, cit., 556-584. This project – addressed to a consistent improvement of the social security system covering both urban and rural areas – can be achieved in the long run only, due also to the fact that the Chinese is an 'aging society'. 'As the aging of the population quickens, the number of elderly people is becoming very large. This trend will reach its peak in the 2030s' (p. 558). However, the number of the employed people beneficiary of a social security program in 2003 in the various areas – as emerging from the Chinese governmental survey – is very limited as compared to the global population and the economic benefits are much lower than those guaranteed by the EU or US welfare system.

67. Alber, 'Social dumping, catch-up or convergence?' [2001] Journal of European Social Policy, Special Issue, 10, p. 2. Alber considers each of the different forms of social dumping, stressing that it is only indirectly connected with governmental policies most of the times, since the lead actors are private parties, such as investors, manufacturers or consumers.
68. Golub, *International Labour Standards and International Trade, Working Paper of the International Monetary Fund*, 1997, p. 5.
69. The main effects of social dumping are: (i) the determination of national tax rates is constrained because of threats of capital flight and loss of foreign investments, which results in a shift from a direct and progressive system of taxation to an indirect and regressive system; (ii) the pressure to limit public debt is reinforced, which results, generally, in public spending cuts and, in

An effort to establish international labour standards was made by the creation of the International Labour Organisation (the 'ILO') as early as 1919.[70]

With its tri-partite structure, the ILO is unique among international organizations. For employers and workers have equal voice with Member States at the *International Labour Conference*, which meets in Geneva in June each year to make decisions on the organization's general policy and work programme. Each member state is represented at the International Labour Conference by four delegates: two government delegates, an employer delegate and a worker delegate, and each delegate has individual, independent rights to voting and to the floor.

The organization's affairs between annual Conferences are managed by a Governing Body, itself a tri-partite structure, with twenty-eight persons representing governments (the ten states of chief industrial importance being permanent members), fourteen representing the employers and fourteen representing the workers. The third body is the *International Labour Office*, which discharges its operating tasks through officials in Geneva and over forty field offices internationally.

The ILO has adopted a number of international conventions over the years, covering matters related to workers' fundamental rights, among which the 'core labour standards' on forced labour (Conventions No 29 and No 105), freedom of association (Conventions No 87 and No 98), equal remuneration (Convention No 100), discrimination, employment and occupation (Conventions No 111), and the worst forms of child labour ((Conventions No 138 and No 182).[71] These Conventions have attracted almost unanimous consensus in terms of ratification by individual governments, save for the two Conventions concerning minimum age for admission to employment.[72]

---

particular, cuts in social protection; (iii) State subsidies are shifted from labour to capital, both in absolute and in relative terms; (iv) the social security system is shifted from the general to the particular; and (v) public resources earmarked for social security are transferred to vocational training programmes. See Alber, 'Social dumping, catch-up or convergence?', p. 5.

70. The ILO was established during the Versailles Peace Conference which, together with the Peace Treaty signed French and English in Versailles on 28 Jun. 1919, put an end to World War I, and is now the only one surviving product of that Treaty, which contained the Covenant of the League of Nations in Part I. Art. 387 et seq., in the first section of Part XIII, contained provisions for the establishment of the International Labour Organisation among the tasks assigned to the prospective League of Nations. See *Traité de Paix/The Treaty of Peace between the Allied and Associated Powers and Germany and Protocol* (Paris, Imprimerie National, 1919), p. 193 ff. Since 1946, the ILO has been the first specialized agency to be associated to the United Nations.

71. The same rights were included in the ILO Declaration on Fundamental Principles and Rights at Work of 18 Jun. 1998.

72. Blengino, 'La dimensione sociale del commercio internazionale', in *Studi di diritto internazionale dell'economia*, Porro ed. (Turin, 1999), p. 227. For it should be noted that, out of an average 160 ratifications (among the 182 countries that were ILO members as at 14 Oct. 2008) for the six Fundamental Conventions, the two Conventions on child labour were ratified by 123 and 135 countries, respectively. (Source: ILO). China has ratified the 'Convention of the Minimum Age for Admission to Employment', the 'Convention on Prohibition and Immediate Action for the Elimination of the Worst Forms of Child Labor', the 'Convention Concerning

With a view to improving the control system provided by the ILO Conventions,[73] a proposal has been made to extend the ILO supervisory procedure to ensure freedom of association to other fundamental principles underpinning the protection of labour. Based on the special procedure for the protection of freedom of association, an ad-hoc Committee reviews complaints concerning violations of freedom of association, whether or not a member State has ratified the relevant convention.[74]

ILO procedures are, however, intrinsically limited by the fact that in practice, even when violation of any Convention has been established, no economic or other penalty is inflicted.[75] The GATT 1947 itself provided for the possibility for any contracting party to apply restrictions on imports only of goods manufactured by prison labour in another member country.[76]

The confrontation on core labour standards has essentially involved economically advanced countries arguing with developing countries in a controversy over the 'international social clause'.[77] The former maintain that any international trade agreement should contain such clause, infringing which should entail retaliatory trade sanctions in the form of quantitative restrictions on imports or even revocation of commercial benefits formerly granted.

Developing countries,[78] however, oppose the use of this clause on the argument that measures such as these are only ostensibly advocated for the protection of their workers, while they are only sought to disguise protectionist purposes.[79] They further contend that, as labour conditions are not a result of deliberate policies but of structural facts, requiring them to observe an international obligation to comply with higher labour standard would greatly increase production costs for the enterprises operating in a less developed country, thus depriving them of their comparative advantage over products manufactured in industrialized countries, and disrupting that country's progression to full economic development.[80]

Equal Remuneration for Men and Women Workers for Work of Equal Value' and the 'Employment Policy Convention'. See 'China's Employment Situation', cit., 458-459.

73. Control over the application of the Conventions is exercised on the basis of annual reports to be furnished by the States. Both complaints and denunciations can be filed against any State alleged to be responsible for violations.
74. Blengino, 'La dimensione sociale del commercio internazionale', p. 248.
75. *Ibid.*, p. 230.
76. See Art. XX(e) of the GATT 1947.
77. Blengino, 'La dimensione sociale del commercio internazionale', pp. 224 ff., maintains that the whole debate about the expediency of introducing a 'social clause' originated from the belief that the ILO's control systems are ineffective in that they do not provide for penalties applicable to violations of Convention rules.
78. According to Leary, 'The WTO and the Social Clause: Post-Singapore' [1997] European Journal of International Law, pp. 118 ff., such view is shared by the United Kingdom.
79. Porro, 'Disciplina del lavoro e commercio internazionale: quali relazioni?', p. 165.
80. Blengino, 'La dimensione sociale del commercio internazionale', p. 235.

Lacking unanimous views on the point, it was impossible to accommodate the *international social clause* either in the various evolutionary phases of the GATT 1947 or even in the WTO/GATT 1994.[81]

A compromise was reached among the contracting parties at the Uruguay Round. In exchange for the non-mention of the international social clause in the Marrakech Ministerial Declaration of 7 April 1994, a commitment was taken by the contracting parties to hold their future discussions of social occurrences apt to distort international trade at WTO meetings.[82] This commitment was re-stated in the Singapore Ministerial Declaration of 13 December 1996 and in the Geneva Ministerial Declaration of 20 May 1998. Both were, in fact, instruments worded in quite unspecific terms, which gave the ILO the power to decide about appropriate standards, while leaving the developing countries' position unaffected and only allowing for corrective actions to be taken in the most outrageous cases. Thus:

> We renew our commitment to the observance of internationally recognized core labour standards. The International Labour Organization (ILO) is the competent body to set and deal with these standards, and we affirm our support for its work in promoting them. We believe that economic growth and development fostered by increased trade and further trade liberalization contribute to the promotion of these standards. *We reject the use of labour standards for protectionist purposes, and agree that the comparative advantage of countries, particularly low-wage developing countries, must in no way be put into question.* In this regard, we note that the WTO and ILO Secretariats will continue their existing collaboration. [*Emphasis added*].[83]

Serious distortions of international trade essentially similar to those discussed above in connection with 'social dumping' may occur where lower production costs are a result of a more or less complete lack of national rules ensuring protection to the *work environment*, the suitability of plant to specific productions and, in particular, workplace security and health. The issue is even more delicate in this respect, since the lack of such rules gives the 'facilitated' producer unfair advantages in international trade and, above all, because the products so manufactured without adequate environmental hygiene protection rules or proper supervision in exporting countries may seriously affect the health of consumers, who are the ultimate recipients of the exported products. The situation is especially dangerous and must be closely watched over in the case of foods and pharmaceuticals exported from countries where health on the workplace is at risk.[84]

---

81. Golub, *International Labour Standards and International Trade, Working Paper of the International Monetary Fund*, p. 15, contends that the United States have unsuccessfully requested since 1953 that a social clause be included in the GATT.
82. Blengino, 'La dimensione sociale del commercio internazionale', p. 224.
83. See paragraph 4 of the Singapore Ministerial Declaration of 13 Dec. 1996.
84. Please refer to the more extensive considerations in my article, 'Limiti alle importazioni dalla Cina fra clausole di salvaguardia ed interventi a tutela della concorrenza' [2005] Dir. Un. Eur., p. 334 f. On the current policy of the Chinese Government see above footnote 66 of this Chapter.

7. THE EUROPEAN UNION AND 'SOCIAL DUMPING'

The European Commission expressly considered 'social dumping' in two Communications to the Council in 1996.[85]

In the first Communication, the Commission specified that:

> If it is unthinkable to deprive developing countries of the comparative advantage of low-cost labour, however such practices as *the prohibition of free association* or *employment of forced labour* cannot be justified on grounds of economic development. [*Emphasis added*].

In the second Communication, the Commission insisted that:

> Political Authorities should not overlook *non-observance of human rights in labour relations* in any forms of deprivation of fundamental freedoms, such as slavery or forced labour, employment of children or the prohibition of the rights to freedom of association and to collecting bargaining,

and stressed that:

> the interest of the Union in the matter of internationally recognised labour standards arises from *the Union's own social foundations.* [*Emphasis added*].

Faced with the objective difficulty of dealing with social dumping within a multilateral context,[86] the European Union has chosen to implement the core labour standards in its bilateral trade relations.[87] Hence, for example, the inclusion of a clause on the respect of human rights in the Association Agreements between the European Union and 6 Central and Eastern European Countries,[88] and in the Association Agreements, as superseded by the Accession Agreements, with Latvia, Lithuania and Estonia.[89]

A similar clause is contained in the bilateral Trade Agreement with South Korea signed on 29 February 1996,[90] in the Co-operation Agreement with South Africa

---

85. See Communications of 14 Feb. 1996, COM(96) 53 final, and of 24 Jul. 1996, COM(96) 402 final, both unpublished.
86. Out-and-out 'social clauses' have, in fact, been introduced in multilateral treaties on commodities to which the European Union is a party, See, for example, the International Cocoa Agreement of 1993, approved by Council Decision of 6 Jul. 1998, in [1998] O.J. L220, p. 1.
87. See: Vellano, 'L'Unione Europea ed il social dumping: aspetti interni e relazioni esterne' [1999] *Il diritto dell'economia*, pp. 176 ff.; Commission Communication on Promoting core labour standards and improving social governance in the context of globalization, COM (2001) 416 final, of 18 Jul. 2001, quoted by Balboni, 'Diritti dei fanciulli e commercio equo: clausola sociale o altro?' in *Commercio internazionale sostenibile – WTO e Unione Europea*, L.S. Rossi (ed.) (Bologna, 2003), p. 137. At a European level, the Commission suggested that such instrument as the generalized preference system, bilateral and multilateral cooperation agreements, aid to development and impact assessment on sustainable development should be used more effectively and consistently.
88. The agreements with the Czech Republic, Slovakia, Poland, Hungary and Slovenia were superseded by the relevant Act of Accession [2003] O.J. L236, effective as from 1 May 2004.
89. [1992] O.J. L403, p. 2.
90. See COM (96) 141 final, of 9 April 1996.

signed in Pretoria on 11 October 1999, in the Association Agreement with Chile signed on 3 October 2002, and in the Partnership Agreement signed with the ACP Countries in Cotonou, Benin, on 23 June 2000, as revised in 2005.

Lastly, mention should be made of the '*essential elements clause*' on human rights the European Union now ordinarily incorporated into cooperation and development agreements.[91]

Although the wording of 'social clauses' does not expressly mention workers' rights, and refers more broadly to human rights, the commitments enshrined in such clauses are of a legally binding import, and so, where the other contracting party violates workers' rights, the European Union would be entitled, in the terms of Article 60 of the Vienna Convention on the Law of Treaties, to suspend the operation of the relevant association or trade treaty in whole or in part or even to terminate it.[92]

The European Union enjoys greater latitude in exacting respect for certain of the workers' fundamental rights when it acts unilaterally on the basis of its 'Generalised System of Tariff Preferences'.[93]

In 1968, the United Nations Conference on Trade and Development (UNCTAD) recommended the creation of a Generalised System of Tariff Preferences ('STP') under which industrialized countries should grant trade preferences to all developing countries.

For such system to be implemented in practice, it was necessary to amend Article 1 of the GATT through a derogation from non-discrimination clause.

The European Community was first in implementing an STP scheme in 1971.

A new STP scheme was adopted by the European Union on 27 June 2005, through Council Regulation (EC) No 980/2005,[94] to be applied until 31 December 2008 to any country recognized and classified as a less developed country by the United Nations.[95] Regulation No 980/2005 provides for a general arrangement for the benefit of all beneficiary countries and two special arrangements, one being an incentive arrangement for sustainable development and good governance, the other an arrangement for the treatment of least developed countries, based on terms set out in the Regulation.

---

91. In accordance with this clause, the relevant benefits are frozen or suspended in case such rights are violated. This is the so-called 'aid conditionality policy' about which see Balboni, 'Diritti dei fanciulli e commercio equo: clausola sociale o altro?', p. 138.
92. Vellano, 'L'Unione Europea ed il social dumping: aspetti interni e relazioni esterne', pp. 176-178.
93. Because of their nature as *positive* measures, such mechanisms as *generalized preferences* cannot be deemed to be the same thing as a social clause. Yet, it is clear that the practical effects are quite similar between the two sets of measures, since both amount in fact to a block in the economic relations with the countries concerned. This is why as well the generalized preference system as the social clause has been challenged by developing countries. See the Joint Communication of the Group of Fifteen. Jakarta, Indonesia, 30-31 May 2001, esp.lly para. 22; See also Balboni, 'Diritti dei fanciulli e commercio equo: clausola sociale o altro?', p. 139.
94. [2005] O.J. L169, p. 1. For the period 2009-2011, see Council Regulation (EC) No 732/2008, [2008] O.J. L211, p. 1.
95. For this topic, see paragraph 8 next following below.

The special incentive arrangement for sustainable development and good governance may only be granted to a country which, among other things, 'has ratified and effectively implemented the conventions listed in Part A of Annex III', i.e. as many as sixteen core human and labour rights UN/ILO Conventions.[96]

Special arrangements are granted upon a request the country concerned is expected to make to the Commission. The request must be accompanied by information about the ratification of the Conventions and their implementing legislation and measures.[97]

The Commission is granted special monitoring and verification powers, in that:

> It may ask the requesting country any questions which it considers relevant and may verify the information received with the requesting country or any other relevant sources.[98]

The preferential arrangements provided for in the Regulation may be temporarily withdrawn, in respect of all or of certain products, if: (a) the beneficiary country seriously and systematically violates any of the core human and labour rights Conventions, as established on the basis of the conclusions of the relevant monitoring bodies; (b) that country's national legislation '*no longer incorporates the conventions*' which have been ratified; or (c) that legislation is not effectively implemented, though complying with the relevant international rules.[99]

8. THE GLOBALIZATION PROCESS: THE WIDENING GAP BETWEEN INDUSTRIALIZED COUNTRIES AND LESS DEVELOPED COUNTRIES (LDCs) AND THE DOHA ROUND'S DIFFICULTIES

While China's economic boom described above – which has been followed, albeit at some distance, by India's, and in some respect also by Brazil,[100] if only because of those markets' huge size in terms of present and prospective producers and consumers – has contributed to the gradual, unchecked globalization of the

---

96. See Article 9(1) of Council Regulation (EC) No. 980/2005, Paragraph 2 of Article 9 also provides for certain derogations that may be granted to a country '*which has not ratified and effectively implemented a maximum of two of the sixteen conventions listed in Part A of Annex III*'.
97. See Article 10 of Regulation 980/2005, cit., *ibid.*
98. See Article 11(1) of Regulation 980/2005, cit., *ibid.*
99. See Article 16(1)(a) and Article 16(2) of Regulation 980/2005, cit., *ibid.*
100. Brazil has, for the past few years, succeeded in providing foreign-exchange stability to its national currency and to cut inflation to a considerable extent. In the last four years, it has also attained an average 4.5% growth rate. These economic successes have reinforced its position internationally. See the documents of the European Commission's DG Trade of 7 and 24 Aug. 2007, available on the website http://trade.ec.europa.eu/doclib/docs/2006/september/tradoc_113359.pdf.

economy, it has also deepened the differences between the industrialized, high-technology countries and the developing countries. And the gap between the most developed and the least developed countries has even widened over the last few years.

Article XVIII of the GATT 1947, as amended in 1955, and, later on, Part IV added to the General Agreement in 1994, as well as the decision on the LDCs adopted earlier, on 28 November 1979, at the end of the Tokyo Round, in compliance with the principle of 'compensatory inequality', have all recognized the LDCs' right to depart from the free trade principles in order to maintain their tariff concessions and to introduce quantitative restrictions on imports for the promotion of their blossoming industries.

The 'compensatory inequality' criterion exceptionally allows different measures to be taken by LDCs depending on their economic lag and lower propensity for development.

Hence, an unspecific 'right to development' being recognized to the LDCs, and an as unspecific solidarity duty for countries already enjoying high economic potentials – such right and such duty being also asserted by the United Nations Conference on Trade and Development, the United Nations' permanent intergovernmental body on trade.

Still, in the last few years of the twentieth century and in the early 2000s, the issue of economic underdevelopment has become more acutely felt, especially because of the sudden explosion of the new information technologies applied to trade. In fact, the number of countries lagging considerably behind other countries in growth has increased as a result.[101]

No suitable provision is be found in the Marrakech Agreements (except for the programmatic provision in Article XI, para.1) to help understanding in practicable terms the content of the preferential treatment accorded to the LDCs. Only in the individual Conventions listed on a sector-by-sector basis in an annex to the WTO Agreement can any such provision be found.

The Marrakech Agreements have, however, solved the prior issue of how to establish that a country is indeed a less developed country. This is because, while no firm definition of LDC has been provided, a new sub-category has been introduced – that of 'Less Advanced Countries', the LACs. The list of LACs is identified and regularly updated by the Committee on the United Nations Development Programme according to stated economic and social parameters.

Additional rights are recognized to the LACs, further to those accorded to the LDCs, in the various WTO covered agreements, for example in the WTO Agreements on Agriculture (Article 15(2)), on Technical Barriers to Trade (Article 12(7), and on subsidies (Article 27 (2) (3) and (5)), as well as in Article IV(3) of the GATS and in Article 66 of the TRIPs.

Under the new GATT 1994 rules, only the LACs, as contrasted with the broader LDC category, are *exempted* from the application of the *reciprocity principle* to them. Yet, 'non-reciprocity' may only be pleaded by them as long

101. See UNCTAD, *Trade and Development Report* (Geneva, 1999).

as they remain categorized as less advanced countries. This is because the WTO system tends to the (gradual) full integration of all countries – developing and less advanced alike – into the framework of ordinary arrangements.

In November 2001, under a settled approach to international commercial relations, the revision of international trade agreements was resumed in accordance with an agenda for development the WTO Members adopted at Doha.

The fact is that, however, the Doha Round has now reached a standstill, and its workings were beset with difficulties even before suspension as a result of the stance taken by countries of all categories in disagreement among them on several issues.

The proposal the EU Commission submitted on 28 October 2005, on the sides of the Hong Kong ministerial meeting, was the only one on the table when negotiations were broken. In particular, the European Union had volunteered to cut internal aid to agriculture by 70%, to reduce the highest tariffs by 60%, and to halve the average agricultural tariff rate down to 12%. This offer was made conditional upon significant improvements in respect of non-agricultural market access and the free movement of services, in addition to an agreement on a registry of geographical indications and on their extension. The European Union stressed that the abolition of aid to the agricultural sector was expected to lead up to equal conditions among industrialized countries as well, and renewed its request that the United States, Canada, New Zealand and Australia undertook to abolish their domestic support to the food industry and export credit measures, and to modify the 'blue box' criteria, which are an exception to the general rule that subsidies to agriculture should be reduced or brought within *de minimis* percentages.[102]

Some criticisms on the EU proposal, but, above all – according to European Commissioner Mandelson, whose stance brought about some ill feelings within the European Commission itself – the lack of flexibility shown by the United States, Brazil and China later prevented negotiations from reaching a successfully outcome at the Geneva session of 23 July 2006.

9. THE DSB (DISPUTE SETTLEMENT BODY) AS CONTRASTED WITH THE PREVIOUS SYSTEM OF INTERNATIONAL DISPUTE SETTLEMENT WITHIN THE WTO

The really qualifying element of the WTO system is the 'Dispute Settlement Body'. After operating for almost a half century within the framework of the GATT 1947, this system was extensively reformed following the approval of the Uruguay Round's Final Act.

The contracting parties' agreement on the rules and procedures governing the settlement of international controversies about *trade*, within the broad meaning this term has taken on following the expansion of matter-specific powers under the

102. See Article 6(5) of the Agreement on Agriculture.

GATT 1994, found its way into the Dispute Settlement Understanding ('DSU'), itself an instrument incorporated into the Final Act as Annex II to the Agreement establishing the WTO. With its *twenty-seven articles* and *four appendices*, the DSU provides the most comprehensive set of rules on the matter since the start of the multilateral trade system.

The success of the Dispute Settlement Body is borne out by the fact that as many as 378 *disputes* had been brought before the WTO's new judicial authorities until 20 June 2008,[103] after less than one year's transitional co-existence with the previous litigation system.[104]

The far-reaching revision of the WTO's entire dispute settlement mechanism was a forced passage in the GATT's history.

Originally, the handling of trade disputes between countries was only provided for by two articles of the 1947 General Agreement – Article XXII ('Consultation') and Article XXIII ('Nullification or Impairment'). *Those rules proved inadequate over time*, especially because, following preliminary consultations between the litigants, the *consensus approach* commonly taken by the contracting parties as a substitute for the majority resolution procedure prescribed by the General Agreement, the system allowed either party to the dispute to prevent the institution of groups of experts (the 'panels'), who were expected to assist them by investigating into, and examining, the case under dispute. Further, *the lack of specific, mandatory time limits* to each stage of the procedure would result in delaying the submission of a final report beyond control.

Hence, a proliferation of special regulatory and institutional treatments, and the ensuing much-criticized *forum-shopping* practice.[105]

For these reasons, the main lines of the reform that led to the establishment of the WTO can be summed up in a *unified, coherent and integrated litigation system*, which can be applied uniformly to any question falling within the Organisation's jurisdiction. Such system operates equally for all member countries, in the presence of non-dilatory procedures allowing for the smooth conduct of litigation proceedings, and the enforcement of the determinations contained in the reports

103. The number of disputes is broken down depending on the stage at which the relevant case is litigated: Panel Reports, Appellate Body Reports, Arbitration Report on the implementation period (Art. 21(3)(c)), Compliance Panel Report (Art. 21(5), and Arbitration Report on the Amount of Sanctions (Art. 22(6)). Based on available statistics, it appears that, if the WTO/GATT disputes are classified by type of the products involved, *as many as 42.9% of total cases concerned agricultural products.*

104. Coexistence was made necessary, albeit on a transitional basis, to allow for the settlement of 'older' disputes started under the egid of the GATT 1947 and still pending after the entry into force of the WTO, in respect of which the Understanding on the dispute settlement mechanism could not be applied retrospectively, or even for the settlement of 'newer' disputes started after 1 Jan. 1995 between Contracting States which were already parties to the GATT 1947, so long as even only one of them had not yet become a WTO Member.

105. This had, in particular, occurred as a result of the adoption of the so-called Tokyo Round Codes on technical (non-tariff) barriers to trade. Each such code provided specific dispute settlement rules and procedures administered by special bodies, which did not even represent every party to the GATT 1947, but just a small numbers of Contracting Parties.

and in the DSB's subsequent decisions in a reasonably short time, while ensuring legal certainty and the stability of international trade relations throughout.[106]

10. INSTITUTIONAL AND PROCEDURAL INNOVATIONS UNDER THE URUGUAY ROUND FINAL ACT

Major innovations introduced by the Uruguay Round in the dispute settlement system are:

- An integrated system allowing the Members to apply the rules of the Dispute Settlement Understanding to claims brought pursuant to the consultation and dispute settlement provisions of the agreements listed in Appendix 1 to the Understanding, while a special Dispute Settlement Body[107] is made responsible for determining the rules and procedures to be followed where the parties to a dispute cannot agree on them, establishing panels, adopting panel and Appellate Body reports, maintaining surveillance of implementation of rulings and recommendations, and authorizing retaliation measures against non-complying Members;[108]

---

106. The integration of the system was achieved, first, by making the Understanding cover all the agreements listed in Appendix 1 thereto (DSU, Art. 1(1)). This 'covered agreements' include both the WTO agreements materially governing the various aspects of international trade and the main institutional agreements, such as the Agreement Establishing the World Trade Organization as well as the Understanding on Rules and Procedures Governing the Settlement of Disputes, taken in isolation or in combination with other covered agreements. One excluded instrument was the set of working procedures for the review of trade policies (Appendix 3), which were intended less to ensure control over the lawfulness than to favour the transparency and disclosure of Member States' trade policies.

107. Essentially, the DSB is nothing but a special session of the General Council to be convened to discharge the responsibilities of the Dispute Settlement Body, and it is composed of all the members of the General Council in attendance, Art. VI(3) of the WTO Agreement requires the General Council composed of the representatives of all the Members to set up a standing body, the Secretariat, with its own Director-General, staff, and conditions of service, specifically responsible for discharging the duties formerly discharged by the GATT 1947 General Council in the area of dispute settlement. In particular, pursuant to Art. 2(1) of the DSU, the DSB has specific authority: (i) to administer dispute settlements procedures; (ii) to establish panels; (iii) to adopt panel and Appellate Body reports; (iv) to maintain surveillance of implementation of rulings and recommendations; and (v) to authorize suspension of concessions and other obligations under the covered agreements.

108. The function of Panels is to assist the DSB in discharging its responsibilities with a view to giving final rulings, by making an objective assessment of the matter before it, and submitting reasoned reports of the facts of the case and the applicability of, and conformity with, the relevant covered agreements (DSU, Art. 11). Therefore, Panels do not, at least formally, play a decision-making role, but their function is to provide a streamlined investigation tool in the service of the DSB, which is the only one authority, as the representative of all the WTO Member States' intent, to decide disputes within the Organization. A Panel is composed of three panelists unless the parties to the dispute agree to a panel composed of five panelists (DSU, Art. 8(5)). The Understanding also sets out in detail the requirements for acting as a panelist and guidelines for the selection of panelists in order to ensure the Panels' reputation

- The actual right for any Member allegedly harmed by a violation of any of the WTO/GATT 1994 rules to request the establishment of a panel under specific rules and within specific timeframes;
- Specific time limits set to each stage in the decision-making and enforcement processes;
- The right for each Member which is a party to a dispute to have a voice in the drafting of panel reports and to request that specific points in any one report be revised before it is submitted to the DSB (the 'Interim Review Stage');
- A second adjudicatory tier, the Appellate Body, responsible for reviewing the DBS's first-degree decisions on appeal;[109]
- A rule providing for 'negative consensus' (an unanimous contrary vote) for the rejection by the DBS of Panel or Appellate Body reports, which has reversed the previous rule whereby a Panel report required the Member's consensus for approval;[110]
- Suitable provisions to improve over the original coercion standards of decisions against the loosing party in a dispute;
- Suitable rules allowing the parties to a dispute to resort to arbitration both as an alternative to adjudication by panels and the Appellate Body and in decision-making proceedings or even at the implementation stage.[111]

---

and independence. Panelists are drawn from lists including rosters of 'governmental' and 'non-governmental' individuals meeting the knowledge and experience requirements laid down in Art. 8(1) of the DSU. If there is no agreement on the panelists so indicated, the composition of the panel is determined by the Director-General pursuant to Art. 8(7). Panels are assisted by the WTO Secretariat, which is responsible for providing them with technical support, especially in the legal, historical and procedural aspects of each relevant case, at the assistance of external experts if need be.

109. The Appellate Body is a standing body responsible for hearing appeals from panel cases (DSU, Art. 17(1) and 17(6)), in order to uphold, modify or reverse the legal findings and conclusions of the panel concerned. (DSU. Art. 17(13)). It is composed of seven persons, who remain in office for a four-year term and may be reappointed once (DSU. Art. 17(2)). Three of the standing seven persons serve on any one case. The qualifications and manners of appointment of the Appellate Body's members are closely determined.

110. Until the WTO was established, the rule was unanimous favourable vote or 'consensus', which allowed the losing party to block the adoption of a Panel's report with its contrary vote alone. This is what occurred, for example, in the '*Banana Case*' (DS38/R of 11 Feb. 1994), in the '*Airbus Case*' (SCM 142 of 4 Mar. 1992) and in the '*Importing of Tuna Fish Case*' (DS21/R of 3 Sep. 1991). Several different safety valves had been proposed to overcome the deadlock such a system would generate. In particular, some support was given to the proposal to introduce the rule of 'consensus minus 1' or 'consensus minus 2', i.e. unanimous voting without the participation of the parties to the dispute. The proposal was not, however, followed up because of the possibility for a losing State to block approval anyhow with the assistance of 'friendly' voters.

111. Besides these major innovations, there are *some gaps*, paramount among which is the lack of unequivocal, clearly worded provisions within the WTO system for solving the problem of the conflict of jurisdiction between WTO rules and the rules of any other multilateral trade agreement having the same scope in any one sector. Reference should specifically made to the so-called exclusivity principle of the WTO system, and the resulting obligation to apply both its internal litigation rules and the particular rules of coordination of the so-called

11. SETTLED LEGAL PRINCIPLES IN DSB/WTO CASE-LAW

An appropriate statement has been made with respect to the WTO Dispute Settlement System:

> The Members recognize that it serves to preserve the rights and obligations of Members under the covered agreements, and to clarify the existing provisions of those agreements in accordance with customary rules of interpretation of public international law. [*Emphasis added*].[112]

The nature and functions of the WTO's set of rules has aptly been summarized by the Appellate Body in its report on *Taxes on Alcoholic Beverages* (Japan Appellant/Appellee, United States, Appellant/Appellee, Canada, Appellee, European Communities, Appellee) of 1 November 1996, as follows:

> WTO rules are *reliable, comprehensible and enforceable*. WTO rules are not so rigid or so inflexible as not *to leave room for reasoned judgements* in confronting the endless and ever-changing ebb and flow of real facts in real cases in the real world. They will serve the multilateral trading system best if they are interpreted with that in mind. In that way, we will achieve the '*security and predictability*' sought for the multilateral trading system by the Members of the WTO through the establishment of the dispute settlement system. [*Emphasis added*].[113]

On this basis, some notable legal principles have emerged from Panel and Appellate Body case-law, in particular:

- Full confirmation of the impartiality, autonomy and independence of Panels and the Appellate Body, in WT/DSB/RC/1, *Rules of Conduct for the Understanding on Rules and Procedures Governing the Settlement of Dispute*, 11 December 1996;
- The principle that the burden of proof is to be discharged by the party alleging a fact, be it the complaining or the responding party;[114]
- The principle of the consistency of decisions with claims,[115] and, in particular, the limitations set to panel reports, in the sense that:

> Panels are inhibited from addressing legal claims falling outside their terms of reference. However, nothing in the DSU limits the faculty of a panel freely to use arguments submitted by any of the parties – or to develop its own legal

'external fora'. For a scrutiny on the functioning of the DSB and its balance after ten years of activity, see: Sacerdoti, 'The dispute settlement system of the WTO in action: a perspective on the first ten years', in *The WTO at Ten*, cit., 35, 52 and 55 ff.

112. See Article 3.2 of the Understanding on Rules and Procedures Governing the Settlement of Disputes.
113. See *Japan – Taxes on Alcoholic Beverages*, Docs WT/DS8/AB/Z, WT/DS10/AB/R, WT/DS11/AB/R, para. 122.
114. See Reports WT/DS46/AB/R, *Brazil – Export financing programme for aircraft* of 2 Aug. 1999, paras. 134 to 141, and WT/DS33/AB/R, *U.S.A. – Measure affecting imports of wool-shirts and blouses from India* of 25 April 1997.
115. See WT/DS163/R, *Korea – Measures affecting Government procurement* of 1 May 2000.

> reasoning – to support its own findings and conclusions on the matter under its consideration. A panel might well be unable to carry out an objective assessment of the matter, as mandated by Article 11 of the DSU, if in its reasoning it had to restrict itself solely to arguments presented by the parties to the dispute.[116]

The principle of judicial economy, so that:

> *[n]othing* in [Article 11 of the DSU] or in previous GATT practice *requires* a panel to *examine all legal claims* made by the complaining party [*Emphasis added*];[117]

> and, again:

> (. . .) a panel need only address those claims which must be addressed in order to resolve the matter in issue in the dispute. [*Emphasis added*].[118]

Let me add that the DSB does not hand down decisions for the past, but only for the future: neither a panel's negative report as confirmed by a later, equally negative report by the Appellate Body, nor the DSB's ensuing decision that closes proceedings in both instances, are deemed to be effective *ex tunc*. No final decision may inflict pecuniary penalties on the loosing party, since it may only order that the violation in issue be ceased and the *quo-ante* legal situation restored.[119]

In other words, the loosing party will have to amend or supersede its national measure or related practice to make it compatible with the violated GATT rule, in compliance with the DSB's decision, which the loosing party must closely implement within the time and in the manners prescribed therein.[120]

Further, based on Article 22 of the DSU, if the loosing Member fails to comply with the DSB's recommendations or rulings with a reasonable period of time, the application to the Member concerned of concessions or other obligations may be suspended.[121]

---

116. See Report WT/DS26/AB/R and WT/DS48/AB/R *EC – Measures concerning meat and meat products (hormones)*, para. 156. See also Reports WT/DS22/AB/R *Brazil – Measures affecting desiccated coconut* of 22 Feb. 1997, para. IV, and WT/DS50/AB/R *India – Patent protection for pharmaceutical and agricultural products* of 19 Dec. 1997, para. 88.
117. See WT/DS33/AB/R *U.S.A. – Measure affecting imports of woolshirts and blouses from India* of 25 April 1997, para. 339.
118. *Ibid.*, par. 340. See also WT/DS56 *Argentina – Certain Measures Affecting Imports of Footwear, Textiles, Apparel and Other Items* of 20 Dec. 2002, paras. 181 and 182.
119. Picone e Ligustro, *Diritto dell'Organizzazione Mondiale del Commercio* (Padua), cit., p. 600. Likewise, See Farah, 'Five Years of China's WTO Membership. EU and US Perspectives about China's Compliance with Transparency Commitments and the Transitional Review Mechanism' in *Legal Issues of Economic Integration*, Kluwer, vol. 33, No. 3, p. 263 ff., p. 304.
120. Farah, 'Five Years of China's WTO Membership. EU and US Perspectives about China's Compliance with Transparency Commitments and the Transitional Review Mechanism', in relation to the impact of WTO rules on the People's Republic of China, points out that these characteristics are in accordance with Chinese Great Tradition as reflected in the core Confucian idea that making mistakes and not learning from them would be worse than making mistakes.
121. Cassese, *Oltre lo Stato* (Bari, 2006), p. 25, observes that, in such a situation, 'National States react to other States' decisions or conducts under the control of the global body that decided the

An outstanding example of lawful response to another Member State's dilatory conduct in implementing a DSB ruling is to be found in Council Regulation (EC) No 2238/2003 protecting against the effects of the application of the United States Antidumping Act of 1916, and actions based thereon or resulting therefrom.[122]

The United States Antidumping Act of 1916 contained, *inter alia*, a right of action against the importer, the imposition of treble (punitive) damages, and *penalties* applicable to the enterprises liable for the violation, all of which led the DSB, on request from both the Community and Japan, to hand down a decision in September 2000 declaring:

> the Antidumping Act of 1916 to be incompatible with the US obligations under the WTO agreement.[123]

Still, after acknowledging that the USA had failed to comply with the DSB's ruling, in that 'the Antidumping Act of 1916 [had] yet to be repealed, and claims brought under this Act are pending before US Courts against persons under the jurisdiction of the Member States', which caused the Community undertakings to incur '*substantial litigation costs and may ultimately result in a judgment awarding treble damages*',[124] the European Council issued the Regulation of 2003, whose Article 1 requires:

> No judgment of a court or tribunal and no decision of an administrative authority located in the United States of America giving effect, directly or indirectly, to the Antidumping Act of 1916 or to actions based thereon or resulting therefrom, shall be recognised or be enforceable in any manner.

Article 2 further provides:

> Any person referred to in Article 3 shall be entitled to recover any outlays, costs, damages and miscellaneous expenses incurred by him or her as a result of the application of the Antidumping Act of 1916 or by actions based thereon or resulting therefrom.
>
> Recovery may be obtained as soon as an action under the Antidumping Act of 1916 is commenced.
>
> Recovery may be obtained from the natural or legal person or any other entity that brought a claim under the Antidumping Act of 1916 or from any person or entity related to that person or entity [. . .]. [*Emphasis added*].

Despite the obvious difficulties of a practical (even sooner than legal) nature that hindered the actual implementation of Article 2 – whose deliberate intent to impose a reparatory burden on complainants is quite clear indeed – the European Union's

---

dispute'. It must be remembered, though, that, in this case, the 'global body' is an 'international' body created by States and formed according to rules agreed to by those States.

122. [2003] O.J. L333, pp, 1 and 2.

123. See the third Whereas of the Regulation, cit., *ibid.*

124. See the fourth, sixth and seventh Whereases of the Regulation, cit., *ibid.*

action accomplished the intended aim, and the antidumping act of 1916 was repealed by the US Congress accordingly.[125]

Council Regulation No 2238/2003 is formally still in force, much as the reasons for its application have waned following the repeal of the contested legislation.

Just to provide an example and to make the timetable of the entire procedure patently clear in all of its possible variations, the following diagram shows the full procedure for the settlement of disputes by the DSB in accordance with the DSU provisions. The diagram is sourced from the WTO's official website:[126]

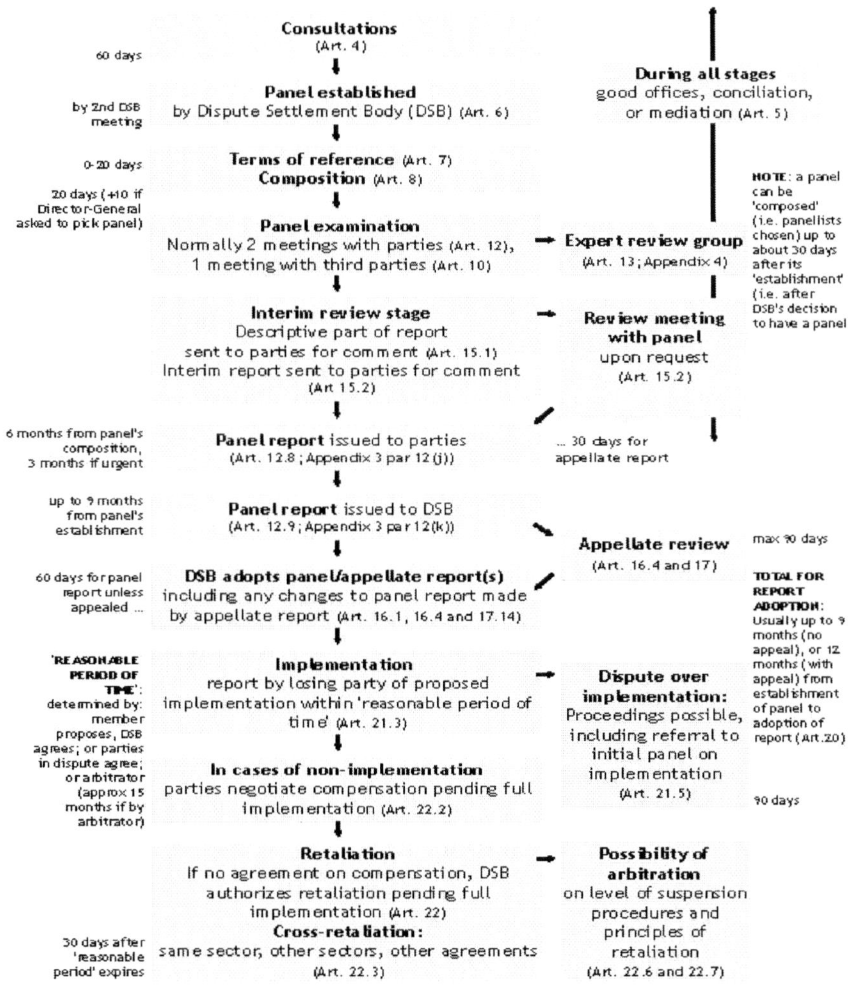

125. For a similar, even more consequential event in a dispute against the United States, which was caused by the 'Byrd Amendment', please refer to paragraph 19 of this Chapter IV.

126. See: http://www.wto.org/images/img_tif/disp_s_e.gif.

12. PROTECTION OF PRIVATE INTERESTS WITHIN THE WTO SYSTEM

Let me now discuss one of the most significant points of the WTO's judicial rules – the role of private traders and non-governmental associations or organizations within the new multilateral system of international trade.

Save for quite few exceptions, as in the case of the Argentinean legal system, in which the WTO's rules seem to be *directly applicable*,[127] the GATT-WTO rules are believed to be generally lacking in provisions for private parties' individual rights or legal duties. As a result, no such rule are actionable direct by private parties before the Member States' judicial authorities, not even in direct or vertical relationships.

This belief does not, however, seem to be entirely correct. It has been pointed out that certain provisions in the TRIPs Agreement, which has been described as 'an outstanding example of the role that private parties are able to play in international law', would be directly applicable[128] based on the argument that Article 41 of the TRIPs Agreement requires Members to ensure that enforcement procedures are available under their law so as to permit effective action against any act of infringement of intellectual property rights – including in respect of relationships between private parties.

This is also thought to be the import of the GATS Agreement,[129] in that the combined application of the most favoured nation clause and the national treatment clause – when applicable to 'providers of services' – would bring about 'substantive economic rights' that could be invoked direct by private parties before their national courts.[130]

Yet, a *negative* approach has been taken by the two leading players in international trade, the United States and the European Union.

---

127. See Report on *Argentina – Measures Affecting Imports of Footwear, Textiles, Apparel and Other Items*, (WTDS56/R para. 3.213), where its clearly stated that national courts in Argentina may rule on the inconsistency of internal acts with the world's trade system, which is the yardstick of their lawfulness.
128. See Esposito, 'International Trade Law and National Legal Orders: The Problem of Direct Applicability of the WTO Law' in Mengozzi (ed.), *International Trade Law on the 50th Anniversary of the Multilateral Trade System* (Milan, 1999), p. 447 ff.
129. Charnowitz, 'The WTO and the Rights of the Individual' [2001] Intereconomics, pp. 99-100.
130. In the matter of dumping and subsidies, the rules contained in the relevant international agreements have been implemented, in full accordance with international principles and rules, in the systems of the major GATT/WTO Contracting States, specifically the United States, the European Union, Canada, Japan and the People's Republic of China. Thus, the rules for the adjustment of those agreements to the GATT 1994 are the direct source of the duties and obligations of the enterprises concerned, in an internal system operating concurrently with the international system, the former necessarily drawing its contents from the latter. In case any difference is found between the national rules and the international agreements, it will obviously be for each Contracting State's courts to determine the consequences of any dispute between private entities in terms of internal law. In this respect, the EU's legal system obviously replaces each of its Member States'.

This approach has even found its way into law in the United States. For the US act implementing the Uruguay Round Agreements specifically requires[131] that no provision of those Agreements may be pleaded in opposition to the national rules. This does, in itself, exclude the possibility for private parties to rely on any of the Uruguay Round Agreement provisions before US Courts.

Obviously, the other WTO Members are fully entitled to challenge any provisions of US law that are in conflict with the Organisation's rules, but they may only do so within the dispute settlement system under the DSU.

As for the European Union, Community case-law has invariably held the view since 1999, with the judgment in *Portugal* v *Council*, that neither the GATT 1947 nor the WTO/GATT 1994 may be deemed to result in any rights or obligations being vested direct in private parties, thereby asserting that mutual rights and obligations pertain to the Contracting Parties alone. Accordingly, neither the GATT nor the WTO rules are deemed to have *direct effects* within the Community legal system.[132]

The negative purport of the Court of Justice's case-law in this matter has clearly emerged in the well-known cases *Parfums Dior* and *Assco Geruste GmbH.*[133] On the one hand, both judgments recognized the Member States' free choice in adopting measures at variance with WTO rules, unless the relevant matters fall within the scope of Community law. On the other hand, both judgments stated that the reciprocity principle is an almost insuperable obstacle to the direct application of the rules laid down in the WTO Agreement and covered agreements.[134]

It is emerged from Community case-law over the years that, however, a private party is entitled to plead GATT/WTO rules as a yardstick against which the legality of Community acts can be assessed either:

(i) where the conformity of a Community act with the international rules referred to is contested in case a Community Regulation expressly refers to GATT/WTO rules;[135]
or

---

131. See Section 102(a)(1) of the *Uruguay Round Agreements Act* in which it is clearly stated: '*No provision of any of the Uruguay Round Agreements, nor the application of any such provision to any person or circumstance, that is inconsistent with any law of the United States shall have effect*'.

132. See Judgment of the Court of 23 Nov. 1999, Case C-149/96, *Portugal* v *Council*, [1999] ECR I-8395, ground 47. In general, on the assumption that, according to the ECJ case-law, the WTO agreements lack any direct effect, see: Rosas, 'The European Court of Justice: sources of law and methods of interpretation', in *The WTO at Ten*, cit., 482 ff., at 485, and Mengozzi, 'The jurisprudence of the Court of Justice and the Court of First Instance of the European Communities', *ibid.*, 474 ff.

133. Cases C-300/98 and C-392/98, both judgments of 14 Dec. 2000, [2000] ECR I-11307.

134. For the study of a dispute in which the problem has recently arisen of the direct applicability of WTO rules within the European Community in relation to the reciprocity principles, see Judgment of the Court of First Instance of 20 Mar. 2001, Case T-30/99, *Bocchi Food.*

135. See Judgment of the Court of Justice of 22 Jun. 1989, Case C-70/87, *Fediol*, [1989] ECR 1781.

(ii) where a Regulation under scrutiny for conformity with the GATT was adopted precisely in order to ensure compliance with an obligation arising from the General Agreement.[136]

These are clearly exceptional occurrences, save for which Community case-law has invariably taken a approach definitely contrary to recognizing direct effects to the GATT/WTO rules.[137]

It should also be noted that the European Court of Justice has long claimed the Community Courts' jurisdiction over the application and interpretation of all GATT Agreements.

It emerges from a review of DSB case-law that some forms of protection of interests not necessarily matching the Organisation's member States' are to be found in the WTO legal order.

Precisely on this basis has DSB case-law often made express reference to private enterprises' and traders' interests, stressing the need for their adequate, effective protection, since the effects of any unlawful state measures ultimately fall upon them.[138]

The result is that the foremost form of protection of 'private' economic and commercial interests is ensured by the correct application of the complex system of agreements annexed to the Agreement establishing the WTO.

For Members States are required to perform the agreements to which they are parties in compliance with the *good faith* principle[139] laid down in the Vienna Convention on the Law of Treaties,[140] specifically in Article 31(1) (on interpretation in good faith) and Article 26 (*Pacta sunt servanda*, on performance in good faith), and expressly referred to in many a DSB report.[141] This is a principle underpinning the entire WTO system, as clearly stated in the Report

136. See Judgment of the Court of Justice of 7 May 1991, Case C-69/89, *Nakajima*, [1991] ECR 2069.
137. See Judgment of the Court of Justice of 5 Oct. 1994, Case C-280/93, *Germany* v *Council*, [1994] ECR I-4973, where the ECJ explicitly ruled out control of conformity of Community law with the GATT/WTO, whether by references for preliminary rulings or by direct infringement procedures.
138. See *US – Definitive Safeguards Measures on Imports of Wheat Gluten from the EC* (WT/DS166/AB/R, para. 10).
139. See *US – Section 301 – 310*, paras 4.30 and 4.265, and *Canada – Patent Protection of Pharmaceutical Products* (WT/DS114/R, para. 7.13).
140. It is so also because of the express provision of Art. 3(2) of the *Understanding on rules and procedures* referred to above.
141. See, for all, *US – Import Prohibition of Certain Shrimps and Shrimps Products* (WT/DS58/AB/R, para. 158), where it is stated: '[t]his principle, at once a general principle of law and a general principle of international law, controls the exercise of rights by states. Once application of this general principle, the application widely known as the doctrine of *abus de droit*, prohibits the abusive exercise of a state's rights and enjoins that whenever the assertion of a right impinges on the field covered by a treaty obligation, it must be exercised bona fide, that is to say, reasonably. An abusive exercise by a member of its own treaty right thus result in abreast of treaty rights of the other members and, as well, a violation of the treaty obligation of the member so acting'.

on *US – Transitional Safeguard Measure on Combed Cotton Yarn from Pakistan* (WT/DS192/AB/R, para. 81):

> The pervasive general principle of good faith underlies all treaties. [*Emphasis added*].

Based on this principle, it can fairly be stated that each WTO Member is fully free to provide different safeguards for the benefit of its own economic operators, but it is also expected to comply with the WTO rules and to secure the effective enforcement of the rights arising therefrom, save for the clear requirement that *the protection of private interests at the international level may only depend on safeguards put in place by the Members' governments alone.*

In other words, *the protection of individual economic operators* within the WTO system becomes a precondition for the protection of free trade and of a level playground for competition between different countries' agricultural and commercial enterprises on individual products. This emerges most clearly from the *Report on US – SECTIONS 301-310*, paragraph 7.73, where it is stated that:

> the purpose of many of these disciplines, indeed one of the primary objects of the GATT/WTO as a whole, *is to produce certain market conditions which would allow this individual activity to flourish.* [*Emphasis added*].

Therefore, the *microeconomic positions* of individual enterprises or private parties generally *are not entirely immaterial* under WTO law, even if the business activity carried on by each of them internationally is but a grain of sand, albeit one that, in its individual marginality, contributes to global demand and global supply as well as to gross national product, gross domestic product and gross national expenditure. These are all macroeconomic factors, and the ones that, alone, are fully relevant to the new global economic order initiated through the establishment of the WTO. For it is quite clear that any country bringing action under the DSU is invariably the holder of *direct interests of its own*, since the asset to be protected is its *national economy*, not any one national undertaking or class of national undertakings. Indeed, a member government that opens an international dispute in this area does not even exercises its right to *diplomatic protection* (and is not, therefore, expected to comply with the rule of prior exhaustion of local remedies).[142]

True, each State is the bearer of interests of its own at an international level, even when it exercises diplomatic protection, but such interests are the reflection of interests of direct concern for specific private entities, so long as the latter are its 'nationals' (within the meaning prescribed by international law for the valid exercise of diplomatic protection).[143] This being the case, the protected asset

142. On 'diplomatic protection' within the scope of the DSU, see Peroni, 'La tutela degli interessi privati nel sistema OMC ed il possibile concorso di giurisdizione con altri ordinamenti ad esso esterni' [2004] Dir. com. int., pp. 740 ff.

143. On 'diplomatic protection', generally, see: Santa Maria, 'La tutela dei soci nel diritto internazionale' [1965] Riv. soc., p. 1088 ff.; Id., 'Il diritto internazionale dell'economia', cit., p. 499 ff.; see also Chapter V of this book., esp.lly paragraph 3.

will be the economic interests directly pertaining to the national parties injured by another State's violation of international rules governing the treatment of foreign natural or legal persons.[144]

13. THE ROLE OF A PRIVATE PARTY, ENTERPRISE CONCERNED OR ASSOCIATION AS AMICUS CURIAE, AND JUDICIAL PROTECTION UNDER THE COVERED AGREEMENTS

A private entity's scope for participating as *amicus curiae* in dispute settlement proceedings, whether before a panel's group of experts in the first instance or before the Appellate Body, is quite narrow (Article 13 of the DSU).

Whether it is a trading enterprise or a non-governmental organization ('NGO'), the private entity may submit briefs to such bodies in order to provide them with suitable elements of fact or law with a view to the drafting of their reports, *so long as, however, the body concerned finds such submission useful* for the sake of full information. This is what has recently emerged from some decisions delivered by the WTO dispute settlement bodies. It has been ruled, for example, that such bodies have:

> no legal *duty* to accept or consider unsolicited *amicus curiae* briefs submitted by individuals or organizations, not Members of the WTO.

On the other hand, they have:

> the legal authority under the DSU to accept and consider *amicus curiae* briefs in an appeal in which we find it pertinent and useful to do so.[145]

In this connection, the multilateral international trade system has highlighted the role of *non-governmental organizations* as an expression of 'civil society'. Much as these entities have no specific identity in international law, precisely in respect of any briefs as may be submitted by them as *amici curiae*, they must be praised for advancing certain values, particularly for environmental protection purposes, although these values may not always be consistent with international law or free market rules.

---

144. About the exercise of diplomatic protection by the 'national' State of a company or, exceptionally, of that company's members, see Santa Maria, 'La tutela dei soci nel diritto internazionale', cit., p. 1088 ff. See also paragraph 3 of Chapter V.

145. See WT/DS138/AB/R of 10 May 2000, *United States – Imposition of Countervailing Duties on Certain Hot Rolled Lead and Bismuth Carbon Steel Products Originating in the United Kingdom*, in particular paras 39-42. For the same approach, see: WT/DS58/AB/R of 12 Oct. 1998, *United States – Import Prohibition of Certain Shrimps and Shrimps Products*, paras 101 and 108-110, and WT/DS231/AB/R of 23 Oct. 2002, *EC – Trade Description of Sardines*, para. 160. On the 'procedural vacuum', which would exist today referring to the filing of the *amicus curiae* brief, see Hughes, 'The WTO dispute settlement system – from initiating proceedings to ensuring implementation: what needs improvement?', in *The WTO at Ten*, cit., 193 ff., at 211 ff.

In the well-known *Bananas* case,[146] the issue was raised as to whether *private lawyers* could be admitted *as a State's legal advisors* to dispute settlement proceedings. The Appellate Body ruled that they could, pointing out that nothing either in customary international law or in the WTO system prevented a WTO Member from determining the composition of its delegation in dispute settlement proceedings.[147]

The most significant application of this approach is to be found in two recent actions brought by the Office of the United States Trade filing two requests with the WTO DSB office in Geneva, on 9 April 2007, for consultation with the People's Republic of China. One such request was based on the alleged infringement by China of Articles 1 and 4 of the DSU, Article XXII of GATT 1994, and Article 22 of the GATS, in respect of 'Measures affecting trading rights and distribution services for certain publications'. The other request was based on the alleged infringement by China of the TRIPs Agreement, specifically the rules on copyrighted works, with respect to imported films for theatrical release, audiovisual home entertainment products (e.g., video cassettes and DVDs), sound recordings, and publications generally, to the detriment of United States manufacturers and distributors.[148]

Consultation between the parties began on 4 June 2007, and, failing a satisfactory settlement agreement within sixty days, i.e. the time period allowed for consultation, proceedings continued according to the DSU rules and timetable set out in the diagram shown in the eleventh paragraph of this chapter.

But the aspect I would like to highlight at this time is that, in view of the economic significance of the United States' complaint about the alleged infringement by China of industrial property rights, and much as:

> [t]he United States believes we have a strong case on IPR protection and a strong case on the market access problems facing our audiovisual and publications industries, and we wile vigorously pursue our rights as a WTO Member.[149]

---

146. See WT/DS27/AB/R *European Communities – Regime For the Importation, Sale and Distribution of Bananas* of 9 Sep. 1997, paras 10-12.
147. In this case, the positive solution was essentially justified on the basis of two arguments. On the one hand, it was noted (see para. 12). that 'representation by counsel of a government's own choice may well be a matter of particular significance – especially for developing-country Members – to enable them to participate fully in dispute settlement proceedings'. On the other hand, '. . . given the Appellate Body's mandate to review only issues of law or legal interpretation in panel reports, it is particularly important that governments be represented by qualified counsel in Appellate Body proceedings'. These arguments were further confirmed in another well-known case in the automotive sector. In this connection, see Reports WT/DS139/AB/R and WT/DS142/AB/R, *Canada – Certain Measures Affecting the Automotive Industry*, of 31 May 2000.
148. The filing of the two US applications opened the infringement procedure. See www.ustr.gov/Document_Library/PressReleases/2007/April/United_States_Files. For an *overview* of trade relations between the US and China, please refer to the *2007 Special 301 Report*, edited by the *Office of the United States Trade Representatives*, p. 18 ff.
149. For the press release from Ms Schwab, as the representative of the U.S. Trade Office, see *Remarks by U.S. Trade Representative Susan C. Schwab, Announcement of Requests for*

the US Trade Office accepted to be joined by lawyers of USA companies and of some trade associations representing private interests in protecting Federal interests.[150] As I have pointed out above, this is not a fact remarkable in itself, because of the convergence of public and private interests in the case. It may become one, however, in the course of the proceedings, if, for example, in the attempt of settlement, preference should be given to the removal of the effects of continuing infringements of TRIPs in exchange for the US's acceptance of predictably moderate results in connection with the issue of excesses.

But the judicial protection of private parties does not end with their participation in government defence. There are additional judicial protection tools at a 'lower level', so to say, namely within the WTO Members' individual legal systems.

Consider the rights a private party enjoys – whether alone or through trade associations out of the implementation of the WTO covered agreements – within each Member State's legal system, specifically the European Union's as far as we are concerned, as a result of the adaptation of internal legislations to the rules of international law embodied in those agreements. Whether it is the complainant or the respondent, that private party will see its interests fully protected, first before the EU Institutions, then before the Community Courts. What really matters is that such outcome is achieved thanks to specific provisions contained in international adaptation instruments.

Major examples are the Antidumping Agreement and the Agreement on Subsidies and Countervailing Measures, each of which expressly provides for private parties' active participation in 'internal' proceedings, if any are instituted.

Think only of the judicial position recognized by the former agreement to the 'domestic industry' or to the 'interested parties' – within the broad notions associated with these phrases – both in Articles 5 and 6 (in respect of written applications for initiating investigations, and of the opportunity to present evidence) and, especially, in Article 13, which requires each Member to maintain judicial, arbitral or administrative tribunals for the purpose of the prompt review of administrative actions relating to final determinations and reviews of determinations within the meaning of Article 11, with respect to duration and review of antidumping duties.

Provisions similar to these can also be found in: Part III of the TRIPs Agreement; Article 2(21) of the Agreement on Preshipment Inspection; Article 23 of the Agreement on Subsidies and Countervailing Measures; Article 2(j) of the Rules of Origin; Article 11 of the Customs Valuation Agreement; and paragraph 1(i) of

---

Consultations with China on IPR and on Certain Market Access Issues for Copyright Intensive Industries, 9 April 2007, *ibid*.

150. In later statements, the US Trade Office Representatives said they had conducted a fully independent preliminary examination of the file on IPR violations, and justified the intervention of counsel for the industry's enterprises and some trade associations (with the private parties' leading counsel J. Bacchus and Greenberg Traurig's Washington-area team) by alleging the US Trade Office's lack of staff. Not all of the US trade associations concerned joined the action, since Business Software Alliance stood neutral. See www.technlawjournal.com/topstories/2007/20070409.asp.

Annex C to the Agreement on the Application of Sanitary and Phytosanitary Measures.

14. THE WTO AND THE EUROPEAN UNION

The European Union has exclusive competence over trade matters (including those related to the WTO) within the scope of the common commercial policy. This means that it acts as a single entity vis-à-vis any parties outside the Community. In other words, it is for the European Commission, in consultation with the Council pursuant to Article 133 of the Treaty Establishing the European Community, to negotiate trade agreements and generally to represent European interests in the name and on behalf of the 27 Member States.

Therefore, as far as the relationships between the GATT and the EU are concerned, the time-worn issue of the compatibility of a regional economic organization such as the original EEC with the GATT principles, particularly non-discrimination, has lastly been set aside – obviously in respect of those countries which, though not members of the European Community, are GATT Members.[151]

Pursuant to Article 133 EC (former Article 113 EEC), it is the European Union which is now entitled, as the successor to its Member States' right and obligations, to participate in the GATT system. Such succession has been accepted in fact by all the other contracting parties to the General Agreement.[152]

---

151. For the relationships between the GATT and the EC, see: Schiavone, *Il principio di non discriminazione nei rapporti commerciali internazionali* (Milan, 1966), p. 199 f.; Imhoof, *Le GATT et les zones de libre échange*, thesis presented at the Law School of the Geneva University (Geneva, La Chaux de Fonds, 1979), esp.lly p. 129 f.; Petersmann, 'Participation of the European Communities in the GATT: International Law and Community Law Aspects' in *Mixed Agreements*, Schermers & Keefe eds. (Deventer, 1983), p. 167 f.; ID., 'Application of GATT by the Court of Justice of the European Communities' [1983] CMLR, p. 397 f.; Venturini, 'La partecipazione dell'Italia e della Comunità economica europea all'Accordo generale sulle tariffe doganali e il commercio' in Venturini, *L'accordo generale sulle tariffe doganali e il commercio (GATT)* (Milan, 1988), p. 14 f. and 30 f. In particular, with regard to the problem of the direct applicability of GATT rules in Italian and Community case-laws. see Venturini, 'Sulla diretta applicabilità delle norme del GATT' [1983] Riv. dir. int., p. 784 f., esp.lly p. 804 f.

152. In this respect, the Court of Justice, in its judgment of 12 Dec. 1972, Joined Cases 21 to 24/72, *International Fruit Company NV and others v Produktschap voor Groenten en Fruit*, [1972] ECR, 1219, observed: 'The Community has assumed the functions inherent in the tariff and trade policy, progressively during the transitional period and in their entirety on the expiry of that period, by virtue of articles 111 and 113 of the treaty. By conferring those powers on the Community, the Member States showed their wish to bind it by the obligations entered into under the General Agreement. Since the entry into force of the EEC Treaty and more particularly, since the setting up of the common external tariff, the transfer of powers which has occurred in the relations between Member States and the Community has been put into concrete form in different ways within the framework of the General Agreement and has been recognized by the other Contracting Parties'. (Grounds 14-16).

In its Opinion No 1/94 of 15 November 1994, given upon the Commission's request in accordance with Article 228(6) ECT (now Article 300(6) EC), the Court of Justice found that, while the European Community had *sole* competence, pursuant to Article 113 ECT (now Article 133 EC), to conclude the multilateral Agreements on trade in goods annexed to the WTO General Agreement, the Community and its Member States were jointly competent to conclude GATS and TRIPs.

The special committee provided for by Article 133 EC ('the Article 133 Committee'), is composed of representatives from the 27 Member States and the European Commission. Its main function is to coordinate EU commercial policy. The Committee meets on a weekly basis, usually on a Friday, in Brussels at the headquarters of the Council of Ministers. During its meetings, it discusses the full range of trade policy issues affecting the Community, from the strategic issues surrounding the launch of rounds of trade negotiations at the WTO to specific difficulties with the export of individual products. In this Committee, the Commission presents and secures endorsement of the Member States on all trade policy issues. The major formal decisions (for example agreement to launch or conclude negotiations) are then confirmed by the Council of Ministers.

What I have described above is, however, just the abstract purview of the relevant rules, because any issues falling within the GATT/WTO competence are handled *de facto* almost exclusively by the Commission, partly by delegation from the Council.

The status of the current WTO Round, the 'Doha Development Agenda' (albeit temporarily suspended) provides an excellent example of how the EU's commercial policy is managed:

> The Commission sets and carries forward the priorities and aims of the EU as laid down in *guidelines* given by the Council of Ministers. *Officials* from the *Commission's Directorate General for Trade*, under the authority of the Commissioner are charged with *actually conducting the negotiations*, and speak on behalf of the EU as a whole. Coordination with Member States is assured at all times through the *133 Committee*, while the Commission regularly informs the Parliament. At the end of the Round, the *Council* has to *agree formally* the outcome. [*Emphasis added*].[153]

15. THE EUROPEAN COMMISSION'S 'EXTERNAL' WEAKNESSES AND CHINA

Let me briefly come back to the impact of globalization – which has ceaselessly gained momentum for a dozen years now, and which I have taken as the starting point to introduce major issues of today's world economy – on international trade and, in particular, on the commercial relations between the European Union and China.

---

153. See *The EU and the WTO*, DG TRADE, on the website of the European Commission.

Clearly enough, the Chinese giant's conversion, sincere as it may be, to the rules of the international free-trade system has been an epochal event.[154] It is equally clear that it abruptly tipped the world's economic balance as we knew it until just a few years ago. A dramatic, sudden reversal has occurred in the traditional juxtaposition of high-technology countries and developing countries, as a result of which the implementation of free trade rules and the simultaneous general abatement of duties or abolition of quotas, far from 'protecting' the 'richer' countries, have become the picklock the two largest formerly 'poor' countries, China and, lagging far behind it, India (two billion four hundred million population between them in 2007) can rely on to reverse their initial economic backwardness in the short run.

The extremely low cost of labour in both countries (a worker's hourly cost approximating US$1 in China, as contrasted with about US$20 in the USA and €20 in Europe, according to currently available statistics),[155] as well as the present lower standard of the working conditions as a consequence of the low tier of social security rules, structurally inadequate hygienic and environmental measures, and, as far as China is concerned, that further unfair competitive device, the yuan's artificial exchange rate – which has been only slightly affected by the recent adjustment of the exchange rate system by way of a currency basket, since it has resulted in a just token re-appreciation of the Chinese currency against the US dollar in the region of 1% to 2%, the heralded revaluation over 6% having been quite short-lived in fact, lasting no longer than the Chinese President's official visit to Washington in April 2006 – have all combined to allow China's GDP to grow at an annual rate close to two digits, far higher than Europe's or the United States'.

China's notification to the WTO in November 2004 of new rules on dumping and subsidies considered by the WTO to be in line with the GATT 1994 prescriptions was the crowning event.[156]

---

154. This conversion is tightly linked to a sensible progress in China of the implementation of human rights. On the declared strong commitment of the Chinese Government to improve the respect of human rights within the country and on the China's active involvement in the formulation of legal comments concerning international human rights see: 'Progress in China's Human Rights Cause in 2003', cit., in *White Papers*, cit., 399-433. On the ten-year programme supporting children's women's rights see 'Progress in China's Human Rights Cause in 2003', cit., in *White Papers*, cit., 420-423. See also, concerning the commitments towards ethnic minorities, 'Regional Ethnic Autonomy in Tibet (May 2004)', in *White Papers*, cit., 510-535.
155. As is frequently the case, statistics have a merely relative value. This has been shown by the figures of hourly labour costs world-wide and by a comparison thereof with the figures prevailing in the United States or in the European Union. This is not only because such statistics reflect average values which may vary even widely depending on the type of business activity they refer to, but also because, for one and the same product, the relevant figures should be related to their proportion to the overall cost and the selling price of that product. Production costs are also affected by the current local legislative deficiencies. In this last respect, production costs in those countries are bound to rise as a result of the local law-makers' greater awareness of environmental issues, with the associated risk that the cost of any amnesty of past faults may be charged to foreign as well as domestic manufacturers.
156. On this subject, see Nardelli, 'Anti-dumping cinese e anti-dumping CE a confronto: una minaccia per le imprese comunitarie', p. 386-389. About differences in applying antidumping

It must clearly be recognized that China is as much entitled as the USA, Canada, Japan and the EU, as well as any other GATT member State willing to do so, to have an *internal* antidumping legislation of its own, so long as it is in line with the GATT/WTO's international rules. Yet, China's ability to produce goods at incomparably low costs is bound to make the other countries' antidumping measures, particularly the EU's, almost unusable against Chinese exported goods as soon as China is given Market Economy Status.[157] There is more to it, though. That same ability will allow China *legally* to shut off foreign imports at any time, whenever it finds that similar goods are produced by its own manufacturers at lower cost, so that any foreign exporter willing to sell its merchandise in China will only be able to do so at less than the normal price in its home country – by dumping, in fact.

That will be the last link in the chain. International free-trade rules will have the distorting effect that, instead of ensuring the free trade of goods *wherever produced* around the world, those rules will force any manufacturer of low-added value products wishing to survive to move out and manufacture its goods in China, India or any other developing country offering adequate guarantees of political stability and proper infrastructure, as a result of which generic manufacturing will be given up *outright*, at least by the largest European countries. The story is different in part for the United States, which has a different response capacity and does not refrain from protectionist interventions when any is deemed necessary in the best national interests.

And this has been the course of things, *pace* the theorists who maintain that those Eastern countries' aggressive attitude in international trade is more than offset by the opening to imports (including from the European Union or the USA) of markets already thriving at a satisfactory economic level today – China's purchasing power appearing to equal Europe's or the USA's for some one hundred fifty million people, with retail sales in continuous growth.[158]

In other words, European governments no longer able to ensure the present domestic economic welfare standards to their own nationals are bound to help in raising the Chinese people's – at least to the extent the Chinese government is more interested in keeping the country's economy growing than in maintaining its conditions of present social unbalance for years on end.

---

rules between China's internal system and the GATT 1994 system, see below, paragraph 24 of this Chapter 4.

157. About China's application, currently the object of the Commission's doubts, and about the impact of such recognition on the EU Member States, see below, the closing part of paragraph 24 of this Chapter 4.

158. In the first eight months of 2008, according to the National Bureau of Statistics, China's retail sales have been growing 21.9 per cent to 6.8 trillion Yuan. These figures may not be explained only by the consumption during the Olympic games and the summer holiday since retail sales in cities jumped 23.9 per cent to 601.5 billion Yuan, but – what is very much impressive – an increase of 21.8 per cent was tracked in rural areas, with sales of 275.3 billion Yuan. In the remainder of the year, however, there is a risk of downturn (Yanlin, 'Jump in retail sales but analysts fear downturn', in *Shanghai Daily*, *Business* of 13 Sep. 2008).

In an unbalanced world market for goods, the most economically advanced countries are focusing on the (even partial) production of high-added value products and are increasingly forced to shift to the tertiary sector, i.e. to the production and exportation of services. Thus, the implementation of the newly introduced GATS rules has become a paramount task in pursuing the goal to restore the world's economic balance.

Faced with such a predicament, the European Commission, though certainly not responsible for it, has taken the wrong approach. It did it wrong at the very beginning, when it failed to consider the full adverse impact of China's trading policy on the European manufacturers (especially small and medium-sized), particularly in the textile sector following the expiry of the Multifibre Agreement. And it was wrong again when it permitted the United States virtually alone to negotiate the conditions of China's accession to the GATT/WTO.

When looking at China's WTO Accession Agreement, it is easy to realize that the specific safeguards against the impact of China's entry into the Organisation are not in fact, quite beyond their broader wording, very different from the general safeguards provided for by the GATT 1994 against any unbalance as might be caused by any of the WTO Members, be it Tunisia, Thailand, Norway or Latvia. There is very little in that Agreement that takes into account the impact of the unprecedented occurrence which is now clear for everyone to see. There are no clauses to protect the industries most at risk, nor is there any provision, beside a twelve-year observation period, for gradual adjustments affording European undertakings time enough to reconvert their operations or, indeed, to safeguard the investments they have made in their home countries over the last few years.

While so patently clear adverse effects escaped the attention of the 'clever' protesters at Seattle and at the subsequent economic summits around the world, they ought not to escape the attention of the Commission of the European Communities.

The Commission is still wrong today, though. Blinded as it is by the holy smoke of free trade, it has not realized that it *must* represent European interests, that free-tradism does not, nor can, have an absolute value, and that, above all, like a game which must be played by applying the same rules, it can only work if compliance with its duties is *exacted* from everybody. Further, the trade balance of as many as twenty-seven States must remain in equilibrium and, when the scales are tilted, *those responsible for government* must necessarily take suitable *political* action if that equilibrium is to be restored, in the awareness that a situation of unbalanced trade can only be withstood for a very brief while.[159]

There are many arguments in support to such action, from 'social dumping' and 'ecological dumping'[160] to the urgency to challenge the abnormal rate of

159. For a discussion of the European Union's political *vacuum* in relation to the monetary Eurosystem, please refer to the considerations in Chapter III of this book, especially paragraphs 7 and 8.

160. Richez-BrumBaum, 'La nouvelle politique commerciale de l'Union européenne: véritable choix on simple conformisme?' [2006] Rev. marché comm., p. 642 f.

exchange for the Chinese currency, much as it is not in conflict with the IMF's admittedly lacking rules.

And yet, the Commission's customary refrain was played again in its Communication of October 2006, 'Global Europe: Competing in the World', in which it reversed the correct methodological approach to the problems discussed here to insist on the need that:

> EU be open so that it can insist on openness from others.[161]

The USA's approach is far more pragmatic: to the US governments, free-trade principles in the land of free trade need be corrected when they harm their country's interests '*seriously*' and '*continuously*'. It is not by chance that the law of adaptation to the GATT 1994 rules provides for the United States' unilateral exit from the Organisation if American interests are prejudiced in the medium term. The entire US system is ready to respond to protect national interests, by imposing quotas in case of excess merchandise inflows, by blocking the entry of goods for sanitary reasons or in order to protect USA industrial property rights or – though this is no good example to follow – by being exceedingly slow in complying with the WTO DSB's negative decisions.

This strong stance has allowed US negotiators to protect American interests sternly in their government's name in any venue and in any situation of trade unbalance. In this connection, mention should be made of the two cases recently opened by the United States against China before the DBS, one concerning China's alleged infringements of intellectual property rights, the other concerning China's alleged difficulties and delays in opening its domestic market.[162]

This is the point, indeed. As far as the EU is concerned, the handling of international trade disputes essentially falls within the European Commission's sole competence. Yet, when European interests are to be protected against any other party around the world, the Commission restricts itself to merely abstract statements, showing its constant worry lest its counterparties should feel offended, probably as a result of its *technical*, not *political*, institutional competence.

European economic policies on international trade now concern as many as twenty-seven countries, and they cannot be managed through public opinion surveys, as is the case with the questions asked in the Commission's Green or White Papers or with the former Commissioner Mandelson's statements to the media.[163] They require clear-cut choices to be made instead. Suffice it to think

161. Available on the website http://trade.ec.europa.eu/doclib/html/130376.htm edited by the Commission's DG Trade.

162. I am referring to Cases DS362, *China – Measures Affecting the Protection and Enforcement of Intellectual Property Rights*, and DS363, *China - Measures Affecting Trading Rights and Distribution Services for Certain Publications and Audiovisual Entertainment Products*, already discussed in paragraph 13 of this Chapter IV.

163. See, for example, the recent Commission Communication: *Global Europe – Europe's trade defence instruments in a changing global economy. A Green Paper for public consultation*, Brussels, 6 Dec. 2006, COM(2006) 763, final. The answers to the questionnaire, which were to be delivered to the Commission by 31 Mar. 2007, were published on the DG Trade's website

of the recent, still unsettled disputes about the European textile industry seriously jeopardized by the unchecked increase in Chinese imports into the EU, which has been the subject matter of *trade defence* actions the European Community has taken in consultation with Chinese authorities. These actions had vociferously been demanded by European manufacturers, and they were followed by as vociferous protests from European traders and importers of goods originating in China on the eve of the expiry of the textile industry agreements (31 December 2007).

The issue clearly has considerable political implications, since it requires a straightforward answer to the basic question as to which interests are to be legitimately protected in priority, within the WTO system, between the European manufacturers' and the European traders' (chiefly large retailers), without forgetting the interests of consumers, who have often been misled by the improper use of the 'CE' marking, meaning 'China Export', on products originating in China – the only difference being that the two initials of the Chinese marking are slightly more apart from each other than the European marking, 'C E' (for 'Comunità Europea' or 'Communauté Européenne'). Well, I do not believe that the Commission could, in this as in another similar situation in the footwear sector,[164] get away with submitting a question to the interested parties about the conflict between manufacturers and traders in trade defence investigations.

Is it not patently clear to everyone that the approach so taken has essentially to do with political considerations, which could well be made beyond the here and now of a specific issue, and take into account prospective economic policies or even, still in macroeconomic terms, the need to get a wider scope for manoeuvring in the game in which what is at stake is the European balance of trade in the face of that big country, China?

If this is the case, these are the motives the Commission is expected to express. The European Commission cannot act as a *super partes* body when it is called upon to confront an *external* party, unlike the case of its discharging supervisory duties within the European Union. In fact, the European Commission can only approach so overriding survival issues as these in the capacity of a government organ protecting 'domestic' interests, by making its *political choices* in matters the Council has delegated it to handle, and then *striving* to attain a useful outcome by using any defensible argument for that purpose.

If the Commission thinks it needs democratic endorsement, let it lay its proposed measures on international trade before the European Parliament, which, though being directly involved in international trade issue by the operation of the European Constitution,[165] seems to be not so directly involved in the terms

---

on 11 Jun. 2007. See also the interview given by Commissioner Mandelson to *Corriere della Sera* of 25 Jul. 2007, p. 23: '*Mandelson: Sarkozy sbaglia. Il protezionismo non serve.*

164. See the *Green Book* cited in the preceding footnote above, *ibid.*, p. 7 f.

165. See Article III-315(3)(3) of the Treaty establishing a Constitution for Europe. I have already observed that it is the Commission's practice, still today, to consult with the European Parliament on international trade issues.

of the present Article 133 EC. But then, let the Commission act *resolutely* and *promptly*.

Failing this – if European manufacturers were left undefended, that is – then we should conclude that this mechanism does not work properly in the present European Union.[166]

It should be acknowledged that the halt given by the negative outcome of the Irish referendum to the Lisbon substitute for the Treaty is a sign of an illness spreading widely across the European public opinion.

A denominator common to Europe should be found, without which a genuine common track can hardly be opened.[167]

The failure of the European Constitution has taught a profitable lesson: it has provided an opportunity to re-write it after the impact of the untimely enlargement of the European Union is digested. Thereupon, the fact will have to be acknowledged that the two functions the Commission has to discharge, one *internal*, the other *external*, are not easily reconcilable or are even incompatible with each other in their being vested in just one body. If the European Union is to progress further to its full accomplishment, new forms of government must be worked out which are conducive to suitable, well-reasoned political choices to ensure full and prompt *political* protection at an international level to the economic as well as other interests of European undertakings and individual citizens alike, with at least the same degree of commitment and quality as they would be accorded by their own national governments.

16. TRADE DEFENCE INSTRUMENTS: (A) SAFEGUARD MEASURES IN GENERAL

It has become clear by now that free trade with all of its corollaries is the general rule in all international treaties and agreements currently in force. Still, as often is the case in the domain of law, general rules leave the door open to exceptions or, rather, to special implementation rules that, under critical circumstances, permit the use of 'exceptional' instruments with a view to the removal of harmful distortions. I am specifically referring to the 'Trade Defence Instruments', which are, in exceptional situations, within the reach of every GATT/WTO Member. These instruments are of two kinds: (a) 'safeguard measures' and (b) 'antidumping and anti-subsidy measures'.

---

166. The President of the French Republic, Mr Sarkozy, has stated that the European Commission '*n'a pas le poids politique pour faire face à des puissances colossales comme le sont aujourd' hui l'Inde, le Brésil, la Chine ou les Etats-Unis*'. And, further: '*C'est pour cela que je me bats, pour de nouvelles institutions en Europe, pour que, notamment à l'OMC, on soit représenté par le président du Conseil européen et non par un commissaire européen, quelles que soient ses compétences*' (see article in *Le Monde* of 29 May 2007: *Nicolas Sarkozy avance la menace d'un veto français dans les négociations agricoles à l'OMC*).
167. See Tremonti, *La paura e la speranza, Europa: la crisi globale che si avvicina e la via per superarla* (Milan, 2008), esp.lly p. 61 ff.

To give an idea of the wide extent of antidumping activities, as exceptional as they may be, let me recall that the EU had imposed more than 194 definitive antidumping measures in just ten years, from January 1996 to December 2005. The countries most frequently responsible for dumping practices were China, the addressee of 38 measures, and India, with 16 measures against it. The EU had 12 anti-subsidy measures and one safeguard measure pending in October 2006.[168]

By contrast, the United States had imposed 201 and India 309 definitive measures over the same decade. The European Union had initiated 294 investigations, the US 352 and India 419 in the period.[169]

The less frequent use by the EU of trade defence instruments, especially antidumping measures, is due to the fact that it is the only GATT/WTO Member to carry out the 'Community Interest Test'[170] before applying antidumping measures.

In the area of Trade Defence Instruments, Article XIX of the GATT 1994 allows a GATT member to take a 'safeguard' action to protect a specific domestic industry from an unforeseen increase of imports of any product which is causing, or which is likely to cause, serious injury to the industry. This provision has been supplemented with the specific provisions set out in Annex 1A to the Agreement establishing the WTO. These new rules prohibit such safeguard measures as self limitation of exports, regulated trading agreements or any other measures having equivalent effects on imports or exports.

Based on the whole set of rules under the General Agreement and in furtherance thereof, the European Union adopted Council Regulation (EC) No 3285/94 of 22 December 1994 on the common rules for imports, specifically concerning safeguard measures.[171] Regulation No 3285/94, still in force albeit somewhat amended, applies to imports of *all* products originating in third countries, *except for*: (i) textile products covered by Regulation (EC) No 517/94; (ii) the products originating in certain non-WTO members listed in Council Regulation (EC) No 519/94; and (iii) products originating in China as provided for by Council Regulation (EC) No 427/2003.[172]

The general rule is the absence of any quantitative restrictions on imports of goods into the Community.[173] But where a disproportionate increase in imports into a specific sector justifies the adoption of surveillance or safeguard measures, the interested Member State(s) may submit information to the Commission to that effect, while individual undertakings are by no means allowed to do so – unlike the case of dumped or subsidized exports.

---

168. See a list of cases and statistics in: http://ec.europa.eu/trade/issues/respectrules/anti_dumping/stats.htm.
169. See *European Commission, Annual Report, DG Trade, Overview of third Country Trade Defence Actions against the Community*, 2006.
170. See below, paragraph 22 of this Chapter IV.
171. [1994] O.J. L349, p. 53, as amended by Regulations (EC) Nos 139/96, 2315/96, 2474/2000 and 2200/2004.
172. See Article 1 of Regulation (EC) 3285/94.
173. See Article 1(2) of Regulation, cit., *ibid.*

Pursuant to Article 10 of Council Regulation (EC) No 3285/94, the examination by the Commission of the trend of imports, of the conditions in which they take place and of *serious injury* or *threat* of serious injury to Community producers resulting from such imports must cover in particular the following factors:

> (a) the *volume of imports*, in particular where there has been a significant increase, either in absolute terms or relative to production or consumption in the Community; (b) the *price of imports*, in particular where there has been a significant price undercutting as compared with the price of a like product in the Community; (c) the *consequent impact on Community producers* as indicated by trends in certain economic factors such as: production, capacity utilization, stocks, sales, market share, prices (i. e. depression of prices or prevention of price increases which would normally have occurred), profits, (. . .); (d) *factors other than trends in imports* which are causing or may have caused injury to the Community producers concerned. (. . .) Where a *threat of serious injury* is alleged, the Commission shall also examine whether it is clearly foreseeable that a particular situation is likely to develop into *actual injury*. In this regard account may be taken of factors such as: (a) the *rate of increase of the exports* to the Community; (b) *export capacity in the country of origin or export*, as it stands or is likely to be in the foreseeable future, and the likelihood that that capacity will be used to export to the Community. [*Emphasis added*].[174]

Consultations may be held within eight working days of the Commission receiving the information so provided for and, in any event, before the introduction of any Community surveillance or safeguard measure.[175]

Such consultations must take place within an Advisory Committee made up of representatives of each Member State with a representative of the Commission as chairman.[176]

Where, after consultations, it is apparent to the Commission that there is sufficient evidence to justify the initiation of an investigation, the Commission must:

(a) initiate an investigation within one month of receipt of information from a Member State and publish a notice in the Official Journal of the European Communities; such notice will give a summary of the information received, and stipulate that all relevant information is to be communicated to the Commission; and
(b) commence the investigation, acting in cooperation with the Member States.[177]

---

174. See Article 1(2) of Regulation, cit., *ibid.*
175. See Article 3 of Regulation, cit., *ibid.*
176. See Article 4 of Regulation, cit., *ibid.*
177. See Article 6(1) of Regulation, cit., *ibid.*

Once the investigation has commenced, the scope of the administrative procedure is enlarged to other participants. The Commission will seek all information it deems necessary and, *where it considers it appropriate*, after consulting the Committee, endeavour *to check this information with importers, traders, agents, producers, trade associations and organizations*, collectively being referred to as 'interested parties'. Each of them and representatives of the exporting country may, upon written request, inspect all information made available to the Commission in connection with the investigation other than internal documents prepared by the authorities of the Community or its Member States. The Commission may, in hearing the interested parties, receive comments in writing from them.

If the Commission considers that Community surveillance or safeguard measures are necessary, it will take the necessary decisions no later than nine months from the initiation of the investigation. In exceptional circumstances, this time limit may be extended by a further maximum period of two months.[178]

Regulation No 3285/94 specifies the manners of adoption of surveillance and safeguard measures in Articles 11 and 16, respectively.

In cases in which safeguard measures take the form of a *quota*, the level of the latter should be set in principle no lower than the average level of imports over a representative period of at least three years.

Where it emerges that the conditions laid down for the adoption of measures are met in one or more regions of the Community, the Commission, after having examined alternative solutions, may *exceptionally* authorize the application of surveillance or safeguard measures *limited* to the region(s) concerned if it considers that such measures applied at that level are more appropriate than measures applied throughout the Community. In any event, these measures must be temporary and must disrupt the operation of the internal market *as little as possible*.[179]

Article 19 requires that no safeguard measure may be applied to *a product originating in a developing country* Member of the WTO as long as that country's share of Community imports of the product concerned does not exceed 3%.[180]

In case safeguard measures are applied throughout the Community, their *duration* must be limited to the period of time necessary to prevent or remedy *serious* injury and to facilitate adjustment on the part of Community producers. In principle, *such period should not exceed four years*, including the duration of any provisional measure.[181]

---

178. See Article 7 of Regulation, cit., *ibid.*
179. See Article 18 of Regulation, cit., *ibid.*
180. It will be so 'provided that developing country Members with less than a 3% import share collectively account for not more than 9 % of total Community imports of the product concerned'.
181. See Article 20 of Regulation, *ibid.*

17. MORE: SAFEGUARD MEASURES WITH REGARD TO THE PEOPLE'S REPUBLIC OF CHINA

As indicated above, no particular conditions or specific clauses are contained in China's WTO Accession Agreement that are conducive to the containment of Chinese unrestricted exports to the world's market for goods.

A twelve-year transitional period (ending on 11 December 2013) has been allowed, during which WTO Members may adopt safeguard measures (duties, quotas or such other instruments as self limitation of exports) to defend specific industries liable to be harmed as a result of their abrupt opening to Chinese competition.

The specific instrument involved is the Transitional Product Specific Safeguard Mechanism ('TPSSM') provided for by Article 16 of the Protocol on China's Accession to the WTO, i.e. a temporary system of safeguard measures intended to protect individual WTO Members' markets from any distortions as may be brought about by massive imports from China.

By the operation of the TPSSM, safeguard measures can be adopted in cases where products of Chinese origin are being imported into the market of any WTO Member in such increased quantities or under such conditions as to cause or threaten to cause disruption to that market's stability.

Where certain stated requirements are met, a WTO Member so affected may request bilateral consultations with the People's Republic of China with a view to seeking a mutually satisfactory solution, provided that any such request shall be notified to the Committee on Safeguards in advance.

If consultations do not lead to an agreement between China and the WTO Member concerned within 60 days of the receipt of a request for consultations, the WTO Member affected shall be free to withdraw exclusive concessions or otherwise to limit imports of such products by way of safeguard measures.

In especially critical circumstances, the WTO Member so affected may *directly* take a *provisional* safeguard measure pursuant to a preliminary determination that imports have caused or threatened to cause market disruption. In this case, notification of the measures taken to the Committee on Safeguards and a request for bilateral consultations shall be effected immediately thereafter. *The duration of the provisional measure shall not exceed two hundred days in any event.*

At a Community level, a new Regulation was adopted specifically providing for safeguard measures and trade diversion measures on certain imports originating in China. Accordingly, on 3 March 2003, the Council adopted Council Regulation (EC) No 427/2003 (on Transitional Product-Specific Safeguard Mechanism, 'TPSSM').[182]

The TPSSM allows product-specific safeguard measures against products of Chinese origin being imported into the Community in cases where such products are imported in such increased quantities or under such conditions as to cause or

182. [2003] O.J. L65, p. 1.

threaten to cause market disruption *to the Community industry affected*. However, safeguard measures can only be used if market disruption has been found to exist throughout the Community.

The relevant proceedings fall within the Commission's *exclusive* competence. In particular, pursuant to Article 10 of Regulation (EC) No 427/2003:

> Where it emerges, primarily on the basis of the factors referred to in Articles 2 and 3, respectively, that the conditions laid down for the adoption of measures pursuant to Articles 7 and 9 are met in one or more Member States, the Commission, after having examined alternative solutions, *may exceptionally authorise the application of safeguard measures limited to the Member State concerned if it considers that such measures applied at that level are more appropriate than measures applied throughout the Community*. These measures must be temporary and must not disrupt the operation of the internal market. The measures shall be adopted in accordance with the provisions laid down in Articles 7 and 9 respectively. [*Emphasis added*].

Therefore, the only way available to a Member State to apply safeguard measures to its own territory is to initiate the special procedure for the application of '*regional measures*' under Regulation No 427/2003, so long as it has been determined that there is a significant cause of market distortion or trade diversion affecting any one product.

It should be noted that textile products (made of natural or artificial fibres), to which Regulation 138/2003 applies,[183] are expressly excluded from the scope of application of Regulation No 427/2003. Although the procedure provided for by Regulation 138/2003 is basically identical with that caught by Regulation No 427/2003, the former instrument *does not afford any opportunity to adopt regional measures*.

18. MORE: (B) 'DUMPING' AND 'SUBSIDIES' AS CAUSES OF DIVERSION OF INTERNATIONAL TRADE

Quite broadly and by reference to a concept of economic doctrine, 'dumping' is deemed to occur where a product manufactured in one country is exported to another country's market (the import market) at a price which is below the price charged for a like or similar product in its home market (the export market).

Much as this definition is only a *prima-facie* description of dumping, which is a far more complex phenomenon, it highlights the nature of dumping as an instrument apt to cause diversion of international trade. Selling in dumping is primarily intended to cause more or less significant distortions to a given industry in the import market. It has the added effect of giving a basic competitive advantage to

183. See Council Regulation (EC) No. 138/2003 of 21 Jan. 2003 amending Regulation (EEC) No. 3030/93 on common rules for imports of certain textile products from third countries [2003] O.J. L23, p. 1.

the exporter over any other foreign or domestic producer operating in the import market.

In principle, similar prejudicial effects are caused by '*export subsidies*', which benefit a country's specific enterprises or groups of enterprises for whatever purpose in whatever manner, whether or not in respect of production processes, in such a way as to create undue advantages to the exporters of a product or class of products being exported to markets other than their home market.

In the latter case, too, prejudice to international trade is one with the prejudice caused to any market sector, along with the corresponding, added effect of an advantage being given to the enterprises or groups of enterprises in receipt of the subsidies over all the other competitors in the same sector in the same market.

Having dumping and subsidies been so defined as factors distorting international trade, it appears entirely logical that the adverse effects just described above have formed the object of the rules set out in Articles VI, XVI and XXIII of the GATT. The matter is currently governed by two separate instruments, the *Agreement on Implementation of Article VI of the General Agreement on Tariffs and Trade 1994* (on dumping), and the *Agreement on Subsidies and Countervailing Measures*, both included in Annex I to the Agreement Establishing the WTO.

On the other hand, it must be pointed out that the unwarranted use of anti-dumping proceedings by any GATT Member State's authorities or even by the EU (which is the only party entitled to act internationally as a proxy for the individual EU Member States, pursuant to Article 133 EC) may change the relevant set of rules into more or less hidden, though certainly effective, forms of protectionism, with all the ensuing distortions of international trade. In other words, deviously using provisions intended to remove the assumedly prejudicial effects of dumped or subsidized exports, as well as the direct application of those provisions beyond the removal of an actual prejudice, may turn out to be an undue advantage for a given national industry, thereby achieving precisely that distorting outcome the General Agreement is intended to avoid.

19. THE NEW INTERNATIONAL RULES ON DUMPING AND SUBSIDIES AND THEIR IMPLEMENTATION WITHIN THE EU

Partly in view of the facts submitted above, the new international agreements signed in Marrakech contain a comprehensive set of rules on dumping and subsidies, with highly innovating provisions covering most aspects of the entire matter.

The Anti-Dumping Agreement makes the imposition of antidumping measures subject to stricter requirements – under detailed rules on the determination of the margin of dumping – regulates the opening and conduct of investigations more closely, and restricts the scope for the imposition of provisional duties and for the application of the rules on the absorption of antidumping import duties.

The Agreement on Subsidies has added closer requirements for the identification of '*subsidy*', by introducing its very notion for the first time in an international instrument. As an overview of the entire Agreement shows, there are basically three distinguishing features to a subsidy.

The first feature is the specificity of subsidies, a requirement based on the assumption that only a subsidy granted to specific entities (enterprises or groups of enterprises) is likely to confer appreciable competitive advantages on the intended recipients.

The second feature is the manner in which a subsidy is granted, i.e. either *directly*, in the form of funds transferred to the beneficiary depending on its activity, or *indirectly*, in the form of government revenue foregone or not collected.

The third and last feature is the distinction between subsidies to exports and subsidies to production. In the former case, government aid granted with a view to increased exports is prohibited outright ('red light'), while, in the latter case, the granting of aid in support to the development of any one or all of a country's domestic industries is only deemed to be prohibited subsidy when it is apt to cause a prejudice to other countries' trade ('yellow light'). In any other case the economic beneficiary is deemed unimportant, and the subsidy permitted as a result ('green light').

Both Agreements contain special provisions in favour of developing countries that are WTO members. Thus, according to Article 15 of the Anti-Dumping Agreement, the application of antidumping duties likely to affect the essential interests of developing country Members may only be permitted after exploring all the possibilities of constructive remedies provided for by the Agreement. Article 27 of the Agreement on Subsidies contains a full set of provisions for a special, differentiated treatment of developing country Members, out of the Members' shared recognition that government aid may play an important role in economic development programmes of developing country Members.

The whole body of the new rules is aimed at achieving that *enhancement of legal certainty* which was the principal objective the European Community had pursued since the beginning of the Uruguay Round negotiations, and which was eventually attained through more closely defined rules, higher transparency and improved respect of the parties' rights.

As I have already noted above, both antidumping and anti-subsidy rules are primarily considered internationally in furtherance of the WTO's DSU provisions. But I have also indicated that, quite beyond the international judicial system, the matter can be considered by any bodies of competent jurisdiction within the individual countries (among which the EU as a single party) that have implemented the GATT/WTO Agreements into their national legal systems.

Depending on which bodies are responsible for applying internal rules based on international agreements on dumping and subsidies in different geographic areas, the national rules (not always identical with one another) for the implementation of international provisions have become all-important elements of relevance to individual situations. This is particularly the case with the EU, the USA, Mexico, Canada (under the North American Free Trade Agreement as well) and, more recently, with the People's Republic of China, each within the scope of its own legislation.

The relevant legal Community instruments currently in force are:

(a) Council Regulation (EC) No 384/96 of 22 December 1995 on protection against dumped imports from countries not members of the European Community (entered into effect on 6 March 1996 pursuant to Article 24), as amended by Council Regulation (EC) No 2331/96 of 2 December 1996, Council Regulation (EC) No 905/98 of 27 April 1998, Council Regulation (EC) No 2238/2000 of 9 October 2000, Council Regulation (EC) No 1972/2002 of 5 November 2002, Council Regulation (EC) No 461/2004 of 8 March 2004, and Council Regulation (EC) No 2117/2005;[184] and
(b) Council Regulation (EC) No 2026/97 of 6 October 1997 on protection against subsidized imports from countries not members of the European Community (entered into effect on 21 October 1997 pursuant to Article 35), as amended by Council Regulation (EC) No 461/2004 of 8 March 2004.[185]

One among the Community instruments implementing international agreements concluded under the GATT is Regulation (EC) No 3286/94 of 22 December 1994, as amended by Council Regulation (EC) No 356/1995 of 20 February 1995,[186] laying down Community procedures in the field of the common commercial policy in order to ensure the exercise of the Community's rights under international trade rules, in particular those established under the auspices of the World Trade Organization (WTO).

The Community antidumping and anti-subsidy investigation procedures are quite similar to each other as summarized in the following table:

Phase	*What happens*	*Timetable*
Complaint	The complaining Community industry submits evidence to the Commission requesting the opening of examination	The Commission has 45 days to take a decision on the opening of examination
Initiating the procedure	The Commission opens an examination against one or more countries if sufficient evidence is provided	Examination is concluded, possibly within one year
Questionnaires	Each exporter must fill in questionnaires and may present views	30 days' time limit to reply to questionnaires (unless extended)

184. Respectively: in [1996] O.J. L56, p. 1; [1996] L317, p. 1; [1998] L128, p. 18; [2000] L257, p. 2; [2002] L305, p. 2; [2004] L 77, p. 12 and [2005] L340, p. 17.
185. [1997] O.J. L288, p. 1, and [2004] O.J. L77, p. 12, respectively.
186. The former is in [1994] O.J. L349, p. 71, the latter in [1995] O.J. L41, p. 3.

Phase	*What happens*	*Timetable*
Verification visits	The Commission makes on-the-spot visits to examine each exporter's disclosures with a view to verifying the accuracy of information submitted	Usually 1 to 3 months following presentation of questionnaires
Provisional duties	Imposed when the following elements have been provisionally estimated: (i) existence of dumping or subsidies; (ii) prejudice to Community industry; (iii) causal link and Community interest test require action	Not earlier than 60 days, nor later than 9 months of opening the procedure. Provisional duties may be imposed for a 6-month period (unless extended for 3 other months) or for a 9-month period In the case of CVDs, provisional duties can only be applied for 4 months
Commitments on prices	Firmed up by the exporter to the Commission	At any time, but not sooner than imposition of provisional duties nor later than imposition of definitive duties
Definitive duties	Definitive measures are adopted if provisional measures are confirmed	
Application of measures	Definitive measures and commitments remain in effect for 5 years, unless expiry review is initiated. Expiry reviews must usually be concluded within 12 months	

20. LEGAL NATURE OF DUMPING: THE REQUIREMENTS

From the point of view of the European Union's applicable legislation, dumping is deemed to occur when:

(a) *sales* of products imported into the Union from the outside have been made at a *price below their normal value*, unless such sales have been just casual or occasional, over a 'prolonged' period of time, usually one year and otherwise not less than six months; the price of an exported product which is below the 'normal value' of a similar product, generally based on the retail price of such similar product in the exporter's domestic market and resulting from the application of complex mathematical formulas following a 'fair comparison', will determine the *margin of dumping* stated as a percentage of the export price;

(b) there is a resulting actual or potential *injury* to the Community industry, which injury must be 'material' and determined on the basis of 'direct positive evidence'; and

(c) there is a *causal link* between the dumped sales in the period and the injury to industry.

The presence of all these three elements together results in the application of special sanctions, i.e. measures in the form of duties which are, in view of the factual circumstances surrounding the relevant case, deemed appropriate to remove the injury caused by dumping (or by *a subsidy*, as the case may be) or to prevent it, albeit less frequently.

A further element has been added by Community law to those listed above: 'Community Interest'.

Save for the exceptional case of an antidumping investigation initiated *ex officio* pursuant to Article 5(6) of Regulation No 384/96 and Article 10(10) of Regulation 2026/97, the burden of proving each of the four dumping elements indicated above must be discharged by the complaining party.

While dumping usually occurs as an unwarranted increase in the market share for certain non-Community products or the failed shrinkage of that market share despite the appreciation of the exporting market's currency against the Euro or any other currency within the EU's non-Euro area, there must invariably be a *causal link* between the dumped or subsidized exports, as the case may be, and the alleged injury.

For example, Commission Regulation (EEC) No 2516/86 of 4 August 1986, imposing a provisional anti-dumping duty on imports of housed bearing units originating in Japan,[187] clearly highlights the importance of determining both the extent of the injury and the existence of the causal link. Whereas 56 of the Regulation expressly states:

> The substantial increase (26 %) in imports of housed bearing units originating in Japan since 1981, the levels of price undercutting (12,11 to 21,61 %) during the period 1 December 1984 to 31 May 1985, the ratio between the market share of housed bearing units originating in Japan and those manufactured by the Community producers concerned (practically 40: 60), and the impact these factors have had on prices for Community-made housed bearing units and the utilization of capacity, profits and return on investment of Community producers in the housed bearing units sector, *have led the Commission to the conclusion that imports at dumped prices of housed bearing units originating in Japan have caused material injury to the Community industry.* [*Emphasis added*].

187. [1986] O.J. L221, p. 16 ff.

At the end of its preliminary examination, the Commission imposed a provisional anti-dumping duty at a rate not below weighted margins of dumping. Interestingly enough, one of the exporters affected by the Commission's decision – alongside *Nippon Saiko KK* affected by a 17.99% duty and other exporters penalized by duties at different rates – was *Nachi Fujikoshi Corp.*, which was hit by a 1.13% duty, a rate exactly corresponding to the margin of dumping it was found to be responsible for, and so moderate a rate had no impact on the determination of the extent of the injury to the Community industry and the ensuing application of the antidumping duty.

For liability is an automatic result of the violation, while the exporter's or possibly the importer's gross negligence or even fraud are entirely immaterial.

It should be stressed again that the addressee of antidumping or countervailing measures is not the entire industry of the exporting country. Duties of both descriptions are imposed *only on non-Community enterprises which have unlawfully exported products to the detriment of the European Union.* Thus, it is a quite common occurrence that, during the proceedings, some enterprises are found not liable, and they are eventually not hit by antidumping or countervailing measures. It is also common for such measures to be applied at different rates even within one and the same proceeding, depending on the margin of dumping each exporter is liable for and in respect of each type of products being investigated.

Ample defence rights are accorded to the parties being investigated and as ample rights are accorded to Community producers applying for remedies, namely the right to submit to the Commission all evidence which they consider appropriate, the right to see all information obtained by the Commission, subject to certain exceptions as to confidential matters, the right to be heard at their request and to have the opportunity of meeting the other parties concerned in the same proceeding, and finally the right to be informed, with at least a summary of the reasons therefor, if the Commission decides not to pursue a complaint both in the case of the proceedings being terminated or on the completion of the stage of preliminary investigation.[188]

In view of the foregoing observations, it is no surprise that, in addition to final or interim reviews of regulations imposing antidumping or countervailing duties, and of Decisions accepting undertakings, and in addition to recovery requests – all the relevant procedures being provided for by Article 8 and 11 of Regulation No 384/96 in respect of dumping, and Articles 18-21 and 13 of Regulation No 2026/97 in respect of subsidies – all the interested parties are entitled, following an interim, challengeable act by the Commission or a Council Regulation closing proceedings, to institute proceedings for annulment, from 15 March 1994 onward, before the Court of First Instance pursuant to the fourth paragraph of Article 230 EC.

As for the parties being investigated, the Court of Justice held, in the case of the 'housed bearing units originating in Japan', that the application lodged by Japanese producers and exporters, and by some importers expressly identified in

188. See Judgment of the Court of Justice of 4 Oct. 1983, Case 191/82, *Fediol* v *Commission*, [1983] ECR 2934.

the relevant instrument, for annulment of the Council Regulation imposing antidumping duties, was admissible, since it was 'a collective decision concerning addressees listed by name', and that the measures so taken 'individually' and 'directly' concerned the interests of the natural and legal persons against whom they were applied.

Obviously, in the case of a regulation imposing antidumping duties on imports of products manufactured by several independent exporting undertakings, each such undertaking can only be deemed to be '*directly*' and '*individually*' concerned to the extent the contested regulation applies to imports of its products into the Community. In its judgment of 10 March 1992,[189] the ECJ dismissed the main application for the annulment of the contested antidumping regulation in its entirety, and only granted the order sought in the alternative, namely the annulment of the contested regulation in so far as it applied to *Ricoh* individually.

Any complaining undertaking or association of undertakings actively involved in the relevant proceeding has the right to lodge a complaint with the Court of First Instance, pursuant to the fourth paragraph of Article 230 EC, if the proceeding is closed without the Community institutions having imposed any of the trade defence measures considered to be appropriate to remove the injury, or even if trade defence measures have been imposed but are deemed to be not up to the claim.[190]

21. CIRCUMVENTION OF ANTIDUMPING DUTIES: THE 'SCREWDRIVER ASSEMBLY' ISSUE

Historically, circumvention of antidumping duties has concerned chiefly the European Union and the United States, on the one side, and Japan on the other side.[191] Circumvention of duties has also been used to a considerable extent by developing countries for several years, as shown by an analysis of the investigations the European Commission has opened in this area.

'Circumvention' is defined as a change in the pattern of trade between third countries and the Community which stems from a practice, process or work for which there is insufficient due cause or economic justification other than the imposition of the duty.[192]

The many different ways of circumventing antidumping duties are all contrived to introduce a product into a market where it would otherwise be liable to antidumping measures, in order avoid duties from being imposed on it.

---

189. This was Case C-174/87, *Ricoh* v *Council*, [1992] ECR 1335, ground 6 f.
190. See Judgment of the Court of Justice of 4 Oct. 1983, Case 191/82, *Fediol*, cit.
191. Ventura, 'L'elusione dei dazi anti-dumping, le norme della Comunità europea e degli Stati Uniti' [1993] Dir. com. int, p. 903 ff.
192. See various Annual Reports by the Commission to the European Parliament on the Community's Anti-dumping and Anti-subsidy Activities, where it can be read: '*An assembly operation in the Community or a third country may fall within this definitio*n (of circumvention, Ed.) *as well as imports from third countries of like products, or parts thereof, when circumvention of the measures in force is taking place*'.

One among the forms of circumvention Japanese producers would put in place, especially around the mid 1980s, as a response to the repeated use of antidumping measures against their products, was the practice of setting up manufacturing facilities in the European and USA markets with a view to making their products appear to have been manufactured there, much as the parts they used for the purpose were imported from Japan. This practice came to be known as 'subassembly dumping'. Since antidumping measures were only applied to imported finished products, the result was the outright failure of trade defence instruments.

Another, newer tool of duty circumvention (one within easy reach for multinational enterprises) was merely assembling products already subject to duties in a country other than that of origin within the European Community ('third country' or 'indirect' dumping). As duties was only applied to products imported from that specific country, completing their production in an intermediate country was enough to make any antidumping measure inapplicable.

Therefore, as early as the later 1980, specific provisions were adopted both in the European Union and in the United States to prevent duty circumvention by this means. As far as the then European Economic Community was concerned, Regulation (EEC) No 1761/87 was adopted to amend the antidumping provisions of Regulation (EEC) No. 2176/84, based on the following considerations:

> Whereas experience gained from the implementation of Regulation (EEC) No 2176/84 (2) has shown that assembly in the Community of products whose importation in a finished state is subject to anti-dumping duty may give rise to certain difficulties; Whereas in particular: – where assembly or production is carried out by a party which is related or associated to any of the manufacturers whose exports of the like product are subject to an anti-dumping duty, and – where the value of the parts or materials used in the assembly or production operation and originating in the country of origin of the product subject to an anti-dumping duty exceeds the value of all other parts or materials used, such *assembly or production is considered likely to lead to circumvention of the anti-dumping duty* (. . .). [*Emphasis added*].[193]

By Regulation No 1761/87 and the ensuing general reform implemented in accordance with Regulation No 2423/88, specific criteria were introduced for the assessment of assembly operations in order to determine the possibility to apply antidumping duties.

The original Community anti-circumvention measures had frequently been applied by the Commission until 1990, when, at Japan's request, Articles 10 and 13(10) of Regulation 2423/88 were declared by a GATT panel to be incompatible with the new GATT and the new GATT antidumping code.[194]

---

193. [1987] O.J. L167, p. 9.
194. See Judgment of 22 Mar. 1990, *Screwdriver Assembly: Japan* v *EEC*, Case L/6657, [1990] Common Market Law Report, 639.

Community antidumping rules in this area had been amended several times[195] until the issuance of Regulation No 384/96 in the text now in force.

Regulation No 384/96 came into effect on 6 March 1996, based, *inter alia*, on the fact that:

> Whereas the multilateral trade negotiations concluded in 1994 have led to new Agreements on the implementation of Article VI of GATT,[196]

and that:

> (. . .) it is therefore appropriate to amend the Community rules in the light of these new Agreements.[197]

Circumvention of antidumping duties is dealt with and provided for in Article 13 of Regulation No 384/96 (as amended by Council Regulation (EC) No 461/2004 of 8 March 2004) the first paragraph of which states:

> Anti-dumping duties imposed pursuant to this Regulation *may be extended to imports from third countries, of the like product, whether slightly modified or not*; or to imports of the slightly modified like product from the country *subject to measures*; or parts thereof, *when circumvention of the measures in force is taking place*. Anti-dumping duties not exceeding the residual anti-dumping duty imposed in accordance with Article 9(5) of this Regulation may be extended to imports from companies benefiting from individual duties in the countries subject to measures when circumvention of the measures in force is taking place. *Circumvention shall be defined* as a change in the pattern of trade between third countries and the Community or between individual companies in the country subject to measures and the Community, which stems from a practice, process or work for which there is insufficient due cause or economic justification other than the imposition of the duty, and where there is evidence of injury or that the remedial effects of the duty are being undermined in terms of the prices and/or quantities of the like product, and where there is evidence of dumping in relation to the normal values previously established for the like product, if necessary in accordance with the provisions of Article 2. The practice, process or work referred to in paragraph 1 includes, *inter alia*, the slight modification of the product concerned to make it fall under customs codes which are normally not subject to the measures, provided that the modification does not alter its essential characteristics; the consignment of the product subject to measures via

195. Following Regulation 1761/87, anti-circumvention rules were introduced by Regulation 2423/88, which reformed the entire anti-dumping and anti-subsidy legislation. Regulation 2423/88 itself was superseded, as from 1 Jan. 1995, by Regulation 3283/94 (and anti-dumping and anti-subsidy duties have been governed by different regulations since then), which was superseded, as from 6 Mar. 1996, by Regulation 384/96 still in force.

196. See the third Whereas of Regulation 384/96 of the Council of 22 Dec. 1995, [1996] O.J. L56, p. 1.

197. *Ibid.*

> third countries; the reorganization by exporters or producers of their patterns and channels of sales in the country subject to measures *in order to eventually have their products exported to the Community* through producers benefiting from an individual duty rate lower than that applicable to the products of the manufacturers; and, in the circumstances indicated below under Article 13(2), the assembly of parts by an assembly operation in the Community or a third country. [*Emphasis added*].

According to the second paragraph of Article 13:

> An *assembly operation* in the Community or a third country shall be considered to circumvent the measures in force where:
>
> (a) the operation *started or substantially increased* since, or just prior to, the initiation of the anti-dumping investigation and the parts concerned are from the country subject to measures; and
> (b) the parts *constitute 60% or more of the total value* of the parts of the assembled product, except that in no case shall circumvention be considered to be taking place where the value added to the parts brought in, during the assembly or completion operation, is greater than 25% of the manufacturing cost; and
> (c) the remedial effects of the duty are being *undermined in terms of the prices and/or quantities* of the assembled like product and there is evidence of dumping in relation to the normal values previously established for the like or similar products. [*Emphasis added*].

Article 13 is completed by paragraphs 3, 4 and 5, which require:

> 3. Investigations shall be initiated pursuant to this Article where the request contains sufficient evidence regarding the factors set out in paragraph 1. Initiations shall be made, after consultation of the Advisory Committee, by Commission Regulation which shall also instruct the customs authorities to make imports subject to registration in accordance with Article 14(5) or to request guarantees. Investigations shall be carried out by the Commission, which may be assisted by customs authorities and shall be concluded within nine months. When the facts as finally ascertained justify the extension of measures, this shall be done by the Council, acting by simple majority and on a proposal from the Commission, from the date on which registration was imposed pursuant to Article 14(5) or on which guarantees were requested. The relevant procedural provisions of this Regulation with regard to initiations and the conduct of investigations shall apply pursuant to this Article.
>
> 4. Products shall not be subject to registration pursuant to Article 14 (5) or measures where they are accompanied by a customs certificate declaring that the importation of the goods does not constitute circumvention [. . .].
>
> 5. Nothing in this Article shall preclude the normal application of the provisions in force concerning customs duties.

Following the opening of an investigation into a duty circumvention case, the Commission may '*extend*' duties to imports of like products or parts of like products from third countries.[198]

22. COMMUNITY INTEREST FALLING OUTSIDE THE SCOPE OF GATT ANTIDUMPING PROVISIONS: CRITICAL REMARKS

One added element should be considered in connection with the Community anti-dumping and anti-subsidy legislation: the imposition of provisional duties or countervailing measures or of definitive duties or countervailing measures is expressly made subject not only to the fulfilment of the three requirements indicated in the paragraph next preceding above, but also to the determination by the competent institution that *Community interest requires community action* to be taken in each relevant case.[199]

It is appropriate to point out that nothing suggesting a 'Community interest test' is anywhere to be found in the articles of the GATT that form the legal basis of the matter, nor can it be found in the later covered agreements which were approved at the Kennedy Round, at the Tokyo Round and at the Uruguay Round, in furtherance of which the 1994 Agreements were implemented by the European Community.

This proposition is by no means impaired by Article 9.1 of the 1979 'Anti-dumping Code', which merely expresses a 'desire' by stating:

> It is desirable that the imposition [of an antidumping duty] be permissive in the territory of all Members.

This phrase, which is nothing more that a mere exhortation, arises from the praiseworthy desire to avoid any country's authorities from taking an exceedingly strict approach to the application of trade defence measures beyond the intended purposes of the relevant international rules, thereby indulging in unwarranted protectionist solutions.[200]

---

198. See various Annual Reports by the Commission to the European Parliament on the Community's Anti-dumping and Anti-subsidy Activities. In particular, see the Twenty-fourth Annual Report by the Commission to the European Parliament (2005) of 10 April 2007, COM(2007) 171 final.
199. Express reference to 'the Community's interests' had already been made in several points of the former Regulation No. 2423/88. Thus, in Art. 5(4), in respect of the suspension of the complaint withdrawal procedure, and in Art. 10(6), in respect of the application of antidumping duties following withdrawal or violation of a commitment. Such reference is also explicit both in Art. 11(1), in respect of the application of provisional duties, and in Art. 12(1), in respect of definitive measures imposed pursuant to the former Regulation.
200. A different view seems to be taken by Stanbrook, *The Impact*, cit., p. 623 f., who refers to this phrase in the 1979 Antidumping Code as a justification for the use of the notion of 'Community interest' in Community legislation.

Nor is there any mention of a corresponding, similar test in the US anti-dumping legislation.[201] This is especially relevant in the light of the fourth Whereas of Regulation 384/96, where it is stressed that:

> in applying the rules [contained in the Antidumping Code and in the Code on Subsidies promulgated in the Uruguay Round] it is essential, in order to maintain the balance of rights and obligations which the GATT Agreement establishes, that the Community take account of how they are interpreted by the Community's major trading partners;

and in the light of the Whereas next following, according to which:

> in view of the extent of the changes and to ensure a proper and transparent application of the new rules, the language of the new agreements should be brought into Community legislation as far as possible.

These consideration primarily implies that the Community interest test ought not be considered in assessing the occurrence of 'dumping' or 'subsidies', and, secondly, they raise serious doubts as to the very legitimacy of such additional requirement to be met in the relations between individual WTO Members and the Community in respect of the application of uniform international rules on dumping and subsidies.[202]

Nor do I believe that supplementing the Community legislation in this way might be justified by anything contained in Article 133 of the EC Treaty. Suffice it to consider that neither the Commission nor the Council might – in cooperating with each other to establish the common general policy in accordance with Article 133, and lacking specific provisions on how Community interest should be assessed – ever refuse to apply any necessary safeguards to remove an injury to

---

201. Only for the purposes of an agreement on the cessation or suspension of antidumping investigations according to the applicable US rules, is the ITA required to establish, *inter alia*, that the relevant investigation should be suspended 'in the public interest' (*Antidumping Statute*, 19 U.S.C., 1673 c, (d), p. 3-A-19). About the administration's wide discretion in connection with the 'public interest' notion, see De Vault, *The efficacy of Antidumping Duties*, cit., p. 11. Favourable to the introduction, in general, of a 'public interest' notion into national legislations as a precondition for the actual imposition of antidumping duties, is Denton, '(Why) Should Nations Utilize Antidumping Measures?' [1989] Michigan Jour. Int. Law, p. 224 f., p. 266 f.

202. A different approach should be taken to Council Regulation (EC) No. 3286/94 of 22 Dec. 1994 laying down Community procedures in the field of the common commercial policy in order to ensure the exercise of the Community's rights under international trade rules, in particular those established under the auspices of the World Trade Organization (WTO), already referred to in paragraph 5 of this study. In that Regulation, both the opening of a Community examination procedure (Art. 8(1)) and the adoption of commercial policy measures (Art. 12(1)) should be based on the existence or non-existence, in the relevant case, of *an interest of the Community*. But this reference is fully lawful in that specific case, since the measure in question is a complementary measure applicable only subject to the other measures considered here, and it does not, unlike such other measures laid down in furtherance of the GATT Codes, have its specific regulatory source in a uniform international instrument, much as it refers to GATT principles.

Community industries merely on the ground that Community interest is lacking in any relevant case.

In a different respect, the Community interest test has introduced such discretion as to baffle the very function of the rules for the application of any necessary trade defence measures to remedy the unbalance caused by dumped or subsidized imports in the European Union.

The rationale behind the Community legislator's action in producing the 1984 acts is even too clear. Since antidumping and anti-subsidy rules were to be introduced within the scope of the common commercial policy, which is a matter to be dealt with solely by the Commission and the Council in cooperation between them under Article 133 EC, the idea was to vest Community authorities, in respect of antidumping and anti-subsidy procedures – as common commercial policy tools – with far-reaching, indisputable discretion with a view to allowing them, where they deem it to be necessary or even only opportune to do so, to devise 'political' responses to violations which should, in fact, be only dealt with by legal means and otherwise referred to the Community Courts for a determination. In other words, the Community legislator's intent was to afford the Community institutions a practicable way out of intractable cases of established dumping practices and injuries to Community industries, in order to avoid being forced to apply the relevant sanctions at all and any times.

A quite different course has been taken in fact. For a review of the practice followed by the Commission and the Council since the earliest antidumping proceedings within the Community shows that both have only seldom given an *independent* weight to the Community interest test, while I have hardly found any case in which, in the presence of the three basic elements pointing to 'dumped' or 'subsidized' imports, the purported lack of Community interest has caused proceedings to be terminated without any protective measures having been taken.

The general impression one can get from an overall examination of the Community institutions' practice is that the Community interest notion is, as a rule, complementary to, or is even incorporated into, the notion of 'injury'. For finding an injury in any relevant case *automatically* results in the necessity to take action in the 'Community interest'. In any such case – a common occurrence indeed – Community interest becomes one and the same thing with the interest of the industry allegedly injured by dumped or subsidized imports, and its mention in the Regulation on protection against dumped imports merely amounts to a hackneyed inconsequential formula.

An example of the Community Institutions' customary line of reasoning about the causal link between injury and Community interest in most cases is Council Regulation (EEC) No 90/82 of 18 January 1982 imposing a definitive antidumping duty on phenol originating in the United States of America,[203] which reads:

> Whereas (. . .) the substantial and sharp increase of imports of dumped phenol (. . .) and the extremely low prices at which the product has been offered for sale in the Community (. . .) has led the Commission to conclude that *the*

203. [1982] O.J. L12, p. 1.

> *injury caused* to the Community industry concerned *by the dumped imports taken in isolation should be regarded as material*; Whereas, in these circumstances, *protection of the Community's interests* call for the imposition of a definitive anti-dumping duty on imports of phenol originating in the United States of America which, having regard to the extent of the injury caused, should be equal to the dumping margins established, and for the definitive collection up to the rates definitely determined, of the amounts secured by way of provisional anti-dumping duty . . . [*Emphasis added*].[204]

My contention still holds, despite the fact that, probably as a result of appeals lodged with the Court of Justice on the point, the problem of whether or not Community interests are jeopardized in any one case is now dealt with in explicit terms in individual Regulations. I am referring to Case 53/83, *Allied Corporation*, already quoted above, which the Court of Justice decided by its judgment of 23 May 1985. In that case, the ECJ declared the challenged antidumping regulation void on various grounds, but ignored the other argument submitted by the applicants, that the test designed to determine the existence of Community interest in that case had been misapplied.[205]

Only in a few particular cases has the existence of Community interest been actually considered under a separate assessment apparently independent of the injury issue. This was the case with Council Regulation (EEC) No 2322/85 of 12 August 1985 imposing a definitive anti-dumping duty on imports of glycine originating in Japan.[206] In that case, it was precisely the determination of Community interest which ultimately decided the applicable antidumping duty rate.

The requesting parties – two Japanese producers and the main Community user concerned – argued, *inter alia*, that:

> the imposition of a definitive anti-dumping duty would not be in the interest of the Community, mainly because it would enable the main Community producer to raise its sale prices unreasonably in a market where there are virtually

---

204. Likewise, see: Council Regulation of 28 Jun. 1984 1825/84 imposing a definitive anti-dumping duty on imports of hardboard originating in the Soviet Union [1984] O.J. L170, p. 68 f., and Council Regulation (EEC) No. 96/85 imposing a definitive anti-dumping duty on imports of pentaerythritol originating in Canada [1985] O.J. L13, p. 1 f., p. 3. In the same sense, see Decision No. 2767/86/ECSC of 5 Sep. 1986 imposing a provisional anti-dumping duty of ECU 68 per 1 000 kilograms on imports of certain sheets and plates, of iron or steel, originating in Yugoslavia [1986] O.J. L254, p. 18 f., p. 20. In particular, paragraph 27 of this instrument states that: 'In view of the particularly serious difficulties facing the Community industry, and in the light of the factors referred to above (paragraphs 22 to 24), the Commission has come to the conclusion that it is in the Community's interest that action be taken. In order to prevent further injury being caused during the remainder of the proceeding, this action should take the form of a provisional anti-dumping duty.' Lastly, see, for example Commission Decision No. 86/232/EEC of 9 Jun. 1986 accepting undertakings given in connection with the anti-dumping proceeding concerning imports of hardboard originating in Argentina, Switzerland and Yugoslavia and terminating the investigation [1986] O.J. L157, p. 61 f., p. 63.
205. On this, see also the Opinion of Advocate General, Verloren van Themaat, in the same case, in ECR, cit., esp.lly p. 1633 f.
206. [1985] O.J. L218, p. 1. *Ibid.*, p. 5. Emphasis added.

only three suppliers or to undercut the Japanese prices so that the Japanese product would disappear from the market.

In this respect, the Council had come to the conclusion that it was in the Community's interest that action be taken. Therefore:

> In view of the probable effect on the competitive situation and structure in the Community market characterized by the presence of essentially one Community producer and two non-Community firms, *it is considered in the Community's interest to take protective measures without fully eliminating the injury* determined to have been suffered by the main Community producer during the period under investigation, but considered *adequate* to enable the said producer to operate economically the plant . . . [*Emphasis added*].[207]

Here again, it is difficult to say whether the reduced rate so applied was, in fact, the adequate minimum rate to remove the injury.

Conversely, in a similar case of imports of potassium permanganate originating in Czechoslovakia, the German Democratic Republic and the People's Republic of China, which was decided by the Commission by Regulation No 2495/86 of 1 August 1986,[208] the express determination by the Commission of the Community's interest in that case resulted in the imposition of a provisional duty fully matching the extent of the injury found. The decision was based on the argument that:

> In view of the economic and social importance of the sole Community producer left and the relatively low incidence of a price increase on the costs of the processing industry and its competitive position, the Commission has, however, come to the conclusion that *it is in the Community's interest that action be taken.* [*Emphasis added*].[209]

In yet another case, which was decided by Commission Regulation (EEC) No 2640/86 of 21 August 1986 imposing a provisional anti-dumping duty on imports of plain paper photocopiers originating in Japan,[210] a detailed scrutiny was made to determine Community interest, following which:

> In conclusion, the Commission, while acknowledging the vulnerable position of OEMs[211] in the proceeding, can see no justification, legal or economic, for according them *special treatment, even if such treatment could be so devised within the provisions of Regulation (EEC) No 2176/84.* [*Emphasis added*].[212]

207. *Ibid.*, p. 5.
208. [1986] O.J. L217, p. 12 f.
209. *Ibid.*, p. 14. Emphasis added.
210. [1986] O.J. L239, p. 5 f.
211. The acronym stands for 'Original Equipment Manufacturers', i.e. firms purchasing photocopiers from unrelated manufacturers to sell them under their own brands. See Regulation No. 2640/86, cit., p. 8.
212. *Ibid.*, p. 21. Emphasis added.

Again, in connection with these last cases, the concept of injury cannot easily be separated from that of Community interest, at least in the substance. Yet, the relevant decisions have clearly pointed up the linkage between the determination of the Community's interests and the issues related the protection of free competition in its internal market.

It should also be noted that, in light of the most recent practice, the reference made by Community legislation on dumping and subsidies to Community interest has brought about a situation now beyond the Community authorities' control. Much as the original purpose was to avoid forcing the Commission or the Council to apply *strictly* trade defence measures where 'superior' reasons would so require to the detriment of contrasting national interests or even of any underlying private interests, the Community interest test allows the investigated parties, too, to appeal to the Court of Justice against the Council's or the Commission's determinations where no adequate grounds had been provided at the time the safeguard measures deemed apt to remove the injury were enacted. Thus, in Case 53/83 (*Allied Corporation*),[213] the applicants complained, *inter alia*, that the Community's interest had not expressly and correctly been determined in the contested Regulation, on the argument that:

> the discretion enjoyed by the competent EC institutions cannot entirely remove the criterion of Community interest from judicial review.[214]

On the same occasion, the Council itself stated that:

> an analysis of the interests of the Community involves a wide discretion in assessing political and economic circumstances and the weighing-up of various factors internal and external to the Community. The interests of consumers and, in particular, their long-term interests, were taken into consideration; the interests of the other categories of persons concerned did not conflict with the imposition of the duties.

And concluded that:

> given such a discretion, the Court must limit its review to determining *whether a manifest error or a misuse of power has been committed.* [*Emphasis added*].[215]

Only in the Commission's view:

> the exercise of the discretion to assess the interests of the Community covers important external aspects and is *even less susceptible to judicial review* than a discretion exercised where only internal elements are involved. [*Emphasis added*].[216]

---

213. The judgment, already quoted above, is published in ECR, cit., p. 1621 f.
214. In ECR, cit., p. 1651.
215. In ECR, cit., p. 1652.
216. In ECR, cit., p. 1652.

In annulling Regulation 101/83 of 17 January 1983 on grounds relating to the determination of injury, the ECJ by no means ruled on the notion of 'Community interest'. And a telling fact is that neither the Council nor the Commission, in their respective defences, nor even the Advocate General in his opinion, considered the problem that the undertakings deemed liable for dumping were entirely precluded from claiming the purported lack of Community interest in enacting the relevant safeguard measures, based on the argument that it was an element otherwise unrelated to antidumping regulations.

Later on, at point 63 of the grounds for its judgment of 14 March 1990 in C 156/87, *Gestetner Holdings*, the Court of Justice ruled on the issue for the first time. Consistent with the approach taken by the Council to *Allied Corporation*, the Court held that it was for it alone to determine the legitimacy of any assessment as to the correct application of the *Community interest test* in the relevant case. The Court further observed that the question whether the interests of the Community call for Community intervention involved appraisal of complex economic situations, and that judicial review of such an appraisal must be limited to verifying whether the relevant procedural rules have been complied with, whether the facts on which the choice is based have been accurately stated and whether there has been a manifest error of appraisal or a misuse of powers.

This principle was re-asserted by the Court in its various judgments of 10 March 1992, already discussed above, relating to the case of antidumping duties imposed on imports of plain paper photocopiers originating in Japan.[217] Thus:

> It must be pointed out in this connection that, according to the institutions, in the absence of anti-dumping duties it would be doubtful whether an independent Community PPC industry could survive although it is necessary in order to maintain and develop the techniques required in manufacturing reprographic equipment and in order to preserve a large number of jobs. That concern arose in particular from the take-over, in the course of the investigation, of the business of one of the Community producers by a Japanese manufacturer. The institutions therefore took the view that *the need to protect Community industry was more important than the need to protect the immediate interests of consumers*, as is explained in paragraph 99 of the preamble to the contested regulation, *and the need to protect importers*. [*Emphasis added*].

This having become settled practice, the express reference to the Community's interests has proved to be a solution useless most of the times, often a thorny one for the Community authorities to handle, and essentially 'harmful' to the Community's interest themselves.

---

217. See judgments dismissing various applications for annulment of Council Regulation (EEC) No. 535/87 of 23 Feb. 1987 imposing a definitive anti-dumping duty on imports of plain paper photocopiers originating in Japan (O.J. L54, p. 12)); Case C-174/87, cit., grounds 68 and 69, in ECR, 1992, cit.; Case C-175/87, cit., grounds 81 and 82, *ibid.*, cit.; Case C-176/87, *Konishiroku Photo Industry Co. Ltd* v *Council*, grounds 43 e 44, *ibid.*, p. 1493 f., p. 1531 f.; Case C-177/87, *Sanyo Electric Co. Ltd* v *Council*, grounds 43 and 44, *ibid.*, p. 1535 f., p. 1571; and Case C-179/87, cit., grounds 58 and 59, *ibid.*, cit., p. 1685.

Therefore, and in view of the broad discretionary power the competent institution already has in assessing the injury, precisely because of the close link established by Community practice between the assessment of injury and the test of Community interest in antidumping and anti-subsidy proceedings, that institution may still attain the intended result even if the 1994 Community acts contained no such express reference to the Community's interests.

Against this background, the Community institutions could well be expected, in adjusting Community legislation to the GATT 1994 Agreements, to remove any reference to *Community interest* from any of their new Regulations. Amending Community rules in this direction would have resulted in closer compliance with the GATT Agreements and in the outright removal of the competent Community authorities' obligation, so clearly set out in the ECJ's judgments discussed above, to assert, and provide grounds for, the existence of Community interest in applying antidumping or countervailing duties against allegedly infringing undertakings in each relevant case.

The opposite has happened, though. The Community has chosen to reinforce the concept of 'Community interest', by introducing explicit rules in Article 21 of Regulation No 384/96 and Article 31 of Regulation No 2026/97, respectively.

These articles primarily require that, whenever the Community authorities are called upon to decide whether or not to take action in the Community's best interests, in accordance with either the antidumping or the anti-subsidy Regulations, they must appreciate 'all the various interests taken as a whole, *including* the interests of the domestic industry and users and consumers'.

Also, it is stressed in those articles that the need to eliminate the trade distorting effects of injurious dumping and to restore effective competition – as is typical of antidumping and anti-subsidy proceedings – should be given special consideration.

Further, the Regulations in question require that a decision as to whether the Community interest exist or does not exist in the relevant case may only be taken if all the parties concerned have been given an opportunity to provide their comments.

Lastly, the nature of 'Community interest' as an essential requirement is expressly acknowledged in the relevant Community Regulations, in the sense that any antidumping or countervailing duties, 'as determined on the basis of the dumping and injury found, *may not be applied where the authorities, on the basis of all the information submitted, can clearly conclude that it is not in the Community interest to apply such measures*'.

Under the heading 'Community Interest', paragraphs 1, 2, 3, 4, 5, 6 and 7 of Article 21 of Regulation No 384/96 require:

> A determination as to whether *the Community interest calls for intervention* shall be based on an appreciation of all the various interests taken as a whole, including the interests of the domestic industry and users and consumers; and a determination pursuant to this Article shall only be made where all parties have been given the opportunity to make their views known pursuant to

paragraph 2. In such an examination, *the need to eliminate the trade distorting effects of injurious dumping and to restore effective competition shall be given special consideration.* Measures, as determined on the basis of the dumping and injury found, may not be applied where the authorities, on the basis of all the information submitted, can clearly conclude that it is not in the Community interest to apply such measures. [*Emphasis added*].

In order to provide a sound basis on which the authorities can take account of all views and information in the decision as to whether or not the imposition of measures is in the Community interest, the complainants, importers and their representative associations, representative users and representative consumer organizations may, within the time limits specified in the notice of initiation of the anti-dumping investigation, make themselves known and provide information to the Commission. Such information, or appropriate summaries thereof, shall be made available to the other parties specified in this Article, and they shall be entitled to respond to such information.

The parties which have acted in conformity with paragraph 2 may request a hearing. Such requests shall be granted when they are submitted within the time limits set in paragraph 2, and when they set out the reasons, in terms of the Community interest, why the parties should be heard.

The parties which have acted in conformity with paragraph 2 may provide comments on the application of any provisional duties imposed. Such comments shall be received within one month of the application of such measures if they are to be taken into account and they, or appropriate summaries thereof, shall be made available to other parties who shall be entitled to respond to such comments.

The Commission shall examine the information which is properly submitted and the extent to which it is representative and the results of such analysis, together with an opinion on its merits, shall be transmitted to the Advisory Committee. The balance of views expressed in the Committee shall be taken into account by the Commission in any proposal made pursuant to Article 9.

The parties which have acted in conformity with paragraph 2 may request the facts and considerations on which final decisions are likely to be taken to be made available to them. Such information shall be made available to the extent possible and without prejudice to any subsequent decision taken by the Commission or the Council.

Information shall only be taken into account where it is supported by actual evidence which substantiates its validity.

It is patently clear that, while the 'Community interest' notion is covered only by the first paragraph of Article 21 of Regulation No 384/96, it retains all the vague and unspecific traits I have highlighted above (and which have characterized it since enactment).

Conversely, the detailed identification of thorough rules of procedure the Commission is required to comply with in the six paragraphs next following in Article 21 for the protection of the defence rights of all the parties concerned seems to be there to allow the Commission to be on the safe side in case the Community Courts are subsequently called upon to review the Commission's own actions for legitimacy.

The wide discretionary powers the Commission and the Council may exercise in their determinations as to whether the Community interest calls for intervention in each relevant case are thereby confirmed.[218]

Further, precisely because of the wide scope for discretion so given to the Community authorities in matters of dumping and subsidies, it is my view that the rules of procedure in question cannot be deemed to be directly applied, thereby attributing any rights to private parties in individual national systems. Therefore, neither the Member States' authorities (which are powerless in this respect also as result of the delegation of exclusive competence to the Community under Article 133 of the Treaty) nor their national courts have jurisdiction as to whether antidumping or countervailing duties are to be applied to non-Community undertakings.

In Part 2, paragraph 2.1, of the Commission's Green Paper of 6 December 2006, significantly headed '*Europe's trade defence instruments in a changing global economy*',[219] the Commission raises a number of questions under the caption 'The Community test', all of which intended to overlook the real essence of the issue I have tried to clarify above. For it by no means asks itself or offers for public consultation[220] the core question, i.e. whether the Community interest test should be maintained or set aside as an essential element of a determination of dumping or subsidies.

---

218. For a recent ruling in the matter of 'Community interests' pursuant to Regulation No. 384/96, see Judgment of the Court of First Instance of 8 Jul. 2003, Case T-132/01, *Euroalliages and others* v *Commission*, [2003] ECR II-2359.
219. See COM (2006) 763 final.
220. The following are the four questions the Commission asked for public consultation on the matter: Question 4: Should the EU review the current balance of interests between various economic operators in the Community interest test in trade defence investigations? Alongside the interests of producers and their employees in Europe, how should we take into account the interests of companies which have retained significant operations and employment in Europe, even though they have moved some part of their production out of the EU? How should we take into account the interests of importers or producers who process affected imports? Question 5: Do we need to review the way that consumer interests are taken into account in trade defence investigations? Should the Commission be more proactive in soliciting input from consumer associations? How could such input be weighted? How could the impact of trade defence measures on consumers be assessed and monitored? Question 6: Should the EU include wider considerations in the Community interest assessments in trade defence investigations, such as coherence with other EU policies? With regard to development policy, should the EU make a formal distinction between least developed countries and developing countries in the application of trade defence measures? Question 7: What kinds of economic analysis might help in making these assessments?

In introducing its questions in paragraph 2.1 of the Green Paper, the Commission states:[221]

> The EU is one of the few trade defence users that applies a public interest test in the form of the Community interest rule before applying Anti-Dumping measures. The Community interest rule states that measures can only be imposed where the Commission determines that imposing them is not against the wider interest of the EU economy. Such a test is not required by the WTO Anti-Dumping Agreement but it has proved a useful factor in weighing the balance of interests in Anti-Dumping cases.

And, further, in concluding the preamble to the questions to the public:

> However, some argue that the Community interest test is too strongly weighted towards EU producers and does not take sufficient account of the impact of measures on importing businesses that have moved some of their production outside the EU. There is also concern that consumer interests are not adequately weighted, especially when trade defence instruments are applied to finished consumer products. While the principal concern of the EU's instruments is responding to the effect of unfair competition, recent cases have also raised the question of using the Community interest test to weigh the impact of measures on the overall coherence of EU policy. For example, the EU might consider whether in some cases Anti-Dumping measures reduce the effectiveness of EU development assistance to a given country.

23. IMPLEMENTING WTO RULES ON DUMPING AND SUBSIDIES: (A) IN THE UNITED STATES OF AMERICA

US law was adapted to the Uruguay Round Agreements on dumping and subsidies by the Uruguay Round Agreements Act of 8 December 1994, *cit.*, Sec. 201-291.

In the US legislation, the antidumping procedure has invariably been a complex procedure falling within the jurisdiction of both the Department of Commerce (the DOC) and the International Trade Commission (the ITC), the latter being an independent governmental agency composed of six members appointed by the president of the USA. Whilst the former is responsible for determining the existence of dumping practices, the latter is competent to determine whether an industry in the United States is materially injured, or is threatened with material injury, or the establishment of an industry in the United States is materially retarded by reason of dumped imports.

The double-track system is in itself a source of difficulties for the enterprises under investigation, since each administering authority's powers can hardly be separated from the other's in practice, and each authority proceeds independently of the other. In general, petitions lodged by American enterprises have a far heavier

221. COM (2006) 763., cit., p. 8.

weight than the defences available to the respondents, irrespective of which party is formally called upon to discharge the burden of proof.

If the double final 'order' is positive, then antidumping duties are applied, provided that each such order may be appealed against before the Court of International Trade. This Court's decision may also be appealed against, according to the general rules, before the US Court of Appeals for the Federal Circuit and ultimately before the Supreme Court.

Further, the Continued Dumping and Subsidy Offset Act of October 2000 (commonly known as the 'Byrd Amendment') even required that the funds from assessed dumping and countervailing duties *be distributed to the US companies that file pricing complaints*, which was in open conflict with many of the WTO agreement provisions. By such ingenious device, US firms would, in fact, receive a double benefit from their national legislation. Through the imposition of antidumping duties, they were protected from foreign imports originally sold at lower prices than cost price in the US, and, at the same time, they were entitled, in their being 'affected domestic producers', to the distribution of the continued dumping or subsidy offset not later than 60 days after the first day of a fiscal year from duties assessed during the preceding fiscal year.[222]

Much as a WTO panel had lodged a recommendation on 16 September 2002 (WT/D234R), as confirmed by the Appellate Body on 16 January 2003 (WT/DS234/AB/R), whereby it acknowledged the unlawfulness of the Act and recommended that the DSB requested the United States to make its legislation consistent with its obligations under the Antidumping Agreement and the Anti-Subsidies Agreement,[223] the United States continued to distribute such funds to its domestic producers. On 13 June 2003, Sole Arbitrator Taniguchi issued his award, in which he determined that the 'reasonable period of time' for the United States to implement the recommendations and rulings of the DSB was finally to expire on 27 December 2003.

The EU reacted by requesting the DSB authorization to suspend tariff concessions and related obligations to the United States under GATT 1994.

The dispute was then referred to arbitration, and, on 31 August 2004, the arbitrator determined that the level of nullification or impairment caused every year to the Community was equal to 72% of the amount of Byrd Amendment disbursements relating to anti-dumping or countervailing duties paid on imports from the Community for the most recent year for which data were available at that time, as published by the United States' authorities.

---

222. To this date, the US authorities have allocated over 1.6 billion dollars to complaining producers. See the *General Overview of Active WTO Dispute Settlement Cases involving the EC as Complainant or Defendant and of Active Cases Under the Trade Barriers Regulation* of 11 May 1997, available on the EU's website.

223. Decisions from WTO judicial bodies had been sought by as many as WTO members (Australia, Brazil, Canada, Chile, the European Community, Korea, Japan, India, Indonesia, Mexico e Thailand), the largest number of complainants ever within the WTO.

Therefore, the Arbitrator concluded that the suspension by the Community of concessions or other obligations not exceeding the amount of nullification or impairment would be consistent with WTO rules.

On 26 November 2004, the DSB granted the European Community the authorization to suspend the application to the United States of tariff concessions and related obligations under GATT 1994 in accordance with the decision of the Arbitrator. Accordingly, the Community adopted Council Regulation (EC) No. 673/2005 of 25 April 2005 establishing additional customs duties on imports of certain products originating in the United States of America.[224] Article 1 requires:

> The tariff concessions and related obligations under GATT 1994 of the Community are hereby suspended in respect of products originating in the United States of America listed in Annex I to this Regulation.

Pursuant to Article 2:

> An *ad valorem* duty of 15% additional to the customs duty applicable under Council Regulation (EEC) No. 2913/92 of 12 October 1992 establishing the Community Customs Code (2) shall be imposed on the products originating in the United States of America listed in Annex I to this Regulation.

Some of the annexes to this Regulation were replaced by Commission Regulation (EC) No 632/2006 of 24 April 2006.[225]

On 8 February 2006, the United States did repeal the Byrd Amendment, but extended its effect *de facto* for an additional period of time. In particular, the repeal contained a transition clause that allowed the US government to continue paying anti-dumping and countervailing duties collected on imports made before 1 October 2007. Since such duties are often collected several years after the import took place, this meant that distribution of funds would continue well beyond 1 October 2007. The US Congressional Budget Office estimated that the repeal of the Byrd Amendment would begin to generate its effects not before 1 October 2009.

The European Union's retaliation measures were therefore made harsher by Commission Regulation (EC) No. 409/2007 for application from 1 May 2007.[226] According to this Regulation, the level of nullification or impairment caused to the Community by distribution under the Byrd Amendment from October 2005 to September 2006 was calculated at 81.19 million US dollars. Accordingly, 32 new products originating in the USA (among which paper products, textiles, pens, footwear and mobile homes) were added to the list of products subject to the additional 15% duty.[227] It is even too clear that such duty is, in fact, substantially made good by a steadily weaker US dollar against the Euro.[228]

224. [2005] O.J. L110, p. 1.
225. [2006] O.J. L111, p. 5.
226. [2007] O.J. L100, p. 16.
227. Japan, too, extended its countervailing measures in Sep. 2006. In 2006, Canada and Mexico stopped their own measures against the United States following a decision by the US Court of International Trade, which ruled that the Byrd Amendment could not be applied against products originating in NAFTA member countries.
228. Please, refer to Chapter III of this volume.

24. MORE: (B) IN THE CHINESE LEGAL SYSTEM

The People's Republic of China filed its application for WTO membership on 7 December 1995.[229] Shortly afterwards, in 1997, it issued an Antidumping and Anti-Subsidy Regulations with extremely vague contents, which were, as such, open to broad discretion in application.[230] It permitted China to make it appear that the successive adjustments it was later forced to make thereto until 2004 to implement the 2001 Accession Protocol were substantial 'concessions'. Although the procedure – now falling within the jurisdiction of the Ministry of Trade and Economic Cooperation as the regulatory body – was designed after the European Community's pattern, it seems that it still exhibits grey areas somewhat at variance with the WTO agreements.[231]

Article 56 of the Regulation expressly provides for retaliatory measures China may take in response to any antidumping duties deemed by it to be discriminatory as may be imposed by other countries on exports from the People's Republic of China. Much as China has represented that the provision in question only concerns non-GATT/WTO members, that provision is so broadly worded as to open the door to its future application within a far wider scope.

If only the essential elements of the Chinese Regulation are considered, it can be noted that one departure from the European pattern is that the procedure to investigate into a Chinese domestic entity's complaint may only be initiated after provisional measures have been taken, which obviously results in a prejudice to the right of defence of the foreign undertakings under investigation, usually following a complaint from competing national undertakings.

Further, the undertakings under investigation are required to fill out certain involved forms written only in Chinese, some of which are lengthy questionnaires that must be replied within, *but not later than*, 37 days from the date of the

229. On the initial China's membership of GATT 1947 see above footnote 9 of this Chapter.

230. See *The Anti-Dumping and Anti-Subsidy Regulations of the People's Republic of China*, promulgated as Decree No. 214 of the State Council of the People's Republic of China on Mar. 25, 1997, with effect as the date of promulgation, published in English in *The Foreign Trade Law of the People's Republic of China*, by Foreign Language Press (Beijing, 2001), p. 21 ff. Art. 1 of Chapter I, under title 'General Provisions' makes express referral to the *Foreign Trade Law of the People's Republic of China* 'in order to maintain proper order and fair competition in foreign trade and protect corresponding domestic industries'. The latter act has been adopted at the Seventh Session of the Standing Committee of the Eighth National People's Congress on May 12, 1994, promulgated by No. 22 Decree of the President of the People's Republic of China on May 12, 1994 and implemented as of 1 Jul. 1994, *ibid.*, p. 1 ff. Under Art. 6, Chapter I, 'General Provisions': 'The People's Republic of China provides most-favored nation and national treatment its counterpart countries or regions in accordance with the international treaties and agreements on foreign trade concluded or joined by the People's Republic of China or in accordance with the principle of equality and mutual benefit', whilst, according to Art. 7, 'the People's Republic of China has the right to adopt corresponding measures against any country or region to counter their discriminatory banning, restrictions or other actions affecting Chinese goods in accordance with the actual circumstances'.

231. Nardelli, 'Anti-dumping cinese e anti-dumping CE a confronto: una minaccia per le imprese comunitarie', p. 388 ss.

notification. Some of the questions concern major aspects of the respondent's business activity, others require complex calculations to be made, and yet others require information about the relevant market which is not readily available most of the times.

Confidentiality about the answers is by no means ensured. In particular, protection of sensitive business information is only discretionary, since it depends on a 'concession' the Chinese regulatory body may issue on a case-by-case basis following receipt of mandatory information, so long as the request therefor is deemed to be 'well-founded'. Thus, foreign enterprises have to face the alternative of whether to disclose sensitive information or to be imposed fictitious calculations and unreasonably high duties based on the 'best information available', as a punitive result of their alleged failure to collaborate.

The duration of proceedings is uncertain, in that the 18 months ostensibly stated as the latest time limit only allowed in exceptional cases is ordinarily applied at all times.

In theory, the parties may appeal to the Intermediate People's Court of Beijing against the imposition of antidumping measures. But, since the jurisdiction of this court is restricted to hearing cases merely to establish legitimacy, while the administrative body is required by law to base its decisions on facts the accuracy and reliability of which need not be proved, it is no surprise that no appeals have been brought to this day. Far more useful are continuing negotiations with the investigating authority in the administrative phase, because of the natural propensity to bargaining, which is considered to be a refined art in China.

For years, China has challenged the manners in which antidumping rules are applied, especially by the United States and the European Union. The entire issue revolves around China's request to be recognized Market Economy Status ('MES') with a view to a more favourable determination of the margin of dumping in respect of merchandise originating in China.

Article 15 of the Protocol on the Accession of the People's Republic of China to the WTO allows Members to regard China as a 'non-market economy' in anti-dumping and anti-subsidy investigations for fifteen years after the date of accession.

The concept of Market Economy Status is only relevant to 'trade defence investigations', specifically to the calculation of margins of dumping in relation to products made in a country which is not considered to be a market economy country. In this case, 'the importing WTO Member may use a methodology that is not based on a strict comparison with domestic prices or costs' in the exporting Member.[232] In other words, the importing Member's authorities will be free to benchmark their determinations to the prices and costs ruling in a market-economy third country which is comparable to the exporting enterprise's.[233] Thus, for example, the European Commission has used production and price information

232. See Article 15(a)(ii), of China's Protocol of Accession to the WTO.
233. See Article 2(7)(a) of Regulation (EC) No. 384/96 of the Council.

from Mexico to determine a 'fair price' for the investigation on imports of *bicycles* from China.[234]

According to the Commission, MES does not have an impact on the number of anti-dumping/anti-subsidy cases. It is deemed to be simply a method to calculate antidumping duties, and one obviously much appreciated by European undertakings in that it permits higher duties to be determined and consequently imposed.[235]

Article 2(7)(b) of Regulation (EC) No 384/96 requires that, in the case of antidumping investigations into imports from the People's Republic of China, Vietnam or Kazakhstan or from any non-market economy country which is a WTO Member at the date of opening investigations, *individual enterprises* should be given an opportunity to show that market economy conditions prevail for the producers in connection with the production and marketing of a like or similar product. Where such prevalence is established, 'normal value' should be determined according to the ordinary criteria. Yet, all the requests by Chinese companies to that effect have invariably been rejected by the Commission.[236]

In June 2003, the People's Republic of China made a formal request to the European Commission for recognition of MES. The Commission issued a 'preliminary assessment' in June 2004, whereby it considered that MES ought not to be granted to China until the following criteria were satisfied:

1. Removal of state interference in the economy and of restrictions on prices and exports.
2. Compliance with corporate governance and accounting standards.
3. No discrimination in bankruptcy proceedings.
4. Respect for intellectual property rights.
5. Transition of the banking sector to market rules.

During the meeting of the European Commissioner, Mr Mandelson, and the Chinese Trade Minister Bo Xilai on 4 November 2005, the Commission, while acknowledging that 'substantial progress towards MES has been made', restricted its commitment to proposing 'to intensify discussions on this issue'.

Time does not seem to be ripe yet. At the end of June 2007, the Commission produced its annual technical report on MES, in which it announced that four out of five MES criteria had not yet fully satisfied by China. Despite the many laws promulgated by China with this view, the Commission had still not received appropriate guarantees as to their actual implementation. Therefore, former

234. The example has been drawn from 'Market Economy Status and the People's Republic of China' of 16 Jan. 2006, edited by the Committee for International Trade (INTA) of the European Parliament.

235. See '*China – Market economy status in trade defence investigations?*' of 28 Jun. 2004, available on the European Commission's website.

236. See 'Market Economy Status and the People's Republic of China' of 16 Jan. 2006, cit., and 'CHINA – *Market economy status in trade defence investigations?*', cit. In Jan. 2006, the Commission rejected an application for '*individual market economy treatment*' Chinese undertakings had filed in an antidumping investigation relating to footwear. The decision was harshly criticized by Beijing authorities.

Commissioner Mandelson promised that the Commission 'will review the situation again in twelve months and continue technical talks in the meanwhile'.[237]

It should be noted that the United Kingdom has been the chief supporter of Chinese requests within the EU.[238]

The United States and Japan, Cina's principal trade partners alongside the European Union, have taken an approach similar to the EU's, and, accordingly, they have not yet granted MES to China.

Still, China has, for the last few years, so eagerly intensified its diplomatic campaign to obtain MES from the largest possible number of WTO Members as to lead to the statement that 'MES has clearly assumed a disproportionate place in China's foreign trade agenda'.[239] A consequence of such activism was that as many as 66 WTO Members had recognized market economy status to the People's Republic of China by 15 January 2007: most African countries, the ten members of the ASEAN (Association of Southeast Asian Nations), New Zealand, Switzerland, and the largest countries of South America (Brazil, Argentina, Chile and Peru). India seems, however, to have not fallen in line.

25. DUMPING AND COMPETITION IN THE EU

The above outline of Community rules resulting from the implementation of the GATT 1994 Agreements confirms that they are primarily and directly intended to remove any trade distorting effects of dumped or subsidized imports into the Community.

Such primary objective can only be achieved through the application of the uniform international rules embodied in the GATT/WTO agreements. In other words, the Community's antidumping and anti-subsidy legislation is a *commercial policy tool* in the first place, designed to protect the internal market from *unlawful* imports from non-Community countries.

Still, it is a tool with another material effect, further to its primary macroeconomic function. For it also operates within the market affected by unlawful imports in order to eliminate any occurrences as may distort competition, by preventing non-Community exporting undertakings and/or Community importing undertakings from enjoying unwarranted competitive advantages over other undertakings, be they national, Community or non-Community entities. Therefore, in this respect, the focus of the problem shifts from the protection of Member States' interests to the protection of the individual interests of undertakings in individual industries.

The close connection of the rules on dumping and subsidies with competition law was already quite clear to the Community law-makers, who included

237. See speech by Commissioner Mandelson at Strasbourg on 10 Jul. 2007.
238. See Minister Pearson's statements of 4 Jul. 2005, in 'UK endorses China bid for market economy status' available on www.ft.com.
239. See 'Market Economy Status and the People's Republic of China' of 16 Jan. 2006, cit.

Sub Article 91 in Section 2 (intra-Community) 'dumping practices' together with the original rules of Section 1, 'Rules applying to undertakings', of Chapter 1, Title VI of the EC Treaty, and Section 3, 'Aid granted by States'.[240] In his Opinion delivered in joined cases 239/82 and 275/82,[241] Advocate General VerLoren van Themaat observed that:

> [d]umping is a phenomenon by nature related to forms of distortion of competition which, under the system established by the EC Treaty, it is normally sought to counter by means of decisions. Dumping is, in particular, a form of cross-frontier price discrimination (made possible by the existence of customs frontiers) which is by nature closely related to the discriminatory practices prohibited by Article 85(1)(d) and Article 86(c) of the Treaty.[242]

Advocate General went on to state:

> [m]oreover, the effects of dumping are comparable to the effects produced by aid measures – which, according to Article 92, are incompatible with the common market – and, in particular, by export aid measures which it is also sought to counter by means of decision.

This is also the import of the provision in the second paragraph of Article 131 in Chapter 4, Title IX ('Common Commercial Policy') of the EC Treaty, the same Title accommodating Article 133(1), which is the legal basis of Community jurisdiction over non-Community dumping practices. The second paragraph of Article 131 EC reads:

> The common commercial policy shall take into account the favourable effect which the abolition of customs duties between Member States may have on the increase in the competitive strength of undertakings in those States.

In fact, competition issues have invariably been considered in Community case-law, especially in the European Union institutions' assessments as to 'injury' and in determining the existence of 'Community interest'. In this respect, both the Council and the Commission have often concerned themselves with the need not only to remove any distortions preventing the Community industry from 'supporting competition with imports', but also to ensure that the introduction of antidumping duties had no adverse impact on competition within the European internal market.

This was the approach taken by the Council in adopting Regulation No 2322/85 of 12 August 1985 relating to imports of glycine originating in Japan, already referred to above, in which the Council's determinations as to *Community interest* reflected the paramount significance it ascribed to the protection of competition in the internal market.[243]

---

240. Article 91 of the Treaty of Rome was deleted by Article 6 of the Treaty of Amsterdam.
241. In Case *Allied Corporation*, in ECR, p. 1005.
242. [1984] ECR 1037.
243. [1985] O.J. L218.

It was on the basis of an assessment of competition issues that, in a similar case relating to the imposition of a provisional anti-dumping duty on imports of potassium permanganate originating in Czechoslovakia, the German Democratic Republic (before unification) and the People' s Republic of China,[244] the Commission ruled that that duty should be applied to an extent exactly equal to the injury.

Momentous consequences can be drawn from these considerations in the case of appeals. Where a country's authorities make a devious use of antidumping and anti-subsidy rules for merely protectionist purposes, a Member State (or the EC, pursuant to Article 133 EC, in case of dumped or subsidized exports from third countries) whose economic interests have been impaired thereby may seek remedy under the GATT, in the terms of Article 17 of the 1994 Antidumping Code, which governs 'consultation and dispute settlement' in dumping cases, or in the terms of Article 30 of the 1994 Anti-Subsidy Code in the case of state subsidies.

In a different domain, from the point of view of the Community's legal system in respect of 'private law' issues, i.e. where a Community industry has been injured by dumping or subsidy events, the close connection already found to exist between antidumping and anti-subsidy rules and antitrust legislation provides further evidence of the fact that it is for the individual parties interested in the relevant case to bring action before the Court of First Instance if they are to protect their interests pursuant to the fourth paragraph of Article 230 EC.

It should also be considered that the same factual elements as are present in any individual case subject to antidumping or anti-subsidy rules may be of relevance in terms of competition law, if a given conduct is found to be a prohibited practice or abuse caught by the provisions of Articles 81 or 82 EC.

For example, a dumping practice could be the result of an agreement between a non-Community producer and a Community importing undertaking which directly or indirectly fix purchase prices. In this case, beside a violation of antidumping provisions, there would be a separate infringement of paragraph 1(a) of Article 81 EC, or it may even be found that the agreement in question was a device by which an undertaking tried to oust a competitor from the market through predatory pricing.

It should finally be observed that the complementarity of competition rules with antidumping rules may come to the fore in a different respect. Just think of unfair competition cases still subject to individual Member States' jurisdiction. For example, from the point of view of the Italian legal system, any breach by a person of his duty to comply with proper standards of professional conduct, as a result of which another's business is injured, is categorized as an act of unfair competition in the terms of Article 2598.3 of the Civil Code. It is now commonly agreed that a person is liable for unfair competition under Article 2598.3 when he takes advantage, in his business activities, of a breach of any provisions of public law – whether by a criminal offence (e.g. contraband) or by a just administrative offence (e.g. cheating the Revenue in value added tax) – i.e. provisions directly

---

244. See Regulation 2495/86 of 1 Aug. 1986, cit., 12 ff.

intended to protect overriding interests. In each such case, it is a commonly accepted view that certain acts considered unlawful under public rules on economic activities may also be treated as acts of unfair competition *where the elements specified in Article 2598.3, Civil Code, are found to exist*. This is the case whenever failure to observe economic rules generates a causal link whereby an undertaking's position becomes *more advantageous* than its competitors', thus inadmissibly altering the 'rules of the game'.

I have no doubts as to the fact that, in case a Community proceeding on dumped or subsidized imports by non-Community undertakings into Italy is closed with the imposition by the competent Community authority of antidumping or countervailing duties, the affected undertakings are fully entitled to bring action for damages, pursuant to Article 2600 of the Italian Civil Code, against such non-Community undertakings before an Italian Court as well, based both on the argument that the duty of proper standards of professional conduct under Article 2598.3, Civil Code, was not complied with, and on the fact that the violation in question was established by the competent Community authority.[245]

245. For this subject, please refer to Chapter VI of this book.

Chapter V

Multinational Enterprises and Globalization

SUMMARY:

1. Methodological preamble.
2. Definitory elucidation.
3. Multinational enterprises and international law in a changing world.
4. Multinational enterprises and the European Union.
5. The features of the phenomenon in general: Unrestricted freedom of choice and the resulting basic distortions of competition.
6. Advantages lawfully acquired by multinationals in some instances of daily practice.
7. Production delocation as a result of globalization.
8. The impact of globalization on financial markets: the USA financial crisis.
9. More: The Sovereign Funds.
10. Unlawful conduct of multinational enterprises.
11. Risk areas: The problem of the 'normal' value of 'transfer prices' and of royalties in intragroup transactions.
12. International cooperation against corruption, pollution, money laundering, financial crimes and the international financing of terrorism.
13. The role of banks in controlling transactions at risk.
14. International cooperation in the supervision of banking groups and the Basel Concordat: The different levels of control.
15. Consolidated supervision over banking transactions in the relationships between legal systems.
16. From the Basel II rules to the present rules of the European Union.
17. Investigations into 'suspicious activities' in context.
18. The universal notion of 'SAR' (Suspicious Activity Reporting).

19. Suspicious activity reporting requirements to prevail over any other requirement of law.
20. The 'Codes of Conduct'.
21. 'Social commitment' and multinational enterprises: Consequences on the relationships with the home State and with third countries.
22. Multinational enterprises' activity in a regional perspective: The limited scope for enforcement of Community rules.
23. The European Union and 'Corporate Social Responsibility'.
24. Community actions in favour of small and medium-sized enterprises.
25. Legal restrictions on third-country-based multinationals' operations in the European Union.
26. Applying competition rules to non-Community businesses.
27. Anti-dumping and anti-subsidy rules as applied to non-Community multinationals (reference).

1. METHODOLOGICAL PREAMBLE

About forty years after the earliest studies on the phenomenon of multinational enterprises in the world of law, it is easy for anyone who has, as I have, worked on the subject since the mid-1970s[1] to observe that the issues that were discussed at that time now appear in a quite different light. It is, in fact, the international environment that has radically changed since then, especially in respect – as I have tried to illustrate throughout this volume – of the dramatic development of international economic and trade relations in the ways they are governed by law and carried on in practice.

It is just too obvious that multinational enterprises themselves were able, from their privileged observatory, to perceive such changes at an early time, with a view to any advantages they could draw from the new environment in making their operational choices. Thus, the basic gap between them and merely domestic firms, which I have identified as a consequence typical of multinationals' activity since the start of my studies on the subject, has by no means been filled. Indeed, it has grown even wider.[2] And that it has been so even as firms operating on a domestic scale can hardly fail to grasp the vital need for them to get 'internationalized', to a greater or lesser degree depending on their business operations, in order for them, too, to take the benefits globalization has to offer, which the multinationals have long been allowed to enjoy – to the point that globalization now appears to have become an essential part of their DNA.

1. Please, refer to my study, 'Imprese multinazionali e Comunità economica europea' [1975] Riv.dir.int., p. 279 ff., and [1975] Riv.soc., p. 924 ff.
2. For the widening gap between most economically developed countries and less developed countries (LDCs) following globalization, please refer to Santa Maria, 'Il diritto internazionale dell'economia', cit., p. 479 ff. For similar considerations, see also section 4 of Chapter V of this volume.

In a dramatically changing business environment, the priority generally assigned by western countries (including those outside the G7) to appropriate measures to combat the financing of international terrorism calls for widespread international co-operation, through which the competent national authorities are enabled on an on-going basis to keep close watch on, and an eye out for, any financial transaction that appears to be 'suspicious' either in itself or because of the intended object or of the identities of the person or persons that are parties to it.

In other words, the fight against international terrorism financing, which inevitably covers any unjustified form of international payments – including, but not limited to, measures against money laundering or bribery in connection with 'international' commercial or industrial deals – has involved a growing number of individual measures within an ever-expanding scope for application. Thus, the 'dedicated' controls applied to multinational enterprises have been supplemented with, or even superseded by, measures applicable to any transactions entered into for unwarranted reasons or falling outside the customary trade standards. As a result, these measures are also applied to traders of any size or description to whose accounts funds are made to flow from the financial institutions of one State to those of another.

Still, because of the materiality of such issues to the present day's international economic life, and because they are of concern for multinational as well as just national enterprises – and because the direct addressees of the rules on the control over cross-border transfers of capital and payments are financial institutions, notably international banking groups – I will discuss the international co-operation in, and the EU regulations relating to, the prevention and suppression of financial crimes in this Chapter V. I will do so in novel terms in the part that, in the previous editions of this volume, was devoted to an examination of the multinational enterprises' 'illegal' activities, i.e. merely contingent activities that are not unique to the phenomenon of multinational enterprises and may clearly reflect the behaviours of any one economic operator.

Substantial changes have also occurred in other aspects of multinational enterprises' operations in the last few years. It is a fact that major multinationals, whether of private or state ownership, operating in a variety of business sectors, are now originated in countries once regarded as developing countries. In the paragraphs below, I will often draw the reader's attention to individual aspects to which this fact and its consequences have acquired special relevance.

2. DEFINITORY ELUCIDATION

The phrase 'multinational enterprise' has been given the most diverse definitions. One especially effective definition identifies the qualifying element of the content of the 'multinationality' concept by reference to an enterprise viewed as a single economic body as contrasted with the plurality of legal entities through which such single economic body performs its entrepreneurial activity: 'An enterprise qualifies as "multinational" in relation to the tangible aspects of its activity, thus to the singleness of the management – or decision-making – body of an economic entity operating in several countries at any one time, irrespective of the legal form (or, rather, forms) used to perform its activity.'[3]

In other words, the physical unity of an economic structure is not matched by a formal unity of its legal status. The contrary is true, in fact. The 'multinational' character of an enterprise emerges from the plurality of companies that are 'nationals' of each of the different counties in which that enterprise's economic processes take place at different times of its life and circumstances as one *single* business concern.

Thus, the phrase 'multinational *companies*' appears inaccurate, since companies are, in fact, invariably 'national'. Only *enterprises* can be 'multinational',[4] precisely because of their operating through a plurality of *national* companies, and the adjective 'national', when attributed to a company, has its usual figurative meaning to indicate the subjection of that company to the laws of the State of which it is a 'national' in this sense.[5]

This does not, however, mean that the life and circumstances of the individual national companies within one and the same multinational enterprise are not somehow predicated upon their being parts of the same 'group' – a legal structure typical of multinational enterprises. Just think of the mother company's liability for its daughter companies' acts determined by the former's own directors within the scope of 'direction and coordination activities'.[6] Another case in point is the

3. See Malintoppi, *Quelques réflexions sur le droit applicable aux entreprises multinationales, Rapport national italien au IX Congrès International de Droit Comparé, Teheran, 1974, Section II,- B – 1* (Milan, 1974), p. 233 f.
4. The term 'multinational companies' is used interchangeably with 'multinational undertakings' in the EC Commission Communication of 7 Nov. 1973, entitled *Multinational Undertakings and Community Regulations*, in *Bull. EC.*, 1973, Suppl. 15/73, p. 15 ff. The document of the United Nations Department of Economic and Social Affairs entitled *Multinational Corporations in World Development, UN, Doc. ST/ECA/190*, New York, 1973, p. 4 f., expressly states that, although the terms 'corporation', 'firm' and 'company' are considered interchangeable in practice, 'multinational enterprise' is somehow preferred, since it patently implies a network of companies or partnerships established in different countries and linked together by ownership connections. The same document further specifies that, in that context, 'corporation' is not used as a legal term, but just in accordance with common usage as reflected in the terminology of the Resolution by the UN Department of Economic and Social Affairs (N. 1721 (LIII)). For this Resolution of 28 Jul. 1972, reproduced in *Multinational Corporations*, cit., Annex 1, p. 106 ff., see Malintoppi, *Quelques réflexions sur le droit applicable aux entreprises multinationales*, cit., p. 233 f., especially fn. 1.
5. Refer to the considerations in my other study, 'Le società nel diritto internazionale privato', cit., p. 7 f., fn. 10. For companies in private international law generally, and for the figurative usage of the adjective 'national' referred to a 'company' for private international law purposes, see also Chapter I of this volume.
6. See the closing paragraph of section 4 of Chapter I above. See also the judgment of the *United States District Court, Northern District of Illinois, Eastern Division* of 18 Apr. 1984 in re *Oil Spill by the 'Amoco Cadiz'*, in which it was held that the US multinational *Standard Oil Co.*, the parent company, was liable for damages from oil spill caused by a crude carrier owned by a subsidiary, *Amoco Transport Co.* and operated by another subsidiary, *Amoco International Oil Co.* [1987] Dir. comm. int., p. 347 f., with a commentary by Bonelli, *La responsabilità della*

impact a parent company's duty to file consolidated financial statements necessarily has on its individual affiliates' financial reporting policies, irrespective of the provisions of law governing each such subsidiary's corporate existence. A third example is a parent company's liability, within the extraterritorial reach of antitrust laws,[7] for acts performed direct by any of its affiliates of a different nationality operating in different relevant product markets.

In international law, too, the economic unity typical of a multinational enterprise has some influence, as discussed further below, on problems relating to the diplomatic protection of limited companies and their shareholders by their home States.

Indeed, the various definitions of the phrase 'multinational enterprises' have one element in common. The 'multinationality' notion is used throughout in the sense that all multinational enterprises *perform their business activities through more than one legal person and in more than one country*, regardless of their respective size in terms of total numbers employed, turnover, product market shares in several geographical areas or total profits.

None of the above considerations denies the methodological statement that the quest for definitions is not an especially useful exercise for the jurist. For the definition suggested above is only intended to provide an appropriate approach to the analysis offered below of the economic circumstances surrounding the multinational enterprises' activities on a global scale, with a view to a convenient assessment of such circumstances with regard to international law, internal law and Community law.

In introducing my study of the problems arising in the world of law from the activities of 'multinational enterprises',[8] let me clarify that this phrase is used

---

società controllante per gli illeciti delle proprie controllate, *op. loc. cit.*, which is here referred to, especially pp. 348 and 350 f., for a comparative analysis in relation to Italian law. The Milan (Criminal) District Court has recently held *Siemens AG* liable for failure to comply with Legislative Decree No. 231/2001, about which more in section 17 of Chapter I hereabove.

7. For this topic, generally, see below, section 21 of this Chapter V, where further references are made to Chapter IV.

8. No comprehensive presentation can be given here of the endless bibliography on so stimulating issues as those typical of multinational enterprises. For there are a number of studies that, since the 1970s, have examined and described the different aspects of the phenomenon, especially in economic and socio-political terms. Therefore, without even the least pretension to completeness, I refer, in addition to the Authors already cited in this section, to the many references contained in the Document of the UN Secretariat, *Multinational Corporations*, cit., especially footnotes at pp. 6 f., and 118 f., See also, essentially, in general terms: Donner, *The World-Wide Industrial Enterprise* (New York, 1967), and Italian translation thereof entitled *L'impresa multinazionale. L'esperienza mondiale della General Motors* (Milan, 1969); Menderhausen, *Transnational Society* v. *State Sovereignity*, in Kyklos (Internationales Zeitschrift fuœr Sozialwissenschaften), 1969, p. 251 f., and references therein; Rolfe, 'Les sociétés multinationales. Leur droits et responsabilités', a report presented to the XXII Congress of the International Chamber of Commerce (Istanbul, 31 May-7 Jun. 1969); Hermanns, 'Multinationale Unternehemen im Vormarsch' [1969] Wirtschaftsdienst, p. 215 f.; Vagts, 'The Multinational Enterprise. A new Challenge for Transnational Law' [1969-1970] Harvard Law Rev., p. 739 f.; Schmitthoff, 'Multi-National Companies' [1970] Journal of Business Law, p. 177 f.; Id., 'Multinationals in

Court', ibidem, 1972, p. 103 f.; Vernon, *Les entreprises multinationales. La souveraineté nationale en péril* (Paris, 1973); Troeller, 'Multinational Corporation in a Changing Europe' [1973] Journal of World Trade Law, p. 293 f.; Galbraith, 'La grande impresa al servizio della collettività', general report presented to the X CIRIEC International Congress in Hamburg, in Economia pubblica, (1974), Nos 8-9, p. 3 f. The Author last cited identified the source of the negative aspects of multinationals' operations in the deficiencies of public control over them in their home States, as well as in the current crisis of corporate structures (especially in the USA). See also: Lazarus, Leben, Lyon-Caen & Verdier, *'L'entreprise multinationale face au droit'* (Paris, 1977); Francioni, *Imprese multinazionali, protezione diplomatica e responsabilità internazionale*, (Milan, 1979), p. 137 ff.; Dunning, *International Production and the Multinational Enterprise* (London, 1981); Wallace, *Legal Control of the Multinational Enterprise* (London, 1982); Lall, *The Multinational Corporations* (New York, 1983); Caves, *Multinational Enterprise and Economic Analysis* (4th ed., Cambridge, 1985); Simmonds, *Multinationals Corporations Law*, (Dobbs Ferry, New York, 1986); Sacerdoti, 'Les codes de conduite sur les entreprises multinationales entre droit international et droit interne, mise en oeuvre et effets juridiques', in *Il diritto internazionale al tempo della sua codificazione*, Studi in onore di Roberto Ago, vol. IV (Milan, 1987), p. 263 f.; Id., 'L'impresa multinazionale come gruppo internazionale di società' [1988] Giur. comm. I, p. 62, Barba Navaretti, Vanables, *Multinational Firms in the World Economy* (Princeton, 2004); Barreveld, *The Enron Collapse: Creative Accounting, Wrong Economics or Criminal Acts?* (San José, 2002); Baxi, Paul, *Mass Disasters and Multinational Liability: the Bhopal Case* (Bombay, 1986); Bazoli, *Mercato e disuguaglianza* (Brescia, 2006); Blumberg, *The Multinational Challenge to Corporation Law: the Search for a New Corporate Personality* (Oxford, 1993); Id., 'Asserting Human Rights against Multinational Corporations under United States Law: Conceptual and Procedural Problems' [2002] AJCL 50, p. 493 ff.; Borzi, *La parabola Enron* (Milan, 2002); Boschiero, 'La lex mercatoria nell'era della globalizzazione: considerazioni di diritto internazionale pubblico e privato' [2005] Sociologia del diritto, p. 83 ff.; Brewer, Young, *The Multilateral Investment System and Multinational Enterprises* (Oxford, 1998); Di Blase, 'La Dichiarazione OCSE sugli investimenti e le imprese multinazionali', in Giardina, Tosato, (a cura di), *Diritto del commercio internazionale* (Milan, 1996), p. 409 ff.; Karl, 'The OECD Guidelines for Multinational Enterprises' in Addo, ed., *Human Rights Standards and the Responsibility of Transnational Corporations* (The Hague, 1999), p. 89 ff.; Malanczuk, 'Multinational Enterprises and Treaty-Making: A Contribution to the Discussion on Non-State Actors and the Subjects of International Law', in Gowland-Debbas, V. ed., *Multilateral Treaty-Making: The Current Status of Challenges to and Reforms Needed in the International Legislative Process* (The Hague, 2000), p. 45 e ff.; Santa Maria, 'Il diritto internazionale dell'economia', cit. p. 499 ff.; Leben, 'L'activité des entreprises dans une économie mondialisée et le droit international public', in *I Rapporti economici internazionali e l'evoluzione del loro regime giuridico, soggetti, valori e strumenti*, XII Convegno, Milan 8-9 giugno 2007, by Boschiero and Luzzatto, Eds. (Naples, 2008), p. 59 ss.

As for the European Union, in addition to the old-dated Commission Communication Multinational Undertakings and Community Regulations, in *Bull. EC.*, 1973, and more recent documents from Community institutions, which are referred to further below, please refer to: Leleux, *Création des sociétés multinationales*, doc. 965/70 (Bruxelles, 1970); Carbone, 'Le imprese multinazionali, area dell'economia comunitaria e ambito di operatività delle regole sulla concorrenza' [1974] Giur. it. IV, c. 197 f.; Campologno e Grisoli, *Le imprese plurinazionali a vocazione europea* (Padua, 1972); Schmitthoff, 'Aspetti giuridici delle imprese multinazionali nell'ambito della CEE' [1972] Dir. scambi int., p. 335 f.; Id., 'The Role of the Multinational Enterprise, in an Enlarged European Community', in Bathurst, Simmonds, Hunnings, Welch, *Legal Problems of an Enlarged European Community* (London, 1972), p. 211 f.; Santa Maria, 'Imprese multinazionali e Comunità economica europea', cit., *loc. cit.*, and, Borgia, *La responsabilità sociale delle imprese multinazionali* (Naples, 2007), p. 139 ff.

below in its broadest meaning, i.e. in the sense of *enterprises of a complex structure controlled by a company national of a given State but established in more than one country.*[9]

Unlike the definition most frequently used elsewhere, the one just given above highlights a major feature of the present-day multinational enterprise. This is less because it is suggestive of the multinational *group* structure in which multinational enterprises have invariably occurred in the legal context, than, and mainly, because it stresses the presence of a 'national' *company* at the top of the group, which is, as such, linked to a given jurisdiction – a factor not without relevance in international law, as will be seen further below.

It is also appropriate to say beforehand that it would be neither correct nor useful to describe multinational enterprises' activities only in negative terms.

As observed in the OECD Guidelines for Multinational Enterprises,[10] first:

> The activities of multinational enterprises, through international trade and investment, have strengthened and deepened the ties that join OECD economies to each other and to the rest of the world. These activities bring substantial benefits to home and host countries,

and, secondly:

> The common aim of the governments adhering to the Guidelines is to encourage the positive contributions that multinational enterprises can make to *economic, environmental and social progress* and to minimise the difficulties to which their various operations may give rise. In working towards this goal, governments find themselves in partnership with the many businesses, trade unions and other non-governmental organisations that are working in their own ways toward the same end. Governments can help by providing effective domestic policy frameworks that include *stable macroeconomic policy, non-discriminatory treatment* of firms, *appropriate regulation and prudential supervision*, an *impartial system of courts and law enforcement and efficient and honest public administration*. Governments can also help by maintaining and promoting appropriate standards and policies in support of sustainable development and by engaging in ongoing reforms to ensure that public sector activity is efficient and effective. [*Emphasis added*].

---

9. See *The OECD Guidelines for Multinational Enterprises, Revision 2000*, 2000 ILM 40, 237 ff., a companion of a sort, which contains recommendations on responsible business conduct addressed to multinationals by the governments of the 29 OECD Member States plus Argentina, Brazil, Chile and the Slovak Republic – thus 33 States overall. Although the OECD Guidelines are based on the assumption that defining 'multinational enterprises' would be pointless, they specify that this phrase should be understood to include 'companies or other entities established in more than one country and so linked that they may co-ordinate their operations in various ways'. This vague definition ignores any reference to an *organic* group and a parent company, and so it appears to favour an *anonymous* type of multinational enterprises which I believe to be no longer of any use. That is why I am inclined to prefer the definition suggested in the narrative above.
10. See *The Guidelines*, cit., *ibid.*, 238.

These statements, which come from one of the most substantial international observatories across the world's industrialized countries, acknowledge the positive role multinational enterprises can play in securing a well-balanced development of world trade. Hence the significance of the phenomenon and the legal scholar's interest in analysing and studying it in its physiological aspects even before looking into its pathology.[11]

3. MULTINATIONAL ENTERPRISES AND INTERNATIONAL LAW IN A CHANGING WORLD

In principle and from a general point of view, it is easy to identify two 'interests' at stake in the international enterprises' activities, both of which deserve protection. One is the obviously pressing need for multinational enterprises to be accorded utmost protection of their investments in a foreign State. The other is such foreign State's need to prevent any power centres, oftentimes even stronger economically than the State itself, from influencing public policies to a more or less consequential extent.

The issue becomes even more difficult to handle when a multinational enterprise has an establishment to conduct organized economic activities in a developing country.[12]

> *Foreign investments* constitute one form of property, rights or interests, and as such *are in principle entitled to the protection of international law*. Since the kinds and methods of such investment are numerous and varied, and since they are still *in the process of expansion and development*, it is inevitable that at the present stage of their evolution *new circumstances and unfamiliar features* will be encountered in the protection of such rights and interests in the international field. But in essence *they all fall within the compass of the general rule of diplomatic and judicial protection of international law*. What is really involved is *the basic principle of protection* (. . .). [*Emphasis added*].[13]

The protection of foreign investments under international law, within the compass, that is, of 'the general rule of diplomatic and judicial protection of international law', as Judge Wellington Koo clearly and effectively put it in the above quotation, gives rise to some complex problems.

---

11. The *Statement by the Chair of the Ministerial*, Jun. 2000, annexed to *The Guidelines*, cit., 5, reads: '*The Guidelines are recommendations on responsible business conduct addressed by governments to multinational enterprises operating in or from the 33 adhering countries*'.
12. See the considerations offered in Chapter IV, on the widening gap between the developing countries that have remained so and industrialized countries as a result of globalization.
13. Thus Judge Wellington Koo in his Separate Opinion in the first judgment in *Barcelona Traction Light & Power Co. Ltd.*, in I.C.J., *Report* (1964), 55.

According to a basic practice first emerged in the mid-1880s and later developed in the early decades of last century,[14] these problems have re-emerged of late in connection with the well-known case of the Canadian company, *Barcelona Traction Light & Power Company Ltd*, which had been declared bankrupt in Spain. The case was finally decided by the International Court of Justice in The Hague at the end of multiyear proceedings in which Belgium, the supposedly offended State, as the national State of the vast majority (about 88%) of the Canadian company's shareholders, sought reparation against Spain, the purportedly offending State.

The case was decided by the International Court of Justice in two orders. The first was an interlocutory judgment dated 24 July 1964,[15] in which two of four preliminary objections raised by Spain were rejected and the remaining two were joined to the merits. In the second, final judgment, entered on 5 February 1970,[16] the Court granted the third preliminary objection according to which Belgium lacked *jus standi* to exercise diplomatic protection of shareholders in a Canadian company. The Court did, however, withhold a ruling on the fourth preliminary objection raised by Spain to the effect that the requirement of the exhaustion of local remedies had not been met.

Prior exhaustion of local remedies is a prerequisite to diplomatic protection under international law.[17] The issue was raised once more before the International Court of Justice in *Elettronica Sicula SpA (ELSI)* (United States of America *v.* Italy), a case decided by a judgment of the Chamber delivered on 20 July 1989.[18]

---

14. For an extensive study of international practice in relation to the diplomatic protection of companies and shareholders, see: Battaglini, *La protezione diplomatica delle società*, (Padua, 1957); de Visscher, 'La protection diplomatique des personnes morales' [1961] Rec. des cours I, vol. 102, p. 399 f.; Santa Maria, 'La tutela dei soci nel diritto internazionale' [1965] Riv. società, p. 1088 f.; Francioni, *Imprese multinazionali*, cit., p. 57 f. See also: Gianelli, 'La protezione diplomatica di società dopo la sentenza concernente la Barcelona Traction' [1986] Riv. dir. int., p. 726 f.; Seidl-Hohenveldern, *Corporations in and under International Law* (Cambridge, 1987), especially p. 7 f.; Amerasinghe, *Local Remedies in International Law* (Cambridge, 1990).
15. See in *C.I.J., Recueil des arrêts, avis consultatifs et ordonnances* (1964), p. 3 f.
16. See in *C.I.J., Recueil*, cit., 1970, p. 3 f.
17. For this approach, see: Ago, 'La regola del previo esaurimento dei ricorsi interni in tema di responsabilità internazionale' [1938] Arch. dir. pubbl., p. 182 f.; Gaja, *L'esaurimento dei ricorsi interni nel diritto internazionale* (Milan, 1967). It is neither useful nor indispensable at this time to discuss at length the rule of the prior exhaustion of local remedies. Suffice it to refer – along with the proposition offered by Ago and shared by Morelli (Dissenting Opinion on the decision of 24 Jul. 1964 of the International Court of Justice on preliminary objections in *Barcelona Traction Light & Power Company Ltd.*, cit., *C.I. J., Recueil*, cit., p. 114), according to which prior exhaustion of local remedies is a substantive rule of international law – to the opposite scholarly view according to which it is a rule of procedure, i.e. a precondition for the exercise in proceedings of the offended State's right following a violation already perfected since the commission by the offending State of the relevant injurious act or fact. In this last sense, see: Fawcett, 'The Exhaustion of Local Remedies - Substance or Procedure?' [1954] Br. Yearbook Int. Law, vol. XXXI, p. 452 f.; and Law, *The Local Remedies Rule in International Law* (Geneva-Paris, 1961).
18. The ICG's judgment in *Elsi* has already been cited in section 12 of Chapter I of this study.

In that action, Italy had objected to the admissibility of the United States' claim because the two United States corporations, *Raytheon* and *Machlett*, as the only shareholders of the Italian company *Raytheon-Elsi SpA* (one-time *Elettronica Sicula SpA*), declared bankrupt by the Tribunal of Palermo on 16 May 1968, had allegedly failed to exhaust all the local remedies available to them in the Italian judicial system. The United States questioned whether the rule of the exhaustion of local remedies could apply at all in relation to an action brought pursuant to Article XXVI of the Treaty of Friendship, Commerce and Navigation concluded between the two parties in 1948, which made no reference to the local remedies rule. In the view of the United States:

> [I]t seemed right (. . .) to conclude that the parties to the FCN Treaty, had they intended the jurisdiction conferred upon the Court to be qualified by the local remedies rule in cases of diplomatic protection, *would have used express words* to that effect; as was done in an Economic Co-operation Agreement between Italy and the United States of America also concluded in 1948.[19] [*Emphasis added*].

The ICJ took a different view, though, in its judgment of 20 July 1989:

> The Chamber has no doubt that the parties to a treaty can therein either agree that the local remedies rule shall not apply to claims based on alleged breaches of that treaty; or confirm that it shall apply. Yet the Chamber finds itself *unable to accept that an important principle of customary international law should be held to have been tacitly dispensed with*, in the absence of any words making clear an intention to do so. This part of the United States response to the Italian objection must therefore be rejected.[20] [*Emphasis added*].

However, the Court rejected Italy's objection, holding that Italy had apparently failed to give sufficient proof that suitable remedies enforceable before domestic courts were available to the two US corporations at the time the dispute first arose.[21]

Once all possible local remedies have been resorted to, but to no avail, or the private entity concerned is unable to defend adequately before domestic courts (in which case the resulting hindrance would amount to a new, separate violation by the host State of international law, namely a 'denial of justice'), the matter exceeds the domestic scope to turn into an (international) dispute between States.

Thereupon, the offended State, and *it alone*, is accorded the right to choose, at its own discretion, whether or not to exercise diplomatic protection of its citizens

---

19. See *Elettronica Sicula S.p.A. (ELSI), C.I.J. Recueil*, 1989, p. 42 f.
20. *Ibid., loc. cit.*
21. *Ibid.*, p. 47 f. In fact, the Court eventually granted Italy's defence and rejected the USA's claims on the merits. About this case, see: Radicati di Brozolo, 'Protezione diplomatica delle società e degli azionisti e trattato di amicizia Italia-Stati Uniti: il caso Raytheon-Elsi dinnanzi alla Corte internazionale di Giustizia' [1990] Dir. comm. int., p. 385 f., and Kubiatowski, 'The case of Elettronica Sicula S.p.A.: Towards greater protection of shareholders' rights in foreign investments' [1991] Col. Jour. of Transnational Law, p. 215 f.

or nationals, on the ground that customary or treaty-based standards of treatment of aliens in international law were violated. With respect to the offending State, it is only at that time – i.e. if the offended State chooses to defend its national's case as its own – that an 'international' dispute sets in.

Back to the general issue, in its 1970 judgment at the end of the second phase of the *Barcelona Traction* case, the International Court of Justice set some firm points about the right for the State or States of which a company or its shareholders are nationals or citizens, as the case may be, to take up their diplomatic protection, in accordance, in fact, with precedent in international practice.

The ICJ first considered that, unlike violations of such international *erga omnes* obligations as those deriving from the outlawing of acts of aggression and of genocide, as also from the principles and rules concerning the basic rights of the human person, including protection from slavery and racial discrimination, violations of obligations entailing *diplomatic protection* – e.g. when one State, the offending State, violates rights ensured by international law rules on treatment of aliens, thereby harming natural or legal persons citizens or nationals, as the case may be, of another State – create rights *solely* for the national State of the private person so harmed, i.e. the *offended* State, as the only party having *jus standi* against the *offending* State.[22]

4 of the exhaustion of local remedies, for a State to be able to plead diplomatic protection against the second type of violations in international law, an international standard of treatment of aliens must have been violated by one State against another's private individuals. Then, if such a violation has occurred, such other State alone will be the party *offended* by the violation of an international obligation, and, accordingly, the *only one* party entitled to claim reparation on its own behalf against the *offending* State.[23]

As the Permanent Court of International Justice held in its judgment of 28 February 1939 deciding the *Panevezys-Saldutiskis Railway* case:[24]

> This right is necessarily limited to intervention on behalf of its own nationals because, in the absence of a special agreement, it is the bond of nationality between the State and the individual which alone confers upon the State the right of diplomatic protection.

In *Barcelona Traction*,[25] the ICJ, after referring to this judgment of the Permanent International Court of Justice, stated:

> Diplomatic protection deals with a very sensitive area of international relations, *since the interest of a foreign State in the protection of its nationals confronts the rights of the territorial sovereign*, a fact of which the general

---

22. See *Barcelona Traction* judgment of 1970, cit., p. 32 f. of the decision, paragraphs 33, 34 and 35.
23. This was, in fact, the approach taken in the *Advisory Opinion* of the International Court of Justice about *Reparation for Injuries Suffered in the Service of the United Nations*, in *C.I.J., Recueil*, 1949, p. 181 f.
24. See *C.P.J.I.*, Sèrie A/B, N. 76, p. 16 f.
25. See decision of 1970, paragraph 37, p. 33.

law on the subject has had to take cognizance in order to prevent abuses and friction. From its origins closely linked with international commerce, diplomatic protection has sustained a particular impact from the growth of international economic relations, and at the same time from the profound transformations which have taken place in the economic life of nations. *These latter changes* have given birth *to municipal institutions, which have transcended frontiers* and have *begun to exercise considerable influence on international relations.* One of these phenomena which has a particular bearing on the present case is the corporate entity. [*Emphasis added*].

It is a settled rule in international practice that, if an international standard of treatment of aliens in general is violated, it is for the State of which a body corporate is a national – as is the case with private individuals – to exercise diplomatic protection of that body corporate, subject to an express limiting condition, though, in this as well as in the case of natural persons. Since as early as the mid-1800s, a firm requirement has developed in international practice according to which – though without automatically extending the International Court of Justice's specific holding in *Nottebohm*[26] to corporate entities – there must be some degree of 'actuality', *in addition to nationality* as attributed under the internal law, in order to strengthen the relationship of a corporation with its home State, i.e. the 'real link' or 'real bond' that makes that attribution of nationality by a State internationally valid and allows that State, accordingly, to intervene for the protection, and on behalf, of its corporate national.[27]

Thus, as far as past diplomatic practice was concerned, the States would normally refrain from asserting the right to exercise diplomatic protection of their corporate nationals whenever the link of the State with a specific company was merely that internal link, nationality, in the absence, that is, of a real link.[28]

---

26. Please, refer to the well-known judgments of 18 Nov. 1953, and of 6 Apr. 1955, in *C.I.J., Recueil*, cit., 1953, p. 111 f., and *ibid.*, 1955, p. 4 f., especially p. 20, respectively. The Court held that, although conferring Lichtenstein citizenship on an individual of German origin, Mr Nottebohm was lawful in itself, it could not, under international law, be enforced against Guatemala (the State against which the complaint had been filed) because of the lack of a 'real link' between the natural person in question and the complaining State.
27. For an extensive examination of the developments in diplomatic practice and in international arbitration practice, see my study, 'La tutela dei soci', cit., especially p. 1092 f.
28. For the univocal attitude of US diplomacy in this sense, see the cases discussed in Hackworth, *Digest of International Law, United States Government* (Washington, 1943), vol. V, p. 837 f., in particular: *Tai Hongo Co. and American Presbyterian Missionary Society* (U.S. Foreign Relations 1901, p. 64-68); *Guayaquil & Quito Co.* (U.S. Foreign Relations 1912, p. 412-422). A similar position was taken by the British Government in *Orinoco Shipping and Trading Co.* (U.S. Foreign Relations 1908, p. 780 f.; see also The Orinoco Steamship Company Limited, Documents presentés par le représentant du Venezuela devant le Tribunal de la Cour Permanente d'Arbitrage de la Haye, constituée conformément au protocole Vénéquélién-Américain passé à Caracas le 13 février 1909); and *Trading Corporation of Enrique Cortes and Co.* (Mc Nair, International Law Opinions, vol. II, Cambridge, 1956, p. 38).

Arbitral practice would invariably fall into line.[29]

In international practice, another issue emerged beside the general norm of the exercise of diplomatic protection of corporate nationals in the sense just indicated above. The question was whether or not it was for the national State of a company's shareholders to exercise such protection concurrently with the company's own national State.

The first genuine claims ever brought forward by States (Britain and the United States, respectively) to protect their citizens internationally against the harm the latter had incurred as the shareholders of a business company of a different (Portuguese) nationality date back to *McMurdo*, also known as the *Delagoa Bay Railway* case.[30]

The documents and notes the parties exchanged in the initial, diplomatic phase of the proceeding show that the intervention of Britain and the United States against Portugal was primarily based on the belief that their nationals shareholders of a Portuguese railway company had been unjustly harmed in consequence of the seizure by the Portuguese authorities of the company's assets.[31]

Yet, the essential element was deemed to be the real impossibility for the British and American nationals to obtain justice through the Portuguese company, either under the internal legal system – because the company had become *extinguished in fact*, and consequently made unable in practice to protect its own and its shareholders' interests validly through its corporate bodies – or under international law, because the company was a *national of the very offending State*, and did not, as such, have any protection for itself, since the customary law rules on the treatment of *foreign* companies could not be pleaded for its benefit.

On 8 November 1889, in a note of instructions addressed to Mr Loring, the US ambassador in Lisbon, the US Secretary of State, Mr Blaine, founded his government's attitude on the argument that:

> the Portuguese company *finding herself without any action to be brought and having practically closed the activity*, the only option available for those whose ownership have been confiscated is represented by their respective Governments' intervention. [*Emphasis added*].[32]

---

29. Among decisions in case-law, all of them based on the same approach, please refer to: *Compagnie Générale des Eaux de Caracas* (Ralston, *Venezuelan Arbitrations of 1903*, Washington, 1904, p. 271-291); *Panama Star & Herald Company* (U.S. Foreign Relations 1899, p. 218-241); *I'm Alone*, (*N.U. Recueil des sentences arbitrales*, vol. III, p. 1611-18); *George D. Emery Company* (U.S. Foreign Relations 1901, p. 406-467); and *Westhold Corporation* (Am. Jour. Int. Law, vol. XLVII, 1953, 623 f.). For the criteria followed by the commissions instituted for the allocation of global indemnities on the basis of treaties entered into after the nationalizations of the early post-war period, see: Santa Maria, 'La tutela dei soci', cit., p. 1139 f.
30. See *Sentence Finale du tribunal Arbitral de Delagoa concernant le chemin de fer de Lourenço Marques* du 29 mars 1900, Berne, Imprimerie Coopérative, 1900.
31. See in *Parliamentary Papers*,1890, Africa, I, 58.
32. See in U S. Foreign Relations, 1902, 808 ff.

Similar arguments were offered, on the British side, by the Marquess of Salisbury in a note of instructions dated 10 September 1889 to the British ambassador in Lisbon.

The approach taken in *Delagoa* has constantly been adopted in the practice of international arbitration since then.[33]

Thus, in light of settled practice, a fair proposition is that a customary norm has set in according to which the conduct of another State is considered *exceptionally illegal* towards the national State of a company's shareholders for violations of an international rule on treatment of aliens, much as they are perpetrated direct against that company, so long as either of two conditions occurs.

One such condition is that the offending State is the same as the national State of the company. Another occurs where the 'internal' nationality nexus between the State and the company concerned is not matched by an *internationally valid nationality*, precisely because of the lack of a *real* bond, which is, as indicated above, a prerequisite to give the company's *national* State *jus standi* to exercise diplomatic protection in addition to that essential *formal* bond, nationality.[34]

Since it is only in either case that the offending State is liable to the shareholders' home State, the result is that, in international law, the protection of the shareholders, then the legitimate exercise by their national State of their diplomatic protection against damages *directly* incurred by the company having a different nationality, is of a *merely residual import*. For the right of diplomatic protection of the shareholders cannot be pleaded in the face of an internationally relevant right of diplomatic protection pertaining to the company's own national State.

Whether or not the company's national state chooses to rely on its *locus standi* to exercise diplomatic protection has no relevance in this respect. For diplomatic protection is a right which the offended State alone has full discretion to exercise. In exercising a right recognized to the State, not to any of its nationals, from the point of view of international law, it is for the State alone to decide whether or not to exercise diplomatic protection, whether and how to come to a settlement or even to decline to pursue the action, thereby sacrificing its national's individual interest in view of superior political exigencies, without its national having any recourse against it, not even under that State's internal law.[35]

33. See arbitral award by Cleveland, President of the United States, in *Cerruti*, Italy *v* Colombia, in U.S. Foreign Relations, 1909, 245 ff., and 403 ff., and the arbitral award by George V, King of Great Britain, in *Alsop*, United States *v* Chile, in U.S. Foreign Relations, 1911, 38 ff., and, more recently, the award by Arbitrator Sisnett, Judge of British Honduras, in Shufeldt, United States *v* Guatemala, in *Shufeldt Claim, U.S. Govern. Printing Office*, Washington, 1932). For an extensive analysis of these cases, see Santa Maria, 'La tutela dei soci', cit., especially p. 1139 ff.

34. See Santa Maria, 'La tutela dei soci', cit., especially p. 1129 f.

35. The only one example to the contrary at a national legislative level is a provision in the Constitution of the Weimar Republic. On this subject, see Conforti, *Diritto Internazionale*, cit., p. 209.

In fact, the conclusions I have just submitted above with respect to the protection of shareholders in international law are fully in line with the grounds set forth in the 1970 judgment in *Barcelona Traction*.[36]

The International Court of Justice found, on the one hand, that:

> It cannot, however, be contended that the corporate entity of the company *has ceased to exist*, or that *it has lost its capacity to take corporate action*. [*Emphasis added*].[37]

On the other hand, it emphasized the *existence of several real links* of the company involved with its national State, Canada, precisely further to the internal requirement of nationality.[38] In this latter respect, the Court specified that:

> In the present case, it is not disputed that the company was *incorporated in Canada* and has its *registered office* in that country. The incorporation of the company under the law of Canada was an *act of free choice*. Not only did the founders of the company seek its incorporation under Canadian law but *it has remained under that law for a period of over 50 years. It has maintained in Canada its registered office, its accounts and its share registers. Board meetings were held there for many years; it has been listed in the records of the Canadian tax authorities*. Thus *a close and permanent connection* has been established, *fortified by the passage of over half a century*. This connection is in no way weakened by the fact that the company engaged from the very outset in commercial activities outside Canada, for that was its declared object. [*Emphasis added*].

On this basis, the judgment concluded:

> Barcelona Traction's links with Canada are thus manifold.[39]

And, next below:

> Furthermore, the *Canadian nationality* of the company has received general recognition. [*Emphasis added*].

It emerges from the International Court of Justice's examination of the case that it took the view that, not only the company's statutory seat but its *real seat*, i.e. the decision-making centre of corporate action, were in Canada.[40]

In reinforcing its view that Canada had valid title to exercise diplomatic protection of the company, the Court expanded on the terms of previous statements

36. Refer, in particular, to paragraphs 64 f., 74 f. and 92 of the judgment, *ibid.*
37. See *ibid.*, paragraph 66 of the 1970 judgment, cit.
38. See *ibid.*, paragraph 69 f. of the 1970 judgment, cit.
39. See *ibid.*, paragraph 74.
40. For a view contrary to this conclusion, in fact, based on serious arguments, see: the individual opinion of Judge Jessup, *C.I.J. Recueil*, cit., p. 162 f., especially paragraph 44 f., p. 986 f., and that of Judge Gros, *C.I.J. Recueil*, cit., p. 268 f., esp.lly paragraph 22, p. 280 f. For a criticism of the Court's assumption in literature, see: Seidl-Hohenveldern, *Corporations in and under International Law*, cit., p. 9.

made by the Canadian Government, which, much as it had decided at a certain point to cease to act on behalf of the company, had:

> nonetheless retained its capacity to exercise diplomatic protection; *no legal impediment has prevented it from doing so* (. . .). [*Emphasis added*].[41]

In fact, the Court observed that the exercise of diplomatic protection is a right each State so entitled may exercise 'to whatever extent it thinks fit, for it is its own right that the State is asserting',[42] and the State 'must be viewed as the sole judge to decide whether its protection will be granted, to what extent it is granted, and when it will cease'.[43] [*Emphasis added*].

Therefore, the Court's decision on Belgium lacking *jus standing* to bring action to protect the Belgian shareholders of Barcelona Traction rested on a belief based on the Court's own analysis – right or wrong as it might be – of the facts of that specific case, to the effect that it was good right for the company's national State, Canada, to exercise diplomatic protection, which resulted in the *automatic exclusion of any subsidiary liability* to any other international entity.

Finally, in equity:

> The Court considers that the adoption of the theory of *diplomatic protection of shareholders* as such, by opening the door to *competing diplomatic claims*, could create an atmosphere of confusion and insecurity in international economic relations. [*Emphasis added*].[44]

This last observation was certainly correct so long as it implied a general, indiscriminate admissibility of international protection by the shareholders' national State, but it may entail difficulties hardly soluble in practice if a public limited company is involved, that is to say a company whose shares are offered for sale to the general public in a regulated market.[45]

Although, from a general point of view, it is irrelevant whether or not the 'control criterion' is applied to a company in establishing its internationally valid nationality – i.e. a criterion based on the nationality of the share capital owned or effectively controlled by the company's majority shareholders – it must be pointed out that this conclusion appears to be hardly in accordance either with the principle of transparency of ownership, which seems to have governed international practice in the post-war period, largely favourable to a wider protection of shareholders than that accorded by the former arbitral and diplomatic practice,[46] or with the

41. See *ibid.*, paragraph 77.
42. See *ibid.*, paragraph 78.
43. See *ibid.*, paragraph 79.
44. See *ibid.*, paragraph 96.
45. I reached a similar conclusion, before the Court's second judgment in *Barcelona Traction*, in my study frequently cited, 'La tutela dei soci', cit., p. 1144.
46. See Santa Maria, 'La tutela dei soci', cit., p. 1139 f., narrative and footnotes, where extensive references. In the same sense, see the 1970 judgment in *Barcelona Traction*, cit., paragraph 90, p. 79.

many projects to codify the matter[47] or even with the Washington Convention of 18 March 1965 on the Settlement of Investment Disputes between States and Nationals of Other States.

The 1965 Washington Convention was ratified and made enforceable in Italy as well as in the remaining signatory States,[48] and it is now by far the most significant instrument for the protection of foreign investments in other States if only one considers that it was in force in as many as 144 States in May 2007.

The Convention,

> [a]ttaching particular importance to the availability of facilities for international conciliation or arbitration to which Contracting States and nationals of other Contracting States may submit such disputes if they so desire;[49]

provides for a special relationship whereby any national of a Contracting State may take direct action against another Contracting State by lodging a request for the institution of conciliation proceedings (Article 28) or arbitration proceedings (Article 36), with a view to settling an investment dispute, subject to *the parties' consent in writing* to submit such dispute, on a case-by-case basis, to the International Centre for Settlement of Investment Disputes.[50] In fact, according to Article 26:

> Consent of the parties to arbitration under this Convention shall, unless otherwise stated, be deemed consent to such arbitration to the exclusion of any other remedy. A Contracting State may require the exhaustion of local administrative or judicial remedies as a condition of its consent to arbitration under this Convention.

---

47. Santa Maria, *op. ult. cit.*, p. 1145.
48. The Convention was ratified and made enforceable by Italy on 29 Mar. 1971, when the ratification was filed. The Convention entered into force on 28 Apr. 1971.
49. See the fourth point of the Preamble.
50. It is declared in the last point of the Preamble that: '[. . .] no Contracting State shall by the mere fact of its ratification, acceptance or approval of this Convention and without its consent be deemed to be under any obligation to submit any particular dispute to conciliation or arbitration'. Point 24 of the *Report of the Executive Directors on the Convention on the Settlement of Investment Disputes between States and Nationals of other States (www.worldbank.org/icsid/basicdoc/partB-section05.htm)* reads; 'Consent of the parties must exist when the Centre is seized (Articles 28(3) and 36(3)) but the Convention does not otherwise specify the time at which consent should be given. Consent may be given, for example, in a clause included in an investment agreement, providing for the submission to the Centre of future disputes arising out of that agreement, or in a compromise regarding a dispute which has already arisen. Nor does the Convention require that the consent of both parties be expressed in a single instrument. Thus, a host State might in its investment promotion legislation offer to submit disputes arising out of certain classes of investments to the jurisdiction of the Centre, and the investor might give his consent by accepting the offer in writing'. Out of 134 cases submitted to the Centre for a decision until Jul. 2007, 133 concerned actions brought by private investors against a State, and only one, in 1976, concerned an action brought by a State (Gabon) against a private party (*Société Serete S.A*, Case No. ARB-76/1).

In case a dispute is initiated by a private person, whether natural or juridical, 'national of another Contracting State', against a Contracting State which has given such consent, as provided for by Article 25, diplomatic protection by the former Contracting State is excluded from the proceedings. This is because, pursuant to Article 27(1):

> No Contracting State shall give diplomatic protection, or bring an international claim, in respect of a dispute which one of its nationals and another Contracting State shall have consented to submit or shall have submitted to arbitration under this Convention, unless such other Contracting State shall have failed to abide by and comply with the award rendered in such dispute.

The acceptance by a growing number of Latin American States of the arbitration mechanism set out in the 1965 Convention has emphasized the growing significance of this instrument. At the same time, widespread acceptance by those countries has shown that their aversion to international arbitration in the matter of foreign investments is fading away. Such aversion is essentially due to the 'Calvo Doctrine', which holds that diplomatic protection exercised by a foreign State goes contrary to national sovereignty, and that any dispute with foreign investors must be decided by the national courts under the domestic laws of the investment target country.[51]

In light of the foregoing, some closing remarks can be offered about the issues discussed so far.

It is appropriate to note that *Barcelona Traction* was not a multinational enterprise in the stricter sense. It did not have a structure of one; it was not a holding company nor was it one of a group of companies; it was a Canadian operating company which, at the time of the facts in dispute, had a permanent establishment in Spain through which it ran its operations in the electric power business; and a majority of its shareholders were Belgian nationals.

Therefore, the problems indicated above appear even more complex in relation to genuine 'multinational' enterprises, a phrase which, as specified above, applies to any enterprise operated essentially as one economic whole, with a closely identified parent company, in more than one jurisdiction through a number of companies, each of them being a 'national' of a given State even different from the parent company's home State.

Within this context, in light of the applicable standards of international customary law, as they emerge from the practice discussed above, the question of

---

51. For the text of the Washington Convention in the three official languages, English, French and Spanish, see the five volumes, which also contain preparatory documents, edited by the *International Centre for Settlement of Investment Disputes*, (Washington, 1968-70). The text of the Convention is reproduced in French in [1965] Riv. dir. int., p. 359 f. On the subject, see Sacerdoti, 'La Convenzione di Washington del 1965 per la soluzione delle controversie fra Stati e nazionali di altri Stati in materia di investimenti' [1969] Riv. dir. int. priv. proc., p. 614 f., with many references. See *ICSID, Documents and Publications*, available on the website: www.worldbank.org/icsid/pubs/pubs.com.

whether (i) it is for the national State of the company whose direct interests were harmed by an internationally relevant act or fact imputable to another State to have the right of protecting that company internationally, or (ii) the right of diplomatic protection belongs to the State to which the multinational enterprise appears to be most closely linked – i.e., as a rule, the national State of the parent company holding the company directly harmed – seems to be solved in the former sense.

As a consequence, even in the entirely reasonable assumption that the offending State is the same as the national State of the company in respect of which, also in light of international practice, as confirmed by the ICJ's judgment in *Barcelona Traction*, the right of diplomatic protection is exercised in favour of the national State of the parent of the subsidiary whose interests have been injured directly, the doubt remains, in the case of a complex group of companies, whether the suggested approach may apply to the national State of the 'ultimate' holding company or to the (possibly different) national State of the company having direct control over the subsidiary so harmed. In the other, equally reasonable assumption that the holding company, whichever it may be, intervenes in the proceedings, such intervention may appear problematic if some real link exists between the national State of the subsidiary and the subsidiary itself, thereby giving that State *locus standi* to exercise diplomatic protection, and so to the automatic exclusion of the shareholders' national State. If the subsidiary's national State refrains from exercising diplomatic protection, then the multinational enterprise concerned may actually be deprived of any protection at all under international law.

Still, the significance of these issues in the present state of customary international law, in a matter certainly open to derogation, is somewhat attenuated by the existence of multilateral or bilateral international agreements.

Suffice it to mention that, in defining the phrase 'National of another Contracting State' to determine the extent of jurisdiction of the International Centre for Settlement of Investment Disputes, Article 25(2)(b) of the Washington Convention of 18 March 1965 on the Settlement of Investment Disputes between States and Nationals of Other States specifies that that phrase also means:

> *any juridical person* which had the nationality of a Contracting State other than the State party to the dispute on the date on which the parties consented to submit such dispute to conciliation or arbitration *and any juridical person* which had the nationality of the Contracting State party to the dispute on that date and which, *because of foreign control, the parties have agreed should be treated as a national of another Contracting State for the purposes of this Convention.* [*Emphasis added*].

This prospective approach was confirmed by some hints contained in the ICJ's *Barcelona Traction* judgment:[52]

> Considering the important developments of the last half-century, the growth of foreign investments and the expansion of the international activities of

52. See Judgment of 5 Feb. 1970, *ibid.*, paragraph 89.

> corporations, in particular of holding companies, which are often multinational, and considering the way in which the economic interests of States have proliferated, it may at first sight appear surprising that *the evolution of law has not gone further and that no generally accepted rules in the matter have crystallized on the international plane*. Nevertheless, a more thorough examination of the facts shows that *the law on the subject has been formed in a period characterized by an intense conflict of systems and interests*. It is essentially *bilateral relations* which have been concerned, relations in which the rights of both the State exercising diplomatic protection and the State in respect of which protection is sought *have had to be safeguarded*. Here as elsewhere, a body of rules *could only have developed with the consent of those concerned*. The difficulties encountered have been reflected in the evolution of the law on the subject. [*Emphasis added*].

In the same judgment of 1970, the International Court of Justice went on to invoke a more extensive recourse to stipulated solutions between States or even of direct agreements between States and foreign companies for the protection of the latter's investments:[53]

> Thus, in the present state of the law, *the protection of shareholders requires that recourse be had to treaty stipulations or special agreements* directly concluded between the private investor and the State in which the investment is placed. States ever more frequently provide for such protection, in both bilateral and multilateral relations, either by means of special instruments or within the framework of wider economic arrangements. Indeed, *whether in the form of multilateral or bilateral treaties* between States, or in that of agreements *between States and companies*, there has *since the Second World War* been *considerable development* in the protection of foreign investments. The instruments in question contain provisions as to jurisdiction and procedure in case of disputes concerning the treatment of investing companies by the States in which they invest capital. Sometimes companies are themselves vested with a *direct right to defend their interests* against States through prescribed procedures. No such instrument is in force between the Parties to the present case. [*Emphasis added*].

One last point on the subject is that, more than 35 years after that judgment, the terms of the problem appear to be far different in yet another respect. The present, fast-developing regulatory framework of international trade, by shifting its emphasis to macroeconomic issues about which the States directly confront each other in specifically recognized venues, has softened the significance of the limitations that prevailed at that time. Let me stress that, with respect to all the macroeconomic matters subject to international regulation, the States take action *on their own behalf*, against alleged violations of obligations undertaken by other States to them, before international courts and for the 'general protection' of entire national

53. See Judgment of 5 Feb. 1970, *ibid.*, paragraph 90.

industries, i.e. outside the exercise of the diplomatic protection of one or another private national.[54]

4. MULTINATIONAL ENTERPRISES AND THE EUROPEAN UNION

It must preliminary be said that the problems associated with 'multinational enterprises' are viewed in a special perspective within the European Union in contrast with the general propositions offered above.

For the conflicting interests discussed before are only seldom to be found or can only be found in subdued terms within the European Union.

In fact, there is no or just little anxiety about possible interferences by any highly industrialized Member State with another Member State's public policy, since all of them enjoy equal rights and look forward to political unity.

Nor can be there any anxiety about protecting the investments a company national of one Member State has made in another Member State in a fully fledged legal system such as the one set up in the European Union. For it is a system ideally suited to ensure full observance of the *four fundamental freedoms* in the (single) internal market. In this respect, it is reinforced by a harmonized judicial system and by the free circulation of national courts' decisions in civil and commercial matters.[55] Pursuant to the second paragraph of Article 14 EC (former Article 7 of the Single European Act):

> The internal market shall comprise an area without internal frontiers in which the free movement of goods, persons, services and capital is ensured in accordance with the provisions of this Treaty.

Subject to the limitations indicated below,[56] even companies belonging to third countries may set up establishments within the European Union, whereupon they will be fully entitled, in the presence of the contact factors required by Article 48(1) EC, to receive the same treatment under Articles 43 et seq. and 49 et seq. EC as Community companies and firms, as these are defined in the second paragraph of Article 48 EC, so long as they meet the requirements set forth in the first paragraph of Article 48 EC.

---

54. In this connection, see my considerations in Chapter IV of this volume, *passim*, in particular section 12.
55. The phrase 'four *fundamental* freedoms' has been coined by Monaco, in the article 'Comunità economica europea' in *Enciclopedia del diritto*, vol. VIII, (Milan, 1961), p. 319 f., p. 321. The Author argues that, precisely by virtue of the provisions for the protection of the four fundamental freedoms, 'the contents of the Treaty on the Economic Community rises above not only one on customs union but also one on a common market for the accomplishment of an actual economic union'. A similar approach has been taken by Levi Sandri, in *Commentario C.E.E.* (Chief Editors Quadri, Monaco and Trabucchi), I, cit., p. 380 f. On the subject, see my considerations in Chapter IV of this volume, *passim*.
56. Please, refer to my considerations in section 25 of this Chapter V. For a discussion of the evolution of the right of establishment and the free provision of services within the European Union, see Chapter I of this volume.

5. THE FEATURES OF THE PHENOMENON IN GENERAL: UNRESTRICTED FREEDOM OF CHOICE AND THE RESULTING BASIC DISTORTIONS OF COMPETITION

The starting point of any discourse about multinational enterprises is the fact that enterprises operating in more than one jurisdictions are typically free to take advantage of any differences between domestic legal systems in a variety of sectors, from company to labour, tax and currency laws, by taking the most favourable approach in concrete terms, from time to time, to any problems associated with their business operations, from research to manufacturing, from logistics to sales.[57]

For the sake of clarity, it is appropriate to specify that the *modus operandi* typical of multinational enterprises is not far removed from the methods applied by any enterprise having solely domestic dimensions and interests. The fundamental difference lies with the fact that the any domestic enterprise seeks optimum, then the legally most favourable, conditions in the national context in performing a specific operation. This is why, for example, if a purely national company wants to set up a manufacturing plant, it will tend to do so in an area categorized as depressed within its own national State, in order to take advantage of any extra tax benefits or even State aid as are available under the law. By contrast, whenever multinational enterprises able to rely on a huge amount of its own or third-party financial resources have engaged in similar operations, they have, for forty years or so, invariably tended to make their choices among the many most favourable opportunities available to them *worldwide*, thus avoiding, or at least making up for, any adverse (even if indirect) impact as might affect them in any one country.

The aptitude multinational enterprises have thus shown to move around the folds of individual legal systems is highly consequential. For it entails the taking by them of a *basic economic advantage* over any other enterprise only operating with

57. There could be no doubts on this. See, in particular: *U.N., Multinational Corporations*, cit., p. 2; Carbone, 'Imprese multinazionali', cit., c. 198; Sacerdoti, *Le imprese multinazionali*, cit., p. 24. According to Commission Communication on *Multinational Undertakings and Community Regulations*, cit., the area that best reveals these problems is taxation. For 'the very existence of disparities in tax systems has inevitably led multinational undertakings to attempt to protect themselves and even to use them in a way considered improper by some' (p. 6). About the so-called 'tax havens' in a worldwide perspective, from the tax legislation of Bermuda to those of the Cayman Islands, the Channel Islands of Jersey and Guernsey, Lichtenstein or Luxembourg, see, essentially: Grundy, *Tax Havens* (London, 1972), esp.lly p. 97 f., Langer, *How to Use Foreign Tax Havens* (New York, 1975), and Chambost, *Guida ai Paradisi Fiscali*, ed. it. by Grande Stevens (Milan, 1978). For notions on company law and on tax provisions in the European countries commonly considered to be 'tax havens', see again, essentially: Benini, *Le società civili e commerciali nei paesi minori d'Europa* (Padua, 1964), p. 67 f. and 103 f. for Guernsey; 107 f. and 141 f. for Jersey; 147 f. and 241 f. for Liechtenstein and 251 f. and 307 f. for Luxembourg. I do not believe a better tax treatment is the current main driver of multinationals' *modus operandi*. Although tax rules are a major component of overall corporate choices, other factors seem to be at play, such as the way in which costs are generated as a result of the location of production factors and the organization of logistics and distribution worldwide.

a domestic view. This advantage is protected by law most of the times and, therefore, fortified by the indiscriminate application of the competition laws in force in the relevant market to multinational as well as to national enterprises.

Wherever free competition prevails, a multinational enterprise has a special interest – only limited by the advisability of avoiding monopolistic behaviours or the abuse of dominant positions, within the meaning of European antitrust law – in demanding that the rules of each individual legal system in which it operates be strictly applied. This is because all of its competitors of a purely domestic size and with merely domestic interests are unable to make up, as the multinational enterprise can do, for the disadvantages arising from compliance with one jurisdiction's national law with the advantages of using the most favourable sector-specific rules in force in other jurisdictions.

In other words, the end-result is that, in a given legal system, certain economic interests are more closely protected, in terms of substantive justice, than others of the same nature. The point is that the advantages thus arising to the multinational enterprises are not acquired *unlawfully*, because the favourable 'legislative' treatment the multinational enterprises benefit from is a result of full compliance by them with the rules of law, even mandatory ones, that are in force in each of the legal systems in which their domestic competitors operate 'at a disadvantage'.

As the phenomenon was already quite sizeable in the 1970s, it must be conceded that certain entities have long been granted actual 'freedom of abuse' in fact, in the sense that, by establishing an appropriate vehicle in a country specifically chosen for the purpose – whose rules are strictly abided by, without either the host State's or the home State's laws being breached – any multinational enterprise can place itself in a preferential position from which, thanks to its managers' expedient business choice, it is enabled to carry out any one specific operation under the most advantageous economic and/or regulatory conditions.

In order to identify the phenomenon under scrutiny closely enough, no relevance can be ascribed to the *artificial alteration* of the real terms of trade between a holding company and its subsidiaries or between companies otherwise related to each other and operating in different jurisdictions. This is simply because that would be a case of behaviours *unlawful* in themselves from the point of view of each of the jurisdictions involved, to the extent such behaviours result in violating rules on financial reporting, tax evasion or customs procedures. The fact that these unlawful behaviours may be not easily detected by any one State's authorities, or may otherwise go unpunished, is a direct result of gaps to be found in that State's legislation or law-enforcement system. For there can be no doubt that the case being considered here, i.e. the artificial alteration – by excess or by defect, depending on the needs and purposes of the companies concerned – of invoices for the supply of products or the provision of services between associated companies or other related parties, as the case may be, is in itself a matter expected to have already been provided for in each State's internal system of laws.[58]

58. About this problem, as now thoroughly defined, see below, section 10 of this Chapter V.

Yet, the 'lawful' advantages the multinational enterprises enjoy in the sense indicated above, are not, in fact, unique to bodies corporate. For the option to choose to be protected by a legal system whose norms are most favourable, in any specific respect, in order to achieve a greater competitive advantage, while suitably avoiding the application of the mandatory rules of the relevant law, has invariably been available to any person, whether an individual or a company, who has funds to invest.

Just think of the widespread practice of incorporating pure holding companies overseas, in countries more favourable tax-wise than the home country, specifically in order to de-personalize the ownership of shareholdings in national companies, possibly by circumventing the home-country's internal rules on securities registration, or in order to trim down the immediate burden of direct taxation or else to avoid inheritance taxes at a future time.

Even assuming that the beneficial ownership of a *foreign holding company's* shareholdings is deemed 'lawful' – in that it was acquired by a natural or legal person in compliance with the laws of the State of that person's *residence* for tax purposes, in relation to the most diverse types of tax,[59] and fully in accordance with the rules in force in the holding company's home State – in the absence of any international regulation, the competent authorities of that person's country of residence will encounter serious difficulties, legal as well as practical, in making *actual* checks on that foreign company's operations, ascertaining its actual assets and liabilities or inspecting the actual contents of its portfolio. Nor is any such check or inspection of any concern for the laws of the holding company's home

59. 'Residence' is one of the most widely variable concepts in the world of the law. The meaning assigned to the term may differ even substantially depending on its usage in this or that legal system. Just consider the meaning of 'residence' in Common Law countries as opposed to other legal systems. For example, the word 'residence' is used in English law merely to indicate a person's 'dwelling', while his or her 'domicile' is the place of his or her continuing 'residence' in any one country, with the intention to remain there permanently. Clearly, it is not a mere terminological inversion from the concept current in the Italian legal system, so that the English term 'residence' would be the equivalent of the Italian word '*dimora*' (dwelling, in fact), and 'domicile' would correspond to the Italian civil law concept of '*residenza*'. It is not so because, under English law (see, essentially: Chesire & North, *Private International Law* (11th ed., London, 1987), pp. 141 and 168; Dicey & Morris, *Conflict of Laws* (11a ed., London, 1987), vol. I, p. 122, unlike Italian private law (See Santa Maria, 'Residente e non residente nel sistema valutario italiano' in *Il sistema valutario italiano*, I, *L'ordinamento valutario*, (1981), p. 273 ff., p. 282 ff., body and fn. 22), the presence of the subjective element has been given special value for the purpose of determining a person's 'domicile' in a given place. Therefore, a separate examination is required beside the one intended to establish the continuity of that person's presence in the same place. Even within the Italian legal system the '*residenza*' of a person may mean different things depending on the matter at hand. Thus, *residenza* has a meaning in private law at variance with its meaning under the rules of civil procedure for the purposes of service of process, and yet another meaning when related to the determination of an Italian court's jurisdiction. Yet another different and far broader meaning of *residenza* is to be found in tax law, to the point that it indicates one thing in determining a taxpayer's situation for income tax purposes and another thing for VAT purposes. The notion changes again under foreign exchange law.

State, at least when, if that home State is a 'tax haven', such holding company, in the same way as non-resident or off-shore companies, is not subject to capital gains taxes or withholding taxes on dividends.[60]

In this respect, therefore, the multinational enterprises bring a quantitative, *not qualitative*, differentiation in the usual terms of the problem.[61] It cannot be denied, though, that multinationals' *modus operandi* described above, as well in finance as in trade – specifically through their ability to transfer huge capitals 'lawfully' from one State to another (or from one currency to another), depending on each multinational's contingently greater financial advantage or on the performance of the exchange rate markets – can be so consequential as to alter the balance of payments of one or another developing country and, generally, to affect the very structure of the international economy.

Still, the essence of the phenomenon amounts precisely to the impact such wide discretion afforded to multinational enterprises worldwide can have on competition, precisely because of the position of *economic advantage* they aim to attain, and do attain, in their business activity, over enterprises having merely domestic size and interests.

This asymmetry, as I stressed above, is such – even when it does not entail violation of national or Community antitrust laws – as to cause a radical distortion of the very basis of the competition between the multinationals and enterprises of just a national structure and size in the same market.

This issue was addressed in the judgment the Court of First Instance of the European Communities delivered on 20 March 2001, in *Bocchi-Food*, Case T-30/99. The Court considered the applicant's contention that:

> small and medium-sized businesses do not have the same procurement and marketing opportunities as the multinationals.[62]

Based on this consideration, the CFI specified that:[63]

> such differences in the effects of the rules, which are due to objective phenomena such as *differences in size and market position*, cannot be described as discrimination within the meaning of the Treaty.[64] [*Emphasis added*].

---

60. Please, refer to Chapter I of this study, especially section 14 ff., for the impact of the rules of Community law on 'national treatment' with regard to the examples offered in the narrative above for the purpose of determining the conduct of Community undertakings operating in more than one Member State.
61. In this sense, see Santa Maria, 'Imprese multinazionali', cit. [1975] Riv.dir.int., cit., p. 285; see also Leben, 'L'entreprise multinationale: problèmes de definition' in Lazarus, Leben, Lyon-Caen and Verdier, *L'entreprise multinationale*, cit. 1977, p. 44 ff.
62. See Judgment of the Court of First Instance of 20 Mar. 2001, Case T-30199, 30/99, *Bocchi-Food Trade International Gmbh* v *Commission*, [2001] ECR II-943.
63. See *ibid.*, grounds 76 and 78.
64. In the same sense, see Judgment of the Court of Justice, 18 Mar. 1980, Case C-52/79, *Debauve and others*, [1980] ECR 833, ground 21.

It then added:

> such differences in the effects of the rules, which are due to objective phenomena such as differences in size and market position, cannot be described as discrimination within the meaning of the Treaty. [*Emphasis added*].

An essentially similar view was taken by the European Commission in its defence in the same case, T-30/99, in which it contended that:[65]

> In order to eliminate that difference it is necessary to implement decisions relating to the conduct of market policy *in a way that affords rights to small and medium-sized businesses different from those afforded to the multinationals.* This solution *might*, however, *create unjustified distortion of competition.* [*Emphasis added*].

Globalization has by no means changed the picture. It has, in fact, caused the phenomenon to spread farther, in the sense that it has permitted the small and medium-sized businesses, too, to take the same 'international' approach, by applying the same *modus operandi* of, and enjoying the same advantages as used to be afforded to, the big multinational enterprises alone.[66]

Conversely, although sheer size is no longer enough to qualify an activity as unique to multinational enterprises, in that small and medium-sized enterprises have been afforded the same opportunities as the very large multinationals, the extent of the attendant advantages and the wider and wider use of favourable tools *ratione materiae* increase in geometric progression as a function of the larger size of a 'multinational' enterprise.

6. ADVANTAGES LAWFULLY ACQUIRED BY MULTINATIONALS IN SOME INSTANCES OF DAILY PRACTICE

In order to clarify the observations offered above, let me give some examples of transactions typical of multinational enterprises and apt to give them 'lawful' advantages over competitors merely national in structure and operating scope.

Think, first, of agreements for the sale or licensing of patents, trademarks, processes, know-how or other rights of intellectual property by a company national of a State especially strict tax-wise to a subsidiary, whether incorporated *ad hoc* or already doing business in another State more favourable tax-wise, in order for that subsidiary to sell or sub-license any such patent, trademark, process, know-how or other intellectual property rights to companies based in different States. The relevant transaction, which cannot but appear perfectly lawful from the point of view of the legal system of a third-party purchaser or sub-licensee, will allow the originating multinational enterprise to improve its profit margin on the relevant

65. See the CFI judgment, cit. *ibid.*, ground 71.
66. See my study of 1975, 'Imprese multinazionali', cit. *loc.cit.*

royalties – more favourably taxed – as well as to accumulate currency quite 'lawfully' in a foreign country.

Some criticalities may arise, if ever, in connection with the first transfer of intellectual property rights under the sale or licence agreement between the two related parties – especially in respect of the fairness of the price one party is required to pay to the other.[67] Sure enough, such criticalities would only concern the measure of the resulting advantages, as the substance of the case would remain unaffected. This is because, even if a suitable provision of law is in place in the original home jurisdiction to guarantee the fairness of the selling price in that intragroup transaction, and *even if such provision is fully abided by*, the advantages discussed above would still be obtained in any subsequent transfers from the subsidiary – as the final purchaser or licensee – to a third party.

Another example, and a very topical one, are international procurement contracts. Tender calls for major supplies of materials or for the construction of public works or large industrial facilities are usually responded to by the world's strongest competitors in the industry concerned, which can rely on their strong manpower capacity and, above all, on the specific know-how they have been able to build up over time in similar deals all around the globe. The contract price will necessarily reflect, in addition to the costs to construct the works plus normal mark-up, that specific know-how and the contractor's organizational and financial efforts that made it happen.

Now, nothing is there to prevent a multinational group from participating in the tender and being awarded the contract, in strict compliance with all applicable laws, through a subsidiary under its direct or indirect control which is established in a State that offers more advantageous provisions of company law and tax law. But, likewise, nothing is there to prevent that subsidiary from sub-contracting the whole or any portion of the contract so awarded to it to one or more related companies headquartered in different States. And this will be done at 'normal' (arm's length) prices as well, in order to avoid violations of the laws governing the individual related companies.

For the mechanism involved permits the attainment of a twofold useful result. First, the difference between the *normal (arm's length) value* of mere construction and the total contract price is the profit accruing to the subsidiary at which the economic advantage for the group is the highest. Secondly, such difference is greatly increased by the fact that, in the multinational's *modus operandi* described above, the contracted work is in fact constructed on the production sites in which human and technical resources are the least expensive – even below 'normal' costs.

Yet another example would be a situation of industry-specific hardships caused, in any one State, by a protracted strike wave in connection with involved union negotiations, the duration of which will depend on the occurrence of certain events that can be foreseen sufficiently in advance in terms of both time and extent. If this is the case, the multinational group concerned will always be able to obviate

67. About the issue of the 'normality' of transfer pricing between companies of the same group, see below, section 7 of this Chapter V.

the harmful consequences of such a condition, by timely redirecting any orders – in full compliance with the applicable law – from a subsidiary established in the affected State to another company of the same group established in a different State, thus using a production site where no such industrial strike is expected to occur. It is even too easy to figure out what advantage that multinational can gain in this case over a competitor of a merely 'national' size or having a merely 'national' *modus operandi*. For the latter will, in the meanwhile, see its productive efficiency thwarted or seriously impaired, to say the least, by the need to face and overcome such industrial conflict in a condition of patent weakness.

7. PRODUCTION DELOCATION AS A RESULT OF GLOBALIZATION

Beginning in the mid-1990s, the entry into effect of the new WTO-GATT 1994 system, and the resulting gradual abolition in the short term of export quotas and customs duties worldwide, following the opening-up of the great East Asian markets – most notably the People's Republic of China, thanks to the boom it has enjoyed for the last few years, as discussed elsewhere in this volume[68] – have caused production factors to become widely available to all and any businesses, whatever their size or home country, at considerably lower overall costs than those they would incur in Europe or North America.[69] This applies in particular to generic, low-added value products.

There has been a rush to production delocation from the original (mainly European) sites to countries in which labour costs are so low as to compensate for transport costs or any increase in distribution costs. This has been a one-way trend unprecedented in the world of trade, and one apt to lead up to anomalous effects of the application of the rules of international trade I have already highlighted.[70]

In this respect, globalization has made one of the basic advantages formerly afforded to multinational enterprises *alone* available to all traders, irrespective of where their main centres of business activity are located.

The parallel development of the Internet has extended certain facilities formerly unavailable to small and medium-sized enterprises to trade factors at no cost,[71] thereby shrinking further, at least potentially, any gaps in *modus operandi* between multinational enterprises and other enterprises.

Thus, an observation submitted above has proved correct, in the sense that, in the present-day world, the distinctive feature of a multinational enterprise's *modus*

68. See above, Chapter IV, *passim*.
69. See above, in particular section 1 of Chapter IV.
70. Please, refer to Chapter IV of this book. Clearly enough, this line of reasoning applies irrespective of both counterfeiting and the presentation of products of Chinese origin bearing the marking 'CE' ('China Export'), which is apt to create confusion with the 'CE' marking on goods originating in the European Union.
71. Please, refer again to section 1 of Chapter IV of this study.

operandi is rather the *quantitative* extent of its economic operations and most notably financial transactions than the *quality* of certain efforts that can now be undertaken, *grosso modo*, through equivalent outward projections, by medium-sized or even small enterprises, which are themselves increasingly motivated to move outside the domestic scope.

In another respect, the active presence of developing as well as industrialized countries in addressing international macroeconomic issues, in an attempt to settle all and any disputes within the WTO Dispute Settlement Understanding system, has relegated multinational enterprises to a generally subordinate position, which has been the one really innovating development in the past decade. Against this background, the solution some have proposed,[72] to the effect that multinational corporations should be regarded as 'non-state actors in the international legal order' and even to be recognized as having a 'partial international legal subjectivity' – albeit with a view to achieving better control over the observance by them of international legal obligations – appears unnecessary and hardly realistic in light of the latest developments in the international economy.

8. THE IMPACT OF GLOBALIZATION ON FINANCIAL MARKETS: THE USA FINANCIAL CRISIS

Major aspects of globalization relate to the financial markets because of their close interconnection, which knows no boundaries for the best or for the worst.

At present, any investor is in a position to monitor the daily opening and closing stock market quotes around the world 'on line' in real time. And the performance of the equity markets first to open, from east westward, on any one day invariably affects the markets that follow sequentially in time, in terms of opening and closing quotes, thus creating a 'continuous' marketplace worldwide, much as each of its constituent markets has rules of its own.

Since the early 1990s, the emergence of new markets has brought about unrestricted benefits, giving anyone a chance to allocate his or her securities investments in better ways. Conversely, the proliferation of new financial instruments originally designed for hedging purposes, but latterly used to a far larger extent, has fostered speculation, thereby entailing higher and higher risks for the investor.

Further, as a result of market interconnection, the cost of capital has shrunk, thus favouring growing investments, the expansion of economic activities and wider job availability.

Against this background, new players have come to the fore in the last few years, whose presence is having a deep impact on the international financial market as a whole.

---

72. Fatouros, 'Transnational Enterprise in the Law of State Responsibility' in *International Law of State Responsibility for Injuries to Aliens*, Lillich (ed.), (Charlottesville, 1983), p. 361 f., esp.lly pp. 383 f. and 389; Carbone, 'I soggetti e gli attori nella Comunità internazionale', in Carbone, Luzzatto & Santa Maria, *Istituzioni di diritto internazionale*, cit., p. 37 f.

In fact, individual investors have given way to a number of *institutional* investors, which actively trade securities across the world's regulated markets, relying on large cash amounts, most of which originated by third-party individual investors, and the rest by banks and other financial institutions.

A special group of institutional investors have recently joined the ranks of the other, general-purpose, investment funds already in operation for so many years. The newcomers are the 'Hedge Funds', which engage in highly speculative investments, then at a high risk attenuated in part by portfolio diversification. Alongside operate a vast array of securities investment funds specializing in trading securities of one or another specific sector. They, too, are in a position to invest huge amounts of money on behalf of individual investors, according to pre-established risk profiles acceded or agreed to by individual investors.

Other collective investment vehicles are 'pension funds' supplementing State pension systems, especially active in the industrialized countries, relying on huge capital flows and seeking *lasting* investment opportunities, in accordance with stated terms and conditions, in listed companies (whose securities are usually rated 'investment grade') engaging in manufacturing, commercial or even financial activities of any description anywhere in the world. Another family of institutional investors are the 'private equity funds' (trading securities or real estate assets), which are uniquely structured outside the scope of customary corporate tools and run by highly specialized managers. In taking control of companies not traded on a public stock exchange, they operate according to typically financial rules, with a view to short-to-medium term profits, including through the use of debt leverage. Thus, they are far more aggressive than conventional businesses in terms of the extent and timing of returns on equity.

The growing number of such giant players in the world's interconnected financial markets affords low volatility in normal situations, but not at times of stock market turbulence. This is because turbulence is apt to spread from one market to another in real time and because just one default occurring shortly after a favourable rating has been awarded to the asset involved, will affect all the links in the chain. An added reason is that the choice the experts invariably make to dispose forthwith of portfolio assets suddenly found to be too risky may well trigger a domino effect, propelling volatility and risk out of proportion.

The swift spreading of the news of any event of favourable or unfavourable economic relevance across the web requires the competent national and international authorities to respond promptly to reassure the market. Only immediate responses and considered assessments may work as an effective resonance chamber to dispel unwarranted excesses. Hence, the need for timely actions to be taken in a crisis by the monetary authorities, central banks and governments of the world's major countries. That is why central banks are expected to exercise ongoing knowledgeable control over the banks they are required to supervise.[73]

This conclusion assumes current value in connection with the situation which has been developing over the most important financial market, the USA one, in the

---

73. See below, section 12 ff. of this Chapter V.

last months. More recently, during September 2008, the US financial system has been shaken by a chain of collapses of important banks as well as of the number one of the American insurance companies[74] that evoke the nightmares of the 'Great Depression', in the press.

This financial crisis of an entire system itself seems to have been originated by (not necessarily illegal) use of the so called '*subprime*' and 'Alt-A' loans in the real estate market.[75] *Fannie Mae* and *Freddie Mac* (the former created in the early thirties), in their quality of Government-Sponsored Entities (GSEs) under the Omnibus Reconciliation Act of 1990, thanks to the guarantee of the Government that gave them access to dispose of low cost money, could massively act in the real estate loan market.[76] On September 7, 2008, the US Government has been forced to intervene placing *Fannie Mae* and *Freddie Mac* under conservatorship conducted by the Federal House Finance Agency, 'FHFA', an independent Federal Agency created by the Housing and Economic Recovery Act of 2008.[77] So FHFA took effectively control of the two financial institutions.

The combination of more factors triggers a domino effect. A general overview of the financial market turmoil of September 2008 is clearly depicted in a recent *CRS Report* edited by Congressional Research Service of the Library of US Congress and prepared for Members and Committees of Congress.[78] In particular, responding to the question 'If 97% of borrowers are still current on their mortgage, why is the financial turmoil so large?', it is noticed:[79]

> Several factors magnify the effects of loan defaults on the financial system. *First*, banks are leveraged, which means that for a given dollar reduction in the value of their assets they must either raise additional capital or reduce their lending by a multiple of the loss. *Second*, banks have become less transparent

74. *AIG* was saved receiving a loan of $ 85m by the Federal Reserve Board by agreement with the Treasury Department in application of Section 13(3) of the Federal Reserve Act, the same procedure followed some months earlier by *Bear Sterns*, then absorbed by *JP Morgan*. Meanwhile, *Bank of America* was forced by the Government to merge *Merril Lynch*. The picture is right now even worse with the bankruptcy of *Lehman Brothers*. Nobody knows the future developments of this crisis whilst investors are afraid that the full extent of damage to bank's assets has not yet been revealed.
75. Subprime and Alt-A are two of the problem loan categories since, largely offered into the real estate market, they are disproportionately located in area that had previously experienced rapid price appreciation, such are Florida, California, Arizona and Nevada. In addition, subprime loans are disproportionately located in relatively low income and minority neighbourhoods across the country. See: Darry and Getter, 'Understanding Mortgage Foreclosure: Recent Events, the Process and Costs', *CSR Report RL34232*; Murphy, 'Financial Market Intervention FAQ', *CRS Report for Congress RS22963*, 29 Sep. 2008, p. 2.
76. The two GSEs, under American law, are 'instrumentalities', being subject to the supervision but not to the direct management of the Government. On the notion of 'GSE' and on the difference between GSEs and Agencies, see Kosar, 'Government-Sponsored Enterprises (GSEs): An Institutional Overview', *CRS Report for Congress RS21663*, 23 Apr. 2007.
77. See: http://thomas.loc.gov/cgi-bin/bdquery/z?d110:HR3221.
78. See Murphy, 'Financial Market Intervention FAQ' cit.
79. Murphy cit., *ibidem*, p. 2.

> because of changes in accounting and risk management. This lack of transparency has made it more difficult for banks to raise additional capital as an alternative to reducing lending or selling assets. Third, the use of financial derivatives that should have reduced risk in the banking system may have had the effect of increasing leverage and making it even harder to identify sound counterparties. [*Emphasis added*].

The close interconnection among the principal markets is stiring up deep fears abroad[80] and, by the customary chain reaction, even though the US financial crisis does not touch industrial corporations,[81] it has already caused huge and generalized losses in the stock exchange markets all over the world.

The seriousness of the pending financial crisis of which nobody can predict either the dimension or the end confirms that new international rules are necessary in order to achieve targets more adequate to face systemic crises and their effects on the global economy of the present world.[82]

Besides, notwithstanding the political power vacuum of the EU in the monetary field, as before clarified,[83] in order to face and possibly overcome the present financial crisis coming from abroad and anyhow to prevent the extension of its dangerous effects to the industrial undertakings, the Member States of both the *euro* zone and *non euro* zone are expected to promptly react and try to find altogether consistent solutions (*inter alia*, with the institution of an *ad hoc* fund in order to financially support the small and medium enterprises[84]).

9. MORE: THE SOVEREIGN FUNDS

Alongside the privately-held investment funds discussed above, whether listed or not listed in regulated markets, whatever legal form each has taken, there are other funds called 'sovereign wealth funds' (SWFs) characteristically operating as government arms and enabled, as such, to manage huge amounts of 'public' (state-owned) financial assets, essentially in the capacity of market-makers with one '*single political* principal'.

---

80. Suffice it to remember that the shares of corporations listed at American stock exchanges are owned by foreigners in large quantities to have a clearer idea of the strong impact that the pending US financial crisis (against which around $ 700 bn Government rescue plan, known as 'project Paulson', now converted in the Emergency Economic Stabilization Act of 2008, had been allocated) anyway has on the global saving.
81. It is easy to predict, however, that soon it will become difficult for undertakings which depend on regularly accessing credit markets to get loans; what in turn can affect the broader economy hitting the weaker actors in the industrial activity.
82. On the inadequacy of the existing rules of IMF and on the limited functions of G7 to face the international effects of the American financial crisis, see above Sections 4 and 5 of Chapter IV of this book.
83. See above Section 7 of Chapter III of this book.
84. On Community action *vis-à-vis* SMEs see below Section 24 of this Chapter.

An outstanding feature of sovereign wealth funds – one constituting what has been described as the 'most apparent paradox' of the present-day world financial system – is the reversal of considerable cash flows which are shifted by the SWFs from developing countries to industrialized countries – largely under the control of the developing countries' own governments – as a result of production delocation and at money costs that remain favourable despite the undervaluation of local currencies against the world's major currencies (the US dollar and the euro).

Consider, for example:[85] (i) the recent purchase by entities controlled by the Chinese government of a substantial holding (though not carrying voting rights) in *Blackstone Group*, a leading alternative asset manager, whose subsidiaries provide a major source of employment in the United States; (ii) the Qatar government's attempted bid for control of the UK's *J Sainsbury* retail chain; (iii) the fact that *Gazprom*, a conglomerate controlled by the Russian government, has strategic interests in the energy sectors of several States and ownership interests in *Airbus*; and (iv) the purchase by the stated-owned *China Development Bank* and by *Temasek Holdings*, the Singapore government's investment arm, of more than 3% and 2%, respectively, in the capital of *Barclays Bank*, by reserved subscription of newly issued shares, in the stated attempt to favour *Barclays Bank's* efforts to proceed to a merger with *ABN AMRO*, with a view to starting a larger world-class bank.

In light of these events, some considerations are in order. First, the question of how to protect developing countries against aggression from foreign multinationals seems to be no longer so dramatic as it used to be. In fact, there seems to be a need to adjust currently deficient rules of law to meet the new challenges posed by the international financial environment. This should be done by reversing the present trend, taking into account the (industrial) States' interest in setting up adequate tools for action with respect to changes in the ownership of formerly state-owned enterprises of *national interest*, which have been targeted in privatization plans for the last few years. For anyone can see how the interests of a third State directly or indirectly in control, by whatever means, of a company whose business object is an activity of national interest for another State may well not match, or even clash with, the economic policy of the State in which that activity is performed.

Secondly, in another, equally material respect, quite beyond the case of investments in sectors of public interest, if any investments are made by businesses controlled by foreign States in privately-held companies of other States, then the small investors' best interests must still be protected. This is because the maximization of the returns on, or the value of, corporate stock, which is any private investor's typical and legitimate expectation, may be not the result the State pursues as an entrepreneur, in protecting its own macroeconomic interests even if these are in conflict with such legitimate expectation.

Finally, the arguments offered above clearly highlight that a multinational enterprise's position is essentially identical with its national State's or that, to

85. See the article by Summers, Professor at Harvard University, 'I rischi nascosti dei fondi sovrani', published in *Il Sole 24 Ore* of Sunday, 5 Aug. 2007, at p. 8.

say the least, the former is actually subordinated to the latter. In substance, it is that State which directly or indirectly determines the multinational's operations and destiny. As per the latter's activity overseas, if the State concerned so deems appropriate, it will, as the bearer of interests of its own – albeit rather particular than macroeconomic – oppose other States, not their respective national enterprises competing with that multinational. This is enough to bear out the immateriality of the need, which some feel and I have never shared, for the multinational enterprises to be treated as entities with an international legal personality of their own, while the States are required to exercise close supervision over them, not only to enforce compliance with the general and treaty rules of international law, but also to implement effective measures to protect savings within the framework of internal law.

10. UNLAWFUL CONDUCT OF MULTINATIONAL ENTERPRISES

The fact that a major feature of multinational enterprises' *modus operandi* are the advantages they acquire 'lawfully' in their being active on a global scale by no means excludes that individual multinationals may try to 'expand' the extent of those advantages through *not as lawful means.*

A number of cases of corporate malfeasance have been recorded to this day: from bribing foreign officials, with a view to prospective economic advantages, to so sweeping financial failures as to bring down many companies, even banks, through bankruptcy or other insolvency proceedings, in many different jurisdictions, or to veritable environmental disasters caused by, if nothing else, hazardous activities in hardly suited, heavily inhabited areas.[86]

Specifically, major cases were *Lockheed* in the mid-1970, *Banco Ambrosiano* in the early 1980s, shortly followed by *Icmesa* at Seveso, Italy, and *Union Carbide Corporation* at Bhopal, India. More recently, the US giants *Enron* and *Worldcom* have been swept away – the former by high-risk investments in the energy sector, the latter by the flop of the 'new economy'. Those corporations' collapse has brought about the annihilation of firms of independent auditors disgraced for failing to report accounting misrepresentations (just think of *Arthur Andersen*, obliterated from the global scene) and a veritable earthquake throughout the international banking system. In Italy, signal cases have been the *Cirio* and *Parmalat* bond default crises. All these occurrences bear witness to the actual existence and possible replication of such pathological phenomena.[87]

---

86. Common law scholarship and case-law have long developed a category of liability 'for hazardous activities', in both domestic and international law. See, essentially: Stallybrass, 'Dangerous Things and the Natural Use of Land' [1923] Cambr. Law Jour., p. 376 f.; Jenks, 'Liability for Ultrahazardous Activities in International Law' [1966] Rec. de cours, vol. I, p. 105 f.
87. See Barreveld, *The Enron Collapse: Creative Accounting, Wrong Economics or Criminal Acts* (San Jose, 2002); Borzi, *La parabola Enron* (Milan, 2002).

An actual environmental catastrophe occurred in Seveso, Italy, on 10 July 1976, when the explosion of a reactor for the production of trichlorophenol caused the release of dioxin from a factory of *Icmesa S.p.A.*, a subsidiary of the Swiss multinational group *Hoffmann-La Roche*. Another major environmental disaster occurred in Bhopal, on 3 December 1984, when a toxic gas cloud drifted from a plant owned by *Union Carbide India Ltd*, a company owned by the USA-based *Union Carbide Corporation* by slightly more than 50%, causing more than 2,000 deaths and permanent injuries to more than 200,000 people.[88]

In fact, it must be added that major environmental disasters are also apt to ensue from events that can be blamed direct on States, as in the case of the Chernobyl nuclear catastrophe in the one-time Soviet Union. Further, hazardous operations can also be undertaken as well by domestic companies as by multinationals in their own home countries. For example, consider the number of disasters blamed on the Italian chemical corporation *Montedison* from the early 1980s onward, such as the Scarlino 'red sludge', the poisonous cloud across the Versilia or the toxic release from the Acna plant at Cengio. Finally, political corruption seems, unfortunately, to have long been one of Italy's national prerogatives. A case in point was *Tangentopoli* ('Briberyville') in the early 1990s, a nasty occurrence implicating the entire Italian political class of the time – to the only, ideologically intended, exception of the former 'Italian Communist Party' – which brought about the end of the Italian 'First Republic' and made the *Lockheed* affair appear to be just a *marginal* event.

11. RISK AREAS: THE PROBLEM OF THE 'NORMAL' VALUE OF 'TRANSFER PRICES' AND OF ROYALTIES IN INTRAGROUP TRANSACTIONS

Alongside the major cases of some multinational enterprises' unlawful conduct illustrated above, there are a number of intragroup physiological relationships that deserve a close, case-by-case review, much as they are by no means extraordinary occurrences.

An area especially at risk is that of business transactions and financial flows between different companies belonging to one multinational corporation, in its customary legal status as 'group of companies', having specific regard to cases in which such companies are established in different States.

For the unity of business and financial transactions typical of multinational groups is such that the quest for the optimum transfer pricing of goods and services traded between companies of the same corporate group established in different countries, or for the optimum amount of royalties due on cross-border transfers of industrial property items within the same multinational group, may lead to figures hardly matching the prices or the royalties, as the case may be, that would be

88. See Baxi & Paul, *Mass Disasters and Multinational Liability: the Bhopal Case* (Bombay, 1986).

charged to third parties on an arm's length basis, i.e., in accordance with normal market standards.

The pricing of intragroup trade or financial transactions can be altered for a number of reasons, for example with a view to discouraging demands for wage increases at local companies, by substantially understating profits, or in order to drain profits into the parent's coffer, thus avoiding withholding taxation in the subsidiary's jurisdiction, or by justifying applications to local government authorities for their consent to price rises or for the preservation of some administered product prices without downward adjustments, on grounds of cost increases, or to avoid antidumping duties.[89]

Thus, the phenomenon consists of the possibility for related entities, i.e. companies controlling, controlled by, or under common control with, other companies located in different countries, to fix the transfer prices of goods or services at different, then 'abnormal' (unfair) values, as compared with the prices applied in similar, ordinary commercial or financial transactions between unrelated entities – the latter prices being absolutely assumed to be 'arm's length', i.e. normal or fair market prices.

An especially delicate problem will arise in this connection when the prices for the sale, or the royalties payable on the licence of, industrial property items in transactions between associated companies must be assessed for fairness. In fact, in a merely subjective respect, the scope of risk, then that of the applicable necessary tests and checks, is currently deemed extended to any transactions between 'related parties' within the broadest meaning this term conveys under Italian law.[90]

The transactions involved are transactions 'at risk' as indicated above, but the uncertainty surrounding them is twofold. On the one hand, the domain of 'transfer prices' and 'royalties' is one in which the distorting impact of the multinationals' typical *modus operandi* may be quite material. On the other hand, wherever clear benchmarks are not forthcoming, a difficult situation arises for the enterprise concerned, because of the wide discretion afforded to local tax authorities, especially when they are called upon to conduct tax audits *ex post facto*.

It is not by chance, therefore, that transactions of this type have attracted the attention of international organizations and become regulated by positive law under appropriate internal tax provisions enacted in the most highly developed States.

In particular, I am referring to the OECD Model Double Taxation Convention on Income and Capital (1977), as amended by the 1992 and 2005 Models, to which Italy is a party as a Contracting State.[91]

89. In this respect, refer to the extensive analysis by Maisto, *Il 'transfer price' nel diritto tributario italiano e comparato* (Padua, 1985). With regard to the tax and foreign-exchange causes of the phenomenon, see again: Jans, *Les transferts indirects des bénéfices entre sociétés interdépendantes* (Bruxelles, 1976), p. 29 f. and Kopitis, 'Taxation and Multinational Firm Behaviour. A critical Survey' [1977] Int. Monet. Fund Staff Pap. III, p. 636 f., respectively.

90. For this notion, see above, section 18 of Chapter I of this book.

91. See OCDE publication, Paris, 1977, especially p. 7 f. for a historical overview of the efforts at an international level to abolish double taxation, p. 19 f. for the text of the 1977 model convention,

It is appropriate to stress that, precisely in the matter of transfer pricing, the reason offered by the Italian Government's Report on The President of the Republic Decree (*DPR*) No. 897 of 30 December 1980, amending the last paragraph of Article 75 of *DPR* No. 597 of 1973, was the intent to comply with the non-discrimination principle 'incorporated as a common principle of international tax law into the OECD Model Convention' (paragraph xvi).

The issue was raised again in the OECD report entitled *Transfer Pricing and Multinational: Report of the OECD Committee on Fiscal Affairs*, where suitable criteria were identified to determine 'arm's length values' in the transfer of goods and services between associated enterprises.[92]

On 16 May 1979, the OECD Council approved a Recommendation to Member governments to the effect that they should: (1) advise their tax authorities to take into account, when reviewing transfer prices, the considerations and methods set out in the Report:

> for arriving at arm's-length prices when goods, technology, trademarks and services are provided or supplied, or loans granted, between associated enterprises;

(2) give the Report publicity in their countries and have it translated, where necessary, into their national languages; and (3) develop further cooperation between their tax administrations, on a bilateral or multilateral basis, in matters pertaining to transfer pricing.[93]

The Recommendation was duly followed up by the Italian tax authorities in Ministerial Circular No. 9/2267 of 22 September 1980, adopting the OECD Report. Shortly afterwards, the provision contained in the last paragraph of Article 75 of the President of the Republic Decree No. 597 of 29 September 1973 was reworded in Article 38 of the President of the Republic Decree No. 897 of 30 December 1980.

At present, the entire matter is governed by Article 76(2) and (5) of the President of the Republic Decree No. 917 of 22 December 1986, as amended

---

and p. 45 for a commentary to same, article by article. See the latest version, updated to 15 Jul. 2005, of the *OECD Articles of the Model Convention with respect to Taxes on Income and Capital*, available on the OECD website.

92. On the same Report, see Malherbe, 'Le rapport du comité des affaires fiscales de l'OCDE: prix de transfert et entreprises multinationals' [1979] Jour. dr. fiscal, p. 395 f. The 1979 Guidelines on transfer pricing were revised and updated in 1995. In 1996, new sections were added to account for intangibles and services. In 1977, a new chapter was introduced on cost contribution arrangements (the CCAs). Lastly, an Annex was added in 1999 concerning Guidelines for conducting advance pricing arrangements under the mutual agreement procedure (the MAP APAs). See also *Transfer Pricing Guidelines for Multinational Enterprises and Tax Administration*, 2001.

93. About the limited value of recommendations under international law, refer to Malintoppi, *Le raccomandazioni internazionali* (Milan, 1958), pp. 48 and 347 f.; and Conforti, *Diritto internazionale*, cit., p. 175 f.

(in 76(5)) by Article 1(1) of *DPR* No. 42 of 4 February 1998, and Article 3(1) of Law Decree No. 216 of 15 September 1990. Article 76(5) requires that:

> Income components deriving from transactions with companies not residing in the territory of the State, which directly or indirectly control, are controlled by, or are under common control with, the relevant enterprise shall be valued on the basis of the normal prices of the goods sold, service provided and goods and services received, as determined pursuant to paragraph 2, hereabove, if the enterprise's income is increased thereby; the same provision shall also apply if income is thereby reduced, but only if in performance of agreements made with the competent authorities of foreign States following any of the special 'friendly procedures' provided for by international double taxation conventions. This present provision also applies to goods sold and services provided by companies not residing in the territory of the State, on behalf of which the relevant enterprise engages in activities for the sale and distribution of raw materials or commodities or for the manufacturing or processing of products.[94]

It is my view that subsequent changes in legislation have by no means impaired the interpretative value of the 1980 Ministerial Circular implementing the OECD Report on transfer pricing.[95]

12. INTERNATIONAL COOPERATION AGAINST CORRUPTION, POLLUTION, MONEY LAUNDERING, FINANCIAL CRIMES AND THE INTERNATIONAL FINANCING OF TERRORISM

It should be observed that the suppression or even the prevention of unlawful international activities have long depended on existing internal laws against the corruption of national or foreign State officials,[96] unlawful banking transactions

---

94. This is the latest legislative text following the changes made by Art. 3(1) of Law Decree No. 216 of 15 Sep. 1990.
95. On this subject, see *Projet de code international de conduite sur le transfert de technologie*, being developed within the framework of the Conference on Trade and Development (UNCTAD), (Doc. TD/Case TOT/41). About this project, see Schwamm & Germidis, 'Vers un code international de conduite en matière de transfert techniques (CNUCED)' in *Les codes de conduite pour les entreprises multinationales: qu'en est il?* (Bruxelles, 1977), p. 17 f.
96. Legislative Decree No. 231 of 8 Jun. 2001 ('Decree 231') has provided the Italian legal system with rules on the liability of legal persons, companies, and associations with or without legal personality, for a number of offences initially only including corruption of public officials and later extended under a sequence of legislative amendments to include other offences committed in the interest, or for the advantage, of legal persons, companies or associations. (Decree 231 has been amended by the following provisions: Art. 6 of Law Decree No. 350 of 25 Sep. 2001, as converted, with amendments, into Act No. 409 of 23 Nov. 2001; Art. 3 of Legislative Decree No. 61 of 11 Apr. 2002; Art. 299 of The President of the Republic Decree No. 115 of 30 May

hidden behind any one multinational banking group's operations overseas or any polluting or otherwise hazardous activities a multinational enterprise may run in a foreign country without appropriate and due safety measures. Other appropriate rules of internal law have provided essentially uniform approaches to the tax treatment, within each jurisdiction, of the trade and financial transactions entered into between companies belonging to one multinational group and having relevance to more than one jurisdiction.

Following the dramatic terror attacks on the New York twin towers on 11 September 2001, a new string of terror-fighting actions have been concerted at an international level, as a result of which strict controls have been introduced and universally applied to all financial transactions, including inter-bank transactions entailing major money transfers between economic entities, from one State to another.

2002; Art. 52 of The President of the Republic Decree No. 313 of 14 Nov. 2002; Art. 3 of Act No. 7 of 14 Jan. 2003; Art. 5 of Act No. 228 of 11 Aug. 2003; Art. 9 of Act No. 62 of 18 Apr. 2005; Art. 31 and 39(5) of Act No. 262 of 28 Dec. 2005; Art. 3 of Act n. 7 of 9 Jan. 2006, and Art. 10 of Act No. 38 of 6 Feb. 2006). In particular, Art. 5 of Decree 231 provides for an entity's *administrative liability* for offences committed by: (i) persons having functions of representation, management or direction of that entity or any of its organizational units with financial and operational autonomy (so-called 'apical persons'); or (ii) persons subjected to the direction or supervision of any of the persons under (i). In fact, the penalties threatened by Decree 231 are only applied on the entity concerned in case the prosecutable criminal offence in question was committed in its *interest* or to *its advantage* (terms not used as synonyms). Corporate liability is not assumed to exist where the prosecutable offences are committed in the *exclusive* interest or to the *exclusive* advantage of the perpetrators or of any third party. It is for the prosecutor in *criminal* cases to initiate proceedings to establish an *administrative* violation committed by the entity concerned, and it is for the competent *criminal* court to try and decide the case. The entire proceeding is subject to the rules of criminal procedure. Thus, Decree 231 had introduced a hybrid system of corporate liability, thereby creating a *tertium genus* of a sort, through a combination of the essentials of the criminal and administrative systems, which essentially allows getting around the conventional principle that '*societas delinquere non potest*'. Before the adoption of Decree 231, the Italian system had already provided for corporate liability in relation to certain criminal offences (later treated as administrative violations) committed by natural persons connected with a body corporate. In particular, Royal Law Decree No. 1928 of 5 Dec. 1938 contained provisions for the suppression of infringements of foreign-exchange rules, in addition to the perpetrator's direct liability. Art. 4 required that: 'Where the act constituting violation is committed in the interest of an entity with legal personality . . . or in the interest of commercial companies, that entity or commercial company shall pay a fine jointly with its chairman, directors, statutory auditors and employees who, by their action or omission to act, participated in, or aided and abetted in committing, or hindered detection of, the violation'. The commission by any such person of any of the crimes caught by Decree 231, as amended, does not, however, entail a corporate entity's automatic liability, so long as suitable exonerating measures have been taken, to the extent provided for in the decree, in the form of a code of conduct, prior determination of specific *organization and governance models*, and the creation of an *ad-hoc* internal *supervisory body*. In case such measures are found to be lacking or inadequate, the entity concerned will be punished with *administrative* sanctions of *not only a pecuniary* nature. Please, refer to section 17 of Chapter I of this book for a discussion of the non-applicability of these provisions to foreign companies generally or, more specifically, to companies formed in another EU Member State.

As the measures arising from international cooperation are universally applied to all and any economic operators, quite beyond the scope of the activities typical of multinational enterprises alone, they have largely helped in curbing unlawful corporate practices and, in same cases, in identifying individual wrongdoings. Yet, they have hardly proved satisfactory in international crime prevention.

As for acts of corruption committed abroad, heavy criminal sanctions have been laid down in most countries' internal laws governing the lives and activities of major multinational enterprises. In their being applicable to the misconduct of multinational firms' executives, employees or agents in their relations with foreign State officials, these sanctions provide a powerful deterrent capable to ensure a higher degree of legality to public behaviours, especially in the running and awarding of government procurement contracts.

In connection with the recent financial breakdowns of large enterprises, the 'American model' had prevailed. It is intended, on the one hand, to pursue in any form and manner those directly or indirectly liable for the collapse, primarily the relevant company's governing bodies, the firms responsible for auditing its accounts and any banks responsible for placing its securities in the market, at least because of their failure to act with due care,[97] thereby protecting the small investors' best interests wherever appropriate class action remedies are available.[98] On the other hand, the 'American model' has introduced new rules for even extra-territorial enforcement to impose transparent behaviours on all traders having access to the stock market, partly through suitable measures for the protection of small investors.[99]

The recent collapse, however, of American colossuses of banking and insurance, the two fields normally under special, continuous control, gives full evidence that the present rules were not apt to prevent a 'systemic' crisis.[100]

Internationally, the far-reaching network of treaties to avoid double taxation and to prevent tax frauds worldwide, which provide for the mutual exchange of information between the tax authorities of the Contracting States (on the basis of Article 26 of the 1977 OECD Model Double Taxation Convention), is expected to allow for adequate cross-border audits enabling each State to prosecute evading

---

97. A case in point was *WorldCom Inc.*, which broke out in 2002, when, following the opening of investigations by the US Securities and Exchange Commission (SEC), the company's CEO, Mr Bernard Ebbers (later to be sentenced to 25 years' imprisonment for having orchestrated the biggest financial fraud ever in American history) was forced to resign. Investigations also uprooted the well-known firm of independent auditors, Arthur Andersen, and exposed frauds in excess of 11 billion dollars to the detriment of small investors in the United States and elsewhere around the world. The vicissitudes of *WorldCom Inc.* are effectively described on the website www.worldcomlitigation.com.
98. For a discussion of class actions, refer to Chapter VI of this book, especially paragraph 18.3, narrative and footnotes.
99. See the *Sarbanes-Oxley Act of 2002, 107th Cong. (2002)*, H.R. 3763, and Italian Act No. 262 of 28 Dec. 2005 containing 'Provisions for the protection of savings and the regulation of financial markets', published in the Official Gazette of the Italian Republic No. 301 of 28 Dec. 2005, Ordinary Supplement No. 208.
100. See above section 8 of this Chapter.

taxpayers and, above all, to identify the perpetrators of such non-tax offences as financial misreporting (for example, for failing to record an invoice payable by a shell branch abroad in consideration for services never actually provided).

It should also be noted that, in other cases, it has only been through international cooperation that model uniform regulatory solutions have been developed (e.g. in the case of the treatment of royalties and transfer prices). The resulting arrangements, on the one hand, permit suppressing or even preventing multinational enterprises' unlawful behaviours in fields that used to be quite fruitful for them until a few years ago. On the other hand, they reduce legal uncertainty in the multinational enterprises' internal transactions, which are especially at risk.

As for the very essence of the phenomenon, as historically identified in the multinationals' peculiar aptitude to move around through the folds of different legal systems – by bending individual provisions of law to their own advantage, yet without breaching any of them in daily practice – it is my view that, unless protectionist or, conversely, autarchic measures are indulged in to bar foreign multinationals from operating in any given State (both propositions being hardly practicable or, at least, quite unrealistic nowadays[101]), individual States are unable to solve, and even seem to be not especially interested in solving, problems of that sort with their internal systems of law.

As has been observed, individual national States' deficiencies in dealing with the phenomenon of multinational enterprises are believed to give rise spontaneously to a new uniform set of rules in international trade, based on professional practice outside the scope of individual national laws – the so-called *lex mercatoria*.[102]

In fact, major gaps in international law-making[103] are being gradually filled as a result of the States' widespread efforts in setting up an increasingly effective set of rules to govern the areas most at risk. They are doing so by introducing contextual controls and follow-up checks, basically to be made by banks, in order to prevent, detect and report money laundering and economic or financial activities in support of terrorism, as well as tools capable to prevent or punish violations of any economic sanctions, including embargos, inflicted on any States under UN resolutions or national orders of similar import.

---

101. On this topic, see the EC Commission Communication on *Multinational Undertakings*, cit. p. 8.
102. See Maspetiol, 'Le dépassement de l'Etat par la société civile internationale' [1972] Archives de philosophie du droit, p. 319 f., especially pp. 330 f. and 333 f. Comments of the same gist, albeit without an express reference to multinationals' *modus operandi*, were already offered by Goldman, 'Frontières du droit et "lex mercatoria" ' [1964] Archives de philosophie du droit, p. 177 f., especially p. 185 f.
103. See Malintoppi, *Quelques réflexions*, cit., p. 236, narrative and footnotes. Malintoppi observes: '*. . . il n'y a pas encore de traités internationaux visant expressément les entreprises multinationales sur un plan général, quoi que certaines dispositions conventionnelles existantes peuvent certainement s'appliquer aux entreprises en question*'. By way of example, Malintoppi refers to the Rome Treaty establishing the EEC.

Clearly enough, this discourse about entities involved as principals in 'suspicious' financial transactions goes beyond the issues typically concerning multinational enterprises to cover a global phenomenon, which has little to do with the exercise of economic and trade activities in the stricter sense.

13. THE ROLE OF BANKS IN CONTROLLING TRANSACTIONS AT RISK

In the defence of the international order against the most serious facts and physiological or even pathological behaviours of our times, whichever their authors may be, the basic control function has been entrusted, as indicated above, with *banks*, whether *multinational* or merely *domestic*. Clearly, it is multinational banks which are in a position, because of their very polycentric structure, to perform effective supervision on an ongoing basis through the 'SARs', the suspicious activity reports each of them, whether the parent or just a subsidiary or branch of a foreign bank, is required to file in real time with the competent supervisory authorities about any cross-border capital movements or payments regarded as a 'suspicious activities' because of their nature or mode of implementation or even because of the generic unreliability of one and/or other parties to the relevant transaction. Thus, a financial institution will report any such transaction out of the total number of ordinary transactions involving capital movements or money remittances from one country to another on the basis of certain stated criteria, and identify the particulars of both the remitter and the intended beneficiary.

This control activity is conducted at different levels by skilled personnel relying on highly sophisticated computer-based forms in the three areas most at risk – i.e. money laundering, terrorist financing and transactions with companies in countries subject to economic sanctions internationally (including within the European Union and each of its Member States).

From an *objective* point of view, such control activity entails the enforcement of national laws, Community rules, international treaty rules and even 'soft law' standards, as these are defined under the Basel Concordat and addressed to banks by the Committee of Central Bank Governors.[104]

From a *subjective* point of view, it relates to the bottom-up relationship each bank, bank subsidiary or parent bank of a banking group must maintain both with its Central Bank and with the Central Bank of the head office or branch that carried out, or was requested to carry out, that transaction. These relationships occur in the form of ongoing flows of notices, reports and data based on general instructions addressed to such Central Banks. To do so, the bank concerned will fill out models and forms concerning many aspects of banking operations, promptly reporting

---

104. For the nature of the rules of the Committee of Central Bank Governors, please refer to my study *Consolidated Supervision of Banking Group in the Relations Between Italy and Poland*, in *Comunicazioni e Studi*, vol. XXII (Milan, 2002), p. 299 ff., esp.lly Part IV, p. 327 ff. About the '*soft law*' notion, generally, see fn. 103 below.

each suspicious transaction. Controls are also applied through the top-down internal control relationship between a parent company and its branches and subsidiaries wherever established.

Downstream of, and as a partial limitation to, such complex control system, there are reasonable provisions to protect professional secrecy and bank secrecy, as well as rules for the protection of personal data, whose essential contents of Community interest are indicated in an *ad-hoc* EC Directive of 24 October 1995.[105]

14. INTERNATIONAL COOPERATION IN THE SUPERVISION OF BANKING GROUPS AND THE BASEL CONCORDAT: THE DIFFERENT LEVELS OF CONTROL

Thus, the cooperation between central banks postulated by the Basel Committee on Banking Supervision (BCBS) plays a major role in international banking operations.

Created in 1974, the BCBS is now composed by senior representatives of central banks and bank supervisory authorities from thirteen countries: Belgium, Canada, France, Germany, Italy, Japan, the Netherlands, Luxembourg, the United Kingdom, Spain (from 1 February 2001), Sweden, Switzerland, and the United States.

The BCBS has focused its attention on improving the effectiveness of international banking supervision and the flows of information between central banking authorities.

Its activities are reflected by a number of documents. One document is a set of '*Core Principles*', twenty-five points prepared in a group containing representatives from the Basel Committee and from Chile, China, the Czech Republic, Hong Kong, Mexico, Russia and Thailand, to which nine other countries (Argentina, Brazil, Hungary, India, Indonesia, Korea, Malaysia, Poland and Singapore) are closely associated, with a view to ensuring effective banking supervision. The other documents are to be found in the '*Compendium*', a collection of recommendations, guidelines and standards the Basel Committee has issued in furtherance of the Core Principles.

The Basel Committee's activity has aims similar to those pursued within the European Union for the coordination and harmonization of the Member States' banking systems and banking supervision rules. However, different tools are applied by each of the two entities. The EU authorities issue *directives binding upon the Member States*, whereas the Basel Committee issues mere *recommendations*. Yet, much as the BCBS's recommendations are non-binding instruments, by opposition to laws or international treaties, they are believed to operate as a 'soft law' of a sort, essentially binding on the ultimate addressees, i.e. individual national banks, by virtue of the central bank Governors' authoritative endorsement of such recommendations.[106]

---

105. Directive No. 95/46/EC of 24 Oct. 1995, [1995] OJ L281, p. 31.
106. See Borrello, 'L'organizzazione sovranazionale ed internazionale delle vigilanza sul credito' [1999] Riv. trim. dir. pubbl., p. 427 ff., p. 428.

The Basel Committee's acts are, in fact, certainly binding *de iure* on the signatories to the instruments it issues from time to time, i.e. its Member States' central banks. Any such act which the Governors have signed in the name and on behalf of their respective central banks, under the powers vested in them, is a commitment binding upon the central banks themselves with the same force as any private law agreement, at least until the legislators of their respective countries resolve otherwise or a central bank denunciates one or more provisions thereof on reasoned grounds.[107]

The substantive legal enforceability of the BCBS's instruments in the sense just indicated above – whether or not they are qualified as regulatory sources – is supported on the consideration that:

> the prudential rules developed by the Basel Committee and implemented over the years have become a primary component of the G-10 Member States' regulatory provisions and of non-members' increasingly so.[108]

The Basel Committee develops general supervisory standards, guidelines and recommendations for national banking supervisors' conduct. As one of its major goals is to spread its principles widely beyond the Group of Ten, the BCBS maintains close contacts with, and encourages and coordinates the regulatory activities of, the supervisory authorities of even non-member countries, and promotes an international conference which takes place every two years and in which banking supervisors from all countries participate.

The most emblematic of the BCBS's instruments is what has become known as the 'Basel Concordat' in its original text of 1975, outlining an allocation of tasks among the authorities responsible for exercising supervision over international banking groups.

Specifically, the first Basel Concordat enunciated a cooperation framework designed to eliminate weaknesses in national control systems, laying down the principle that no foreign banking establishment should escape supervision and, accordingly, allocating banking supervisory responsibilities among the different national authorities possibly interested in the exercise.

The Basel Concordat was first revised in 1983 (following the collapse of *Banco Ambrosiano*) and again in 1992 (following the breakdown of the *Bank of Credit and Commerce International*).

On the latter occasion, the Concordat principles were updated with the addition of the so-called 'Minimum Standards' to define the conditions for effective consolidated supervision.[109]

---

107. In connection with the Governors' commitment, see Borrello, *op. cit.*, p. 434, according to whom: 'the approval by supervisory authorities of the initiatives taken at Basel reinforces the commitment to enforce such principles through implementing measures – whether in the form of laws or otherwise – best suited to national realities. A common approach to supervision will be promoted thereby, regardless of the analytical harmonization of the different supervisory techniques being applied in different countries'.
108. See Borrello, *op. cit.*, p. 438.
109. On this subject, see *History of the Basel Committee and its Membership* (Jan. 2007), available on the website www.bis.org/bcbs/history.pdf.

Among the principles laid down in the Basel Concordat, the one most relevant to our discussion is that the home country authority should possess the right, subject to the prior consent of the competent host country supervisory authority, to gather *information from the cross-border banking establishments of the banks or banking groups for which they are the home country supervisor, including through on-site examination.*

The standards for supervision over international banking groups and their foreign subsidiaries entail four core requirements:

1. All international banking groups should be supervised by a *home country authority* on the basis of the home country control principle, according to which that authority has the duty of, and responsibility for, exercising capable consolidated supervision and preventing corporate affiliations or structures that hinder effective supervision.
2. The creation of a cross-border banking establishment should receive the prior consent of both the host country supervisory authority and the bank's home country supervisory authority.
3. Home country supervisory authorities should possess the right to gather information from the cross-border banking establishments of the banks for which they are the home country supervisor.
4. If a host country authority determines that any one of the foregoing Minimum Standards is not met to its satisfaction, that authority could impose restrictive measures, including the prohibition of the creation of banking establishments.

In practice, however, home country supervisors are often confronted with difficulties in gaining access to the necessary information for effective consolidated supervision because of bank secrecy constraints provided for by the laws of the host countries of a bank's branches or subsidiaries. Thus, the Basel Committee has issued recommendations on many an occasion to the effect that supervisory authorities should endeavour to prevent bank secrecy from curbing consolidated supervision anywhere across the international banking system.

It should be remembered that the Minimum Standards have also been subscribed to by countries not members of the G-10, in furtherance of the Basel Committee's purpose to expand its scope for action and strengthen prudential supervision in such countries as well.

On 22 September 1997, it was issued a list of *Core Principles for Effective Banking Supervision*, which are expected to operate as a frame of reference for the activities of bank supervisors and other State authorities in carrying out banking supervision.[110]

Some of the *Principles* expressly apply to international banking operations as well. In particular, the following requirements should be noted:[111]

> Banking supervisors must practise *global consolidated supervision* over their internationally-active banking organisations, adequately monitoring

110. The *Principles* were revised in Oct. 2006. See www.bis.org/publ/bcbs129ita.pdf.
111. Refer to points 23 and 24 of the *Principles*, cit., *ibid.*

> and applying appropriate prudential norms to all aspects of the business conducted by these banking organisations worldwide, *primarily at their foreign branches, joint ventures and subsidiaries*.
>
> A key component of consolidated supervision is establishing *contact and information exchange* with the various other supervisors involved, primarily host country supervisory authorities. [*Emphasis added*].

The *Principles* closely follow the Basel Concordat standards as constantly amended, all of which are contained in Volume III of the Compendium.

In the Supplement to the Concordat, 'Information Flows between Banking Supervisory Authorities', it is specified that the principal requirement of the parent supervisor is to ensure that a routine is laid down for the regular flow of information to the parent bank, and from the parent bank in consolidated form to the parent authority. This calls for a sound system of reporting from foreign establishment to head office or parent bank, for the adequate working of the system to be capable of verification, and for practical solutions to be found for dealing with particular areas of concern. This is followed by a number of recommendations made to ensure the adequate working of the first level of supervision by the bank's head office based on regular reports from its foreign establishments.

One of the latest documents in the Compendium was the Report on 'The Supervision of Cross-Border Banking', prepared by the Basel Committee in cooperation with the Offshore Group of Banking Supervisors. The principles set out in that report were endorsed by 130 countries attending the Ninth International Conference of Banking Supervisors in June 1996.[112]

The Report contains twenty-nine recommendations intended to overcome obstacles to effective consolidated supervision. These recommendations are subdivided into three sections covering the following issues:

(i) improving the access of home supervisors to information necessary for effective consolidated supervision;
(ii) improving the access of host supervisors to information necessary for effective host supervision; and
(iii) ensuring that all cross-border banking operations are subject to effective home and host supervision.

In particular, the recommendations in the first section presuppose that the necessary information for consolidated supervision has correctly been delivered within the banking group concerned. They deal, in fact, with the second supervisory level: the home supervisors are entitled to request and obtain information from host supervisory authorities in order to verify that the aggregate information (quantitative information) received by banking organizations in respect of subsidiaries and branches in other jurisdictions is accurate and to reassure themselves that there are no supervisory gaps.

112. Available on the website http://www.bis.org/publ/bcbs27.pdf?noframes=1.

A quite innovative feature is the two-way information flow recommended in the next two sections, where provision is made for extensive tests and checks the host supervisor should be permitted to conduct on a foreign bank's subsidiary or branch established in the host jurisdiction.

Both the host supervisor and the home supervisor will apply their controls primarily through quantitative examination, though the host supervisor may only do so in respect of transactions entered into by or through the relevant bank's local subsidiary or branch. This does not, however, exclude that, pursuant to special rules – e.g. those on money laundering or terrorism, and those contained in the USA Patriot Act,[113] in EU Regulations[114] or in any national provision implementing UN sanctions – identity-protecting rules may be disapplied, and depositors' names and account information, as well as any qualitative information about their activities, may be scrutinized accordingly.

As for the nature of information flows, there are many channels through which the home supervisor and the host supervisor can receive information, based on the assumption that effective consolidated supervision essentially rests on proper information flows from the local banking activity to the home country supervisor.

For example, information should be capable of flowing:

- from the subsidiary or branch to the head office or parent bank;
- from the parent bank or the head office to the home supervisor;
- from the subsidiary or branch to the host supervisor;
- from the host supervisor to the home supervisor.[115]

Thus, early enough, effective consolidated supervision can only be ensured if two supervision levels are implemented. One allows information to flow direct from the subsidiary (or branch) to the parent. The other gives the home country supervisor adequate tools to *verify* the accuracy of the data received from the parent in a consolidated form.

The host country supervisor has a role to play precisely to this end. In fact, the Basel Committee has urged host supervisors to address adequate rules to foreign banks' subsidiaries or branches and to endeavour to enforce compliance therewith and to sanction any violations thereof as they may detect.

The loop closes with the information flow from the host country supervisor to the home country supervisor.

In Italy, the Consolidating Banking Act requires banking authorities to exercise their powers '*in harmony*' with EU rules, by enforcing EU regulations and decisions and ensuring compliance with EU recommendations in credit and finance matters.

---

113. See the *Uniting and Strengthening America by Providing Appropriate Tools Required to Intercept and Obstruct Terrorism Act* (by acronym: USA Patriot Act), HR 3162 RDS, 10th *Congress, 1st Session*, HR 3162, of 25 Oct. 2001.
114. See Council Regulation (EC) No. 423/2007 of 19 Apr. 2007 concerning restrictive measures against Iran, [2007] OJ L103, p. 1, as amended by Commission Regulation (EC) No. 219/2008, [2008] OJ L68, p. 5.
115. See *The Supervision of Cross-Border Banking*, cit., *loc. cit.*

The European Union' prudential supervisory framework is based upon the *principle of subsidiarity*. For:

> the rules on the Economic and Monetary Union require *national authorities to retain responsibility for conducting supervisory policies*, while the European System of Central Banks (ESCB) *has only been assigned support tasks*, except that the European Central Bank may eventually be assigned specific prudential supervision tasks.[116] [*Emphasis added*].

15. CONSOLIDATED SUPERVISION OVER BANKING TRANSACTIONS IN THE RELATIONSHIPS BETWEEN LEGAL SYSTEMS

It should preliminary be observed that globalization has also, for the past few years, influenced such issues as the allocation of responsibilities among the Central Banks and the controls to be applied direct by individual banks as well as by parents of banking groups to capital flows, both domestically and internationally.

Such responsibilities relate both to such physiological positions as the 'high risks' within any one banking group or the parent's ability in preparing consolidated financial statements, and to such pathological conditions as misreporting or the use of incorrect entries to account for intra-group transfers, all of which may result in a failure to make appropriate disclosures to the competent authorities and – often unawares – in the risk to aid and abet in committing such offences as money laundering or favouring support for terrorism.

Therefore, it is hardly surprising that the rules that govern economic and financial relations have *essentially similar* contents across the most highly developed countries in respect of the behaviours of economic operators (customers and banks alike), the controls applied to them by the competent authorities, the object of such controls and the manners in which they are carried out.

In such a setting of regulatory quasi-uniformity across different legal systems, whichever examining authority is at work in relation to any one transaction or set of homogeneous transactions within any one banking group, whether the home authority or the host authority, is scarcely relevant in principle. Yet, safe for the general observations submitted below, there can be no doubt that, *in the specific area of banking supervision*, it is for the enquiring authority to apply its own law in all respects, under the rules on investigation and the protection of the enquiree that are applicable in that legal system.

The enquirer will also have to ensure, on a case-by-case basis, that any requests from foreign supervisors are accurate and specific, as opposed to mere 'fishing expeditions'. It will also establish whether the entire process may result in costs for the investigated entity that are excessively high relative to the intended

116. For this view, see Borrello, 'L'organizzazione sovranazionale ed internazionale della vigilanza sul credito', cit., p. 427.

results and whether or not there are alternative remedies available that are less onerous, more respectful of people's rights and, above all, not 'out from the point', i.e. beyond the scope for investigation the relevant authority is expected to carry out in that specific instance.

Such an investigation may not, in fact, be an end to itself, but it is also intended to allow the investigating authority to understand the precise contents and scope of the controls the bank being investigated must physiologically conduct *in the future*.

Alongside these solid blocks of converging rules in each legal system, as they have developed especially in banking matters, through the evolution of the common principles of 'soft law'[117] laid down from time to time by the Basel Committee[118] and by the Central Bank Governors' subsidiary committees, whose resolutions and reports are endorsed by the G7 and G8 finance ministers and by the Central Bank Governors at their regular meetings,[119] there are other, soft law rules intended to limit the application of the general provisions on preventive or subsequent controls in relation to bank secrecy, professional secrecy and the protection of personal data. However, these other rules are continuously compressed and more and more applied for a quite different purpose, i.e. as *limitations* – if and when applicable – set in *derogation from the general principles* of correctness and transparency in capital movements and inter-bank payments, as these principles are increasingly and more and more effectively applied at an international level.[120]

---

117. 'Soft law' is taken to mean 'a plurality of acts and occurrences in practice, [without] binding legal effects; . . . [it is a set of] propositions (described as semi-regulatory by some) having the same logical structure as veritable binding provisions of law: any one behaviour is indicated as dutiful upon the fulfilment of certain requirements. Yet, such dutifulness occurs at a level different from that of legal obligations; either because the entity originating the proposition has no power to issue binding rules of conduct or because the relevant assessment is expressly carried out in terms other than strictly juridical terms, in that it amounts to an indication of behaviours that are merely recommended or deemed to be dutiful from a moral, social or political standpoint'. See Luzzatto, 'Il diritto internazionale generale e le sue fonti', in Carbone, Luzzatto & Santa Maria, Istituzioni di diritto internazionale, cit., p. 78 f.; see also Santa Maria, Il diritto internazionale dell'economia, cit., p. 512 f.
118. For the proceedings of the Basel Committee, and the evolution and value of the relevant rules and principles, please refer to my other study, Consolidated Supervision of Banking Group, cit., p. 327 ff., body and footnotes.
119. In the view of Borrello, 'L'organizzazione sopranazionale ed internazionale della vigilanza sul credito' [1999] Riv. trim. dir. pubbl., p. 427 ff., p. 434, 'the approval by supervisory authorities of the initiatives taken at Basel reinforces the commitment to enforce such principles through implementing measures – whether in the form of laws or otherwise – best suited to national realities. A common approach to supervision will be promoted thereby, regardless of the analytical harmonization of the different supervisory techniques being applied in different countries'.
120. For similar considerations, see also Chapter III of this volume, especially section 13. In particular, since the home supervisors have often been met with problems in accessing necessary information to exercise consolidated supervision because of bank secrecy constraints imposed by national legislative measures, the Committee has, on several occasions, issued recommendations for supervisory authorities to undertake to prevent bank secrecy from hindering consolidated supervision in the international banking system.

Obviously, an entirely different status is that of any violation which skips the regulatory level and still provides aid in an underlying transaction prohibited by the criminal law of the relevant legal system. As any such occurrence amounts to a criminal offence, it may result in *criminal* proceedings entirely separated from, and independent of, any administrative procedures as the regulatory authority may initiate against the banking institution involved or any person acting on its behalf. For example, consider Legislative Decree No. 231/2001, as amended,[121] which introduced provisions in the Italian legal system for companies or other corporate entities' 'administrative liability', subject to public prosecutors in criminal proceedings and to criminal courts. Also consider Section 311 of the USA Patriot Act, or the rules relating to the supervisory responsibilities of the Office of Foreign Assets Control (OFAC) both in State legislations and in the Federal legislation of the United States,[122] or to the duties of district attorneys and of the Department of Justice in respect of violations investigated and prosecuted by State authorities or by Federal authorities, as the case may be.

16. FROM THE BASEL II RULES TO THE PRESENT RULES OF THE EUROPEAN UNION

Within the area of the twenty Member States of which the *single* market of the European Union is comprised, in relation to the issues under scrutiny, in connection with the bank's control obligations, nothing has changed in the usual relationship between the general rules on aggregate reporting and the regulatory exceptions requiring specific disclosures. The difference from the Basel II soft law principles is to be found in the 'quality' of the two sets of rules, which are both *fully binding* in the European Union and accordingly have uniform

---

121. For this legislative decree, see above, fn. 88 of this Chapter V and, in broader terms, Chapter I of this volume, section 17.

122. See the *USA Patriot Act*, cit. in fn. 105 above. The OFAC is responsible for watching over compliance with the US rules on economic and embargo sanctions in any transactions involving money flows 'passed at, by or through' a bank or a bank branch established in the United States, when such flows are directed to foreign States affected by resolutions of the UN Security Council or national restrictive measures, among which Iran, North Korea, Sudan and Cuba. Hence, the OFAC's authority to test the lawfulness of any transactions in US dollars cleared by authorized banks in New York. In this respect, if any New York branch of a European bank is assumed to be concerned with these rules, because each such transaction is subject to 'suspicious activity reporting' (SAR) to the Federal Reserve Bank of New York (FRBNY) and to the New York State Bank Department (NYSBD), then such bank branch may well concurrently be subjected to administrative investigations by such two authorities and, in case it fails to comply with such reporting obligation, it may be punished with administrative sanctions, even including withdrawal of the authorization to carry out banking operations in the State of New York. It may also be subjected to criminal investigations by the relevant State or federal authorities into possible major infringements of the rules on payments in trafficking weapons, weapon components or apparently non-prohibited product which may be the object, in practice, of 'dual use'. Investigations of the latter type may entail criminal proceedings being brought against that bank branch's officers.

regulatory contents of an absolute value under both EU law and each Member State's national law.

In other words, the primary norms set out in the Maastricht Treaty about the free movement of capital and payments, and especially the provisions of secondary law issued in the form of directives and regulations based on the Basel II standards and international recommendations, have led to specific rules on the delivery of data and documents and the filling-out of the related questionnaires by individual banks and the parents of banking groups, with a view to making consolidated supervision homogeneous, thus more effective.

These rules govern the data a parent bank and the group's individual foreign subsidiaries and branches are expected to report to the competent authorities. At a different level, within any one group, they also provide for the data and documents each subsidiary and each branch are required to deliver to its parent bank.

Along with the general requirements just described above, there are other Community rules – themselves based on the Basel Committee's standards and recommendations – which have been set in derogation from such general requirements, i.e. the rules on the protection of bank secrecy, professional secrecy and personal data. The relevant provisions are intended to prevent unnecessary abuse, not to curb the effects of controls if any are prescribed.[123]

In this last respect, it is quite clear that such forms of protection implied in ordinary controls, which are generally based on the *exchange of consolidated information*, have nothing to do with controls over pathological cases that may even involve the commission of offences, in respect of which the relationship between the rule and the exception is clearly reversed, so that the acquisition and the transmission to criminal authorities of any direct and personal data become an obligation.

Back to the question of ordinary relationships between each Central Bank and banking institutions, it can be assumed that, for example, difficulties in reporting unconsolidated data at the request of a British, a German or an Italian parent bank are alleged by a Luxembourg or Russian branch, or by a Polish subsidiary listed in Poland. Without venturing any specific comments about Luxembourg law, Polish law or, even the less, Russian law, let me note that Luxembourg has been a Member State of the European Union since the very start, and that, accordingly, only the Community rules of uniform law can apply to the relationships between the Luxembourg subsidiary and its Italian parent bank. (Or it may be enough, in support to this contention, to look at Article 39 and 40, not Article 41 alone, of the Luxembourg Act dated 5 April 1993, as recently amended). The same reasoning applies to Poland, itself a Member State of the EU in its own right. Russia itself, albeit not a party to the Basel II Accord – to which it has undertaken to accede formally, commencing in 2009 – is one of the founding members of the

123. It is enough to read Whereas 43 of Directive 2004/39/EC of the European Parliament and of the Council of 24 Apr. 2004 ([2004] OJ L145, p. 5), which expressly refers to Directive 95/46/EC of the European Parliament and of the Council of 24 Oct. 1995 ([1995] OJ L281, p.31) for the protection of 'the right to privacy of natural persons'.

Group of Banking Supervisors from Central and Eastern European Countries, some of which have become members of the European Union and all of which are working in full agreement with the Basel Committee.

In fact, the instrument entitled 'The Supervision of Cross-Border Banking' was a report authored by a working group comprised of members of the Basel Committee and the Offshore Group of Banking Supervisors and it was endorsed by the Central Bank Governors of the 130 countries attending the Ninth International Conference of Banking Supervisors. This bears out the nearly universal application of the Basel Committee's standards and recommendations.

Thus, in this respect, the European banking group's Russian subsidiary is caught within the same international regulatory framework as the subsidiaries established in the other jurisdictions considered in our assumption.

17. INVESTIGATIONS INTO 'SUSPICIOUS ACTIVITIES' IN CONTEXT

Further, let us assume that another, New York-based, subsidiary or branch of an European banking group is being investigated by the bank supervisory body, the FED, and that, therefore, the ultimate recipient of the information flow addressed by the US subsidiary or branch to its parent company is the FED. The purpose of that particular information flow is to trace back the transactions and payments made 'at, by or through' the US subsidiary or branch over the relevant period. Such an investigation necessarily involves several different jurisdictions: the parent bank's home country, the host country of the foreign subsidiary under investigation, and each of the same group's other foreign subsidiaries' host country. The object of each relevant request will be unconsolidated information and documents to be forwarded, through the parent bank, to the authorities of the first host country.

The resulting trilateral relations are *per se* in line with the present status of international practice. Following the evolution of soft law rules and of the Basel II international standards,[124] supervision over the banking group in question *is not* the exclusive responsibility of the central bank of the parent's home country. As noted above, in furtherance of the general principle of subsidiarity, the basic control to be exercised by that central bank will be supplemented with the control also exercised by the Central Bank or any different authorities specifically set up in the State in which each subsidiary or branch is established, for the shared purpose of enhancing all-round control over the entire banking group in all and any relevant respects.[125]

124. See *Home-Host Information Sharing for Effective Basel II Implementation* of Jun. 2006.

125. Likewise, specific obligations have been laid down for extensive ongoing cooperation between the parent's Central Bank and the Central Bank of any of its branches or subsidiaries established within the European Union. See Whereas 32 of Directive 2004/39/EC, cit., which reads: '*By way of derogation from the principle of home country authorisation, supervision and enforcement of obligations in respect of the operation of branches, it is appropriate for the*

In any event, as the data collection hub will be the parent bank, it will be up to it – albeit with some departures from the rules of private international law governing groups of undertakings subject to Community law – to determine and govern the requirements, contents, manners and timing of the transmission of information and documents from each subsidiary or branch to the parent bank, i.e. 'outside-in', from the periphery to the centre, in compliance with the existing requirements of law.

As indicated above, this level of supervision operates along with the other level – equally recognized internationally and mandatory in itself – that requires that ordinary and extraordinary information and documents be delivered by each bank subsidiary or bank branch to the supervisory authority of the relevant host country.

Apart from a bank's foreign subsidiary or branch's duty to report and convey data to the host country supervisor, subject to the latter's cooperation in whatever direct form with the home country supervisor, the parent bank *must* discharge the duty, among its ordinary responsibilities, to coordinate the relationships among all of its subsidiaries or branches and to enable each of them, to the extent necessary, to comply in full with the obligations such subsidiary or branch (and it alone) is required to perform under its host country's own laws.

18. THE UNIVERSAL NOTION OF 'SAR' (SUSPICIOUS ACTIVITY REPORTING)

Much as the above comments generally apply to physiological situations, they are especially relevant to any investigation in which the host supervisor of a bank's foreign subsidiary or branch calls into question the compliance by it of the applicable rules in any case of 'suspicious activities'.

In the above example of a bank subsidiary established within the United States, 'suspicious activities', within the meaning assigned by the Office of the Controller of the Currency (OCC) of the US Department of Treasury, must be reported whenever a national bank (or a foreign bank's subsidiary, which is treated as a national bank under the US laws) detects a 'known or suspected violation of Federal law or a suspicious transaction related to a *money laundering activity* or *a violation of the Bank Secrecy Act*'.[126] Thus, in any case of

---

competent authority of the host Member State to assume responsibility for enforcing certain obligations specified in this Directive in relation to business conducted through a branch within the territory where the branch is located, since that authority is closest to the branch, and is better placed to detect and intervene in respect of infringements of rules governing the operations of the branch'.

126. See 12 CFR § 21.11, *Minimum Security Devices and Procedures, Reports of Suspicious Activities, and Bank Secrecy Act Compliance Program*, available at www.occ.treas.gov/sar.htm.

'suspicious activity', the bank involved is required promptly to file an SAR (Suspicious Activity Report).[127]

In Community law, Directive 2005/60/EC of 26 October 2005, which is the third anti-money laundering directive (the 'Third Directive'),[128] applicable to, *inter alia*, 'credit and financial institutions',[129] has superseded Directive 91/308/EEC.[130] The Third Directive has consolidated all the qualifying elements of the Community's previous regulatory acts in the matter, but it also contains provisions reflecting some approaches recently emerged at an international level (of which more below).

Directive 2005/60/EC explicitly refers to the notions of '*money laundering*'[131] and '*terrorist financing*'.[132]

Further, the Third Directive has widened the range of the so-called 'serious crimes', i.e. any offences arising from a 'criminal activity', which are accordingly deemed to be 'conduct regarded as money laundering' within the meaning of Article 1 of the Directive.[133]

Pursuant to Article 20 of the Third Directive:

> Member States shall require that the institutions and persons covered by this Directive pay *special attention* to any activity which they regard as

---

127. Id., letter C). In particular, the reporting obligation arises under a number of circumstances: (1) *insider abuse involving any amount*; (2) *violations aggregating $5,000 or more where a suspect can be identified*; (3) *violations aggregating $25,000 or more regardless of potential suspects*; (4) *transactions aggregating $5,000 or more that involve potential money laundering or violate the Bank Secrecy Act.*
128. [2005] OJ L309, p. 20. Directive 2005/60/EC was supplemented with 'implementing measures' by Commission Directive 2006/70/EC of 1 Aug. 2006. However, such measures only covers a narrow range of matters, none of which is relevant to the case in point.
129. See Article 2 of Directive 2005/60/EC.
130. [1991] OJ L166, p. 77, as amended by Directive 2001/97/EC of 4 Dec. 2001, [2001] OJ L344, p. 76. Member States were given time for implementing the Third Directive until 15 Dec. 2007. Italian law is fully in line with the provisions of this directive with regard to terrorist financing (Legislative Decree No. 109 of 22 Jun. 2007). As for the other provisions, a draft legislative decree has been laid before the Justice Commission of the Italian Chamber of Deputies. Let me point out that the principles laid down therein are by no means in contrast with those already in force in the Italian system pursuant to previous Community Directives – except that they are even more stringent.
131. Initially, 'money laundering' was only defined in relation to crimes connected with drug trafficking. A new approach has been taken in recent years, which tends to provide a *far broader definition*, based on a wider range of basic offences, thereby enhancing suspicious activity reporting and international cooperation in this area. In this respect, see Art. 1 of the Third Directive, cit. It should also be noted that money laundering is categorized as such even when the activities that generated assets to be laundered were carried out in the territory of another Member State or of a third country. Also essentially consistent with the money laundering notion under Community law is the Italian Anti-money Laundering Act, which defines the money laundering offence by reference to Art. 648-*bis* of the Italian Criminal Code.
132. For the purposes of Directive 2005/60/EC, 'terrorist financing' means the provision or collection of funds, by any means, directly or indirectly, with the intention that they should be used or in the knowledge that they are to be used, in full or in part, in order to carry out any of the offences within the meaning of Art. 1 to 4 of Council Framework Decision 2002/475/JHA of 13 Jun. 2002 on combating terrorism ([2002] OJ L164, p. 3).
133. See Article 3(5) of Directive 2005/60/EC.

> particularly likely, by its nature, to be related to money laundering or terrorist financing and in particular complex or unusually large transactions and all unusual patterns of transactions which have no apparent economic or visible lawful purpose.[134]

Directive 2005/60/EC has introduced a distinction between 'simplified customer due diligence' and 'enhanced customer due diligence' requirements.

Article 11 allows for both simplified customer due diligence in some cases (e.g. where the customer involved is a credit or financial institution situated in another Member State or in 'a third country which imposes requirements equivalent to those laid down in this Directive', or the customer is the owner of pooled accounts held by notaries or other independent legal professionals), and even exemptions in situations representing a low risk of money laundering because just negligible amounts are involved.

Article 11 is mirrored by Article 12, which contemplates three areas regarded as especially at risk in fighting money laundering: (i) where the customer has not been physically present for identification purposes; (ii) in respect of cross-frontier correspondent banking relationships with respondent institutions from third countries; and (iii) in respect of transactions or business relationships with politically exposed persons residing in another Member State or in a third country. Enhanced customer diligence is required in each such area.

Lastly, as far as the manners of reporting are concerned, the Third Directive requires that suspicious transactions should be reported to a Financial Intelligence Unit (FIU), which serves (in each Member State) as a *national centre to collect* suspicious transaction reports.[135] Article 21 of the Directive specifies that each FIU[136] is responsible for receiving (and, to the extent permitted, *requesting*), analysing and disseminating suspicious transaction reports to the competent

---

134. Further, in the same way as the US law, the Third Directive provides a list of cases in which banks must take 'customer due diligence measures', to wit: (a) when establishing a business relationship; (b) when carrying out occasional transactions amounting to EUR 15 000 or more, whether the transaction is carried out in a single operation or in several operations which appear to be linked; (c) when there is a suspicion of money laundering or terrorist financing, regardless of any derogation, exemption or threshold; (d) when there are doubts about the veracity or adequacy of previously obtained customer identification data. See Art. 7 of Directive 2005/60/EC. 'Customer due diligence measures' are defined in Art. 8.
135. The obligation for Member States to set up FIUs had already been set forth in Council Decision No. 2000/642/JHA of 17 Oct. 2000 ([2000] OJ L271, p. 4). The United Nations Convention against Transnational Organized Crime adopted in New York on 15 Nov. 2002 required 'each State Party' to consider 'the establishment of a financial intelligence unit to serve as a national centre for the collection, analysis and dissemination of information regarding potential money laundering'. (Art. 7(1)(b)).
136. In Italy, the establishment of a FIU within the Italian Foreign Exchange Office (*UIC*) had formerly been provided for under Act No. 388/2000. Thereafter, such responsibility has been assigned to the Bank of Italy under Art. 6 of a legislative decree currently being implemented, while the *UIC* – which was described as a 'provisional body' in the Lieutenant of the Kingdom's Legislative Decree No. 331 of 17 May 1945 – is expected to be ultimately abolished after sixty years' provisional existence.

authorities. In substance, the Third Directive calls for the necessary coordination of the FIU established within each Member State with the competent authorities, which retain their supervisory powers (under Articles 25 and 37 of the Directive) and sanctioning powers (under Article 39).

Some conventions against money-laundering and terrorist financing have been endorsed internationally. In particular:

- the United Nations Convention against Illicit Traffic in Narcotic Drugs and Psychotropic Substances, adopted in Vienna on 19 September 1988;[137]
- the United Nations Convention against Transnational Organized Crime, adopted in New York on 15 November 2000,[138] whose Article 6 contains a list of activities amounting to offences for the 'laundering of proceeds of crime', and whose Article 7 emphasizes the need for 'a comprehensive domestic regulatory and supervisory regime for banks' based on the following activities: (i) customer identification, (ii) record-keeping and (iii) the reporting of suspicious transactions;
- the International Convention for the Suppression of the Financing of Terrorism, adopted in New York on 9 December 1999;[139] and
- the Council of Europe Convention on Laundering, Search, Seizure and Confiscation of the Proceeds from Crime, done at Strasbourg on 8 November 1990.[140]

Further, let me stress the role played by the Financial Action Task Force ('FATF'), an inter-governmental body developing uniform standards and remedies to combat money laundering and terrorist financing.[141] In 1990, the FATF adopted 'The Forty Recommendations of the Financial Action Task Force on Money Laundering'.[142] Much as the Recommendations are not binding upon FAFT members, they have been received into a number of national legislations. Recommendations 13 through 16 expressly provide for the reporting by financial institutions of their 'suspicions' about funds believed to stem from criminal activities.

---

137. This Convention has been in force among 170 Contracting States since 11 Nov. 1990, and it was ratified and made enforceable in Italy under Act No. 328 of 5 Nov. 1990.
138. The New York Convention has been in force among 138 State Parties since 29 Aug. 2003, and it was ratified and made enforceable in Italy under Act No. 146 of 16 Mar. 2000.
139. This Convention has been in force among 154 States since 10 Apr. 2002, and it was ratified and made enforceable in Italy under Act No. 7 of 14 Jan. 2003.
140. The Council of Europe Convention has been in force among 48 States since 1 Sep. 1993, and it was ratified and made enforceable in Italy under Act No. 328 of 9 Aug. 1993.
141. The FATF was set up during a G7 Summit held in Paris in 1989. Initially the Task Force included sixteen members (seven of whom were representatives of G7 States, one a member of the European Commission, while the others represented Australia, Austria, Belgium, Luxembourg, The Netherlands, Spain, Sweden and Switzerland). The FAFT's currently includes thirty-four members, the Russian Federation among them.
142. The Recommendations were revised in 1996 and in 2003. It should be noted that there is a second set of nine Recommendations, categorized as 'special', on terrorist financing, which the FATF issued on 31 Oct. 2001.

Along the lines of, and in full accordance with, the international and Community rules discussed above, the notion 'suspicious activities' is also present in the Italian legal system. This notion and the related provisions of law are obviously to be found at a different level from information flows relating to 'physiological' situations, such as reporting about the preparation of consolidated financial statements or banks' 'high risks', or even 'pathological' situations, such as violations of the rules on the determination of capital requirements or risk ratios, both set of rules being provided for generally by the Consolidating Banking Act relating to Bank of Italy's reporting, regulatory and auditing responsibilities, including consolidated supervision.

Without expanding here on specific rules relating to specific cases provided for in matters of 'anti-money laundering' or 'anti-usury', within the scope of the broader financial crime prevention and suppression responsibilities assigned to the Italian Foreign Exchange Office (the *UIC*), Act No. 197 of 5 July 1991 (the 'Anti-money Laundering Act'), implementing Directive No. 91/308/EEC of 10 June 1991, has introduced rules for the prevention of the laundering of proceeds from criminal activities.[143]

Under the Italian legal system, too, information flows generated in compliance with anti-money laundering or anti-usury laws *are by no means limited to the Italian supervisory authority* but *are intended for supranational circulation to its foreign counterparts*, thus entering the loop of cooperation and information sharing that was first set up within the Community to be then extended outside it.[144]

19. SUSPICIOUS ACTIVITY REPORTING REQUIREMENTS TO PREVAIL OVER ANY OTHER REQUIREMENT OF LAW

Pursuant to Article 26 of Directive No. 2005/60/EC, disclosure by the bank concerned:

> shall not constitute a breach of any restriction on disclosure of information imposed by contract or by any legislative, regulatory or administrative

---

143. On this, see Urbani, *Disciplina Antiriciclaggio e ordinamento del credito* (Padua, 2005), and *Normativa antiriciclaggio della criminalità economica*, Brina & Picchio Forlati eds. (Padua, 2002).

144. In order to comply with the provision of Article 2(3) of Council Decision No. 2000/642/JHA of 17 Oct. 2000 concerning arrangements for *cooperation between financial intelligence units of the Member States* in respect of exchanging information (i.e. the FIUs I referred to above in discussing the relevant Community directives), the Italian Finance Act 2001 had already provided for the institution of a FIU in Italy within the structure of the Italian Foreign Exchange Office (the *UIC*), and required the Ministry for the Treasury, Budget and Economic Planning to notify the Secretary General of the European Union Council in writing of the establishment of such unit (Act No. 388 of 23 Dec. 2000). The Finance Act 2001 also required the investigatory bodies responsible for the matter (as they were identified in Art. 3(4)(f) of the Italian Anti-money Laundering Act) to provide the *UIC* with any information available to them as might be necessary to supplement the information to be transmitted to *counterparts in other States* (Art. 3(10) of the Italian Anti-money Laundering Act, as amended by Act No. 388/2000).

> provision, and shall not involve the institution or person or its directors or employees in liability of any kind.[145]

In other words, *reporting a suspicious activity* to the competent authority will not amount to a violation of privacy requirements under civil or criminal laws.

In fact, this provision was *already* caught by Article 9 of Directive 91/308/EEC and it has an all-important role to play in the prevention of international crime.

For the sake of completeness, it must be pointed out that Article 26 of Directive No. 2005/60/EC quoted above fully reflects FATF Recommendation 14, according to which:

> Financial institutions, their directors, officers and employees should be [...] protected by legal provisions from criminal and civil liability for breach of any restriction on disclosure of information imposed by contract or by any legislative, regulatory or administrative provision, if they report their suspicions in good faith to the FIU, even if they did not know precisely what the underlying criminal activity was, and regardless of whether illegal activity actually occurred.

The Community legislator was fully aware that money laundering and terrorist financing are international problems and must, as such, be combated on a global scale. Thus, it has specifically required that:

> Where Community credit and financial institutions have branches and subsidiaries located in third countries where the legislation in this area is deficient, *they should, in order to avoid the application of very different standards within an institution or group of institutions, apply the Community standard or notify the competent authorities of the home Member State if this application is impossible.*[146] [*Emphasis added*].

Both Community law[147] and the national laws patterned after it, and US law[148] require financial institutions *to maintain* a set of supporting documents and records

---

145. The same principle was laid down in the UN Conventions of 1999 and 2000 (Art. 12 and 18, respectively). For the States Parties to those Conventions *may not* decline to render mutual legal assistance on the ground of *bank secrecy*. On this point, the Joint ECOFIN/JHA Council meeting of 17 Oct. 2000, with a view to completing the process of cooperation in the fight against organized crime, the laundering of proceeds from crimes, and financial crime, reaffirmed the significance of the bar to pleading bank secrecy before judicial authorities, as a core principle to allow criminal investigations at financial institutions to contribute useful evidence within the framework of national legislations.
146. Whereas 35 of Directive No. 2005/60/EC. See also Art. 31 thereof.
147. See Article 30 of the Third Directive. See also Art. 25 of (MIFID) Directive 2004/39/EC of 21 Apr. 2004 on market in financial instruments, also including transactions carried out by investment firms on behalf of clients, as already provided for by Council Directive 91/308/EEC of 10 Jun. 1991 on prevention of the use of the financial system for the purpose of laundering proceeds from unlawful activities. In Italy, this provision has been received into Legislative Decree No. 164 of 17 Sep. 2007, which amended Art. 65 of the *TUF* (Consolidating Financial Services Act).
148. The obligation to maintain a copy of any SAR filed and supporting documentation *for a period of five years* from the date of filing the SAR is set forth in 12 CFR, Sec. 21.11 (g).

for a period of five years for use in any investigation by the FIU or by other law enforcement agencies into possible cases of money laundering or terrorist financing.[149]

It clearly emerges from the necessarily synthetic picture outlined above that the point I made to begin with is correct, i.e. that the rules against money laundering and terrorist financing just discussed are essentially equivalent to one another in contents, scope and reach across a wide range of different jurisdictions.

In light of the regulatory instruments and requirements illustrated above, it clearly appears from the foregoing comments that the prompt application of investigations or controls whether by the home supervisor over a banking group's parent or by the host supervisors over the group's subsidiary A or branches B or C is of paramount public law relevance.

Further, the exceptions intended to impose SARs are constantly expanding, while the rule on consolidated reporting appears to be compressed as a result of the *unanimous recognition*, whether at a Community, national or international level, that the rules on detecting and curbing suspicious activities *far prevail* over any other public law rules for the protection of personal rights, as important as the latter may be.

It is the very picture of substantially equivalent contents and manners of implementation which allows for an oversimplified approach in methodological terms. Beyond and above the many concurrent laws – about which no great differences are, in fact, to be found – and failing material conflicts of laws, I believe one can assume that, in respect of any one international situation, the conflict between, on the one hand, the rules requiring disclosure of disaggregate information, *in cases of suspicious activity*, by subject and by object, in relation to a given bank transaction, and, on the other hand, any objections as might be raised to such disclosure requirements on individual or cumulative grounds of bank secrecy, professional secrecy or privacy, can be viewed and correctly dealt with within any one single legal system – e.g. the Italian system as well as any other national system. An obvious result would be full recognition – albeit in accordance with the order of priority among public law provisions and mandatory rules of law – of the overriding importance of the core rules laid down for the collective protection of international public interests versus the rules protecting individual persons' interests.

As indicated above, the Italian legal system itself has introduced a number of specific, stringent rules to ensure the implementation by banking groups of homogeneous procedures, effective internal audit systems and enhanced information and data flows from branches and subsidiaries, *even if situated overseas*,[150] to the parent company and from the parent company to the competent supervisory authorities. This is also required, in particular, in respect of such pathological situations as those here under scrutiny, in relation to which enhanced reporting

149. The EU provisions are similar to those applied in the United States. (See fn. 136 next preceding above).

150. See *Istruzioni di Vigilanza per le Banche* (Supervisory Directions for Banks), Title I, Chap. 2, Section II. (Circular No. 229 of 21 Apr. 1999 as amended).

requirements have, in fact, been introduced along with material derogations from privacy protection rules, precisely because of the intrinsic priority of the intended purposes and of the 'closed and qualified' nature of the reporting loop within which such information and data are caused to flow.[151]

These conclusions apply even in more technical terms, i.e. in terms of private international law. If appropriate emphasis is placed on the fact that modern legal scholarship, in recognizing the validity of foreign laws, has gone beyond the distinction of old between private rules and public rules of foreign law – based on which only the former were to be recognized outside their home jurisdiction, through the customary remission mechanism under private international law – then the linkage between the two types of rules, now appears to be so strong as to justify the idea that, for a correct reference to be made to a foreign law, a global view must be taken in order to account for a comprehensive assessment of the foreign law so referred to, in addition to strictly private law considerations even on issues of public law.[152]

---

151. Some among the most consequential provisions in this respect, both in general and in specific terms, are the following: (i) General provisions on group-level supervision in the three forms of disclosure supervision (Art. 66 of the *TUB*, the Consolidating Banking Act), regulatory supervision (Art. 67 of the *TUB*), and auditing supervision (Art. 68 of the *TUB*), involving Italian parent companies (Art. 60 and 61 of the *TUB*), any banking, financial and services companies controlled by them (Art. 60, 61 and 65 of the *TUB*), and the Bank of Italy, each at a different level; (ii), in particular, Art. 61(4) of the *TUB* on parent companies' guidance, coordination and direction powers, and the corresponding duties of subsidiaries' directors; (iii) the rules contained in the *Istruzioni*, Title VI, Chap. 2, Sec. II (*Consolidated Supervision*), with regard to Art. 65 of the *TUB*, on consolidated reporting by parent companies; (iv) Art. 54(4) of the *TUB* on *audits to be made at Italian banks' subsidiaries established in non-EU States*; (v) Title VI, Chap. 4, Sec. II of the *Istruzioni*, on *audits* in respect of *entities subject to consolidated supervision* to be made, as a rule, *at the parent company through which information is collected about its subsidiaries*, then in reliance on *the parent company's direction powers in connection with reports to be made to it by consolidated entities*; and (vi) Title IV, Chap. 11, Sec. II of the *Istruzioni*, on Internal Audit Systems, and, at paragraph 5, on '*Audits at foreign subsidiaries*', where *peculiar auditing needs* are recognized with respect to *Italian banks' foreign subsidiaries*, and certain areas are identified in which the parent is required to perform such audits at such subsidiaries, having regard, *inter alia*, to *documental audits of all aspects of such subsidiaries' operations*. As for 'suspicious activities' and the banking system's relations with the Italian Foreign-Exchange Office (the *UIC*), reference should be made to paragraph 4.5 of the Bank of Italy's *Istruzioni Operative* (Operational Directions) of 12 Jan. 2001. For the sake of completeness, it should be noted that, whereas Art. 28 of the Third Directive prohibits the bank concerned from disclosing to the customer concerned or to other third persons the fact that information on suspicious activities has been transmitted, nonetheless it expressly allows disclosure thereof between institutions (from Member States or from third countries) *belonging to the same group*. The entire picture is not expected to change, not even following the ultimate approval of the draft legislative decree still laying before the Justice Commission of the Italian Chamber of Deputies, which requires that the prohibition laid down in Art. 46 of the draft *shall not prevent disclosure* between financial intermediaries *belonging to the same group, even if established in third countries*.
152. See, for all, Palaia, 'L'efficacia extraterritoriale del diritto pubblico' in *La disciplina giuridica della licenza di commercio. Atti Amministrativi economici e misure sui prezzi nell'ambito della CEE* (Milan, 1975), p. 532 ff., esp.lly p. 543 ff.

In summary, what needs to be stressed here is that, depending on the parent's governing law referred to as a whole in the Luxembourg, Polish or Russian legal systems – to keep to the example made above – the acts the parent bank is required to perform in compliance with the public law rules of its own jurisdiction as well as of any other competent foreign jurisdictions (the US system in the case in point) are relevant, at least in principle, to each of those three legal systems as well.

All in all, the rules relating to the prevention of international crime take priority, in the hierarchy of public law rules or of those for mandatory application, over the rules on the protection of individuals in various forms, so that it is quite immaterial whether the applicable public law rules are those of the forum or those of the system to which reference is made.[153] Thus, it is only in this sense that Whereas 43 of the MIFID Directive can be read:

> Member States shall protect the right to privacy of natural persons with respect to the processing of personal data in accordance with Directive 95/46/EC of the European Parliament and of the Council of 24 October 1995 on the protection of individuals with regard to the processing of personal data and of the free movement of such data.[154]

20. THE 'CODES OF CONDUCT'

Since the last decades of 1900, international organizations have tended to develop 'codes of conduct' intended not so much for sovereign States as, and above all, for private entities – multinational or transnational corporations in particular. In fact, where a code of conduct is expressly addressed to sovereign States, its provisions are merely intended as 'recommendations'. In this case, they amount to instruments internationally *non-mandatory* by definition, essentially aimed at providing broad guidelines or 'behavioural standards' expressly described as 'voluntary' for non-state entities as the ultimate addressees.[155]

---

153. I reached the same conclusions, *mutatis mutandis*, in *Consolidated Supervision*, cit., *loc. cit.*, in connection with the primacy of the rules on control over banking groups under the law governing each parent company over the rule concerning the right of each shareholder of a listed company to equal treatment (disclosure) in respect of any price sensitive transaction entered into by that company, without any preferential treatment being accorded to the controlling shareholder, irrespective of whether or not that rule is contained in the law governing the foreign branch or subsidiary concerned.
154. See Directive 2004/39/EC of the European Parliament and of the Council of 21 Apr. 2004 on markets in financial instruments ([2004] OJ L145, p. 1) as amended.
155. The most comprehensive codes of conduct of general content on multinational enterprises prepared by international organizations are: *Déclaration de principes tripartite sur les entreprises multinationales et la politique sociale* dell'*Organization Internationale du Travail (OIT)* of 16 Nov. 1977 (in Picone & Sacerdoti, *Diritto internazionale dell'economia*, cit., p. 745 f.); the OECD's *Principes directeurs à l'intention des entreprises multinationales* of 1976, as revised and updated in 1982 and 1984 (in OCDE, *Les principes directeurs de l'OCDE à l'intention des entreprises multinationales*, Paris, 1986), and the UN *Projet de code de conduite sur les entreprises multinationales*, a project still to be implemented (doc. *ECOSOC*

Clearly, I am referring to codes described as 'external' as opposed to 'internal' (or 'corporate') codes, the latter being standards arising from a need for 'business ethics', so deeply felt for the last few years, even when the relevant instrument is dictated by the need to comply with requirements of law.[156]

In internal (corporate) practice, the belief is spreading widely that observance of ethical, social and environmental values embodied in correct corporate policies is rather an advantage to be pursued than a gap to be filled.[157] Anyone failing to comply with the behavioural standards contained in such codes, when imposed by law and brought to the knowledge of a company's employees and directors, may even be subject to disciplinary sanctions so long as this is expressly provided for by that company.

As indicated above, external 'ethical codes' or 'codes of conduct' are not binding, in that they are 'suggested' by international entities. They are aimed at regulating private parties' conduct without requiring domestic laws to be adjusted to merely 'recommended' international standards.

In general, though some support is provided by national rules of law, the present state of things in this domain is hardly stimulating, in its being the result of a compromise between the interests of the industrialized countries with the developing countries', The approach taken by the former has been to promote the multinationals' positive contribution to economic advancement, by reducing any risks or difficulties as might arise to both the multinational enterprises and to

---

E/C. 10/1982/6). For an analysis of general issues, see: Schwamm e Germidis, *Les codes de conduite*, cit., pp. 1 f. e 52 f.; Francioni, *Imprese multinazionali*, cit., p. 144 f. Francioni emphasizes the exceptionally binding scope of Decision No. 24 of the Commission of the Andean Community of 31 Dec. 1970 (in *Registro Oficial* No. 264, p. 1, and, in English [1971] Int. Legal Mat., p. 152 f.). This decision did not, in fact, specifically concern multinationals' activities, but it contained common rules on foreign investments in the Andean Community, subject to controls by each 'State of investment' (or home State) and ceilings on the annual amount of repatriated profits, along with common provisions on divestures and the definition of sectors exclusively reserved to national enterprises. For an analysis of the contents and scope of the 'non-binding' codes referred to above, see Sacerdoti, 'Les codes de conduite sur les entreprises multinationals', cit., p. 267 f. On the subject, see also: Sanders, 'Implementing International Codes of Conduct for Multinational Enterprises' [1982] American Journal of Comparative Law, Vol. 30, p. 241 f.; Id., 'Codes of Conduct and Sources of Law', in *Etudes offertes à Berthold Goldman – Le droit des rélations économiques internationales* (Paris, 1987), p. 281 f.; Salerno, 'Il nuovo codice comunitario per le imprese europee operanti in Sud Africa' [1986] Riv. dir. int. Vol. 69, p. 58 f.; Lansing and Rosaria, 'An Analysis of the UN Proposed Code of Conduct for Transnational Corporations' [1990] World Competition Law and Economics Review, Vol. 14, n. 1, pp. 35-50; Sprôte, 'Negotiations on a UN Code of Conduct on Transnational Corporations' [1990] German Yearbook of International Law, vol. 33, p. 331 f., and Nguyen, 'Les codes de conduite: un bilan' [1992] Revue Générale de Droit International Public, vol. 96, n. 1, p. 45 f.

156. For a breakdown of internal ('private') codes and external codes, see Perulli, 'Diritti sociali e mercato globale' [2000] Riv. giur. lav., I, p. 951. In Italy, the adoption of an 'ethical code' by each company is prescribed by Act 231/1001, as amended, to which I refer at footnote 84 of this Chapter V.

157. See Coda, 'Codici etici e liberazione dell'economia', paper presented to the meeting on Codici etici e cultura di mercato (Milan, 1993).

their home States. In this perspective, it is common belief that the introduction of a set of even not binding rules governing multinationals' overall activity would, in return, require at least the acceptance by the host state of the principles of non-discrimination and equal treatment in favour of multinational corporations.

Conversely, the developing countries would have ethical codes recognized as actual international treaties, with a view to getting the multinational enterprises to comply with certain standards of conduct to be regarded as mandatory rules of law guaranteed by the industrialized countries in which the major multinationals have traditionally[158] been supposed to have their decision-making centres.[159]

Therefore, although it cannot be denied that the steps taken so far at an international level in this area must be praised for having successfully distinguished, by widespread agreement, between lawful and unlawful activities in multinational enterprises' operations, one cannot but concur with the statement in a Recommendation of the EU Commission, according to which 'the problems raised could not be solved by adopting a few spectacular measures or a code of good conduct which, by definition, would be binding only on undertakings of good will'.[160]

21. 'SOCIAL COMMITMENT' AND MULTINATIONAL ENTERPRISES: CONSEQUENCES ON THE RELATIONSHIPS WITH THE HOME STATE AND WITH THIRD COUNTRIES

In late 1900, with growing intensity in the 1990s, large-scaled enterprises themselves have taken the lead in an attempt to improve their corporate images worldwide, partly as a response to the global reverberation of the scandals caused by the 'forward' conduct of some multinationals.

Thus, a number of veritable advertising campaigns have been launched to regain favourable public opinion, whereby businesses engaging in hazardous or polluting activities have passed themselves off as champions of the environment or defenders of mankind. Alongside, major corporations have developed codes of conduct addressed to their most senior executives down through all other ranks, among whom officers assigned to foreign operations, whether established in the corporation's home State or seconded to establishments abroad. They have expressly been prohibited in both the home and the host countries from acting or behaving in any way apt to result in violations of either national or foreign laws or to put the corporation's image in bad light in either its home country, the host country or both.

The effects of that complex phenomenon, globalization, as well recent developments in international terrorism, have laid the foundations of a silent 'moral

158. See above, section 7 of this Chapter V.
159. See Sacerdoti, 'Les codes', cit., p. 273.
160. EC Commission, *Multinational Undertakings*, cit., p. 8.

compact' between multinationals and their home States, thus reversing the mounting tide of ill will between multinational enterprises and national Sates that was a major feature of globalization in the early 1970s. At critical times for business and financial relations around the world, 'multinational enterprises' have turned into 'national companies' for the occasion and, in return for a commitment to proper conduct both at home and abroad, they have sought their home State's factual support with a view to achieving adequate economic results abroad to make up for their difficulties at home, and to being afforded more effective 'protection' of their business operations against foreign competitors' products in their domestic markets.

This attitude has brought about a growing number of economic conflicts between States in handling even trivial as well as big issues in international trade.

Thus, the problems affecting multinational enterprises have turned into economic disputes between States.

As early as the last period of application of the GATT 1947, trade controversies were rife, especially between the United States and the European Communities, in the most diverse sectors, from steel to edible pasta, plastics, manmade fibres, clothing, footwear and even chestnuts and dried fruits.[161]

This is illustrated by some meaningful episodes of the trade war already underway in the early 1980s between US and Community undertakings in the synthetic, acrylic and polyester fibres. At that time, many US-based corporations relied on internal laws providing them with such an array of administered prices, export bars and drawing rights as to afford them lower internal prices of crude oil and naphta – core raw materials for the production of aromatics, themselves indispensable feedstock for synthetic fibres – than the prices then ruling in the international market. In this reliance, those corporations had significantly increased their manmade fibre exports to the Community's member countries (notably Italy, where acrylic fibre imports grew by over 100%, and polyester imports by nearly 1000% in 1979 from 1978).[162] As a result, these American products were sold across the European Community at far lower prices than any Community competitor could afford, thus contravening Article XX(i) of the GATT 1947.[163]

In support for the attitude so favoured in itself by the US internal legislation, there was a vast range of stimulating publications arranged by the US Department of Commerce, Industry and Trade Administration under such titles as *Apparel in Belgium*, *Apparel in Great Britain*, and *Apparel in Italy*, each of them being

161. Please see Chapter IV of this book, *passim*, esp.lly section 2, for the origin and evolution of the GATT.

162. For this case, which was decided in an urgency by a decree by the Chief Judge of the Milan District Court of 2 Apr. 1980, granting the claims of the applicants, *Snia Viscosa* SpA and other Community (Italian, French and UK) companies v *American Cyanamid Co., Cyanamid International Sales* e *Carter Moore and Co. Inc.*, see the 2nd edition of my book, *Diritto commerciale comunitario*, cit., p. 509 ff.

163. For the connection of infringements of antidumping rules with competition, refer to section 25 of Chapter IV of this study.

intended for every clothing market within the Community. And each of them amounted to a veritable handbook for the American fibre manufacturer and its European dealers about how to address European customers most effectively.

An especially meaningful booklet concerning Italy[164] contained general data about the potentials of the Italian clothing and textile industries, base product market, and distribution and marketing networks, and even such specific details, especially in Appendices 3, 4 and 5, as the addresses, telephone numbers and names of possible contacts at the largest Italian apparel manufacturers, retailers and textile importers.[165]

The observations offered above are borne out by an examination of the statistics on dumping cases within the European Community, which point to an actual explosion of the phenomenon in the early 1980s.

In situations such as the one just described above, the international community has reacted by placing growing emphasis on the activities of international organizations, as clearly evidenced by the large number of States participating in the GATT Uruguay Round.

It is in the context of the WTO-GATT 1994 that the contracting parties have embarked on intense cooperation efforts to provide more uniformity and transparency to those norms of national legislations most likely to have adverse protectionist effects on foreign economic or trade relations. Two instruments that were negotiated with this view during the Tokyo Round of the GATT were the Agreement on Technical Barriers to Trade and the Agreement on Government Procurement,[166] both of which were superseded by a number of multilateral agreements on trade in goods included in Annex 1A to the Agreement Establishing the World Trade Organization, which was the concluding act of the Uruguay Round.[167]

22. MULTINATIONAL ENTERPRISES' ACTIVITY IN A REGIONAL PERSPECTIVE: THE LIMITED SCOPE FOR ENFORCEMENT OF COMMUNITY RULES

It has already been observed that the complex issues involved in the operation of multinational enterprises could adequately be solved only through general international cooperation, i.e. through multilateral conventions or a web of bilateral international agreements designed to allow anyone to engage in business activities at equal terms in the most diverse industries or markets.

---

164. CMS-804, Aug. 1979.
165. See also the volume prepared by the US Department of Commerce on the occasion of a visit made by an American mission of fibre manufacturers to Belgium, France, the Federal Republic of Germany and the United Kingdom: *Besuch der Handelsmission in Europa* (5-16 Nov. 1979).
166. See Comba, *Il neo liberismo internazionale*, cit., p. 182 f.
167. See above, section 2 of Chapter IV of this book.

Now, this remark seems to show that, within the European Union, the position of all business concerns, including multinational enterprises, must be viewed in a different perspective: for the EU is a union of sovereign States and is conducive, as such, to a substantial attenuation of any selfish attitudes as may hamper the conclusion of agreements between States for the solution of at least the most disquieting issues among those considered so far.

In practice, the achievement of the economic and monetary union, albeit with its present deficiencies,[168] and the gradual harmonization of the Member States' legislations in a variety of sectors. and even more the latest Community approach to antitrust regulatory issue,[169] seem to make it possible to curb discriminatory measures and to enhance the control of the unlawful activities discussed above throughout the European Union and in its single market.

In principle, fiscal harmonization is one of the tools available to prevent the inequalities between different Member States' tax systems from causing economic distortions that cannot possibly be removed by other means.[170] The need for a wide harmonization of both indirect and direct taxation appears to be a logical complement of, on the one hand, the removal of obstacles to the free movements of persons, services and capital between Member States and, on the other, the creation of a suitable statutory framework to eliminate anticompetitive barriers between enterprises of different Member States operating within the internal market. Indeed, these objectives also set limits to the scope for harmonization, because, for it to achieve a useful effect Community-wide, it is enough that fiscal harmonization only deals with levies most likely to bring about distortions of competition or to obstruct the full realization of the four fundamental freedoms.[171]

The observation just made above by no means imply that the phenomenon of multinational enterprises and its consequences can, by this way, be thoroughly provided for and regulated within the European Union. For the problem to be solved on a global scale, albeit in a 'regional' perspective, a wide external projection would be needed, through the conclusion of number of international agreements should be entered into by the EU – and not with the most industrialized countries alone.

The Commission Communication on multinational undertakings acknowledged that:[172]

> Nevertheless, it is quite obvious that the activities of the Community will be fully effective only to the extent that *identically inspired rules are imposed at*

168. Please, refer to sections 7 and 8 of Chapter III of this book.
169. Please, refer to my considerations in the next section of this Chapter V and, in broader terms, to the survey offered in Chapter VI of this book.
170. See Stammati, 'Presupposti e condizioni per l'armonizzazione dei sistemi fiscali nell'ambito della CEE' in *Problemi fiscali della Comunità economica europea, Atti del II Convegno di studi, Roma 30 maggio 1961* (Milan, 1961), p. 191 f.
171. Sacchetto, 'L'armonizzazione fiscale nella Comunità europea' [1989] *Dir. prat. trib.*, p. 281 f., also to be referred to for a review of all the draft directives still being prepared on the matter. For a thorough presentation of the Community's tax laws, please refer to the website http://ec.europa.eu/taxation_customs/common/legislation/legislation/taxation/index_en.htm
172. EC Commission, *Multinational Undertakings*, cit., p. 8.

> *world level* with a view to ensuring a homogeneous framework for the operations of multinational undertakings *whatever their origin and their geographic field of activity*. The Community will work on this both in the appropriate international bodies such as the OECD and the United Nations, and, for certain points, within the framework of any bilateral negotiations. [*Emphasis added*].

It is also appropriate to stress that essential parties to the international treaties in this area are precisely those States of a lighter political weight, which have introduced measures exceedingly favourable to the most diverse sectors in their legal systems. This issue has aptly been considered by the European Parliament, which, in its opinions on the Commission's Communication on Multinational Undertakings to the Council just referred to above:[173]

> would like to see increasing and more thorough application of the procedures for exchange of information between the anti-trust authorities of the European Community and the corresponding bodies in the other OECD countries. [Paragraph 13].
>
> Supports the idea of co-operation agreements with the developing countries designed to encourage the kind of private investment best suited to their priorities, and to define longterm conditions for receiving these investments and possibly the provisions applicable in the event of transfer of ownership of industrial plant. [Paragraph 14].
>
> Feels it essential that a better dissemination of information about the operations of multinational undertakings should be aimed at. [Paragraph 15].
>
> Considers that the collection and periodic publication of increasingly accurate quantitative and qualitative information about multinational undertakings over a certain size would constitute a particularly effective means of making their activities more transparent in future. [Paragraph 16].
>
> Would like to see the Commission regulate the specific content of annual accounts, ensure their uniformity and adopt the idea of requiring all undertakings or companies above a certain size, whatever their statutes, to publish their annual accounts, as provided for in the proposal amending the fourth Directive on the annual accounts of limited liability companies. [Paragraph 17].
>
> In view of the world dimensions of the problems raised by the multinational companies, would like the Commission and the Council, while incorporating the provisions listed above in Community law, to take the initiative of undertaking negotiations with the governments and the various international organisations with a view to their universal application. The aim would be to arrive at a general agreement on taxes and investment, similar to GATT, and the

173. See *European Parliament Resolution* of 12 Dec. 1974, paragraphs 13, 14, 15, 16, 17 and 18, respectively [1975] OJ C5, p. 37 ff.

> creation of an international body responsible for its implementation and authorised to carry out investigations and make recommendations. [Paragraph 18].[174]

Again, the European Parliament, in a later resolution on the principles to be observed by undertakings and governments in international economic activities, resolved on 19 April 1977:[175]

> having regard to the fact that international undertakings have a beneficial effect on productivity, technology and management methods while, on the other hand, there are no international legal Regulations to solve the problems caused by their size, massive liquid resources and centralisation of economic power,
>
> having regard to the need to ensure equal opportunities and prevent discrimination in competition between national and international undertakings,
>
> 1. applauds the establishment by the OECD of international guidelines for the conduct of governments and international undertakings based on voluntary implementation of the rules adopted but stresses that binding and legally enforceable norms must gradually be laid down for international undertakings and a framework for their activities be defined in one or more international agreements;
> 2. calls on the Council and Commission to establish one or more legally binding agreements through negotiations with the parties concerned – governments and international organisations and undertakings;
> 3. feels that these negotiations should use as a basis the declarations by the governments of the OECD Member States on international investments and multinational undertakings and take into account as working document the 'Draft Code of Principles for multinational enterprises and governments' annexed to this resolution.[176]

In the face of an essentially favourable view of the overall impact of multinational enterprises' operations, the above comments indicate some concern that it might be impossible, at an economic level, to prevent multinationals from conducting their trade or financial operations elsewhere, outside the Community, only to exploit the basic advantages so acquired over other undertakings of merely Community scale and interests within the European Union.

As early as 1977, the Parliament's comments had a prospective value, in the sense that, already at that time, a widespread belief was that, in a global perspective, even after the completion of European integration, it would be realized that the problem would remain unsolved despite the wider territorial size the European Union had already reached by then.

---

174. [1975] OJ C5/37.
175. See *European Parliament Resolution* of 15 Apr. 1977, paragraphs 1, 2 and 3, respectively [1977] OJ C118/15.
176. [1977] OJ C118/15.

For the European Union as a whole is now suffering from the basic distortions of competition I have described as the most typical consequences of the phenomenon of multinational enterprises in its ordinary occurrences within each national State.

Yet, in such different perspective, the inadequacy of the European Union, so similar to any individual national State's, to cope alone with the many issues considered above, is worsened by the risk – a very real one in a global economy – that it may, by its very action, impose so vast an array of bars and bans on Community enterprises, whether or not multinational, under strongly invasive prescriptions in the most diverse industries, as to make them weaker than non-Community enterprises.

23. THE EUROPEAN UNION AND 'CORPORATE SOCIAL RESPONSIBILITY'

Within this context, the European Union has, for the last few years, embarked on an actual advertising campaign addressed *not only to large-sized enterprises but to SMEs* and cooperative societies operating within the EU as well, with a view to promoting the observance of a broad concept of corporate 'social' responsibility. The goal the Union set itself, as specified in the Presidency Conclusions at a special meeting held by the Lisbon European Council,[177] is:

> to become the most competitive and dynamic knowledge-based economy in the world, capable of sustainable economic growth with more and better jobs and greater social cohesion. [*Emphasis added*].

Still, corporate social responsibility is essentially viewed less as an object of Community rules than as a result of 'voluntary' decisions companies are expected to take *of their own accord* in order to 'contribute to a better society and a cleaner environment'.[178] According to the Commission:

> Although the prime responsibility of a company is generating profits, (. . .) corporate social responsibility (. . .) *should be treated as an investment, not a cost, much like quality management.*[179] [*Emphasis added*].

Businesses are not alone in these efforts, though:[180]

> Public policy also has a key role (. . .) in establishing a framework to ensure that businesses integrate environmental and social considerations into their

177. The Lisbon Summit was held on 23-24 Mar. 2000. See also the Presidency Conclusions at the Göteborg European Council of 15-16 Jun. 2001.
178. See EC Commission, *Green Paper on promoting a European framework for corporate social responsibility* of 18 Jul. 2001, COM(2001) 366, final, paragraphs 8 ff., and 20 ff.
179. Id., paragraph 12.
180. See Commission Communication concerning *Corporate Social Responsibility: A business contribution to Sustainable Development* of 2 Jul. 2002 (COM/2002/0347 final).

> activities (. . .). Business should be encouraged to take *a proactive approach to sustainable development* in their operations both within the EU and elsewhere. [*Emphasis added*].

The European Commission was well aware that the initiative it supported in its Communication could not be an end to itself. Thus, it specified that:[181]

> At the international level, through policies such as trade and development cooperation, the European Union is directly involved in issues concerning market behaviour. A European approach to corporate social responsibility must thus reflect and be integrated in the broader context of various international initiatives, such as the UN Global Compact (2000), the International Labour Organisation (ILO's) Tripartite Declaration of Principles concerning Multinational Enterprises and Social Policy (1977/2000), the Organisation for Economic Cooperation and Development (OECD) Guidelines for Multinational Enterprises (2000). While these initiatives are not legally binding, in the case of the OECD guidelines they benefit from the commitment of adhering governments to promote their actual observance by business. The European Commission is committed to the active promotion of the OECD guidelines. Observance of the core ILO labour standards (freedom of association, abolition of forced labour, non-discrimination and elimination of child labour) is central to corporate social responsibility; their monitoring and compliance should be strengthened.

In May 2002,[182] in calling for new Community legislation to require companies to publicly report annually on their social and environmental performance, to make Board members personally responsible for these practices, and to establish legal jurisdiction against European companies' abuses in developing countries, the European Parliament also voted:

> to set up a European CSR Forum to give rights to stakeholders such as consumer and activist groups to oversee policies alongside business and trade unions;
>
> to set up a European Social Label to endorse products where there is respect for human and trade union rights;
>
> to introduce the wider social and environmental impact of companies' performance in to European negotiations between employers and trade unions;
>
> to make all EU financial assistance to business subject to compliance with basic standards, including setting up a blacklist against companies guilty of corruption;
>
> to mobilise the EU's trade and development programmes to tackle abuses by companies in developing countries.

---

181. See EC Commission, *Green Paper on promoting a European framework*, cit., para. 17.
182. European Parliament, *European criteria for European companies operating in developing countries (LDCs): towards a European code of conduct* [2003] OJ C39/2.

It should be noted that, in environmental matters, the Single European Act first introduced far-reaching rules on environmental protection under the heading 'Environment' in Title XVI (as renumbered from Title VII by the Maastricht Treaty).[183]

The European Community's action on environment has also been projected to an international scale. Paragraph 4 of Article 174 EC states that, within their respective spheres of competence, the Community and the Member States shall co-operate with third countries and with the competent international organizations.

Thus, on 14 October 1988, the Council, on the Commission's proposal and following consultations with the Parliament and the Economic and Social Committee, adopted Decision No. 88/540/EEC,[184] relating to the implementation of the Vienna Convention for the protection of the ozone layer,[185] signed on 22 March 1985, the Montreal Protocol on Substances that Deplete the Ozone Layer, signed on 16 September 1987, and Council Regulation (EEC) No. 3322/88 of 14 October 1988[186] on certain chlorofluorocarbons (CFC) and halons which deplete the ozone layer. At the same time, the Council adopted a decision to reduce the use of chlorofluorocarbons and halongenated hydrocarbons.

The two international instruments mentioned above (the Vienna Convention and the Montreal Protocol) and the limitations set out therein, provide for common actions to be taken by several countries to protect the ozone layer from a gradual deterioration capable to cause serious consequences for human health and ecosystems. The Decision required that both instruments be simultaneously ratified by the Community and its Member States, which was done on 17 October and 16 December 1988, respectively, thereby allowing the two agreements to *enter into effect on 1 January 1989.*

In full awareness of the growing significance of international cooperation in environmental matters, the European Commission has participated, on behalf of the Community and in close cooperation with its Member States, in the OECD negotiations on draft conventions for enhanced control on cross-border hazardous waste shipments to third countries.

On 21 December 1988, the Council adopted a resolution on cross-border hazardous waste shipments to third countries.

In June 1988, a Council Regulation entered into effect concerning export from and import of certain dangerous chemicals into the Community.[187] Then the

183. Thieffry, 'Les nouveaux instruments juridiques de la politique communautaire de l'environnement' [1992] Rev. trim. droit europ., p. 669 ff.; London, 'Droit communautaire de l'environnement' [1994] Rev. trim. droit europ., p. 291 ff.; Hession, Macrory, 'Maastricht and the Environmental Policy of the Community : Legal Issues of a New Environmental Policy' in O' Keefe, Twomey, *Legal Issues of the Maastricht Treaty* (London, 1994), p. 151 ff.; Amadeo, 'Art. 174' in Tizzano, *Trattati dell'Unione Europea e della Comunità Europea* (Milan, 2004), p. 871 ff.
184. [1988] OJ L297, p. 8.
185. [1988] OJ L297, p. 8 f., p. 10 f. for the text of the Convention, and p. 21 f. for the text of the Protocol.
186. [1988] OJ L297, p. 1 f.
187. [1988] OJ L155, p. 2 f.

Commission, in connection with the management of the notification system suggested by the Council therein, proposed that the Council Regulation should be amended in view of the discussions at an international level about the system described as 'informed prior consent'.

Lastly, the Commission's attitude to environmental issues appears to be dictated by the principle of the highest possible level of environmental protection. This is the view conveyed by the provisions contained in the second sub-paragraph of paragraph 4 of Article 174 EC and in Article 176 EC.

Pursuant to the former provision, it is expressly acknowledged that the European Union's own efforts in the field of environmental protection:

> shall be without prejudice to Member States' competence to negotiate in international bodies and to conclude international agreements.

In the latter provision, it is specified that the protective measures adopted by any of the Community's authorities:

> shall not prevent any Member State from maintaining or introducing more stringent protective measures. Such measures must be compatible with this Treaty. They shall be notified to the Commission.

True, the call for 'ethics' addressed to all economic operators certainly deserves full support. But it cannot be 'unilateral' least 'utopian' propositions should ensue. When the Commission deals with issues concerning businesses, but even when it takes a formal stance on general economic issues in exercising economic policies, it cannot but expect other States to require their own national enterprises to behave in accordance with the social commitments imposed on Community-based businesses or, in fact, to comply with international rules.[188]

Therefore, the European Union's ultimate goal cannot be just an attempt at providing a uniform framework to govern the behaviours of the enterprises, of whether a national or a multinational scale, operating within the EU or at recommending them, irrespective of size, to observe a 'social' policy in the sense specified above.

Precisely because of the global reach of the multinational enterprise phenomenon and of the fact that it implies rather quantitative issues than operations quantitatively different from the national companies', there is a need for further and different efforts to be taken by the Commission to protect the positions of Community-based multinationals aligned on 'virtuous' behaviours as contrasted with other enterprises, based whether within or outside the European Union, which fail to fall in line.

188. Please, see my objections to the Commission's performance in economic policy, especially section 15 of Chapter IV of this book.

24. COMMUNITY ACTIONS IN FAVOUR OF SMALL AND MEDIUM-SIZED ENTERPRISES

In light of the impossibility to eradicate the internal-market distorting effects of the type of multinationals' activities I have described as 'lawful', the Community has tended to offset the *basic economic advantage* I have indicated as the most significant effect of the *modus operandi* typical of multinational enterprises by advancing a policy favourable to small and medium-sized enterprises in many respects.

The approach so taken has primarily found its way into a set of plans and programmes on facilitating SMEs' investments.[189]

The Council itself set up the first action programme for small and medium sized enterprises (SMEs) under its Resolution of 3 November 1986,[190] where the Council:

> Considering the objectives of integration, completion of the internal market and the implementation of the Community's policy on economic convergence and of the cooperative growth and employment strategies; Considering the important role which the creation and development of SMEs can play in the creation of employment and the specific problems they face in the various Member States call for a Community strategy covering SMEs which will complement national action in this area; Noting that the development of SMEs is an essential part of Community policies and initiatives under examination by the Council, for example in the framework of employment-creating measure; *Approves* in principle the main lines of the policy followed and the strategy in the [Commission's] action programme.

The definitions of 'micro-', 'small-' and 'medium-sized' enterprises are now contained in the Commission Recommendation of 6 May 2003.[191]

---

189. For this topic, see *The activities of the European Union for small and medium-sized enterprises (SMEs)*, 1988 ed., (Brussels and Luxembourg, 1989), pp. 74 f, and 91 f.
190. The Resolution of 3 Nov. 1986 is in [1986] OJ C287, p. 1.
191. [2003] OJ L124, p. 36. This Recommendation replaced that of 3 Apr. 1996, in [1996] OJ L107, p. 4. See also the European Charter for Small Enterprises approved by the Santa Maria Da Feira European Council of 19 and 20 Jun. 2000. No specific definition of 'small and medium-sized enterprises' had been given theretofore within the framework of Community law. The 1988 edition of the handbook edited by the Commission, *The activities of the European Union for small and medium-sized enterprises*, provided a definition based on essentially quantitative elements. For it stated that, with regard to Community structural grants and loans, SMEs had always been taken to be businesses with up to 500 employees on their payroll, net fixed assets of less than ECU 75 million, and no more than one third of their capital in the hands of a larger company, while lower ceilings were often used for sectors requiring special policies. See also the publication *The New Definition of SMEs*, published by the Commission (2006), which, with respect to applications for Community grants or loans, contains (i) explanations about the new definition of SMEs in Recommendation 2003/361/EC, which entered into force on 1 Jan. 2005, and (ii) a model for a voluntary enterprises' status self-declaration, is available on http://ec.europa.eu/enterprise/enterprise_policy/sme_definition/sme_user_guide_en.pdf

The reference to the independence criterion has been removed. Thus, instead of the abstract prescription of 'independence' set out in the previous, 1996 Recommendation, the 'types of enterprise taken into consideration in calculating staff numbers and financial amounts' have been distinctly identified, depending on whether they are autonomous, whether they have holdings which do not entail a controlling position (partner enterprises), or whether they are linked to other enterprises. This has been done with a view to providing an accurate identification of the data being considered by the Commission in determining enterprise categories.[192]

The ceilings defined for SMEs after the introduction of the revised Regulation can be summarized as follows:[193]

Criteria	*Micro*	*Small*	*Medium-sized*
Number of employees	less than 10	less than 50	less than 250
Annual turnover or balance sheet total	unspecified $\leq$ €2 mn from 2005	€7 mn $\leq$ €10 mn from 2005	€40 mn $\leq$ €50 mn from 2005
	unspecified $\leq$ €2 mn from 2005	€5 mn $\leq$ €10 mn from 2005	€27 mn $\leq$ €43 mn from 2005

The notion of small and medium-sized enterprise does not necessarily match that of companies operating within a merely national scope, which I have, in fact, contrasted with multinational enterprises, irrespective of size, much as, in the typical occurrence of the phenomenon, the multinational enterprise pattern most often matches that of large-sized enterprises.

In a different respect, it should be noted that one of the initiatives intended to improve cooperation among small and medium-sized enterprises within the European Union has been the introduction of the cooperation instrument known as 'European Economic Interest Grouping' (EEIG), an entity whose maximum numbers employed must not exceed 500.[194]

A step forward was taken by the Council in its subsequent Resolution of 30 June 1988 on the improvement of the business environment and action to

192. In the case of *partner enterprises* or *linked enterprises*, the voluntary declaration required to be filed, commencing in 2000, by enterprises wishing to apply for grants available to SMEs, must also provide information about linked or sister companies. What is really material to the definition of micro, small and medium-sized enterprises is the whole of numbers employed, annual turnover or annual balance sheet.

193. It should be noted that, since the approval by the Santa Maria Da Feira European Council in Jun. 2000 of the European Charter for Small Enterprises, a further distinction has been introduced between small enterprises and 'microenterprises'.

194. For the EEIGs, see above, section 12 of Chapter II of this volume.

promote the development of enterprises, especially small and medium-sized enterprises, in the Community.[195] By that Resolution, the Council *undertook*, 'in full agreement with the Commission, to provide a favourable business environment and to promote small and medium-sized enterprises in the Community'.

The Council's undertaking was based on the acknowledgement that:

> the completion of the internal market represents at the same time a major opportunity and a challenge for businesses and that small and medium-sized enterprises will be increasingly drawn into the process of integration of the European economies; (. . .) the development of the spirit of enterprise and the creation of new firms in the Community must be encouraged; (. . .) the development of small and medium-sized enterprises is of great importance in increasing the competitiveness of the European economy, for employment growth and for economic and social cohesion in the Community; (. . .) the economic and regulatory environment should favour the development of firms and should not impose unnecessary costs on them; (. . .) small and medium-sized enterprises require adequate financial resources, especially risk capital, a highly qualified workforce and management capable of meeting new challenges in an ever more rapidly changing world and access to new technology and marketing skills which enable them to operate successfully on the European internal market and to meet competition from third countries; (. . .) at Community level the availability of relevant information on the Community and cooperation between firms in different Member States are of particular importance.

Thus, the Council undertook to provide a policy in favour of small and medium-sized enterprises to be worked out in consultation between the Member States and the Commission and based on the following guidelines:

(a) the promotion of small and medium-sized enterprises must be achieved through a strengthening of market forces;
(b) the cost to enterprises of compliance with Community legislation must be minimized and unnecessary regulations avoided;
(c) existing legislation should be reviewed with a view to appropriate simplification;
(d) measures at Community level should not duplicate those at the level of the Member States; they should, as far as possible, make use of existing structures rather than create new ones;
(e) the opportunities for small and medium-sized enterprises in the Structural Funds, in the Community's research and development programmes and in other Community programmes should be increased;
(f) at Community level specific services with a European dimension are of importance to small and medium-sized enterprises, *inter alia* the provision

195. The Resolution of 30 Jun. 1988 is in [1988] OJ C197, p. 6 f.

of information and the promotion of transfrontier cooperation between enterprises and with other private and public organizations;

(g) at Community level the exchange of experiences from the various parts of the Community and the demonstration of concrete measures can help to improve the efficiency of programmes to support small and medium-sized enterprises; the Commission will take up, develop and encourage these initiatives;

(h) Community measures should be taken in close consultation with the social partners;

(i) the action should take account of the variety of institutional and cultural structures in the Community, which gives rise to different needs (. . .).

The approach so taken seems to have not been confined to mere statements of intent, though. In the last Resolution cited above, the Council already underlined:

> *the need for simple legal and fiscal regulations for small and medium-sized enterprises* and in this context urges in particular that the Fourth Company Law Directive be examined with a view to its further substantial simplification.

Precisely with this view, the Council approved Directive No. 90/604 of 8 November 1990 aimed at streamlining the administrative procedures imposed on small and medium-sized undertakings by the Fourth Directive (No. 78/660) on limited companies' annual accounts, and the Seventh Directive (No. 83/349) on their consolidated accounts.[196]

As for competition rules, i.e. one of the areas in which the basic disadvantage of merely domestic enterprises versus multinational enterprises is the strongest, the Commission has chosen the approach of a 'favourable' application of competition rules to SMEs. In the 'Conclusion' of the volume entitled *Operations of the European Community Concerning Small and Medium-Sized Enterprises*, the Commission released in 1986 it is stated that:

> so as to strengthen the position of SMEs, which, in difficult periods, are an important source of employment and a factor in adaptation to the necessary structural changes, the Commission of the Communities is working towards the practical expression of its *favourable* attitude to the various forms of co-operation between such enterprises. In general terms certain types of understanding will no longer be forbidden, particularly agreements on specialisation or research and development, *which will enable SMEs to meet competitive pressure from larger enterprises more successfully*. [*Emphasis added*].[197]

196. For the sentence quoted in the narrative, see the Resolution of 30 Jun. 1988, cit., p. 7 (*Emphasis added*). Directive No. 90/604 is in [1990] OJ L317, p. 57 f. For the administrative simplification in favour of small and medium-sized enterprises, see also: the Council Resolution of 3 Dec. 1992, [1992] OJ C331, p. 3, and the Council Recommendation of 28 May 1990, [1990] OJ L141, p. 55 f.

197. See *Operations of the European Community Concerning Small and Medium-Sized Enterprises*, 1986 edition, (Brussels and Luxembourg, 1987), p. 135 (*Emphasis added*). For the

On 28 July 1989, the Council supplemented the Resolutions of 3 November 1986 and 30 June 1988 with a decision on the improvement of the business environment and the promotion of the development of enterprises, in particular small and medium-sized ones, in the Community.

By this instrument,[198] the Community went beyond plans to decide as follows:

> Article 1. In order to improve the business environment and encourage the creation and development of enterprises, and in particular small and medium-sized enterprises (SMEs), measures shall be implemented at Community level.

The measures referred to in Article 2 were to include:

- removal of undue administrative, financial and legal constraints which check the development and creation of enterprises, and in particular SMEs,
- information and assistance to enterprises, and in particular SMEs, on Community policies, regulations and activities and those of each Member State which concern or are likely to concern them,
- encouragement of cooperation and partnership between enterprises, and in particular SMEs, from different regions of the Community.

Article 3 stated that:

> In order to achieve the objectives and carry out the measures referred to in Articles 1 and 2, the Commission will propose the necessary action to the extent that it cannot be undertaken better at Member State level.

Further, the Commission was to be assisted by a committee composed of the representatives of the Member States and chaired by the representative of the Commission, and:

> The Commission shall adopt measures which shall apply immediately. However, if these measures are not in accordance with the opinion of the committee, they shall be communicated by the Commission to the Council forthwith. In that event the Commission shall defer application of the measures which it has decided for a period of three months from the date of communication.
>
> The Council, acting by a qualified majority, may take a different decision within the time limit referred to in the previous subparagraph. (*Article 4.1*).

Of late, the DG Enterprise and Industry of the European Commission has set up a specific SME portal 'to provide a single entry point to information on all European Union policies, programmes, projects, tools and services aimed at SMEs'.[199]

Commission's discretion specifically with regard the application of Art. 85(3) of the Treaty, please refer to Chapter III of this study.

198. Published in [1989] OJ L239, p. 33 f.

199. Available at http://ec.europa.eu/enterprise/sme/about_it.htm See also the recent publication '*Le PMI al primo posto*' (2007), available at http://ec.europa.eu/enterprise/entrepreneurship/docs/sme_pack_it.pdf.

Further, the Commission has appointed an 'SME Envoy' to act as an interface between SMEs and the EU institutions to ensure that the SMEs' best interests be taken into due account in working up Community policies and norms at any level of government.[200]

25. LEGAL RESTRICTIONS ON THIRD-COUNTRY-BASED MULTINATIONALS' OPERATIONS IN THE EUROPEAN UNION

Yet another aspect of the entire issue remains to be scrutinized, i.e. the European Union's attitude to non-Community multinational enterprises.

The Commission Communication of 7 November 1973 I have frequently referred to above preliminarily showed a preliminarily open attitude to non-Community multinational companies, especially those whose home countries were Japan or the United States. For the Communication expressly stated that: '[T]he Community's aim in this field as in others is not to apply restrictive or discriminatory measures but to make liberalization measures more widespread'.[201]

In fact, precisely in light of the need so strongly felt within the European Community to put some restraints on the then increasingly keen competition from non-Community businesses, the Community's attitude to them was initially not especially receptive. Indeed, the Community has invariably tried to prevent companies incorporated in any Member State, but belonging to non-Community economic groups[202] from establishing within the European internal market, i.e. from taking on Community status while they belonged to third countries in terms of sources of capital or effective seats of management, by excluding them from certain benefits afforded by the Treaty of Rome to companies belonging to Member States.

Thus, Article 43 EC – which requires nationals of a Member State to be 'established in the territory of any Member State' for them to enjoy freedom of establishment in setting up agencies, branches or subsidiaries – has been relied on to require that, *in this case*, companies or firms formed in accordance with the law

200. Mention should also be made of Commission Regulation (EC) No. 70/2001 of 12 Jan. 2001 on the application of Art. 87 and 88 of the EC Treaty to State aid to small and medium-sized enterprises, [2001] OJ L10, p. 33, the period of application of which was later extended to 30 Jun. 2008 by Commission Regulation (EC) No. 1976/2006 of 20 Dec. 2006, [2006] OJ L368, p. 85.

201. See *Multinational Undertakings and Community Regulations*, cit., p. 12.

202. Please, refer to the introductory section of this Chapter V for the concept of 'multinational' as an attribute of 'enterprise' in the economic meaning of the term – as contrasted, that is, to the legal phrase 'group of companies' – and for the correlation existing between an enterprise, which can be 'multinational', and a company, which is invariably 'national'. For this reason, talking of 'Japanese' or 'American' multinational enterprises appears incorrect, although it cannot be ignored in practice that that phrase accomplishes the purpose of identifying the groups of companies that are known to have their driving engine in Japan or in the United States, as the case may be.

of a Member State, but having only their registered (statutory) office within the Community should also have an 'effective and continuous link' with the economy of a Member State.[203]

Further, Article 49 of the Rome Treaty expressly restricts the application of the provisions on freedom to provide services within the Community to nationals of Member States who are '*established* in a State of the Community other than that of the person for whom the services are intended'.[204]

For this reason, it has aptly been maintained that companies having only their registered office in any one Member State may only benefit from these provisions so long as they show an additional connection with Community law *in any event*, i.e. so long as they have an 'effective and continuous link' with the economy of a Member State.[205]

Therefore, the approach so taken to companies having Community status, but being essentially 'non-Community' enterprises, merely results in denying them certain benefits in terms of freedom of establishment and freedom to provide services.

It should also be noted, at a more general level, that the radical solution of withholding recognition of foreign companies in any one legal system appears to be hardly conducive to useful results. For such an attitude would essentially lead the European Union to take up that protectionist stance the Commission has consistently opposed as impracticable in the present course of the international economy.

Further, such an approach could hardly be really effective in itself in any of the more and more frequent cases of 'indirect' exploitation of the European internal market area, i.e. whenever business transactions are entered into by non-Community multinationals from outside that area.[206]

It is appropriate to stress that the 'non-recognition' of a foreign company in a given jurisdiction may even result immediately and directly in the very 'non-existence' of that company in that jurisdiction.[207]

---

203. In this respect, see the considerations offered in Chapter I of this book, *passim.*
204. In particular, refer to section 2 of Chapter I of this book.
205. It should be remembered that the General Programme for the abolition of restrictions on freedom to provide services of 18 Dec. 1961, cit., p. 32 f. contains a declaration to the same effect. Both such General Programme and the General Programme for the abolition of restrictions on freedom of establishment only negatively define the *additional connection* with Community law. Both state that such connection must not depend on citizenship, in particular that of the shareholders, members of managing or supervisory bodies, or persons holding a majority of the company's capital, so that the so-called 'control factor' is ruled out. Still, no positive contribution is given by either General Programme to the solution of the problem.
206. For cases of indirect exploitation of the European market from the outside, though the conclusion of licence agreements for the manufacturing of any product within the Community area, see Carbone, 'Imprese multinazionali', cit., c 199 f.
207. For this issue, see my study, 'Le società nel diritto internazionale privato', cit., pp. 46 f., fn. 81, and 199 f., in particular p. 201, narrative and fn. 7.

This would be the case not only when it is the foreign company so denied recognition – then 'non-existing' in that jurisdiction – which brings action as claimant against that State's nationals before local courts, but even in the opposite case, when the company is sued as an insolvent debtor. In this respect, the Tribunal of Trieste, in its judgment of 27 February 1974 in *Ubaldanstalt di Vaduz* v *Credito Romagnolo S.p.A.*,[208] made known its view about the year-long issue of the recognition or non-recognition of a Liechtenstein *Anstalt* in Italy, as follows:

> (...) if a bank among those that, unlike Defendant, customarily maintain relationships with *Anstalten* without suspecting their non-existence lend moneys to any of them, then it could hardly claim repayment of the sums so lent or payment of interest accrued thereon by contract from the non-existing *Anstalt*. At best, what it could do is to turn to the natural person who is the *Anstalt*'s *'falsus procurator'*, to claim repayment of the sum so lent without cause, plus interest at just the legal rate. And this would certainly be an unpleasant consequence.

In this perspective, the foreign company itself might even plead its own 'non-existence' to avoid bankruptcy or just withhold payment of a debt.[209]

Thus, 'non-recognition' is certainly not the right approach to be taken by the European Union.[210]

In the alternative whether to allow for the straightforward, formal establishment of foreign multinationals, whatever their investments, within the European internal market, or to bar their establishment, without the Community authorities being in a position to prevent those multinationals from achieving the same practical results by other, less blatant means, the former approach is certainly the more advisable. It is, in fact, the one better suited to the essential purpose of keeping non-Community multinationals' activities within the EU under closer watch.

26. APPLYING COMPETITION RULES TO NON-COMMUNITY BUSINESSES

The European Union's actions to protect Community interests against non-Community companies, i.e. multinationals which, while not being statutorily based within the Union, directly or indirectly carry out business activities in its territory, are implemented most logically and naturally by enforcing Community competition rules on non-Community undertakings.

---

208. See in [1975] Riv. dir. int. priv. proc., p. 90 f., p. 92.

209. See Judgment of the Milan District Court of 14 Sep. 1978, in re *Idera Business A.G.* v *Fallimento Soc. Idera Business A.G.* and others, [1979] Riv. dir. int. priv. proc., p. 125 f.

210. The pointlessness of using 'non-recognition' of companies as a means to prevent tax frauds is emphasized by Schnitzer, 'Le trust et la fondation dans les conflits de lois', [1965] Rev. crit. dr. int. privé, p. 479 f., p. 491. On this topic generally, refer to Chapter I of this study, *passim*.

This approach is highly advisable in that it makes such undertakings' activities of any description within the European internal market, whether on an on-going or a just occasional basis, subject to the competent EU authorities' control when it comes to compliance with competition rules.[211]

In view of the predictable entrenchment of the latest rules of competition law within the Community, this approach is also expected to ensure full compliance with them in any transaction as may be carried out or even generate effects of any sort in the territory of the European Union.[212]

The 'effects doctrine', a mechanism long established in US antitrust law, on which the extra-territorial application of competition rules is primarily based, is now finding its way into less and less timid rulings by EU courts.[213]

In fact, at least in principle, the opposite approach, i.e. widespread harmonization of antitrust rules on a global scale would appear to be a far more effective solution in this area as well.[214]

---

211. About the Commission's practice and the CFI's and the ECJ's case-law in this field, please refer to my considerations in section 8 of Chapter VI of this book, *passim*.
212. Underlying the evolution of Community antitrust rules in case-law is the gradual development of a unified economic concept of 'undertaking' as one increasingly independent of, and unrelated to, the formal legal concept. See, essentially, Commission Decisions No. 69/195 of 18 Jun. 1969, *Christiani & Nielsen*, [1969] OJ L165, p. 12 f., and No. 70/332 of 30 Jun. 1970, *Kodak*, [1970] OJ L147, p. 24 f. The same view was taken in the judgments of the Court of Justice of the European Communities of 8 Jun. 1971, Case 78/70, *Deutsche Grammophon GmbH* v *Metro-SB-Grosmarkte GmbH & Co. KG*, [1971] ECR, p. 487 f., and of 14 Jul. 1972, Case 48/69, *Imperial Chemical Industries (ICI)* v *Commission*, the most important of all cases concerning the cartel of aniline-based dyes [1972] ECR, p. 619 f. Trabucchi, 'Sviluppo della giurisprudenza e suo significato nella disciplina comunitaria della concorrenza', [1973] Riv. dir. civ., p. 497 f., p. 504, has aptly observed: 'In the face of such a huge phenomenon (that of multinational enterprises), it would have been inadequate for an effective application of antitrust rules to refer to the traditional notion of legal personality alone in order to identify the enterprise as an economic operator capable to determine its own line of conduct in the economic field'. The notion of 'economic unit' was the foundation of the Commission's view and, later, of the ECJ's ruling in the landmark case *Continental Can*, which is extensively discussed in Chapter III of this book, to which reference is made here. Both institutions used that notion to conclude that an infringement of competition rules within the Community area by a subsidiary can be charged *directly* on its parent company established outside the common market. See Commission Decision of 9 Dec. 1971, cit., and the ECJ's judgment of 21 Feb. 1973, cit., p. 215 f. For a similar case-law approach to the application of Art. 85 of the EC Treaty, please refer to Carbone, 'Imprese multinazionali', cit., c. 203, narrative and footnotes 15-23.
213. On this subject, please refer to Chapter VI of this book.
214. Reflections in this sense can be found in Fikentscher, *Wirtschaftskontrolle und Weltinnenpolitik*, in *Gewerblicher Rechtsschutz und Urheberrecht, Internationaler Teil, Festschrift fuær Eugen Ulmer zum 70 Geburtstag*, 1973, pp. 478 f., and 485 f. Favourable to a coordination of national antitrust rules was the OECD Council Recommendation of 15 Oct. 1977, [1979] Int. Legal Mat., p. 1309 f. This was the context in which an attempt was made by the EC Commission and the US Government through the conclusion of the Washington Agreement of 23 Sep. 1991, which, following the unfortunate events described in section 6 of Chapter III of this book, was finally entered into by the Council and the Commission under their joint decision of 10 Apr. 1995 ([1995] OJ L95, p. 45 f).

Let me add that the Council Regulation on the control of concentrations between undertakings, in the text currently in force, together with the related Commission Regulation on its implementation, plays a major role in respect of non-Community multinationals as well.[215]

27. ANTI-DUMPING AND ANTI-SUBSIDY RULES AS APPLIED TO NON-COMMUNITY MULTINATIONALS

Finally, the Community's regulatory actions against non-Community multinational also include an involved set of anti-dumping and anti-subsidy rules introduced for adjustment to the norms that have been adopted under the GATT over the years. In this connection, reference should be made to the analysis presented elsewhere in this book.[216] For the time being, let me stress that Community measures in this matter have gradually been refined over time, with a view to preventing non-Community undertakings from resorting to circumventing techniques. This is evidenced by the frequent revision of EU anti-dumping and anti-subsidy regulations above and beyond the necessary adjustments to be made in compliance with international texts developed at the *Kennedy Round* (1967), the *Tokyo Round* (1979) and the *Uruguay Round* (1994).

It is enough, in this respect, to mention Council Regulation No. 1761/87 of 22 June 1987, dealing with the phenomenon of the so-called 'screwdriver plants', i.e. merely assembling factories established, especially by Japanese multinational enterprises, in any of the EU Member Countries, in order to make a product appear to have been 'manufactured' within the Community, even if it is actually of foreign origin and already hit by antidumping duties, thus circumventing their actual application.[217]

215. For the evolution of the Council Regulation of 21 Dec. 1989, and for Regulation (EC) No. 139/2004 of 20 Jan. 2004 and Commission Implementing Regulation (EC) No. 802/2004 of 7 Apr. 2004, see Chapter VI of this book generally, and especially section 17.

216. In particular, see Chapter IV, *passim*, in particular sections 18-22.

217. The provisions in question have remained essentially unchanged in the present regulations both on dumping and on subsidies in the ambit of the far wider problem of 'circumvention'. On this, see Chapter IV of this book.

Chapter VI

Competition Law between General Theory and Actual Implementation

SUMMARY:

1. The peculiarities of the rules on competition in general.
2. Protection of interests under European competition law.
3. Competition law rules as an essential part of EU formation. The legal basis of European rules. The limited scope of this study.
4. Objectives and aims of EU competition law rules.
5. The 'relevant' market and the significance of economic analysis.
6. The Commission's role in the EU competition law system.
7. Some aspects of the cumulation of the Commission's functions in administrative proceedings.
8. Immediate and direct applicability of Commission decisions.
9. Public enterprise and competition: Transparency of financial relations between Member States and public undertakings.
10. The Alitalia bailout and the European rules.
11. A criticism of the extensive application by the Commission of Article 87 EC, specifically in respect of State aid.
12. State aid by legislative Act under US law and new possible approaches in EU law.
13. Recovery decisions and rights of defence.
14. The Community Courts' control over Commission Decisions.
15. The scope of application of the Community's rules of competition law.

16. Direct applicability of the European rules on competition and the Member States' authorities' competence to apply them.
17. Relationships between Community rules and national rules.
18. Applying the subsidiarity principle having regard to the 'one-stop shop', and the multi-State examination of mergers.
19. Damages awarded for losses arising from infringements of antitrust rules.
20. Actions for damages brought by competing undertakings.
21. Actions for damages in consumer protection.
22. A new collective redress action: the so-called 'Italian class action'.
23. Italian courts' jurisdiction in collective redress actions and Community law.
24. Assessment of loss in antitrust cases.

1. THE PECULIARITIES OF THE RULES ON COMPETITION IN GENERAL

Whatever legal system is considered, the rules governing free competition have been set out very broadly with a view to their applicability to any possible situation. This peculiarity hardly matches the usual contents of any rules designed to place obligations or prohibitions on the intended addressees.

In principle, the rules on competition are addressed to 'undertakings', a quite relative concept indeed, which changes from one system to another, but one that can roughly be taken as referring to *autonomous entities organized for the actual operation of an economic activity.*

The meaning of 'undertaking' under EU competition law emerges, for example, from the judgment of the ECJ of 10 January 2006, Case C-222/04, *Ministero dell'Economia e delle Finanze* v *Cassa di Risparmio di Firenze, Fondazione Cassa di Risparmio di San Miniato* and *Cassa di Risparmio di San Miniato,*[1] where it was stated:

> In the field of competition law, the concept of 'undertaking' covers any entity *engaged in an economic activity*, regardless of its legal status and the way in which it is financed. [*Emphasis added*].

The same judgment also specified the extent of the notion of 'economic activity', as follows:

> Any activity consisting in offering goods or services on a given market *is an economic activity*. Whilst, usually, the economic activity is carried on directly on the market, *that may, however, be the case* both of an operator in direct contact with the market and, indirectly, of another entity controlling that operator as part of an economic unit which they together form.

1. [2006] ECR I-289, grounds 107-113.

> In that regard, the mere fact of holding shares, even controlling shareholdings, is insufficient to characterise as economic an activity of the entity holding those shares, *when it gives rise only to the exercise of the rights attached to the status of shareholder or member*, as well as, if appropriate, *the receipt of dividends*, which are merely the fruits of the ownership of an asset. On the other hand, an entity which, owning controlling shareholdings in a company, actually exercises that control *by involving itself directly or indirectly in the management thereof*, must be regarded as taking part in the economic activity carried on by the controlled undertaking and must therefore itself, in that respect, be regarded as an undertaking [in the field of competition law]. [*Emphasis added*].

The nationality or place of establishment of an undertaking is, however, entirely irrelevant, whatever its legal status, it being sufficient that it operates, even just sporadically, in any one market or that *just* the effects of its activity operate in such a way as to alter the normal course of competition in that market. As is discussed in more details below, even the way in which the 'effects theory' is understood is apt to vary from one country to another, For example, its use has a significant extension in the US antitrust system, to the point that 'extraterritorial application' of the rules on competition could be a phrase aptly used in that respect. Within Europe, however, the Court of Justice has, over the years, insisted on pointing out the 'territoriality' requirement in each relevant case, also when confirming the implementation by the Commission of the effects theory.

What is certain is that, in this area as well, the phenomenon of globalization, which entails the concentration of the means of production on countries where their costs are the lowest, brings about disparities at an 'international level' between competing undertakings, thereby raising entirely new problems which cannot easily be solved in relation to any single market.

In technical terms, from the point of view of any one system, national rules on competition fall within the class of 'mandatory rules of law', i.e. rules that mandatorily apply in respect of the private parties to which they are addressed in connection with any legal situation, irrespective of any provisions of private international law chosen by them to govern their contractual relations.[2]

The rules governing competition within the European Union must apply in each of the Member States' legal systems in relation to any issue of Community relevance on the basis of whether primary or secondary provisions of Community law, thus resulting in the general primacy of the European Union's law over national laws in the sense now widely accepted and with the specific adjustments to be made from time to time, as discussed further below.

Competition law rules are, however, more likely to generate conflicts in connection with their applicability in cases involving undertakings belonging to non-EU countries, although even they are undoubtedly bound by the obligations and

---

2. Refer, in particular, to paras 15 and 16 of Ch. I, and to para. 8 of Ch. III of this book.

prohibitions provided by Community law in relation to the European internal market and are consequently exposed to any penalty threatened by the European Commission whenever the effects of a breach of those obligations or prohibitions occur within the internal market.

In fact, the question of the protection of free competition essentially arises to its fullest extent in the industrial countries' legal systems, whose economies are based on free trade standards.

In countries characterized by a command economy or even in developing countries, central authorities may be less interested in laying down comprehensive rules on competition. This occurs essentially for ideological reasons in the former systems, and, in the latter systems, because subjection of economic activities to free competition rules would ultimately benefit any foreign multinationals that happen to operate in those countries' markets.

Yet, the role of competition rules in market economies is not only to balance economic relations between competing entities within the State's territory. Competition law provisions are also intended to guarantee compliance with free market rules and, above all, to work as a *driver* of the national economy. In a system of healthy competition, observance of the rules of the game in any sector of a market economy urge undertakings to endeavour to sell, and otherwise to trade in, goods and services at increasingly competitive prices.[3] And so, full compliance with competition rules also operates as a powerful anti-inflationary device.

This having been said, one of the most obvious consequences of the very broad formulation of competition rules is that the authorities called upon to enforce them are given very broad scope of discretion. Thus, anyone who investigates into pro- and anti-competitive phenomena may express judgments of just a relative import most of the times, and often mutually conflicting opinions, under the influence of a wide range of frequently understated implications of a socio-political type.[4]

This common connotation of the rules for the protection of competition is made more noticeable by the close connection the specific cases subject to them usually have with ever-changing economic factors. In fact, except in matters relating to currency or foreign exchange controls,[5] which are usually dealt with according to

3. These aspects have aptly been highlighted by Ms Diana Bracco, President of the Regional Employers Association of Lombardy, Assolombarda, in the Report she presented to the Association on 23 Jun. 2008 (p. 2): 'Competitive pressures force enterprises to rethink themselves; racing against, and confronting, others help developing forms of intelligent adaptation; and competition generates a drive to improvements in all areas relevant to this Country's life'.
4. About the strong ideological connotation of competition law, see Bork, *The Antitrust Paradox* (New York, 1993), p. 3 f.
5. See Chs III and IV, respectively, of this volume. For the purpose and functions of foreign exchange control systems, see also Santa Maria, 'Les critères d'application des règles italiennes des changes', cit.; Id. 'Disciplina valutaria, sanzioni penali e certezza del diritto', cit., p. 603 ff.

macroeconomic criteria, or even to the rules on dumped or unlawfully subsidized exports, closely associated as they are with international law issues, no sector of legal life appears to be more linked to economic factors than the protection of free competition.

The entire problem of free competition is compounded by globalization, a phenomenon often referred to or discussed in details elsewhere in this volume.

Yet, the strong economic characterization considered here cannot – as is the case in relation to antidumping proceedings wherever any is brought – have an absolute value, as it is necessarily linked to a relevant market, whichever it may be, in relation to that specific area, the 'relevant' market in fact. And the *relevance* of the market involves two different profiles, examining which is equally preparatory to a delimitation of the scope for assessing an undertaking's conduct as *pro-* or *anti*-competitive. Therefore, the necessary yardsticks against which the actual occurrence of a competition-distorting effect should be scrutinized are the relevant product market and the relevant geographic market.

No serious line of reasoning can be offered in such scrutiny, unless it is quite specific and to the point, without any accurate delimitation of the market in question, as determined against the two yardsticks indicated as ideally suited to identify and fix the boundaries of the 'playground'.

Both at a juridical level and in general terms, depending on the characteristics of the system of competition rules just highlighted above, irrespective of the legal system in question, because of the specificity of any one case, the authority responsible for assessing an undertaking's actual or alleged conduct should use precedent warily enough, refraining from resorting to the comfortable quotation of individual sentences outside a genuinely equivalent context.

2. PROTECTION OF INTERESTS UNDER EUROPEAN COMPETITION LAW

In an article[6] following the judgment whereby the Court of First Instance confirmed the Commission's decision in *Microsoft*,[7] Neelie Kroes, as the European Commissioner for Competition, followed her predecessor Mario Monti's practice of communicating by press releases to pour oil on troubled waters in connection with differences in approach allegedly leading to differences over similar cases

6. In The Wall Street Journal of 26 Sep. 2007.
7. The *Microsoft* judgment is dated 17 Sep. and it has not been published yet in ECR. The Commission's Decision was adopted on 24 Mar. 2004, and it was published in [2007] O.J. L32, p. 23.

between the competent US antitrust authorities and the European Commission, as follows:

> Both in Europe and America the objective is to find the *best solution for consumers*, the best way to solve competition problems so as *to increase consumer welfare*. [*Emphasis added*].

In particular, she stated:

> *By breaking up international cartels*, it saves European consumers at least $ 6 billion every year. [*Emphasis added*].

And further specified:

> Sound rules, rigorously applied, benefit European consumers every day, for competition usually *induces companies to offer the best products at the lowest prices*. [*Emphasis added*].

Ms Kroes then added some examples showing the usefulness for consumers of the Commission's most recent actions in such areas as telephony, the energy industry, the mail services market and the pharmaceuticals market. In particular, in referring to the pharmaceuticals market, she noted:

> The European Commission has acted against the drug company AstraZeneca for misuse of the patent system and the drug authorization system, which delayed market entry by generic drug manufacturers.[8]

As for the big question, underlying the entire matter, of whether or not competition rules are intended to protect law-abiding undertakings first, and consumers only as a result, the European Commissioner for Competition seemed to attach no special importance to a direct answer to such question, and to incline toward the belief that the basic objective is consumer protection, well aware as she was that observance by every undertaking of the rules of the game is conducive to enhanced protection of the undertakings themselves and of the market in any event. Thus:

> *Antitrust law opens markets and keeps them open for companies to compete*; it does not choose who wins. Inevitably, however, when a *monopolist's abusive*

8. The title of the press release of 15 Jun. 2005 (19/05/237) is self-explanatory in this respect: *Commission fines AstraZeneca € 60 million for misusing patent system to delay market entry of competing generic drug*. In fact, on the same date, the Commission issued a decision in which it found the Anglo-Swedish group responsible for serious abuses of its dominant market position in relation to its ulcer drug *Losec* (omeprazole), a proton pump inhibitor, by misusing its patents with different periods of protection in different countries to block or even only to delay market entry of competing generic drugs and to prevent 'parallel' imports. The decision was challenged by *AstraZeneca* before the Court of First Instance on 25 Aug. 2005, Case T-231/05, and it is still pending. The case reflects the Commission's will to pursue consumer protection in furtherance of Art. 82 EC. In that specific case, *AstraZeneca*'s conduct, in addition to violating Article 82 EC, also violated Art. 54 of the Agreement on the European Economic Area, since, in the Commission's view, it also concerned the Norwegian market.

> *behaviour* is stopped, chances are that its competitors will have a stronger position on the market afterward. So when *differences of opinion emerge across the Atlantic* as to what to do in a particular case we need to move beyond the simplistic rhetoric of whether one side protects consumers or competitors. [*Emphasis added*].

Because of the role of their author, these statements deserve serious consideration, although it is my view that they fall short of a full coverage of the area of competition issues.

Consumers' wellbeing cannot be the only ultimate interest to be protected in any relevant case in any of the many sectors in which competition rules are to be enforced. Were it so, any behaviour of one or more undertakings that does not involve an increase in the price of a good or service or does not artificially prevent its reduction in any one market would never be regarded as anti-competitive, whereas any opposite behaviour would always be so.

This conclusion sounds simplistic and it is at least in contrast, in fact, with the system of the derogations generally allowed, by category or on a case-by-case basis, in relation to restrictive agreements. It also appears to be in contrast with the system of commitments, conditions or undertakings relating to the various issues (such as the granting of a permit or the mutually agreed closure of an antitrust investigation) in respect of which they may come into play.

For example, in the area of State aid, as will be discussed in details below, the ultimate objective seems to be market protection or non-discrimination between traders based in different Member States, whereas consumer protection appears to be an intermediate objective of a sort. Especially in this last respect, there can be no reasonable doubt that the relevant rules should be revised or, at least, applied by taking into due account the effects of globalization – as remote as they can be from the conventional view of competition rules.

In fact, the rules intended to protect free competition under Community law are addressed to undertakings in the sense indicated above, and pertain to their behaviours, which must be assessed (though while taking into account the consumer's interest) as to whether, and to what extent, they 'may affect trade between Member States' or 'have as their object or effect the prevention, restriction or distortion of competition within the common market'.

Lastly, in a different respect, also in light of the obvious uncertainties attaching to the application of competition law rules by the Commission as well as by the competent national authorities, the essential factor to ensure the unbiased use of such rules is judicial scrutiny, the only one device capable by itself to provide 'certainties' or to curtail 'uncertainties' in any field of this complex matter, with a view to the protection of both the undertakings affected by acts of unfair competition and the consumers. And, as judicial scrutiny in each relevant case *can only be carried out ex post*, it must be as strict, but also as unbiased as possible.

3. COMPETITION LAW RULES AS AN ESSENTIAL PART OF EU FORMATION. THE LEGAL BASIS OF EUROPEAN RULES. THE LIMITED SCOPE OF THIS STUDY

The European rules on competition are laid down in Part Three ('Community Policies') of the Treaty of Rome, Chapter I of Title VI, under the heading 'Rules on Competition', and include the provisions from Article 81 through Article 89 EC. The relevant provisions are grouped into two sections. One is headed 'Rules applying to undertakings', and contains Articles 81 to 86. The other is headed 'Aids granted by States', and contains Articles 87 to 89.[9]

Broadly speaking, the European Union's competition rules follow as many as five different main routes.

The legal basis of four of them is to be found direct in the EC Treaty, namely: the provision in Article 81, which prohibits all *agreements* affecting trade between Member States or restricting competition within the common market; the provision in Article 82, which prohibits undertakings having a *dominant position* within the common market from *abusing* such position; the provision of Article 86, which addresses the case of public undertakings or of any undertakings entrusted by the State with *the operation of services of general economic interest*; and the provisions in Articles 87 et seq., which regulate Member States' interventions in the economy in the form of *aid* to undertakings, which may distort competition and is, therefore, prohibited, so long as any such aid meets certain stated standards and unless the Commission finds that a derogation is applicable.

Implementation of the framework rules contained in the Treaty is now ensured chiefly by Council Regulation (EC) No. 1/2003 of 16 December 2002 on the implementation of the rules on competition laid down in Articles 81 and 82 of the EC Treaty,[10] and by the so-called 'Modernisation Package' consisting of six Commission Communications and Commission Regulation (EC) No. 773/2004 of 7 April 2004 relating to the conduct of proceedings by the Commission pursuant to Articles 81 and 82 of the EC Treaty.[11]

The last, but by no means the least, of these main routes relates to the control of *concentrations between undertakings*, which has its regulatory basis in Council Regulation No. 4064/89 of 21 December 1989, as amended by Regulation No. 1310/1997,[12] and eventually superseded, effective from 1 May 2004, by Council Regulation No. 139/2004 of 20 January 2004.[13]

9. Article 91 of the Rome Treaty on 'internal dumping' is no longer part of Chapter 1, as it was repealed by the Amsterdam Treaty.
10. [2003] O.J. L1, p. 1.
11. [2004] O.J. L123, p. 18.
12. Regulation No. 4064/89 is in [1989] O.J. L395, as amended for *corrigenda* in [1990] O.J. L257. Regulation No. 1310/97 is in [1997] O.J. L180.
13. Regulation No. 139/2004 is in [2004] O.J. L24, p. 1.

This was because the original text of the Rome Treaty lacked a specific provision to regulate concentrations between undertakings. As a result, complicated interpretational issues arose, which the Commission's changed approach and subsequent judgments of the Court of Justice compounded further over the 1980s, until the a complex set of rules were issued on 21 December 1989.[14] These rules, as modified in progress and superseded in 2004, after more than fifteen years of revising efforts, now provide a model of functionality.

On this basis, topics such as these, each of which would require a sizeable monograph, cannot be discussed here at any length.

Therefore, for sheer lack of space, leaving aside not only specific issues[15] but also the institutional aspects of the classic subjects of competition law, such as those relating to the basic notions of control over restrictive agreements and the abuse of dominant positions, I will only offer some considerations about general criticalities, chiefly in the areas of public undertakings and State aid. For the former issue is closely linked with privatization, a phenomenon already covered in the third chapter of this book, in connection with the free movement of capital, and the latter issue has clear implications in terms of globalization.[16]

---

14. On the evolution of practice in preparation to Regulation No. 4064/89, see my study 'Il Regolamento comunitario n. 4064/89 sul controllo delle concentrazioni' [1990] Riv. Dir. Comm. Int, p. 127 ff., containing an extensive review of the Commission Decisions and the Judgments of the ECJ leading up to the regulatory definition of 21 Dec. 1989.
15. For the regulations on transports and agriculture not considered in this chapter, because of their special character, see *Commission, Competition Law in the European Communities*, Vol. I-A, *Rules applicable to undertakings* (Brussels-Luxembourg, 1994), pp. 301 f. and 445 f, respectively.; Casanova, Brignardello, *Diritto dei trasporti. Infrastrutture e accesso al mercato* (Milan, 2004); Munari, *Il diritto comunitario dei trasporti* INT. III – 22; Various Authors, *Principio di sussidiarietà e politica dei trasporti nell'unione europea.*
16. The vast literature on EC competition law rules cannot certainly be reviewed in this book. Therefore, without any pretension of completeness, and only in respect of the most recent studies, in addition to the authors cited in the footnotes to this chapter, see chiefly:

    a) About general problems, Bernini, *Le regole di concorrenza nei trattati comunitari* (Rimini, 1982); Costa, *Il diritto CEE anti-trust, nella giurisprudenza della Commissione e della Corte Comunitaria* (Naples, 1984); Korah, *Competition Law of Britain and the Common Market* (3ª ed., The Hague, Boston, London, 1982); Korah, Pavesio e Zanon di Valgiurata, *Il diritto della concorrenza nella CEE* (Milan, 1984); Pescatore, 'Public and Private Aspects of Community Competition Law' [1986] Ann. Proc. Fordham Corp. L. Inst. (Hawk ed., 1987), p. 383 f.; Mertens de Wilmars, 'Statement of Reasons and Methods of Interpretation in the Case Law of the EC Court of Justice Relating to Art. 85 and 86' [1987] ibid. (Hawk ed., New York, Oakland, Albany, 1988), p. 607 f.; Schroter, 'Antitrust Analysis under Art. 85 (1) and (3)', ibid., p. 645 f.; Waelbroeck, 'Antitrust Analysis under Art. 85 (1) and (3)', ibid., p. 693 f.; Bernini, *Un secolo di filosofia antitrust* (Bologna, 1991); Floridia-Catelli, *Diritto antitrust* (Milan, 2003); Tosato-Bellodi, *Il nuovo diritto europeo della concorrenza* (Milan, 2004); Moavero Milanesi, *Diritto della concorrenza dell'Unione Europea* (Naples, 2004); Ritter & Braun, *European Competition Law: A Practitioner's Guide* (The Hague, 2004); Whish, *Competition Law* (Oxford, 2004); Idot, *Droit communautaire de la concurrence* (Brussels, 2004); Van Bael & Bellis, *Competition Law of the European Community* (The Hague, 2005); Kerse & Khan, *EC Antitrust Procedure* (London, 2005); Ortiz Blanco, *European*

The rest of this chapter will be devoted to the EU Courts' review of Commission decisions, to the relationship between European and national rules on the matter and to issues relating to compensation for damages.

Community Competition Procedure (Oxford, 2006); Various Authors, *La concorrenza*, Frignani & Pardolesi, Eds (Turin, 2006); Bellamy & Child, *European Community Law of Competition* (London, 2007); Faull & Nikpay, *The EC Law of Competition* (Oxford, 2007); Pappalardo, *Il diritto comunitario della concorrenza – Profili sostanziali* (Turin, 2007).

b) For a comparison of the EU system with US rules, and extra-territorial application of competition rules generally, Fox, 'Abuse of a Dominant Position under the Treaty of Rome – a Comparison with U.S. Law' [1983] Ann. Proc. Fordham, cit. (Hawk ed., 1984), p. 367 f.; Stockmann, 'Foreign Application of European Antitrust Laws' [1985] ibid., (Hawk ed. 1986), p. 251 s.; van der Esch, 'Some Aspects of "Extra-Territorial" Infringement of EEC Competition Rules', ibid., p. 285; Fox, 'Extraterritoriality and Antitrust – is "Reasonableness" the Answer?' [1986] ibid., (Hawk ed. 1987), p. 49 f.; Id., 'EC Rules on Undistorted Competition and U.S. Antitrust Laws: the Limits of Comparability' [1988] ibid., (Hawk ed. 1989), p. 18-1; Denozza, *Antitrust – Leggi monopolistiche e tutela dei consumatori nella CEE e negli USA* (Bologna, 1988).

c) About the relationships of EU rules with national rules on competition, Stockmann, 'EEC Competition Law and Member State Competition Laws' [1987] Ann. Proc. Fordham, cit. (Hawk ed. 1988), p. 265 f.; Joliet, 'National Anti-Competitive Legislation and Community Law' [1988] ibid., (Hawk ed. 1989), p. 16-1 f.; Various Authors, *Diritto antitrust italiano – Commento alla legge 10 ottobre 1990, n. 287*, Frignani, Pardolesi, Patroni Griffi & Ubertazzi, Eds. (Bologna, 1993); Various Authors, *L'antitrust italiano – Le regole della concorrenza* (Milan, 2003); Fattori-Todino, *La disciplina della concorrenza in Italia* (Bologna, 2004); Guerri, *L'applicazione del diritto antitrust in Italia dopo il regolamento CE n. 1/2003* (Turin, 2005); Various Authors, *L'applicazione del diritto comunitario della concorrenza – Commentario al regolamento (CE) n. 1/2003 del Consiglio del 16 dicembre 2002*, Adinolfi, Daniele, Nascimbene & Amadeo, Eds. (Milan, 2007).

d) On public undertakings and State aid, Minervini, 'Lo Stato italiano e le imprese pubbliche. Ricerca preliminare ai fini dell'applicazione dell'art. 90 del Trattato C.E.E.' [1967] Riv. dir. int. priv. proc, p. 759 f.; Gilmour, 'The Enforcement of Community Law by the Commission in the Context of State Aids: the Relationship between Art. 93 and 169 and the Choice of Remedies' [1981] Com. Market Law Rev., p. 63 f.; Brothwood, 'The Commission Directive on Transparency of Financial Relation between Member States and Public Undertakings' [1981] ibid., p. 207 f.; Hellingman, 'State Participation as State Aid under Art. 92 of the EEC Treaty: the Commission's Guidelines' [1986] ibid., p. 111 f.; Quigley & Collins, *EC State Aid Law and Policy* (Oxford-Portland, 2003); Various Authors, *Aides d'Etat*, Dony & Smits, Eds. (Bruxelles, 2005); Various Authors, *Concorrenza e Aiuti di Stato*, Santa Maria Ed. (Turin, 2006); Hancher, Ottervanger, Slot, *EC State Aids* (London, 2006); Various Authors, *The EC State Aid Regime: Distortive Effects of State Aid on Competition and Trade*, Sanchez & Rydelski Eds. (London, 2006); Various Authors, *Competition and State Aid*, Santa Maria Ed. (The Hague, 2007).

e) About EU rules on concentrations, Various Authors, *Il fenomeno delle concentrazioni di imprese nel diritto interno e internazionale* (Padua, 1989); Mestmäcker, 'Merger Control in the Common Market: between Competition Policy and Industrial Policy'[1988] Ann. Proc. Fordham, cit. (Hawk ed., 1989) p. 20-1 f.; Schwarz, 'New EEC Regulation on Mergers, Partial Mergers and Joint Ventures', ibid., p. 21-1; Bellamy, 'Mergers outside the Scope of the New Mergers Regulation – Implications of the Philip Morris Judgment', ibid., p. 22-1; Fox, 'Federalism, Standards, and Common Market Merger Control', ibid., p. 23-1; Scherer, 'European Community Merger Policy: why? why not?', ibid., p. 24-1; Goyder, 'U.K. Merger Law and Policy in the Wake of the EEC Regulation – a British View', ibid., p. 26-1; Hirsch, 'Member State Merger Law and Policy in the Wake of the EEC Regulations – a German View', ibid., p. 27-1; Rossi, 'Control of Concentrations: the Wake of the EEC Regulations

As discussed in details below, the rules on restrictive agreements, abuse of dominant positions, control over concentrations, public undertakings and State aid are as many aspects of a general policy of the European Union based on the 'free market' notion, which includes the whole of Member States' territories, with the corollaries of the protection of the *free operation* of any undertaking, whether public or private, *without discriminations* between nationals and 'Community' foreigners or between residents and non-residents of any one Member State, within the EU market as a whole.

4. OBJECTIVES AND AIMS OF EU COMPETITION LAW RULES

The starting assumption is that antitrust rules provide one of the most dynamic and significant parts of Community law with a view to 'establishing the economic and political integration of Europe'.

There can be no doubt that, even before the entry into force of the Maastricht Treaty, the Community's aims were not merely political, but social as well. It is sufficient, in this respect, to mention the challenging contents of the Treaty establishing the European Economic Community in its original version. Article 2 stated:

> It shall be the aim of the Community, by establishing a Common Market and progressively approximating the economic policies of Member States, to promote throughout the Community a harmonious development of economic activities, a continuous and balanced expansion, an increased stability, an accelerated raising of the standard of living and closer relations between its Member States.

Article 3, in the wording used before the amendments introduced by the Treaty establishing the European Union:

> For the purposes set out in the preceding Article, the activities of the Community shall include, under the conditions and with the timing provided for in this Treaty: ... (f) the establishment of a system ensuring that competition shall not be distorted in the Common Market ...

Thus, since the very beginning, ensuring fair play in competition was understood as a 'device' essential to the progressive establishment of the common market.

---

and the Debate in Italy', ibid., p. 28-1; de Mello, 'French Merger Law and Policy in the Wake of EEC Regulation – a French View', ibid., p. 29-1; Cook & Kerse, *EC Merger Control* (London, 2005); Lindsay, *The EC Merger Regulation: Substantive Issues* (London, 2006); Levy, *European Merger Control Law* (Newark, 2007).

Community competition law has become more and more important over time, at the same pace as the gradual development of the Union. In a first draft of the Lisbon Treaty, the matter was treated as a primary 'objective', even indicated among the fundamental aims to be pursued.[17]

Moreover, the fact that, upon French pressures, the topic was later formally downgraded from a text in the Treaty to an annex, has not substantially affected the import of the entire matter. Competition has been made the subject matter of Protocol 6 annexed to the Treaty on European Union and the Treaty on the Functioning of the European Union, which reads:

> The High Contracting Parties, considering that the internal market as set out in Article 2 of the Treaty on European Union *includes a system ensuring that competition is not distorted*, have agreed that, to this end, the Union shall, if necessary, take action under the provisions of the Treaties, including under Article 308 of the Treaty on the Functioning of the European Union. [*Emphasis added*].

In fact, the closer the European Union comes to an actual union of States, the more essential becomes due observance of the rules on competition for the proper operation of an effective *single market*.

The very fact that implementation of competition rules at Community level has been made a matter for the Commission of the European Union – on an exclusive basis by the Lisbon Treaty as well – in one of the institutional functions the Commission is called upon to discharge in relation to the internal market over an extent equal to the summation of all Member States' domestic markets, affects the contents of those rules in two respects: firstly, in respect of the progressive establishment of the European Union; secondly, and chiefly, in respect of the impact the other rules and the principles laid down in the EU Treaties have on the interface between default rules of contract law and competition.

As for the latter profile, consider the *non-discrimination* principle underlying the implementation of each of the four fundamental freedoms within the EU, a principle which becomes also highly relevant to the implementation of the rules of competition law.

Also consider the case-law principle according to which the granting of any derogation under Article 81(3), in the matter of prohibited agreements, or under Article 87(2) and (3), with regard to the recognition of State aid as 'compatible', cannot even be proposed, in the Commission's view, if the relevant case constitutes an infringement of a different rule of Community law.[18]

---

17. See Tesauro, *Diritto comunitario* (5th ed., Padua, 2008), pp. 24 and 629-30.
18. On this approach, see Judgments of the ECJ of 21 May 1980, Case C-73/79, *Commission of the European Communities* v *Italian Republic*, [1980] ECR, p. 01533, ground 11, and of 15 Jun. 1993, Case C-225/91, *Matra SA* v *Commission*, [1993] ECR I-3203, ground 41. See also Judgment of the Court of First Instance of 31 Jan. 2001, *Weyl Beef Products BV, Exportslachterij Chris Hogeslag BV and Groninger Vleeshandel BV* v *Commission*, [2001] ECR II-303, ground 75. The Commission has interpreted this case-law extensively, and has accordingly taken the view that no aid can be found compatible *even* where the measure appears, at first

Finally, the framework provisions on State aid also include Article 96 EC (originally Article 101 of the Rome Treaty) in the chapter dealing with 'approximation of laws'.

The first paragraph of Article 96 reads:

> Where the Commission finds that a difference between the provisions laid down by law, regulation or administrative action in Member States is distorting the conditions of competition in the common market and that the resultant distortion needs to be eliminated, it shall consult the Member States concerned. [*Emphasis added*].

The second paragraph of the same article, itself kept unchanged except for the numbering, reads:

> If such consultation does not result in an agreement eliminating the distortion in question, the Council shall, on a proposal from the Commission, acting by a qualified majority, issue the necessary directives. *The Commission and the Council may take any other appropriate measures provided for in this Treaty.* [*Emphasis added*].

Only in this context, and just because of the principle of *legal certainty*, can any justification be accorded to the choice taken by the Commission and endorsed by the EU Courts in case-law – though almost entirely neglected by Member States in implementing Article 96 EC – to accept the even deep disparities still existing in material law,[19] as well as in tax law,[20] between Member States in respect of undertakings. These are key disparities, which, *per se*, make competing enterprises' performance unequal across the European market.

---

examination, to be contrary to secondary rules (i.e. Directives). See Invitation to submit comments pursuant to Art. 88(2) of the EC Treaty, in Procedure C 70/03 (ex NN 72/03) – *Measure in favour of professional sports clubs* – '*Decreto Salva Calcio*', cit., in particular point 26. In that case, the Commission took the view that Art. 3(1-*bis*) of Law Decree No. 282 of 24 Dec. 2002, as converted into Act No. 27 of 21 Feb. 2003, in addition to qualifying as State aid, entailed violation of the Fourth and Seventh Accounting Directives. This violation of the accounting directives was alleged by the Commission (DG Internal Market) as a separate act from the procedure opened by DG Competition alleging State aid (Letter 2003/2172, C(2003) 4211 of 11 Nov. 2003 from Commissioner Bolkestein). The State aid procedure was closed by Commission Decision pursuant to Art. 7(3), Reg. 659/99 of 22 Jun. 2005, since the measure at issue was not recognized to be State aid. The Commission reached this conclusion following action by the Italian Parliament, which on the former's request removed the phrase '. . . *for tax purposes* . . .' from the text of the original decree in question (even though such a phrase had no concrete influence on the application of the law at issue). See Commission Press Release IP/05/777 of 22 Jun. 2005. At a closer scrutiny, the measure should not be qualified as 'aid' in the first place, since the requirement of 'State resources' was already non-existing before the amended text was introduced in 2005. See Santa Maria, 'Professional Sport and Competition' in Aa.Vv., *Competition and State Aid*, cit., p. 291 ff.

19. Refer to Chapter I, *passim.*
20. See, among many, Judgments of the ECJ of 11 Dec. 2003, Case C-364/01, *Barbier*, [2003] ECR I-15013, and of 12 Sep. 2006, Case C-196/04, *Cadbury Scweppes*, [2006] ECR I-7995.

While a Member State in which business income is generally taxed, including social and insurance contributions, at a rate around 30%, is unlikely to issue 'selective' measures qualifying as *aid* in the form of tax exemptions, another Member State in which a far wider gap exists, with business tax rates nearly twice as high than the rates applied to other incomes, is far more likely to do so.[21]

As for the impact of the new rules introduced through Treaties amending the Treaty of Rome over time, consider the provision of Article 163(1) EC introduced by the European Single Act, as amended by the Maastricht Treaty, which specifies:

> The Community shall have *the objective of strengthening the scientific and technological bases of Community industry and encouraging it to become more competitive at international level....* [*Emphasis added*].

It is even too obvious that this provision has introduced both a new assessment criterion, normally foreign to competition law, and a clear recommendation that any assessment in this field should be made with a wider view. Therefore, neither indication ought to be taken into account by the Commission, for example when reviewing a concentration deal or when assessing an aid measure for compatibility.

In relation to privatization operations, which have frequently taken place in several Member States over the last few years, the Commission has imposed severe restrictions on the use of 'golden shares'.[22] On the other hand, by referring to the principle of the neutrality of the system of property ownership, private or public, under Article 295 EC – within the mesh of substantive law and competition law provisions – the Commission has shown scanty interest in the *pro*-competition aspects inhering *per se* in the market following a privatization, and has, instead, emphasized any *anti*-competition aspects as might be found in that privatization, and categorized them as State aid because of the tax exemptions granted by statute to the 'public' undertakings of the State concerned in order to facilitate privatization.[23]

As irrelevant to the implementation by the Commission of competition law rules remain the disparities between undertakings depending on whether the undertaking concerned operates in a Member State participating in 'euro zone' or in a Member State not participating in it, whether because of its failure to meet the Treaty requirements or at its own free choice.

---

21. Nonetheless, EU Courts tend to take an attitude of unyielding neglect in this respect. See Judgment of the Court of 22 Mar. 1977, Case C-78/76, *Steinike & Weinlig*, [1977] ECR 595, ground 24, where it is finally stated that: '*[T]he effects of more than one distortion of competition on trade between member states do not cancel one another out but accumulate and the damaging consequences to the common market are increased*'.
22. See Chapter III, paras 11 ff. of this book.
23. See Commission Decision No. 2002/581/EC of 11 Dec. 2001 on the tax measures for banks and banking foundations implemented by Italy [2002] O.J. L184, p. 27 ff; and Commission Decision No. 2003/193/EC of 5 Jun. 2002 on State aid No. C 27/99 (ex NN 69/98) granted by Italy in the form of tax exemptions and subsidized loans to public utilities with a majority public capital holding [2003] O.J. L77, p. 21 ff.

The undertakings based in non-participating States will, as already observed in Chapter III, benefit from flexible rates of exchange to the euro or even to the US dollar, as is the case with the British pound, a less strong currency than the euro. As a result, the UK undertakings enjoy a competitive edge over the undertakings operating in the euro area in the sales of goods and services outside the United Kingdom, but within the EU 'single' market, depending on the exchange rate fluctuations as regards Euro which, because of the competent UK authorities' unilateral choice, ranged within a wide band close to 30% from early 2002 to 30 June 2008.

Hence, an additional advantage arises to those undertakings in their exports to countries outside the European Union, if only because the national Member State concerned, unlike the Member States within the Eurozone ESCB, is in a position to manage almost at will its exchange rate to the US dollar, which remains the benchmark currency for the vast majority of international trade transactions.

The fact that the Commission has invariably, in its assessment of competition issues, overlooked the various basic competitive advantages certain undertakings have over others within the European Union is hardly consistent with the 'single market' notion, which is, in fact, the mainstay of a full implementation of the core European Treaty rules in actual practice.

In other words, I wonder whether, in a legal system unitarily originating from the same common international agreements, it is correct to 'presume' that a 'single' market can be fully established without basic disparities being kept between undertakings within it, whatever their Member States of origin, or whether such real disparities should, instead, be taken into account with a view to achieving substantive justice, at least in reviewing State aid schemes or State aid granted by legislative measures.

It is appropriate to mention that, in principle and save for derogations accorded under the *subsidiarity* principle, it is for the Commission to decide whether or not certain behaviours of Community relevance qualify as prohibited agreements or decisions (negative opinion) and, above all, whether or not it may, pursuant to Articles 81(3) and 87(3) EC, authorize *prima-facie* prohibited behaviours (under exemptions) by category or on a case-by-case basis, depending, in the latter case, on factors regarded as favourable because of their *pro*-competition potentials, and eligible, as such, for derogations by exception from the general prohibition. It is also for the Commission to impose penalties, the extent of which may vary following a necessarily discretional scrutiny of the gravity and the duration of the infringement, albeit subject to the application of certain rules and based on the value of the infringing undertaking's turnover or on the sum of the sales of the members of an infringing association of undertakings.[24]

The observations offered above confirm that peculiarity of Community competition law, because of which, unlike any similar set of rules in any national legal

24. See, in particular, Article 23 of Regulation No. 1/2003 [2003] O.J. L1 and the Guidelines on the method of setting fines imposed pursuant to Art. 23(2)(a) of Regulation No. 1/2003 [2006] O.J. C210.

system, the EU's competition rules are not, for the reasons set forth above, an end to themselves, but are unavoidably influenced by their coexistence with the constitutional principles laid down by international treaties on which they are based.

As a result, the flexible and discretionary character typical of the application of national rules on competition is compounded by the fact that otherwise normal interpretations and applications may go by unattended, and apparently similar situations may be treated far differently from one another, if *Community interest* so demands, depending on the view taken of such interest by the Community, which is, in fact, the only one body institutionally responsible therefor under EU law.

5. THE 'RELEVANT' MARKET AND THE SIGNIFICANCE OF ECONOMIC ANALYSIS

It has become clear by now that any antitrust scrutiny necessarily entails a comparison between a *real* situation and the *ideal* model on the basis of a specific, *microeconomic* analysis to be conducted by the authority responsible for ensuring compliance with competition law rules. In addition to presenting an X-ray image of the undertaking or category of undertakings, irrespective of whether it is the applicant or the party under investigation, such analysis must identify the main competitors, their market shares and related markets, while duly distinguishing vertical from horizontal transactions, in relation to a specific business sector within a specific geographical area.

This complex logical process is *per se* of a clearly relative value. This also explains why many States' authorities called upon to examine the same transaction or the same behaviours – but always and only in relation to the *effects* generated by the markets over which they have jurisdiction – may express a plurality of views even in conflict with one another.[25]

Therefore, the Commission is called upon to conduct an economic analysis of each case brought to its scrutiny for any reason, and to do so from a *relative* point of view, which may be *different* depending on the features of that individual market – the *concretely* 'relevant' market, in fact – irrespective of the area of competition being considered.

In other words, quite beyond an abstract determination of the interests at stake that are deemed to deserve most legal protection[26] – either by those who favour the protection of the market and of the undertakings, even if only potentially

25. See the different view taken by the European Commission from the US authorities' in connection with Microsoft Corporation's pattern of conduct (refusal to supply and conditional licensing). See, in particular, Commission Decision of 24 May 2004, Case COMP/C-3/37.792.

26. For a bibliography about the purposes pursued by antitrust law, see the fundamental study by Denozza, *Antitrust – Leggi monopolistiche e tutela dei consumatori nella CEE e negli USA*, cit., p. 25, fn. 12.

competing among them,[27] or by those who consider the protection of the overall freedom of the system and of its individual participants, through consumer protection, to be the primary and overriding objective of antitrust rules,[28] or else by those who identify such primary objective in the pursuit of economic efficiency[29] – it is always in concrete, and depending on economic findings and assessments relating to any one undertaking competing with other undertakings in the same market at any one time, that the same virtuous patterns of conduct are ultimately determined as distinguished from those implying wrongful behaviours.

Obviously, the economic factor comes to the fore in relation to each relevant case not only from an objective point of view, in relation, that is, to the economic features of a product or a set of products or services in the relevant market, depending on the general and sectoral economic status of that market, but also from a subjective point of view, i.e. with regard to the economic power of the individual enterprises involved and to how some of them uses that power to disrupt the market. Only think, in this respect, from the point of view of EU competition law, of that misconduct prohibited by Article 82 EC, 'abuse of dominant position'.

Nonetheless, it is the very variety of the situations to be protected, depending on undertakings' individual competition-distorting behaviours, which, together with the ways in which competition rules are typically formulated, as discussed above, grants the competent authorities the power to scrutinize such behaviours – a discretional power, in fact, which has no equal in any other field of the law.[30] Nor would it make any sense to supplement this discretional power with the power arising from allowing the Commission, in relation to an investigation in any one of the areas in which competition is protected under EU law, to resort to presumptions or, which is the same, to assert anti-competition liabilities by merely using hackneyed phrases or just expedient case-law references restricted to isolated sentences, thereby saving itself the trouble to engage in an adequate preparation of the case.

What can hardly be understood is the Commission's foibles for economic analysis, especially in cases of alleged State aid, if only one considers that State aid is a matter almost entirely outside the Court of First Instance's scope for review of Commission decisions,[31] while the absence or shortage of economic assessments are quite apt to open the door to challenges.

---

27. See Frignani & Waelbroeck, *Disciplina della concorrenza nella CEE* (Turin, 1996), p. 6 ff.
28. Cfr. Denozza, *Antitrust – Leggi monopolistiche*, cit., *passim*, and especially, p. 9 f., 15 f., 153 f.
29. I refer to the 'Chicago School', about which see chiefly: Bork, 'The Antitrust Paradox', cit.; Posner, 'The Chicago School of Antitrust Analysis' [1979] Un. Penn. Law Rev., p. 925 f. For a criticism, see Denozza, 'Chicago, l'efficienza e il diritto antitrust' [1988] Giur. comm. I, p. 5 f., Id., *Antitrust*, cit., pp. 19 and 23 f.
30. Only in the matter of currency rules alone, can similar traits of unspecificity and flexibility be found, which, in relation to a now-repealed Italian regulatory system in force until the primary Act of 1989, ill matched the seriousness of the sanctions applicable to violations. See Santa Maria, 'Disciplina valutaria, sanzioni penali e certezza del diritto', cit., p. 603 ff. On the topic, generally, see Santa Maria 'Les critères d'application des règles italiennes des changes' in *Comunicazioni e Studi*, cit., pp. 221-299, *passim*.
31. Please, refer to section 10 ff. on State aid in this Chapter VI.

Hence, the pressing need for the Commission to conduct adequate investigations for the identification and classification of the *relevant market*, and the consequent correct positioning of the undertaking(s) being investigated.

True, economic analysis may have a rationale of its own when it is used in the matter of prohibited agreements or concerted practices, as opposed to abuses of dominant position or, if only potentially, to the authorization procedure involved in merger control or even to the procedure – a 'hybrid' one, because of its 'trilateral' quality – for the assessment of State aid cases, with respect to which the need for economic analysis is deemed, on not entirely convincing grounds, to be 'less immediate' than in respect of the other areas of competition law.[32] Nevertheless, economic analysis cannot be missing as the *common denominator* in an anti-trust investigation,[33] because of the relativistic function such an investigation must have anyhow, in its being intended, through the closing *decision*, rather to restore the correct rules of the game in a *given market* in which such rules were breached, than to address teachings or warnings to third parties or, even worse, to give everyone an indication of laudable behaviours for the future.

The Commission Notice of 1997 on the definition of relevant market refers direct to cases entailing the application of Articles 81 and 82 EC and of Regulation (EC) 139/2004 on merger control.[34]

In this connection, the Court of First Instance observed that the definition of relevant market has not the same function depending on whether Article 81 EC or Article 82 is to be applied. According to the CFI:

> In the context of the application of Article 81 EC, the reason for defining the relevant market is to determine whether the agreement, the decision by an association of undertakings or the concerted practice at issue is liable to affect trade between Member States and has as its object or effect the prevention, restriction or distortion of competition within the common market. That is why, for the purposes of Article 81(1) EC, the objections to the definition of the market adopted by the Commission cannot be seen in isolation from those concerning the impact on trade between Member States and the impairing of competition. Thus, the objection to the definition of the relevant market is of

---

32. See Commission Notice on the definition of relevant market for the purposes of Community competition law [1997] O.J. C372, 5. In the Commission's view, the notion of relevant market and the attendant economic approach may serve as a basis for the assessment of State aid case only '*when consideration of market power and therefore of the relevant market are raised in any particular case*'.
33. An opening to the introduction of economic analysis in State aid cases as well can be found in the *State Aid Action Plan* of 7 Jun. 2005, COM(2005) 107 final, especially para. 22: '*Making more use of a refined economic approach is a means to ensure a proper and more transparent evaluation of the distortions to competition and trade associated with state aid measures. This approach can also help investigate the reasons why the market by itself does not deliver the desired objectives of common interest and in consequence evaluate the benefits of state aid measures in reaching these objectives*'.
34. See point 1 of Commission Notice on the definition of relevant market for the purposes of Community competition law (97/C 372/03) [1997] O.J. C372, 5-13.

no consequence provided that the Commission has rightly concluded, on the basis of the documents referred to in the contested decision, that the agreement in question distorted competition and was liable to have an appreciable effect on trade between Member States.[35]

Footnote 1 to the Commission Notice on the definition of relevant market specifies that:

> The focus of assessment in State aid cases is the aid recipient and the industry/sector concerned rather than identification of competitive constraints faced by the aid recipient.

The Commission has always been up to such self-limitation. In assessing State aid cases, unlike other cases, it has tended to keep prior investigation to a minimum, and even to abstain from any economic analysis of the market, and has only offered formal references deprived of genuinely substantive contents when taking a decision at the end of administrative proceedings. In that context, in a decision concerning State aid, the *relevant product market* is defined on the basis of the PRODCOM product list,[36] whilst the *relevant geographic market* is nearly automatically identified with that of the whole European Union and made to coincide with the European Economic Area.[37]

However, having taken this approach, the Commission invariably fails to analyse the impact of alleged aid on both the recipient's competitive position and its competitors', as if violation of competition rules were *in re ipsa*. In fact, in doing so, the Commission essentially ends up in breaching the letter and the spirit of Article 87 EC, as discussed in more details further below.[38]

Basically, the Commission's changed attitude in this respect, although it acknowledged its propriety in the *Action Plan*[39] – partly following the Community Courts' 'permissive' precedent in relation to the Commission's pattern of conduct in this area – has essentially remained a dead letter. Only recently has the Court of First Instance, when seised of challenges to Commission decisions on State aid, at last emphasized the significance that the definition of relevant market has in this field of Community competition law as well, by annulling any decisions in

35. See Judgments of the Court of First Instance of 14 Dec. 2006, Joined Cases T-259/02 to T-264/02 and T-271/02, *Raiffeisen Zentralbank Österreich AG and Others* v *Commission*, [2006] ECR II-5169, ground 172, and of 11 Dec. 2003, Case T-61/99 *Adriatica di Navigazione* v *Commission*, [2003] ECR II-5349, ground 27.
36. See Council Regulation (EEC) No. 3924/91 of 19 Dec. 1991 on the establishment of a Community survey of industrial production [1991] O.J. L374, 1. See also Commission Regulation (EC) No. 317/2006 of 22 Dec. 2005 establishing for 2005 the Prodcom list of industrial products provided for by Council Regulation (EEC) No. 3924/91 [2006] O.J. L60, 1.
37. Crocioni, 'Can State Aid Policy Become More Economic Friendly?' [2006] World Competition 89.
38. See section 10 below.
39. See the *State Aid Action Plan* of 7 Jun. 2005, cit., and the Communication from the Commission of 20 Apr. 2004 (COM(2004) 293 final), 'A proactive Competition Policy for a Competitive Europe'.

preparation for which the Commission had failed to carry out adequate investigation in order to correctly identify the relevant market.[40]

Precisely because 'State aid' amounts to a *trilateral* relationship in which the State plays the necessary role of a granting party in favour of the recipient undertaking(s), and the Commission acts as the regulatory authority, especially in cases in which aid arises from a legislative act, the fundamental principle of reference is legal certainty, while it would be overly simplistic to assume at all and any times that the recipient is in the same position as the granting State, as if it were the holder of the same interests as the State's.

Only consider the frequent occurrence of a statute addressed to a specific class of undertakings, such as banks, 'municipal' utilities or sports clubs, in order to provide those undertakings with genuine or assumed tax benefits as an incentive to their 'choice' to enter into certain transactions for modernization or even for the 'cleaning' of their accounts. Once any such transaction is completed, the State has an obvious interest in recovering the tax benefits so granted by it, and so its position clearly becomes one of conflict with the recipients, which only feel themselves harmed by such recovery being made mandatory in compliance with the relevant Community rules.

This is the peculiarity which makes the rules on State aid unique among all rules of competition law. For the regulatory authority's discretion in applying the rules in this area is bound to be seriously jeopardized and to give way to a necessarily uniform application.

In other words, the presuppositions and manners of application of such rules must be clear and transparent, and the investigated undertakings' rights of defence must be observed in the first place. That another Member State's competing undertakings, which alone are the parties Community rules intend to protect from the State aid scheme under scrutiny, almost never intervene either in the administrative phase – while the Commission does nothing to change the picture, not even in terms of information, as it does instead with respect to other sectors of competition law – or, even the less, in the judicial phase, does certainly not help the occurrence of a genuine adversarial procedure.

Therefore, no discounts can be granted to the Commission in this context. Moreover, the Community Courts' precedent that *de-facto* makes the *principle of legitimate expectation*, as the discriminating factor in recovery, inapplicable – based on the absurd assumption, also pleaded by the Commission in somewhat absolute terms, that the recipient could not, by itself, but identify a scheme as unlawful or even only incompatible in respect of a State's legislative measure, *even before* a decision by the Commission has categorized and sanctioned it as State aid – really makes no sense at all. As a consequence, the undertaking involved, whether or not the Commission's administrative procedure has been opened and, if this is the case, irrespective of the stage at which such procedure

40. See CFI Judgment of 28 Feb. 2002, Case T-155/98, *SIDE* v *Commission*, [2002] ECR II-1179, ground 71. See also CFI Judgment of 22 Feb. 2006, Case T-34/02, *EURL Le Levant 001* v *Commission*, [2006] ECR II-267, grounds 123-124.

is being conducted, will have to disapply the relevant national legislative measure favourable to it, just in case the Commission should take a negative decision – one to be read in the crystal ball for the time being.

6. THE COMMISSION'S ROLE IN THE EU COMPETITION LAW SYSTEM

Thus, the formulation of rules with extremely broad contents, whether in the form of obligations, prohibitions, derogations, commitments or otherwise, the variety of the underlying principles and the consequently wide scope for discretion in applying them, which I have already pointed out as characteristics typical of any body of antitrust rules,[41] are especially apparent in EU competition law.

This domain of EU law had initially been kept within a few articles, from 81 to 89 EC (in the new numbering, which has left the contents unchanged from the Rome Treaty). Thereafter, it has gradually expanded into Council Regulations, consistently issued upon the Commission's recommendations, and the Commission's own Regulations, chiefly issued for enforcement, and the Commission's interpretative Communications,[42] but it has also been enhanced following decisions by the Commission, the body responsible for the entire matter, through the exclusive exercise by it of decision-making powers – though under judicial control, with contents and limitations discussed further below, which was once entrusted with the Court of Justice and is now exercised by the Court of First Instance[43] subject to appeal to the Court of Justice itself.

---

41. Only in the matter of currency rules alone, can similar traits of broadness and flexibility be found, which, in relation to a now-repealed Italian regulatory system in force until the primary Act of 1989, ill matched the seriousness of the sanctions applicable to violations. See Santa Maria, 'Disciplina valutaria, sanzioni penali e certezza del diritto', cit., p. 603 ff. On the topic, generally, see Santa Maria, 'Les critères d'application des règles italiennes des changes' in *Comunicazioni e Studi*, cit.
42. True, in principle, as the Commission itself has oftentimes pointed out, Commission Communications merely have information purposes, and are binding on it alone. Nonetheless, their import exceeds this qualification to provide guidelines addressed to everyone, including the undertakings. Just consider the many communications issued in the matter of State aid and the recent consolidating Communication of 10 Jul. 2007 on jurisdiction over merger control.
43. In this connection, it should be recalled that, by Council Decision 88/591/ECSC, EEC, Euratom of 24 Oct. 1988, the Council, in furtherance of Articles 168A and 140A – as introduced in the EC Treaty and in the Euratom Treaty, respectively, by Art. 11 of the European Single Act – established 'a Court of First Instance of the European Communities' and, accordingly, made some amendments to the Statute of the Court of Justice (see Decision No. 88/591 [1988] O.J. L319, p. 1 f.). Later on, Council Decision No. 94/149/ECSC, EEC of 7 Mar. 1994 amending Decision 93/350/Euratom, ECSC, EEC (see [1993] O.J. L144, p. 21 f.), which had, in turn, amended Decision 88/591 (see [1994] O.J. L66, p. 29 f.) set forth the duties and powers of the Court of First Instance. Pursuant to Art. 3 of that Decision, in the amended version effective as from 15 Mar. 1994, pursuant to Art. 1 of Decision 94/149, the scope of the CFI's jurisdiction now coincides with the entire area of judicial protection accorded by the EC Treaty to private parties against the Community institutions' acts, thus covering the whole matter of competition

There is no doubt that the Council Regulations that have been issued in the matter over time have had a great impact on Community competition law, from Regulation No. 17 of 6 February 1962, as amended, or the Regulation of 21 December 1989, which paved the way for the rules on merger control, to the recent Regulations No. 1 of 16 December 2002 and No. 139 of 20 January 2004. But the true driver has been, and still is, the Commission.

The whole system of Community competition law essentially revolves around the Commission, which takes action beyond and above its own regulations and communications and the Council's regulations, in forming which it plays a major role *in the implementation stage*, through its own case-law – the only one recognized precedent *on the merits*.

In this respect, a question must be raised. Is it really correct that a body vested, though in conjunction with the Council, with executive powers in governing the European Union, should also be the *sole* holder of the general power to watch over the implementation of primary and secondary rules of the Treaties, while actively participating, along the lines indicated above, in the formation of competition rules, and even be the one body responsible – *on an exclusive basis Community-wide* – for applying, and taking decisions on, those very rules?

It should be remembered that a 'Commission decision' in this domain has a peculiar significance *per se*, in light of its *immediate and direct effect*, partly because it is almost impossible, in the CFI's practice, to obtain stay of enforcement of Commission decisions in an urgency.[44] As a consequence, even where any such decision is reversed mainly on grounds of law, following review by either Court acting upon ordinary challenge, it would still leave an indelible mark on the party to which a transaction has been permitted or prohibited (by the Commission) or by which a fine has been paid, irrespective of the amount, possibly following an enforcement action sought by the Commission before a national court.

Only *ex post*, after (too) many years, may the undertaking concerned seek redress from the Community Courts, although the latter are often influenced by a 'deference' of a sort, which may well amount to a veritable complex of submission to the undoubtedly high skills recognized to the Commission in matters of competition.[45]

(including merger control) as well as that of dumping and subsidies. In this sense, see Condinanzi, 'Ampliate le competenze del Tribunale di primo grado delle Comunità europee' [1994] Corr. giur., p. 797 f. Art. 5 of the Decision has introduced amendments to Art. 46 f. of the Statute of the Court of Justice regarding the CFI's organization, appeals to the ECJ against the CFI's decisions 'only on grounds of law', the relevant procedure before the ECJ and the ECJ's decisions on appeals.

44. See *Judicial Statistics 2007 – Statistics of judicial activity of the Court of First Instance, Miscellaneous*, para. 13, available on the ECJ's website. In 2007, only 4 of 41 expedited procedures acted upon by the CFI were granted. None of those four related, however, to competition (or State Aid). Moreover, in practice, interim decisions are only seldom appealed against before the Court of Justice, for obvious reasons of time. In 2007, only two such appeals were brought, and both were dismissed. (See *Judicial Statistics 2007 – Statistics of judicial activity of the Court of Justice, Miscellaneous*, para. 16).

45. This is a recurring theme of strong criticism in this chapter. In my view, this feeling of submission to the Commission could be overcome both before the competent Community judicial

The end result is that, even in case a challenge raised in ordinary proceedings is successful – except where a fine unduly paid is restored and unless compliance with the obligation to pay it has brought about irreparable consequences on the business life of the undertaking so unjustly fined – it has become settled practice that, because of the passing of time, the prohibited transaction can no longer be carried out, and the undertaking concerned, may only, as the successful party, bring a new action seeking compensation for damages from the Commission.[46]

With these facts in mind, the concentration of powers on the Commission alters the balance of relationships between the Commission and the undertakings at the time the rules are to be applied, and it cannot, because of the crystal-clear asymmetry of the rights of defence, offer suitable guarantees of impartiality.

Therefore, if flexibility of rules is *in re ipsa* in this matter, their application to any one real case should be the outcome of an objective balancing of interests. The Commission is, however, in the conflicting position of an authority which, wearing too may hats – among which the substantive management of the EU's economic policy towards the outside, thus the handling of the relations with both third States and the WTO/GATT bodies on *macroeconomic* issues, despite the Council's merely formal powers – 'might' be led to use its intervention in any one antitrust case as a device for general admonishment (a veritable sound box, in fact, the range of which will be the wider as the interest arisen in the relevant case among the public opinion spreads wider) addressed to a market, to Member States or even to Third States, in the same way as it 'might' tend to *exalt other Community interests*, which it considers more important than those closely relating to that case. Or it 'might' even consider an explicit assessment of its own to be inappropriate in either direction, because, at that time, it believes such assessment to be conflicting with one or another of its economic policies, as a result of which it might choose *inaction* as the proper approach.[47]

---

bodies and before national courts through specialized chambers whose members are fully conversant with the economic analysis of law.

46. By way of illustration only, an interesting case appears to be *Schneider Electric*, a case recently decided by the CFI by its judgment of 11 Jul. 2007 (case T-351/03). It is appropriate to note that the Commission, (i) by its decision of 10 Oct. 2001, had found the merger between *Schneider* and *Legrand* incompatible with the common market, and (ii) by its decision of 30 Jan. 2002, had ordered *Schneider* to separate from *Legrand*. *Schneider* brought an action for annulment of each of these two decisions. By its judgments of 22 Oct. 2002, the CFI overturned the incompatibility decision and, accordingly, the separation decision. In particular, the CFI found that the Commission had failed to have regard to Schneider's rights of defence. Following the annulment of both decisions, the Commission reopened its investigation into the merger. However, the investigation procedure was closed by the Commission on 13 Dec. 2002 after its persistent doubts as to the suitability of Schneider's corrective measures to make the merger compatible with the common market had led Schneider to *abandon* the merger. *Schneider* then sued the Commission for damages, seeking *compensation for the loss* caused to it due to the illegal merger prohibition decision. By its decision of Jul. 2007, the CFI found that such illegality entailed an obligation for the Commission to pay damages.

47. Notwithstanding the possibility to bring action for 'failure to act' pursuant to Art. 232 EC against the Commission, this device seems to have been used by private entities to a quite low extent.

The Commission conflicting position in this respect may well have an adverse impact on the rule-abiding player, who is entitled anyhow to play his cards at equal terms and in the shortest time afforded by a free market.

The timeliness of this outcome is, in fact, the main reason that justifies the *immediate applicability* of any *decision* by the Commission.

The issue of the Commission's conflict of powers was already raised in the late 1970s in connection with the Commission's administrative procedure in competition matters, when decisions by the Commission were challenged before the Court of Justice for its alleged infringement of the rules on 'due process of law' under Article 6(1) of the European Convention on Human Rights, whereupon the Commission successfully claimed the inapplicability of that article to itself. It had based this contention on the argument that the 'executive power of the Community was vested in it', which excluded *per se* that it could constitute a 'tribunal' within the meaning asserted by ECJ precedent.[48,49]

In my view, however, the real problem goes beyond the incompatibility for the Commission, as the body vested with 'the Community's executive power', also to manage competition matters in the capacity of a judicial body of first instance, albeit with the correctives intended to attenuate the present asymmetries as discussed in the paragraphs below.

In a future perspective, hopefully not too far away in time, greater doubts arise as to the powers the Commission has as a government body, as the guarantor of compliance with Treaty rules, and as the exclusive holder of the right of legislative initiative.

As long as the task at hand is to make a community in progress grow to become a genuine union of States, the executive power may well be shared with a technical body designed to protect Community interests and to ensure compliance, also and especially by Member States, with the primary and secondary rules of the Treaties.

Anyone knowledgeable of the origin and the gradual development – quite peculiar in the international society – of Community law, from the Treaty of Rome to the subsequent amendments and supplements made to it over time, is perfectly aware of the key role the Commission has constantly played in the *Community's interest*, precisely through its institutional powers, both by cementing cohesion among the ever-increasing number of member States, and by operating as the true driver of the entire Community, relying on the support, at the most controversial times, of the Court of Justice's converging and yet ever-evolving case-law.

Nevertheless, when the entire process is completed with the eventual creation of a federal State, the Commission's multiform powers of today would no longer be

---

48. See Judgments of the ECJ of 29 Oct. 1980, Joined Cases 209 to 215 and 218/78, *Fedetab*, [1980] ECR 3125, and of 7 Jun. 1983, Case 100-103/80, *Musique diffusion francaise*, [1983] ECR 1825, ground 7.
49. About compliance with the rights of defence of the parties investigated by the Commission since the preliminary phase, see ECJ Judgment of 9 Nov. 1983, Case 322/81, *Michelin*, [1983] ECR p. 3461, ground 7.

justified.[50] Under the customary separation of powers, the Commission, whatever its new name might be, is bound to be substituted for by a governmental body which is the democratic expression of the Member States' peoples, and the general task to ensure compliance with EU law can only be entrusted with the Court of Justice acting as a federal court suitably coordinated by the Advocate General's office discharging new and different functions, typical of an attorney general's, while the legislative power in federal matters can only be vested in the European Parliament as the genuine expression of the European peoples.

Thereupon, the Commission may well discharge functions typical of a (federal) authority responsible for the correct application of competition rules or of Community rules on international trade, if you will. In both cases, it will have to manage administrative proceedings, obviously in full compliance with the rules of 'a fair hearing' pursuant to Article 6(1) of the European Convention for the Protection of Human Rights.

7. SOME ASPECTS OF THE CUMULATION OF THE COMMISSION'S FUNCTIONS IN ADMINISTRATIVE PROCEEDINGS

In the present-day's institutional unbalance discussed so far, another observation is that, in competition cases, the European Commission 'cumulates' diverse functions within itself, i.e. both *investigation* and *prosecution* tasks in addition to the *decision-taking* function, without any clear distinction having been made.

In theory, but just in theory, final decisions in matters of competition are taken by the Commission sitting as a panel, while the preceding stages, investigation and referral, are the responsibility of DG Competition.

In fact, the Commission's collective decision-taking system is such that, in far the greatest majority of cases, decisions are taken according to the view offered by the competent directorate general, without such view being even laid before the panel for a discussion.

It has been observed that, when a proceeding for the alleged infringement of any competition rule is managed by a branch of the executive instead of by dedicated independent judicial or even administrative bodies, there is no guarantee as to the necessary fairness and impartiality of the whole process.[51]

---

50. It would be as if the US government's powers were, *mutatis mutandis*, vested in the Federal Trade Commission.
51. Van Bael & Bellis, *Competition Law of the European Community*, § 10.3.; Brent, 'The Binding of Leviathan? – The Changing Role of the European Commission in Competition Cases' [1995] ICLQ 44, p. 255; Montag, 'The Case for a Radical Reform of the Infringement Procedure Under Reg. 17' [1996] ECLR 8, p. 428; Van Bael, 'A Practitioner's Guide to Due Process in Antitrust and Antidumping Proceedings' [1984] Int. Law 8, p. 841. See also House of Lords, Session 1981-1982, *8th Report*, and House of Lords Select Committee, Session 1993-1994, *1st Report*.

In this respect, the European Parliament[52] has suggested:

> the Commission should, within its internal procedures, make a distinction between its investigatory, examinatory and decision-making functions regarding restrictive agreements and abuses of dominant position.

Yet, in *Shell*, the Court of First Instance[53] held that:

> the fact that certain Commission officials acted in the administrative procedure both as investigators and rapporteurs [did] not render the Decision unlawful.

Community Courts tend to downplay the significance of this blend of tasks, although they have oftentimes held that, during administrative proceedings before the Commission, the Commission is under an obligation to comply with the procedural safeguards provided for by Community law. In other words, it must, through *due process of law*, ensure compliance with the accusatorial principle and the principles of legal certainty, proportionality and legitimate expectations, as the case may be.[54]

It is appropriate to stress that the *only one* procedure 'on the merits' in this matter takes place before the Commission, and that, despite its being labelled 'administrative procedure', its characteristics are, in fact, typical of an inquisitorial procedure. This is even more so where the object of the examination is a purported *cartel*, or the charge at issue is *abuse* of dominant position, while those characteristics are less apparent in the case of any application for clearance or derogation – yet on an almost absolute presumption of incompatibility, because of the approach the Commission has elected to take to any procedure it opens in each case of undeclared State aid, which is, as such, invariably deemed unlawful.

Moreover, the procedure in question is handled by DG Competition's officials. It is settled practice that, during the proceedings, the parties concerned do not even meet the Commissioner for Competition, *nor do they have an opportunity to argue their cases before the Commissioners sitting as a panel* to arrive at their decision, which is itself packaged by the Commission's staff and submitted to the Commissioner for Competition even in *exceptional* cases of 'automatic' non-clearance. And yet, those same parties, or some of them, may be hit, if need be, by even substantial economic sanctions capable to condition the very future survival of a party so hit.

In this context, the misgivings of the undertakings being investigated can hardly be soothed by the knowledge that, pursuant to Regulation 1/2003, as severe as the fines for infringements of competition rules could be, they 'shall not be of a criminal law nature'.[55]

---

52. *XXth Report on competition policy*, point 89.
53. See Judgment of the Court of First Instance of 10 Mar. 1992, Case T-11/89, *Shell* v *Commission*, [1992] ECR II-757, ground 39.
54. See Judgments of the Court of First Instance of 29 Jun. 1995, Case T-30/91, *Solvay*, [1995] ECR II-1775, grounds 59 and 98, and of 22 Oct. 1997, Cases T-213/95 and T-18/96, *SCK* e *FNK*, [1997] ECR II-1739.
55. This is expressly stated in Art. 23(5) of Regulation (EC) of the Council No. 1/2003 of 31 Dec. 2002 [2003] O.J. L1, p. 1. This statement was already contained in Article 15(4) of Regulation

Against this background, a palliative seems to have been provided by the post of 'Hearing Officer' the Commission has instituted with a view to making its performance transparent and independent in conducting administrative proceedings in competition cases. The Hearing Officer is not a member of the staff of, but administratively reports to, the Directorate-General for Competition,[56] away from the team of investigating officers in charge of any one case, which restricts his real scope for action.

A Hearing Officer's duties have aptly been summarized as follows:

> his duties are now extensive, but essentially are directed at ensuring that the rights of the defence are respected and draft decisions take due account of the relevant facts.[57]

All form and only form, once again!

8. IMMEDIATE AND DIRECT APPLICABILITY OF COMMISSION DECISIONS

When the European system of competition law is assessed as a whole, the rules on 'due process of law' do not seem, for the time being, to inform administrative proceedings before the Commission. In fact, although the investigating officers' behaviours and assessments invariably comply with formal prescriptions, they seem to be based, most of the times, on presumptions of guilt and even on impatience with assessments in point of law contrary to their views.

What worries more, though, is the extent of the actual unbalance, compounded as it is by the *immediate enforceability* of the possibly punitive 'decision' by which the Commission closes the procedure.

The problem is by no means mitigated by, but it becomes even more open to criticism through, the Community Courts' settled case-law already referred to above, whereby the Commission's decisions have been stayed only in quite

---

(EEC) No. 17/62. This qualification was introduced in response to Member States' objections in point of constitutional lawfulness with regard to the European Community's criminal law jurisdiction. A dissenting view was tendered by Mr Advocate General Darmon in his Opinion in Case *Pasta di legno*, point 451, where he stated: '*A Commission decision in the field of competition [. . .] is manifestly of a penal nature*'. For a similar view, see also Mr Advocate General Vesterdorf's Opinion of 10 Jul. 1991, Joined Cases T-1/89 to T-4/89 and T-6/89 to T-15/89, *Rhone Poulenc* v *Commission*, [1991] ECR II-867. For a view favourable to equating fines in competition cases to criminal penalties, see Kerse & Khan, *EC Antitrust Procedure* (London, 2005), § 7-008.

56. The Commission created the post of hearing officer in 1982, and defined the attendant duties in its Decision 94/810/ECSC, EC of 12 Dec. 1994 on the terms of reference of hearing officers in competition procedures before the Commission ([1994] O.J. L330, p. 67). See also Commission Decision of 23 May 2001 on the terms of reference of Hearing Officers in certain competition proceedings ([2001]O.J. L62, p. 21) and Art. 14(1) of Regulation (EC) No. 773/2004.
57. Kerse & Khan, *EC Antitrust Procedure*, § 4-014. For a criticism, see also Van Bael & Bellis, *Competition Law of the European Community*, § 10.3.

exceptional cases – so few, in fact, as to be almost entirely deprived of statistical significance.

An emblematic case in this respect has been that of a company of the *Leali* group, subject to *insolvency proceedings*, which had applied to the Court of First Instance in urgency, and was denied suspension of the pecuniary sanction imposed by the Commission following an agreement prohibited by Article 65 of the extinguished ECSC Treaty.[58] The ground for rejection was that, in the relation to the test as to the existence of *periculum in mora*, the company's counsel had failed to show that there were no banks willing to issue suitable guarantees on behalf of the *insolvent* company, pending insolvency proceedings, to ensure immediate payment of the fine upon the European Courts' judgment confirming the Commission Decision becoming *res judicata* – a way out the Commission had 'generously' offered to the insolvent company as an alternative to immediate payment of the fine.[59]

58. The measure in question was Commission Decision of 17 Dec. 2002 relating to a proceeding under Art. 65 of the ECSC Treaty (in COMP/37.956, the 'reinforcing bars' case), not published in the *Official Journal*. The Decision was based on investigations and inspections the Commission had conducted pursuant to Art. 47 of the ECSC Treaty at some producers of concrete-reinforcing bars and at Federacciai, their trade association, in Oct. through Dec. 2000. Subsequently, the Commission had notified the relevant charges to the addressees on 27 Mar. 2002. On 13 Aug. 2002, twenty days *after the extinction of the ECSC Treaty on 23 July 2002*, the Commission served a supplemental notification of charges on the addressee, where it *failed*, in fact, to notify any charges new or different from those already notified, but attempted to convey the idea of an impossible 'relay' from the ECSC procedure, which had become extinguished upon the expiry of the ECSC Treaty, failing an agreement among the States that were parties to the ECSC Treaty, to a new EC procedure under Council Regulation No. 17/62, as amended. In conclusion, the Decision was solely based on the provisions of the ECSC Treaty, specifically Art. 65, which provisions had, in fact, been no longer in force for over five months at the time the Decision was notified. The addressees of the Decision filed an application for annulment with the Court of First Instance, which, by its judgment of 25 Oct. 2007 in Joined Cases T-27/03, T-80/03, T-46/03, T-58/03, T-79/03, T-97/03 e T-98/03, and Cases T-45/03, T-77/03 and T-94/03, albeit on minimalist grounds, annulled the Decision (issued nearly five years earlier), which the Commission had already enforced in full and whose sole legal basis was a provision of a treaty already expired. The peculiarity of this case is that, in the face of the crystal-clear unlawfulness of the Decision, all of the undertakings involved had either to pay the fine or to ask a bank to guarantee payment.
59. In *Leali I*, the President of the Court of First Instance incredibly dismissed the application for interim measures, even as, '*in the present case, in order to show the impossibility of setting up a bank guarantee, the applicant had exhibited three letters in which two banks had, in general terms, expressed their refusal to grant the guarantees so requested. In the letter [. . .], the bank in question, which is the applicant's habitual bank, restated its refusal and expressly indicated that the total amount of the credits reached by the applicant thus far made any new increase in credit impossible*'. According to the CFI, Leali had failed to show indisputably that its plant and equipment could not have been tendered as collateral for bank guarantees. It was so, even as the applicant had claimed that its plant and equipment had an almost negligible technological or commercial value. About two years later, Leali again filed an application for suspension with the President of the CFI, and exhibited *new letters* in which three banks refused to grant any guarantee irrespective of the creation of specific collateral (see the CFI President's Order of 24 Jan. 2006, Case T-46/03 R II, *Leali II*, in *ECR* 2006, II-9). One bank expressly refused to

9. PUBLIC ENTERPRISE AND COMPETITION: TRANSPARENCY OF FINANCIAL RELATIONS BETWEEN MEMBER STATES AND PUBLIC UNDERTAKINGS

The starting point is the observation, considered to be just obvious,[60] that the writers of the Treaty of Rome intentionally refrained – because of the existence of different concepts in different Member States' internal laws about the reach and structure of public undertakings, and also in light of the different significance of public undertakings in different Member States – from giving a definition of 'public undertaking'. Nevertheless, it is as obvious that Community competition law rules apply to any undertaking, be it 'private' or 'public'.

This is borne out by Article 86(1) EC, which requires:

> In the case of public undertakings and undertakings to which Member States grant special or exclusive rights, Member States shall neither enact nor maintain in force any measure contrary to the rules contained in this Treaty, in particular to those rules provided for in Article 12 and Articles 81 to 89.

The rationale behind this provision is to place public authorities' influence in economic matters under the Commission's supervision in order to prevent such influence from being misused lest it should have an adverse impact on the proper functioning of the internal market through discrimination (reference being made to Article 12 EC) or distortion of competition (reference being made to Articles 81 through 89 EC).

The phrases used in Article 86(1) EC, 'public undertakings' and 'undertakings to which Member States grant special or exclusive rights' are Community law notions and must accordingly be construed uniformly by all Member States, in light of the meaning and purpose of that provision.[61]

In this perspective, with regard to the definition of the content of the 'public undertaking' concept, appropriate support was given by Commission Directive No. 80/723 of 25 June 1980 on the transparency of financial relations between Member

---

grant any guarantee, not even if covered by a pledge on equipment. The Court's President ruled that just one letter of refusal from just one bank, notwithstanding the offer to pledge plant and equipment, was inadequate proof (point 72 of *Leali II* Order, cit.). This case is also quite meaningful in relation to the conduct of the Commission, which had imposed heavy fines.

60. See the Commission's position in the report for the hearing in Judgment of the ECJ of 16 Jun. 1987, Case 118/85, *Commission of the European Communities* v *Italian Republic*, ([1987] ECR 2599 f.) in respect of the nature of the Amministrazione Autonoma dei Monopoli di Stato for the purposes of the application of Commission Directive No. 80/723 of 25 Jun. 1980 ([1980] O.J. L195, p. 35 f.) on the transparency of financial relations between Member States and public undertakings.
61. A statement to this effect was made by the Commission in its report for the hearing for the facts of Case 118/85 quoted in the footnote next preceding above, p. 2600 f.

States and public undertakings, later repealed and superseded by Directive No. 2006/111/EC of 16 November 2006.[62] Whereas 10 of this Directive requires:

> It should be made clear what is to be understood by the terms 'public authorities' and 'public undertakings'.

Accordingly, Article 2 states a follows:

> 'public undertakings' means any undertaking over which the public authorities may exercise directly or indirectly a dominant influence by virtue of their ownership of it, their financial participation therein, or the rules which govern it.

In the light of the same article of Directive No. 2006/111, *public authorities* must be taken to mean all public authorities, including the State and regional, local and all other territorial authorities.

For 'dominant influence' on the part of the public authorities over undertakings is presumed when these authorities, as defined above, directly or indirectly, in relation to an undertaking, hold the major part of the undertaking's subscribed capital or control the majority of the votes attaching to shares issued by the undertaking or can appoint more than half of the members of the undertaking's administrative, managerial or supervisory body.

The Commission further stressed that:

> Public undertakings play a substantial role in the national economy of the Member States. (Whereas 2 of Directive 2006/111).

And it added:

> Article 295 of the Treaty provides that the Treaty is in no way to prejudice the rules in Member States governing the system of property ownership. *There should be no unjustified discrimination between public and private undertakings* in the application of the rules on competition. This Directive should apply to both public and private undertakings. (Whereas 4 of Directive 2006/111, *emphasis added*)

Article 1 of the Directive requires the Member States to ensure that financial relations between public authorities and public undertakings are transparent so that the following emerge clearly:

(a) public funds made available directly by public authorities to the public undertakings concerned;
(b) public funds made available by public authorities through the intermediary of public undertakings or financial institutions;
(c) the use to which these public funds are actually put.

---

62. Directive No. 80/723 had already been amended by Commission Directives No. 85/413, of 24 Jul. 1985, No. 93/84, of 30 Sep. 1993, No. 52/2000, of 26 Jul. 2000, and No. 81/2005 of 28 Nov. 2005 on the same matter, all of them with legal basis on Art. 86(3) EC. Directive No. 2006/111/EC is in [2006] O.J. L318, p. 17.

This provision ensure transparency both in case public resources are made available *directly* and in case they are so made available *indirectly*, and it also allow for adequate knowledge of the actual use to which they are put.

Moreover, Article 3 of the Directive is intended to give the Commission accurate knowledge of the reasons for any such grant of public resources, specifying, in a listing by no means mandatory, that:

> The transparency referred to in Article 1(1) shall apply in particular to the following aspects of financial relations between public authorities and public undertakings:
>
> (a) the setting-off of operating losses;
> (b) the provision of capital;
> (c) non-refundable grants, or loans on privileged terms;
> (d) the granting of financial advantages by forgoing profits or the recovery of sums due;
> (e) the forgoing of a normal return on public funds used;
> (f) compensation for financial burdens imposed by the public authorities.

In connection with the former Directive No. 80/723 (superseded by Directive 2006/111, as indicated above), the Court made some statements still valid today:

> It should be noted, as the Court stated in its Judgment of 6 July 1982 (Joined Cases 188 to 190/80 *French Republic, Italian Republic* and *United Kingdom of Great Britain and Northern Ireland* v *Commission*) that the essential purpose of Directive 80/723 is to promote the effective application to public undertakings of the provisions contained in Articles 92 and 93 of the treaty concerning state aid. As can be seen from the recitals in the preamble to the directive, the complexity of the relations between national public authorities and public undertakings tends to hinder the performance by the Commission of its supervisory duties with the result that a fair and effective application of the aid rules in the EEC treaty is possible only if those financial relations are made transparent. In particular, the sixth recital in the preamble states that with regard to public undertakings, such transparency should enable a clear distinction to be made between the role of the State as public authority and its role as proprietor. [*Emphasis added*].[63]

Therefore, the problems considered here are also related, because of the disclosure requirements so stated, to those typical of *the supervision over the lawfulness of State aid* according to competition rules pursuant to Articles 87 and 88 EC discussed further below.

Article 6 of Directive No. 2006/111 also requires the Member States to ensure that information concerning the financial relations with public undertakings controlled by them be kept at the disposal of the Commission for five years from the

63. This was the express wording of Judgment of 16 Jun. 1987, Case 118/85, cit., ground 6.

end of the financial year in which the public funds were made available to the public undertakings concerned.

In implementing the 1980 Directive in practice, the Commission had established that a significant proportion of the financial flows between a State and its public undertakings passed though a variety of forms of financial transfers and did not simply take the form of capital or quasi-capital injections. It had also found that it was predominantly in the manufacturing sector that a considerable amount of aid had been granted to undertakings, but not notified pursuant to Article 88(3) EC (fifth and sixth Whereases of Directive No. 93/84). It had, therefore, taken remedial action by introducing a number of duties in Article 5(b) of Directive No. 93/84 of 30 September 1993. These duties were restated in Article 8 of Directive No. 2006/11, requiring Member States to supply the Commission with financial information for each undertaking on an annual basis in respect of all public undertakings in the manufacturing sector whose turnover for the most recent financial year was more than EUR 250 million. Obviously by reference to the provisions of the Fifth Directive on companies, the information to be so provided are the annual report and annual accounts, which include the balance sheet and profit/loss account, explanatory notes, together with other financial reporting statements and 'more specific information'; all of which intended to present a *true and fair view* of the economic and financial position of the company or public body concerned and to allow the Commission to rely, in receiving such information, on an economic language common to all Member States. With this view, the Member States are required, pursuant to Article 8(7) of Directive No. 2006/111, to 'furnish the Commission with any additional information that it deems necessary in order to complete a thorough appraisal of the data submitted'.

Paragraph 2 of Article 86 EC requires, by way of exception to the general rule contained in paragraph 1 of that same article, that undertakings entrusted with the operation of services of general economic interest or having the character of a revenue-producing monopoly shall be subject to the rules contained in the Treaty, in particular to the rules on competition, but only 'in so far as the application of such rules does not obstruct the performance, in law or in fact, of the particular tasks assigned to them'. The exception in question is, however, qualified as follows: 'The development of trade must not be affected to such an extent as would be contrary to the interests of the Community.'

In the Court of Justice's view, the phrase 'undertakings entrusted with the operation of services of general economic interest' must be construed in the sense of undertakings expressly so entrusted under an administrative act.[64]

64. See Judgment of the ECJ of 30 Jan. 1974, Case 127/73, *Belgische Radio en Televisie* e *Société belge des auteurs, compositeurs et éditeurs* v *SV SABAM e NV Fonior* (*BRT* c. *SABAM* I), [1974] ECR, 51, ground 56. In the same sense, see Judgment of the ECJ of 11 Apr. 1989, Case 66/86, *Ahmed Saeed*, [1989] ECR 803, ground 55.

In furtherance of the foregoing, the Commission has, in Article 5 of Directive No. 2006/111, provided that the Directive will not apply to:

(a) public undertakings, as regards services the supply of which is not liable to affect trade between Member States to an appreciable extent;
(b) central banks;
(c) public credit institutions, as regards deposits of public funds placed with them by public authorities on normal commercial terms;
(d) public undertakings whose total annual net turnover over the period of the two financial years preceding that in which the funds referred to in Article 1(1) are made available or used has been less than EUR 40 million.

10. THE ALITALIA BAILOUT AND EUROPEAN RULES

In Italy, Law Decree No. 134/2008, as converted into Law No. 166/2008, containing '*Urgent provisions on the restructuring of large firms in difficulty*' has extended, and accordingly modified, the insolvency procedure under Law Decree No. 347 of 23 December 2003, as converted, with amendments, into Act No. 39 of 18 February 2004 (the 'Marzano Act'), to large undertakings operating in the sector of *essential public services*. Thus, the provisions so newly introduced also apply to Alitalia, the Italian State-controlled air carrier.

Even though no express reference is made therein to such European rules as Article 16 EC introduced by the Amsterdam Treaty, or Articles 73, 86(2) or 87 EC[65] as referred to therein, the Italian legislator's patent intention in making such extension was to emphasize the 'public' significance of the Alitalia case and, therefore, to affirm the need for a mitigated application of competition rules to the complex operation that entails the split-up of Alitalia into two separate businesses. This has been done so that, while the 'bad company' undergoes liquidation, the 'good company' emerging from the operation should not be prevented, in law or in fact, from perpetuating the mission originally entrusted with Alitalia.

---

65. Although the Italian legislator has not used the same phrase, 'services of general economic interest', as is used in the provisions of Art. 16 and 86(2) EC, I doubt that the phrase 'essential public services' could be taken to mean anything else: Whether or not this is the case, it is still quite clear that the provisions so newly introduced to amend the Marzano Act, the implied reference is to Alitalia, precisely because it is regarded as a 'large firm in difficulty' operating in the sector of 'essential' public services or 'services of general economic interest'. Quite beyond terminological issues, the event of insolvency affecting the Italian national airline may well be caught by the national or Community notion that would make the new decree applicable to the case, although, in technical terms, the essential services provided by Alitalia account for a tiny proportion of its total turnover, in that they only amount to certain air links with Italian islands and the national air mail service. What actually characterizes the case as one of 'public interest' are its political and social implications, which could, in fact, trigger the applicability of special measures. Yet, as discussed below, the real issue is one of a different nature, i.e. the extension of the provisions for the bailout and protection of Alitalia to its merger with AirOne, a transaction only complementary to the rescue operation.

The approach taken to the case by subjecting Alitalia to the insolvency procedure provided for by the Marzano Act, as amended,[66] seems to have met expectations long voiced both in Italy and in Brussels. This seems to be substantiated by the 'can do' view taken of the peculiarities of the Alitalia case by European Commissioner Almunia a day after Alitalia sought bankruptcy protection, when he stated: '*Alitalia must find a solution that is in accord with European regulations and that is also good for the company, passengers and employees*'. This amounts to not only advocating free competition, but also to acknowledging profiles crucially material to national policy.

The decree newly adopted in Italy raises two issues under Community law, overcoming both of which is necessary for the Alitalia bailout plan to be carried through.[67] The first issue is to establish whether or not the decree, obviously entailing State aid, can be authorized by derogation by the Commission, which has *exclusive* jurisdiction over the case. The second issue relates to the merger with AirOne, itself falling within Community jurisdiction (under the one-stop shop principle), so that reference must be made to both companies' threshold turnover amounts as reported in their annual accounts as at 31 December 2007. The question may well, however, be referred to the national authorities of Italy and of other Member States for an examination based on more recent turnover figures emerging from later financial reporting data, which reflect the abandonment by Alitalia of its takeoff and landing slots at the Malpensa airport and its resulting lower revenues from operations in and outside Italy. Also, the proposed merger deal may as well be referred to the Italian Authority on Trade and Competition (the '*AGCM*'), should the so-called 'top-down referral' approach be accorded in furtherance of the subsidiarity principle.[68]

The two procedures are independent of each other only in theory since they exhibit several points of mutual interference, both because of the general scope of the State aid procedure and because the applicability of the new Regulation on merger control is predicated upon full cooperation between the Commission and the competent national authorities.

For the time being, the proposed rescue plan seems – because of its structure, the quality and 'private' nature of the good company, and the provision for

66. It should be noted that the Marzano Act was not the object of an *ad-hoc* decision by the Commission, but of just a press release dated 28 Jan. 2004 by Mr Mario Monti, the Commissioner for Competition then in office, according to whom the procedural changes from Legislative Decree No. 270/99 (the 'Prodi-*bis* Act') did not seem to raise problems in connection with the European rules on State aid. In fact, not even the Prodi-*bis* Act had been examined by the Commission, which had only expressed its view about the original Italian instrument (Act No. 95/79, the 'Prodi Act'). In its Decision of 16 May 2000 – then after the Prodi-*bis* Act had been adopted – the Commission declared some elements thereof incompatible with the common market. In fact, no such element was included in either the Prodi-*bis* Act or the Marzano Act, and they are otherwise immaterial to the newest provisions on the matter. For these issues, see Biscaretti di Ruffia, 'State Aid and Insolvency Proceedings', in *Competition and State Aid*, cit., pp. 123 ff.
67. For the time being, it can only be assumed that the trade unions' present reckless attitude obstructing the definition of an entrepreneurial solution – the only one available under Community law – will change, thereby allowing the completion of the operation in question, since this appears to be the only solution still practicable to avoid the cessation of Alitalia's business activity.
68. On this issue generally, see below, section 18 of this Chapter VI.

an independent expert to appraise the transfer price (Article 4.4-*quater* of the decree) – to meet the three requirements of paragraph 76 of the Community guidelines of 2004 on State aid for rescuing and restructuring firms in difficulty.[69]

Moreover, the Italian Treasury's claims on the bad company (approximating 450 million euros), if waived by the State, as well as any costs arising from re-employing redundant employees, should be treated as aid exempted under Article 87(3)(b) EC, since the plan for the restructuring of Alitalia qualifies as '*an important project of common European interest*', intended '*to remedy a serious disturbance in the economy*' of Italy. In the alternative, another suitable device could be a derogation under Article 87(3)(c) (to be read in conjunction with paragraph 37 et seq., of the 1994 Guidelines concerning transport in the aviation sector[70]).

Far more sensitive appears to be the issue arising in connection with the provision of Article 4.4-*quinquies* of Law Decree No. 134/2008, which, with respect to undertakings operating 'essential public services', *exceptionally*, though subject to any substantive, time-related restrictions as the Italian Competition Authority might impose, excludes the need for antitrust clearance of *merger operations connected or concurrent with, or otherwise envisaged in, the plan authorized* under a decree of the President of the Council of Ministers or of the Minister for Economic Development, and delegates all decision-making powers in respect thereof to the competent political authorities. This is a clear reference to the part of the merger that concerns AirOne.

The contents of such new provision are not dissimilar from that in Article 42 of the *Gesetz gegen Wettbewerbsbeschränkungen* (*GWB*).[71] The result so achieved by the Italian instrument had already been envisaged, albeit only in prospect, by Article 25(1) of Act No. 287/1990, which made the Council of Ministers, acting upon a proposal from the Minister for Industry Trade and Crafts, responsible for determining the general prior criteria according to which the Italian Competition Authority may:

> *exceptionally* authorise merger operations otherwise prohibited by Article 6, because of *overriding general interests of the national economy* within the context of European integration.

This provision has never been applied, though.[72]

---

69. See in [2004] O.J. C244, p. 2.
70. See in [1994] O.J. C350, p. 5.
71. In the English version published in the *Bundeskartellamt* website, this provision requires that: 'The Federal Minister of Economics and Labour shall, upon application, authorize a concentration prohibited by the Bundeskartellamt if, in a specific case, the restraint of competition is outweighed by advantages to the economy as a whole following from the concentration, or if the concentration is justified by an overriding public interest. In this context the competitiveness of the participating undertakings in markets outside the scope of application of this Act shall also be taken into account. Authorization may be granted only if the scope of the restraint of competition does not jeopardize the market economy system'. It should be noted that the last sentence specifies market protection as the core standard, which considerably narrows the scope for application of the rule.
72. Nonetheless, the provision has been further qualified by the *AGCM*. In particular, the Italian Authority's Annual Report on activities performed in 1992 specifies that the government's

Underlying paragraph 4-*quinquies* of Article 4 is the principle that the Italian Competition Authority has *exclusive* cognizance over mergers, while, as indicated above, no event of merger may occur as far as Alitalia and AirOne are concerned.

Moreover, at a closer look, the new provision of Italian law merely *resembles* the general provision set forth in Article 25(1) of Act No. 287/1990. The differences between the two are patently clear. Under the new rule, the *AGCM* is no longer responsible for deciding antitrust cases, while the previous rule allowed the Authority to disapply the general law, by 'exceptionally' authorizing merger deals otherwise prohibited in the ordinary course of law, so long as the merger in question had a direct relevance to public interests.

Further, the new provision far exceeds the scope of application of its predecessor. For it concerns, by definition, transactions *ancillary* to operations of general interest. This is the problem. In order to have its scheme granted by the Community institutions, the Italian government should first get the Commission to accept the inescapable premise that Alitalia is an undertaking operating in the sector of essential public services,[73] and then to show that the AirOne deal is not only necessary to rescue Alitalia, but is itself an operation of overriding public interest.

Undoubtedly, within the context of the Alitalia case, the AirOne deal clearly plays a *complementary* role, intended to let Alitalia retain and freely transfer its remaining routes (slots) to another air carrier[74] and to allow the 'good company' to rely on the options for the purchase of aircraft in the next few years as a *pre-requirement* for its very survival and future operations. In other words, the entire operation, as presented and currently structured, could not be carried through without AirOne.

Therefore, it is in light of the ultimate purpose and of its public-policy implications that the issues of monopoly and dominant position arising from the proposed merger in relation to the main national routes (the individual relevant markets) will have to be considered. This is a penalty which, if suffered over a

---

powers on mergers are limited by the requirement to identify the exceptional conditions under which, in the presence of overriding general interests of the national economy within the context of European integration, any otherwise prohibited operations may be authorized by the Authority, and the criteria according to which any such authorization may be granted should be fixed in general terms in advance. The 2004 Report further specifies that any such action which has Community relevance must be agreed upon with the European Commission, but in no event can it be an offhand or particular measure, which would only result in distorting market rules, bringing about imitative and emulative effects and a disastrous impact on the entire economy.

73. It should be noted that, however, the argument of the 'need to ensure the public service provided by Alitalia for reasons of public policy and territorial continuum' had already been submitted at the time of the preliminary examination of the EUR 300 million bridge loan in Apr. 2008, and the Commission seems to have not deemed it well-grounded in its invitation to submit comments (State Aid C 26/08, para. 44, in [2008] O.J. C184, p. 34).

74. According to Article 8a(1) of Regulation (EEC) No. 95/1993 of 18 Jan. 1993, slots may be exchanged, one for one, between air carriers or transferred to another air carrier 'in the case of a total or partial takeover when the slots are directly related to the air carrier taken over'.

comparatively short timeframe (the three years indicated as the 'floor' in the decree appearing, in fact, to be the 'cap'), can be accepted, so long as the users are given necessary side protection in the form of clear prior criteria to safeguard service continuity and fair ticket prices.

There are many technical and logical arguments in support to the uniqueness of the Alitalia case as a whole,[75] such as the elongated geography of the country, population density across a number of provincial capitals, the need to provide links, mostly at a loss, with the Italian islands on an ongoing basis, and the need to make suitable arrangements for the renovation of the Malpensa airport with a view to the Expo 2015 to be hosted by Milan. All these arguments appear to provide firm ground on which to base the Italian government's negotiations with the Commission to obtain appropriate authorization, albeit under the commitments and subject to the conditions which the very text of Article 4.4-*quinquies*) requires the Italian Competition Authority to provide for.

What is unlikely, though, is that the Commission may, in its capacity of regulatory body in matters of competition, grant so wide and absolute a derogation, in connection with the AirOne issue, from the rules on merger control, even if direct jurisdiction over the case were recognized to the Italian Authority on Trade and Competition. (What remains to be seen is, in fact, whether the *AGCM* may only acknowledge an authorization already automatically granted by a national legislative measure for reasons of public policy, without assessing its legality and without acting in conjunction with the Commission).[76] It should further be observed that, if a multi-state examination is required, the merger at issue may well be subjected to scrutiny by other national authorities.

---

75. Let me point out that the operation may not necessarily be prohibited by the competent authority (whether the Commission or the *AGCM*), but it could be *conditionally authorized*, subject to obligations or commitments to be undertaken by Alitalia and AirOne (see Art. 6(2) of Act No. 287/1990). This has been the case with both the Commission's and the Italian Authority's previous decisions on mergers between airlines. For example, in its Decision on *Air France/ KLM*, the Commission required the parties to surrender a number of slots on nine intra-Community routes and on several long-haul routes. (See Commission Decision of 11 Feb. 2004, *Air France/KLM*, para. 154 et seq. See also Commission Decision of 4 Jul. 2005, *Lufthansa/ Swissair*, para. 190 et seq.). In *Air France/Alitalia*, the Commission made exemption subject to several commitments, among which the surrender of slots at the Paris airports Charles De Gaulle and Orly and at the Milano Linate Airport. (See Commission Decision COMP/38.284/D2, *Air France/Alitalia*, para. 52 et seq.). It should be noted that the Commission frequently makes its authorizations subject to the parties' commitment to maintain a fixed number of flights on critical routes for a specified number of years. A negative precedent has been, however, the decision on *RyanAir/Air Lingus* of 27 Jun. 2007, in which the Commission held the view that the acquisition by Ryan Air of Air Lingus was incompatible with the common market, pursuant to Art. 8(3) of Regulation No. 139/2004, in that the operation would have created a monopoly or dominant position on as many as 35 air routes.
76. By Decision rendered on 3 Dec. 2008, the *AGCM* acknowledged that the new airline will have a dense network of routes covering the whole country and on individual routes will have, if not a monopoly, certainly a leading position in terms of frequency of currently available flights. However, the Authority – being precluded from assessing the legality of the merger – limited itself to set out a few measures necessary for avoiding the risk of unfair prices being imposed on consumers.

The provision of law in question may even turn out a boomerang when reference is made to the ECJ's case-law according to which a State aid measure which may not – because of certain of the manners of, or provisions for, its implementation, be held to be conflicting with other rules of the Treaty (or with any derivative rules in Regulations or Directives) – be admitted to examination for compatibility.[77] In other words, if the Commission confirms its view that the general cooperation obligation under Article 10 EC and/or the Regulation on merger control have been breached through the application of Article 4(4-*quinquies*) to the involved Alitalia case, then the Commission might be led to refrain altogether from assessing the aid for exemption, thereby making the whole operation founder at the onset.

11. A CRITICISM OF THE EXTENSIVE APPLICATION BY THE COMMISSION OF ARTICLE 87 EC, SPECIFICALLY IN RESPECT OF STATE AID

As the European internal market has, for many years now, been regarded as an 'area without frontiers', in which the four fundamental freedoms are, or should be, fully implemented, a State's intervention in the economy, as lawful as it may be pursuant to Article 295 EC in relation to ownership of property, is most likely to have an adverse impact on the harmonious functioning of such internal market when it aims at essentially favouring certain (usually 'national') undertakings or production sectors.

It is the unanimous assessment by the European institutions, the Commission and the Courts alike, of this situation of unbalance – caused by a choice made in the original Treaty of Rome (unchanged in the various amendments made over time) expressly to link '*aid*' from a public source (the *State*, in fact, *lato sensu*) to competition law – that, as discussed more extensively in the following section, seems to be no longer capable to provide a useful, balanced solution of the whole set of problems considered in this book.

The question of State aid, above and beyond its connection with competition law, lies astride *macro-* and *micro-economics*, and is one of the issues to solving which the Commission has ascribed great significance for the purposes of the full achievement of a united Europe.

Conversely, the gradual establishment of the principles of legal certainty, proportionality and legitimate expectations in the Community system calls into question the wide scope for discretion afforded to the Commission in the matter of State aid, a matter over which the Commission has exclusive jurisdiction,[78] except

77. See the case-law referred to at footnote 18 of this Chapter.

78. The Commission's excess discretion in applying the rules on aid, which has essentially been endorsed by the European Courts, is clearly highlighted in a volume I have edited, *Concorrenza e aiuti di Stato. Un osservatorio sulla prassi comunitaria*, cit., especially Chapter VII, 'La fase giurisdizionale', by Gambaro, p. 245 ff.

for a specific, only temporary situation. I am referring to a situation of 'unlawful' aid, i.e. one sourced, in Community language, by an act of '*public*' origin (one issued, that is, by the State or by any governmental, even local, authority or body), for the granting of *public resources*, that has not been notified in advance and has not yet been made the object of a decision of the Commission, in respect of which, pursuant to the last sentence of Article 88(1) EC, national courts have concurrent jurisdiction with the Commission's until the Commission takes a decision.[79]

On the other hand, the need for compliance with the freedoms of establishment and provision of services throughout the internal market, with the necessary, now deeply rooted, complement of free capital movements, has given the ECJ, when properly applied to by the Commission, direct jurisdiction over cases the Commission has so far categorized solely as State aid.

The Commission's Directorate General for Trade has made liberal use of the rules on State aid for the last few years. This deliberate choice dates back, if I am not mistaken, to 1964, when the Commission took the decision to suspend the aid granted in the *Ford Tractor Belgium* case,[80] which was followed by just thirteen 'negative' decisions until 1980, and by the same number in 1981 alone. This fact, along with the approach taken by the Commission to subsequent cases in the same matter, with a view to expanding the scope of application of the rules on State aid quite beyond the boundaries set by Article 87(1) EC, has led me, admittedly against conventional wisdom, to call into question the very rationale behind the current use of those rules, at least in connection with the so-called 'aid schemes' or aid by *administrative measures*.

I am referring to *legislative*, even *tax-related*, measures intended not to grant '*individual*' aid in support to individual positions, but to favour *certain categories of undertakings* or the *production of certain goods*, often in connection with, or in preparation for, privatization transactions. To avoid possible misunderstandings, it must be said that any measures of a '*general*' nature addressed, that is, to the *generality* of recipients in the same situation, do not fall within the State aid category. Precisely because of their *general nature*, measures of this type are lawful *per se* or, in the words of the Treaty of Rome, '*compatible with the common market*', for the simple reason that the aid so granted is not capable to affect free trading and competition.

In principle, the rules in question, applicable to whether *individual cases* or *aid schemes*, are quite complex in many one respect, in that they can only be applied if certain criteria, all equally essential, are met at the same time, such as: the imputability of the aid measure to public authorities (including, but not limited to, the State) and its impact on the State budget, its '*selectivity*', and its capability to distort competition or to affect trade between Member States.[81]

---

79. On the direct enforceability of this provision, its rationale and its correct application, please refer to Chapter VIII of the volume *Competition and State Aid*, cit.
80. See Commission Decision 64/651/EEC of 28 Oct. 1964.
81. For an more extensive analysis of each of these criteria, all of which must be met at the same time for an aid to be categorized as prohibited 'State aid', refer to *Competition and State Aid* by various authors, cit., especially Chapter I, 'The Notion of State Aid', p. 16 f.

Moreover, since 'State aid' is a matter of competition law, and amounts, as such, to an indissoluble trilateral relationship the parties to which are the State granting the aid, the Commission, which must enforce compliance with the relevant rules, and both the recipient undertakings and those allegedly harmed by that aid. Thus, if the intended beneficiaries are not '*undertakings*', as the Commission found in its decision on the Italian banking foundations in relation to the Ciampi Act,[82] the matter exceeds the boundaries of competition law, and Article 87 et seq. EC are not applicable as a result.[83]

For the Commission's resulting assessment to make any sense, it must be related to the '*relevant market*' in the usual meaning this phrase has in antitrust law, both in terms of geography and in terms of products.

Lastly, in case the Commission adopts a *negative* decision, recognizing the existence of incompatible aid, it will require the State involved, pursuant to Article 14(1) of Regulation No. 659/99, to take all necessary measures *to recover* the entire aid forthwith from the beneficiary undertakings.

Yet, the *recovery/repayment* is not, at least in theory, a punitive measure, since it is only intended to restore the former conditions of free competition in the market that were impaired by the act so recognized by the Commission to be unlawful State aid in its *directly enforceable decision*.

In fact, the end result of a 'recovery decision' is a heavier burden for the beneficiary, and quite unexpectedly so most of the times (notwithstanding the presumption to the contrary Community case-law has recognized in almost absolute terms). And its application is contingent only in theory, since it has been the Commission's settled practice, both before and after Regulation No. 658/1999, that a negative decision containing an order of recovery is the rule, and the opposite case is only a rare exception.

But it was not so at the beginning, mind you. Nothing was provided in the Community primary law (now represented by Articles 87 et seq. EC) that required recovery of unlawful State aid. Only in 1973 did the Court of Justice, in order to give *practical effect* to the Commission's negative decision in *Kohlengesetz*,[84] recognize the Commission's power to require the State involved to abolish or alter an aid found incompatible, which abolition or modification '*may include an obligation to require repayment of aid granted in breach of the Treaty*'.[85]

---

82. See Commission Decision No. 2003/146 of 22 Aug. 2002, on the tax measures for banking foundations implemented by Italy [2003] O.J. L55, p. 56.
83. That decision was confirmed, at least in part, by the Judgment of the ECJ of 10 Jan. 2006, Case C-222/04, *Ministero dell'Economia e delle Finanze* v *Cassa di Risparmio di Firenze SpA an others*, not yet published in ECR, following reference from the Italian Supreme Court for a preliminary ruling pursuant to Art. 234. On the topic, see also *Competition and State Aid*, cit., Chapter I.
84. Judgment of the Court of Justice of 12 Jul. 1973, Case 70/72, *Commission* v *Germany*, [1973] ECR 813.
85. *Ibid.*, ground 13.

The power so vested in the Commission was implicitly or explicitly confirmed by a number of ECJ judgments until 1985,[86] and, again in *Alcan*[87] and *Siemens*[88] decided by the ECJ and the CFI, respectively, as an inescapable result of the Commission finding an aid measure to be *unlawful* (i.e. a measure not notified by a Member State's government in advance, thus one adopted without the Commission's prior authorization), and by a Judgment of the Court of Justice of 21 March 1990 in *Tubemeuse* (*Belgium v Commission*).[89] As noted above, this precedent has found its way into the recovery obligation expressly provided for in Regulation No. 659/99.

Against this background, it should not come as a surprise that undertakings, as the ultimate addressees of the obligation to repay unlawful aid, are now playing a major role in the administrative procedure to which they are active parties before the Commission pursuant to the 1999 Regulation.

There is a misunderstanding which must be disposed of, though. State aid is an essentially technical matter, which has nothing to do with more or less explicit hints at 'obviousness' or 'common sense'. Only consider that it has been the Commission's practice – fully endorsed by the Community Courts' unanimous case-law – that, in determining the necessary anticompetitive nature of an aid, any initial disadvantages caused by the differences in structural rules still existing between different EU Member States are taken into no account, either in categorizing an aid as lawful or compatible or in granting exemptions from the recovery obligation. Nor is any consideration given to any basic penalties imposed on undertakings operating in any given Member State, in the case of alleged aid in the form of tax benefits, because of the even deep differences, already discussed above, in the overall taxation of corporate income generally applicable within different Member States.

The argument on which this approach is based, as it is often offered by the Commission and the Courts, is quite simple. Since measures of a general nature are never categorized as 'aid', it is for each Member State alone, obviously in compliance with the other Treaty rules, to modify any less favourable provisions of national law, unless such provisions restrict the full exercise by Community foreigners of any of the fundamental freedoms in that Member State.

From the point of view of the undertakings receiving allegedly unlawful aid granted by national legislative measures, they could hardly understand why any basic unbalances and asymmetries existing in national law should be deemed entirely immaterial.

86. See, among others, Judgments of the ECJ of 15 Jan. 1986, Case 52/84, *Commission* v *Belgium*, [1986] ECR 89, and of 6 Feb. 1986, Case 310/85, *Deufil* v *Commission*, [1987] ECR 901.

87. Judgment of the Court of Justice of 20 Mar. 1997, Case C-24/95, *Land Rheinland Pfalz* v *Alcan*, [1997] ECR I-1591.

88. Judgment of the Court of First Instance of 8 Jun. 1995, Case T-459/93, *Siemens* v *Commission*, [1995] ECR II-1675, ground 66.

89. See Judgment of the Court of Justice of 21 Mar. 1990, Case C-142/87, *Belgium* v *Commission*, [1990] ECR I-959, ground 66.

This is even more so as there is no guarantee as to the actual *general* application of State aid rules, since the relevant procedures can be opened or not opened depending on *the Commission's exclusive discretion* in taking the relevant decision.

Quite irrelevant in this respect is the distinction between *lawful* aid, i.e. measures duly notified in advance, and *unlawful* aid, i.e. measures not so notified to the Commission. This difference in qualification entails merely procedural consequences most of the times.

An essential part of the State aid procedure is the recovery decision. In 1983, the Commission had, based on the finding that '*illegal aid grants* [*were*] *becoming increasingly common*', already issued a Communication (*OJ*, C 318, 24 November 1983) whereby it '*informed*':

> potential recipients of State aid of the risk attaching to any aid granted to them illegally, in that any recipient of an aid granted illegally, i.e. without the Commission having reached a final decision, may have to refund the aid.

The fact is, however, that Commission Communications of this type are only intended for those familiar with the specific field of State aid, and usually fail to reach undertakings, especially if small or medium-sized. And this has an even heavier impact today, with twenty-seven Member States.

Further, because of the complexity of the very State aid notion, and taking into account the Commission's wide scope for discretion even in respect of the crucial choice whether or not to open a procedure, especially in cases of aid or aid schemes granted by unnotified legislative measures, how could a beneficiary undertaking be expected spontaneously to 'disapply' a more favourable national measure just because the recipient has 'scented' incompatible aid before the Commission takes a decision? And it should be considered that, in a recent case of national legislative measures that, at least *prima facie*, appeared to qualify outright as 'State aid' and had been notified in details by one or more 'interested' parties, the Commission decided to dismiss the case on the argument that the complaining party *was not a competitor* of the defendant's. (Yet., one should wonder, was it not an *ex officio* procedure?).[90] A further allegation was that there was no discriminatory effect (and then, one should wonder, where is any such effect provided for in Article 87 EC?).[91]

The very rules on State aid, as they have developed over time as a result of case-law developments and of the prescriptions contained in secondary regulatory instruments discussed above, irrespective of whether or not prior notification has been given, are essentially intended to govern two situations far different from each other: individual aid and aid schemes. Only in the former situation does the Commission apply, or believe it dutiful to apply, competition rules, albeit in softer manners and with more subdued contents than in the latter situation.

---

90. See 10 Mar. 2008 letter to SEA SpA, CP 169/07, concerning Act No. 248/2005 on 'system requirements'.
91. *Ibid.*

In recent times, the Commission appears to have tried to downplay the disputes over aid schemes granted by legislative measures as they were just *bilateral relationships* between the Commission and the State assumedly granting aid, *with the exclusion* of the purportedly recipient undertakings from any legal protection of their interests.[92] It has also tried – with the endorsement occasionally provided by generic statements in one or another ECJ judgment – to analyse the purported State aid without relating it to a given geographic or product market. Clearly enough, lacking any such logical exercise, there remains no other standard of reference for an even passing assessment as to the competition-distorting nature of the legislative measure in question.

It should also be noted that the Commission does by no means, with the Community Courts' occasional endorsement, try to establish whether, in any relevant case, the legal measure in dispute has or has not an actual *adverse impact* on trade between Member States. In fact, it only makes generic references, in its decisions, to a presumed harm to trade, without the support of even the least element of fact to show such harm.[93]

Thus, two of the essential requirements of the 'State aid' notion – the two most relevant to antitrust matters – can be found to exist in any relevant case merely as a result of the Commission using hackneyed phrases contained in primary provisions of law or in articles of Regulation No. 659/99, as substitutes for sound reasons based on a serious preparatory investigation intended to identify actual competition-distorting elements in the disputed measure.[94]

In my view, the Commission's statement as to the substantive differences presumably existing – even in the field of competition – between the rules on unlawful agreements, those on dominant position and those on merger control, and between these rules as a whole and the rules on State aid, because of the necessary presence of a State or a public authority as the acting party in State aid procedures alone, cannot possibly account for a presumption of guilt *iuris et de iure* in the case of 'illegal' aid later to be categorized by the Commission as unlawful or incompatible.

---

92. See Chapters V and VII of the volume *Competition and State Aid*, cit.
93. See the considerations offered in Chapter I of the volume *Competition and State Aid*, cit., para. 2.4, especially p. 30 f.
94. Indeed, case-law is not unequivocal in this respect. See para. 2.3.2 of Chapter VII, Gambaro, 'La fase giurisdizionale' in *Concorrenza e Aiuti di Stato*, cit., p. 245 ff., also for an examination of a ECJ Judgment on State aid under the Ciampi Act, in *Unicredito* v *Agenzia delle Entrate* of 15 Dec. 2005, Case C-148/04. Let me also point out the procedural deficiency of that judgment, in which the Court, *in its preliminary ruling* by reference from the Commissione Tributaria Provinciale di Genova, acceded to a preliminary objection raised *in limine* by the Commission intervening in the hearing of 3 Feb. 2005, and, without even mentioning in the judgment either such (ungrounded) objection or the Court's own choice, in breach of the adversarial principle, utterly disregarded the arguments relating to the huge deficiencies in the Commission's line of reasoning about the competition-distorting aspects of the disputed measure, as already dealt with by Unicredito's counsel in their written statements and only more specifically discussed in the oral address.

Beyond and above any considerations about the homogeneity of the rules in connection with the structure in which, by comparison with the rules on prohibited agreements, the general rule of prohibition and the derogations thereto under Article 87 are so close, even at first sight, to those under Article 81 EC, a decisive consideration is that *the impact on trade between Member States* and *the effect of distorting or threatening to distort competition* are stated among the essential requirements for a State aid measure to be categorized as unlawful, with both articles meaningfully using the same wording.

Nor can the Commission's wide scope for discretion be placed, as the Commission would like it to be, above or outside any effective judicial control.

How can the Commission – I wonder – even assess the actual presence or possibly the absence of such requirements in any one real case without using the crucial yardstick of the *relevant market*, albeit by an 'attenuated' determination,[95] against which that specific case can be measured in comparison with the ideal model?

Nor can I possibly share the Commission's statement that a genuine, effective verification of the competition-distorting effects of an unnotified legislative measure would give an unjust advantage to an unlawful aid over a notified aid. It is just appropriate to mention the scrutiny with similar prognostic contents the Commission is required to conduct in a merger control case irrespective of whether the deal has or has not already been carried out. It can hardly be seen why the examination of an aid, whether notified or not, should have different contents. In either case the Commission's scrutiny cannot, in principle, but be based on the same type of hypothetical judgment about the effects that a legislative measure as well as a merger agreement may have on the relevant market.

The contrary would be true, in fact. It is the Commission which has an advantage in case an unnotified aid has already been implemented, since it can, in addition to the usual hypothetical judgment, more easily refer to the anticompetitive effects that measure has already had on competing undertakings. When no such effects have materialized, assuming that they exist anyhow would even seem to amount to abuse.

But the very approach the Commission has taken to the most recent cases, probably because of the difficulties it has had in analysing State aid in the form of legislative measures under competition law draws attention to a novel aspect, never emerged so clearly so far, which is, in my view, the point of arrival of the very notion of unlawfulness of a '*State aid scheme*' for violation of free competition rules.

The Commission's latest decisions have clearly shown that the unlawfulness of State aid granted by a national legislative measure would arise, in fact, from the

---

95. The way out of the problem the Commission has consistently chosen to take is the lower significance it ascribes to the identification of the relevant market. In fact, the assessments it usually makes or is expected to make in any one case are rather 'absent' than 'attenuated', in that they are often unsupported on any economic analysis. See para. 2.4 of Chapter I of the volume *Competition and State Aid*, cit.

discrimination made to the advantage of the recipient undertakings operating in that State and to the disadvantage of the *competing* undertakings operating in the same or in another Member State. In an '*internal*', now single, market – then a highly competitive one by definition – it is discrimination that would by itself, in the Commission's view, make State aid unlawful, so that any further scrutiny would be unnecessary.

This is the point, though. Within a competitive context, discrimination has not, nor could it have, the absolute character it is bound to have if compliance with the four fundamental freedoms is at stake. This is because, in terms of competition law, only if *the assumed discriminatory effect* of a national law intended to favour some category of (possibly national) undertakings in any way occurred in *the same relevant (geographic) market*, could the competition-distorting element be deemed to exist as one of the requirements that must necessarily be met under Article 87(1) EC in the filed of State aid for a legislative measure to be categorized as aid scheme. If, however, the discrimination between national and foreign undertakings, both of them Community-based, were to generate its effects outside the relevant market, there would be no violation of competition law rules and, accordingly – lacking one of the stated requirements – there would be no unlawful State aid.

Therefore, if the real issue were outright discrimination by any one Member State between its own nationals and foreign Community citizens within its territory, then the competition rules on State aid would be immaterial. What would really be at stake would be the granting State's compliance (or, rather, failure to comply) with one or more of the four fundamental freedoms, all of which are ensured by a whole set of primary and derivative Community rules, specifically those specifically concerning the free provision of services or the right of establishment, as the case may be, along with that complementary requirement, free movement of capital.

However, if this is this case, the Treaty prescribes quite another procedure – that under Article 226 EC, which *by no means* vests the Commission with decision-making powers, but only empowers it to refer a Member State's failure to fulfil its obligations under the Treaty to the Court of Justice, after delivering a reasoned opinion.

12. STATE AID BY LEGISLATIVE ACT UNDER US LAW AND NEW POSSIBLE APPROACHES IN EU LAW

At this point, one could even wonder if State aid by a legislative act, as the Commission understands it, still has anything to do, in itself, with competition law.

It is not by chance that no such provisions as the Community rules on State aid are to be found among the antitrust rules in the US legal system, which is the world's most consequential '*federal*' system and is still the most highly advanced system in competition matters – in addition to its having been the earliest system ever to govern competition by law.

Under US federal law, the issue of unlawful subsidies is primarily dealt with in terms of *export subsidies*, which are hit because, in their being granted by third countries, they unduly favour imports by those countries' manufacturers into the United States market – in breach of the US internal rules now implementing the GATT 1994/WTO Agreements, specifically the Agreement on Subsidies and Countervailing Duties.[96]

Further, in the US federal system, the adoption of governmental measures in support to specific categories of enterprises, in the form of whether subsidies, tax breaks or protective tariffs, is not treated as matter of competition law and it falls outside the jurisdiction of the Federal Trade Commission (and of the Department of Justice, when competent). Therefore, the entire problem should be analysed in light of the US constitutional law, which is a matter falling under the Federal Courts' direct and exclusive jurisdiction.

This is because, much as State protectionist measures are abstractly viewed as conducts prohibited by the Sherman Act and by the other federal antitrust laws, it is settled case-law that the governmental acts of any one State of the Union in exercising its sovereignty ('*act*[*s*] *of government by the State as sovereign*') are not subject to federal antitrust rules, but to constitutional precepts (according to the Supreme Court's 'State action doctrine'). Thus, in this latter respect, subsidies are dealt with in light of the so-called 'dormant' or 'negative commerce clause', a case-law doctrine arising from a negative converse of Article I, § 8, of the US Constitution, which requires that 'The Congress shall have the power . . . to regulate commerce with foreign nations and among the several states.' The dormant commerce clause, however, prohibits a State from passing legislation that grants firms monetary incentives through State revenues or by laying duties or taxes which entail 'a visible burdensome impact on out-of-state producers' or *discriminate against interstate commerce*.

In this latter profile, the analogy of European laws with the US system is also quite apparent in the way their respective rules are worded. This can be seen, for example in Community case-law on golden shares at the implementation stage. The matter has already been discussed here in terms of European constitutional law in connection with the *non-discrimination obligation* and the related duty of full compliance with fundamental freedoms.[97]

As for the former profile, it should be noted that the question relates to that body of international rules which (under an efficient judicial system for the settlement of trade disputes at an international level, with two judicial instances within the WTO) are currently binding upon the European Union, as a direct single addressee separate from its individual Member States, as well as upon the one hundred fifty-three States that are currently parties to the GATT/WTO. On the other hand, beyond the international rules on *macroeconomic* relations, there is a set of concurrent 'internal' rules in the European Union as well as within the United States. As for the European Union, these rules have been the outcome of the

96. Please, refer to Chapter IV of this book for a discussion of this topic.
97. See above, Chapter III, section 10 ff.

adjustment of Community law to those same 1994 international agreements on world trade, and they have been introduced in the form of Community regulations pursuant to which the active parties are as well the Council, the Commission and the Member State or States concerned as undertakings interested for whatever reasons – be they non-European firms being investigated for dumped imports to an importing Member's market or for the improper advantage accorded to them by government subsidies, or else Community undertakings claiming to have been '*harmed*' thereby.[98]

In compliance with these rules at the two different, international and (European) internal levels at which they operate, nobody would ever blame a State member of whether the European or the American Union for having in force a less stringent legislation in matters of environmental protection or workplace safety, thus one less burdensome for the local firms, than that in force in any third country. Nor would anyone blame another State member of either Union for adopting legislative measures favouring its entire manufacturing industry, or any one sector thereof, then in a 'selective' way. Nor would any Member State be blamed for attracting commercial companies to its own territory through simplified rules of company law or an especially favourable tax treatment.[99] In fact, when any such situation is viewed in the light of a union of States or of intra-union relations, it clearly appears to promote a competition of a sort among member States, which eventually results in a full advantage for consumers throughout that union's internal market.

Thus, quite beyond international considerations, a Member State's legislative act providing subsidies should not be assumed to be an outright State aid scheme in any event, but *either* it falls under a third country's rules implementing the GATT 1994/WTO Agreements (in the same way as dumping), in the case of the United States – then solely in relation to *subsidy schemes* granted by a European State to its national undertakings for the ultimate purpose of unduly favouring exports to the United States to the detriment of United States enterprises – *or* a Member State's measure favouring certain Community (national) undertakings to the detriment of other Community undertakings would not fall under 'competition' rules and should only be disciplined by the Commission to the extent it *discriminates* against such other Community undertakings, in which case Article 226 EC would come into play, if it is correct to assess any such measure in relation to the single market at all and any times.

Once observance of the four fundamental freedoms within the European Union is acknowledged to be now the main pillar of the entire Community construction, I believe that the approach to be taken against any discrimination introduced by a legislative act can only be that just indicated above in relation to the latter assumption.

---

98. See above, Chapter IV, section 18 ff., and section 23 in relation to the United States of America.
99. For the evolution of Community case-law on full freedom of choice in exercising the right of establishment, see above, Chapter I, sections 9-13.

In conclusion, if the lawfulness or unlawfulness of a State aid scheme were assessed outside the scope of competition law – something which is already entirely practicable today – the Commission would achieve the intended result to have as its only one necessary counterparty, in a procedure pursuant to Article 226 EC, the Member State that adopted the disputed legislative measure, to the exclusion of any private parties, which would accordingly have no say in the matter.

As for the protection of private parties' rights, such exclusion would be made good by the different role the Commission has to play under Article 226 EC. Since the Commission would, in this case, act outside the rules of competition law, it would not have the power to deliver a *decision* immediately and directly applicable in itself, but, after having notified the Member State concerned to no avail, it should deliver a reasoned opinion, i.e. a non-binding instrument in itself, on the existence of an infringement or of an incorrect application of a Community norm, with the power to bring the matter before the Court of Justice against the non-complying Member State. It will then be for the ECJ – in a role not too far removed from the Federal Court's under Article I, § 88 of the US Constitution – to deliver a declaratory judgment about the actual existence or non-existence of the alleged infringement.

In this case, only the *recovery-and-repayment* obligation would be lacking, but it should not be forgotten that – as the Commission has expressly maintained in an attempt to exclude the undertakings concerned from an action brought to challenge one of its decisions on State aid – recovery is not prescribed by a primary norm and is only contingent, and it would be for the competent national authorities to assess both any relevant excluding causes and the amount to be repaid.

Moreover, it should be noted that, in any of the (frequent) cases in which a Member State does not spontaneously enforce the Commission's relevant decision on State aid – irrespective of whether or not the decision has been challenged before the ECJ or the CFI – the Commission is still required to bring the matter against the non-complying Member State before the Court of Justice in a procedure under Article 226 EC.

After all, the approach I venture to suggest would have the added positive effect, in a judicial system greatly burdened in itself, to anticipate the ECJ's intervention, thereby considerably curtailing the overall time required to decide the case.

There is a specific reason why the entire body of Community rules on 'State aid' also deserves second thought in the light of the US pattern.

In opening all of the world's markets to any undertakings, irrespective of size, globalization has a powerful impact on this matter as well.

In this context, outside the international rules that uniformly govern export subsidies, the rigid, relentless application by the Commission of the Community rules on State aid, notwithstanding their being solely applicable within the internal market, in prosecuting European undertakings, takes into no account the prejudice possibly arising to the undertakings concerned, in their competition with non-Community undertakings, not only in international, non-Community markets, but within the common market as well. I am not really sure that, in doing so, the Commission has any chance to accomplish:

> the objective of . . . encouraging [Community industry] to become more competitive at international level,

an objective most clearly laid down in Article 163(1) EC.

Nor can the Commission delude itself into thinking that it may apply the provisions of Article 87 EC to non-Community undertakings, by calling into question third countries' acts or laws intended to favour such third countries' national firms, and still demand recovery by a negative decision based on the effects theory.

The Commission's bashful attempt to take action in relation to the recent salvage of *Bears Stearns* by the Fed does certainly not alter my assumption.

In fact, that would be wishful thinking, to say the least, on the part of a institution as the Commission, which is forced by its stated need to drive Member States' governments into self-denunciation to resort to the presumption technique against undertakings that are the beneficiaries of a purported State aid scheme, thereby trying to make good its recurring inability to pick out by itself any cases of unlawful aid granted by Member States.

Internationally, the Commission's action could readily be defeated by any third country by reference to the GATT rules, along the same logical lines I submitted above in relation to the US system, thereby drastically repulsing any different approach the Commission might attempt to take.

13. RECOVERY DECISIONS AND RIGHTS OF DEFENCE

I have already observed that providing for recovery orders in State aid cases, now a natural consequence of a Commission decision determining State aid, though not under any primary norm and only the result of the Commission's view being upheld in case-law, obviously requires, in exchange, that any private undertaking in receipt of that aid must have standing in their own right to participate as well in the administrative procedure as in any subsequent judicial stages, for them to be able to challenge the Commission's negative decisions before the European Courts.

For I am convinced that, in any case of individual aid or aid under an aid scheme, expecting that the beneficiaries should only be allowed to institute proceeding subject to the requirement of '*individual concern*' in the literal sense of the phrase, in one with that other requirement, '*direct concern*', under Article 230(4) EC, would make no sense at all. If such view were granted, as the Commission has forcefully requested for some time now, it would eventually result in individual undertakings being denied standing to bring action, then in their being deprived of their rights of defence on the primary issue, the existence or non-existence of State aid, through an assessment preparatory to a discussion about the recovery issue.

The Commission's request is also in contrast with the '*formal*' interpretation it has adopted, and the European Courts have endorsed so far, of the principles of *legitimate expectation, legal certainty* and *proportionality* as the discriminating factors for a recovery order to be granted. It is not enough to enable a private operator to plead one or more of these principles if their use is only allowed in extreme cases, on the case-law assumption that '*the private operator could not help but know that an unnotified law qualified as State aid*' – apparently hinting at an objective liability of a sort.

One of two propositions must be true. Either the private operator is a party to the procedure *optimo iure*, in which case only when the Commission's bar to a national law is adequately publicized[100] can that private operator be correctly assumed to be aware thereof, or, if the latter has no standing to participate in the procedure, knowledge can *never* be presumed, in compliance with the right to defence, and the general rule must prevail that it is for the Commission to discharge the duty of proof if and when it intends to order recovery by its decision.

The Commission has objected that each of the beneficiaries lacks *individual concern* because a decision against an *aid scheme* instituted by a legislative measure, i.e. an act of general application *per se*, would itself be of general application. Therefore, the Commission has alleged that the beneficiaries of unlawful aid granted on the basis of an aid scheme found to be incompatible could not plead individual concern to challenge that decision in case recovery is ordered.

This is an entirely groundless argument, if one only considers that the legislation in dispute is by no means 'general' because, were it so, there would be no aid and, even if it were so, it could not automatically entail the 'general application' of a decision and prevent any undertaking, whether a beneficiary or a non-beneficiary competitor, from participating in the challenge.

In fact, the Community Courts' most recent approach has been to consider the beneficiaries of national aid schemes to have standing to contest a decision categorizing such measures as incompatible.[101]

The fact that, pursuant to Article 14 of Regulation 659/99, it is for the authorities of the Member State concerned to enforce a recovery decision cannot deprive a beneficiary of the alleged aid of its rights of defence before the Community

---

99. This cannot come as a surprise, since, when the Commission wants to publicize one of its acts or positions it does so by press releases.

101. See Judgments of the Court of First Instance of 15 Jun. 2000, Joined Cases T-298/97, T-312/97, T-313/97, T-315/97, T-600/97 to 607/97, T-1/98, T-3/98 to T-6/98, and T-23/98, *Alzetta and others*, [2000] ECR II-2319, grounds 24-25, and Judgment of the Court of Justice of 19 Oct. 2000, *Sardegna Lines*, [2000] ECR I-8855, grounds 31-35. In this last case, the Court held the applicant to be *individually concerned* by the decision in question not only as a shipping company in Sardinia and, as such, *a potential beneficiary* of the aid scheme granted to Sardinian ship owners, but also '*by virtue of being an actual beneficiary of individual aid granted under that scheme, the recovery of which has been ordered by the Commission*'. The *Sardinian Lines* precedent was later applied by the Court to *Alzetta*, on appeal brought by the Italian Government (Judgment of 29 Apr. 2004, grounds 38-39), when the ECJ confirmed admissibility of appeals brought by private operators. The same approach was further stated by the Court of First Instance in its recent judgments of 20 Sep. 2007, Case T-136-/05, *EARL Salvat père & fils*, [2007] O.J. C269, p. 47, ground 70, and of 12 Sep. 2007, Joined Cases T-239/04 and T-323/04, *Italy and Brandt Italia*, [2007] O.J. C247, p. 20, ground 44.

Courts on the underlying issue, that of the assessment of compatibility of a national legislative measure. This conclusion is supported on ECJ case-law, which has denied the application of the *legitimate expectation principle* to the beneficiary of an aid under an aid scheme where that principle is pleaded to cripple a recovery decision, on the argument that an *individual businessman* is expected, even in a case of unnotified aid, to have knowledge since the very beginning of the risk that the aid measure in question may be deemed unlawful, and to refrain from relying on it in his behaviour even before the Commissions takes a decision.[102]

Likewise, there appears to be no ground for the view the Commission has taken for some time on the matter of aid schemes, according to which the protection of persons affected by a decision of incompatibility of an aid scheme is supposed to be ensured *indirectly* by the competent national court, rather than *directly* by the Community Courts. According to the Commission, both mechanisms – the application for annulment and national remedies – are expected to provide '*adequate judicial protection*'.

This view can be readily rebutted on the argument that there is no equivalence between the *direct* protection available under Article 230 EC and the *indirect* protection afforded by Article 234 EC, in that the protection offered to the private parties to a reference for a preliminary ruling is merely *contingent* and it is 'enfeebled' because of the characteristics typical of a reference for preliminary ruling, which is a procedure of an *incidental* rather then contentious nature. *Initiating a reference procedure for a preliminary ruling is precluded to the parties*, which are not allowed to file claims of their own and are only allowed to submit statements of case in the preparatory phase or to make specific proposals as to how the relevant questions should be answered.[103]

Moreover, from a strictly procedural point of view, in proceedings pursuant to Article 234 EC, unlike ordinary Community proceedings: (i) following the initial written observations to the Court pursuant to Article 23 of the Statute of the Court of Justice, neither answers nor supplements in writing are allowed; and (ii) only one judicial instance is available to the parties.

In fact, reference may even be 'barred' by a previous judgment of the Court confirming the Commission's decision at the end of the proceedings in the case between the Member State concerned and the Commission, in the absence of the 'interested' private parties.

It should be noted that the Commission's 'invitation' to the applicants in receipt of an alleged aid for them to press for a reference for a preliminary ruling as to validity in case the recovery decision is challenged (thereby avoiding direct resort to the Court of First Instance) is in conflict with the ECJ's judgment of 9 March 1994 in *TWD*, based on which a recipient of State aid is not permitted to plead the unlawfulness of the Commission decision against the Member State

---

102. See among many, Judgment of 20 Sep. 1990, Case C-5/89, *Commission* v *Germany*, [1990] ECR I-3437, ground 14.
103. This is the gist of Advocate General Alber's Opinion in *Alzetta*, cit., point 89, where he referred to Mr AG Jacobs' Opinion in *UPA*, point 36 ff.

granting the aid, whereby the Commission ordered recovery, in proceedings before a national judge. And this precisely because, though the recipient in question could have brought an action against that decision under Article 173 of the Treaty (now Article 230 EC), *it did not bring action, or did not do so within the period prescribed by that same article.*[104]

Even a trade association is allowed to challenge a decision by the Commission so long as it does so in the capacity of agent of one or more of its members, who were themselves permitted to bring an admissible action.[105]

At ground 60 of its *AITEC* judgment, the Court of First instance considered that:

> the collective action brought by the association presents procedural advantages, since it obviates the institution of numerous separate actions against the same decisions, whilst avoiding any risk of Article 173 of the Treaty [now Article 230 EC] being circumvented by means of such a collective action.

In any event, an action for annulment brought by an association of undertakings *is admissible in its own right*, according to the judgments of the Court of First Instance in *Van der Kooy, CIRFS* and *AIUFFASS/AKT*, so long as its negotiating position *vis-à-vis* the Commission is affected by the measure which it seeks to have annulled.[106]

14. THE COMMUNITY COURTS' CONTROL OVER COMMISSION DECISIONS

As observed above, control over Commission decisions in matters of competition, when any such decision is challenged by an interested party, is entrusted with the Court of First Instance and, if need be, with the Court of Justice in case an appeal is brought.

In principle, I state again my view that the European Court's control over any Commission decision is one *as to legality, not as to the merits.*

By way of exception, Article 229 EC gave the Community Courts jurisdiction *on the merits* as well, though only in respect of that part of a decision which concerns the application of the penalties provided for in regulations on competition and the determination of the amount of any such penalty. This rule later found its way into Article 31 of Regulation (EC) No. 1/2003, and Article 16 of Regulation (EC) No. 139/2004, pursuant to which the European Courts are empowered to

---

104. The judgment in *TWD* is in [1994] ECR I-833.
105. See Judgments of the Court of First Instance of 22 Oct. 1996, Case T-266/94, *Skibsvaerftsforeningen*, [1994] ECR II-1399, ground 50; *CETM*, cit., grounds 24-25; of 6 Jul. 1995, Joined Cases T-447/93, T-448/93 and T-449/93, *AITEC and others* v *Commission*, [1995] ECR II-1971, ground 62; and of 13 Sep. 2006, T-210/02, *British Aggregates Association*, [2006] ECR II-2789, ground 47.
106. See the Judgment of the CFI of 12 Dec. 1996, Case T-380/94, *AIUFFASS and AKT* v *Commission*, [1996] ECR II-2169, ground 50.

cancel, reduce or increase any fine or periodic penalty payment imposed by the Commission.

It is also fair to point out that, in respect of the complex assessments typical of the matter, distinguishing between legality and merits is by no means and easy task in itself.

On the other hand, the role the Commission has to play under Community law in its capacity as guarantor of free competition – as is the case, in fact, with the powers of any independent national administrative authority – requires special consideration to be given to judicial decisions. Hence, the essential bias of the European Courts' rulings in favour of the Commission over the other parties to challenge proceedings as well – even over Member States, each of which is always entitled anyhow to intervene in Community proceedings on competition as well as on other issues.[107]

Thus, at least in principle, the Community Courts' control could be deemed to be a *weak* one in the sense conveyed by the distinction made by the Italian Council of State between 'weak' and 'strong' controls, according to which the former include the review by administrative judicial bodies of decisions taken by the *Autorità Garante della Concorrenza e del Mercato* (*AGCM*, the Italian Office of Fair Trading).[108]

In fact, the Court of First Instance seems to exercise a more stringent control over the Commission's decisions also in connection with the rules on free competition relied upon in any such decision.

The Court of First Instance has clarified the scope of its own control in a judgment recently delivered *in an action for the annulment* of a Commission decision on a *prohibited agreement* between undertakings, as follows:

> In that regard, the [Community] Court hearing an application for annulment of a decision applying Article 81(1) EC must undertake a *comprehensive review* of the examination carried out by the Commission . . . unless that examination entails *a complex economic assessment*, in which case review by the Court *is confined* to ascertaining that there has been *no misuse of powers, that the rules on procedure and on the statement of reasons have been complied with, that the facts have been accurately stated and that there has been no manifest error of assessment of those facts* . . . Furthermore, that review is carried out solely by reference to the elements of fact and of law existing on the date of adoption

---

107. In particular, this principle must be implemented in Italy 'through *ad-hoc* administrative structures having special standing and competence' (Council of State, VI, 5287/01, cit., and Council of State, VI, 2199/2002, cit.) and 'having regard to how the Law has configured the Authority and its powers and measures, outside the loop of political guidance, as an organ placed in a position of unique independence . . . For the Law is intended to provide a special guarantee for any subjective, constitutionally protected situations related to the protection of competition (Constitution, Article 41)'. (Council of State, 5156/02, cit.).

108. Council of State, VI, 2199/2002, cit. and Council of State, 5156/02, cit. However, in its judgment of 27 Jan. 2004, No. 926, the Council of State deems preferable to go beyond the formal categories of 'weak' and 'strong' control. See also Council of State, VI, 10 Mar. 2006, No. 1271.

> of the contested decision . . . without prejudice to the possibility afforded to the parties, in the exercise of their rights of defence, of supplementing them by evidence established after that date, but for the specific purpose of contesting or defending that decision. [*Emphasis added*].[109]

Now, the Court of First Instance's control will be especially 'weak' – in which case it has been referred to as *marginal control as to legality*[110] or *narrow control* – where the decision is taken by the Commission pursuant Article 81(3) EC,[111] or where the Commission has dismissed a complaint from a third party in relation to an alleged infringement of Article 81(1) or Article 82 EC.[112]

For in each such case the CFI's task is only to establish whether the evidence relied on is factually accurate, reliable and consistent, whether it contains all the information which must be taken into account for the purpose of assessing a complex situation and whether it is capable of substantiating the conclusions drawn from it by the Commission in the decision. Conversely, *it is not* for the Court of First Instance *to substitute its own economic assessment* for that of the Commission.[113]

This by no means implies that the Commission's examination if definitive in this respect. In an action in which the Commission's decision in a case of a '*conglomerate-type concentration*' had been challenged, the Court of Justice held that:

> Whilst the Court recognises that the Commission has a margin of discretion with regard to economic matters, that does not mean that the Community Courts must refrain from reviewing the Commission's interpretation of information of an economic nature.[114]

More recently, the Court of First Instance again stressed that the Commission has *a wide margin of discretion* in the field of merger control, and added that the CFI's *test of manifest errors alone* is justified by the *prospective nature* of the economic analysis the Commission carries out to establish whether or not the transaction under scrutiny creates or strengthens a dominant position.[115]

---

109. See CFI Judgment of 27 Sep. 2006, Case T-168/01, *GlaxoSmithKline Services* v *Commission*, [2006] ECR II-2969, grounds 57-58.
110. Gattinara, 'La tutela giurisdizionale in sede europea' in *Il nuovo diritto europeo della concorrenza*, Tosato & Bellodi Eds. (Milan, 2004), p. 457.
111. See, of many, Judgments in *GlaxoSmithKline Services*, cit., grounds 241-245, and of 21 Mar. 2002, Case T-131/99, *Hamilton Shaw* v *Commission*, [2002] ECR II-2023, ground 38. *Contra*, Ortiz Blanco & Jörgens, '*Antitrust Rules*' in *EC Competition Procedure*, Ortiz Blanco Ed. (Oxford, 2006), § 15.18, who argue that the direct applicability of Art. 81(3) EC, as introduced by Regulation 1/2003, requires the CFI to conduct a review similar to that used for an examination pursuant to Art. 81(1) EC.
112. See, of many, Judgment of the Court of First Instance of 27 Sep. 2006, Case T-204/03, *Haladjian Frères* v *Commission*, [2006] ECR II-3779, ground 30.
113. See Judgment in *GlaxoSmithKline Services*, cit., ground 244.
114. See Judgment of the ECJ of 15 Feb. 2005, Case C-12/03 P, *Commission* v *Tetra Laval*, [2005] ECR I-987, ground 39.
115. See Judgment of the Court of First Instance of 11 Jul. 2007, Case T-170/06, *Alrosa Company Ltd* v *Commission*, not yet published in ECR, ground 109. See also Judgment of the Court of First Instance of 30 Sep. 2003, Case T-158/00, *ARD* v *Commission*, [2003] ECR II-3825,

The ECJ's judicial review of a judgment of the CFI that has been challenged in a competition case decided by the Commission is one *in point of law* alone, not *in point of fact*. The limits to the Court of Justice's jurisdiction even over the CFI's powers indicated above, have aptly been described by the ECJ itself in *John Deere* as follows:

> [A]n appeal [against a judgment of the CFI] may be based only on grounds relating to the infringement of rules of law, to the exclusion of any appraisal of the facts. The Court of First Instance has exclusive jurisdiction, first, to establish the facts except where the substantive inaccuracy of its findings is apparent from the documents submitted to it and, second, to assess those facts. When the Court of First Instance has established or assessed the facts, the Court of Justice has jurisdiction under Article [225] of the Treaty to review the legal characterisation of those facts by the Court of First Instance and the legal conclusions it has drawn from them . . . The Court of Justice thus has no jurisdiction to establish the facts or, in principle, to examine the evidence which the Court of First Instance accepted in support of those facts. Provided that the evidence has been properly obtained and the general principles of law and the rules of procedure in relation to the burden of proof and the taking of evidence have been observed, it is for the Court of First Instance alone to assess the value which should be attached to the evidence produced to it . . . The appraisal by the Court of First Instance of the evidence put before it does not constitute, save where the evidence has been fundamentally misconstrued, a point of law which is subject, as such, to review by the Court of Justice. [*Emphasis added*].[116]

The difference in jurisdictional powers between the Community Courts results in essential differences between their respective procedures. This, among other things, explains why the CFI may, as it usually does between the written phase and the oral phase in the proceedings, put questions to the parties and ask them either to submit explanations in writing or to produce documents. It also explains why the Judge-Rapporteur may, as he usually does between the various parties' arguments and their answers in the hearing before the CFI, ask the parties' representatives more specific questions, not so much in point of law as in point of fact.

---

grounds 328 and 329. Already in *Tetra Laval*, cit., grounds 42-43, had the Court specified that: 'A prospective analysis of the kind necessary in merger control must be carried out with great care since it does not entail the examination of past events – for which often many items of evidence are available which make it possible to understand the causes – or of current events, but rather a prediction of events which are more or less likely to occur in future if a decision prohibiting the planned concentration or laying down the conditions for it is not adopted. Thus, the prospective analysis consists of an examination of how a concentration might alter the factors determining the state of competition on a given market in order to establish whether it would give rise to a serious impediment to effective competition. Such an analysis makes it necessary to envisage various chains of cause and effect with a view to ascertaining which of them are the most likely'.

116. See Judgment of the ECJ of 28 May 1998, Case C-7/95 P, *John Deere Ltd.* v *Commission*, [1998] ECR I-3113, grounds 21-22.

15. THE SCOPE OF APPLICATION OF THE COMMUNITY'S RULES OF COMPETITION LAW

The scope for application of the European Union's competition law must be considered, as well with regard to the place of occurrence of the harmful effects of infringements of competition rules – irrespective of the nationality or seat of any of the undertakings concerned – as in relation to the 'Community' and/or 'national' relevance of their behaviours in cases found to distort competition under Community law and/or under any Member State's domestic law.

Another aspect, which has extensively analysed in the past, is the relationship between the rules on competition contained in the ECSC Treaty and in the EAEC Treaty, an issue which now appears to have just marginal relevance as a result of the extinction of the ECSC Treaty on 23 July 2002.

The principle of independence of the Community treaties has resulted in the *substantive autonomy* of the assessments contained in each treaty with regard to competition rules as well as to the rules on dumping and subsidies. This was especially true for the provisions of Articles 65 and 66 of the extinguished Treaty establishing the ECSC and for the related implementing acts.

As for the Treaty establishing the EAEC (Euratom), its lack of organic rules on competition is such that, beyond the special rules to be found in individual provisions relating to aspects somehow related to competition – such as those subjecting the supply of ores and nuclear fuels to *non-discrimination* requirements (Articles 2(d) and 52(2) of the EAEC Treaty) or those *prohibiting discrimination* among users in pricing practices (Articles 68 and 69 of the EAEC Treaty) – it is the general provisions in the EC Treaty which must also be applied to restrictive practices relating to goods and services in the *common nuclear market* as provided for in Annex IV to the Treaty establishing the Euratom.[117]

The problems associated with the spatial scope of application of Community competition law *vis-à-vis* third countries' undertakings have been solved by applying the 'effects theory' originated in the United States.[118]

The starting consideration is that the European rules on the different aspects of competition essentially refer to restrictions imposed on competition 'within the common market' or 'in the common market or in a substantial part of it', respectively. In other words, as have observed above, what matters in this respect is not the domicile, registered office or nationality of any undertaking allegedly responsible for infringing Community rules, but solely the place of the 'damaging event', i.e. the place where the effects of a prejudicial conduct amounting to a violation of competition rules have occurred. In other words, the damaging event is relevant

---

117. See Commission Decisions of 23 Dec. 1975, Cases *United Reprocessors GmbH*, 76/248, and *Kewa*, 76/249, [1976] O.J. L51, p. 7 f. and p. 15 f., respectively.

118. See Luzzatto, *Stati stranieri e giurisdizione nazionale* (Milan, 1972), p. 89 f.; van der Hesch, 'Some Aspects of "Extra-Territorial" Infringement of EEC Competition Rules', cit., p. 287; Picone, 'L'applicazione extraterritoriale delle regole sulla concorrenza e il diritto internazionale' in *Il fenomeno delle concentrazioni*, cit., pp. 110 f., 115 f. e 156 f.

less as a physical consequence of the action than as an element constituting the violation which, if occurring 'within the common market', triggers the Commission jurisdiction over the matter.

As early as in Decision No. 69/243 of 24 July 1969, in *Dyestuffs*, the Commission stated, at point II, paragraph 40, that, since the treaty rules on competition applied to any restrictions on competition that generate the effects provided for in Article 85(1) within the common market, there was no reason why an assessment should be made as to whether the undertakings responsible for such restrictions on competition had their registered offices *within* or *outside* the Community.[119]

In the other well-known judgment in Continental Can of 21 February 1973, Case 6/72, the Court of Justice ruled that 'the circumstance that Continental does not have its registered office within the territory of one of the Member States is not sufficient to exclude it from the application of Community law'.[120]

The problem was dealt with by the Court of Justice in *Boehringer Mannheim GmbH* v *Commission* (*Boehringer II*), Case No. 7/72, in its judgment of 14 December 1972.[121] The dispute was over a double fine that had been imposed on the German pharmaceutical company by the Commission for infringement of Article 85 of the Treaty (now Article 81 EC) and by a New York District Court for infringement of the US Federal Law on Competition. Based on the core principle prohibiting double penalties for the same action, *Boehringer* had asked the Commission to set the amount of the fine paid in the United States against that imposed by the decision of the Commission of 16 July 1969. The company had brought appeal before the Court of Justice against a new decision of 25 November 1971, whereby the Commission had rejected such request. Then the ECJ endorsed the Commission's decision by referring to a judgment rendered in previous proceedings between the same parties, and stated, *inter alia*, that:

> in accordance with Article 85 of the Treaty, that judgment took account only of such instances *of application of the cartel* as may have affected *trade between Member States* or have distorted competition *within the common market.* [*Emphasis added*].[122]

In connection with the relationships between the Community antitrust legislation and the US laws, Advocate General Mayras stated in quite clear and specific terms, in his Opinion of 29 November 1972 in *Boehringer II*,[123] that:

> By virtue of the principle of territoriality, legislation against activities in breach of competition rules limit their scope to the territory of the State in which the *effects* of those activities have been established; this is also the case in the Community: Article 85(1) of the Treaty of Rome *is limited to acts likely*

119. See this Commission Decision in [1969] O.J. L195, p. 11 f. English version not available.
120. The *Continental Can* judgment is in [1973] ECR, cit. See para. 16, p. 242, cit.
121. The judgment in 7/72 (*Boehringer II*) is in [1972] ECR, p. 1281 f.
122. See *Boehringer II* judgment, cit., ground 6, p. 1290.
123. The Opinion is in [1972] ECR 1281 f. cit.

> *to restrict competition in the common market*; in the same way, American antitrust legislation, although it is directed as much against interference with both the external and the internal trade of the United States, *is limited in its territorial scope*; it is only directed against interference with competition which bears upon persons trading in the United States.[124]

Therefore, belonging to third countries outside the Community does not prevent undertakings from being subject to the Community's competition law when the effects of violations occur within the common market.

This proposition was restated by the Court of Justice in its judgment of 25 November 1971, Case 22/71, *Beguelin Import Co.* v *SAGL Import Export*, in which it expressly ruled:

> The fact that one of the undertakings which are parties to the agreement is situated in a third country does not prevent application of that provision since the agreement is operative on the territory of the common market.[125]

Statements of this type have become settled Commission practice. By mere way of example, reference should be made to Commission Decision No. 82/860 of 10 December 1982 in *Cafeteros de Colombia.*[126] The Commission, having found that a contractual clause restricting the sale of Colombian green coffee by coffee toasters and distributors was contrary to Article 85(1) (now 81) EC and entailed prejudice to trade between Member States, ordered the Bogota-based *Federación Nacional de Cafeteros de Colombia* to refrain from including such clause in any contract which it was to conclude thenceforth with coffee toasters in the EEC. The decision was notified to the seat of the *Federación* in Bogota, Colombia.

In a case concerning the distribution by *Fillisdorf*, a Swiss firm, of hygienic and cosmetic products of a French company, *Grosfillex*, in Switzerland, under a contractual prohibition of re-import into the Community, in connection wherewith an application for negative clearance had been submitted, the Commission took the view, in its Decision 64/233 of 11 March 1964, that such application should be granted, but just because, by virtue of the circumstances surrounding the case, no 'substantial limitation' of competition had occurred within the common market.[127]

Similar considerations had been offered by the Commission as grounds for the negative clearance granted by Decision 64/344, of 1 June 1964, to *Anciens Etablissements Mertens et Straet*, a Belgian limited company, for a contract concluded by it with *Bendix International Division of the Bendix Corporation* based in New York State.[128] Similar conclusions were reached by the Commission in granting negative clearance to *Transocean Marine Paint Association*, an association of eighteen manufacturers based in as many European and non-European States,

---

124. [1972] ECR 1302, cit., p. 1302 (Emphasis added).
125. See ground 12 of the judgment in *Beguelin* [1971] ECR, p. 949 f., p. 958.
126. [1982] O.J. L360, p. 31 f.
127. [1964] O.J. 58, p. 915 f.
128. [1964] O.J. 92, p. 1426 f.

by two consecutive decisions, one of 27 June 1967,[129] the other of 21 December 1973 (No. 74/16).[130]

In fact, it may well happen that an agreement between residents of EC Member States is not deemed to be prohibited under Article 81(1) where all of its effects occur outside the common market.

In its Decision No. 64/599 of 22 October 1964 in *Dutch Engineers and Contractors Association (DECA)*,[131] in response to an application for negative clearance, the Commission took the view that Article 85(1) (now Article 81) was inapplicable to an agreement between a group of French undertakings and its associated undertakings based in other Member Countries, which provided for cooperation among such associates solely outside the common market, because, much as all the parties to the agreement resided in the common market, the resulting restriction on competition generated its effects in third countries alone.

Likewise, in Decision No. 68/276 of 6 November 1968, in *Rieckermann AEG – Elotherm*,[132] also concerning an application for negative clearance, an agreement for exclusive concession with territorial protection for sales in non-European countries was deemed to fall outside the purview of Article 85 (now Article 81).

The actual implementation of the effects theory raises the sensitive issue of the international limitations to the Community's jurisdiction over this matter. The issue is related to a problem which is widely discussed, especially in US legal literature, and usually referred to as the '*extraterritorial application*' of antitrust laws.

In particular, an analysis of US case-law on the *extraterritorial application* of the Sherman Act[133] has shown that:

> on the basis of international law, it would not be legal, under certain conditions, to impose on foreign citizens a conduct in a foreign country that contradicts the rules of law in force in that country.

In a different respect,

> the need should be stressed to avoid any interference in other States' juridical lives through the application of contrasting rules.[134]

Relevant to the same issue are also the OECD Council's recommendations, especially that of 21 May 1986, which revised and superseded the previous recommendation of

---

129. [1967] O.J. L163, p. 10 f.
130. [1974] O.J. L19, p. 18 f.
131. [1964] O.J. 173, p. 2761 f.
132. [1968] O.J. L276, p. 25 f.
133. See Luzzatto, *Stati stranieri e giurisdizione nazionale*, cit., pp. 51 f. and 89 f.
134. See Luzzatto, *Stati stranieri e giurisdizione nazionale*, pp. 105 and 125. For these issues, particularly with regard to the evolution of US law until the *Restatement of the Law Third, Foreign Relations Law of the United States*, approved in 1986 (St. Paul, 1987), edited by the *American Law Institute*, which has laid down rules which can be referred to by State courts and administrative authorities in examining cases exhibiting problems of international law in relation to the limits posed by international law to State jurisdiction in matters related to competition law, See also Picone, 'L'applicazione extraterritoriale', cit., pp. 110 f. and 151 f.

25 September 1979 (itself modifying and superseding the recommendations of 5 October 1967 and of 3 July 1973) concerning the cooperation between OECD Member Countries on restrictive trade practices affecting international trade. Also relevant to the point is the OECD Council's recommendation of 23 October 1986 on the cooperation between OECD Member Countries in the area of potential conflicts between competition policies and trade policies.[135]

The problem of the *extraterritoriality* of laws and the protection of free competition appears especially important in case there is a conflict between an assessment of illegality made under the law of the country in which the effects of a specific conduct occurred and an assessment of legality made under the law of the place in which that conduct occurred and in which it may well have effects.

In this connection, reference should be made to Commission Decision No. 69/243 of 24 July 1969 in *Dyestuffs*,[136] whereby penalties were imposed on undertakings which were parties to an allegedly unlawful agreement, even including a British company, *Imperial Chemical Industries Ltd (ICI)* – at a time prior to the United Kingdom's accession to the European Economic Community. Article 4 of that decision stated that notice of that measure could have been served on ICI at the registered office of any of its subsidiaries in the common market.

Thereupon, the British Governments addressed a note to the Commission, explicitly declaring that, in accordance with the British interpretation of the rules of international law on the matter, it did not want to take a position for or against that decision, and expressing its view about the *extraterritorial* application of rules protecting free competition.[137]

The conditions indicated by the UK Government for the exercise of national jurisdiction over foreign undertakings in competition cases seemed to be more restrictive than those considered by the Commission in its decision.

In the UK Government's view, admissibility was based on the territoriality principle and on the nationality criterion. The relevant factor in terms of territoriality was the place in which the illegal conduct had occurred, then to the exclusion of any reference to the place where just some prejudicial effects had been generated. The nationality criterion could itself provide a valid jurisdictional basis in relation to actions carried out abroad only insofar as its application did not lead the citizens of the State of competent jurisdiction to act in contrast with the laws of the State in which the alleged prejudicial actions had been carried out.

About the British note, described as a 'confidential letter', Mr Glimme addressed Written Question No. 219/70 to the Commission before the European Parliament on 24 August 1970.[138] The question was worded in eleven points about the 'Commission's right to impose fines on third countries' undertakings'.

---

135. See OCSE, *Mise en ouvre du droit de la concurrence, Coopération internationale pour la collecte de renseignements* (Paris, 1984).
136. [1969] O.J. L195, 11, cit.
137. See Luzzatto, *Stati stranieri*, cit., p. 125.
138. [1970] O.J. C138, p. 8 f.

In its written answer, the Commission reserved its view on the ground that the undertakings in question had appealed to the ECJ and the proceeding was still pending. Yet, in concluding its answer, the Commission specified that no conclusions could be drawn from Commission Decision No. 69/240 of 16 July 1969 on the issue of the so-called extraterritorial application of competition rules, since such decision was only addressed to undertakings having their registered offices within the Community, and the amount of the fines had been established on the basis of the reasons set forth in the Commission's decision of 24 July 1969.[139]

In an opinion as to whether imports of Japanese products into the Community could be deemed to fall within the scope of application of Article 85(1) of the Treaty of Rome (now Article 81(1) EC),[140] the Commission observed that the fact that many, if not all, of the participating undertakings had their registered offices outside the Community did not prevent this provision from being applied insofar as the effects of the agreements, decisions or concerted practices extended to the Community's territory.

This confirmed the Community's view that the effects theory is adequate to give the Community's territorial jurisdiction.

A weary approach has, however, been taken by the Community institutions to illegal conducts occurring entirely 'outside' the EC. In fact, the Community authorities have failed so far to provide a generally applicable solution. They have, instead, tried to solve the problem by asserting the applicability of the territoriality principle to each relevant case in the sense specified above. Thus, both in Cases No. 48-49 and 51-57/69 (*Dyestuffs*) of 14 July 1972[141,142] and in *Istituto Chemioterapico Italiano SpA (ICI) – Commercial Solvents Corporation (CSC)* v *Commission* (Joined Cases 6-7/73 of 6 March 1974),[143] the ECJ granted the Commission's suggestion and chose to get around the problem, by merely ruling that, in each relevant case, the parent company (situated outside the Community) constituted just one economic unit with its subsidiaries (established within the Community), and, accordingly, the acts at issue were not 'external behaviours', but normal unlawful conducts of undertakings 'within' the EC, which were, as such, subject to the antitrust rules of the Treaty.

This basic approach was also taken by the Court of Justice in its judgment of 27 September 1988 in Joined Cases 89/85, 104/85, 114/85, 116/85, 117/85, 125/85, 126/85, 137/85, 128/85 and 129/85 (*Wood pulp*), concerning 'Concerted practices between undertakings established in non-member countries affecting selling prices to purchasers established in the Community', in which cases A. Ahlström

139. *Quinine Cartel* [1969] O.J. L192, p. 5. No English version is available.
140. [1972] O.J. C111, p. 13. No English version is available.
141. These are the cases commonly referred to as *I.C.I., Basf, Bayer, Geigy, Sandoz, Francolor, Cassella, Hoechst* and *Acna* v *Commission*.
142. These were judgments the ECJ delivered in separate cases recorded in [1972] ECR 619 f.
143. [1974] ECR 223 f.

Osakeyhtiö and eleven other Finnish undertakings and a number of US, Canadian and Swedish companies had filed applications against the Commission.[144]

Thereupon, the applicants brought action pursuant to Article 173 of the Rome Treaty (now Article 230 EC), for the annulment of Commission Decision No. 85/202 of 19 December 1984,[145] whereby the Commission, having discovered a number of infringements, notified fines to the different addresses. The alleged infringements amounted to agreements among the addresses to concert on the prices announced on a quarterly basis to customers established in the Community and on the actual transaction prices (paragraphs 1 and 2 of Article 1 of the Decision), by recommendations addressed by the Pulp, Paper and Paperboard Export Association of the United States, former Kraft Export Association (KEA), grouping a number of producers established in the United States, to its associates, recommending prices for the relevant deliveries (Article 1(3)). Another addressee of the Decision was *Finncell*, the common sales organization of twelve producers established in Finland, which were allegedly responsible for concerting on announced and actual transaction prices and exchanging information within the framework of the Research and Information Centre for the European Pulp and Paper Industry run by the trust company Fides of Switzerland (Article 1(4) of the Decision).

Based on these facts the ECJ delivered its judgment on 27 September 1988, in Joined Cases 89/85, 104/85, 114/85, 116/85, 117/85, 125/85, 126/85, 137/85, 128/85 and 129/85 (*Wood pulp*), whereby it confirmed the Commission Decision against each of the addressees, and only declared the Decision void in so far as it concerned the trade association *KEA*, on the argument that KEA's price recommendations could not be distinguished from the pricing agreements concluded by undertakings which were members of the Pulp Group, and that KEA had not played a separate role in the implementation of those agreements.

Again on this occasion, in the face of the applicants' allegation that the Commission had taken the wrong view on the scope of territorial application of Article 81 EC, and that the Decision was incompatible with international law, the Court of Justice relied on the effects theory to restate the applicability of a territoriality principle to the relevant case.

For ground 16 of the 27 September 1988 judgment of the ECJ reads as follows:

> It should be observed that an infringement of Article 85, such as the conclusion of an agreement which has had the effect of restricting competition within the common market, consists of conduct made up of two elements, the formation of the agreement, decision or concerted practice and the implementation thereof. If the applicability of prohibitions laid down under competition law were made to depend on the place where the agreement, decision or concerted

144. The judgment is published in [1988] ECR 5193 f. Pursuant to point (4) of the operative part of the judgment, the Court assigned the case 'to the Fifth Chamber for consideration of the other submissions'. The Fifth Chamber handed down its final judgment in the case (C-125/85 and C-129/85) on 31 Mar. 1993 (published in [1993] ECR 1307 f.

145. [1985] O.J. L85, p. 1.

> practice was formed, the result would obviously be to give undertakings an easy means of evading those prohibitions. *The decisive factor is therefore the place where it is implemented.* [*Emphasis added*].

The next ground further specified:

> The producers in this case implemented their pricing agreement *within the common market.* It is immaterial in that respect whether or not they had recourse to subsidiaries, agents, sub-agents, or branches within the Community in order to make their contacts with purchasers within the Community. [*Emphasis added*].

An the conclusion was, at ground 18, that:

> Accordingly the Community' s jurisdiction to apply its competition rules to such conduct *is covered by the territoriality principle* as universally recognized in public international law. [*Emphasis added*].

The Court of First Instance, too, handed down a judgment in furtherance of the 'effects theory' on 28 February 2002, Case T-395/94, *Atlantic Container* v *Commission*,[146] as follows:

> In that regard, the Court of Justice has held that where producers established outside the Community sell directly to purchasers established in the Community and engage in price competition in order to win orders from those customers, that constitutes competition within the common market, so that concertation between those producers on the prices to be charged to their customers in the Community has the object and effect of restricting competition within the common market within the meaning of Article 85 of the Treaty.

It also appropriate to note that, in *Wood Pulp II*, the Court also rejected another argument submitted by the applicants in relation to the alleged non-compliance

146. [2002] ECR II-875, ground 72. The ECJ had already ruled likewise in its judgment of 27 Sep. 1988, in *Ahlström Osakeyhtiö and Others v Commission* ('*Wood pulp I*'), grounds 12 and 13. At grounds 16-18 of the *Wood pulp I* judgment, the ECJ had aptly observed that: '[A]n infringement of Art. 85, such as the conclusion of an agreement which has had the effect of restricting competition within the common market, consists of conduct made up of two elements, the formation of the agreement, decision or concerted practice and the implementation thereof. If the applicability of prohibitions laid down under competition law were made to depend on the place where the agreement, decision or concerted practice was formed, the result would obviously be to give undertakings an easy means of evading those prohibitions. *The decisive factor is therefore the place where it is implemented*' (Emphasis added). For an application of the effects theory in relation to merger control, see the Judgment of the CFI of 25 Mar. 1999, Case T-102/96, *Gencor*, [1999] ECR II-753, ground 89 ff. ('Application of the Regulation is justified under public international law when it is foreseeable that a proposed concentration will have an immediate and substantial effect in the Community', ground 90). In that specific case, the Commission had prohibited the formation of a joint venture between a South African and a British company because of the creation of a dominant position in *non-European markets*.

with the provisions of Article 23 and 27 of the Free Trade Agreement then in force between Finland and the Community, which were purported by the applicants to provide a prior consulting procedure within the Joint Committee instituted under that Agreement. In this respect, the ECJ stated, at ground 32 of the judgment, that:

> It should be pointed out finally that in this case the Community applied its competition rules to the Finnish applicants not because they had concerted with each other but because they took part in a very much larger concertation with United States, Canadian and Swedish undertakings which restricted competition within the Community. It was thus not just trade with Finland that was affected. In that situation reference of the matter to the Joint Committee could not have led to the adoption of appropriate measures.

On 23 September 1991, the Commission of the European Communities and the US Government signed an agreement in Washington regarding the application of their competition laws. The Washington Agreement entered into force on the same date. It is a highly detailed instrument intended to regulate, 'in the international context', the old issue of the *extraterritorial* application of competition laws between the world's most important authorities, those of the US and of the Community. The Agreement covers the entire field of competition, including, but not limited to, the rules on merger control, and it is by no means restricted to the rules on information exchange and mutual consultations to be held at least twice each year (Article III). It also establishes forms of close cooperation and coordination (Article IV) and even a 'positive comity', in the sense that, if either contracting party believes that anticompetitive activities carried out on the territory of the other party are adversely affecting its important interests, the first party may notify the other party and may request that the other party's competition authorities initiate appropriate enforcement activities (Article V). In this connection, it is appropriate to observe that the Commission and the United States Government supplemented the 1991 Agreement on 4 June 1998, by entering into an Agreement on the application of positive comity principles in the enforcement of their competition laws.[147]

The 1991 Agreement also specifies 'traditional comity' as an obligation to consider the other party's 'important interests' in decisions as to whether or not to initiate an investigation or proceeding, the scope of an investigation or proceeding, the nature of the remedies or penalties sought and in other ways as appropriate (Article VI). In the course of their enforcement activities, the parties must take account of certain principles listed in Article VI. Procedures have been provided for consultation regarding any matter related to the Agreement (Article VII), and provisions have been made for communications between the parties' competent authorities (Article X), i.e. between the Commission's competent Directorate-General, for the European Union, and the Department of Justice and the Federal Trade Commission for the United States.

---

147. The Agreement was adopted by a Decision of the Council and of the Commission of 29 May 1998, and it is published in [1998] O.J. L173, p. 28 ff.

As it happens, the French Republic – whose views were soon concurred with by the Dutch and Spanish Governments – challenged that Agreement before the Court of Justice of the European Communities on 13 December 1991, alleging that the Agreement had been concluded in breach of the Community rules on jurisdiction over the conclusion of contracts, i.e. in breach of Article 228 of the Treaty. The French Government also complained for lack of grounds, violation of the legal certainty principle and violation of Community competition law.

In its judgment of 9 August 1994 in Case C-327/91, *French Republic v Commission*,[148] the ECJ endorsed the Advocate General's Opinion and upheld the plea alleging lack of competence on the part of the Commission to enter into the disputed agreement, in the belief that the matter fell within the Council's jurisdiction (ground 42).

That was not the end of the story, though. On 10 April 1995, following a proposal from the Commission and the European Parliament's favourable opinion, the Council and the Commission approved the Agreement with the United States on antitrust measures with contents essentially identical with those of the instrument previously concluded by the Commission.

According to Article 2 of that decision, the Agreement in question became applicable and entered into force on 23 September 1991.[149]

16. DIRECT APPLICABILITY OF THE EUROPEAN RULES ON COMPETITION AND THE MEMBER STATES' AUTHORITIES' COMPETENCE TO APPLY THEM

It should be specified that the problem of the direct applicability of the European antitrust rules must be viewed in a special light.

Article 88 of the original version of the Rome Treaty (now Article 84 EC) envisaged the direct applicability of Articles 85 and 86 (now Articles 81 and 82 EC, respectively) by the authorities in Member States, including internal courts,[150] on a temporary basis, specifically 'up to the time of entry into force of the regulation

---

148. The judgment is published in [1994] ECR I-3641. Advocate General Tesauro's Opinion was submitted on 16 Dec. 1993, and recorded in [1994] ECR I-3641. The ECJ's judgment of 9 Aug. 1994 had not annulled the Washington Agreement which, pursuant to Article 46 of the 1969 Vienna Convention on treaty law, remained valid under international law. The ECJ had only ruled that 'the act whereby the Commission sought to conclude the Agreement with the United States regarding the application of the competition laws of the European Communities and the United States must be declared void'. (Point 43).

149. See Article 2 and 1, respectively, of the decision of 10 Apr. 1995 in O.J., [1995] L95, p. 47 ff. In the United States, the 1991 Agreement has been published in 30 ILM, 1991, p. 1487. On the subject generally, see 'U.S. International Antitrust Enforcement Assistance Act' of 2 Nov. 1994 in [1995] ILM. 34, p. 494 f.

150. For this view, see Judgment of the ECJ of 6 Apr. 1962 on the implementation of Art. 85 of the Treaty, Case 13/61, *Kledingverkoopbedrijf De Geus en Uitdenbogerd* v *Robert Bosch GmbH e Maatschappij tot Voortzetting Van De Zaken der Firma Willem van Rijn N.V.* (*De Gens* v *R. Bosch GmbH*), [1962] ECR, p. 87 f. Art. 88 was also made the object of Article 23 of

envisaged in article 87, in conjunction with article 85 [now Article 83] of the Treaty . . . ', i.e. until the issuance of the first implementing regulation as provided for by the Treaty.

At that initial stage, therefore, the implementation of both Article 85(1) and Article 85(3) was provisionally made the responsibility of the Member States' authorities.

Thereafter, the problem was approached in a new light as a result of Regulation 17/1962, as the 'First Regulation implementing Articles 85 and 86 of the Treaty'. Article 1 of this Regulation provided:

> Without prejudice to Articles 6, 7 and 23 of this Regulation, agreements, decisions and concerted practices of the kind described in Article 85 (1) of the Treaty and the abuse of a dominant position in the market, within the meaning of Article 86 of the Treaty, shall be prohibited, *no prior decision to that effect being required.* [*Emphasis added*].

Article 6 and 7 concerned the implementation of the provision in Article 85(3), which was made the Commission's *exclusive* responsibility to decide upon. Article 23 contained transitional provisions applicable to the decisions of the Member States' authorities before the entry into force of Regulation 17/62. Article 9(3) of the Regulation itself required:

> As long as the Commission has not initiated any procedure under Articles 2, 3 or 6, the authorities of the Member States shall remain competent to apply Article 85(1) and Article 86 in accordance with Article 88 of the Treaty; they shall remain competent in this respect notwithstanding that the time limits specified in Article 5(1) and in Article 7(2) relating to notification have not expired.

The Court of Justice was called upon to rule on the matter, and it did so by its judgment of 30 January 1974, in Case No. 127/73, *BRT* v *SABAM-I*, where it affirmed the national court's jurisdiction on the ground that Articles 85(1) and (2) and 86, which produce direct effects in relations between individuals, conferred rights upon individual undertakings which the national courts must protect.[151] As a result, unlike the conventional scope of the principle of direct effects of Community rules, based on which individuals have the right to demand compliance by each Member State of any one rule of Community law, this principle is deemed to amount, when it comes to implementing Community rules on competition, to an individual's right only to demand that his home Member State ensure the implementation of his legal relationships with other private individuals in compliance

---

Regulation No. 17/62, which dealt with the 'transitional provisions' applicable to decisions of authorities of the Member States.

151. See Judgements of the ECJ of 30 Jan. 1974, Case 127/73, *BRT* v *SABAM*, [1974] ECR, p. 51, ground 6; of 18 Mar. 1997, Case C-282/95, *Guérin Automobiles*, [1997] ECR I-1503, ground 39; del 20 Sep. 2001, Case C-453/99, *Courage*, [2001] ECR I-6297, ground 23.

with specific Community rules – the antitrust provisions, in fact.[152] In the judgment just referred to above, the Court of Justice ruled:

> to deny, by virtue of the aforementioned Article 9, the national courts' jurisdiction to afford this safeguard, would mean depriving individuals of rights which they hold under the treaty itself. [*Ground 17*].

The Commission view was that:

> In this way, national courts are able to ensure, at the request of the litigants or on their own initiative, that the competition rules will be respected for the benefit of private individuals. In addition, Article 85(2) enables them to determine, in accordance with the national procedural law applicable, the civil law effects of the prohibition set out in Article 85(3).[153]

The Community system then current for the implementation of competition rules was drastically reformed by Regulation 1/2003. The new rules abolished the system of prior notification by the undertakings concerned to the Commission of any agreements apt to fall within the scope of application of Article 81 EC, and a 'directly applicable exception system' was introduced in its stead. As a result of this change, any agreements not meeting the requirements stated in Article 81(3) EC were prohibited outright, without a prior decision being required to that effect. Concurrently, any agreements meeting those requirements were not prohibited *per se*, lacking a prior decision to the contrary.

Still, through the abolition of the duty of prior notification to the Commission, the undertakings concerned were made responsible *prima facie* for assessing the agreements involved for compatibility with Community law. Thus, it is for each undertaking to carry out any such agreement directly where it believes that the requirements of Article 81(1) and (3) have been met.

Whether Article 81(1) is applicable or Article 81(3) is inapplicable in each relevant case may only be established *ex post* in an *ad-hoc* procedure in which the legality of the agreement is called into question.

Another substantial change was introduced by Regulation 1/2003 in respect of the applicability of Article 81(3), which was removed from the Commission's exclusive jurisdiction to that of the national courts and antitrust authorities.

---

152. See Luzzatto, *La diretta applicabilità*, cit., p. 92 f.
153. See Notice on cooperation between national courts and the Commission in applying Art. 85 and 86 of the EEC Treaty [1993] O.J. C39, p. 5 f., cit., para. 6. This conclusion is, in fact, in line with the principles the Commission relied on in the Notice, para. 4 of which lays down the general principle that distinguishes between the two positions, in the sense that 'The Commission is the administrative authority responsible for the implementation and for the thrust of competition policy in the Community and for this purpose has to act in the public interest. National courts, on the other hand, have the task of safeguarding the subjective rights of private individuals in their relations with one another'. (Cf. Judgment of 28 Feb. 1991, Case 234/89, *Delimitis* c. *Henninger Brau*, [1991] ECR, p. 935, ground 44; and Judgment of 17 Sep. 1992, Case T-24/92, *Automec* v *Commission*, [1992] ECR II-2223, grounds 73 e 85).

The abolition of the duty of prior notification has had the heaviest impact at a substantive level. For the relationship of the first to the third paragraph of Article 81 EC has changed, in the sense that those paragraphs must be read *in conjunction with* one another, and their direct applicability must, pursuant to Article 5 and 6 of Regulation 1/2003, be decided by the Member States' national antitrust authorities or courts, as the case may be.[154]

An observation should be made in this connection, though. A judgment by a national ordinary court granting an objection based on Article 81(3) EC cannot rest on the same basis as that on which a decision for individual exemption is taken by whether the Commission under Regulation 1/2203 or by a national antitrust. For a decision by the latter bodies acting as antitrust judges is oftentimes the result of discretional assessments and – especially when it is taken by the Commission – it also takes into account factors of a broadly political or even dirigist nature in relation, for example –where assessments are made as to compatibility – to the advisability of coordinating competition policies with other Community interests or policies, i.e. factors that cannot be considered in a judgment rendered by an ordinary court, which is bound to apply the law.

In fact, quite beyond such 'departures', the entire approach may raise some doubts when it comes to a correct implementation of the norm. For it is appropriate to mention that an exemption decision is expected to last as long as the stated exemption period and possibly to contain any conditions on which it is predicated, compliance with which is assessed by the competent authority at subsequent times, in addition to imposing any adjustment to the relevant agreement as may be deemed necessary or useful to make it compatible.

Conversely, an 'ordinary' court's judgment can only, because of that court's own nature, establish the applicability or inapplicability of Article 81, without any of the reasonable adjustments the very nature of an exemption would require.

In its Notice on the handling of complaints filed with the Commission under Articles 81 and 82 of the EC Treaty,[155] the Commission reaffirmed its *responsibility*,

---

154. Still, it should be noted that, even before Regulation 1/2003 entered into force, national courts could apply the Commission's *decisions* and *regulations* relating to Art. 81(3). For the ECJ has confirmed the direct applicability of these instruments on more than one occasion. See Judgments of 3 Feb. 1976, *Fonderies de Roubaix* v *Fonderies Roux*, Case 63/75, [1976] ECR, p. 111 f., and of 28 Feb. 1991, *Delimitis* v *Henninger Brau*, Case C-234/89, [1991] *ibid.*, p. 935. This fact has expressly been confirmed by Commission Notice 2004/C 101/04 on the co-operation between the Commission and the courts of the EU Member States in the application of Art. 81 and 82 EC [2004] O.J. C101, p. 54 ff. Para. 7 of the Notice specifies: 'Apart from the application of Art. 81 and 82 EC, national courts are also competent to apply acts adopted by EU institutions in accordance with the EC Treaty or in accordance with the measures adopted to give the Treaty effect, to the extent that these acts have direct effect. National courts may thus have to enforce Commission decisions or regulations applying Art. 81(3) EC to certain categories of agreements, decisions or concerted practices'.

155. In O.J. C101, p. 65 ff.

which the ECJ has recognized in case-law,[156] *for defining and implementing the orientation of the Community competition policy.* In the wording of paragraph 8 of that Notice:

> While national courts are called upon to safeguard the rights of individuals and are thus bound to rule on cases brought before them, public enforcers cannot investigate all complaints, but must set priorities in their treatment of cases. The Court of Justice has held that the Commission, entrusted by Article 85(1) of the EC Treaty with the task of ensuring application of the principles laid down in Articles 81 and 82 of the Treaty, *is responsible for defining and implementing the orientation of Community competition policy* and that, in order to perform that task effectively, it is entitled to give *differing degrees of priority* to the complaints brought before it. [*Emphasis added*].

According to the Commission, its actions had been restricted by then, as it clarified in paragraph 11 of the 2004 Notice:

> In this new legislative framework, the Commission *intends to refocus* its enforcement resources along the following lines:
>
> – enforce the EC competition rules in cases for which it is well placed to act(9), *concentrating its resources on the most serious infringements*;[157]
> – handle cases in relation to which the Commission should act with a view *to defin*[ing] *Community competition policy and/or to ensure coherent application of Articles 81 or 82.* [*Emphasis added*].

Nevertheless, at paragraph 16 of the Notice, the Commission stated some points which, in its view, would make the recourse to national courts attractive. Indeed:

> Action before national courts has the following advantages for complainants:
>
> – National courts may *award damages for loss* suffered as a result of an infringement of Article 81 or 82.
> – National courts may rule on *claims for payment* or contractual obligations based on an agreement that they examine under Article 81.
> – It is for the national courts to apply the civil *sanction of nullity* of Article 81(2) in contractual relationships between individuals. They can in particular assess, in the light of the applicable national law, the scope and consequences of the nullity of certain contractual provisions under

---

156. See Judgments of the ECJ: *Masterfoods*, Case C-344/98, [2000] ECR I-11369, ground 46; *Union française de l'express (Ufex)*, Case C-119/97 P, [1999] ECR I-1341, ground 88; and *Automec*, Case T-24/92, cit., grounds 73-77.

157. In this sense, see Whereas 3 of Regulation 1/2003, laying down the rationale of the reform as follows: 'The centralised scheme set up by Regulation No. 17 no longer secures a balance between those two objectives. It hampers application of the Community competition rules by the courts and competition authorities of the Member States, and the system of notification it involves prevents the Commission from concentrating its resources on curbing the most serious infringements [. . .]'.

Article 81(2), with particular regard to all the other matters covered by the agreement.
- National courts are usually better placed than the Commission *to adopt interim measures.*
- Before national courts, it is possible *to combine* a claim under Community competition law with other claims under national law.
- Courts normally have the power *to award legal costs to the successful applicant.* This is never possible in an administrative procedure before the Commission. [*Emphasis added*].

Thus, it is most evident that the system so newly set up by Regulation No. 1/2003 even provides the institutionalization of that *concentration of roles* – of both the body dictating the rules and the body responsible for applying them – on just one body, the Commission, which I have expressly criticized in these pages because of the utter disregard for the undertakings' individual rights under this approach.

This is because, within the new context, the Commission has openly retained its guiding role, even through its power of delegation to national authorities, which it has promoted, in fact, with a view rather to relieving itself of the burden of the least significant issues than to applying the *subsidiarity principle.* And yet, it reserves the right to take *direct* action on any actual case as it may deem fit in order 'to define and implement the orientation of Community competition policy' or to ensure application of the principles laid down in Articles 81 and 82.

The use of any relevant case to address 'general warnings' to the market has thus been even legally permitted, in the face of the protection of individual interests.[158] The absurdity the approach so taken in the new Regulation can hardly come as a surprise, if only because the draft of the Regulation had been developed, in this as in every other case, by the Commission's own staff, as a result of which the Regulation itself was filled, as usual, with references, concepts and phrases conveniently drawn from individual ECJ judgments.

158. This approach was reflected, for example, in an action for private enforcement recently brought by the Commission's DG ADMIN before the Brussels *Tribunal de Commerce*, for private enforcement, against some manufacturers of lifts and escalators which were found by the Commission to be liable for price fixing, as stated in the Commission's own decision of 2007, because of damages suffered by the Commission itself from installing and maintaining such lifts in its own buildings. See Press Release IP/08/998 of 24 Jun. 2008. Commission Vice-President Kallas stated: '*This case represents an important example of a coherent attitude of the Commission in acting both as market regulator and as diligent administrator of EU taxpayers' money. As a result of the anticompetitive behaviour of these companies, the EU institutions, and so the European taxpayer, have suffered financially by paying over the odds for the installation and maintenance of lifts and escalators*'. On the same occasion, Ms Kroes, Commissioner for Competition added: '*the Commission is doing its utmost to encourage and facilitate actions for damages before national courts by victims of anticompetitive behaviour. In this case, we are leading by example*'. Quite beyond official proclamations, initiatives such as this may also foster criticisms from many parties about the Commission's 'hybrid' role in its capacity of 'prosecutor and judge', mingling public interests with partisan interests in frequently inconsistent ways.

On the basis of the principle empowering national courts and competent authorities to apply Articles 81 and 82 EC, what must now be done is to define their respective scopes for action. The initiation by the Commission of a procedure under Regulation 1/2003 cannot exempt a national court before which the direct effect of article 81 or 82 EC is pleaded from giving judgment. What the national court can do in such a case, if it considers it necessary for reasons of legal certainty, to stay the proceedings before it while awaiting the outcome of the Commission's action.[159]

Any judgment by a national court is not, however, binding upon the Commission, which remains free to take a different decision.[160]

Still, some limitations to the application by national courts of Community competition law can be found in the Commission's 2004 Notice on the cooperation between the Commission and the courts of the EU Member States.[161] In particular, paragraph 8 of the Notice specifies:

> When applying EC competition rules, national courts are bound by the case law of the Community courts as well as by Commission regulations applying Article 81(3) EC to certain categories of agreements, decisions or concerted practices. Furthermore, the application of Articles 81 and 82 EC by the Commission in a specific case binds the national courts when they apply EC competition rules in the same case in parallel with or subsequent to the Commission. Finally, and without prejudice to the ultimate interpretation of the EC Treaty by the Court of Justice, national courts may find guidance in Commission regulations and decisions which present elements of analogy with the case they are dealing with, as well as in Commission notices and guidelines relating to the application of Articles 81 and 82 EC (20) and in the annual report on competition policy. [*Emphasis added*].

Regulation No. 1/2003 does not specify the criteria according to which cases should be allocated between the Commission and the *national competition authorities*, but it provides for cooperation between them within the European network of competition authorities (the 'ECN').

However, Article 11(6) of Regulation No. 1/2003 states that the initiation by the Commission of proceedings for the adoption of a decision in antitrust matters shall relieve the competition authorities of the Member States of their competence to apply Articles 81 and 82 of the Treaty.

The Commission Notice on cooperation within the Network of Competition Authorities[162] specifies that cases should be dealt with: (i) by a single national

159. See the ECJ's judgment of 10 Jul. 1980, Case 37/79, *Anne Marty SA* v *Estée Lauder SA*, [1980] ECR, cit., p. 2500, grounds 13 e 14.
160. However, the Commission Notice on the cooperation between national courts and the Commission, cit., introduced broad forms of cooperation capable to ensure as a uniform application of competition law as possible, by laying down obligations for fair cooperation between the institutions involved.
161. See Commission Notice on the cooperation between national courts and the Commission, cit.
162. [2004] O.J. C101, p. 54 ff.

competition authority, possibly with the assistance of national competition authorities of other Member States; or (ii) by several national competition authorities acting in parallel; or (iii) by the Commission.

Points 8 et seq. of the Notice are intended to add clarity to the question of the allocation of cases, as follows:

> An authority can be considered to be well placed to deal with a case *if the following three cumulative conditions* are met:
>
> 1. the agreement or practice has substantial direct actual or foreseeable effects on competition within its territory, is implemented within or originates from its territory;
> 2. the authority is able to effectively bring to an end the entire infringement, i.e. it can adopt a cease-and-desist order the effect of which will be sufficient to bring an end to the infringement and it can, where appropriate, sanction the infringement adequately;
> 3. it can gather, possibly with the assistance of other authorities, the evidence required to prove the infringement.
>
> The above criteria indicate that *a material link between the infringement and the territory of a Member State must exist* in order for that Member State's competition authority to be considered well placed. It can be expected that in most cases the authorities of those Member States where competition is substantially affected by an infringement will be well placed provided they are capable of effectively bringing the infringement to an end through either single or parallel action unless the Commission is better placed to act.
>
> *Parallel action* by two or three NCAs may be *appropriate* where an agreement or practice has substantial effects on competition mainly in their respective territories and the action of only one NCA would not be sufficient to bring the entire infringement to an end and/or to sanction it adequately.
>
> *The Commission is particularly well placed if one or several agreement(s) or practice(s),* including networks of similar agreements or practices, *have effects on competition in more than three Member States* (crossborder markets covering more than three Member States or several national markets).
>
> Moreover, the Commission is particularly well placed to deal with a case if *it is closely linked to other Community provisions which may be exclusively or more effectively applied by the Commission, if the Community interest requires the adoption of a Commission decision* to develop Community competition policy when a new competition issue arises or to ensure effective enforcement. [*Emphasis added*].

The question of direct applicability also arises in connection with the *rules on State aid*. Their structure and the fact that they are not addressed direct to the undertakings, but to the Member States, exclude in principle and generally that they could *per se* have direct effect.

One exception is the prohibition on the Member States from putting their proposed measures into effect '*up to the final decision where the Commission sets in motion the contentious procedure*'. This prohibition appears to be direct and unconditional, and such that it can be pleaded by the undertaking concerned before national courts.[163] In this sense, the direct effect of Article 88(3) comes into play.[164]

An infringement of this rule can be brought before the Member States' courts, each of which has jurisdiction to rule, by a precautionary order if need be, that a measure put into effect *before* the Commission's final decision is in contrast with Community law. Conversely, a national court is not allowed to assess an aid for compatibility on the merits, since this can only be established by the Commission on an exclusive basis, although subject to further review (if any) by the Community Courts.

The provision of Article 86(2) EC is not directly applicable. In this respect, the fact that:

> Undertakings entrusted with the operation of services of general economic interest or having the character of a revenue-producing monopoly shall be subject to the rules contained in this Treaty, in particular to the rules on competition,

but only

> in so far as the application of such rules does not obstruct the performance, in law or in fact, of the particular tasks assigned to them,

places that provision within such a wide scope for discretion that it cannot possibly have direct effect. This proposition is further borne out by that other requirement, that '[t]he development of trade must not be affected to such an extent as would be contrary to the interests of the Community'.[165]

There can be no doubt, however, about the direct effect of Article 86(1) under Directive No. 80/723 for implementation, as amended, which was discussed above.

---

163. In this sense, see the three judgments of the ECJ of 11 Dec. 1973, Case 121/73, *Markmann* v *Fed. Rep. of Germany*, Case 122/73, *Nordsee Deutsche Hochseefischerei* v *Fed. Rep. of Germany*, Case 141/73, *Frits, Lohrey* v *Fed. Rep. of Germany and Land Assia*, [1973] ECR 1495 f., 1511 f., and 1527 f., respectively.

164. Community case-law has long considered the last sentence of Art. 88(3) to be directly applicable by the Member States' national courts. It has been so since the Judgment of the ECJ of 15 Jul. 1964, Case 6/64, *Costa* v *ENEL*, [1964] ECR 1127, on the wake of which: Judgments of the ECJ of 11 Dec. 1973, Case 120/73, *Lorenz*, [1973] ECR 1741 and of 21 Nov. 1991, Case 354/90, *Fédération nationale commerce extérieur des produits alimentaires e syndicat national des négociants et trasformateurs de saumon* v *France* (Judgment '*FNCE*', the so-called '*Salmon Judgment*'), [1991] ECR I-5505, and 1992 *Foro it.* IV, 471, with commentary by Roberti.

165. In this sense, see Judgment of the Court of Justice of 14 Jul. 1971, Case 10/71, *Ministère public luxembourgeois* v *Madeleine Muller, Veuve J.P. Hein and others*, [1971] ECR p. 723 f. For the notion of 'Community interest' under antidumping and anti-subsidy rules, please refer to Chapter V, section 11 of this book.

Jurisdiction over the applicability of Article 86(1) and (2) is vested in the Commission, which may, where necessary, address appropriate directives or decisions to Member States (Article 86(3) EC).[166]

In light of the considerations offered above, it is appropriate to stress that it is settled Community case-law that, until the Commission has expressed its intention to adopt a decision under the aforesaid articles, Member States' authorities, thus national courts as well, have jurisdiction over the *direct applicability* of the rights and duties arising from Community competition rules. For denying jurisdiction to any national court would be tantamount, in the ECJ's view, to depriving individuals of their rights under the Treaty.

From a statistical point of view, it should be noted that about one hundred twenty judgments had been handed down by national courts in applying the rules of Community competition law from the date of entry into force of Regulation 1/2003 through 2006.

Such application had been sought before national (notably German and French) courts, especially by competing undertakings injured by the conduct of other undertakings within the EU market, which the former alleged to be unlawful under Community law.

Although only three cases of direct application by national judges of Articles 81 and 82 were litigated in Italy in 2006, the area is expanding at a fast pace. In 2006, according to the statistics contained in the Annual Report on Competition Policy, the Commission was informed of some one hundred fifty new case investigations launched by national competition authorities.

So far, rules of Community competition law have chiefly been pleaded before national courts either in seeking orders in urgency or other interim measures or in defending actions for breach of contract.

There are still few cases of national courts awarding damages to competing undertakings allegedly harmed by a breach of Articles 81 or 82 of the Treaty.[167] A study by the Commission on the conditions of claims for damages in case of infringement of EC competition rules up to 31 August 2004[168] mentions some sixty judgments handed down by national courts, twelve of which were delivered on the basis of Community law alone.

---

166. On this subject, generally, see: Lamberti Zanardi, 'La competenza degli organi nazionali nell'applicazione delle norme comunitarie sulla concorrenza' [1979] Riv. dir. int. priv. proc., p. 609 f.; Luzzatto, *La diretta applicabilità*, cit., p. 91 f.; Temple lang, 'EEC Competition Actions in Member States's Courts – Claims for Damages, Declarations and Injunction for Breach of Community Antitrust Law' [1984] Annual Proceedings of the Fordham Corporate Law Institute, cit., p. 219 f; Steindorff, 'Common Market Antitrust Law in Civil Proceedings before National Courts and Arbitrators' [1986] Annual Proceedings of the Fordham, cit., p. 409 f.
167. On this subject, see the Commission's recent White Paper of 3 Apr. 2008 on compensating consumer and business victims of breaches of the competition rules, COM (2008) 165 final, in http://ec.europa.eu/comm/competition/antitrust/actionsdamages/index.html. In this connection, see the considerations offered in section 20 of this Chapter VI.
168. At: http://ec.europa.eu/comm/competition/antitrust/actionsdamages/study.html.

17. RELATIONSHIPS BETWEEN COMMUNITY RULES AND NATIONAL RULES

When the relationship of the competition provisions of Article 81 and 82 EC to national antitrust rules is considered, the discriminating factor is, in principle, that the alleged cartel or purported abuse of dominant position must be such as to 'affect trade between Member States'.[169] In other words, where this is the case, the question will still be material to Community law even if a given conduct is assumed to be prohibited by a Member State's domestic legislation, since a cumulation of prohibitions is hardly expected to occur in any one actual case.[170]

In light of Regulation No. 17 of 6 February 1962, lacking specific provisions in the matter, the *Walt Wilhelm* judgment had laid down the principle that a case falling within the scope of application of Articles 85 and 86 (now Articles 81 and 82 EC) should not, for this reason alone, be removed from the scope of application of national rules on competition (according to the 'double barrier' theory). Parallel application of both sets of rules to the same case could, in the Community Courts' view, only be allowed, in furtherance of the principle of the *primacy of Community law*,

> in so far as it does not prejudice the uniform application throughout the common market of the community rules on cartels and of the full effect of the measures adopted in implementation of those rules.[171]

---

169. In 2004, the Commission adopted a Notice to clarify the reach of the 'effect-on-trade concept' in order to clarify further the content and scope of the Community competition rules as contrasted with national rules. See Commission Notice No. 2004/C 101/07, 'Guidelines on the effect on trade concept contained in Art. 81 and 82 of the Treaty', in [2004] O.J. C101, p. 86 ff. As for the different scope for application of Community rules versus national rules, see Judgments of the ECJ of 10 Jul. 1980, Joined Cases 253/78 and 1 to 3/79, *Giry and Guerlain*, [1980] ECR 2327, ground15, and of 9 Sep. 2003, Case C-137/00, *Milk Marque*, [2003] ECR I-7975, ground 61.

170. Goldman, *Droit commercial européen*, cit., p. 760; Frignani & Waelbroeck, *Disciplina*, cit., p. 35 f., especially p. 39 f.

171. See Judgment of the Court of Justice of 13 Feb. 1969, Case C-14/68, *Walt Wilhelm and others* v *Bundeskartellamt*, [1969] ECR, cit. (Reference to the Court under article 177 of the EEC Treaty by the *Kammergericht (Kartellsenat) Berlin* for a preliminary ruling). The facts in dispute were the following. The *Bundeskartellamt* of Berlin had relied on certain provisions of the *GWB* – the German Act of 27 Jul. 1957 against restrictions on competition – to impose fines on German manufacturers who, together with other aniline-based dye manufacturer within the Community and in third countries, had agreed to increase aniline prices. The fines so imposed were intended to punish a conduct held to be unlawful under the German rules of competition law. The decision had been challenged by the addressees in an action then pending before the *Kammergericht Berlin*. Nearly at the same time, the Commission had opened a procedure under Art. 3 and 9(3) of Regulation No. 17 against four of the German undertakings that were the addressee of the fines and against other Community undertakings and third countries' aniline producers. In the Commission's view, repeated and uniform increases in the aniline price had led to *an assumption of concerted practices* prohibited, as such, by Art. 85(1) of the Treaty. Within this context, the *Kammergericht Berlin*, in its reference for a preliminary ruling, asked the Court of Justice whether, *inter alia*, 'when a procedure has already been initiated by the Commission under

The problem of the *double*, national and Community, *barrier* in relation to the competition-distorting impact of any economic activity carried out within the Community by no means arises, in principle, in connection with Italian Act No. 287 of 10 October 1990 containing 'rules for the protection of competition and trading'.

In defining the *scope of application* and the *relationship with Community law* of Act No. 287, Article 1(1) under Title I, which specifically contains 'provisions on cartels, abuse of dominant position and merger transactions', states that the Italian rules have a function *subsidiary* to the Community's. This means that the provisions of Italian antitrust law apply to cartels, abuses of dominant positions and mergers not falling within the scope of either Article 81 or Article 82 of the EC Treaty, of Community Regulations or other Community acts with similar or comparable regulatory effects.

Article 1(2) of Act No. 287 further requires that, where the Italian Authority on Competition and Trading finds that a specific case brought to its scrutiny does not fall within the scope of application of the Act pursuant to Article 1(1) thereof, then it is required to notify the EC Commission to that effect, and to transmit all information available to it to the Commission. Moreover, pursuant to Article 1(3), in

---

Art. 14 of Regulation No. 17 of 6 Feb. 1962, it is compatible with the Treaty for the national authorities to apply to the same facts the prohibitions laid down by the national law on cartels' (first question). The *Kammergericht* further asked whether 'the risk of its resulting in a double sanction imposed by the Commission of the European Communities and by the national authority' should be avoided (second question). The first question was supplemented with the third question 'relating to the risk of a different legal assessment of the same facts and to the possibility of distortions of competition in the common market'. The first and third questions were answered by the Court in the sense that 'Community and national law on cartels consider cartels from different points of view. Whereas Art. 85 regards them in the light of obstacles which may result for trade between Member States, each body of national legislation proceeds on the basis of the considerations peculiar to it and considers cartels only in that context [. . .]. The distinction between community and national aspects [. . .] implies that one and the same agreement may, in principle, be the object of two sets of parallel proceedings, one before the community authorities under Art. 85 of the EEC Treaty, the other before the national authorities under national law'. Moreover, according to the ECJ, 'if the ultimate general aim of the Treaty is to be respected, this parallel application of the national system can only be allowed in so far as it does not prejudice the uniform application throughout the common market of the community rules on cartels and of the full effect of the measures adopted in implementation of those rules. Any other solution would be incompatible with the objectives of the treaty and the character of its rules on competition'. 'Consequently, *conflicts between the rules of the Community and national rules in the matter of the law on cartels must be resolved by applying the principle that Community law takes precedence*. It follows from the foregoing that, should it prove that a decision of a national authority regarding an agreement would be incompatible with a decision adopted by the Commission at the culmination of the procedure initiated by it, the national authority is required to take proper account of the effects of the latter decision. [. . .]. Consequently, [. . .] national authorities may take action against an agreement in accordance with their national law, even when an examination of the agreement from the point of view of its compatibility with community law is pending before the commission, subject however to the condition *that the application of national law may not prejudice the full and uniform application of community law or the effects of measures taken or to be taken to implement it*'. (*Emphasis added*)

cases in respect of which the Commission has initiated a procedure, the Italian Authority must stay investigations 'except into any aspects of exclusive national relevance'.[172]

Lastly, according to Article 1(4) of Act No. 287/1990:

> The rules contained in this present Title shall be interpreted on the basis of the principles of the European Communities' provisions of law on competition.

Article 3 of Regulation 1/2003 concerns the relationship between Articles 81 and 82 of the Treaty and national competition laws. In fact, it by no means restricts the scope of application of either set of rules, but it only deals with the issue from the special point of view of the concurrent application of both legislations to that same matter, distortion of competition, as follows:

> Where the competition authorities of the Member States or national courts apply national competition law to agreements, decisions by associations of undertakings or concerted practices within the meaning of Article 81(1) of the Treaty which may affect trade between Member States within the meaning of that provision, they shall also apply Article 81 of the Treaty to such agreements, decisions or concerted practices. Where the competition authorities of the Member States or national courts apply national competition law to any abuse prohibited by Article 82 of the Treaty, they shall also apply Article 82 of the Treaty. (Paragraph 1).
>
> The application of national competition law may not lead to the prohibition of agreements, decisions by associations of undertakings or concerted practices which may affect trade between Member States but which do not restrict competition within the meaning of Article 81(1) of the Treaty, or which fulfil the conditions of Article 81(3) of the Treaty or which are covered by a Regulation for the application of Article 81(3) of the Treaty. Member States shall not under this Regulation be precluded from adopting and applying on their territory stricter national laws which prohibit or sanction unilateral conduct engaged in by undertakings.
>
> Without prejudice to general principles and other provisions of Community law, paragraphs 1 and 2 do not apply when the competition authorities and the courts of the Member States apply national merger control laws nor do they preclude

---

172. For a discussion of Article 1 of the Italian Act in general, see Frignani, in Frignani & others, *Diritto antitrust*, p. 93 f., and, for an examination of the application of the double barrier principle in other Member States, p. 125 f. See also: Alessi, in Alessi & Olivieri, *La disciplina della concorrenza e del mercato (commento alla L. 10 ottobre 1990, n. 287 ed al Regolamento CEE n. 4064/89 del 21 dicembre 1989)* (Turin, 1991), p. 3 f.; Afferni, *Concorrenza e mercato, Commento alla legge 10 ottobre 1990, n. 287 e al decreto legislativo 25 gennaio 1992, n. 74* (Padua, 1994), p. 4 f. About the procedural character of the phrase and its connection with Art. 9(3) of Regulation No. 17/62, see the commentary by Frignani, in Frignani & others, *Diritto antitrust*, vol. I (Art. 1-7) (Bologna, 1993), p. 135 f.

the application of provisions of national law that predominantly pursue an objective different from that pursued by Articles 81 and 82 of the Treaty.

At a closer look, it emerges from these provisions, which takes it for granted that both Community law and national competition laws can be applied to the same type of cases, that the relationship between the two sets of rules is still based, as for the past, on the 'double barrier' theory.[173]

Thus, Article 3(1) imposes an *obligation* on national competition authorities and national courts, requiring them to apply Articles 81 and 82 concurrently with their own rules. In other words, whenever they decide to apply national law to a case also falling within the scope of application of Articles 81 or 82 EC, they *must also* apply the rules of Community law.

This obligation of concurrent application of the rules of both systems arises as soon as a procedure or an action is initiated pursuant to domestic legislation, but it no longer operates if the Commission initiates proceedings under Article 11(6) of Regulation 1/2003 for the adoption of a decision on the same relevant case.[174]

The norm being discussed here does not deal with cases falling within the scope of application of Community rules, though *not* within that of national legislations. In each such case, the obligation directly to apply Articles 81 and 82 as a whole arises, as observed above, from the provisions of Articles 5 and 6 of Regulation 1/2003.[175]

Article 3(2) concerns any differences in outcome as may arise from the concurrent application of both national and Community provisions to the same case. Pursuant to Article 3(2), applying the national provisions *cannot* entail the prohibition of agreements which are not prohibited by Article 81, as much as such agreements may affect trade between Member States.

This is the so-called *convergence obligation*, in line with the principle of Community law primacy laid down by the ECJ as early as in *Walt Wilhelm*. Although this obligation satisfies an understandable need for consistency and certainty in the relationships between the two legal systems, it reduces the national competition authorities' interest in applying both national and Community rules to the same case.

Theoretically, the national authorities might well apply their own internal legislations to an agreement likely to affect intra-Community trade, then one falling within the scope of application of Article 81. In fact, should they do so, they

173. The Commission had proposed, instead, that: 'Where an Agreement (. . .) within the meaning of Art. 81 of the Treaty or the abuse of a dominant position within the meaning of Art. 82 may affect trade between Member States, Community competition law shall apply to the exclusion of national competition laws.'

174. As indicated above, Article 11(6) of Regulation 1/2003 requires that: 'The initiation by the Commission of proceedings for the adoption of a decision under Chapter III shall relieve the competition authorities of the Member States of their competence to apply Articles 81 and 82 of the Treaty.'

175. Article 5 requires: 'The competition authorities of the Member States shall have the power to apply Articles 81 and 82 of the Treaty in individual cases.' Art. 6 merely provides that: 'National courts shall have the power to apply Articles 81 and 82 of the Treaty.'

would be forced to apply the Community rules *as well* and, what is more, they would be prevented by law from ruling that any restrictive agreement prohibited by their national legislation, but not by Community law, is unlawful.[176]

Just reading the second sentence of Article 3(2) seems to indicate that such *convergence obligation* does not operate either in cases of abuse of dominant positions under Article 82 EC or, more generally, in cases of competition-distorting conduct engaged in by undertakings. Indeed, in each such case, national authorities are free to discipline behaviours not prohibited by Community law.

Independent choice by national authorities is, however, only allowed in the sense that stricter national rules than those of Community law are permitted, not to permit less stringent treatment. In other words, as expressly indicated in paragraph 6 of the Commission Notice on cooperation between national competition authorities and the Commission, the former are precluded from authorizing practices that are unlawful under national law but not under Community law.

Lastly, it should be observed that neither the obligation of *concurrent application* under Article 3(1) of Council Regulation No. 1/2003 not the *convergence obligation* under Article 3(2) provide for the application by national authorities of either the rules on merger control or any rules pursuing objectives other that those laid down in Articles 81 and 82 EC.

18. APPLYING THE SUBSIDIARITY PRINCIPLE HAVING REGARD TO THE 'ONE-STOP SHOP', AND THE MULTI-STATE EXAMINATION OF MERGERS

The process to reform the Community system on merger control was started by the European Commission in December 2001, when it released the Green Paper on the review of Council Regulation (EEC) No. 4064/89, at about the same time as the Community system on merger control began to be criticized by the US antitrust authorities[177] and by the economic operators concerned, in addition to the annulment by the Community Courts of some of the Commission's decisions.[178]

176. The norm only deals with the case of a conduct prohibited by the relevant domestic legislation but not by Community law, without dealing with the opposite case, when a conduct is prohibited by Community law but not by the domestic legislation. In the latter case, in furtherance of the core principle of primacy of Community law, national authorities are prevented from authorizing any agreements or abuses of dominant positions that are prohibited by Community law but not by national laws. (See Guidelines on the application of Art. 81(3) of the Treaty, in [2004] O.J. C101, p. 97 ff., para. 14).
177. Chiefly following the prohibition by the Commission of the merger between General Electric and Honeywell in 2001, after the transaction had already been approved by the US authorities.
178. See Judgment of the Court of First Instance of 6 Jun. 2002, Case T-342/99, *Airtours plc* v *Commission*, [2002] ECR II-2585, Case T-310/01, *Schneider Electric SA* v *Commission*, [2002] ECR II-4071 and of 25 Oct. 2002, Case T-5/02, *Tetra Laval BV* v *Commission*, [2002] ECR II-4381. The judgment last cited was endorsed by the ECJ in judgments rendered on 15 Feb. 2005, Case C-12/03 P, *Commission* v *Tetra Laval BV*, [2005] ECR I-987.

This reform process ended with the adoption of Regulation (EC) No. 139/2004[179] (the 'New Merger Regulation'), which replaced Council Regulation (EEC) No. 4064/89 on the control of concentrations between undertakings (the 'Old Merger Regulation') effective as from 1 May 2004.[180]

The New Merger Regulation was supplemented with regulatory and interpretational measures, specifically:

(a) The Commission's Guidelines on the assessment of horizontal mergers under the New Council Regulation on the control of concentrations between undertakings;[181]
(b) DG Competition Best Practices on the conduct of EC merger control proceedings;[182] and
(c) Commission Regulation (EC) No. 802/2004 of 7 April 2004 implementing the New Merger Regulation,[183] which has attached to it; (i) the new version of Form CO relating to the notification of a concentration pursuant to the New Regulation; (ii) a new short form for the notification of concentrations eligible for a simplified procedure; and (iii) a new Form RS relating to reasoned submissions pursuant to Articles 4(4) and 4(5) of the New Regulation.[184]

This innovating thrust has also led up to a re-organization of the Directorate-General for Competition, through the appointment of a Deputy Director-General for mergers and antitrust, the appointment of a Chief Economist assisted by a dedicated staff, the dissolution of the 'Merger Task Force' – whose staff has been redeployed among seven different units of the Directorate-General for

---

179. Regulation (EC) No. 139/2004 of the Council of 20 Jan. 2004 on the control of concentrations between undertakings, in [2004] O.J. L24, p. 1.
180. Regulation (EEC) No. 4064/89 of the Council of 21 Dec. 1989 on the control of concentrations between undertakings in [1989] O.J. L395, p. 1, as amended by Regulation (EC) No. 1310/97 of the Council of 30 Jun. 1997, [1997] O.J. L180, p. 1.
181. Guidelines on the assessment of horizontal mergers under the Council Regulation on the control of concentrations between undertakings, in [2004] O.J. C31, p. 5.
182. See *DG Competition Best Practices on the conduct of EC merger control proceedings*, published on the Commission's website.
183. See Commission Regulation (EC) No. 802/2004 of 7 Apr. 2004 implementing Council Regulation (EC) No. 139/2004 on the control of concentrations between undertakings in [2004] O.J. L133, p. 1, which, effective from 1 May 2004, replaced Commission Regulation (EC) No. 447/98 of 1 Mar. 1998 on the notifications, time limits and hearings provided for in Council Regulation (EEC) No. 4064/89 on the control of concentrations between undertakings, in [1998] O.J. L61, p. 1.
184. The Implementing Regulation provides in details for the manner in which a notification is to be submitted to the Commission, and the beginning, expiry, and suspension of time limits under the new Regulation. The Implementing Regulation also specifies the parties having the right to be heard at the hearings of the administrative procedure, the contents of such right and the conduct of hearings before the Commission. It further defines the manners of access to the file and treatment of confidential information, and the time limits and manners the notifying parties must observe in the submission of commitments.

Competition, each with special responsibilities for a specific sector[185] – and the institution of a new Phase II Peer Review Panel, whose members are not members of the case team seised of the examination of the relevant concentration.[186]

Three more Commission Notices were prepared: (i) one on the allocation of cases between the Commission and the National Competition Authorities (the 'NCAs') on case referral, (ii) one on ancillary restrictions, and (iii) yet another on short-form notifications for certain concentrations.[187]

The New Regulation introduced major changes in the mechanism of concentration case referrals both from the Commission 'top-down' to the national competition authorities, and from the NCAs 'bottom-up' to the Commission, by providing for pre-notification referrals and allowing the notifying parties to request such referrals.

Yet, the 'one-stop shop' principle was retained, with a view to avoiding multiple notifications.[188]

Under Article 4(4) and (5) of the New Regulation, the parties concerned may request that a concentration transaction be referred by the Commission to any Member State's national competition authorities or by one or more such authorities to the Commission as early as at the pre-notification stage, and the conditions to be fulfilled for a concentration to be referred have been simplified.

The case allocation system has thereby become far more flexible than under the rules of the Old Merger Regulation. Further, by the introduction of the referral mechanism, the reform is intended both to accomplish better case allocation between the Commission and the NCAs and to reduce the number of cases in which multiple notifications are in order. As for referrals of concentrations of a Community dimension *from the Commission to an NCA*, Article 4(4) provides

---

185. In case a transaction involves several sectors, the case is allocated according to the 'centre of gravity' principle, in the sense that it is allocated to the unit responsible for the sector on which that transaction has the greatest impact.
186. I has been objected that, although the creation of such a review panel must be regarded as a positive step forward, it has failed to result in substantially altering the existing situation, in which the Commission still acts as both an investigator and a decision-maker throughout the procedure. See, among others, Berg & Ostendorf, 'The Reform of EC Merger Control: Substance and Impact of the Proposed New Procedural Rules' [2003] ECLR 594.
187. [2005] O.J. C56, pp. 2-35. Two years later, the Commission issued (a) the Consolidated Notice on jurisdictional criteria of 10 Jul. 2007, and (b) the *Guidelines on the assessment of non-horizontal mergers* of 28 Nov. 2007.
188. See Whereases 8 and 11 of Regulation No. 139/2004 and para. 20 of the Notice on referrals. Specifically, Whereas 8 of the Regulation requires that concentrations of Community dimension 'should, as a general rule, be reviewed exclusively at Community level, in application of a "one-stop shop" system and in compliance with the principle of subsidiarity'. Whereas 11 specifies that 'The rules governing the referral of concentrations from the Commission to Member States and from Member States to the Commission should operate as an effective corrective mechanism in the light of the principle of subsidiarity; these rules protect the competition interests of the Member States in an adequate manner and take due account of legal certainty and the 'one-stop shop' principle.'

that, prior to notifying any such concentration, the persons or undertakings concerned:

> may inform the Commission, by means of a reasoned submission, that the concentration may significantly affect competition in a market within a Member State which presents all the characteristics of a distinct market and should therefore be examined, in whole or in part, by that Member State.

An obvious consequence of the change made to the compatibility test is that, in order to obtain a top-down referral, it is no longer necessary, contrary to a provision in the Old Merger Regulation, to show that:

> a concentration threatens to affect significantly competition in a market within that Member State, which presents all the characteristics of a distinct market.[189]

This means that it is now sufficient for the transaction in question to have a significant impact on competition within a Member State.

To this end, both Whereas 16 of the 2004 Regulation and the Commission Notice on case referral in respect of concentrations clarify that:

> the undertakings concerned should not (. . .) be required to demonstrate that the effects of the concentration would be detrimental to competition.[190]

Thus, the requesting parties are only required to point to indicators which are generally suggestive of the likelihood that the transaction is liable to have a potential impact on competition.[191]

The ultimate objective of the reform under scrutiny is to facilitate the use of this form of referral with a view to making the Commission's workload less burdensome. And yet, certain new provisions may make such use less attractive to the parties concerned.[192]

Firstly, for a party to request a top-down referral from the Commission, it is required to submit a reasoned request on Form RS, in which highly detailed information must be given, specifically in respect of the markets likely to be affected by

---

189. Article 9(2)(a) of the Old Merger Regulation.
190. Whereas 16 of the New Merger Regulation.
191. In particular, the Commission Notice clarifies that, in general, showing the existence of one or more markets affected by the transaction will, as a rule, be enough to meet the substantive requirement of Art. 4(4) of the New Merger Regulation. The Notice further specifies that indications of possible competitive impact may be no more than preliminary in nature, and would be without prejudice to the outcome of the investigation into the transaction.
192. Submissions pursuant to Article 4(4) have been quite few: just 38 of the total 1,432 cases notified in 2004 through 2008. Still, none of these 38 cases appears to have been dismissed by the Commission. See *European Merger Control Council Regulation 139/2004 – Statistics – 21 September 1990 to 30 April 2008*, available on the EU Commission's website. See also Mr Monti's speech of 17 Sep. 2004, *Private litigation as a key complement to public enforcement of competition rules and the first conclusions on the implementation of the new Merger Regulation.*

the concentration. This clearly amounts to an exceedingly time-consuming and costly exercise for the parties concerned.

Secondly, the timing of the procedure is such that it becomes poorly beneficial for the requesting parties. For they may request a top-down referral only in relation to a transaction which can already be notified in itself. And this, along with the fact that the Commission has an additional period of twenty-five working days from the date of receiving Form RS to decide to refer the case, implies that the length of the concentration approval procedure may be extended considerably.

Thirdly, the parties will have in any event – whether their requests are acceded to or rejected – to notify the transaction in question to the NCAs of the Member State concerned or to the Commission (or to both, in case of partial referral).

Pursuant to Article 4(5) of the New Merger Regulation, the parties to a concentration which does not have a Community dimension – and which is, therefore, capable of being reviewed under the national competition laws of *at least three Member States* – may, before any notification is made to the competent authorities, inform the Commission by means of a reasoned submission that the concentration should be examined by the Commission as a 'substitute' for such authorities.

The Commission must transmit this submission to all Member States without delay. Where none of the Member States competent for examining the concentration under their own national laws has expressed its disagreement as to the request to refer the case within fifteen working days, the transaction is deemed to have a Community dimension and must be notified to the Commission *alone*.

Even in respect of a bottom-up referral are the parties required to submit a reasoned request on Form RS, albeit within the scope of a far simpler procedure than in a top-down referral and without any discretionary assessment being warranted.

The usefulness of the device provided for by Article 4(5) of the New Merger Regulation is shown by the fact that the Commission received as many as one hundred forty-one requests for bottom-up referrals in the first four years of application of the Regulation.[193]

The new wording of Articles 9 and 22 of the 2004 Regulation still provides for the option to submit requests for top-down or bottom-up referrals with regard to concentrations *after* notification, while only some procedural requirements have been altered.

In the same way as in pre-notification referrals, the procedures for both top-down and bottom-up referrals have been streamlined. The requesting Member State is no longer required to show that 'a transaction threatens to create or to strengthen a dominant position', but only that it 'threatens to affect competition within its territory'.

---

193. See *European Merger Control Council Regulation 139/2004 – Statistics – 21 September 1990 to 30 April 2008*, cit. In the 2004-2008 period, the Commission rejected a request for a bottom-up referral on just four occasions.

19. DAMAGES AWARDED FOR LOSSES ARISING FROM INFRINGEMENTS OF ANTITRUST RULES

In the well-known *Courage* judgment,[194] the ECJ stated:

> *The full effectiveness* of Article 85 of the Treaty and, in particular, *the practical effect* of the prohibition laid down in Article 85(1) *would be put at risk if it were not open to any individual to claim damages for loss* caused to him by a contract or by conduct liable to restrict or distort competition. [*Emphasis added*].

The Court had no doubts as to the *dissuasive* effect of actions for damages brought against infringers of antitrust law:

> Indeed, *the existence of such a right* strengthens the working of the Community competition rules and *discourages agreements or practices*, which are frequently covert, which are liable to restrict or distort competition. From that point of view, *actions for damages* before the national courts *can make a significant contribution to the maintenance of effective competition* in the Community. [*Emphasis added*].

In the same judgment, the Court of Justice went on to rule:

> [...] in the absence of Community rules governing the matter, *it is for the domestic legal system* of each Member State to designate the courts and tribunals having jurisdiction and to lay down the detailed procedural rules governing actions *for safeguarding rights which individuals derive directly from Community law*, provided that such rules are not less favourable than those governing similar domestic actions (*principle of equivalence*) and that they do not render practically impossible or excessively difficult the exercise of rights conferred by Community law (*principle of effectiveness*) in the absence of Community rules governing the matter, it is for the domestic legal system of each Member State to designate the courts and tribunals having jurisdiction and to lay down the detailed procedural rules governing actions for safeguarding rights which individuals derive directly from Community law, provided that such rules are not less favourable than those governing similar domestic actions (principle of equivalence) and that they do not render practically impossible or excessively difficult the exercise of rights conferred by Community law (principle of effectiveness). [*Emphasis added*].

In its more recent judgment in *Manfredi*,[195] the ECJ referred back to its on arguments in *Courage* to rule that:

> [...] *any individual* can claim compensation for the harm suffered where there is a causal relationship between that harm and an agreement or practice prohibited under Article 81 EC. [*Emphasis added*].

194. Judgment of the Court of Justice of 20 Sep. 2001, Case C-453/99, *Courage*, [2001] ECR I-6297, ground 26 ff.

195. Judgment of the Court of Justice of 13 Jul. 2006, Joined Cases C-295/04 to C-298/04, *Manfredi*, [2006] ECR 6619, grounds 61 and 63.

And it stressed again that, in the absence of Community rules governing the matter, it is for the domestic legal system of each Member State to determine the manners in which such right should be exercised.

The same core concept was clearly laid down in Whereas 7 of Regulation No. 1/2003, which states that national courts have an essential part to play in applying the Community competition rules, i.e. to protect subjective rights under Community law in disputes between private parties, in particular by awarding *damages to the victims of infringements*. In the White Paper on Damages actions for breach of the EC antitrust rules of 2 April 2008,[196] the Commission stressed the need to extend the right to bring actions for damages before national courts as far as possible, with a view to protecting individual *consumers*, but also *small businesses*, i.e. *any* individuals who have suffered 'scattered and relatively low-value damage, who are often deterred from bringing an individual action for damages by the costs, delays, uncertainties, risks and burdens involved'.

Therefore, the scope for protection advocated in the White Paper includes 'all victims' of infringements of the antitrust rules contained in the EC Treaty.[197] In other words, the issues addressed in the White Paper concern:

> *all* categories of victim, *all* types of breach of Articles 81 and 82 and *all* sectors of the economy.[198] [*Emphasis added*].

20. ACTIONS FOR DAMAGES BROUGHT BY COMPETING UNDERTAKINGS

In the Italian legal system, while the powers to adjudicate infringements of *Community* rules under Articles 81 and 82 EC are allocated according to the ordinary provisions on jurisdiction, Article 33 of Act No. 287 of 10 October 1990, relating to breaches of the *national* antitrust law, requires that:

> actions for annulment and damages, as well as motions seeking urgent measures in relation to breaches of the provisions in Titles I to IV, shall be brought before the *Court of Appeal of competent territorial jurisdiction*.

---

196. See Document COM(2008) 165 final.
197. It should be noted that, in the *Courage* judgment, the ECJ went to the point to concede that even an *undertaking which is party* to a competition restrictive agreement is full entitled to claim for damages. According to the Court, 'There should not therefore be any absolute bar to such an action being brought by a party to a contract which would be held to violate the competition rules.' Relying on this principle, the ECJ recognized that a party to a restrictive agreement which is 'in a markedly weaker position than the other party' is entitled to claim damages for losses incurred as a result of such agreement. In the Italian system, the Turin Court of Appeal (Judgment of 6 Jul. 2000, *VHF Ventana Incentive House* v *Juventus F.C.*), while acknowledging in principle that even a party to a restrictive agreement which has incurred a loss and has not passed it on to a third party (see below for the issue of loss pass-on) is entitled to bring action for damages, ruled out compensation in the relevant case, on the ground that the deciding factor was that party's misconduct, in that it was well aware it was participating in a violation.
198. See para. 1.2 of the White Paper cited above.

Any actions concerning infringements of competition rules under Article 2598 *et. seq.* of the Italian Civil Code must be brought in accordance with the ordinary rules on jurisdiction.

It should be noted that, in the area of infringements of national competition laws,[199] there is *no* relationship of priority, consequentiality or accessoriality between an administrative proceeding before the AGCM, the Italian competition authority – including the two phases of the subsequent action (if any is brought) to challenge the AGCM's decision before an administrative court – and a civil action brought by a competitor before the Court of Appeal.[200]

The mutual independence of the two types of action arises from the fact that different interests are at play in each of them.

The tasks of the AGCM cannot be mistaken for those of an ordinary court. While the former is responsible for establishing and suppressing anticompetitive conducts prejudicial to public interests (*public enforcement*), the latter is required to protect individual rights (*private enforcement*).[201]

The jurisdiction vested by Article 33 of Act 287/1990 in the Courts of Appeal expressly covers the civil consequences of infringements of competition rules. A Court of Appeal may adjudicate even in the absence of a decision by the AGCM's, and independently assess whether all the elements falling under the Italian competition rules are present in any one relevant case.

In theory, a Court of Appeal seised of the consequences of infringements of national laws, and a District Court or Justice of the Peace dealing with the civil

199. Unlike the clear-cut choice taken by the Italian Court of Cassation, Joint Chambers, in Judgment No. 2107 of 4 Feb. 2005 – which is discussed further below, in particular in this Chapter VI – the phrases 'antitrust law' and 'antitrust violation' are taken to mean the same thing as 'competition law' and 'competition violation'. respectively, without distinction, even in the awareness of the different weight public interests may have in the different areas in which each of antitrust law and competition law operates, thus of the different role public interests may play in respect of each specific breach of antitrust law or competition law, as the case may be.

200. This is the view taken by most Italian law scholars: Vettori, *Concorrenza e mercato* (Padua, 2005), 176; Scuffi, 'Orientamenti consolidati e nuove prospettive nella disciplina italiana antitrust' [2003] Riv. dir. ind. I, 95; Tavassi – Scuffi, *Diritto processuale antitrust* (Milan, 1998), 173; Toffoletto, *Il risarcimento del danno nel sistema delle sanzioni per la violazione della normativa antitrust* (Milan, 1996), 31; Barone, 'Danni da abuso di posizione dominante e giurisdizione ordinaria' [1996] Foro it. I, 277. The same view has been taken by Italian Courts of Appeal in case-law: Rome Court of Appeal, 20 Jan. 2003, *WIND/Telecom* [2003] Riv. dir. ind., 548; Milan Court of Appeal, 18 Jul. 1995, *Telsystem/Sip* [1996] Foro it., 276, with commentary by Barone, 'Danni da abuso di posizione dominante e giurisdizione ordinaria'; Rome Court of Appeal, 20 Jan. 1993, *Gruppo Sicurezza/Aeroporti di Roma* [1993] Foro it., 3377, with commentary by Valdina.

201. In the relationship between the two types of proceeding, not even the rule can be pleaded according to which civil proceedings must mandatorily be stayed pending a decision on a dispute in another action pursuant to Art. 295 of the Code of Civil Procedure. For this article only provides for a case in which another proceeding is pending in another *judicial* proceeding, as opposed to an *administrative* proceeding before the AGCM. Art. 33 envisages no link between administrative investigations and judicial proceedings brought before a Court of Appeal. See La China, *Concorrenza e mercato, commento alla legge 10 ottobre 1990, n. 287* (Padua, 1994), 647.

consequences of infringements of *Community* antitrust rules may well deliver decisions conflicting with a measure taken by the Competition Authority in relation to the same case, by which *neither is legally bound*. But such a conflict appears quite unlikely in practice because of the indisputable value as 'precedent' the Italian Competition Authority's decisions have in the eyes of civil judges.[202]

Therefore, in the Italian legal system, the actions for damages provided for by the national antitrust legislation are viewed as judicial remedies independent of, and concurrent with (under a 'binary' approach of a sort), any administrative actions as may be brought before the Italian Competition Authority.

Although no formal cooperation between adjudicating bodies has been provided for, the AGCM's decisions on similar cases operate as 'authority' and represent a fundamental point of reference for ordinary courts' decisions as well.[203]

The distinction between 'public enforcement' and 'private enforcement' has aptly been highlighted in a recent judgment by the *Tribunale Amministrativo Regionale* (*TAR*, regional administrative court) of Lazio,[204] in which the administrative judges stressed the diversity of public protection requirements versus an ordinary court's tasks. The latter is expected to decide a party's claims for the protection of private interests, whilst the Competition Authority acts on its own motion in the primary public interest of primary Community relevance, with a view to protecting a competitive market.[205]

---

202. Let me refer again to the 'deference complex' I have discussed elsewhere in this Chapter VI, from which judicial authorities seem to suffer, in whatever legal system, whenever they are faced with a specialist authority's decision. In para. 2.3 of the White Paper on Damages actions for breach of the EC antitrust rules, cit., the Commission proposed that the possible adverse effects of the separateness between the two investigatory levels in some national legislations, including Italian law, be overcome on the following argument: 'Whenever *the European Commission* finds a breach of Art. 81 or 82 of the EC Treaty, victims of the infringement can, by virtue of established case law and Art. 16(1) of Regulation 1/2003, rely on this decision *as binding proof* in civil proceedings for damages. For decisions by *national competition authorities* (*NCAs*) finding a breach of Art. 81 or 82, similar rules currently exist in only some Member States. . . . ' (Emphasis added) Therefore, the Commission suggested the following rule: 'National courts that have to rule in actions for damages on practices under Art. 81 or 82 on which *an NCA* in the ECN has already given a *final decision* finding an infringement of those articles, or on which a review court has given a *final judgment* upholding the NCA decision or itself finding an infringement, *cannot take decisions running counter* to any such decision or ruling. This obligation should apply without prejudice to the right, and possible obligation, of national courts to seek clarification on the interpretation of Art. 81 or 82 under Art. 234 of the EC Treaty. The rule set out above confers *binding effect only on decisions that are final*, i.e. where the defendant has exhausted all appeal avenues, and relates only to *the same practices* and *same undertaking(s)* for which the NCA or the review court found an infringement.' [*Emphasis added*].
203. Scuffi, *Diritto processuale antitrust*, p. 95; Vettori, *Concorrenza e mercato*, p. 176; Meli, *Autonomia privata, sistema delle invalidità e disciplina delle intese anticoncorrenziali* (Milan, 2002), 137.
204. *TAR Lazio*, First Chamber, Judgment No. 1713/2006, *Merck (Principi Attivi)*.
205. On this subject, see also Cassinis, 'Rapporti tra public e private enforcement' in Atti del VII Convegno UAE-LIDC *Antitrust between EC and national law* (Treviso 18–19 May 2006).

A quite different approach, more in line with the Commission's views, has been taken in Germany. Paragraph 33(4) of the *Gesetz gegen Wettbewerbeschrankungen* (*GWB*) requires the German courts seised of actions for damages to comply with the decisions not only of the German competition authority, but also of any of the latter's counterparts in other Member States, subject to references to the ECJ for preliminary rulings.[206]

Likewise, in actions for damages brought before either ordinary courts or the *Competition Appeal Tribunal* in England and Wales, the judges are bound by the decisions taken by the Office of Fair Trading or by the Competition Appeal Tribunal, as the case may be, in accordance with both the national rules and the Community rules on competition.

As for the competitors of an undertaking (or undertakings) liable for infringing antitrust rules, there can be no doubt as to their standing to bring actions for damages. A competitor's interest to be protected is to retain its competitive position in the relevant market, which interest is harmed by the total or partial *exclusion* of the competitor from the market or by the competitor being forced to access the market *under less advantageous conditions.*

In the Italian judicial system, competing undertakings' standing to bring actions for damages was confirmed by the Court of Cassation in Judgment No. 17475/2002,[207] whereby the Italian Supreme Court ruled that antitrust law is intended, because of its public law nature, to protect businesses and, therefore, businesses have full *locus standi* to bring action under Article 33 of Act No. 287 of 10 October 1990.

In fact, the protection accorded to competitors had already been affirmed in precedent, when it was stated that, according to Article 2043 of the Civil Code, relating to general actions for non-contractual liability, or according to Article 2598 of the Civil Code relating to unfair competition, the breach by an undertaking of an antitrust rule should give its competitors standing to sue that undertaking for damages.[208]

---

206. Cassinis, 'Rapporti tra public e private enforcement' p. 9. For more details, see section 18.4 below. The same German law also requires that the limitation period for seeking compensation be suspended not only by the national courts, but by the other Member States' judges as well, in case a procedure is opened pursuant to Art. 81 or 82 EC.

207. *Cass, civ,, Sez. I*, of 9 Dec. 2002 [2003] Foro it. 1, I, p. 1121.

208. *Cass, civ,, Sez. I*, No. 827 of 1 Dec. 1999 [1999] Giur. it., 1223, holding that 'any one conduct may be deemed to be a violation under Articles 2598 or 2597 of the Civil Code, though not under antitrust law. Likewise, any one conduct may be found to be multi-offending, because it harmed both an individual undertaking's interests and the public interest contemplated by Act No. 287/1990'. A different approach has been taken by some Italian judges on the merits, who, in furtherance of the principle of the speciality of the norms, have ruled that antitrust law prevails over the general rules on unfair competition, thus conforming to the criterion of the just seeming concurrence of the norms. (See Rome District Court Order of 23 Dec. 1999 [2000] Giur. it., p. 2333). For the relationship between the Italian rules on unfair competition and those contained in the Italian antitrust law, see below, the view held by the Court of Cassation, Joint Chambers, in Judgment No. 2207 of 4 Feb. 2005.

An especially meaningful example was an action brought for liability arising from *abuse of dominant position*, which resulted in damages being awarded to the complainant, one of the defendant's *competitors*. That was the judgment handed down by the Milan Court of Appeal in *Telesystem* v *SIP (Telecom)*,[209] whereby *Telecom* was ordered to pay damages for using an 'excluding practice' against a competitor (*Telesystem*).

The Milan judges held that:

> *Telecom* abused its dominant position in the market for voice transport line leases, by obstructing or otherwise delaying *Telesystem*'s entry into the market for closed-user group telephone services, and *Telecom* must therefore pay damages pursuant to Articles 3 and 33 of Act No 287/90.

In *Wind (Albacom)* v *Telecom*,[210] the Rome Court of Appeal ordered Telecom to pay damages for the losses incurred by an undertaking which had been denied entry into the data-transmission market with access to DSL and SDH technologies.

21. ACTIONS FOR DAMAGES IN CONSUMER PROTECTION

A far more complex issue appears to be the *consumers' locus standi* to bring action for damages for losses incurred as a result of breaches of competition law. The issue was analysed by the Commission in some depth in its 2008 White Paper on damages actions for breach of the EC antitrust rules. Paragraph 2.1 of the paper reads:

> [T]he Commission welcomes the confirmation by the Court of Justice that '*any individual*' who has suffered harm caused by an antitrust infringement must be allowed to claim damages before national courts. This principle also applies to *indirect purchasers*, i.e. purchasers who had no direct dealings with the infringer, but *who nonetheless may have suffered considerable harm because an illegal overcharge was passed on to them along the distribution chain.*[211] [*Emphasis added*].

In this context, the Commission proposed the adoption of a mechanism of *collective redress* 'allowing aggregation of the individual claims of victims of antitrust infringements (...) who have suffered scattered and relatively low-value damage'.[212] In Paragraph 2.1 of the White Paper, the Commission then

209. Judgment of the Milan Court of Appeal of 18 Jul. 1995, *Telesystem S.p.A. c. SIP S.p.A*, [1996] Foro it. I, p. 276.

210. Rome Court of Appeal, 20 Jan. 2003 [2003] Foro it. 9, I, 2474.

211. In its judgment in *Bluvacanze*, the Milan Court of Appeal awarded damages to a travel agency that had been 'boycotted' by a cartel of undertakings which, though not being direct competitors of the complainant, came upstream of it along the business and distribution chain. See Milan Court of Appeal, 11 Jul. 2003 [2004] Diritto Ind. 2, p. 157.

212. See *White Paper on damages actions*, cit., para. 2.1.

distinguished between cases in which a consumer had direct dealings with the infringer and cases in which a chain of other entities came in between the infringer and the consumer.[213]

When the injured person enters into direct dealings with the infringer of antitrust rules, there can be no doubt as to the standing to bring action for damages. Thus, in the case of contracts *downstream of a cartel* of insurers, the persons who took out policies with the members of the cartel must be deemed to be *direct victims* of the infringement, contrary to the view initially taken by the Italian Supreme Court's in Judgment No. 1745/2002 of 9 December 2002.[214] In that case the trade 'loop' had come to an immediate close, and, accordingly, there could have been no 'passing-on' of the loss but only a contractual relationship that was flawed at the very start.

A more complex reasoning is in order when the harmful effects of a restrictive agreement reverberate through the whole or any part of the distribution chain. For the undertaking that was the first to incur an overcharge as a result of the prohibited agreement may well try to pass on the effects of such overcharge to its customers, in an attempt to maintain its profits unchanged. In this connection, the Commission observed:

> If the direct customer of the infringer fully or partially passed on the illegal overcharge to his own customers (the indirect purchasers), several legal issues can arise. At present, these create a great degree of legal uncertainty and difficulties in antitrust damages actions. (*White Book*, para. 2.6)

In this connection, the Commission suggested that two measures should be taken, the first of which for the benefit of the defendant, as follows:

> (. . .) infringers should be allowed to invoke the possibility that the overcharge might have been passed on. Indeed, to deny this defence could result in *unjust enrichment* of purchasers who passed on the overcharge and in undue *multiple compensation* for the illegal overcharge by the defendant. The Commission therefore suggests that: *defendants* should be *entitled to invoke the passing-on defence against a claim for compensation of the overcharge*. The standard of proof for this defence should be not lower than the standard imposed on the claimant to prove the damage. [*Emphasis added*].

---

213. Vettori, *Concorrenza e mercato*, p. 249 ff. The notion of 'consumer' in the broad sense accepted under antitrust law includes both final users and any entities in intermediate positions along the trade chain. According to the Commission Notice containing Guidelines on the application of Article 81(3) of the Treaty, 'the concept of "*consumers*" encompasses all direct or indirect users of the products covered by the agreement, including producers that use the products as an input, wholesalers, retailers and final consumers, i.e. natural persons who are acting for purposes which can be regarded as outside their trade or profession. In other words, consumers within the meaning of Article 81(3) are the customers of the parties to the agreement and subsequent purchasers. These customers can be undertakings as in the case of buyers of industrial machinery or an input for further processing or final consumers as for instance in the case of buyers of impulse ice-cream or bicycles'.

214. [2003] Danno e responsabilità 4, p. 390.

The second measure was intended to favour claimants as indirect purchasers:

> Difficulties also arise, on the other hand, if an *indirect purchaser* invokes the passing-on of overcharges as a basis *to show the harm suffered*. Purchasers at, or near the end of the distribution chain are often those most harmed by antitrust infringements, but given *their distance from the infringement* they find it particularly difficult to produce sufficient proof of the existence and extent of passing-on of the illegal overcharge along the distribution chain. If such claimants are unable to produce this proof, they will not be compensated and the infringer, who may have successfully used the passing-on defence against another claimant upstream, would retain an unjust enrichment. To avoid such scenario, *the Commission* therefore *proposes to lighten the victim's burden* and suggests that: indirect purchasers should be able to rely on *the rebuttable presumption that the illegal overcharge was passed on to them in its entirety*. [*Emphasis added*].

The very approach to the issue has been taken in different terms in the US legal system. Because of the *sanctionatory and deterring function* of actions for damages in antitrust cases under US law, the awardees of *damages* in such cases – 'punitive damages', in fact[215] – are identified very narrowly.

There is no question as to the right to stand in court of a *consumer* who has entered into *direct* dealings with the infringer and has suffered a loss as a result.[216] *Jus standi* was, however, denied to the final consumers where there was an intermediary who had been *first* to incur the injury, since the latter was the only person entitled to bring action even in case he had passed on the resulting loss on the final consumers.

In fact, beginning with *Hanover Shoe* (392 *US* 481) of 1968, the US Supreme Court has consistently held that the victim's conduct after suffering the injury from a violation of antitrust rules *is not relevant in the assessment of damages*, and that it cannot otherwise be shown that an intermediary would have refrained from overcharging *in any event*. This is the argument on which the so-called 'passing-on theory' has been deemed to be outdated.[217]

215. For the notion of 'punitive damages', refer to the extensive monograph by F. Benatti, *Correggere e punire dalla Law of Torts all'inadempimento del contratto* (Milan, 2008), *passim*, in particular in relation to *The Restatement (Second) of Torts § 908* (1978), p. 33 ff.

216. See *Chattanooga Foundry and Pipe Works v. Atlanta*, 203 US 390, 1906.

217. By contrast, in the Italian system, a defence based on the 'passing-on theory' was granted by the Turin Court of Appeal in its judgment of 6 Jul. 2000, *VHF Ventana Incentive House* c. *Juventus F.C.* In that case, the Court of Appeal held that a company that had purchased tourist packages for away football matches lacked standing to bring action because it had passed on the loss to the final consumers. In particular, the Court held: 'In our system, actions for damages have rather a compensatory function than the sanctionatory or deterring functions typical of other systems, and, accordingly, the party having standing to bring action is the person that has actually incurred the loss. Conversely, substantive standing is denied to a party that has aided in passing on the loss to other persons, thus to final consumers.'

In a later case, *Illinois Brick*, the US Supreme Court confirmed its restrictive approach by stating that the complexity of damages suits, in which the courts would be called upon to avoid duplication of damages and, at the same time, to allocate awarded damages fairly among different injured parties, would undermine the deterring effectiveness of such suits.[218]

The Italian Supreme Court, too, had initially taken a restrictive approach to the issue of consumers' *locus standi* in damages actions, albeit on arguments different from the US Supreme Court's in *Illinois Brick*.

In a judgment of 9 December 2002,[219] which was much criticized as appearing to be in conflict with the Community Courts' precedent, the Italian Supreme Court *excluded* that consumers who had concluded contracts downstream of competition-restrictive agreements had any standing, at first sight, to bring actions for damages.

More specifically, the plaintiffs were natural persons who had entered into insurance contracts with undertakings participating in a *cartel* and had brought action for having being forced to pay exceedingly high premiums precisely because of a restrictive agreement. The Supreme Court had been called upon to give a ruling on the different issue of whether a Court of Appeal or a Justice of the Peace were competent to hear damages suits, under Article 33 of Act No. 287/90 and the ordinary rules on jurisdiction, respectively. Then it held that the Italian antitrust law *only concerned businesses and competition*, and that, accordingly, *the sanctions provided for in Article 33 were not applicable to the case being heard*. In fact, the actions for damages contemplated in Article 33:

> appear to have been conceived with regard to the undertakings alone.

As a consequence, such actions for damages:

> cannot but lead to the belief that the type of losses for which compensation is sought are closely connected with issue concerning undertakings and their presence in the market.

Thus, by this ruling, final consumers were excluded from the number of parties having standing to bring action under Article 33. According to the Court, consumers would not remain without legal remedies, since they were allowed to bring ordinary actions for damages under Article 2043 of the Civil Code, so long as they could give proof of a injury to a specific subjective right.

---

218. *Illinois Brick Co. v. Illinois*, 431 U.S. 720, of 1977. The Court, *by way of exception*, identified two typical situations in which the indirect purchaser can positively prove the use of pass-on: (a) when a supply contract is entered into, prior to the infringement of competition law, between the direct purchaser and the indirect purchaser, whereby the price of re-selling from the former to the latter is arrived at according to the cost-plus method; and (b) when the direct purchaser is an entity belonging to the same group as its customer's.
219. *Cass. civ. No. 17475* of 9 Dec. 2002, cited in footnote 214.

Later on, quite the opposite was held by the Italian Court of Cassation, Joint Chambers, in Judgment No. 2207 of 4 February 2005.[220] What is relevant to the issue in question is the part of the judgment in which it is stated that:

> antitrust law is not the law of undertakings alone, but is the law concerning all the parties in the market, thus *any individual* who is interested in preserving its competitive quality. [*Emphasis added*].

Therefore, this ruling also counts *final consumers* among the holders of legally relevant interests.[221]

Hence, the conclusion that any violation of antitrust rules amounts, at least potentially, to an 'unjust injury' within the meaning of Article 2043 of the Italian Civil Code. Therefore, according to the Italian Supreme Court:

> a person who has incurred an injury as a result of a contract allowing for no alternative because of upstream collusive arrangements, even if that person is not a party to a competitive relationship with the makers of such arrangements, can rely on the remedies provided for in Article 33 of Act No 287/1990.

In other words, if and as long as a consumer's claim for damages is based on an injury allegedly caused to its interest by a cartel between undertakings, that claim abstractly falls among the actions contemplated by Article 33 of Act 287/1990. Accordingly, jurisdiction to decide actions brought by consumers – and this was the true *thema decidendum* in the Supreme Court's second judgment as well – is

220. *Cass. civ., sez. un., No. 2207* of 4 Feb. 2005 [2005] Corr. giur. 8, p. 1093. The Joint Chambers had been prompted to act by the Court's Chamber III, which, by Decree No. 15538/03 of 17 Oct. 2003, had pointed to the conflict, by offering views opposite to those the Supreme Court had reached just one year before. See *Cass. civ., sez. III*, Decree No. 15538 of 17 Oct. 2003 [2003] Foro it. I, 2938. The Court had stated in that order that 'even different suggestions could be drawn from the layout of Act No. 287 of 1990 about jurisdictional issues and the consumer's *jus standi*' since 'the person seeking voidance of the agreement or compensation for losses arising from a competition-restrictive practice has full standing to bring action under Article 33(2)(1) of Act 287/90'. It is so because 'it is the matter which identifies jurisdiction, while it is for the competent judge to consider whether or not the party bringing suit has standing [. . .]. In brief, where the consumer is believed to have standing to act under Art. 33, it should be concluded that the Court of Appeal has jurisdiction over the case'.

221. This conclusion is also warranted by such provisions of law as Art. 4 of Act 287/90, which expressly states the consumer's benefit among the criteria according to which the lawfulness of agreements is to be assessed. In this connection, due consideration should be given to the very origin of Italian antitrust law, specifically to the objectives of Draft Bill No. 1012, which are laid down at the beginning of the accompanying Report as follows: 'Any law on market protection which contains rules traditionally governing monopolist practices has acquired a specific political value by general agreement, based on which that law should be changed into device to govern the economy. Therefore, it is appropriate to specify that this is not the core purpose of the Draft Bill now being submitted, since it is intended solely for the protection of consumers.' More recently, the Communication from the Commission on 'A pro-active Competition Policy for a Competitive Europe' has stated: 'A further element which will underpin the new EU competition regime is the better integration of consumers' interests in the competition regulatory structure.'

vested in the Courts of Appeal, not in any courts as might be identified in accordance with generally applicable criteria.

In reaching such conclusions, the Italian Supreme Court made a clear-cut distinction between the antitrust rules in Act 287/1990 and Articles 81 and 82 EC, on the one hand, and the Civil Code rules on unfair competition on the other. In the Court's view, while the code-based rules on unfair competition retain their fundamental quality as a device to protect correct competitive relationships between undertakings, and damages are to be awarded to compensate losses incurred by the competitors *alone*, the antitrust rules are there to protect free competition for the 'public' purpose of ensuring the market's competitive quality. Thus, in case the rules of the latter type are infringed, and because anticompetitive behaviours have 'multi-offensive force' – capable, that is, to prejudice the assets of *all* parties in the market, whether or not competitors of the infringer – *any individual* who has suffered such prejudice is entitled to compensation.

This approach, which the Joint Chambers of the Italian Supreme Court have taken in ruling on the consumers' entitlement to damages for losses incurred 'downstream' of restrictive agreements, as discussed above, seems to have been endorsed in recent case-law, both on the merits[222] and in point of law.[223]

In summary, it can be stated that, in the Italian legal system, as well as in major EU Member States' systems, the *redressing function* of damages actions entails compensation for *all the losses caused* by the relevant infringement, regardless of the complainant's position along the chain of the injured parties.

Yet, for the party at the upper end of the chain to plead *jus standi*, it must have not, at least in the Italian system, passed on its losses to other parties.[224] Hence, no solution is conceivable that accords standing to act to persons who have not actually been injured, in that they have passed on their losses to other parties along the same distribution chain.

22. A NEW COLLECTIVE REDRESS ACTION: THE SO-CALLED 'ITALIAN CLASS ACTION'

Through Act No. 244 of 24 December 2007, relating to the approval of Finance Act 2008 (Article 2(445) to (449)), provisions were 'rashly' introduced in the Italian legal system for an *azione collettiva risarcitoria* (roughly, collective redress action) under the first six paragraphs of Article 140-*bis* of the Consumer Code. The device so made available was initially treated by the Italian press, including trade media, as the 'Italian class action', with more critical than favourable

---

222. See, of many, the judgment of the Naples Court of Appeal, Chamber I, of 13 Jul. 2006.
223. See *Cass. civ. No. 2305* of 2 Feb. 2007 [2007] Resp. civ. e prev., pp. 7-8, with a commentary by Bianchi, *Cass. civ. No. 4104* of 21 Feb. 2007, and *Cass. civ. No. 9205* to *No. 9212* of 20 Apr. 2006.
224. In this sense, see the Turin Court of Appeal's judgment of 6 Jul. 2000.

overtones. The date of entry into force of the new provisions was then postponed from the end of June 2008, as originally stated, until 1 January 2009.[225]

In fact, the 'general' collective redress device introduced by Article 140-*bis* of the Consumer Code, appears to be less a 'class action', of which it is just a remote imitation, than a result of the general scheme for the generalization and extension of the 'Continental European' model of procedural rules, which is already governed in Italy by Article 139 et seq. of the Consumer Code. This model was first imported into Italy, essentially in the area of consumer protection, as a consequence of the obligation to adjust to, and implement, Community legislation in compliance with the present Title XIV (former Title XI) of the EC Treaty relating to consumer protection.

Whether the term 'class action' is used for the sake of simplification or for propagandistic ends in defining the contents of the Italian rules of procedure so newly introduced, it is ultimately bound to generate confusion and to foster expectations or fears, depending on the circumstances.

It was not by chance that the authors of the new Article 140-*bis* of the Consumer Code chose the phrase '*azione collettiva risarcitoria*' as the heading of that article. That was a more appropriate wording in technical terms, and one well known to the Italian system,[226] to designate a proven procedural mechanism already provided for by the Italian domestic legislation: the collective or associative action of German origin (the *Verbandsklage* on the general terms of contract of 1976, which served as the model for the present-day Community legislation in this domain).

There are many reasons, arising from the general differences between the US and the Italian rules of civil procedure, why the procedural device of a 'genuine' class action can hardly be transplanted into the Italian legal system.[227]

Firstly, a major role is played by the far broader scope for discretion available to the US courts under procedural rules, which, specifically in class actions, allow the judges, thanks to their high skills in economic analysis, to manage wholly on their own, and even to direct 'according to justice', the entire pre-trial stage in a court case until the crucial time of 'category' or 'class' 'certification'.

Moreover, the rule of 'discovery' in the US system requires each party, in the pre-trial phase – the timing and contents of which will be determined by the judge, who will closely supervise it, including by issuing any timely orders as the parties

---

225. See Law Decree No. 112 of 25 Jun. 2008 in [2008] GURI (Italian Official Gazette) 147. A further postponement to 30 June 2009 was provided by a Law Decree on 18 Dec. 2008.
226. See the heading of Article 13 of Legislative Decree No. 185 of 22 May 1999 on the '*implementation of Directive 97/7/EC on the protection of consumers in respect of distance contracts*', now incorporated into the Italian Consumer Cod.
227. For the huge difficulties encountered in finding appropriate legal terms in Italian to translate the US notion of 'class action', because of the great 'system-specific' differences between the two legal frameworks, see the extensive and deep analysis by C. Consolo, 'Class actions fuori dagli USA? (Un'indagine preliminare sul versante della tutela dei crediti di massa: funzione sostanziale e struttura processuale minima)' [1993] Riv. dir. civ. I, 609 ff., passim. About the same issue and by the same author (together with R. B. Cappalli), see 'Class Action for Continental Europe: A Preliminary Inquiry' [1993] 6 Temple Int'l and Comp. L.J., 217.

may have moved for – to produce all the documents available to it in relation to the case, and not only those that party believes it appropriate to produce in its own best interests. Therefore, the process is capable in itself to afford full knowledge of the relevant documents to the party on which the burden of proof is placed – which results in considerable benefits for complainants in a class action.

Major procedural aspects of US civil actions are: the questioning of witnesses by each party's at its unobstructed discretion about any admissible issue in direct and cross-examination; the possibility that, by the judgment rendered at the end of the proceedings, 'punitive damages' can be awarded against the party liable for the violation in issue, so long as that party's is found to have acted out of fraud or gross negligence; the fact that a civil action for damages is decided by jury trial; and the challenge system in which, where appeal is expressly admitted following a preliminary examination by the judge into its 'possible' grounds, it is usually limited to just one further stage, resulting in considerable time savings throughout the proceeding, as contrasted with the average length of an Italian lawsuit (i.e. two to three years in the USA versus ten or more years in Italy).[228]

Specifically, the Italian collective redress mechanism, in addition to be poorly efficient for the reasons offered above, is also far less effective than a genuine class action both in terms of the parties to the action and *ratione materiae*. For eligible complainants may only be trade associations or committees representing 'consumers' or 'users',[229] under a norm intentionally incorporated into the Consumer Code, and the defendant may only be an individual 'undertaking' or a 'group of undertakings', while only certain matters, precisely because of the limited range of issues in respect of which collective actions are available.

The *exclusion* of collective actions against *public administrations* in Italy is removed even farther from the US type of class actions.[230] This exclusion is open to criticism even in light of the Italian legal system, because of the constitutional

228. See Santa Maria, 'Proposta senza appigli comunitari', article published in *Il Sole 24 Ore* of 24 Dec. 2007, p. 32. In highlighting such deep structural differences, I also pointed out in that article that the European Commissioner for consumer protection, Ms Meglena Kuneva, in her speech '*Healthy markets need effective redress*' delivered in Lisbon on 10 Nov. 2007, stated her opposition to the introduction of any form of class action in Europe. She added that, if any form of action for collective redress were otherwise allowed within the Community, it ought not to have the punitive thrust of a class action American-style, and the introduction of 'unmeritorious claims' should suitably be discouraged anyhow.

229. Such dual identification can hardly be found in relation to class actions brought by counsel on behalf of actual or potential clients having *collective* or *class* interests. In this respect, the competent court is required to take special precautionary steps, first among which the verification and assessment, within the full scope of the court's discretion, of the counsel's entitlement adequately to represent the defence of the *collective interests* at stake.

230. A well-known federal class action was *Brown v. Board of Education of the City of Topeka* (1951-1954), 347 U.S. 483 (1954), which originated the US Supreme Court's decision that put an end to racial segregation in the educational institutions across the nation. It all began as an action brought by the parents of some coloured students before the Federal District Court of Kansas against the Board of Education of Topeka responsible for applying racial discrimination in the local schools in contrast with the Federal Constitution, albeit in furtherance of an older decision delivered by the US Supreme Court (in *Plessy v. Ferguson* 163 U.S. 537, 1896)

principle of the equal treatment of all citizens before the law and of the *inviolable* right of defence, and of the right to bring action, including against acts of administrative agencies, for the judicial protection of *legitimate interests* (Articles 3, 24 and 113, respectively, of the Italian Constitution). If one considers that a subjective right to be awarded damages has been recognized in Italy, at least since 1999, in respect of losses incurred as a result of a public administration violating their constituencies' legitimate interests, it is just fair to wonder why no attempt has been made to provide for an '*azione collettiva risarcitoria*' in this area as well. For cases of unlawful conduct by public agencies may well occur which could be treated as cases of private liability for violations. (Just think of the competition authority's possible joint liability for failure to act in the case of a violation committed by a listed company, or of the Bank of Italy's failure to exercise due supervision in the case of violations committed by a credit organization or by any other financial institution).

In this respect, the 'Italian choice' appears to be as reductive as short-sighted. One example is a phenomenon which has only recently highlighted by the media, although it has been a chronic disease for some fifteen years, i.e. the inability to carry out adequate waste disposal in the urban areas of Campania. A collective legal action for damages may well be brought by *ad-hoc* committees or environmental protection associations, in relation to injuries caused to health or to the environment, against the (poorly solvent) public, private or mixed undertakings responsible for the collection and destruction or consolidation of urban waste, but not against the public bodies (municipal, provincial, regional or State agencies) that must ultimately be blamed as the real perpetrators of such a catastrophic predicament.

Still, the *Italian collective redress device* has the underlying rationale in common with the American class action,[231] i.e. the best possible protection of *collective interests*.

---

and of certain state laws endorsing the practice of 'separate but equal' schools on racial bases. The possibility to bring a class action against an administrative agency, whether at a local, state or federal level, dated, in fact, further back in time, since one of the predecessors of the present-time class action was the 'taxpayer's suit', which could (and still can) be brought by any individual whose income is subjected to charges imposed by the state or federal government, for the benefit of that individual *and others* in order to prevent the unlawful diversion of public funds.

231. In recent years, two major reforms have been introduced at a federal level in the United States, with a view (hopefully) to curbing any real or assumed 'abused' of the class action device. More specifically, one such reform was the result of the many amendments and additions made on 1 Dec. 2003 to Rule 23 Fed. R. Civ. Proc., (the general federal rule of procedure that defines the requirements and regulate the peculiarities of class actions brought before federal courts), and of the subsequent Class Action Fairness Act of 2005, whereby the US Congress, after over ten years' efforts and parliamentary debates, approved a reform of the criteria for the internal allocation of class action cases between state and federal courts. In particular, the Amendments of 2003 concerned: (a) the pre-trial phase of 'class certification' (the stage at which the federal court seised of the case assesses whether the class action in question can lawfully and conveniently proceed as such), by regulating in details the selection of the class counsel;

In brief, the final text of Article 140-*bis* of the Consumer Code[232] provides for:

- legal actions for 'the protection of consumers' and users' collective interests', intended to '*establish individual consumers or users' right* to be awarded damages or to recover sums of money', which can be brought against any '*undertaking*' within the framework of 'legal relationships relating to *contracts concluded under Article 1342 of the Civil Code* or as a result of non-contractual unlawful acts, *improper trade practices* or *competition-restricting behaviours*', so long as there has been an *injury to 'the rights of a plurality of consumers or users*' (Article 140-*bis*(1));
- subject-matter jurisdiction of district courts, which are required to sit each as a panel (Article 2(448) of the Finance Act amending Article 50-*bis* of the Code of Civil Procedure by adding a paragraph 7-*bis*);
- territorial jurisdiction of the 'forum *of the undertaking*' so sued, so that the relevant complaint must be filed with 'the district court of the place in which the undertaking has its registered office' (Article 140-*bis*(1));
- *locus standi* to bring action accorded to consumerist associations registered in the Ministerial Registry provided for by Article 139 of the Consumer Code, and to the '*other entities specified in paragraph 2*', i.e. any other

---

(b) provisions for the non-contentious decision of the case (by settlement, voluntary dismissal or compromise), by specifying the forms thereof and adequate guarantees for absent class members; and (c) provisions for awarding attorney fees and non-taxable costs, by increasing the court's supervisory and review powers. The Class Action Fairness Act of 2005 dealt with federal rules on jurisdiction outside the body of the federal rules of civil procedure, and extended federal district courts' jurisdiction, by according them jurisdiction of any civil action in which the matter in controversy exceeds the sum or value of $5,000,000, and in which any member of a class of plaintiffs is a citizen of a State different from any defendant, any member of a class of plaintiffs is a foreign state or a citizen or subject of a foreign state and any defendant is a citizen of a State, or any member of a class of plaintiffs is a citizen of a State and any defendant is a foreign state or a citizen or subject of a foreign state. The Act also vested federal district courts with the power to decline to exercise jurisdiction in favour of state courts based on subjective and objective factors of close connection of the controversy with a specific state forum, and such surrender of jurisdiction was made mandatory in cases of even closer connection. The Act further introduced certain provisions for the protection of 'consumers' in collective settlements entailing awards 'in kind' ('coupon settlements'), in order to subject attorney fees to restrictions and judicial supervision, to avoid discrimination based on the geographic location of class members, and to favour the enforcement of general or legislative measures to solve any collective issues originating the controversy.

232. See the text proposed by the Government and signed by Minister Bersani in Jul. 2006 (AC 1495), which was used as a script – through the Bordon-Manzione Amendment adopted by the Senate on 15 Nov. 2007 – for the provisions being commented below. See also, 'Disposizioni per l'introduzione della class action' (Benvenuto, AS 679); 'Modifiche all'art. 140 del codice del consumo' (Maran, AC 1289); 'Nuove norme in materia di azione collettiva' (Fabris AC 1330); 'Disciplina dell'azione giudiziaria collettiva' (Poretti e Capezzone AC 1443); 'Introduzione dell'art. 141-bis del codice di cui al decreto legislativo 6 sett. 2005' (Buemi, Turci, Fluvi, Tolotti e altri, AC 1662), based on a draft bill released by the Chamber of Deputies in Jul. 2004; and 'Introduzione del sistema processuale dell'azione collettiva risarcitoria' (Pedica, Grillini, Crapolicchio, AC 1834, AC 1882, AC 1883).

association or committee '*adequately representing the collective interests so pleaded*' (*ibid.*, paras 1 and 2);

- the right of individual consumers or users wishing to rely on the collective protection defended by representative associations or by any of the 'other entities' mentioned above to notify the complaining entity in writing of '*their accession to the collective action*', which may be conducted across the two stages of the proceedings on the merits '*until the hearing of qualified claims*' on appeal (second sentence of para. 2);
- the capability both of the writ introducing a collective action and of the acts of any individual consumers or users wishing to accede as indicated above to cause the suspension of the applicable period of limitations '*pursuant to Article 2945 of the Civil Code*' (third sentence of para. 2);
- preliminary summary cognizance by the competent 'district court' (without any indication as to whether sitting as a panel or as a single examining judge) at the first hearing, with a view to a ruling on the admissibility of the application for collective protection according to the (somehow unspecific) criteria of *manifest groundlessness, conflict of interests* or *non-existence 'of a collective interest eligible for adequate protection under this Article 140*' (first sentence of para. 3);
- the right to apply to a Court of Appeal (sitting in Chambers) against an order whereby a district court has ruled on the admissibility of the action (*ibid.*, second sentence);
- the competent court's discretion '*to defer a ruling while the same issue is being examined by an independent authority*' (*ibid.*, third sentence);
- the duty of the entity bringing collective action to give '*suitable publicity*' to the contents thereof in case the collective action has been admitted to proceedings on the merits (*ibid.*, fourth sentence);
- rules on the contents of the collective judgment granting the complaint, which, *in assessing the unlawfulness of the sued undertaking's conduct*, must '*determine the criteria according to which the amounts to be awarded to, or to be recovered by, the individual consumers or users that have acceded to the collective action shall be calculated*', including an indication, so long as this is allowed under the findings reached in the proceedings, as to the minimum amount each injured party is entitled to receive from that undertaking (first and second sentences of para. 4);
- the option accorded to the undertaking found liable for the collective violation to propose, by a notice in writing to be served on the parties concerned and to be filed with the court clerk within 60 days of 'the judgment being notified', to pay each entitled party an amount, the acceptance of which, '*in any form*', by the consumer or user concerned will be treated as '*an enforceable title*' (third sentence of para, 4);
- an express rule whereby a judgment delivered in a collective action '*is enforceable*' not only between the complaining association or committee and the defending undertaking, but also '*in respect of the consumers and users who have acceded to the action*', without prejudice for any action as

may be brought by any individual consumers or users who were not involved in the action, whether because they had not acceded to it at the very start or because they had not acceded at any time thereafter (para. 5);

- the duty of the adjudging district court, in case the responsible undertaking has failed promptly to submit the voluntary proposal indicated above, or the recipients thereof have not accepted it within 60 days of the relevant notice, to set up an *ad-hoc* 'single' conciliation panel of counsel designated by the parties to the action, standing on an equal footing with one another, and chaired by a Supreme Court barrister appointed by the President of the competent district court, with the task of '*determining the amounts to be awarded to, or to be recovered by, the individual consumers or users that have acceded to the collective action*' (para. 6);
- the 'quantification' by the conciliation panel, in a record signed by the Chair and to be treated as an enforceable title, of the details of the amounts awarded to the individual injured parties, regardless of whether each had acceded at the start or during cognizance proceedings, so long as they '*have filed an application to that effect*' (second and third sentences of para. 6); and
- in the alternative – upon a motion from the complainants and the defendant in agreement between them, and by an order issued by the relevant district court's President – a procedure of '*non-contentious settlement . . . before one of the conciliation bodies*' provided for in the legislative decree relating to the so-called 'rules of company law procedure' (Articles 38, 39 and 40 of Legislative Decree No. 5 of 17 January 2003), which conciliation body must have its seat in the municipal area in which the relevant district court is sited (fourth and fifth sentences of para. 6).

In its recent White Paper often referred to in this Chapter VI, the European Commission considered that there was a clear need for mechanisms allowing aggregation of the individual claims of victims of antitrust infringements. In this connection, it suggested a combination of two complementary mechanisms of collective redress:

- *representative actions*, which are brought by *qualified entities*, such as consumer associations, state bodies or trade associations, which are either officially designated in advance or certified on an *ad hoc* basis by a Member State for a particular antitrust infringement to bring an action on behalf of identified or, in rather restricted cases, identifiable 'victims'; and
- '*opt-in*' *collective actions*, in which victims *expressly decide* to combine their individual claims for harm they suffered *into one single action.*

In the Commission's view, considering that qualified entities will not be able or willing to pursue every claim, it is necessary that these two types of action complement each other to ensure effective collective redress for victims of antitrust infringements.

In addition, the Commission considered it was important that victims are not deprived of their right to bring an *individual action for damages* if they so wish, except that safeguards should be put in place *to avoid that the same harm is compensated more than once*.

As for Italian law, the newly introduced Article 140-*bis* provides that a 'collective redress action' can be brought, *inter alia*, as a result of '*improper trade practices or competition-restricting behaviours*', so long as there has been an injury to '*the rights of a plurality of consumers or users*'.

Thus, the provisions of Italian law so newly introduced expressly contemplate a form of protection described as 'redress' also in cases falling within the scope of the White Paper, i.e. with regard to infringements of antitrust rules.

As for the entities having standing to act, Article 140-*bis*(1) accords the right to bring action for '*the protection of consumers' and users' collective interests*' to the associations contemplated in Article 139 of the Consumer Code, thus to any representative entities 'qualified' by proven indicators of due representation and registered, as such, in a special registry maintained at the Italian Ministry for Productive Activities. The underlying criterion is the 'traditional' *jus standi* principle, fully in line with the suggestion submitted by the White Paper – though by using that hardly appropriate phrase, '*representative actions*' – which is most likely to lead up to misunderstandings (especially in respect of the first of the two eligibility requirements).

Further, the new Italian provisions give standing to 'other entities' as well, i.e. '*associations and committees adequately representing the collective interests being pleaded*', whose *locus standi* cannot be assessed *ex ante* and in general terms at the time of being entered into a ministerial registry, which is not provided in their case, but only *ex post*, specifically by the court applied to collectively, in the 'screening' hearing required to be held under Article 140-*bis*(3) of the Consumer Code.

In fact, at a closer look, even actions brought by 'other entities' can be categorized as 'representative actions' within the meaning of the White Paper, where the entities to be considered as having good standing include entities:

> certified on an *ad hoc* basis by a Member State for a particular antitrust infringement to bring an action on behalf of some or all of their members.

Moreover, if one considers that the new Article 140-*bis*(5) of the Consumer Code explicitly states that judgments delivered in 'collective redress actions' shall have 'the effect of being also enforceable with respect to any consumers and users who have acceded to the collective action', *without prejudice to any individual actions* as might be brought by non-acceding parties, the reach of the so-called 'collective redress actions' can be deemed to be limited by law to *the acceding parties alone*. If this is the case, there are many similarities with the second eligibility requirement stated in the White Paper, which suggests the introduction of:

> opt-in collective actions, in which victims expressly decide to combine their individual claims for harm they suffered into one single action. [*Emphasis added*].

In light of the foregoing observations about *ius standi*, specifically as to the close adherence of the Italian 'collective redress action' to the device suggested by the

EC Commission in the White Paper, it is clear that neither has introduced a mechanism somehow similar to the genuine USA 'class action' into the Italian system or in the Community system, respectively.

For the structure suggested in the White Paper appears to be patterned after either (i) the 'traditional' model of the so-called '*representative actions*' (which should more aptly be termed 'associative actions' or 'collective actions' *stricto sensu*) allowed to be brought by collective, not-for-profit entities or even by governmental institutions, or (ii) that different model, the 'opt-in collective action', which more closely resembles a form of class action that was, in fact, cast off in the United States over forty years ago.

Thus, the *azione collettiva risarcitoria* introduced by the Italian law-makers appears to be partly a collective action of the kind suggested in the White Paper (the 'opt-in' action) and to fall almost entirely within the continental category of actions brought by representative entities qualified either *ex ante* or *ex post factum*.

Generally, based on Rule 23(b)(3) of the US Federal Rules of Civil Procedure, a class action *automatically includes all* members of the class, who must be adequately represented and informed, *except* those who voluntarily and timely choose to opt out (so-called 'individual opt-out right') – a nonsense that rules out the very possibility of individual 'exits'.

Indeed, the class defined by class certification is mandatory in two specific instances of class action (as provided for by Rule 23(b)(1) and (b)(2), Fed. R. Civ. Proc.), in the sense that individual 'exits' are prohibited.

Therefore, if opting-out is the rule under the US federal system of civil procedure (which provides the benchmark for most of the state statutes in the matter), the exception is by no means opting-in (the opt-in mechanism having been abandoned as early as 1966), but the 'closed' class action, which allows for no exits at any time.[233]

Only the laws of Denmark, Portugal and The Netherlands, among the EU Member States, have provided for actions intended to protect the rights of an entire class save for voluntary 'defections' (opt-out system), although each such law is far removed from the others both in its subjective scope for application and *ratione materiae*. For example, the Portuguese collective action, which is based on similar Brazilian rules, can only be brought by a public prosecutor.

The White Paper on damages actions for breach of the EC antitrust rules was presented as 'part of the Commission's wider initiative to strengthen collective redress mechanisms in the EU'.[234]

In general terms, the Commission's so-called 'DG SANCO' (Health and Consumers) *expressly stated its disagreement* on the introduction in Europe of any

233. For this issue viewed as one arising in 'mass tort litigations', refer to Benatti, *Correggere e punire*, p. 42 ff., narrative and footnotes, especially fn. 137 for the four core requirements of a class action under Rule 23, and fn. 138 for an examination of the earliest Italian literature on the subject.
234. See para. 2.1 of the *White Paper*, and paras 62-64 of the *Commission Staff Working Paper*.

form of class action patterned after the USA device.[235] According to Commissioner Kuneva, any collective action as might be introduced in the Community should not have the punitive thrust of a class action American-style, and the introduction of 'unmeritorious claims' should suitably be discouraged anyhow.

In fact, the Commission itself is considering the advisability for the Community to introduce a 'collective redress mechanism' (a vague, unspecific concept indeed[236]) by year-end 2008, with a view to protecting consumers against infringements of rules on consumer protection or on competition.[237]

For the sake of completeness, it should be noted that there are already specific instruments of Community legislation which provide for the collective protection of consumers.[238] One is Directive 98/27/EC of the European Parliament and of the Council of 19 May 1998, relating to the approximation of the Member States' laws through the provision of *uniform injunctions* for the protection of consumers' interests, as already provided for in a number of specific directives.[239] Another instrument is Regulation (EC) No. 861/2007 of the European Parliament and of the Council of 11 July 2007 establishing a European Small Claims Procedure.[240]

Under the new Italian rules on 'collective redress actions', the protection of collective interests contemplated in Article 140-*bis* of the Consumer Code is solely the protection of '*the rights of a plurality of consumers or users*', where any '*improper trade practices or competition-restricting behaviours*' have harmed such rights. In this respect, Article 140-*bis*(1) is quite clear in requiring that there must have been an injury to '*the rights of a plurality of consumers or users*'.

The protection by 'redress' provided for by Article 140-*bis* of the Consumer Code, whatever its actual scope and contents may be, is intended to ensure 'the *compensation for loss and the repayment of the sums owing to individual consumers and users*', who, as a rule, are *only indirectly and reflectively affected* by an undertaking's competition-restricting behaviours. In this respect, the provisions so

235. Please, refer to the speech on '*Healthy markets need effective redress*' addressed by Commissioner (Ms) Meglena Kuneva to the *Conference on Collective Redress* in Lisbon on 10 Nov. 2007.
236. In her speech of 10 Nov. 2007, Ms Kuneva indicated the ten benchmarks that effective and efficient redress systems should respect.
237. See the Commission Communication of 13 Mar. 2007 (*EU Consumer Policy Strategy 2007-2013*), especially p. 11. See also Commissioner Kuneva's speech of 10 Nov. 2007 quoted above, and her speech at the seminar on Collective Redress, Leuven, of 29 Jun. 2007. See Commission's Green Paper on Consumer Collective Redress published on 27 Nov. 2008, COM (2008) 794 fin.
238. By its Green Paper of 8 Feb. 2007 on the Review of the Consumer Acquis, the Commission proposed to review eight EU consumer protection directives (85/577/EEC, 90/314/EEC, 93/13/EEC, 94/47/EC, 97/7/ EC, 98/6/CE, 98/27/ EC and 99/44/ EC) with a view to the creation of the so-called '*consumer internal market*'. At the end of the exercise, the Commission maintained, it should, ideally, be possible to say to EU consumers 'wherever you are in the EU or wherever you buy from it makes no difference: your essential rights are the same'.
239. [1998] O.J. L166, p. 51, as repeatedly amended. Annex I to Directive 98/27/EC refers to the following directives on consumer protection: 85/577/EEC, 87/102/EEC, 89/552/EEC, 90/314/EEC, 92/28/EEC, 93/13/EEC, 94/47/EC, 97/7/EC, 99/44/EC, 2000/31/EC, 2002/65/EC, 2005/29/EC and 2006/123/EC.
240. [2007] O.J. L1999, p. 1.

newly introduced by the Italian Parliament appear to be stricter than those proposed at a Community level.

When the complex – though certainly not organic or even the less exhaustive – set of rules in the six paragraphs of Article 140-*bis* of the Consumer Code is compared with the suggestions offered in the White Book, the first finding is that the new Italian 'collective redress action' is not a veritable redress action, since its outcome is a judgment not actually providing an enforceable title for the benefit of the individual complainants, who will, therefore, have either to take action for conciliation *post sententiam*, under Article 140-*bis*(6) of the Consumer Code, or to seek individual redress in court, perhaps through an injunction if the judge in the collective action has fixed the minimum amount of damages to be awarded pursuant to Article 140-*bis*(4) of the Consumer Code. In this, the Italian device departs from the clear, albeit vague, suggestions offered by the Commission.

The most apparent weaknesses of the new Italian procedural system as contrasted with the Community framework seem to be the rules on evidence, the relationship of the damages judgments with any declaratory measures *de eadem re* as may be taken by antitrust authorities, and costs.

For the Italian body of rules in this matter stands out for its 'deafening' silence both as to the manners of collecting, receiving and assessing evidence (whereas the White Book has suggested a tentative and wary form of discovery) and as to assessment of costs – which is, in fact, a crucial requirement for a collective action not to amount to a 'dead-letter right'.

As for the rules on the relationships with antitrust authorities, the Italian system's departure from the European project is most apparent. Article 140-*bis*(3), second part, of the Consumer Code grants discretion to the judge in a collective action:

> to defer a ruling on the admissibility of claims while the same issue is being examined by an independent authority.

Further to utter silence on the effects of an administrative decision already taken by the antitrust authority on the same unlawful conduct, the discretion so granted exposes the Italian law-maker's deliberate choice to depart from the Community model, which tends to make administrative decisions automatically binding in subsequent civil proceedings for damages.

This is an unprecedented approach in the Italian legal system, and it seems to be inspired by Article 16(1) of Regulation (EC) No. 1/2003 (now fully mirrored by paragraph 2.3 of the White Paper), which specifically requires national courts to conform to any decisions on competition which the Commission has adopted or contemplates in proceedings it has initiated.

However, Regulation (EC) No. 1/2003 does not place a similar duty to stay proceedings on national courts when such proceedings *are pending* before the relevant NCAs in compliance with the rules of Community competition law.[241]

241. The *White Paper* itself confers 'binding effect only on decisions that are final, i.e. where the defendant has exhausted all appeal avenues'.

23. ITALIAN COURTS' JURISDICTION IN COLLECTIVE REDRESS ACTIONS AND COMMUNITY LAW

A parenthetical sentence in Article 2(445) of the Italian Finance Act refers, as has become customary for the Italian Parliament to do in law-making, to the '*principles laid down in Community law*' to which the new act expressly states it is intended to conform.

There can be no doubt within the EU framework as to the fact that the Italian courts' jurisdiction over 'collective actions', as the first issue the Italian legislator ought to have correctly dealt with, must be determined on the basis of Regulation (EC) No. 44/2001 of 22 December 2000 of the Council ('Brussels I'), as amended with *corrigenda*.[242] For the new form of legal action obviously falls within the scope for application of that Regulation (Article 1(1)) and cannot possibly be deemed to be one of the exclusions provided for in Article 1(2).

Therefore, the core principle of the 'domicile' or 'seat' of the defendant, be it a natural or a legal person, as both terms are defined in Article 59 and Article 60, respectively, of the Regulation, must apply to collective actions.

Yet, beside the general forum, there are special forums available by derogation from the general and other alternative forums.

In the first respect, jurisdiction covers *any 'contract' concluded by a 'consumer'* 'for a purpose which can be regarded as being outside his trade or profession', in the broad sense emerging from the Regulation just cited, if:

(a) it is a contract for the sale of goods on instalment credit terms; or
(b) it is a contract for a loan repayable by instalments, or for any other form of credit, made to finance the sale of goods; or
(c) in all other cases, the contract has been concluded with a person who pursues commercial or professional activities in the Member State of the consumer's domicile or, by any means, directs such activities to that Member State or to several States including that Member State, and the contract falls within the scope of such activities. (Article 15(1)).

Pursuant to Article 16(1) and (2) of the Regulation, a consumer has a *choice* to bring proceedings against the other party to a contract either in the courts for the place where *he is domiciled* or in the courts of the Member State in which that other party *is domiciled*, whereas such other party may bring proceedings against the

---

242. Published in [2001] O.J. L12, p. 1. *Corrigendum* in [2001] O.J. L307, p. 28, as amended by Regulation (EC) No. 1496/2002 of 21 Aug. 2002 of the Commission ([2002] O.J. L225, p. 13), of the Act concerning the conditions of accession of the Czech Republic, the Republic of Estonia, the Republic of Cyprus, the Republic of Latvia, the Republic of Lithuania, the Republic of Hungary, the Republic of Malta, the Republic of Poland, the Republic of Slovenia and the Slovak Republic and the adjustments to the Treaties on which the European Union is founded ([2003] O.J. L236, p. 33), by Regulation (EC) No. 1937/2004 of 9 Nov. 2004 of the Commission ([2004] O.J. L334, p. 3), and by Regulation (EC) No. 2245/2004 of 27 Dec. 2004 of the Commission ([2004] O.J. L381, p. 10).

consumer 'only in the courts of the Member State in which the consumer is domiciled'.[243]

As, 'any legal relationships relating to contracts concluded by consumers or users pursuant to Article 1342 of the Civil Code', in the words of the new Italian law, are among those provided for by Regulation 44/2001, the indication of the undertaking's forum in a collective redress action or in an action brought for losses arising from such legal relationships against a foreign 'Community' defendant, may quietly be disregarded by any consumer association or committee, which will be fully entitled to sue that undertaking in Italy before the courts of the place in which just *one* of the consumers represented by it is domiciled.

As used in the text of Article 140-*bis* of the Consumer Code, the phrase '*consumers or users*' should not be misunderstood, though, since it refers to any legal relationships concerning consumers *lato sensu.*

In point of terminology, the distinction is justified in that the former word refers to 'consumers of goods' and the latter to 'users of services'. But such a distinction has been introduced merely for purposes of lexical accuracy.

For it appears quite clearly both from the comprehensive formulation of Article 15 of Regulation (EC) 44/2000 and from the various directives in the matter[244] that the phrase 'consumer contracts' plainly includes contracts envisaging an *offer-and-purchase* of services.

In fact, this is the sense both of the ECJ's judgments in *Benincasa* and in *Gruber* and of Advocate General Jacobs' Opinion in the latter case.[245] In particular, in many a ground for the *Gruber* judgment, the Court of Justice referred to the treatment invariably applied to consumers in cases of 'use of the goods or services concerned'.[246]

That the Italian legislator, in drafting the provisions for the new collective action, underrated – not to say utterly disregarded – the existence of Italian rules of civil procedure interlocked with Community regulatory norms, which, as such, prevail over, and override, any rules of domestic law conflicting therewith, is shown once again by the introduction in Regulation 44/2001 of *ad-hoc*

---

243. For the notion of domicile of natural persons or companies or other legal persons, please refer to Art. 59 and 60 of the Regulation in question.

244. See, for example, Council Directive 93/13/EEC of 5 Apr. 1993 on unfair terms in consumer contracts [1993] O.J. L95. In particular, see Art. 2 and 4 and some Whereases thereof, from which it can be inferred that the notion of '*consumer contracts*' also includes the provision of services. Likewise, see Directive 97/7/EC of the European Parliament and of the Council of 20 May 1997 on the protection of consumers in respect of distance contracts, in [1997] O.J. L144, p. 19 (see Art. 2(1), definition of '*distance contract*').

245. Judgment of the ECJ of 3 Jul. 1997, Case C-269/95, *Benincasa*, grounds 11-19; AG Jacobs's Opinion of 16 Sep. 2004, Case C-464/01, *Gruber*, paras 20-28, and the judgment of 20 Jan. 2005 in Gruber, in particular ground 36 ff. These instruments provide an interpretation of '*consumer contracts*' within the meaning of Art. 13-15 of the Brussels Convention (now Art. 15 ff. of Regulation (EC) 44/2001). On this point, see also Gambaro & Landi, 'Consumer Contracts and Jurisdiction, Recognition and Enforcement of Judgments in Civil and Commercial Matters' [2006] European Business Law Review 5, 1355.

246. See, in particular, grounds 41, 42 and 45 of the *Gruber* judgment, cit.

provisions for matters relating to insurance contracts among the special criteria on jurisdiction.

One such provision is that an insurer may be sued, at the plaintiff's election, as well before the courts for the place where the plaintiff is domiciled, be it the policyholder, the insured or a beneficiary (Article 9(1)(b)), as before the national courts of the place where the harmful event occurred, in respect of liability insurance or insurance of movable and immovable property, if covered by the same insurance policy, or else before the courts for the place where proceedings for damages have already been brought against the insurer (Article 11 of Regulation 44/2001).

Thus, once again, in the case of 'cross-border' collective actions brought within the European Union in matters relating to insurance contracts, applying the special jurisdiction criteria laid down in Articles 9 to 11 of Regulation (EC) No. 44/2001, which certainly prevail over any conflicting rules of national law, seems to displace the choice of the sued undertaking's 'seat' as the exclusive jurisdiction criterion in the domain of collective actions.

In light of this umpteenth case of 'legislative absentmindedness' in the face of the *practical* consequences of national law rules increasingly interlocking with rules of Community law, all the statements of principle and impassioned references to Community law and its developments that are contained in the 'preamble' to the set of rules so newly introduced in the Italian system appear to be just hackneyed and empty phrases.

In connection with Community law, the other collective actions provided for in the new Italian rules of procedure – i.e. actions brought against a defendant, whether a natural or a legal person, who is a 'Community' foreign national, '*as a consequence of non-contractual unlawful acts, improper trade practices or competition-restricting behaviours*' – are also subject to *special jurisdiction*.

This is because, pursuant to Article 5 of Section 2 of Regulation 44/2001, a person domiciled in the territory of one Member State may alternatively be sued, at the plaintiff's election, either in another Member State, specifically:

> in matters relating to tort, delict or quasi-delict, in the courts for the place where the harmful event occurred or may occur [para. 3];

or:

> as regards a civil claim for damages or restitution which is based on an act giving rise to criminal proceedings, in the court seised of those proceedings, to the extent that that court has jurisdiction under its own law to entertain civil proceedings [para. 4].

As noted above, the 'unbreakable'[247] jurisdiction of the consumer's or the insured's courts in the terms indicated above, or the special jurisdiction of the *forum commissi delicti* – both provided for by a Community Regulation – will prevail

247. Subject to the departures allowed under Article 17 of Regulation 44/2001.

over any conflicting national rule, even if introduced at a later time. The obvious consequence is that, within the European Union, the criterion laid down in the first paragraph of Article 140-*bis* of the Italian Consumer Code merely (and unnecessarily) operates as a reference to the general criterion of the domicile (seat) of the undertaking being prosecuted, without otherwise ruling out that the other criteria specified above can be resorted to insofar as the relevant requirements are met.

An examination of the ordinary rules on jurisdiction would not bring about results any different from those emerging in respect of Community rules, because of the express reference made to Sections 2, 3 and 4 of Title II of the Brussels Convention of 22 September 1986, as amended, in Article 3(2) of Italian Act No. 218 of 31 May 1995 on a reform of the Italian private international law system. This is because, pursuant to Article 68 of Regulation No. 44/2001, 'in so far as this Regulation replaces the provisions of the Brussels Convention between Member States, any reference to the Convention shall be understood as a reference to this Regulation'.

Now, as indicated above, Sections 2, 3 and 4 of Chapter II of Regulation No. 44/2001 provide for special jurisdiction, jurisdiction in matters relating to insurance and jurisdiction over consumer contracts, respectively. Therefore, the reference made to the Brussels Convention in Article 3(2) of Act No. 218/1995, must be deemed automatically superseded by an appropriate reference to Regulation No. 44/2001, as a result of which the general rules are made identical to those for *direct* applicability between EU Member States under the Community law provisions examined above.

It should further be noted that identifying Italian district courts, each sitting as a panel, as the authorities of competent jurisdiction over collective claims for judicial protection is quite appropriate, because of the likely complexity of collective actions – not only in objective, but also in subjective terms, because of the individual parties' unaltered right to intervene by voluntary accession in *inter-alios* proceedings, a right affirmed rather unwisely in the second sentence of Article 140-*bis*(2), second sentence, of the Italian Consumer Act.

Lastly, it is my view that the choice of the ordinary cognizance procedure under Article 163 et seq. of the Italian Code of Civil Procedure, as now generally allowed in collective actions for the protection of consumers and users – much as certain rather humour-inclined draft bills demanded the application of company law rules of procedure to such actions, thereby dooming consumers' collective protection to unwarranted additional complications and costs – has resulted in a pressing need to asses the Constitutional legitimacy of the applicability of company law rules of procedure only to controversies:

> in matters provided for by Legislative Decree No 385 of 1 September 1993, when the controversy is brought by [. . .] associations representing consumers [. . .]

as Article 1(e) of Legislative Decree 5/2003 quite insensibly requires.

24. ASSESSMENT OF LOSS IN ANTITRUST CASES

In principle and in general terms, the issue of how to assess damages is a quite sensitive one.

The European Court of Justice has stressed that the victims of an antitrust infringement must be awarded compensation for *the full real value* of the loss suffered.[248] The entitlement to 'full' compensation should therefore extend not only to the actual loss caused by an anti-competitive price increase, but also to the loss of profit resulting from a reduction in sales, and it encompasses a right to interest.[249]

Well aware of the involved issues to be encountered in this domain, the Commission, in paragraph 2.5 of its White Paper on damages actions, observed:

> This calculation, implying a comparison with the economic situation of the victim in the *hypothetical scenario* of a competitive market, is often a very cumbersome exercise. It can become *excessively difficult* or even practically impossible, if the idea that the exact amount of the harm suffered must always be precisely calculated is strictly applied. Moreover, far-reaching calculation requirements can be disproportionate to the amount of damage suffered. [. . .]. *To facilitate the calculation of damages*, the Commission therefore intends to draw up a framework with pragmatic, non-binding guidance for *quantification* of damages in antitrust cases, e.g. by means of *approximate methods of calculation or simplified rules on estimating* the loss. [*Emphasis added*].

As for the Italian system, in the face of the terse wording of Article 33 of Act 287/1990, it is reasonable to believe that assessment of losses is subject to code-based rules, specifically the provisions of Article 2056 of the Civil Code[250] (headed '*assessment of loss*'), of Article 1223, Civ. Code (relating to the distinction between *damnum emergens* and *lucrum cessans*), of Article 1226, Civ. Code (relating to equitable assessment of losses) and of Article 1227, Civ. Code (relating to participation in a creditor's act of quasi-delict).

Yet, in the matter of losses from antitrust infringements, both case-law and literature have developed at least three theories: (i) the '*Asl Ob*' theory; (ii) the 'before and after' theory; and (iii) the 'yardstick' theory.

(i) The '*Asl Ob*' ('as if') theory is of German origin, entailing a comparison between the harmed person's *patrimonial situation* as it is following the infringement, and his purely hypothetical patrimonial situation as it would be had the infringement not been committed. It is a merely

248. See the *Manfredi* judgment, grounds 95 and 97.

249. On this, see also the judgments of the ECJ of 8 Mar. 2001, Joined Cases C-397/98 and C-410/98, *Metallgesellschaft*, [2001] ECR I-1727, ground 91, of 5 Mar. 1996, Joined Cases C-46/93 and C-48/93, *Brasserie du Pêcheur*, [1996] ECR I-1029, ground 87, and of 2 Aug. 1993, Case C-271/91, *Marshall*, [1993] ECR I-4367, punto 31.

250. Genovese, *Il risarcimento del danno da illecito concorrenziale* (Naples, 2005), 196; Bastianon, 'Violazione della normativa antitrust e risarcimento del danno' [1996] Danno e Resp., 555.

hypothetical kind of comparison, which calls on the court to identify the market conditions (such as prices or market shares) that would have prevailed if there had been no competition-restrictive behaviour.[251]

(ii) The 'before and after' theory is of North-American origin. The harmed enterprise's profits before the harmful event are compared with those after the event, so long as the two periods are comparable with each other. This method is the most widely used by the EU Member States' national courts in calculating antitrust damages.[252] Still, it must be pointed out that other occurrences (such as general changes across the market or the victim's conduct) may well affect the victim's financial position, thereby making the identification of the causality nexus between the violation and the harm very difficult.[253]

(iii) The 'yardstick' theory is based on a criterion, itself of American origin, according to which the profits posted by the harmed enterprise after the violation are compared with those of another enterprise with similar characteristics, which, though engaging in a comparable business activity, has remained unaffected by anticompetitive practices.[254]

Each of the three loss assessment technique just outlined above has some hit-and-miss elements, since they are based on comparisons with just assumed situations and on such financial information relating to competitor or third parties which can hardly be collected unless it is made available to the general public.

---

251. The '*Als Ob*' theory is useful in quantifying losses incurred by consumers as a consequence of an overcharge. See: Nivarra, 'Il 2° comma dell'art. 33. La tutela civile: profili sostanziali' in *Diritto antitrust italiano* (Pardolesi, Patroni Griffi, Ubertazzi) (Bologna 1993), 1457; Guizzi, 'Mercato concorrenziale e teoria del contratto' [1999] Riv. dir. comm. I, 124. See Telsystem/SIP, a case decided by the Milan Court of Appeal, in which damages were awarded under an order of 26 Nov.-24 Dec. 1996, in [1997] Danno e resp. 5, p. 602.
252. See Ashurst, Study on the condition of claims for damages in case of infringement of EC competition rules, 31 Aug. 2004; Prosperetti, 'Antitrust damages in Europe: an economic perspective' in Acta of the VII UAE-LIDC Conference on '*Antitrust between EC and national law*' (Treviso 18-19 May 2006). See Milan Court of Appeal, 30 Apr. 2003, *Bluvacanze c. Ventaglio/Turisanda.*
253. The 'Before and After Theory' is quite effective in establishing losses caused by boycott. See: Hovenkamp, *Federal Antitrust Policy* (St. Paul, Minn., 1999), 605; Gavil, Kovacic, Baker, *Antitrust law in prospective: cases, concepts and problems in competition policy* (Howard, 2002), 1049; Jones, *Private Enforcement of Antitrust Law in the EU, UK and USA* (Oxford, 1999), 202; Bastianon, 'Violazione della normativa antitrust e risarcimento del danno'; Bastianon, 'Abuso di posizione dominante e risarcimento dei danni' [2003] Danno e Resp., 1215; Page, *Proving antitrust damages* (Chicago, 1996), 37.
254. This theory could usefully been applied in assessing the losses incurred by an undertaking which was denied entry into the relevant market, by benchmarking its profits to the profits of another undertaking in the same market. See Hovenkamp, *Federal Antitrust Policy*, 619; Gavil, Kovacic, Baker, *Antitrust Law in Prospective*, 1051; Jones, *Private Enforcement of Antitrust Law in the EU, UK and USA*, 215; Bastianon, 'Abuso di posizione dominante e risarcimento dei danni'; Roma Court of Appeal of 20 Jan. 2003 [2003] Foro it. 9, I, 2474.

Still, because of their value as circumstantial indicators, these theories may prove useful, especially where damages are to be calculated on an equitable basis, for example under Article 2056 or 1226 of the Italian Civil Code. In fact, resorting to quantitative assessment of damages may even become necessary, because of the clear difficulty of determining each item of loss to any degree of accuracy. However, for equitable assessment not to be left to each judge's individual insight, it will have to be 'anchored' in each case to as detailed economic analyses as possible and to market indicators relevant to the case being assessed.[255] The findings so arrived at can be used by the judge, first to establish the *existence* of the alleged loss, then equitably to quantify the loss the existence of which has been shown.

For an Italian court to be able to quantify losses, the starting point is Article 1223 of the Civil Code, in which the two traditional elements of *damnum emergens* and *lucrum cessans* are identified and provided for.

The former element is the easier to be determined, since it is accounted for by the costs the complaining undertaking has incurred at a loss.

A more difficult exercise is to prove *lucrum cessans*. The difficulty lies in how to establish the difference between the affected undertaking's current condition and its 'but-for condition', i.e. the condition in which it would have found itself had the anticompetitive practice not been entered into.

Both legal literature and case-law have tended to view *lucrum cessans* as also including 'opportunity loss'[256] (itself a claim to be duly grounded and proved, in fact), i.e. any loss arising from gains the undertaking affected could have earned or, rather, contributed to earning, in the absence of the wrong complained for.

In other words, *lucrum cessans* consists in an enterprise's foregone profits. Still, all depends on a number of variables, and identifying the loss incurred or the gain foregone as a result of, and caused by, the infringement is by no means an easy task. For example, a mere reduction in turnover cannot be capable, by itself, to show a prejudice to the enterprise's competitive strength.[257]

The difficulty of arriving at an accurate determination of the loss suffered could be overcome, as indicated above, by the court's *equitable assessment* under Article 1226 of the Civil Code. Equitable assessment is a merely supplemental device, though. Thus, in addition to showing that the loss incurred was the result of the unlawful conduct (causality nexus), the amount of such loss must also be shown, even if only to an approximate extent.

---

255. 'In other words, in the sector under scrutiny, great care should be taken to avoid mistaking the mere difficulty to quantify the loss accurately for the impossibility to do so, because, since such difficulty is *in re ipsa*, so to say, the court may be led to an indiscriminate use of its power to adjudicate the case equitably.' See Bastianon, 'Abuso di posizione dominante e risarcimento dei danni', p. 563.
256. Milan Court of Appeal Order of 24 Dec. 1996 in *Telsystems v SIP* [1996] Danno e resp., 602, with commentary by Bastianon.
257. Nivarra, 'Il 2° comma dell'art. 33. La tutela civile: profili sostanziali', p. 1452; Vettori, *Concorrenza e mercato*, p. 230.

Any equitable quantification of damages will not release the plaintiff of the duty to provide grounds to, and give proof of, the amount of damages claimed. For the court may well equitably correct or alter the amounts stated by the parties, but it cannot disregard the legal principle that *it is for the plaintiff to show valid grounds for its claim.*[258]

258. Genovese, *Il risarcimento del danno da illecito concorrenziale*, p. 276.

List of Binding Acts of the EC Institutions

(a) Regulations

Council Regulation of 18 January 1982, No. 90/82, in [1982] O.J. L12/1
Commission Regulation of 28 June 1984, No. 1825/84, in [1984] O.J. L170/68
Council Regulation of 14 January 1985, No. 96/85, in [1985] O.J. L13/1
Council Regulation of 25 July 1985, No. 2137/85, in [1985] O.J. L199/1
Council Regulation of 12 August 1985, No. 2322/85, in [1985] O.J. L218/1
Commission Regulation of 1° August 1986, No. 2495/86, in [1986] O.J. L217/12
Commission Regulation of 21 August 1986, No. 2640/86, in [1986] O.J. L239/5
Commission Regulation of 4 September 1986, No. 2516/86, in [1986] O.J. L221/16
Council Regulation of 23 February 1987, No. 535/87, in [1987] O.J. L54/12
Council Regulation of 14 October 1988, No. 3322/88, in [1988] O.J. L297/1
Council Regulation of 11 July 1988, No. 2423/88, in [1988] O.J. L209
Council Regulation of 19 December 1991, No. 3924/91, in [1991] O.J. L374/1
Council Regulation of 7 March 1994, No. 517/94, in [1994] O.J. L67/1
Council Regulation of 7 March 1994, No. 519/94, in [1994] O.J. L67
Council Regulation of 22 December 1994, No. 3283/94, in [1994] O.J. L349
Council Regulation of 22 December 1994, No. 3285/94, in [1994] O.J. L349/53
Council Regulation of 22 January 1996, No. 139/96, in [1996] O.J. L21
Council Regulation of 25 November 1996, No. 2315/96, in [1996] O.J. L314
Council Regulation of 9 November 2000, No. 2474/2000, in [2000] O.J. L286/1
Council Regulation of 22 December 1994, No. 3286/94, in [1994] O.J. L349, p. 71
Council Regulation of 22 December 1994, No. 3320/94, in [1994] O.J. L350/27
Council Regulation of 20 February 1995, No. 356/95, in [1995] O.J. L41/3
Council Regulation of 22 December 1995, No. 384/96, in [1996] O.J. L56/1
Council Regulation of 2 December 1996, No. 2331/96, in [1996] O.J. L317/1

Council Regulation of 17 June 1997, No. 1103/97, in [1997] O.J. L162/1
Council Regulation of 30 June 1997, No. 1310/97, in [1997] O.J. L180/1
Council Regulation of 6 October 1997, No. 2026/97, in [1997] O.J. L288/1
Commission Regulation of 1° March 1998, No. 447/98, in [1998] O.J. L61/1
Council Regulation of 27 April 1998, No. 905/98, in [1998] O.J. L128/18
Council Regulation of 3 May 1998, No. 974/98, in [1998] O.J. L139/1
Council Regulation of 31 December 1998, No. 2866/98, in [1998] O.J. L359/1
Council Regulation of 29 May 2000, No. 1346/2000, in [2000] O.J. L160
Council Regulation of 29 May 2000, No. 1348/2000, in [2000] O.J. L160
Council Regulation of 9 October 2000, No. 2238/2000, in [2000] O.J. L257/2
Council Regulation of 27 November 2000, No. 2596/2000, in [2000] O.J. L300/2
Council Regulation of 22 December 2000, No. 44/2001, in [2001] O.J. L12/1
Commission Regulation of 12 January 2001, No. 70/2001, in [2001] O.J. L10/33
Council Regulation of 28 May 2001, No. 1206/2001, in [2001] O.J. L174/1
Council Regulation of'8 October 2001, No. 2157/2001, in [2001] O.J. L294/1
Council and European Parliament Regulation of 19 July 2002, No.1606/2002, in [2002] O.J. L243/1
Commission Regulation of 21 August 2002, No. 1496/2002, in [2002] O.J. L225/13
Council Regulation of 5 November 2002, No. 1972/2002, in [2002] O.J. L305/2
Council Regulation of 16 December 2002, No. 1/2003, in [2003] O.J. L1/1
Council Regulation of 21 January 2003, No. 138/2003, in [2003] L23/1
Council Regulation of 3 March 2003, No. 427/2003, in [2003] O.J. L65/1
Council Regulation of 22 July 2003, No. 1435/2003, in [2003] O.J. L207/1
Council Regulation of 27 November 2003, No. 2201/2003, in [2003] O.J. L338/1
Council Regulation of 15 December 2003, No. 2238/2003, in [2003] O.J. L333/1
Council Regulation of 20 January 2004, No. 139/2004, in [2004] O.J. L24/1
Council Regulation of'8 March 2004, No. 461/2004, in [2004] O.J. L77/12
Commission Regulation of 7 April 2004, No. 773/2004, in [2004] O.J. L123/18
Commission Regulation of 7 April 2004, No. 802/2004, in [2004] O.J. L133/1
Council and European Parliament Regulation of 21 April 2004, No. 805/2004, in [2004] O.J. L143/15
Commission Regulation of 9 November 2004, No. 1937/2004, in [2004] O.J. L334/3
Council Regulation of 13 December 2004, No. 2200/2004, in [2004] O.J. L374
Commission Regulation of 27 December 2004, No. 2245/2004, in [2004] O.J. L381/10
Council Regulation of 25 April 2005, No. 673/2005, in [2005] O.J. L110/1
Commission Regulation of 28 April 2005, No. 659/2005, in [2005] O.J. L108/17
Council Regulation of 27 June 2005, No. 980/2005, in [2005] O.J. L169/1
Council Regulation of 21 December 2005, No. 2117/2005, in [2005] O.J. L340/17
Council Regulation of 21 December 2005, No. 2169/2005, in [2005] O.J. L346/1
Commission Regulation of 22 December 2005, No. 317/2006, in [2006] O.J. L60/1
Commission Regulation of 24 April 2006, No. 632/2006, in [2006] O.J. L111/5
Council Regulation of 7 November 2006, No. 1647/2006, in [2006] O.J. L309/2
Council and European Parliament Regulation of 12 December 2006, No. 1896/2006, in [2006] O.J. L399/1

Commission Regulation of 20 December 2006, No. 1976/2006, in [2006] O.J. L368/85
Commission Regulation of 16 April 2007, No. 409/2007, in [2007] O.J. L100/16
Council Regulation of 10 July 2007, No. 835/2007, in [2007] O.J. L186/1
Council Regulation of 10 July 2007, No. 836/2007, in [2007] O.J. L186/3
Council and European Parliament Regulation of 11 July 2007, No. 861/2007, in [2007] O.J. L199/1
Council and European Parliament Regulation of 11 March 2008, No. 297/2008, in [2008] O.J. L97/62

(b) Directives

Council Directive of 11 May 1960, in [1960] O.J. 43/921
Council Directive of 18 December 1962, No. 63/21, in [1963] O.J. 9/62
Council Directive of 30 July 1963, No. 63/474, in [1963] O.J. L125/2240
Council Directive of 9 March 1968, No. 68/151, (First Directive), in [1968] O.J. L65/8
Council Directive of 15 October 1968, No. 68/360, in [1968] O. J. L257/13
Council Directive of 17 July 1969, No. 69/335, in [1969] O.J. L249/25
Council Directive of 21 March 1972, No. 72/156, in [1972] O.J. L91/13
Council Directive of 21 May 1973, No. 73/148, in [1973] O.J. L172/14
Council Directive of 13 December 1976, No. 77/91, (Second Directive), in [1977] L26/1
Council Directive of 17 May 1977, No. 77/388, in [1977] O.J. L145/1
Council Directive of 25 July 1978, No. 78/660, (Forth Directive), in [1978] O.J. L222/11
Council Directive of 9 October 1978, No. 78/855, (Third Directive), in [1978] O.J. L295/36
Council Directive of 25 June 1980, No. 80/723, in [1980] O.J. L195/35
Council Directive of 20 October 1980, No. 80/987, in [1980] O.J. L283/23
Council Directive of 17 December 1982, No. 82/891, (Sixth Directive), in [1982] O.J. L378/47
Council Directive of 13 June1983, No. 83/349, (Settima Directive), in [1983] O.J. L193/1
Council Directive of 27 November 1984, No. 84/569, in [1984] O.J. L314/1
Council Directive of 24 July 1985, No. 85/413, in [1985] O.J. L229/20
Council Directive of 20 December 1985, No. 85/611, in [1985] O.J. L375/3
Council Directive of 20 December 1985, No. 85/583, in [1985] O.J. L372/39
Council Directive of 17 November 1986, No. 86/566, in [1986] O.J. L332/22
Council Directive of 8 December 1986, No. 86/635, in [1986] O.J. L372/1
Council Directive of 22 March 1988, No. 88/220, in [1988] O.J. L100/31
Council Directive of 24 June 1988, No. 88/361, in [1988] O.J. L178/5
Council Directive of 21 December 1989, No. 89/666, (Eleventh Directive), in [1989] O.J. L395/36
Council Directive of 21 December 1989, No. 89/667, (Twelfth Directive), in [1989] O.J. L395/40

Council Directive of 23 July 1990, No. 90/434, in [1990] O.J. L225/1
Council Directive of 23 July 1990, No. 90/435, in [1990] O.J. L225/6
Council Directive of 8 November 1990, No. 90/604, in [1990] O.J. L317/57
Council Directive of 8 November 1990, No. 90/605, in [1990] O.J. L317/60
Council Directive of 10 June 1991, No. 91/308, in [1991] O.J. L166/77
Council Directive of 19 December 1991, No. 91/674, in [1991] O.J. L374/7
Council Directive of 23 November 1992, No. 92/101, in [1992] O.J. L347/64
Council Directive of 15 March 1993, No. 93/6, in [1993] O.J. L141/1
Council Directive of 5 April 1993, No. 93/13, in [1993] O.J. L95/29
Council Directive of 21 March 1994, No. 94/8, in [1994] O.J. L82/33
Council Directive of 22 September 1994, No. 94/45, in [1994] O.J. L254/64
Council and European Parliament Directive of 24 October 1995, No. 95/46, in [1995] O.J. L281/31
Council and European Parliament Directive of 20 May 1997, No. 97/7, in [1997] O.J. L144/19
Council and European Parliament Directive of 19 May 1998, No. 98/27, in [1998] O.J. L166/51
Council Directive of 17 June 1999, No. 99/60, in [1999] O.J. L162/1
Council and European Parliament Directive of 20 March 2000, No. 2000/12, in [2000] O.J. L126/1
Commission Directive of 26 July 2000, No. 2000/51, in [2000] O.J. L198/41
Council and European Parliament Directive of 27 September 2001, No. 01/65, in [2001] O.J. L283/1
Council Directive of 8 October 2001, No. 2001/86, in [2001] O.J. L294/22
Council Directive of 22 July 2003, No. 2003/72, in [2003] O.J. L207/25
Council and European Parliament Directive of 18 June 2003, No. 2003/51, in [2003] O.J. L178/16
Council and European Parliament Directive of 15 July 2003, No. 2003/58, in [2003] O.J. L221/13
Council and European Parliament Directive of 21 April 2004, No. 2004/25, (Thirteenth Directive), in [2004] O.J. L142/12
Council and European Parliament Directive of 21 April 2004, No. 2004/39, in [2004] O.J. L145/1
Council Directive of 17 February 2005, No. 2005/19, in [2005] O.J. L58/19
Council and European Parliament Directive of 26 October 2005, No. 2005/56, in [2005] O.J. L310/1
Council and European Parliament Directive of 17 May 2006, No. 2006/43, in [2006] O.J. L157/87
Council and European Parliament Directive of 14 June 2006, No. 2006/46, in [2006] O.J. L224/1
Council and European Parliament Directive of 14 June 2006, No. 2006/48, in [2006] O.J. L177/1
Council and European Parliament Directive of 14 June 2006, No. 2006/49, in [2006] O.J. L177/201
Commission Directive of 1° August 2006, No. 2006/70, in [2006] O.J. L214/29

Commission Directive of 10 August 2006, No. 2006/73, in [2006] O.J. L241/26
Council Directive of 6 September 2006, No. 2006/68, in [2006] O.J. L264/32
Commission Directive of 16 November 2006, No. 2006/111, in [2006] O.J. L318/17
Council Directive of 20 November 2006, No. 2006/98, in [2006] O.J. L363/129
Council Directive of 20 November 2006, No. 2006/99, in [2006] O.J. L363/137
Commission Directive of 8 March 2007, No. 2007/14, in [2007] O.J. L69/27
Commission Directive of 19 March 2007, No. 2007/16, in [2007] O.J. L79/11
Council and European Parliament Directive of 13 November 2007, No. 2007/63, in [2007] L300/47
Council and European Parliament Directive of' 11 March 2008, No. 2008/30, in [2008] O.J. L81/53

(c) Decisions

Commission Decision of 11 March 1964, No. 64/233, *Grosfillex* v. *Fillistorf*, in [1964] O.J. 58/915
Commission Decision of 1° June 1964, No. 64/344, *Anciens Etablissements Mertens et Straet*, in [1964] O.J. 92/1426
Commission Decision of 22 October 1964, No. 64/599, *Dutch Engineers and Contractors Association* (*D.E.C.A.*), in [1964] O.J. 173/2761
Commission Decision of 6 November 1968, No. 68/276, *Rieckermann AEG – Elotherm,* in [1968] O.J. L276/25
Commission Decision of 18 June 1969, No. 69/195, *Christiani & Nielsen,* in [1969] O.J. L165/12
Commission Decision of 16 July 1969, No. 69/240, *Intesa della chinina,* in [1969] O.J. L192/5
Commission Decision of 24 July 1969, No. 69/243, *Materie coloranti,* in [1969] O.J. L195/11
Commission Decision of 30 June 1970, No. 70/332, *Kodak*, in [1970] O.J. L147/24
Commission Decision of 21 December 1973, No. 73/16, *Transocean Marine Paint Association,* in [1974] O.J. L19/18
Commission Decision of 10 December 1982, No. 82/860, *Cafeteros de Colombia,* in [1982] O.J. L360/31
Commission Decision of 19 December 1984, No. 84/202, *Wood Pulp*, in [1985] O.J. L85/1
Commission Decision of 9 June 1986, No. 86/232, accepting undertakings given in connection with the antidumping proceeding concerning imports of hardboard originating in Argentina, Switzerland and Yugoslavia and terminating the investigation, in [1986] O.J. L157/61
Commission Decision of 5 September 1986, No. 2767/86, imposing a provisional anti-dumping duty on imports of certain sheets and plates, of iron or steel, originating in Yugoslavia, in [1986] O.J. L254/18
Council Decision of 14 October 1988, No. 88/540, approved the 1985 Vienna Convention for the protection of the ozone layer which provided a framework for international cooperation in the research of and agreement on measures for the protection of the ozone layer, in [1988] O.J. L297/8

Council Decision of 28 July 1989, No. 89/490, on the improvement of the business environment and the promotion of the development of enterprises, and in particular small and medium-sized enterprises, in the Community, in [1989] O.J. L239/33

Council Decision of 7 March 1994, No. 94/149, amending Decision 93/350/Euratom, ECSC, EEC amending Decision 88/591/ECSC, EEC, Euratom establishing a Court of First Instance of the European Communities, in [1994] O.J. L66/29

Council Decision of 24 October 1988, No. 88/591, establishing a Court of First Instance of the European Communities, in [1988] O.J. L319/1

Commission Decision of 12 December 1994, No. 94/810, on the terms of reference of hearing officers in competition procedures before the Commission, in [1994] O.J. L330/67

Council and Commission Decision of 10 April 1995, concerning the conclusion of the Agreement between the European Communities and USA regarding the application of their competition laws, in [1995] O.J. L95/45

Council and Commission Decision of 29 May 1998, Agreement between the European Communities and USA regarding the application of «*comitas gentium*» principles in the enforcement of their Competition Laws, in [1998] O.J. L173/28

Council Decision of 6 July 1998, No. 98/489, concerning the conclusion of the International Cocoa Agreement, 1993, on behalf of the Community, in [1998] O.J. L220/1

Council Decision of 17 October 2000, No. 2000/642, concerning arrangements for cooperation between financial intelligence units of the Member States in respect of exchanging information, in [2000] O.J. L271/4

Commission Decision of 23 May 2001, No. 2001/462, on the terms of reference of Hearing Officers in certain competition proceedings, in [2001] O.J. L162/21

Commission Decision of 11 December 2001, No. 2002/581, on the tax measures for banks and banking foundations implemented by Italy, in [2002] O.J. L184/27

Commission Decision of 5 June 2002, No. 2003/193, on State aid granted by Italy in the form of tax exemptions and subsidised loans to public utilities with a majority public capital holding, in [2003] O.J. L77/21

Commission Decision of 22 August 2002, No. 2003/146, on the tax measures for banking foundations implemented by Italy, in [2003] O.J. L55/56

Council Decision of 27 April 2006, No. 2006/326, concerning the conclusion of the Agreement between the European Community and the Kingdom of Denmark on the service of judicial and extrajudicial documents in civil or commercial matters, in [2006] O.J. L120/23

List of the Rulings of the EC Courts and of the Opinions of the Advocates General

(a) Judgments of the Court of Justice

Judgment of 6 April 1962, Case 13/61, *Kledingverkoopbedrijf De Geus en Uitdenbogerd v. Robert Bosch GmbH e Maatschappij tot Voortzetting Van De Zaken der Firma Willem van Rijn N.V.* (*De Gens* c. *R. Bosch GmbH*), in [1962] ECR 87

Judgment of 5 February 1963, Case 26/62, *van Gend en Loos*, in [1963] ECR 3

Judgment of 15 July 1964, Case 6/64, *Costa v. ENEL*, in [1964] ECR 1127

Judgment of 13 February 1969, Case 14/68, *Walt Wilhelm and others v. Bundeskartellamt*, in [1969] ECR 1

Judgment of 8 June 1971, Case 78/70, *Deutsche Grammophon GmbH v. Metro-SB-Grosmarkte GmbH & Co. KG*, in [1971] ECR 487

Judgment of 14 July 1971, Case 10/71, *P.M. lussemburghese v. M. Mìller vedova J.P. Hein and others*, in [1971] ECR 723

Judgment of 25 November 1971, Case 22/71, *Beguelin Import Co. v. S.A.G.L. Import Export,* in [1971] ECR 949

Judgment of 14 July 1972, joined Cases 48-49 and 51-57/69, *I.C.I., Basf, Bayer, Geigy, Sandoz, Francolor, Cassella, Hoechst* and *Acna v. Commission,* in [1972] ECR 619

Judgment of 12 December 1972, joined Cases 21-24/72, *International Fruit Company NV and others v. Produktschap voor Groenten en Fruit*, in [1972] ECR 1219

Judgment of 14 December 1972, Case 7/72, *Boehringer Mannheim GmbH v. Commission* (*Boehringer II*), in [1972] ECR 1281
Judgment of 21 February 1973, Case 6/72, *Continental Can,* in [1973] ECR 215
Judgment of 12 July 1973, Case 70/72, *Commission v. Germany*, in [1973] ECR 813
Judgment of 11 December 1973, Case 120/73, *Lorenz*, in [1973] ECR 1741
Judgment of 11 December 1973, Case 121/73, *Markmann v. Germany,* in [1973] ECR 1495
Judgment of 11 December 1973, Case 122/73, *Nordsee Deutsche Hochseefischerei v. Germany,* in [1973] ECR 1511
Judgment of 11 December 1973, Case 141/73, *Frits, Lohrey v. Germany and Land Assia*, in [1973] ECR 1527
Judgment of 30 January 1974, Case 127/73, *Belgische Radio en Televisie and Société belge des auteurs, compositeurs et éditeurs v. SV SABAM and NV Fonior* (*BRT v. SABAM* I), in [1974] ECR 51
Judgment of 6 March 1974, joined Cases 6-7/73, *Istituto Chemioterapico Italiano S.p.A. (I.C.I.) – Commercial Solvents Corporation (C.S.C.) v. Commission*, in [1974] ECR 223
Judgment of 21 June 1974, Case 2/74, *Jean Reyners v. Belgian Government*, in [1974] ECR 631
Judgment of 12 November 1974, Case 32/74, *Friedrich Haaga GmbH*, in [1974] ECR 1201
Judgment of 3 December 1974, Case 33/74, *Johannes Henricus Maria van Binsbergen v. Bestuur van de Bedrijfsvereniging voor de Metaalnijverheid*, in [1974] ECR 1299
Judgment of 4 December 1974, Case 41/74, *van Duyn v. Home Office*, in [1974] ECR 1337
Judgment of 3 February 1976, Case 63/75, *Fonderies de Roubaix v. Fonderies Roux*, in [1976] ECR 111
Judgment of 7 July 1976, Case 118/75, *Watson*, in [1976] ECR 1985
Judgment of 15 December 1976, Case 41/76, *Donckerwolcke in Criel and Henri Schou v. Procuratore della Repubblica*, in [1976] ECR 1921
Judgment of 1° February 1977, Case 51/76, *Verbond van Nederlandse Ondernemingen v. Inspecteur der Invoerrechten en Accijinzen*, in [1977] ECR 113
Judgment of 22 March 1977, Case 78/76, *Steinike & Weinlig*, in [1977] ECR 595
Judgment of 14 July 1977, Case 8/77, *Sagulo and others*, in [1977] ECR 1495
Judgment of 30 November 1977, Case 52/77, *Cayrol*, in [1977] ECR 2261
Judgment of 18 January 1978, joined Cases 110/78 and 111/78, *van Wesemael*, in [1979] ECR I- 35
Judgment of 9 March 1978, Case 106/77, *Amministrazione Finanze v. S.p.A. Simmenthal (Simmenthal)*, in [1978] ECR 629
Judgment of 22 November 1978, Case 33/78, *Somafer S.A. v. Saar-Ferngas AG,* in [1978] ECR 2183
Judgment of 23 November 1978, Case 7/78, *Regina v. Thompson and others*, in [1978] ECR 2247

Judgment of 5 April 1979, Case 148/78, *Ratti*, in [1979] ECR 1629
Judgment of 27 June 1979, Case 105/79, *Hayange* (I), in [1979] ECR 2257
Judgment of 18 March 1980, Case 52/79, *Debauve and others,* in [1980] ECR 833
Judgment of 21 May 1980, Case 73/79, *Commission v. Italy*, in [1980] ECR 1533
Judgments of 10 July 1980, joined Cases 253/78 and 1-3/79, *Giry and Guerlain*, in [1980] ECR 2327
Judgment of 10 July 1980, Case 37/79, *Anne Marty SA v. Estée Lauder SA*, in [1980] ECR 2481
Judgment of 29 October 1980, joined Cases 209-215 and 218/78, *Fedetab,* in [1980] ECR 3125
Judgment of 11 November 1981, Case 203/80, *Casati*, in [1981] ECR 2595
Judgment of 19 January 1982, Case 8/81, *Ursula Becker v. Finanzamt Mìnster – Innenstadt*, in [1982] ECR 53
Judgment of 9 June 1982, Case 95/81, *Commission v. Italy,* in [1982] ECR 2187
Judgment of 6 July 1982, joined Cases 188-190/80, *France, Italy and United Kingdom v. Commission*, in [1982] ECR 2545
Judgment of 12 October 1982, Case 136/81, *Commission v. Italy,* in [1982] ECR 3547
Judgment of 25 January 1983, Case 126/82, *D.J. Smit Transport BV v. Commissie Grensoverschrijdend Beroepsgoederenvervoer*, in [1983] ECR 73
Judgment of 3 February 1983, Case 29/82, *van Luipen*, in [1983] ECR 151
Judgment of 22 March 1983, Case 34/82, *Martin Peters Bauemternehmung GmbH v. Zuid Nederlandse Aaunemers Vereniging*, in [1983] ECR 987
Judgment of 7 June 1983, joined Cases 100-103/80, *Musique diffusion française*, in [1983] ECR 1825
Judgment of 22 September 1983, Case 271/82, *Vincent Rodolphe Auer v. Pubblico Ministero*, (*Ordre National des Vétérinaires de France and others*), in [1983] ECR 2727
Judgment of 9 November 1983, Case 322/81, *Michelin*, in [1983] ECR 3461
Judgment of 13 December 1983, Case 218/82, *Commission v. Council*, in [1983] ECR 4063
Judgment of 15 December 1983, Case 5/83, *Criminal Proceeding against H.G. Rienks*, in [1983] ECR 4233
Judgment of 26 January 1984, Case 301/82, *SA Clin Midy v. Kingdom of Belgium*, in [1984] ECR 251
Judgment of 31 January 1984, joined Cases 286/82 and 26/83, *Giuseppe Carbone and Graziana Luisi v. Ministero del Tesoro,* in [1984] ECR 377
Judgment of 21 February 1984, joined Cases 239 and 275/82, *Allied Corporation*, in [1984] ECR 1005
Judgment of 10 April 1984, Case 14/83, *Sabine von Colson and Elisabeth Kamann v. Land Nordrhein – Westfalen*, in [1984] ECR 1891
Judgment of 10 April 1984, Case 79/83, *Dorit Harz v. Deutsche Tradax GmbH*, in [1984] ECR 1921
Judgment of 15 January 1986, Case 52/84, *Commission v. Belgium Government*, in [1986] ECR 89

Judgment of 28 January 1986, Case 270/83, *Commission v. France*, in [1986] ECR 273
Judgment of 6 February 1986, Case 310/85, *Deufil v. Commission*, in [1987] ECR 901
Judgment of 26 February 1986, Case 152/84, *Marshall*, in [1986] ECR 723
Judgment of 10 July 1986, Case 79/85, *Segers*, in [1986] ECR 2375
Judgment of 4 December 1986, Case 205/84, *Commission v. Germany*, in [1986] ECR 3755
Judgment of 16 June 1987, Case 118/85, *Commission v. Italy*, in [1987] ECR 2599
Judgment of 27 September 1988, joined Cases 89/85, 104/85, 114/85, 116/85, 117/85, 125/85, 126/85, 127/85, 128/85 and 129/85, *Ahlström v. Commission* ("*Wood Pulp*"), in [1988] ECR 5193
Judgment of 27 September 1988, Case 81/87, *Daily Mail*, in [1988] ECR 5483
Judgment of 2 February 1989, Case 22/87, *Commission v. Italy*, in [1989] ECR 143
Judgment of 2 February 1989, Case C-186/87, *Cowan*, in [1989] ECR 195
Judgment of 11 April 1989, Case 66/86, *Ahmed Saeed*, in [1989] ECR 803
Judgment of 22 June 1989, Case 103/88, *Costanzo*, in [1989] ECR 1839
Judgment of 22 June 1989, Case C-70/87, *Fediol*, in [1989] ECR 1781
Judgment of 14 March 1990, Case C-156/87, *Gestetner Holdings v. Council and Commission,* in [1990] ECR I-781
Judgment of 21 March 1990, Case C-142/87, *Belgium Government v. Commission*, in [1990] ECR I-959
Judgment of 19 June 1990, Case C-213/89, *Factorame Ltd. v. Secretary of State for Transport*, in [1990] ECR 2433
Judgment of 20 September 1990, Case C-5/89, *Commission v. Germany*, in [1990] ECR I-3437
Judgment of 18 October 1990, joined Cases C-297/88 and C-197/89, *Massan Dzodzi v. Belgium Government*, in [1990] ECR 3763
Judgment of 13 November 1990, Case C-106/89, *Società Marleasing v. Società La Commercial International de Alimentation*, in [1990] ECR 4135
Judgment of 26 February 1991, Case C-180/89, *Commission v. Italy*, in [1991] ECR I-709
Judgment of 26 February 1991, Case C-198/89, *Commission v. Greece,* in [1991] ECR I-727
Judgment of 28 February 1991, Case C-234/89, *Delimitis* c. *Henninger Brau*, in [1991] ECR 935
Judgment of 21 March 1991, Case C-305/89, *Italy v. Commission*, in [1991] ECR I-1603
Judgment of 7 May 1991, Case C-69/89, *Nakajima*, in [1991] ECR 2069
Judgment of 30 May 1991, joined Cases C-19/90 and C-20/90, *Marina Karella and Nikolaos Karellas v. Ypourgoviomichanias, energias & technologias and Organismo Anasygkrotiscos Epicheiriscon AE (Case Velka)*, in [1991] ECR 2691
Judgment of 25 July 1991, Case C-76/90, *Säger v. Debbemeyer,* in [1991] ECR I-4221

Judgment of 19 November 1991, joined Cases C-6/90 and C-9/90, *Francovich v. Italy and Bonifaci and others v. Italy*, in [1991] ECR I-5357

Judgment of 21 November 1991, Case C-354/90, *Fédération nationale commerce extérieur des produits alimentaires and syndicat national des négociants et trasformateurs de saumon v. France* (*Case "FNCE"*), in [1991] I-5505 and in [1992] Foro italiano IV, 471

Judgment of 28 January 1992, Case C-204/90, *Hanns-Martin Bachmann v. Belgium Government*, in [1992] ECR 249

Judgment of 10 March 1992, Case C-174/87, *Ricoh v. Council*, in [1992] ECR 1335

Judgment of 10 March 1992, Case C-175/87, *Matsushita v. Council,* in [1992] ECR I-1409

Judgment of 10 March 1992, Case C-176/87, *Konishiroku Photo Industry Co. Ltd v. Council*, in [1992] ECR I-1493

Judgment of 10 March 1992, Case C-177/87, *Sanyo Electric Co. Ltd v. Council*, in [1992] ECR I-1535

Judgment of 10 March 1992, Case C-179/87, *Sharp Corporation v. Council,* in [1992] ECR I-1635

Judgment of 10 March 1992, Case C-214/89, *Powell Duffryn Ple v. Wolfgang Petereit*, in [1992] ECR 1745

Judgment of 7 July 1992, Case C-370/94, *The Queen v. Immigration Appeal Tribunal and Surinder Singh, ex parte Secretary of State for Home Department,* in [1992] ECR I-4265

Judgment of 16 July 1992, Case C-83/91, *Meilicke v. ADV-ORGA F.A. Meyer AG*, in [1992] ECR I-4871

Judgment of 16 December 1992, Case C-169/91, *B & Q*, in [1992] ECR 6635

Judgment of 31 March 1993, Case C-19/92, *Kraus*, in [1993] ECR I-1663

Judgment of 15 June 1993, Case C-225/91, *Matra SA v. Commission*, in [1993] ECR I-3203

Judgment of 1° July 1993, Case C-20/92, *Hubbard*, in [1993] ECR I-3777

Judgment of 2 August 1993, Case C-271/91, *Marshall,* in [1993] ECR I-4367

Judgment of 12 October 1993, Case C-37/92, *Criminal proceeding against J. Vanacker and A. Lesage*, in [1993] I-4947

Judgment of 16 December 1993, Case C-334/92, *Wagner Miret v. Fondo de Garantia Salarial*, in [1993] ECR 6911

Judgment of 14 July 1994, Case C-91/92, *Paola Faccini Dori v. Recreb S.r.l.*, in [1994] ECR I-3325

Judgment of 9 August 1994, Case C-327/91, *France v. Commission*, in [1994] ECR I-3641

Judgment of 9 August 1994, Case C-43/93, *Vander Elst v. Office des migrations internationales*, in [1994] ECR I-03803

Judgment of 5 October 1994, Case C-280/93, *Germany v. Council*, in [1994] ECR I-4973

Judgment of 10 May 1995, Case C-384/93, *Alpine Investments,* in [1995] ECR I-1141

Judgment of 30 November 1995, Case C-55/94, *Gebhard*, in [1995] ECR I-4165
Judgment of 1° February 1996, Case C-177/94, *Perfili*, in [1996] ECR I-161
Judgment of 5 March 1996, joined Cases C-46/93 and C-48/93, *Brasserie du Pêcheur*, in [1996] ECR I-1029
Judgment of 28 March 1996, Case C-272/94, *Guiot*, in [1996] ECR I-1905
Judgment of 13 June 1996, Case C-144/95, *Criminal proceeding against J.L. Maurin*, in [1996] ECR I-2909
Judgment of 12 December 1996, Case C-3/95, *Reiseburo Broede*, in [1996] ECR I-6511
Judgment of 18 March 1997, Case C-282/95, *Guérin Automobiles,* in [1997] ECR I-1503
Judgment of 20 March 1997, Case C-24/95, *Land Rheinland Pfalz v. Alcan*, in [1997] ECR I-1591
Judgment of 15 May 1997, Case C-250/95, *Futura Participations SA*, in [1997] ECR I-2471
Judgment of 5 June 1997, Case C-398/95, *Syndesmos ton en Elladi Touristikon kai Taxidiotikon Grafeion v. Ypourgos Ergasias*, in [1997] ECR I-3091
Judgment of 3 July 1997, Case C-269/95, *Benincasa v. Dentalkit,* in [1997] ECR I-3767
Judgment of 9 July 1997, Case C-222/95, *Parodi v. Banque de Bary*, in [1997] ECR I-03899
Judgment of 18 December 1997, Case C-402/96, *EITO*, in [1997] ECR I-7515
Judgment of 28 May 1998, Case C-7/95P, *John Deere Ltd. v. Commission*, in [1998] ECR I-3113
Judgment of 16 July 1998, Case C-264/96, *ICI*, in [1998] ECR I-4695
Judgment of 9 March 1999, Case C-212/97, *Centros Ltd v. Erhvers – og Selskabs-styrelsen*, in [1999] ECR I-1459
Judgment of 29 April 1999, Case C-317/97, *Royal Bank of Scotland,* in [1999] ECR 2651
Judgment of 21 September 1999, Case C-307/97, *Saint-Gobain ZN*, in [1999] ECR I-6161
Judgment of 23 November 1999, Case C-149/96, *Portugal v. Council*, in [1999] ECR I-8395
Judgment of 9 March 2000, Case C-355/98, *Commission v. Belgium Government*, in [2000] ECR I-1221
Judgment of 9 March 2000, Case C-358/98, *Commission v. Italy,* in [2000] ECR I-1255
Judgment of 13 April 2000, Case C-251/98, *Baars v. Inspecteur der Belastingen Particulieren/Oondernemingen Gorinchem,* in [2000] ECR I-2287
Judgment of 23 May 2000, Case C-58/99, *Commission v. Italy,* in [2000] ECR I-3811
Judgment of 3 October 2000, Case C-58/98, *Corsten*, in [2000] ECR I-7919
Judgment of 19 October 2000, joined Cases C-15/98 and C-105/99, *Sardegna Lines*, in [2000] ECR I-8855
Judgment of 14 December 2000, Case C-300/98, *Parfums Dior,* in [2000] ECR I-11307

Judgment of 14 December 2000, Case C-344/98, *Masterfoods*, in [2000] ECR I-11369

Judgment of 14 December 2000, Case C-392/98, *Assco Geruste GmbH,* in [2000] ECR I-11307

Judgment of 20 February 2001, Case C-205/99, *Asociación Profesional de Empresas Navieras de Líneas Regulares (Analir) and others v. Administración General del Estado*, in [2001] ECR I-1271

Judgment of 8 March 2001, joined Cases C-397/98 and C-410/98, *Metallgesellschaft and others*, in [2001] ECR I-1727

Judgment of 29 May 2001, Case C-263/99, *Commission v. Italy*, in [2001] ECR I-4195

Judgment of 20 September 2001, Case C-453/99, *Courage*, in [2001] ECR I-6297

Judgment of 15 January 2002, Case C-439/99, *Commission v. Italy*, in [2002] ECR I-305

Judgment of 24 January 2002, Case C-164/99, *Portugaia Construções*, in [2002] ECR I-787

Judgment of 7 February 2002, Case C-279/00, *Commission v. Italy*, in [2002] ECR I-1425

Judgment of 4 June 2002, Case C-483/99, *Commission v. France*, in [2002] ECR I-4781

Judgment of 4 June 2002, Case C-503/99, *Commission v. Belgium Government*, in [2002] ECR I-4809

Judgment of 5 November 2002, Case C-208/00, *Überseering BV v. NCC Nordic Construction Company Baumanagement GmbH*, in [2002] ECR I-9919

Judgment of 13 May 2003, Case C-98/01, *Commission v. United Kingdom*, in [2003] ECR I-4641

Judgment of 9 September 2003, Case C-137/00, *Milk Marque*, in [2003] ECR I-7975

Judgment of 30 September 2003, Case C-167/01, *Kramer van Koophandel en Fabrieken voor Amsterdam and Inspire Art Ltd*, in [2003] ECR I-10155

Judgment of 11 December 2003, Case C-364/01, *Barbier*, in [2003] ECR I-15013

Judgment of 11 March 2004, Case C-9/02, *Hughes de Lasteyrie du Saillant*, in [2004] ECR I-2409

Judgment of 5 October 2004, Case C-442/02, *Caixa Bank France,* in [2004] ECR I-8961

Judgment of 5 October 2004, joined Cases C-397/01 to C-403/01, *Pfeiffer and others*, in [2004] ECR I-8835

Judgment of 21 October 2004, Case C-445/03, *Commission v. Luxemburg,* in [2004] ECR I-10191

Judgment of 20 January 2005, Case C-464/01, *Gruber*, in [2005] ECR I-439

Judgment of 15 February 2005, Case C-12/03P, *Commission v. Tetra Laval*, in [2005] ECR I-987

Judgment of 13 December 2005, Case C-411/03, *SEVIC Systems AG*, in [2005] ECR I-10805

Judgment of 13 December 2005, Case C-446/03, *Marks & Spencer plc*, in [2005] ECR I-10837

Judgment of 10 January 2006, Case C-222/04, *Ministero dell'Economia e delle Finanze v. Cassa di Risparmio di Firenze and others*, in [2006] ECR I-289

Judgment of 2 May 2006, Case C-341/04, *Eurofood IFSC*, in [2006] ECR I-3813

Judgment of 13 July 2006, joined Cases C-295/04 to C-298/04, *Manfredi*, in [2006] ECR 6619

Judgment of 12 September 2006, Case C-196/04, *Caldbury Schweppes plc and Caldbury Schweppes Overseas Ltd. v. Commissiones of (UIC) Inland Revenue*, in [2006] ECR I-7995

Judgment of 3 October 2006, Case C-452/04, *Fidium Finanz*, in [2006] ECR I-9521

Judgment of 23 October 2007, Case C-112/05, *Commission c. Germany,* in [2007] ECR I-8995

Judgment of 6 December 2007, joined Cases C-463/04 and C-464/04 *Federconsumatori and others and Assoc. Azionariato Diffuso dell'AEM S.p.A. and others v. Comune di Milano,* in [2007] ECR I-10419

Judgment of 14 February 2008, Case C-274/06, *Commission v. Spain*, not published

(b) Judgments of the Court of first instance

Judgment of 11 February 1992, Case T-16/90, *Anastasia Panagiotopoulon v. European Parliament*, not published

Judgment of 10 March 1992, Case T-11/89, *Shell v. Commission*, in [1992] ECR II-757

Judgment of 17 September 1992, Case T-24/92, *Automec v. Commission*, in [1992] ECR II-2223

Judgment of 9 March 1994, Case T-188/92, *TWD,* in [1994] ECR I-833

Judgment of 8 June 1995, Case T-459/93, *Siemens v. Commission*, in [1995] ECR II-1675

Judgment of 29 June 1995, Case T-30/91, *Solvay,* in [1995] ECR II-1775

Judgment of 6 July 1995, joined Cases T-447/93, T-448/93 and T-449/93, *AITEC and others v. Commission*, in [1995] ECR II-1971

Judgment of 22 October 1996, Case T-266/94, *Skibsvaerftsforeningen*, in [1994] ECR II-1399

Judgment of 12 December 1996, Case T-380/94, *AIUFFASS and AKT v. Commission*, in [1996] ECR II-2169

Judgment of 22 October 1997, joined Cases T-213/95 and T-18/96, *SCK and FNK*, in [1997] ECR II-1739

Judgment of 25 March 1999, Case T-102/96, *Gencor*, in [1999] ECR II-753

Judgment of 4 April 1999, Case C-119/97P, *Union française de l'express (Ufex)*, in [1999] ECR I-1341

Judgment of 15 June 2000, joined Cases T-298/97, T-312/97, T-313/97, T-315/97, T-600/97 to 607/97, T-1/98, T-3/98 to T-6/98 and T-23/98, *Alzetta and CETM*, in [2000] ECR II-2319

Judgment of 31 January 2001, Case T-197/97, *Weyl Beef Products and others v. Commission*, in [2001] ECR II-303

Judgment of 20 March 2001, Case T-30/99, *Bocchi – Food Trade International Gmbh v. Commission,* in [2001] ECR II-943

Judgment of 28 February 2002, Case T-395/94, *Atlantic Container v. Commission* in [2002] ECR II-875

Judgment of 28 February 2002, Case T-155/98, *SIDE v. Commission*, in [2002] ECR II-1179

Judgment of 21 March 2002, Case T-131/99, *Hamilton Shaw v. Commission*, in [2002] ECR II-2023

Judgment of 6 June 2002, Case T-342/99, *Airtours plc v. Commission*, in [2002] ECR II-2585

Judgment of 22 October 2002, Case T-310/01, *Schneider Electric SA v. Commission*, in [2002] ECR II-4071

Judgment of 25 October 2002, Case T-5/02, *Tetra Laval BV v. Commission*, in [2002] ECR II-4381

Judgment of 8 July 2003, Case T-132/01, *Euroalliages and others v. Commission,* in [2003] ECR II-2359

Judgment of 30 September 2003, Case T-158/00, *ARD v. Commission*, in [2003] ECR II-3825

Judgment of 11 December 2003, Case T-61/99, *Adriatica di Navigazione v. Commission*, in [2003] ECR II-5349

Judgment of 24 January 2006, Case T-46/03 R II, *Leali II*, in [2006] ECR II-9

Judgment of 22 February 2006, Case T-34/02, *EURL Le Levant 001 v. Commission*, in [2006] ECR II-267

Judgment of 4 July 2006, Case C-212/04, *Adeneler and others*, in [2006] ECR I-6057

Judgment of 13 September 2006, Case T-210/02, *British Aggregates Association,* in [2006] ECR II-2789

Judgment of 27 September 2006, Case T-204/03, *Haladjian Frères v. Commission*, in [2006] ECR II-3779

Judgment of 27 September 2006, Case T-168/01, *GlaxoSmithKline Services v. Commission*, in [2006] ECR II-2969

Judgment of 14 December 2006, joined Cases T-259/02 to T-264/02 and T-271/02, *Raiffeisen Zentralbank Österreich AG and others v. Commission*, in [2006] ECR II-5169

Judgment of 11 July 2007, Case T-351/03, *Schneider Electric,* in [2007] ECR II-2237

Judgment of 11 July 2007, Case T-170/06, *Alrosa Company Ltd v. Commission*, in [2007] ECR II-2601

Judgment of 12 September 2007, joined Cases T-239/04 and T-323/04, *Italy and Brandt*, not published

Judgment of 17 September 2007, Case T-201/04, *Microsoft v. Commission*, in [2007] ECR II-3601

Judgment of 20 September 2007, Case T-136/05, *EARL Salvat père & fils*, in [2007] ECR II-4063

Judgment of 25 October 2007, joined Cases T-27/03, T-80/03, T-46/03, T-58/03, T-79/03, T-97/03 and T-98/03, T-45/03, T-77/03 and T-94/03, *SP/Commission,* in [2007] ECR II-4331

(c) Opinions of the Advocates General

Opinion of the Advocate General Mayras presented on 29 November 1972, Case 7/72, *Boehringer* II, in [1972] ECR 1281

Opinion of the Advocate General Capotorti presented on 7 July 1981, Case 203/80, *Casati,* in [1981] ECR 2621

Opinion of the Advocate General Verloren van Themaat presented on 10 January 1984, joined Cases 239 and 275/82, *Allied Corporation and others v. Commission,* in [1984] ECR 1005

Opinion of the Advocate General Verloren Van Themaat presented on 21 November 1984, Case 53/83, *Allied Corporation, Transcontinental,* in [1985] ECR 1621

Opinion of the Advocate General Vesterdorf presented on 10 July 1991, joined Cases T-1/89 to T-4/89 and T-6/89 to T-15/89, *Rhone Poulenc v. Commission,* in [1991] ECR II-867

Opinion of the Advocate General Tesauro presented on 8 April 1992, Case C-83/91, *Meilicke v. ADV-ORGA F.A. Meyer AG,* in [1992] ECR I-4871

Opinion of the Advocate General Darmon presented on 7 July 1992, joined Cases C-89/85, C-104/85, C-114/85, C-116/85, C-117/85 and C-125/85 to C-129/85, *Ahlström v. Commission ("Wood Pulp"),* in [1993] ECR I-1307

Opinion of the Advocate General Tesauro presented on 16 December 1993, Case C-327/91, *France v. Commission,* in [1994] ECR I-3641

Opinion of the Advocate General La Pergola presented on 16 July 1998, Case C-212/97, *Centros Ltd v. Erhvers – og Selskabsstyrelsen,* in [1999] ECR I-1459

Opinion of the Advocate General Ruiz-Jarabo Colomer presented on 4 December 2001, Case C-208/00, *Überseering BV v. NCC Nordic Construction Company Baumanagement GmbH,* in [2002] ECR I-9919

Opinion of the Advocate General Jacobs presented on 21 March 2002, Case C-50/00P, *Unión de Pequeños Agricultores / Conseil (UPA),* in [2002] ECR I-6677

Opinion of the Advocate General Ruiz-Jarabo Colomer presented on 13 June 2002, Case C-206/01, *Arsenal Footbal Club* plc., in [2002] ECR I-10273

Opinion of the Advocate General Ruiz-Jarabo Colomer presented on 6 February 2003, Case C-463/00, *Commission v. Spain,* in [2003] ECR I-4581

Opinion of the Advocate General Alber presented on 15 May 2003, Case C-298/00P, *Alzetta,* in [2004] ECR I-4087

Opinion of the Advocate General Stix-Hackl presented on 30 March 2004, joined Cases C-346/02 and C-347/02, *Commission/Luxemburg,* in [2004] ECR I-7517

Opinion of the Advocate General Jacobs presented on 16 September 2004, Case C-464/01, *Gruber,* in [2005] ECR I-439

Opinion of the Advocate General Tizzano presented on 7 July 2005, Case C-411/03, *SEVIC Systems AG,* in [2005] ECR I-10805

Opinion of the Advocate General Léger presented on 2 May 2006, Case C-196/04, *Cadbury Schweppes*, in [2006] ECR I-7995

Opinion of the Advocate General Ruiz-Jarabo Colomer presented on 13 February 2007, Case C-112/05, *Commission v. Germany,* in [2007] ECR I-8995

Opinion of the Advocate General Poiares Maduro presented on 23 May 2007, Case C-438/05, *International Transport Workers' Federation and Finnish Seamen's Union,* in [2007] ECR

Opinion of the Advocate General Ruiz-Jarabo Colomer presented on 6 November 2008, Case C-326/07, *Commission v. Italy*, not published.

List of Authors Cited in this Volume

ABRAHAMS
ADRION
AFFERNI
AGO
ALBER
ALESSANDRI
ALESSI
ALLEGRI
AMADEO
AMERASINGHE
ANGELICI
ANZILOTTI
ARMINJON
AUBERT
AUBRI
BACCANI
BADR
BAKER
BALBONI
BALLARINO
BALOSSINI
BÄRMANN
BARATTA
BARBA
BARBASO
BARIATTI
BARONE
BARREVELD
BASTIANON
BATIFFOL
BATHURST
BATTAGLINI
BAXI
BAZOLI
BENINI
BEITZKE
BELLAMY
BELLIS
BELLODI
BENATTI
BENEDETTELLI
BERAUD
BERG
BERNARD
BERNINI
BIANCHI
BINI SMAGHI
BISCARETTI DI RUFFÍA
BISCOTTINI
BLANQUET
BLENGINO
BLOCH
BLUMBERG
BOERNER
BONELL
BONINO
BORGIA
BÖRK
BORRELLO
BORSARI
BORZI
BOSCHIERO
BOSSERT
BRACCO
BRANSBURY
BRAUN
BREDIN
BRENT
BREWER
BRIGNARDELLO
BROTHWOOD
BRUHL
BUCHERE
BUTTARO
CABERLOTTO
CAEN
CAFARI PANICO
CALERO
CAMPOLOGNO
CAPOTORTI
CAPPALLI
CARBONE
CARRERA
CARUSO

Casanova
Casella
Cassese
Cassinis
Castelli
Cavaglieri
Caves
Cavour
Cera
Cerexhe
Chesire
Chambost
Charnowitz
Cheli
Chesire
Chiaraviglio
Child
Clayton
Comba
Cook
Coda
Collins
Colombo
Condinanzi
Conforti
Conlon
Consolo
Corapi
Costa
Costi
Covelli
Crespo
Crocioni
D'Alessandro
David
Daniele
Danieli
Davi
De Cesari
De Gennaro
De Guttry
De Mello
De Nova
Denozza
Denton
Despagnet
De Vault
De Vergottini
De Visscher
Di Blase
Dicey
Diena
Dieu
Di Giovine
Di Sabato
Donner
Draetta
Drobnig
Dukgeun
Dunning
Ehlermann
Embid Irujo
Enriques
Esposito
Esteban Velasco
Fadda
Farah
Fatouros
Fattori
Faull
Fawcet
Fenghi
Ferrari
Ferri
Fikentscher
Fiore
Fischer
Flores
Floridia-Catelli
Foglia
Fortunato
Fox
Francioni
Frignani
Frigo
Fumagalli
Fusco
Gabba
Gaetano
Gaja
Galbraith
Galgano
Gambaro
Gambino
Gattinara
Gavil
Genovese
Gennai
Gerbino
Gerini
Germidis
Gianelli
Gianviti
Gianzana
Gilmour
Giral
Gismondi
Giuliani
Gleichmann
Goldman
Goldsmith
Golub
Goyder
Graveson
Grisoli
Groeben
Grossfeld
Grundy
Guarino
Guerra
Guerri
Guizzi
Gulotta
Gurrado
Guyenot
Hackworth
Hancher
Haug
Hellingman
Hermanns
Hession
Hirsch
Hohenveldern
Houin
Hovenkamp
Hunnings
Hunter
Iannuzzi

IDOT
IMMENGA
IPSEN
IRACE
ISAAC
ISRAEL
IUDICA
JAEGER
JANS
JENARD
JENKS
JEULAND
JOLIET
JONES
JÖRGENS
KAMINSKI
KARL
KERSE
KEUTGEN
KHAN
KNOBBE
KOHLER
KOLLEWIJN
KOPITIS
KORAH
KOVACIC
KROES
KUBIATOWSKI
KUEK
KUSTERMANN
LA CHINA
LAGARDE
LAINE
LALIVE
LALL
LAMBERTI ZANARDI
LANDI
LANDOLFI
LANDRUT
LANFRANCHI
LANGER
LANSING
LANZA
LAURIA
LAZARO
LAZARUS
LAW
LEARY
LEBEN
LECOURT
LEFEBVRE D'OVIDIO
LELEUX
LEROYER
LEVEN
LEVY
LIBONATI
LIGUSTRO
LINDSAY
LONDON
LOQUIN
LOUISS
LOUSSOUARN
LYON
LUPONE
LUTTER
LUZZATTO
MACRORY
MAESTRIPIERI
MAISTO
MALANCZUK
MALATESTA
MALESCI
MALHERBE
MALINTOPPI
MANN
MARCHAL
MARIANI
MARLETTA
MARTENS
MARZIALE
MASCARDI
MASPETIOL
MATSUSHITA
MELI
MENGOZZI
MÉGRET
MENDERHAUSEN
MERTENS DE WILMARS
MESTMÄCKER
MESTRE
MEYER
MIGLIAZZA
MINERVINI
MIOLA
MOAVERO MILANESI
MONACO
MONGIELLO
MONTAG
MONTANELLI
MONTELLA
MORRIS
MOSCO
MOSCONI
MUNARI
NAMUR
NAPOLETANO
NASCIMBENE
NARDELLI
NAVARETTI
NGUYEN
NIEMEYER
NIESSEN
NIKPAY
NIVARRA
NORTH
NOTARI
NYBOYET
ORTIZ BLANCO
OSTENDORF
OTTERVANGER
PAGE
PAILLIET
PALAIA
PANICO
PAOLOZZI
PAPPALARDO
PARDESSUS
PARDOLESI
PARODI
PATRONI GRIFFI
PAUL
PAVESIO
PAVONE LA ROSA
PENNINGTON
PERNAZZA
PERONI
PERRET
PERRIN

PERULLI
PESCATORE
PETITE
PEVTEHIN
PICONE
PIETROBON
PIVATO
POCAR
PONTANI
PONZANELLI
PORRO
PORTALE
POSNER
POZZOLI
PREDIERI
PROSPERETTI
PROTO
PROVASOLI
QUEIROLO
QUIGLEY
RADICATI DI BROZOLO
RALSTON
RAUSTIALA
RAU
RAZZANTE
RENAULD
RICHEZ-BAUM
RITTER
ROLFE
RORDORF
ROSARIA
ROSSI
RUHLAND
RUTTEMAN
SACERDOTI
SACCHETTO
SALAFIA
SALERNO
SANCHEZ
SANDERS
SANDRI
SANTAGATA
SANTA MARIA
SARKOZY
SARMET
SAVIGNY
SBISÀ
SCARLI
SCHERER
SCHLITZER
SCHMITTHOFF
SCHNITZER
SCHOLTEN
SCHROTER
SCHWAMM
SCHWARZ
SCORDINO
SCUFFI
SEIDL
SEGRÈ
SERENI
SERICK
SILVA
SIMMONDS
SIMONETTO
SLOT
SPINDLER
SPRÔTE
SPOLIDORO
STALLYBRASS
STAMMATI
STANBROOK
STARACE
STEIN
STEINDORFF
STOCKMANN
SUMMERS
SUPERTI FURGA
TAVASSI
TEDOLDI
TELCHINI
TEMPLE LANG
TESAURO
THIEFFRY
THIESING
THOMPSON
TIZZANO
TODINO
TOFFOLETTO
TOSATO
TOSCANO
TRABUCCHI
TRAVERSI
TREMONTI
TREVES
TRIMBLE
TROELLER
TROPLONG
TRUMAN
UBERTAZZI
URBANI
VAGTS
VAGUE
VALLOIS
VAN BAEL
van der ESCH
van GERVEN
van HECKE
van HULLE
van OMMESLAGHE
van RYN
VARDI
VELLANO
VENABLES
VENTURA
VENTURINI
VERDIER
VERNON
VETTORI
VIGANÒ
VIVANTE
VISENTINI
VISMARA
VITALI
von BAR
von der GROEBEN
YOUNG
WAELBROECK
WALLACE
WEISS
WELCH
WERLAUFF
WHISH
WYATT
ZANON DI VALGIURATA
ZICCARDI
ZONCA

Index

A

Abuse of dominant position
  'dominant position'   353, 420-423, 429
  geographical market   431
  predatory pricing   328
  'relevant market'   429
  repression of   430
Action for damages. *See also* Law No 287/90
  collective redress action   506-516. *See also* 'class action'
  competitor's interest   500
  consumer's interest   515. *See also* White Paper (2008)
  damages awarded, and   496-497
  evaluation
    'public enforcement' and 'private enforcement'   499
Alitalia case   445-450
  aid exempted under Article 87(3)(b) EC Treaty   447
  Community guidelines of 2004 for rescuing and restructuring firms in difficulty   447
  Marzano Law   445
Allied Corporation case   313, 315, 327. *See also* Community interest
Antitrust rules
  application to non-Community undertakings   410-412
  breach of antitrust rules. *See* Action for damages
  derogations   447
  excess of powers (criticism on)   453-459, 470-477, 481-484
  exemptions   480
  general principles   414-419
  investigative powers of Commission   430
  negative clearances   470-471
  potential competition   428-429
  powers of inspection   354-355
  prohibited agreements   502
  verifications   456

B

Banks
  bank secrecy   375
  banking group   373-378
  CONSOB
    Italian legislative decree No. 58/98 (TUF)   98, 99
  directives   88, 157, 373
  documentary control   373
  ECB inspections and supervision   204-205
  freedom of establishment   36, 196
  freedom to provide services   36, 196
  holding companies   157, 211, 363, 391

internal regulations 88
Italian banking law 219
multinational groups 369
Barcelona Traction case 338, 339, 341, 345, 346, 348, 349-350
Basel Committee on Banking Supervision (BCBS)
Basel II regulations 380-382
Home Country control 375
Host Country control 375
supervision of banking groups 373-378
supervision over banking transactions 378-380
Bhopal disaster 364, 365
Brussels Convention on jurisdiction and enforcement of judgments
'agreement conferring jurisdiction' 104
'any other establishment' 105
criteria of competence 102-106
'exclusive jurisdiction' 105
free movement of judgments 102-103
jurisdictional competence 102, 105
'matters relating to a contract' 105
prorogation of jurisdiction 105
recognition of foreign court judgments 102-106
'seat' 103
'single competence' 288
Brussels Convention on mutual recognition
Article 58, Treaty of Rome, and 10
capacity of companies 10
coordination of Article 52 EC Treaty, impact 121
Interpretation 9
'legal' person and 'natural' person 24
lex societatis 103
location of head office of company
'company's real seat or real registered office' 11
place of incorporation and place of central administration 11
public policy 11
reservations 117
scope of application 116-117
shift of statutory seat of company, single member companies 103-104
treatment/recognition of foreign companies 12-24, 31-37

C

Cadbury Schweppes case 45, 67, 70, 425
Centros case 41, 44, 48, 51, 53, 67, 68, 69, 70, 741, 87
China
anti-dumping and anti-subsidies regulations 323-326
European Commission, and 288-294, 325
Foreign Trade Law of the People's Republic of China 323
implementation of WTO rules 323-326
safeguard measures, and 298-299
White Papers of Chinese Government 263, 264, 289
China Accession Protocol (2001) 323
Citizenship of European Union xiv, 36
Class Actions
EC Commission's White Paper, and 513-514
entities having standing to act 513
new Italian statute on collective redress 506-516
principle of the 'domicile' or 'seat' of the defendant 517
Commission
China, and 288-294, 325
court's control 464
cumulation of functions 437-439
decision's effect 434
directorate-general for competition 439, 492-493
'external' weaknesses 288-294
hearing officer 439
role in competition field 433-437
Shell case 438
Community interest 310-320. *See also* dumping
Companies
activities of foreign entities in Italy, authorisation 55
administrative liability for criminal violations
Italian Legislative Decree 231/2001 79-88
Articles 52 *et seq.* of EC Treaty 133
automatic recognition 15, 55, 112
Brussels Convention 9-12

conflict of laws between controlling and controlled entities 95-96
dispute in Italian court 134
group of 89, 97, 365
international law, and 338-351
Italian law 76-79, 89-97
jurisdiction on 102-106
legal personality 5, 43-44
meaning of recognition 24-28
mutual recognition and treatment 12-24, 31-37
navigation, and 28-31
private international law, and 2-6, 46-51, 71-72
treaties of establishment, and 28-31
treaties of friendship, commerce and 28-31
treatment of EC companies 32
treatment of foreign companies 31-37
Treaty of Rome, and 2-9
'unitary management' 334
Company law
Company directives 139, 144, 164
legal basis 126-129
'corporate purpose' 73
damage to individuals 137, 138
direct applicability 129-138
divisions of joint stock companies 123, 124, 127, 140, 141, 154, 161, 162, 164
domestic mergers of joint stock companies 161
European Company 167-172
European Economic Interest Grouping (EEIG) 172-180
harmonisation. See Harmonisation of company law
highest level of environmental protection 402
horizontal relationships 133
implementation of Directives in Member States 130, 141, 144
internal mergers 123, 140, 141
international cooperation in environmental field 401-402
joint stock companies
capital requirements 387
mergers
companies subject to laws of different Member States 157-162
date from which effective 150, 161
disclosure 140, 161
draft terms 140, 161
fiscal rules 406
internal laws 61
nullity 150
obstacles to 159
procedures 160-161
referral technique 446, 493-495
withdrawal of partners 8, 62, 126, 160
rights of parent company 166
single-member companies 153-154
social liability 45. *See also* European Council of Lisbon
Competition
Alitalia case. *See* Alitalia case
American and European rules 420-423
Article 81 EC Treaty 420, 430, 456, 469, 471, 474, 479, 480, 481, 483, 487, 488, 489, 490, 499, 500
Article 82 EC Treaty 418, 420, 429, 430, 466, 480, 481, 483, 487, 488, 490, 491, 499, 500
Article 87 EC Treaty 431, 450, 452, 456, 461
basic characteristics of rules 417
benefit of private individuals, and 479
breach of competition rules 469. *See also* Action for damages
'class action' 506-516
Commission decisions, and 439-440, 464-467
Commission Notice on cooperation between competition authorities 483-484, 491
Commission's role and functions (criticism on), and 433-437, 453-459, 470-477, 481-484
Community Courts' control 464-467
competence of national authorities, and 490-491
consumer's interests 419
Continental Can case 411, 469
co-operation between national courts and Commission 479, 483
direct effect, and 478, 483
direct effect of EC Rules 485
'doctrine of effects' 411

domestic jurisdiction over foreign firms 409-410
domestic rules of Member States 468
'double barrier' theory and convergence obligation 490-491
dumping. *See* dumping
economic issues, and 429-430, 435
enforcement of rules 476
Euratom Treaty 433, 468
exercise of powers by Commission 433
extra-territoriality of rules, and 411
illegal conduct outside EC 473
legal basis 420-423
objectives and aims 423-428
possibility of distortion 488
private undertakings 442
protection of free competition 416
public undertakings, and 441-445
exceptionality 448
'relevant' market 428-433
scope of application of Community provisions, and 468-477
state aid. *See* State aid
subsidiarity principle 491-495
survey of Community Regulations 431
territorial scope of rules 470
territoriality 415, 472
third countries outside Community 470
'traditional comity' 476
transparency in financial relations with Member States 441-445
Comune di Milano case 235, 236, 237, 238
art. 2449 of the Italian Civil Code 239
Concentrations
antitrust rules, and 411-412
Commission practice 470
cumulative application of Articles 81 and 82 EC Treaty 483
financial structure of operation 444
'group effect' 420
initial position of Commission 435
'one-stop shop' principle 491-495
Philip Morris Case
applications of principles by Commission 422
prior supervision by Commission 441
purchase of minority shareholdings 158
Regulation governing
ancillary restraints 493
application 415
banking and insurance activities 426
boundaries of rules 451, 452
'Community dimension' 495
control 492
definition 415
'German clause' 487, 500
joint ventures 475
'ordinary activities' 480-481, 497-499
powers of Commission 429, 433, 435-437
procedure
Community and national rules 487-491
'Wood pulp' case 473, 474, 475
Contract of duration
principle of the continuity of contracts 214-215
relation with Euro, and 213-219
Courage case 478, 496, 497
Cross-border mergers. *See also* Transfer of seat.
Directive No 2005/56 8, 57-64, 140, 160
EC case law 57-64
in general 76, 126, 161

D

Daily Mail case 6, 12, 39, 51, 52-56, 58, 65
Delagoa Bay Railway case 343, 344
Delors Report 197-200, 201
Diplomatic protection
Barcelona Traction case 338, 339, 341, 345, 346, 348, 349-350
on companies 335
Delagoa Bay Railway case 343, 344
ELSI case 339-340
multinational corporations 341-344
previous exhaustion of local remedies 339-340
on shareholders 335, 346
Washington Convention 349
Dispute settlement body (DSB). *See* WTO
Dispute settlement understanding (DSU). *See* WTO

Doha Round 252, 260, 272. *See also* WTO, GATT
Doha development agenda 288
Domestic jurisdiction 250
Draft Directive on groups 162-166
Dumping. *See also* subsidies, anti-dumping duties
Agreement on implementation of article VI of the GATT 1994 252, 300
Appeals 321, 324
prohibited practices in Articles 81-82 EC Treaty 328
causal linkage with injury 315
circumvention of antidumping duties 306-310
commercial policy, and 312, 326
Community rules implementing GATT 308, 317, 326
comparison with State aid 459-460
competition, and 326-329
confidentiality 324
'constructed normal value' 294-297
consultation and dispute settlement 328
definition 299, 303, 304
EC Dumping Regulation 313
immateriality of Community interests 305
injury, and 252, 304, 311-314, 317, 328
the Chinese system, in 323-326
the United States of America, in 320-322
intra-Community 327
legal status 365
liability 305
margin 304, 305, 324
meaning 299
multinational enterprises, and 412
'normal value' 303, 325, 365
practised by third countries 459
price comparison 260-261
rules in US and EC 320-322
selling in dumping, definition 299
services 244, 247
source of distortion in international trade, as 299-300
'subassembly dumping' 307
'third country' dumping 307
'undertakings' 278, 306, 326
US legislation 320
US rules 278, 312-313

E

Economic activity
definition 414
Economic and monetary policy of Member States
economic integration process, and 195-197
Resolution of 22 March 1971 197
Werner Report 196-197
Economic and Monetary Union. *See* also European Monetary Snake and European Monetary System.
Article 2 EC Treaty 201
'balances of payments' 190
criteria for suitability 213, 271, 275
institutional context 209, 251
Maastricht Treaty, and 200-208
monetary integration 202, 203
second stage 203
single European currency 193
subsidiarity 378
'transitional stage' 203
Economic integration process
economic and monetary policy of Member States, and 195-197
Economy
economic development 198, 199, 254
macroeconomic issues 435
market economy 202
market economy status 324-326
microeconomic issues 283, 428
State-planned economy 243
statistics 242, 245
Eleventh Directive 166-167
ELSI case
previous exhaustion of local remedies 339-340
Treaty of Friendship, Commerce and Navigation between USA-Italy (1948) 30, 90
Establishment
abuse of the right 50, 71
Articles 43 *et seq.* EC Treaty 47
Article 293 EC Treaty xv, 3, 4, 5, 6-9, 33, 61, 159
Centros case 41, 44, 48, 51, 53, 67, 68, 69, 70, 71, 87

companies and other entities
definition of 5
criterion of 'direct link' 50
cross-border mergers. *See* cross-border mergers
Daily Mail case 6, 12, 39, 51, 52-56, 58, 65
derogations provided in Article 46 EC Treaty 86, 223
direct applicability of rules of the Treaty 38-41
disapplication of national provisions 129
disclosure requirements in respect of branches (Eleventh Directive) 65, 77, 125
freedom of establishment and freedom to provide services 5, 12, 31, 34, 38, 46, 50-51, 74, 101, 106
insolvency proceedings 106-113
Inspire Art case 51, 68, 69, 70, 78, 79, 85, 87
letterbox company 71
national treatment principle 66-71
notion 33, 41-44
requirements 30, 46, 48, 49
restriction admitted by ECJ 33-34
restrictions prohibited by Article 48 EC Treaty 67
right to incorporate new autonomous companies in a MS 64
right to open branches in a MS 26
scope of Article 48 EC Treaty 32, 66
tax system shopping 45
transfer of seat 57, 65
Überseering case 2, 6, 7, 26, 36, 39, 41, 45, 49, 53, 55, 56, 60, 61, 67, 69
EU's exclusive competence (over trade matters)
Article 133 EC Treaty 287-288
Euro Zone 209, 244, 362
European Central Bank 204-205
European Community Law
relationship with international law xv, 2, 4, 7, 54, 383
relationship with national laws xv, 487-491
European Company (statute) 167-172
European Economic Interest Groupings (EEIG) 172-180. *See also* SMEs
competitive bidding for public works 175
contract 173
creditors 179
direct taxes 178
functions 172
internal operations 177
legal basis 174
legal personality 179
legal structure 173
mandatory rules 173
members 173, 177
profits 175, 178
protection of third parties, purposes 173
European Monetary Snake 197-200
European Monetary System
derogations provided in Article 58 EC Treaty 222
European Currency Unit (ECU) 198
full liberalisation of capital and payments movements 198. *See also* Maastricht Treaty
vacuum of powers 209-210
European Single Act (1986) 192, 201
European System of Central Banks 204-205
European Union
'Corporate social responsibility', and 399-402
international origins xiii-xviii
multinational enterprises, and 351
community law and national law 487-491
substantive law 116-118
WTO, and 287-288
Exhaustion (previous) of local remedies 339-340
Exportation of banknotes
free movement of capital, and 184-189

F

Financial Action Task Force (FATF) 386
Financial crisis 359-364
Fannie Mae and Freddie Mac 361

Financial integration
  financial services 198, 199
  liberalisation 198
  re-launch 198
Foreign companies
  mutual recognition and treatment 12-24, 31-37
  right of establishment 42, 44, 51, 77, 84
Forum non conveniens 510
Free movement of capital
  complexity of regime 229
  criticalities of the European system 208-210
  double standard 211-213
  exchange control, and 196
  exportation of banknotes, and 184-189
  fiscal issue 396
  'full liberalisation' 198
  implementation 185, 200, 223
  Italian rules on special powers. *See* 'Golden Share'
  safeguard measures 202-203
  'services', and 189, 190, 211
  Treaty of Rome 189-194
  UK case 211-213
Free movement of goods 191, 223, 290
Free movement of services
  nature of 34
  derogations provided in Articles 46 and 55 EC Treaty 86, 223
Freedom of payments 191
  complexity of regime 229-230
  criterion of nationality 32
  criterion of residence 32
  criterion of 'the place where capital is invested' 32
  exchange control, and 196
  fiscal issue 183-184
  'full liberalisation' 198
  implementation 185
  safeguard measures 203
  Treaty of Rome, and 189-194

G

G7 Finance 262-263
GATT
  development of Community rules to implement 326
  international agreements 301-302
  international bidding, and 253-254
  international co-operation to resolve problems 250-256
    principles 253
  international law 250
  international obligations, and 281, 322
  legal protection of foreign investments 246
  legally acquired advantages, and 356-358
  limits of efficacy of Community rules 281-284
    lis alibi pendens 278
  multinational enterprises, and 182
  unlawful forms of behaviour 260, 263, 282, 321, 326, 329
GATS Agreement
  substantive economic rights 280
Globalization 252, 270-272, 332-333, 356, 358-364, 378, 393-394
'Golden share'
  direct investment 226, 227
  financial or portfolio investment 226, 227
  national law on, and 227
  ECJ's guiding principles 229
  special powers 232
Green Paper 'Europe's trade defence instruments in a changing global economy' 319-320. *See also* trade defence instruments

H

Harmonization of company law
  affiliation contract 146
  aim 174
  annual financial statements
    'clarity and accuracy' 156
    true and fair view 144, 156
  application of national law 135, 136
  Article 94 EC Treaty 119, 126, 128, 141
  authority of Commission 133
  banking 157
  case law of ECJ 122, 129, 131
  Commission's 'White Paper', and 162-163
  common tax system 178
  competition rules 139
  concentrations 158

consolidated accounts (Seventh Directive) 162-166
consolidated group balance sheets 156
consultation with workers 152
contracts of affiliation 146
cooperation between companies 160
council's resolution 128
direct applicability of harmonisation directives 129-138
'direct effect' principle 122
directives 123-125, 129-138, 139-143
directives affecting general complex of rules 149-157
discretionality of Member States 131, 137, 154
dispute between private citizens
Eleventh Directive. *See* disclosure requirements
exemptions 131-132
fiscal provisions 128
general considerations 120-126
groups of companies (Draft Directive) 162-166
interpretative issues, and 139-147
Italian law
co-ordination with local authorities
judicial bodies, and 133
legal basis 126-129
legal certainty 148
legal supervision of accounting documents 124
limits of directives 142
majority decisions of Council, mergers 111
minimal standards 178
multinationals 144
national jurisdictions 141, 159
non-coincidence between Community rule and domestic law of adaptation 126
private international law 116-118
problems of coordination 106
problems of implementation in Italian law 125
protection of subordinated workers 152
protection of third parties 143, 173
protection of workers' rights 140, 141, 152
right of establishment, and 126-127, 139
social policy 140
State authorities liability in implementing Community directives 133
stock exchanges 144-145
transitional period 120-122
uniformity 115-120
'unitary direction' 174
vertical relationships 133
Havana Charter 251
Human Rights
'essential elements clause' 269
European Convention on Human Rights 436
'generalised system of tariff preferences' (STP) 269

I

Injury (dumping)
meaning 312-313
Insurance companies
administrative authorization 85
common treatment for agents and brokers 21
freedom of establishment 44, 85
freedom to provide services 85
protection of consumers 520
protection of policy-holders 519
Inspire Art case 51, 68, 69, 70, 78, 79, 85, 87
International Labour Organization (ILO)
Core Labour Standards 265-266
International Social Clause, and 267
International Monetary Fund (IMF) 251, 256-262. *See also* WTO
fundamental tools 258
International public policy 82, 184
Italian Legislative Decree 231/2001 79-88, 368-369, 380

J

Jurisdiction
Brussels Convention 102, 105
competition
division of powers between EC Commission and NCAs 493
locus standi of private parties 501, 510
Regulation (EC) 44/2001 7, 102, 104, 517-520

K

Kennedy round 252, 412

L

Labour law 263-267
Less developed countries (LDCs) 270-272
  definitions 271
  industrialised countries 271, 272
  Less advanced countries (LACs), and 271-272
  principle of compensatory inequality 271
  principle of 'non-reciprocity' 271-272
  unspecific 'right to development' 271
Lobbies 249
Lockheed case 364-365
  possibility of harmful behaviour 364
  Seveso disaster 365

M

Maastricht Treaty
  Economic and Monetary Union 200-208
  free competition 202, 205
  Maastricht Criteria 184, 206, 207, 208, 212
  open market economy 202, 205
Manfredi case 496, 521
Market Economy Status
  China and 324-326
Marrakesh Agreement 182. *See also* WTO
Mergers. *See* Company law, Concentrations, Harmonisation of company law.
Money laundering
  Directive No 2005/60 384-385, 388
Monetary dumping 256-262
Monetary exchange. *See* Economic and Monetary Union, European Monetary System and IMF.
  the case of UK pound 207, 211
Morality general principles 184
Multinational enterprises
  advantages, lawful and unlawful 354, 356-358, 364
  antitrust rules 355
  Banco Ambrosiano case 364, 374
  Bank control of transactions 372-373
  Barcelona Traction case 338, 339, 341, 345, 346, 348, 349
  Basel II regulations 380-382
  Basel Concordat 374-375, 376
  Bhopal disaster 364, 365
  cases of abuse 364-365
  codes of conduct 391-393
  criterion of control
    'national' companies 346
  diplomatic protection on companies, and 335
    shareholders 335, 341-344, 346
  distortions of competition 355-356
  double taxation, and 366, 370
  Elettronica Sicula case 339-340
  European Union, and 351
  exclusion of any subsidiary liability 346
  exhaustion of local remedies 339-340
  'hedge' funds 360
  international cooperation, against
    corruption 370
    financial crimes 370
    money laundering 371
    pollution 369
    terrorism 369
  International Law, and 338-351
  non-Community Multinationals
    application of dumping and subsidies rules 412
  normal value of transfer prices and royalties in intragroup transactions 365-368
  'pension' funds 360
  principle of protection 338
  private equity funds 360
  'social commitment', and 393-395
  'sovereign wealth funds' 362-363
  'suspicious' activity control 372, 382
  third-country-based multinationals (activity) 408-410
  transfer price 366-367
  USA financial crisis 359-362
Mutual recognition and treatment of foreign companies 12-24, 31-37. *See also* Brussels Convention, Establishment

N

North American Free Trade Agreement (NAFTA) 301

O

OECD Guidelines for Multinational Enterprises 337, 400
OECD Model Double Taxation Convention on Income and Capital 366
One-stop shop principle 491-495
Opinion No 1/94 288

P

Predatory pricing. *See* Abuse of dominant position and Dumping
Price dumping 261
Principle of Community law primacy 55, 415, 490, 491
Principle of good faith 282, 283
Principle of legal certainty 69, 116, 117, 144, 230, 425, 432, 450, 462, 477, 487
Principle of national treatment 60, 63, 66, 143, 189, 253, 355
Principle of non-discrimination 31, 32, 37, 188, 211, 253, 287, 424, 458, 468
Principle of proportionality 187, 188, 238, 438, 462
Principle of subsidiarity 378, 382, 427, 446, 482, 493
Private international law
  application and disapplication of Article 25(1) of Law No 218/1995 74
  application of Legislative Decree 231/2001 to community foreign companies 79-88
  auditing companies 100
  companies, and 2-6, 46-51, 71-72
  conflict of laws and harmonizing law on companies 116-117, 118
  disapplication of Article 25(3) of Law No 218/1995 76
  domicile 103
  exclusive jurisdiction 103, 106
  foreign companies with secondary establishments in Italy 77
  group of companies 89
  incorporation criteria 11, 25, 57, 103
  Italian reforming law 27
  jurisdiction criteria 103, 106
    lex societatis 103
  listed companies 98-101
  mandatory rules of *lex fori* 82
  mandatory rules of foreign law 82
  member state's nationality 103
  mergers 58, 63, 161
  multinational groups 89
  place of administration or place of principle object 73
  residence 4, 56
  subsidiary liability of sole shareholder 89
  transfer of seat 57, 65
  uniformity 116-117
Protection of personal data
  bank secrecy 373
  privacy 391
Public undertakings
  competition, and 441-445
  meaning 442
  Directive No 2006/111/CE 442-445
  public authorities 238-239, 442-443
  State aid 443
  transparency 443

R

Regulation (EC) No. 3285/94 295-297
Regulation (EC) No 384/96 302, 304, 305, 308, 311, 317, 318, 325. *See also* Dumping
Regulation (EC) No 2026/97 302, 304, 305, 317
Regulation (EC) No 659/99 452, 453, 455, 462. *See also* State aid
Regulation (EC) No 1346/2000 71, 106-113
  Eurofood case 111
  decision to open insolvency proceedings
    member state's refusal of the decision 111
  insolvency proceedings definition 107
  limited universality approach 109
  scope of application 107
  subsidiary's centre of main interests 109, 111, 112
  winding up proceedings 109
Regulation (EC) No 44/2001 3, 7, 102, 104, 106, 107, 517, 518, 519, 520. *See also* Private international law
Regulation (EC) No 1/2003 420, 427, 438, 464, 466, 479, 480, 481, 482, 483, 486,

489, 490, 491, 497, 516. *See also* Antitrust
Regulation (EC) No 139/2004 63, 420, 430, 464, 492, 493, 494, 495. *See also* Concentrations
'Relevant' market 428-433, 452
Commission Notice 97/C 372/03 430
Reyners & Van Bisbergen case 38, 40, 122
Royalties 357, 365, 366, 371

S

Safeguard measures. *See also* WTO
China, and 298-299
provisional safeguard measures 298
'regional measure' 299
Regulation (EC) No 3285/94 295, 297
transitional product-specific safeguard mechanism (TPSSM) 298
Services. *See also* Establishment, Free movement of services
establishment distinguished 35
direct applicability of the Treaty rules 38-41
Seventh Directive on consolidated accounts 144, 162-166
Seveso disaster 365
SEVIC case 51, 58, 60, 65
SGEI (services of general interest) 225
Small/Medium-sized enterprises (SMEs) 403-408
Social dumping 263, 268. *See also* ILO
Soft law 259, 379
State aid
competition, and 424-425, 431-432
comparison between other competition rules 456
co-ordination principles 476
economic activities, and 423
extensive application of Article 87 EC Treaty 450-457
Ford Tractor Belgium case 451
lawful aid and unlawful aid 451, 454
provision by private investor, and 225
recovery (decision) 452, 461-464
preliminary ruling *ex* Article 234 EC Treaty, and 463
'relevant' market 429-432, 452, 456
State Aid Action Plan (SAAP) 430, 431
the US system, in 460-461
Stock exchanges
Directives 144-145
Subsidies. *See also* dumping
Agreement on Subsidies and Countervailing Measures 252, 286, 300
amount 312-313, 341-342
commercial policy, and 312, 326
'Community interest' (dumping) 310-320
Community rules implementing GATT 308, 317, 326
countervailing duties 317, 321
definition 300-301
EC Regulation 3285/94 295, 296, 297
'government' 301, 458
immateriality of Community interests 305
injury, and 252, 304, 311-314, 317, 328
the United States of America, in 320-322
the Chinese system, in 323-326
practised by third countries 459
prohibitions 301
rules in US and EC 320-322
source of distortion in international trade, as 299-300
'specificity' 301
'undertakings' 305-306, 323, 326-327, 328, 329
US legislation 320
Suspicious activity
the Italian legal system, in 387
supervision and Suspicious Activity Reports (SARs) 372, 389

T

Tarification 253, *See also* GATT
Third-country-based multinational enterprises
application of EU Competition law 470
'effective and continuous link' 409
'effects doctrine' 411
freedom of establishment and to provide services 409
trade defence measures. *See* dumping, subsidies, safeguard measures
Tokyo Round 252, 271, 310, 412

Trade defence instruments 294-300. *See also* antidumping, subsidies, safeguard measures
Trade policy review mechanism (TPRM) 254
Transfer of seat 57, 65
Transfer price 368-372, 447
Treaties of establishment
  companies, and 28-31
Treaties of friendship, commerce and navigation
  companies, and 28-31
TRIPS Agreement 271, 280, 285-286

U

Überseering case 2, 6, 7, 26, 36, 39, 41, 45, 49, 53, 55, 56, 60, 61, 67, 69
Undertaking
  definition 414
  multinational 396-397
  remedies in competition law 444
Uniformity
  national law, and 141-142
  private international law, and 116-117
United Nations. *See* WTO
United States Anti-dumping Act 278
Uruguay Round
  Byrd Amendment, and 321-322
  Uruguay Round Agreements Act 320
US financial crisis 362

V

Vienna Convention on the Law of Treaties 269, 282, 477

W

White paper on damages actions for breach of the EC Antitrust rules (2008) 497, 501, 514
World Trade Organisation (WTO)
  Community interest 311, 320
  customs duties (abating) 182
  Dispute settlement body (DSB) 272-274
  Dispute settlement understanding (DSU) 254-255, 273, 274, 359
  European Union, and 287-288
  free trade rules and principles 182, 290
  'global' market 182
  judicial rules 280
  legal principles 276-279
  nature and functions of the WTO's rules 276
  other International Economic Organisations, and 256-267
    G7 Finance, and 262-263
    International Labour Organisation, and 263-267
    International Monetary Fund, and 256-262
    United Nations, and 56
  Panels 255, 274-275
  pleading GATT/WTO rules 281
  private party, role of 284-287
  protection of private enterprises' and traders' interests 282
  quotas (equalizing) 182
  role of private entity as *amicus curiae* in dispute settlement proceedings 284
  'sovereign funds', and 182
    trade defence instruments 294-300
      dumping
        circumvention of antidumping duties 306-310
        nature 303-306
    safeguard measures 294-297
    subsidies
      implementation in
        China 323-326
        EU 300-303
        USA 320-322
Washington Convention (1965) 347-348, 349